I0352347

听见瑞金：地方民歌中的文化记忆与跨代传承

Listening to Ruijin: Cultural Memory and Intergenerational Transmission in Folk Songs

编著：刘晨

Author and Editor: Chen Liu

编著：刘晨
原著手稿：钟同荣（1933–2018，笔名钟同荥）
学术顾问（审阅与校订）：刘方，钟键
手稿整理与保存：林美娟

Author and Editor: Chen Liu
Original Manuscripts by: Zhong Tongrong (1933–2018, pen name: Zhong Tongying)
Academic Advisors (Review and Proofreading): Liu Fang, Zhong Jian
Manuscript Custody and Preparation: Lin Meijuan
出版发行：出版
地址：
出版日期：2025 年 10 月
ISBN：
美国印刷

Published by:
Publisher Address:
Publication Date: 2025.10
ISBN: 978-1-970316-05-6
Printed in the United States of America

作者简介

刘晨，美国哥伦比亚大学东亚研究所研究学者，主要从事跨文化传播的研究工作。

毕业于中国中央戏剧学院表演系音乐剧方向，获音乐剧表演文学学士学位与戏剧戏曲学学术型文学硕士学位，参与电影、音乐剧与文化艺术项目的制作、策划与跨文化创意实践，关注叙事与艺术在不同文化语境中的传播方式。

其学术与创作工作结合档案整理、文本翻译与数字技术探索，关注地方文化如何在全球语境中被重新理解与传播。《听见瑞金》基于其家族保存的大量瑞金民歌手稿与田野记录，并在哥伦比亚大学研究期间完成系统整理与跨文化阐释，是其在文化记忆与非物质遗产研究中的重要成果。

除学术研究外，她亦担任多项国际文化与传媒项目的战略与创意工作，致力于融合学术视野、艺术创作与国际制作体系，推动艺术、技术与叙事在不同文化语境中的呈现与对话。

Author Introduction

Chen Liu is a research scholar at the Weatherhead East Asian Institute of Columbia University, where she conducts research in cross-cultural communication.

She holds a Bachelor of Literature in Acting (Musical Theatre) and a Master of Literature in Theatre Studies from the China Central Academy of Drama. Her professional experience spans film, musical theatre, and cultural arts projects, encompassing production, creative planning, and cross-cultural creative practice. Her work focuses on how narrative and artistic expression circulate across different cultural contexts.

Integrating archival reconstruction, textual translation, and digital methodologies, her academic and creative practice examines how local cultures are reinterpreted and transmitted within global frameworks. Listening to Ruijin draws upon a substantial collection of folk song manuscripts and fieldwork materials preserved by her family, which she systematically organized and interpreted during her research at Columbia University. The book represents a significant contribution to her ongoing exploration of cultural memory and intangible heritage.

Beyond her academic research, Liu also contributes to strategic and creative work across several international cultural and media initiatives. She is committed to integrating scholarly perspectives, artistic practice, and global production systems, fostering dialogue across cultures through the intersection of art, technology, and narrative expression.

《听见瑞金》书稿摘要

《听见瑞金》是一部中英文对照的学术文献与研究著作，汇集了中央苏区核心区——瑞金——最重要的一批民歌手稿，是目前所存最完整的地方声音档案之一。本书基于 20 世纪 80 年代田野采录的一手材料，系统呈现了那个时代乡土社会的声音景观、民间叙事与文化想象。

本项目在我于哥伦比亚大学东亚研究所的研究期间得以深化，并置于文化记忆、民族音乐学与跨文化传播的学术框架之中。通过历史分析与原始手稿的文本解读，本书探讨了民歌如何在特定历史时期承担情感表达、社区记录与政治叙事的功能，呈现其作为“活态档案”的文化价值。

通过将传统档案整理、翻译研究与 AI 智能数字化研究方法相结合，《听见瑞金》尝试在过去与当下之间重建对话，使瑞金的文化记忆得以进入国际学术语境，并为非物质文化遗产与跨文化研究提供新的视野。同时，从情感价值判断与传承的角度，对未来人工智能时代下的文化研究提供了新的范式与启承。

Abstract of the Book Manuscript Listening to Ruijin

Listening to Ruijin is a bilingual scholarly volume that brings together one of the most extensive surviving collections of folk song manuscripts from Ruijin, the cultural center of the 1930s Central Soviet Area. Based on fieldwork materials preserved by my family for decades, the book offers rare primary sources that document everyday soundscapes, oral traditions, and the cultural imagination of a pivotal historical era.

Developed during my research affiliation at Columbia University's Weatherhead East Asian Institute, this project situates Ruijin folk songs within broader conversations in cultural memory, ethnomusicology, and cross-cultural translation. Through historical analysis and manuscript-based interpretation, the book explores how folk songs functioned as emotional expression, community record, and political storytelling, revealing their role as living archives of local society.

By integrating traditional archival compilation, translation-based analysis, and emerging AI-driven digital methodologies, Listening to Ruijin seeks to reconstruct a dialogue between the past and the present. This approach enables the cultural memory of Ruijin to enter the global scholarly discourse and offers new perspectives for the study of intangible cultural heritage and cross-cultural transmission. At the same time, from the standpoint of emotional valuation and cultural continuity, it proposes a new paradigm—and a new point of departure—for cultural research in the era of artificial intelligence.

作者导言　Author's Introduction

二十世纪三十年代的中央苏区，瑞金是中国革命的重要发源地之一。这里的山川河谷间，流淌着无数民歌。这些歌谣既是百姓日常生活的自然记录，也是时代风云的生动见证。它们从田间地头流出，穿过村落小径，成为民众心声与集体记忆的回响。

本书所汇集的资料，主要源于二十世纪八十年代由钟同荣（笔名钟同荥,1933—2018）先生及同仁展开的大规模田野采录。他们跋山涉水三万余里，访谈六百余位乡村歌手与乡民，用录音机采录并手抄保存了千余首民间歌曲，其中包括三百余首中央苏区时期的革命历史民歌。这些资料不仅是音乐学的宝贵财富，也是研究中国社会文化与地方史的重要文献。本书所收录的全部历史手稿与歌谣文献，均依法统一授权，以原貌形式完整呈现，未作删改或现代化处理。其目的在于为学界提供第一手史料，以便开展历史学、民俗学与音乐学等多领域的深入研究。这些歌谣作为二十世纪三十年代地方社会的声音档案，承载着特定历史语境与集体记忆，既展现了民众的日常经验，也反映了民间文化的生成与流传。保持原貌的呈现方式，旨在凸显其史料价值，使学界后续研究得以建立在真实文献之上，开展多角度的解释与分析。

本书的学术意义在于，它并不仅仅呈现一批歌词与曲谱，而是为当下和未来的研究提供了一种可能性：如何在跨文化的语境中理解这些民间声音？如何通过翻译、数字化、人工智能等方法，让它们在全球学界与公众领域被重新聆听？因此，本书既是文献集，也是学术对话的起点。

未来，我们计划尝试利用 AI 技术还原田野场景，将手稿与歌声结合，建立开放的声音档案库，使这份无形遗产得到新的延展和再生。

In the early 1930s, Ruijin stood as one of the most important cradles of the Central Soviet Area. Amid its mountains and valleys flowed countless folk songs. These songs were not only natural records of daily life, but also vivid witnesses to the turbulent tides of history. Emerging from the fields and spreading through village paths, they became the voice of the people and the echo of collective memory.

The materials collected in this volume originate primarily from a large-scale fieldwork project conducted in the 1980s by Mr. Zhong Tongrong (pen name Zhong Tongying,1933-2018) and his colleagues. Traveling more than 30,000 li across mountains and rivers, they interviewed over 600 villagers and folk artists, and recorded with tape recorder and hand-copied more than one thousand folk songs—among them, over 300 revolutionary historical songs from the Central Soviet period. These documents are not only invaluable treasures for ethnomusicology, but also essential texts for the study of Chinese social culture and local history. All historical manuscripts and folk song texts included in this volume ,which rights have been lawfully authorized by his heirs are presented in their original form, without deletion or modernization. The purpose is to provide primary materials for scholarly research in history, folklore, and ethnomusicology. As sonic archives of local society in the 1930s, these songs embody a specific historical context and collective memory, reflecting both the everyday experiences of the people and the processes of folk cultural transmission. Preserving them in their original form underscores their value as historical evidence and enables future research scholarship to be conducted on the basis of authentic documents, allowing for diverse perspectives and interpretations.

The academic significance of this book lies in the fact that it does not merely present a collection of lyrics and notations. Rather, it provides a possibility for present and future research: How can we understand these folk voices within a cross-cultural framework? How can translation, digitalization, and artificial intelligence allow these voices to be heard anew in global academia and the public sphere? Thus, this book is both a compilation of documents and a starting point for scholarly dialogue.

Looking ahead, we envision the use of AI technologies to recreate the fieldwork context, combining manuscripts with reconstructed singing, and building an open sound archive. In doing so, this intangible heritage will find new extensions and new life.

致谢 Acknowledgements

在整理与编纂这部《听见瑞金》的过程中，我心中最深的感触，不是我们今天能够交出的成果，而是那些在岁月风尘里默默守护、执着坚持的人。本书得以付梓，凝聚了数代人的心血与努力。

首先，我要向已故的外祖父钟同荣（笔名钟同荥，1933—2018）先生致以深深的敬意。正是他数十年的田野采录与手稿整理，才使得这些珍贵的民歌文献得以完整保存。他用脚步丈量乡土，用心血守护声音，为我们留下了不可替代的文化遗产。

我要感谢我的外祖母林美娟女士。正是她在那个动荡不安的年代里，作为老一辈教育工作者把这些手稿视若生命般守护。她没有留下宏大的誓言，却以平凡的方式承担了非凡的使命：一页页纸张不被遗失，一个个名字不被遗忘。若没有她数十年的坚持，今日的《听见瑞金》或许早已无从谈起。她的守护构成了本书最初也是最深沉的基石。

感谢父亲刘方教授，作为音乐家，他以严谨的学术态度和六十余载的音乐教育经验，为本书的校订与完善倾注大量心力。感谢母亲钟键教授，亦以四十余载的声乐与钢琴教学的专业视角，为本书的理论与实践提供了坚实的支撑，并将其信念传递给一代又一代学子。

此外，还要感谢瑞金及赣南地区的无数民间“老乡”。没有他们在田间地头倾情吟唱，就不会有这些在独特历史时期，对抗动荡而饱含泥土芬芳的歌谣。

谨向哥伦比亚大学东亚研究所致以诚挚的谢意，感谢其在本研究过程中提供的学术支持与重要的学术交流平台。特别感谢著名政治经济学家吕晓波教授，他的指导与深刻洞见，使我能够在跨文化的分析框架语境下开展并推进本项研究。

在跨文化研究与出版过程中，我也得到了学界同仁与家人朋友们的关怀与指点。感谢他们在学术交流、方法论探讨以及出版推进等方面给予的帮助。

本书的出版，不仅是对前辈努力的延续，也是对未来研究的期许。谨以此书，致敬所有为文化记忆与非物质遗产保护而付出的人们。

In the process of compiling and editing Hearing Ruijin, what moved me most was not the outcome we can now present, but the memory of those who, through the dust of time, guarded and persevered in silence. The publication of this book is the fruit of several generations' dedication and effort.

First and foremost, I pay my deepest respect to my late grandfather, Mr. Zhong Tongrong (pen name Zhong Tongying, 1933-2018). Through decades of fieldwork and meticulous manuscript compilation, he preserved these precious folk song materials in their entirety. He measured the land with his footsteps and safeguarded its voices with his devotion, leaving us with an irreplaceable cultural legacy.

I wish to thank my grandmother, Mrs. Lin Meijuan. In those turbulent years,as an older generation of educators, she protected these manuscripts as if they were her very life. Without solemn declarations, she bore an extraordinary mission in an ordinary way: ensuring that no page was lost, and no name forgotten. Without her decades of quiet perseverance, *Listening to Ruijin* would hardly be possible today. Her guardianship forms the earliest and deepest foundation of this book.

I am also grateful to my father, Professor Liu Fang. As a musician, he dedicated immense effort to the proofreading and refinement of this volume, with the rigor of his scholarship and over sixty years of experience in music education. I also thank my mother, Professor Zhong Jian, whose expertise in vocal and piano pedagogy over forty years ,provided invaluable support to both the theoretical and practical dimensions of this book, passing her conviction on to generations of students.

My gratitude also extends to the countless villagers of Ruijin and the greater Gannan region. Without their heartfelt singing in fields and villages, these songs—born of turbulence yet rich with the fragrance of earth—would not have come into being.

I would like to express my sincere gratitude to the Weatherhead East Asian Institute at Columbia University for its academic support and for providing an essential platform for scholarly inquiry and exchange. I am especially indebted to Professor Xiaobo Lü, a distinguished political economist, whose guidance and intellectual insight have been instrumental in enabling me to pursue and advance this research within a cross-cultural analytical framework.

In the course of this work, I also received generous care and insightful advice from colleagues and families and friends in academia. Their contributions in scholarly exchange, methodological discussion, and publication guidance have been invaluable.

The publication of this book is not only a continuation of the work of earlier generations but also a promise for future research. I dedicate this book to all who have contributed to the preservation of cultural memory and the safeguarding of intangible heritage.

目录 / CONTENTS

第三章　艺术特征与表现手法

Chapter Three: Artistic Characteristics and Modes of Expression

第四章　《瑞金民歌歌曲集手稿》总目录（五册本）

Chapter Four: Listening to Ruijin: Complete Table of Contents (Five Volumes Edition)

第五章　七大类歌种的学术解读与影印呈现

Chapter Five: Academic Interpretation and Facsimile Presentation of the Seven Categories of Folk Songs

第二节　象征与隐喻的艺术语言
Section Two: The Artistic Language of Symbol and Metaphor

第三节　即兴与口传的创作机制
Section Three: The Creative Mechanism of Improvisation and Oral Transmission

01

第一章　瑞金民歌的历史与文化背景

Chapter One: The Historical and Cultural Context of Ruijin Folk Songs

01 瑞金的地理与人文环境

GEOGRAPHY AND CULTURAL SETTING OF RUIJIN

瑞金位于江西省东南部赣南地区，东邻福建，南接广东，地处武夷山与南岭余脉之间。境内群山环绕，河谷纵横，丘陵与盆地交错，形成了典型的山地农业社会。村落依山傍水而建，田畴环绕，稻作农业和多样化的副业构成了民众的生计方式。

这种地理环境造就了瑞金文化的独特性。由于交通不便和相对封闭，当地居民长期保持着自给自足的生产生活方式，同时也保留了丰富的口头传统与民间艺术。歌谣在田间地头自然生成，成为人们交流情感、传递经验的方式。

此外，瑞金自古以来是客家人聚居之地。客家先民自中原南迁，带来了北方的语言、习俗与宗族制度，与当地民俗融合，逐渐形成了独特的客家文化。方言的声腔、祠堂建筑、农耕礼俗，以及聚落的群体性格，无不体现出客家文化与地方环境的交融。

Ruijin is located in the southeastern part of Jiangxi Province, bordering Fujian to the east and Guangdong to the south. Nestled between the Wuyi Mountains and the Nanling ranges, its terrain is characterized by mountains, valleys, and interspersed basins, giving rise to a classic mountain-based agrarian society. Villages were typically built alongside rivers and hills, with rice cultivation and diversified subsistence activities forming the foundation of local livelihoods.

This geographical setting nurtured Ruijin's cultural distinctiveness. Owing to its relative isolation and poor transport links, local communities maintained self-sufficient ways of life and preserved a rich body of oral traditions and folk arts. Songs arose naturally from the rhythms of farming life, serving as vehicles for communication and emotional expression.

Ruijin has also been historically settled by the Hakka people. Migrating southward from the Central Plains, the Hakka brought with them northern linguistic features, customs, and clan structures. These gradually blended with local traditions, giving rise to a distinctive Hakka cultural identity, reflected in the tonal inflections of dialects, ancestral halls, agrarian rituals, and communal solidarity.

02 民歌的生活功能

THE SOCIAL FUNCTIONS OF FOLK SONGS

在瑞金，民歌不仅仅是艺术娱乐的形式，而是与日常生活紧密相连的文化实践。农耕劳动中的号子，节庆祭祀中的歌舞，男女青年在山野间的对唱山歌，都是民众日常生活的组成部分。

这些歌谣承载着多重功能。首先，它们是劳动的节奏器，在插秧、打谷、修堤等集体劳动中，号子统一了动作，增强了协作效率。其次，它们是社会交流的媒介，山歌对唱常常成为青年男女表达爱情、结识伴侣的重要方式。再次，民歌具有教育和记忆的功能，许多歌谣以简练的句式传递道德规范，或以歌声记录村落间的事件，使其成为“口头档案”。

In Ruijin, folk songs were not merely forms of artistic entertainment but cultural practices intertwined with daily life. Work chants accompanied farming, songs and dances enlivened rituals and festivals, while mountain songs—sung antiphonally by young men and women in the hills—were integral to social life.

These songs carried multiple functions. First, they served as rhythmic regulators of labor; chants unified movements and boosted efficiency in transplanting rice, threshing grain, or repairing dikes. Second, they acted as channels of social interaction, with antiphonal mountain songs providing young people with opportunities to express affection and form bonds. Third, folk songs fulfilled pedagogical and mnemonic roles; concise verses transmitted moral norms, while others preserved accounts of village events, rendering them an “oral archive” of communal memory.

03 革命年代的文化转折

CULTURAL TRANSFORMATIONS IN THE REVOLUTIONARY ERA

二十世纪三十年代，瑞金成为中央苏区的政治中心。随着社会与政治的剧烈变动，民歌的内容与功能也发生了转折。传统以爱情、劳动、自然为主题的歌谣，逐渐吸纳了革命叙事，形成了一批“红色民歌”。这些歌曲或记录红军，或描绘苏区新生活，或以歌声动员群众，成为革命宣传的重要工具。

这种转折说明，民间艺术并非静止的传统，而是与历史语境相互作用的动态产物。一方面，革命运动为民歌提供了新的题材与社会使命；另一方面，民歌作为民众最熟悉的艺术形式，也成为革命得以深入乡村的重要媒介。

In the 1930s, Ruijin became the political heart of the Central Soviet Area. Amidst the turbulence of social and political transformation, the content and functions of folk songs underwent a dramatic shift. Traditional songs about love, labor, and nature absorbed revolutionary narratives, giving rise to a repertoire of “red folk songs.” These depicted the Red Army, depicted the new life in the Soviet areas, and mobilized the populace through song, becoming vital instruments of revolutionary communication.

This transformation demonstrates that folk art was not a static tradition but a dynamic product shaped by historical contexts. On the one hand, the revolutionary movement furnished new themes and purposes for the songs; on the other, folk songs, being the art form most familiar to the masses, became crucial channels through which revolutionary messages permeated rural life.

04 田野采录与手稿的学术价值

THE SCHOLARLY VALUE OF FIELDWORK AND MANUSCRIPTS

二十世纪八十年代，钟同荣（笔名钟同荥）先生及其团队在瑞金及赣南地区展开了大规模田野采录。他们行程三万余里，访谈六百余位乡村歌手与艺人，手抄保存了一千余首民歌。这些手稿，既保留了地方民间艺术的原貌，也保存了三百余首中央苏区时期的革命歌曲。

手稿的学术价值体现在三个方面：第一，它们是民间口传文化的重要载体，保存了濒危的歌谣；第二，它们提供了历史研究的第一手资料，尤其是关于苏区社会生活的文化证据；第三，它们是跨学科研究的资源，涉及音乐学、人类学、社会史与翻译研究。

In the 1980s, Zhong Tongrong (pen name ZhongTongying) and his colleagues carried out extensive fieldwork in Ruijin and the wider Gannan region. Traveling over 30,000 li (approximately 15,000 kilometers), they interviewed more than 600 village singers and artists, and hand-copied over 1,000 songs. These manuscripts preserved both the original forms of local folk traditions and more than 300 revolutionary songs from the Soviet era.

The scholarly significance of the manuscripts lies in three areas: first, they serve as vital repositories of endangered oral traditions; second, they provide firsthand historical evidence, particularly cultural insights into Soviet area social life; and third, they constitute interdisciplinary resources, bridging musicology, anthropology, social history, and translation studies.

05 民歌与当代研究的对话

FOLK SONGS IN DIALOGUE WITH CONTEMPORARY SCHOLARSHIP

进入二十一世纪，随着跨文化研究、数字化与人工智能的发展，瑞金民歌的学术意义获得了新的延展。如何在跨语言语境中翻译与传播这些歌谣？如何利用数字技术建立声音档案，使之进入全球学术与公众视野？这些问题成为本书的重要出发点。

因此，本书不仅仅是文献的汇编，而是一个学术对话的平台。通过翻译与注释，民歌得以进入跨文化语境；通过数字化与出版，地方声音得以进入全球文化流通体系。这也是《听见瑞金》作为项目的核心追求。

In the twenty-first century, with the rise of cross-cultural studies, digitization, and artificial intelligence, the scholarly significance of Ruijin folk songs has been newly extended. How can these songs be translated and disseminated across linguistic boundaries? How can digital technologies be employed to build sound archives, bringing them into global scholarly and public view? These questions form a central point of departure for this book.

Thus, this work is not merely a compilation of documents but also a platform for scholarly dialogue. Through translation and annotation, the songs enter cross-cultural contexts; through digitization and publication, local voices become part of global cultural circulation. This is the core pursuit of the *Listening to Ruijin* project.

小结 / Summary

综观瑞金民歌的历史源流与地域特色，我们不难发现，它们既是乡土生活的自然回响，也是文化身份的集体铭刻。民歌在田野间生长，却在历史的激荡中获得了超越日常的意义。它们承载着语言的节奏、情感的肌理与社会的记忆，既连接了个体与土地，也联结了群体与历史。

本章所呈现的民歌谱系，不仅是地方文化的艺术印记，更是后续章节展开具体分析与影印呈现的基础。可以说，它为我们理解瑞金民歌的精神底色与文化逻辑奠定了坐标，也提示我们：唯有在历史与现实的对话中，这些歌声才会真正焕发生命的回响。

A survey of the historical origins and regional characteristics of Ruijin folk songs reveals that they are both the natural echoes of rural life and the collective imprints of cultural identity. Rooted in the soil of everyday existence, these songs have acquired meanings that transcend the ordinary through the turbulence of history. They embody the rhythm of language, the texture of emotions, and the memory of society—linking individuals to the land and communities to their shared past.

The folk song lineage outlined in this chapter serves not only as an artistic hallmark of local culture but also as the foundation for the detailed analyses and manuscript reproductions in the following chapters. In this sense, it establishes the coordinates for understanding the spiritual essence and cultural logic of Ruijin folk songs, reminding us that only through dialogue between history and the present can these voices truly resonate with vitality.

02

第二章　文艺运动的条件与特点

Chapter Two: Conditions and Characteristics of the Cultural Movement

01 社会文化基础

SOCIAL AND CULTURAL FOUNDATIONS

20 世纪 30 年代初，瑞金及其周边地区的社会结构与文化传统为文艺活动的展开提供了坚实土壤。以农耕为主的乡村社会，依靠血缘与地缘维系，形成了稳定的村落网络与礼俗秩序。民间音乐、舞蹈与口头叙事深嵌于日常生活：从农事节令到婚丧嫁娶，从集体劳作到节庆聚会，“以歌言志、以歌言情”成为常态。口耳相传的机制让作品具备了高度的可扩散性；而村社内部的共同记忆，则为文艺提供了持续的受众与在场性。在此意义上，文艺不是外加的装饰，而是乡土社会运行方式的一部分。

In the early 1930s, the social structure and cultural traditions of Ruijin and its neighboring areas provided fertile ground for the development of cultural activities. Predominantly agrarian villages, bonded by kinship and locality, formed stable networks and ritual orders. Music, dance, and oral narratives were embedded in daily life—from agricultural seasons to life-cycle ceremonies, from collective labor to festive gatherings. Oral transmission ensured wide diffusion, while communal memory supplied a consistent audience and a sense of presence. Cultural practice was thus not an external embellishment but integral to the functioning of rural society.

02 群众性与参与度

MASS PARTICIPATION AND INCLUSIVITY

这一时期的文艺活动呈现出显著的群众性。表演者多为普通村民：农人、手工业者、青少年皆可即兴参与；“旧曲新词”“你唱我和”“问答对歌”等形式降低了参与门槛并提升了互动密度。文本来源贴近日常经验，场景多在田头、圩日、庙会、祠堂等公共空间。由于“创作—表演—再传播”常在同一社会场域内快速循环，作品能在短期内获得较高的可见度与记忆度，形成带有地方风格的“公共曲库”。

Cultural activities displayed a distinctly mass-oriented character. Performers were ordinary villagers—farmers, artisans, and youth—who participated spontaneously. Practices such as “new lyrics to old tunes,” call-and-response, and antiphonal singing lowered barriers and enhanced interaction. Texts drew directly from everyday experience, and performances took place in fields, markets, temples, and ancestral halls. Because creation, performance, and re-circulation occurred rapidly within the same social milieu, pieces achieved visibility and memorability in a short time, forming a localized “public repertoire.”

03 地方语言与艺术风格

LOCAL LANGUAGE AND ARTISTIC STYLE

瑞金地区以客家方言为主，语音的声调与节律深刻影响旋律走向与分句方式。民歌多以五声音阶为骨架，旋律线条简洁而可延展，常见“拖腔”“回环”等唱法，便于山地环境中的远距离传唱。歌词语言口语化却富诗性，擅用比兴、对偶、顶真与排比；意象多取自身边山川草木与农事器具，呈现“以景寓情、以物达意”的表达传统。舞蹈、说唱、灯戏等地方元素的互渗，使整体风格既统一又多样。

Hakka dialects predominant in Ruijin shaped melodic contour and phrasing through tonal and rhythmic features. Most songs are pentatonic, with succinct yet extensible lines and techniques such as sustained notes and circular phrases, suitable for long-distance singing in mountainous terrain. Lyrics are colloquial yet poetic, employing metaphor, parallelism, anadiplosis, and gradation. Imagery is drawn from local landscapes and agrarian tools, embodying an expressive tradition that projects feeling through scenery and meaning through objects. Interpenetration with regional dance, narrative singing, and lantern theatre yields a style that is both coherent and diverse.

04 历史语境中的功能转换

FUNCTIONAL SHIFTS WITHIN THE HISTORICAL CONTEXT

随着社会环境的深刻变化，文艺的功能发生了显著转换。除娱乐与抒情之外，作品逐步承担信息沟通、群体认同与历史记述的任务：现实处境、价值观念与共同经验以口头文本的方式被快速汇集和扩散。“传统形式 + 新的叙述主题”的组合，使既有曲调获得新生命。功能转换并非对传统的断裂，而是传统在新情境中的延续性重构：沿用熟悉的旋律与表演程式，纳入当下经验与集体议题，从而实现文化表达的历史更新。

As the broader environment changed, the functions of cultural expression shifted. Beyond entertainment and sentiment, works increasingly mediated information, fostered group identity, and recorded collective experience. The combination of traditional forms with new narratives gave established tunes renewed life. This transformation did not sever tradition; rather, it reconstituted continuity by embedding contemporary concerns within familiar melodies and formats, producing historical renewal in cultural expression.

05 艺术与社会的互动机制

MECHANISMS OF INTERACTION BETWEEN ART AND SOCIETY

文艺与社会现实之间形成了循环互动：

1. 题材供给——日常生活与重大事件源源不断地为文本与表演提供素材；

2. 情感整合——共同演唱与群体观看促进情绪共鸣与价值协商；

3. 记忆固化——高频演唱与礼俗嵌入使作品成为地方公共记忆的一部分；

4. 版本演化——口耳传播导致句式增删、意象替换、调式微调，生成地方“变体链”。

由此，文艺既是社会生活的镜像，也是推动地方社会沟通与整合的媒介。

The relationship between art and society operated through cyclical interaction:

1.Thematic supply—everyday life and major events continually furnished material;

2.Affective integration—communal singing and shared spectatorship generated emotional resonance and value negotiation;

3.Mnemonic consolidation—frequent performance and ritual embedding turned pieces into elements of public memory;

4.**Variant evolution**—oral transmission produced additions and omissions, imagery substitutions, and modal tweaks, generating chains of local variants.

Thus, cultural practice mirrored social life while serving as a medium for communication and integration.

小结 / Summary

本章基于乡土社会结构、语言—音乐耦合与公共空间的在场性，说明了瑞金地区文艺实践的“高参与—强互动—快扩散”的机制，以及在历史语境中完成的功能转换。这一框架为后续的艺术分析、类型谱系与文本导读提供了方法论支点。

Grounded in rural structures, the coupling of language and music, and the presence of public spaces, this chapter has outlined mechanisms of high participation, strong interaction, and rapid diffusion, alongside functional shifts within historical settings. This framework underpins the subsequent analyses of artistic form, typological mapping, and guided readings of the manuscripts.

03

第三章　艺术特征与表现手法

Chapter Three: Artistic Characteristics and Modes of Expression

01 旋律与音调结构

MELODIC AND TONAL STRUCTURES

瑞金民歌的旋律以五声音阶为基础，整体音域偏窄，多在六度至八度之间。旋律线条简洁而富于张力，常通过“上行渐进—下行收束”的结构制造情绪张弛。由于客家方言的声调特征，曲调与语言之间呈现“声腔同构”的关系：句末常用长音或滑音，以呼应语音的降调趋势。拖腔、倚音、倚拍等装饰性唱法丰富了旋律层次，使得同一旋律在不同场合可延展为多样化的表达。

Ruijin folk songs are fundamentally pentatonic, with a relatively narrow range spanning about a sixth to an octave. The melodic contour is succinct yet tension-filled, often shaped by “ascending progression–descending closure” patterns to balance expansion and resolution. Influenced by Hakka tonal features, melodies display “phonetic-musical isomorphism,” with final syllables elongated or glided to echo falling tones. Ornamentations such as sustained notes, appoggiaturas, and anticipatory rhythms enrich the melodic texture, allowing flexible adaptation across different performance contexts.

02 节奏与律动

RHYTHM AND METER

节奏多为自由散板，依歌手呼吸与语义自然延展，兼有一定的均拍性。劳动歌与行军歌则强调节拍规整，与动作节律密切结合，形成“声—身”同步的韵律系统。多声部与呼应式演唱常在节奏层面制造张力：领唱者以自由节拍铺陈，合唱部分则用齐整节奏回应，形成“松—紧—松”的节奏张力。这样的律动机制既保证了歌曲在山野间的传播力，又强化了集体行动的协同性。

Rhythm is frequently free and speech-based, extending according to breath and semantics while retaining traces of regular meter. Work songs and marching songs, however, stress strict beats synchronized with bodily motion, creating a system of “voice–body” rhythm. Antiphonal and multi-part singing generate rhythmic tension: leaders employ freer pacing while the chorus responds with strict meter, yielding a dynamic cycle of relaxation and tightening. This rhythmic mechanism not only facilitated transmission in open landscapes but also enhanced coordination in collective labor or mobilization.

03 歌词与修辞

LYRICS AND RHETORICAL STRATEGIES

歌词语言口语化而富于诗意，善于借助比兴、对仗与顶真等修辞手法。

- 比兴：通过自然意象暗喻人事，如“青山不老”寓意坚贞。
- 对仗：多见于对歌场景，两句平行句式形成思维与音声的平衡。
- 顶真：句末与句首的衔接，制造连环效果，增强记忆性。

此外，象征性意象频繁出现：山川草木常寓友情与爱情，农具器物折射劳动与生活。修辞功能不仅在于审美装饰，更在于帮助歌者在即兴演唱中快速组织文本，维持表演的流畅性。

The lyrics are colloquial yet poetic, frequently employing metaphor, parallelism, and anadiplosis.

- Metaphor (bixing): Natural imagery is used to symbolize human affairs, e.g., “evergreen mountains” implying loyalty.
- Parallelism: Common in antiphonal contexts, where paired structures balance thought and sound.
- Anadiplosis: Linking the end of one line with the beginning of the next, creating a chain effect that strengthens memorability.

Symbolic imagery abounds: landscapes signify friendship or love, while agricultural tools reflect labor and livelihood. Such rhetorical devices serve not merely as ornament but also as improvisational aids, allowing singers to compose fluently in performance.

04 表演空间与互动形式

PERFORMANCE SPACES AND INTERACTIVE FORMS

瑞金民歌的表演往往与特定空间紧密相连：

- 田间地头：劳动歌以节奏统一劳动动作，声音在开阔环境中远距离传播。
- 圩场庙会：对歌与灯歌常在临时搭建的戏台或集市空地展开，观众可随时加入。
- 祠堂与家屋：婚丧仪礼中的歌唱与说唱具有仪式性，强调社会秩序与伦理规范。

互动形式上，常见“你唱我和”“男女对唱”“群体合唱”三种模式。表演空间与互动形式的结合，使民歌不仅是艺术事件，更是社会关系的在场实践。

Performance is closely tied to specific spaces:

- Fields: Work songs synchronized labor actions, projecting voices across open landscapes.
- Markets and Festivals: Antiphonal songs and lantern songs occurred on makeshift stages or open squares, where audiences could spontaneously participate.
- Ancestral Halls and Homes: Ritual songs in weddings and funerals reinforced social order and ethical norms.

Interactive modes included solo–chorus response, male–female duets, and group unison singing. The convergence of space and interaction rendered folk songs not only artistic events but also enactments of social relations.

05 即兴性与变体生成

IMPROVISATION AND THE MAKING OF VARIANTS

瑞金民歌具有高度即兴性。歌者可根据现场情境与听众反应调整歌词与旋律：

- 歌词变体：常见于对歌场合，因应语境而改换人名、地名与事件。
- 旋律变体：在保持基本骨架的前提下，拖腔长短与节拍松紧因人而异。
- 表演策略：歌手之间的“攻防”互动往往推动文本向更复杂或更机智的方向发展。

这种即兴性使民歌成为“开放文本”，在传唱中不断衍生变体，形成庞大的语料链条。这种“生成性传统”正是瑞金民歌的核心艺术特质之一。

Ruijin folk songs are highly improvisational. Singers adapt lyrics and melodies to situational contexts and audience responses:

- Textual variants: Names, places, and events are substituted to match the immediate setting.
- Melodic variants: Within a stable framework, sustain lengths and rhythmic elasticity vary by performer.
- Performance strategies: Antiphonal “attacks and defenses” often propel texts toward greater complexity and wit.

This improvisational quality renders folk songs “open texts,” continually generating variants through performance. Such generative tradition constitutes one of the core artistic characteristics of Ruijin folk culture.

小结 / Summary

本章从旋律、节奏、歌词、表演空间与即兴机制五个维度，揭示了瑞金民歌的艺术特征与表现手法。其核心特质在于：旋律的声调化、节奏的动作化、歌词的修辞化、空间的社会化与文本的生成性。这些特征不仅构成地方艺术风貌，也奠定了民歌在社会功能中的独特价值。

This chapter has examined five dimensions—melody, rhythm, lyrics, performance spaces, and improvisation—to uncover the artistic characteristics of Ruijin folk songs. Their defining traits include tonalized melody, action-based rhythm, rhetorical lyrics, socialized performance spaces, and generative textuality. These features not only define local aesthetics but also underpin the distinctive social functions of the folk tradition.

04

第四章 《瑞金民歌歌曲集手稿》总目录（五册本）

Chapter Four: Listening to Ruijin: Complete Table of Contents (Five Volumes Edition)

本章所呈现的，是钟同荣（笔名钟同荥）先生在二十世纪八十年代整理的《瑞金民歌歌曲集手稿》原始五册编次与目录。

其目的在于展示史料保存的原貌与整体框架，便于学术研究者理解手稿的历史编目方式。

需要说明的是，本章仅提供“总目录”，不附手稿影印。完整的手稿影印，将结合学术分类，统一收录于第五章。

This chapter presents the original five-volume arrangement and catalog of the *Ruijin Folk Song Manuscripts* compiled by Mr. Zhong Tongrong (pen name Zhong Tongying) in the 1980s.

Its purpose is to display the archival structure and original preservation format, enabling researchers to better understand the historical organization of the manuscripts.

It should be noted that this chapter provides only the “catalogue” and does not include manuscript facsimiles. The full facsimile reproductions are integrated with scholarly classification in Chapter Five.

第一册 • 传统民歌集 | VOLUME I · TRADITIONAL FOLK SONGS I

《瑞金民歌》

前　言

瑞金县地处赣省南端，接壤于闽，毗邻粤山，四季常绿，又有绵水西汇赣江，故环境秀丽，气候宜人。第二次国内革命战争时期，这里是中央民主政府所在地。

上述特定的自然环境和历史条件，使我县产生了大量的革命历史民歌和传统民歌。据历史查考，我县民歌的沿革大概起于嘉靖年间。据《瑞金县志》记载："采子桂林处人集于亭庭或歌窈窕之章，或为幽兰白雪之曲，或咏秋风黄竹之辞，莫不同祖风骚，妙谐音律。"从此勤耕苦作的农夫从庭院到山野，到处唱歌，以歌传情，以声传意，抒发自己的内心感情和意志。它是封建社会制度下农民反抗统治阶级的剥削压迫，反对旧封建，旧礼教向往新生活，进行阶级斗争和生产斗争的纪实。也是他们遭受黑暗与痛苦生活的真实写照。

瑞金民歌从调性上说，以五声羽调式为多，徵调式的也不少，商调式的也有一部分，宫调和角调式的较少见。所以曲调比较抒情，对于联系实，形象的比喻手法比较多，往往是借景说情，寄言寄意，上句起兴，下句点题，画龙点睛。如郑坊山歌："过了一窝又一窝，这窝竹子尾拖拖，竹子低头食露水，妹子低头寻情哥"等。在创作手法上与其他文艺作品有不同之处。歌词大都是用民间语言组成，既通俗又形象。说起就起，一开头就是用形象反映内容，说落就落，不受任何束缚，语言生动、活泼，理性说教很少，感情朴实、真挚，唱起来朗朗上口，听起来娓娓动人，易教易唱，易学易记，易于普及。

在作曲的技法上，与学院派的作曲法有很大差异，曲式结构不是那么规整，一般以四句式二段体的为多，也有五句式和六句式三段体的。节奏安排比较灵活。在同一曲调中常常反复出现 2/4 3/4 或 4/4，音程跳跃有时比较特殊，有时旋律重复很巧妙，自然。它与人民群众的生活习俗非常接近，笑语言谈，喜怒哀乐，融合在一起，形成了音乐形象上的地方特色。

瑞金民歌分布很广，遍及整个瑞金城乡。但是由于山地、平原、河流和毗邻县的影响，民歌的格调、流行都有些不同。绵江沿岸的平原地带，民歌比较多，山区，高亢辽阔的山歌多，民歌小调少。文化比较发达的集镇如九堡、壬田等公社则小调较为流行，山歌茶歌较少，而铜钵山盛产茶叶附以方圆数十里茶歌（茶灯）比较盛行。而靠近宁都的瑞林大柏地等公社则三角班的采调颇为流传。壬田的罗汉岩，云石山的猫子寨，九堡的九龙岩，叶坪的东华山等地都有庵堂庙宇和道法，这一带地方还不同程度的流行道教音乐。

解放以来，由于党和政府对民间艺术的重视，在上级党委的领导下，由文化馆组织力量，对这些民歌、小调等进行过二次搜集和整理，分别于1960年和1962年油印上报。虽然搜集不够全面，遗漏很多，但仍然取得一定的成绩。曾经一度，由于林彪、"四人帮"极左路线的干扰破坏，把这些优秀的民间艺术遗产污之为"情郎妹子"、"庸俗"、"低级"、"下流"，最后以毒草定罪付之一炬。使我县民歌搜集整理工作遭到严重破坏。

现在，根据中央文化部、中国音协和省、地文化主管部门下达的文件指示精神，在县委县革委的直接领导下，为了发掘整理民族文化遗产，使之更好地"为人民服务，为社会主义服务"。我们又重新组织力量深入下去进行采风、挖掘。迄今为止已搜集了革命历史民歌127首，传统民歌59首，小调60首，山歌31首，灯歌41首，共318首。革命历史民歌已于1979年付印。现将传统民歌、小调、山歌和灯歌等共计191首，汇集成册，定名"瑞金民歌选（第一集）"。这是一部民族历史资料。依据上级指示"要尽量保持民歌原貌"的精神，我们只作少量的整理和修改，尽量做到"保持原词原曲"精华糟粕相杂共同，内容也很不完整。有多段词的我们都只采用一、二段，漏选的还有很多，因此仅作内部参考之用。加之人手不足，水平不高，缺点错误一定不少。望广大音乐专门家、民间艺人、民间歌手和音乐工作者，希多提宝贵意见，使瑞金民歌选（第二集）的整理出版更为完善。

本歌选承蒙音乐专门家刘天浪、解策励、李镇华、杨襄铭等同志和民间艺人欧可银、民间歌手刘发娇、江桂英以及业余音乐工作者杨德坡、方德林、刘先梯、马秉仁、钟盛琳、钟时祥等同志大力帮助，共同搜集整理，在此一并表示感谢！

瑞金文化馆
一九八〇年七月一日

注：凡歌名右上角标有△者均有音响资料。

目录

民歌

小 调

山 歌

灯 歌

茶 灯

花 鼓 灯

迎 亲 灯

民歌 / Folk songs

导读

“民歌”是民众在日常生活与社会交往中自发创作、口耳相传的歌唱形式，具有地方性与口语化的特征。它们既是劳动与生活的写照，也是情感与文化的表达。赣南地区的民歌以真挚质朴、旋律自由、即兴性强著称，常见于田间劳作、山野对唱、节庆场合。民歌的内容广泛，既有表现自然风光与乡村风情的抒情曲调，也有青年男女即兴唱和的爱情歌谣。这些作品不仅是群众生活的艺术再现，更是研究当地社会历史与文化心理的重要材料。

Introduction

Folk Songs are spontaneous forms of singing created and orally transmitted by ordinary people in the course of daily life and social interaction. They are marked by their regional flavor, colloquial style, and improvisational nature. In southern Jiangxi, folk songs are known for their sincerity, simplicity, and flexible melodic patterns, often sung in the fields, in the mountains, or during festive gatherings. Their themes are wide-ranging, from lyrical depictions of natural landscapes and rural scenery to love duets improvised by young men and women. These songs are not only artistic reflections of communal life but also valuable sources for understanding the local social history and cultural psychology.

小调 / Xiaodiao – Minor Tunes

导读

曲调轻快，内容多与日常生活、娱乐、嬉戏相关。常见于节庆或集镇，具有雅俗共赏的特征。

Introduction

Light and playful tunes reflecting everyday life and festive entertainment, popular in market towns and communal gatherings.

山歌集 / Shan’ ge – Mountain Songs

导读

山歌多为青年男女对唱，抒发爱情、友情，具有即兴性与机智的语言特征。旋律以五声音阶为主，简洁流畅，充满地方色彩。

Introduction

Shan'ge are antiphonal love songs among young men and women, marked by improvisation, wit, and lyrical simplicity, often in pentatonic scales.

灯歌 / Dengge – Lantern Songs

导读

多在节庆、庙会和灯节中传唱，曲调明快，常带有表演性和热闹气氛。

Introduction

Performed during lantern festivals and temple fairs, featuring lively rhythms and performative elements.

1. 劳动茶歌 / Tea-Picking Labor Songs

导读

“劳动茶歌”是流行于江西、福建、湖南等地茶区的一种民间歌谣。它多在采茶、制茶的劳动过程中即兴唱出，既有调动劳动节奏、驱散疲倦的功能，也寄托了茶农的情感与生活智慧。茶歌常以男女对唱的形式出现，内容涉及劳动场景、自然风物以及青年男女的爱情情愫，兼具实用性与抒情性。

Introduction

Tea-Picking Labor Songs are a type of folk singing tradition popular in tea-growing regions such as Jiangxi, Fujian, and Hunan. They are usually improvised during tea-picking and tea-making work, serving both to regulate the rhythm of labor and to relieve fatigue. These songs often take the form of antiphonal singing between men and women, with lyrics that depict scenes of agricultural life, the surrounding natural landscape, and romantic feelings among young people. They embody both practical and lyrical functions, blending everyday labor with cultural expression.

2. 花鼓灯歌 / Flower Drum Lantern Songs

导读

“花鼓灯歌”源自中原地区的民间歌舞形式，后来在赣南与闽粤交界一带也广为流传。它往往与舞蹈、灯会、节庆活动结合，具有浓厚的表演性和娱人性。歌声明快，节奏感强，多在元宵、庙会、婚庆等场合演唱，以渲染喜庆气氛，表达吉祥祝愿。歌词内容丰富，既有对民间生活的描绘，也包含幽默风趣的调侃。作为民俗仪式歌的一支，花鼓灯歌既展现了地方性的艺术特征，又反映了社区共同体的文化认同。

Introduction

Flower Drum Lantern Songs originated from folk singing-and-dancing traditions in central China and later spread widely in the border regions of southern Jiangxi, Fujian, and Guangdong. Closely tied to festive performances, lantern fairs, and communal celebrations, they are highly performative and entertaining in nature. Characterized by lively melodies and strong rhythmic patterns, these songs are frequently sung during the Lantern Festival, temple fairs, and weddings, creating an atmosphere of joy and auspicious blessing. Their lyrics are diverse, ranging from depictions of everyday folk life to humorous banter. As a branch of ritual and festive songs, Flower Drum Lantern Songs embody distinctive regional aesthetics while reinforcing the cultural identity of local communities.

3. 迎亲灯歌 / Wedding Procession Lantern Songs

导读

“迎亲灯歌”是传统婚嫁礼俗中一种独特的表演性民歌，常与舞灯、花鼓等民俗表演结合，营造热烈、喜庆的氛围。在赣南与周边地区，迎亲仪式不仅是家庭与家族的婚礼庆典，也是整个村落共同参与的文化活动。迎亲灯歌多在迎亲队伍行进过程中演唱，伴随灯火、锣鼓与舞蹈，歌词既有祝福新人和婚姻幸福的内容，也包含调侃、即兴对唱等成分，充满生活气息与民间智慧。它在音乐形态上多为节奏鲜明、旋律流畅的曲调，便于集体合唱，烘托仪式的庄重与热烈。

Introduction

Wedding Procession Lantern Songs are a distinctive type of folk song performed during traditional marriage ceremonies, often accompanied by lantern dances, flower drum performances, and other festive rituals to create a lively and jubilant atmosphere. In southern Jiangxi and surrounding regions, the wedding procession was not only a family event but also a communal celebration involving the entire village. These songs were typically sung along the wedding route, accompanied by lanterns, drums, and dancing. The lyrics conveyed blessings for the bride and groom, hopes for marital happiness, as well as humorous banter and improvised exchanges that reflected the wit of the community. Musically, they feature clear rhythms and flowing melodies suitable for group singing, amplifying both the solemnity and festivity of the ritual.

第二册 • 传统民歌集 II / VOLUME II · TRADITIONAL FOLK SONGS II

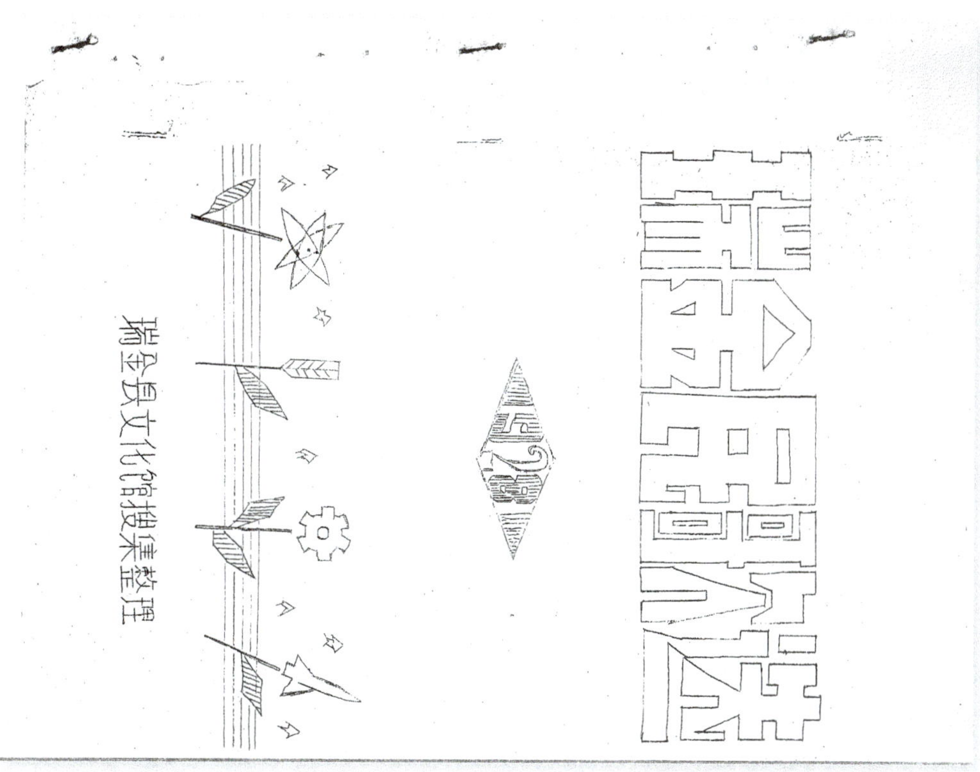

《瑞金民歌》第二集说明

在县委、县政府的领导下，我们派出专人搜集到各类民歌400首，已于1980年编印成册印《瑞金民歌》第一集。现将新搜集的100多首精选部分刻印为《瑞金民歌》第二集。本集共选编各类民歌55首，其中：山歌27首，灯歌2首，茶歌3首，小调12首，劳动号子1首，风俗歌9首，生活音调1首。因水平所限，一定存在不少缺点，请广大音乐工作者指正。

瑞金民歌分布很广，由于人手少，时间短，我们未全面普查收集，有待今后继续完成。

瑞金县文化馆

1981.12.1.

附：瑞金行政区划图（草）

瑞金民歌歌种分布图

瑞金民歌色彩区图

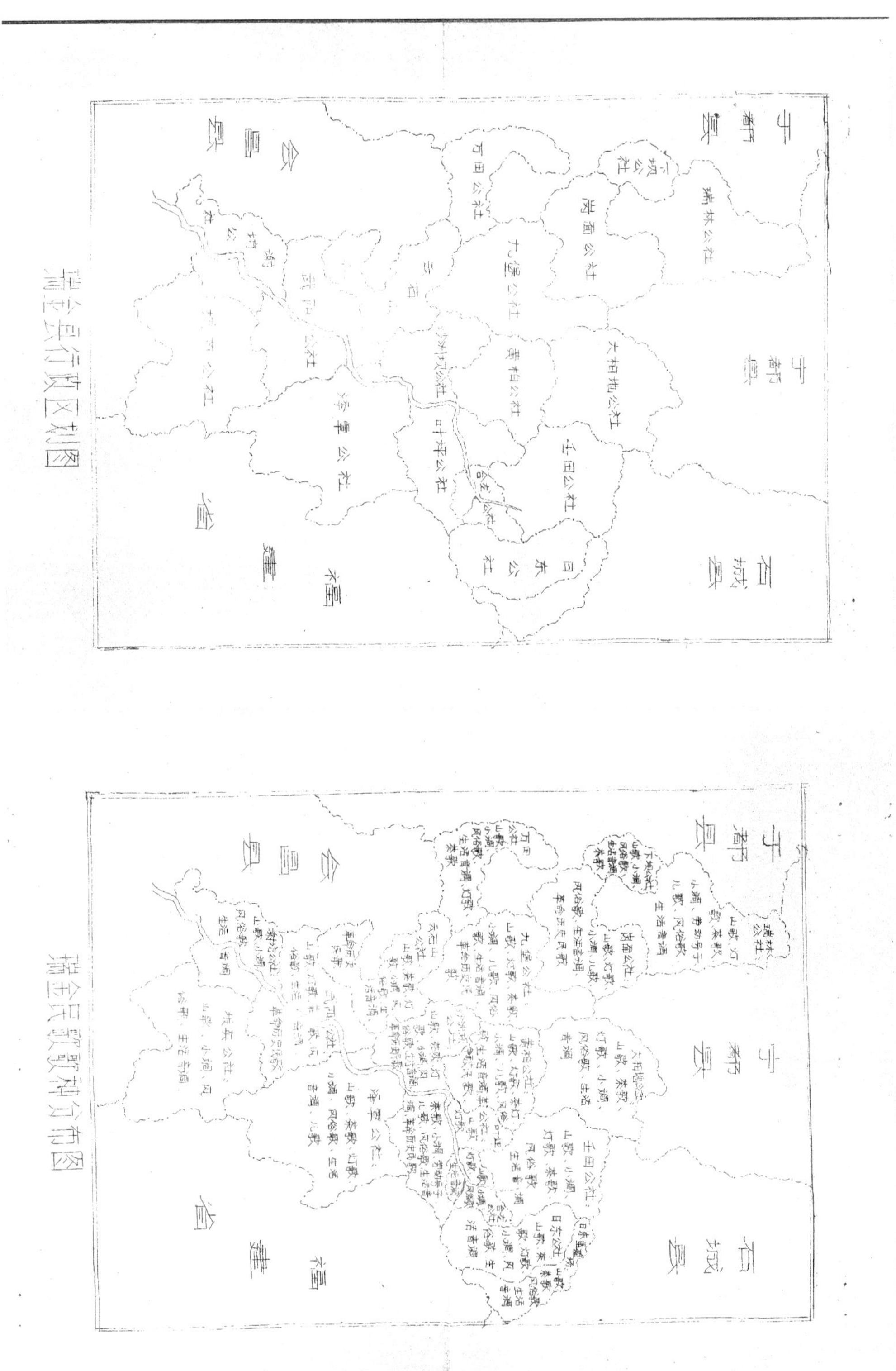

瑞金县行政区划图

瑞金县民歌歌种分布图

瑞金民歌色彩区图

《瑞金民歌》第二集目录

一、山歌

山歌 / Shan'　ge – Mountain Songs

灯歌 / Dengge – Lantern Songs

茶歌 / Cha'　ge – Tea Songs

小调 / Xiaodiao – Minor Tunes

劳动号子 / Labor Cries and Chants

导读

号子类歌谣，常见于搬运、打桩等体力劳动，声调高亢有力，具有协调与鼓舞功能。

Introduction

Work chants used in heavy labor, with forceful rhythms to synchronize effort and boost morale.

风俗歌 / Ritual and Custom Songs

生活音调 / Everyday Tunes

导读

贴近日常生活的即兴小唱，往往生动幽默，表现百姓的生活智慧。

Introduction

Improvised songs rooted in daily life, humorous and vivid, reflecting folk wisdom.

第三册 · 传统民歌集 III / VOLUME III · TRADITIONAL FOLK SONGS III

瑞金民歌

（第三集）

1982.12.

瑞金县文化馆搜集整理

编者的话

遵照中央文化部、中国音乐家协会和省、地、县各级党和政府的指示，我们继搜集整理《瑞金民歌》第一集、第二集之后，对本县的一部分社、队进行了民歌普查。现又搜集到各类民歌100多首，经过筛选，整理出山歌29首，灯歌1首，小调37首，风俗歌15首，生活音调5首，共87首，刻印为《瑞金民歌》第三集分送上级有关单位。因时间和水平的局限，缺点在所难免，望音乐工作者订正。同时为了更好挖掘民间音乐资料，抢救民族文化遗产，希广大群众和音乐工作者共同帮助我们，继续对我县民间音乐进行搜集和整理。

瑞金县文化馆

一九八二年十二月三十一日

目录

一、山歌

二、灯歌

三、小调

山歌 / Shan’ ge – Mountain Songs

灯歌 / Dengge – Lantern Songs

小调 / Xiaodiao – Minor Tunes

风俗歌 / Ritual and Custom Songs

导读

“风俗歌”是与特定民间习俗、社会礼仪和生活仪式相联系的歌谣，通常在婚嫁、节庆、岁时祭祀以及村落公共活动中演唱。这类歌谣不仅具有娱乐与抒情的功能，更承担着社会教育与文化传承的作用。歌词往往包含祝福、规训、劝诫或叙事内容，体现了民间社会的价值观与伦理秩序。赣南地区的风俗歌与地方信仰、节令习惯紧密相连，既是社区日常生活的一部分，也构成了民众认同与集体记忆的重要载体。

Introduction

Customary Songs are folk songs associated with specific local customs, social rituals, and communal practices, often performed during weddings, seasonal festivals, ancestral worship, and village gatherings. Beyond entertainment and lyrical expression, these songs serve as vehicles of social instruction and cultural transmission. Their lyrics frequently include blessings, admonitions, moral guidance, or narratives, reflecting the values and ethical order of folk society. In southern Jiangxi, customary songs are closely intertwined with local belief systems and calendrical traditions, forming an integral part of everyday communal life and serving as vital carriers of collective memory and cultural identity.

生活音调 / Everyday Tunes

第四册 • 传统民歌集 IV/ VOLUME IV · TRADITIONAL FOLK SONGS IV

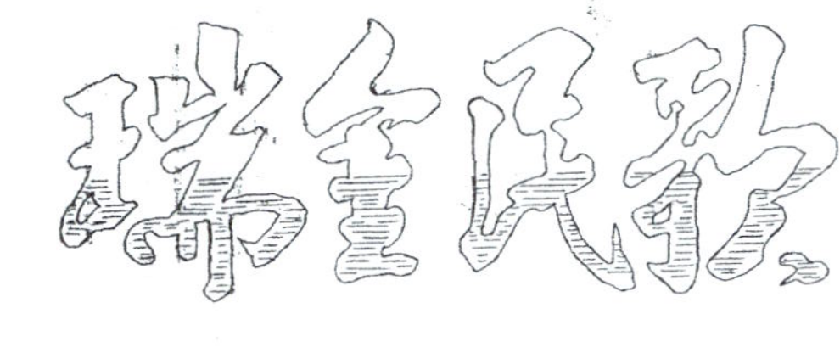

（第四集）

《内部资料》

1983.12.

瑞金县文化馆搜集整理

编辑说明

按照中央文化部、中国音乐家协会和省、地、县文化主管部门关于民歌普查的工作部署，我县继《瑞金民歌》第一、二、三集编辑付印上送之后，为了善始善终地完成这一工作，我们又继续派出专人下去对未普查的公社、大队、山乡、村镇进行了普查工作。搜集到各类民歌近300首，经过鉴别整理出山歌56首，灯歌50首，小调79首，风俗歌25首，生活音调13首，共222首。附印成册，称《瑞金民歌》第四集，分别呈送上级有关单位审查存档和作为民间音乐借鉴参考。因为时间、人力、水平所限，整理粗糙，缺点难免，祈请广大音乐行家、音乐爱好者批评订正。

瑞金县文化馆

一九八三年十二月

目　录

一、山　歌

（1

二、灯 歌

三、小　调

13

四、风俗歌

五、生活音调

山歌 / Shan’ ge – Mountain Songs

灯歌 / Dengge – Lantern Songs

小调 / Xiaodiao – Minor Tunes

风俗歌 / Ritual and Custom Songs

生活音调 / Everyday Tunes

第五册 · 革命历史民歌集 / VOLUME V · REVOLUTIONARY FOLK SONGS

以下内容均为 1930 年代苏区流传版本，保持原貌，以供研究。

The following **materials** are preserved in their original form as they circulated in the Central Soviet Area during the 1930s, and are presented here for research purposes.

目　　录

1

2

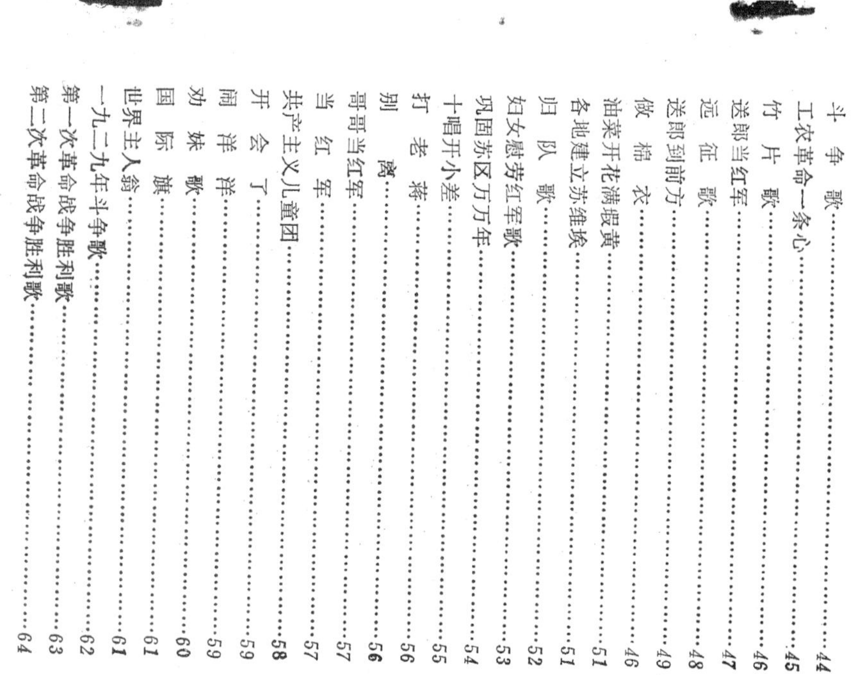

编者的话

为了隆重纪念伟大领袖毛主席率领中国工农红军向赣南闽西进军和中华苏维埃政府成立，两个五十周年，我们搜集整理了这本一百三十首的《苏区革命歌曲选》。

这些歌曲在第二次国内革命战争时期，我县武阳、沙洲坝、叶坪、大柏地、泽谭、云石山、九堡、壬田等地广为流传。当时它紧密配合政治运动，充分利用文艺这一武器，激发了苏区人民对敌人的仇恨和斗争，鼓午了红军的士气。描绘了红军的坚强、果敢和革命的乐观主义精神。五十年来瑞金人民没有忘却这些革命歌曲，即使在国民党反动派横行的白色恐怖日子里，他们仍然暗暗地传唱。谢秀英、谢柳贤等苏区老演员和许多人民群众，还冒着生命危险，千方百计地在墙洞里把苏区歌本保存了下来。解放后，我们对这些苏区革命歌曲分别在一九五八年和一九六〇年作过两次搜集整理和出版。可是由于"四人邦"的干扰破坏，他们以破"四旧"为名把这些慷慨激昂、富有革命英雄气魄的苏区革命歌曲也夷为灰尘。打倒"四人邦"，文艺大解放。在英明领袖华主席的亲切关怀下，苏区革命歌曲这朵鲜花才重放异采。

《苏区革命歌曲选》是在中共瑞金县委宣传部、瑞金县文化教育局的直接领导下，由革命老前辈和广大业余音乐工作者的大力协助整理出来的。因为时间匆促和水平的限制，缺点错误在所难免，望广大工农兵群众和文艺工作爱好者提出宝贵意见，并继续提供有关音乐资料，使之更加完善。我们所搜集整理过程中曾得到赣南师专中文科的师生和江西大学中文系老师的大力支持和帮助，在此表示感谢。

瑞 金 文 化 馆

导读

“革命历史民歌”产生于二十世纪三十年代的中央苏区，是在土地革命、工农武装斗争及长征等特定历史语境中流传的民间歌谣。这些作品以口耳相传的方式记录社会变迁与集体经验，既反映了普通民众的生活与情感，也承载了革命历史的集体记忆，是红色文化遗产的重要组成部分。

Introduction

Revolutionary Folk Songs of the Central Soviet Area emerged in the 1930s during **a historically specific context** of the Central Soviet Region. Rooted in the Land Reform, workers' and peasants' armed struggles, and the experiences of the Long March, these songs were orally transmitted among the populace. They document social transformation and collective experience, reflecting both the everyday lives and emotions of ordinary people as well as the shared memory of revolutionary history, making them a significant component of China's revolutionary folk heritage.

05

第五章　七大类歌种的学术解读与影印呈现

Chapter Five: Academic Interpretation and Facsimile Presentation of the Seven Categories of Folk Songs

本章以七大类民歌为框架，结合学术导读与手稿影印，系统呈现《瑞金民歌》资料的全貌。

以下内容均为 1930 年代苏区流传版本，保持原貌，以供研究。

与第四章依据原始手稿的分册目录不同，本章采用研究分类的视角，将手稿依其题材与功能划分为七大类型：山歌、民歌、小调、灯歌、风俗歌与茶歌、生活音调、革命历史民歌。

每一类均由中英文导读开篇，阐述其艺术特征与社会功能；其后附完整的手稿影印，以保持史料原貌与阅读便利的统一。

因此，本章既是学术分析的主体，也是手稿影印的主要载体。它将理论阐释与史料展示结合，为后续的艺术特征研究奠定基础。

This chapter adopts a seven-category framework to present the *Ruijin Folk Songs* in their entirety, combining scholarly introductions with manuscript facsimiles.

The following **materials** are preserved in their original form as they circulated in the Central Soviet Area during the 1930s, and are presented here for research purposes.

Unlike Chapter Four, which followed the original five-volume catalog of the manuscripts, this chapter reorganizes the materials from a research perspective, classifying them into seven types: Mountain Songs, Songs of Labor, Wedding Songs, Children's Rhymes, Ritual and Custom Songs, Minor Tunes and Lantern Songs, and Revolutionary Folk Songs.

Each category begins with a bilingual introduction that outlines its artistic characteristics and social functions, followed by the complete manuscript facsimiles (formatted as "two pages per sheet" for clarity and convenience), preserving both authenticity and accessibility.

Thus, this chapter constitutes both the scholarly core of the book and the main repository of manuscript reproductions, integrating theoretical interpretation with archival presentation to lay the foundation for the subsequent study of artistic features.

01 第一类 · 山歌集

CATEGORY I · SHAN'GE – MOUNTAIN SONGS

导读

山歌是瑞金民歌传统中最为广泛、最具代表性的一类。其演唱形式多为青年男女对唱，常在山间、田头、劳作或集会之际即兴唱和。歌词内容以爱情、友情和生活感悟为主，形式自由，语言质朴，常带有机智的对答与即兴创作的张力。旋律多为五声音阶，曲调婉转流畅，具有鲜明的地方色彩与口语化特征。作为一种“在场的文化”，山歌不仅承载了个体情感，也反映了瑞金社会风俗与乡土文化的深厚底蕴。

Introduction

Shan'ge (Mountain Songs) are among the most widespread and representative genres of the Ruijin folk tradition. Typically performed as antiphonal duets between young men and women, they were often sung in the mountains, in the fields, or during communal gatherings. The lyrics revolve around themes of love, friendship, and reflections on daily life, marked by spontaneity, wit, and improvisation. Melodies are predominantly pentatonic, flowing and lyrical, with a distinct local flavor and colloquial style. As a form of "culture in presence," *Shan'ge* embody both personal emotion and the collective ethos of Ruijin's social customs and rural heritage.

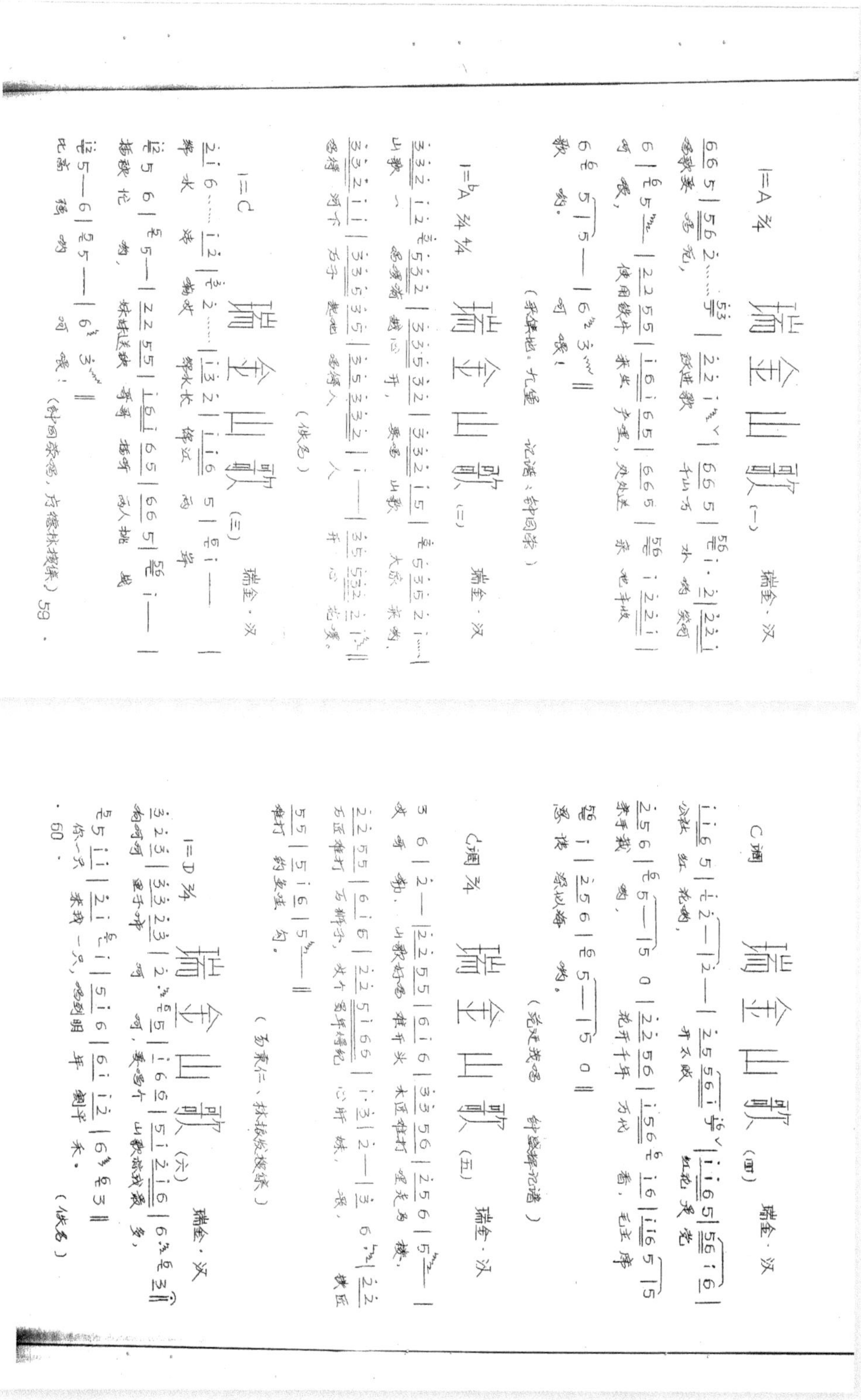

瑞金山歌（一）

1=A 2/4　　瑞金·汉

山歌要唱花，跃进歌　千山万水哟　笑呵
呵　喂，使用铁牛　来出　产量，处处送　来　也丰收
歌　哟。　呵　喂！

（采集地：九堡　记谱：钟同荣）

瑞金山歌（二）

1=♭A 2/4 4/4　　瑞金·汉

山歌　一　唱嗳满　越心　开，要唱　山歌　大家　来哟，
唱得　河下　万子　起也　唱得人　人　开　心　花嗳。

（佚名）

瑞金山歌（三）

1=C　　瑞金·汉

绵　水　涛　滔哎　绵水长　饶江　两　岸
插秧　忙　哟，妹妹送秧　哥哥　插呀　两人挑　战
比高　强　哟　呵　喂！（钟同荣唱，疗德林搜集）

· 59 ·

瑞金山歌（四）

C调　　瑞金·汉

公社　红　花哟，开不败　红花　是党
亲手栽　哟，花开千年　万代　香，毛主　席
恩　情　深似海　哟。

（范廷茂唱　钟盛辉记谱）

瑞金山歌（五）

C调 2/4　　瑞金·汉

丈　哥　勤，山歌好唱　难开头　木匠难打　哩龙凤　楼，
石匠难打　石狮子，丈个　习年媳妇　心肝　妹，　喂，　铁匠
难打　钓鱼　钩。

（刘秉仁、林振发搜集）

瑞金山歌（六）

1=D 3/4　　瑞金·汉

的呵呵　里子呀　呵　呵，要唱个　山歌就我　最　多，
你一只　来我　一只，唱到明　年　割　禾。

（佚名）

· 60 ·

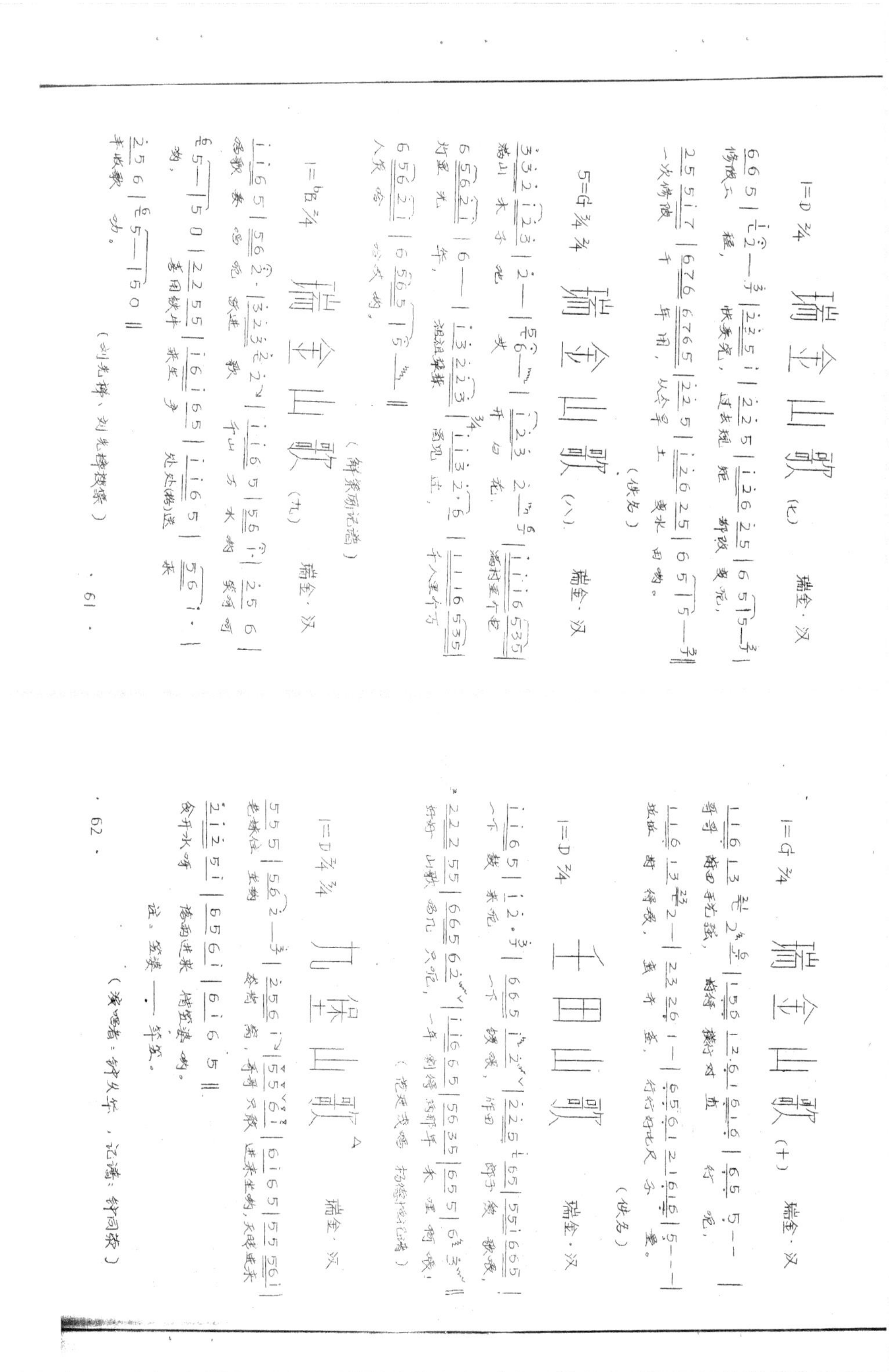

瑞金山歌（七）

1=D 2/4　瑞金·汉

6 6 5 | 2 — | 2 3 5 i | 2 2 5 | i 2 6 2 5 | 6 5 | 5 — |
修防工 程， 快要完， 过去规 矩 都改 变呢，

2 5 5 i 7 | 6 7 6 6 7 6 5 | 2 2 5 | i 2 6 2 5 | 6 5 | 5 — ||
一次修被 千 年用， 从今早 土 变水 田哟。

（佚名）

瑞金山歌（八）

5=G 3/4 2/4　瑞金·汉

3 3 2 i 2 3 | 2 — | 6 — | i 2 3 2 — | i i i 6 5 3 5 |
满山 木 子 地 艾 开 白 花， 满村里个也

6 5 6 2 i | 6 — | i 3 2 2 3 | i i 3 2· 6 | 1 1 1 6 5 3 5 |
灯里 光 华， 祖祖辈辈 团见 过， 千人里个万

6 5 6 2 i | 6 5 6 5 | 5 — ||
人笑 哈 哈大 哟。

（解策励记谱）

瑞金山歌（九）

1=♭B 2/4　瑞金·汉

i i 6 5 | 5 6 2· | 3 2 3 2 | i i 6 5 | 5 6 i | 2 5 6 |
唱歌 要 唱 呢 跃进 歌 千山 万 水 哟 笑呵 呵

5 — | 5 0 | 2 2 5 5 | i 6 i 6 5 | i i 6 5 | 5 6 i· |
哟， 喜用铁牛 来生 产 处处(都)送 来

2 5 6 | 5 — | 5 0 ||
丰收歌 声。

（刘先梯、刘先棒搜集）

· 61 ·

瑞金山歌（十）

1=G 2/4　瑞金·汉

1 1 6 1 3 2 | 1 5 5 1 2 6 1 6 1 6 | 6 5 5 — — |
哥哥 崩田 手光强， 崩得 横行对 直 行 呢，

1 1 6 1 3 2 — | 2 3 2 6 1 — | 6 5 6 1 2 1 6 1 6 | 5 — — |
妹妹 时 得很， 直 齐 齐， 行行好也尺 子 量。

（佚名）

壬田山歌

1=D 2/4　瑞金·汉

i i 6 5 | i 2· 3 | 6 6 5 i 2 | 2 2 5 6 5 | 5 5 i 6 6 5 |
一下 鼓 来呢 一下 锣哦， 昨日 郎子 叙 歌哦，

2 2 2 5 5 | 6 6 5 6 2 | i i 6 6 5 | 5 6 3 5 | 6 5 5 | 6 3 ||
好好 山歌 唱几 只呢， 一年 割得 两那年 禾 哩 何 哦！

（范廷茂唱　杨德梅记谱）

九堡山歌△

1=D 2/4 3/4　瑞金·汉

5 5 5 | 5 6 2 — | 2 5 6 i | 5 5 6 i | 6 i 6 5 | 5 5 5 6 i |
老妹住 坐哟 大岗 窝， 哥哥 只敢 进来坐哟，天晴进来

2 i 2 5 i | 6 5 6 i | 6 i 6 5 ||
食开水呀 落雨进来 借笠婆 哟。

注：笠婆——斗笠。

（演唱者：钟久华，记谱：钟同荣）

· 62 ·

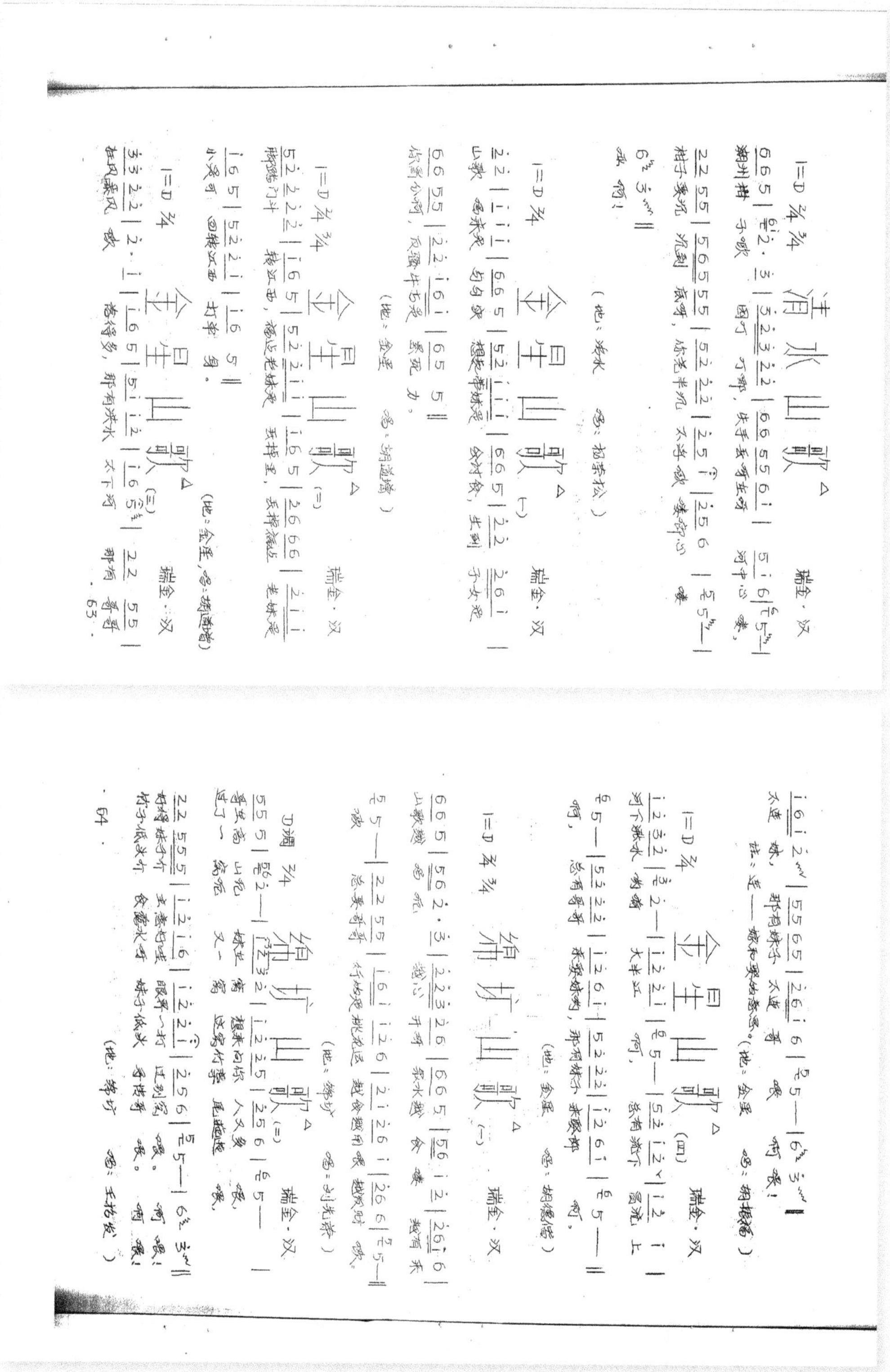

清水山歌△

1=D 2/4 3/4　　瑞金·汉

665 | 6i 2 · 3 | 5 2 3 2 2 | 66 55 6 i | 5 i 6 | 6 5 — |
湖州柑子喲　　囡仃仃啷，失手丢呀在呀　河中心　喽，

22 55 | 56 5 55 | 5 2 2 2 | 2 5 i | 2 5 6 | 5 5 — |
柑子要氹　氹到　底呀，你若半氹　不浮啾　喽仰心　喽

6 3 ||
哪　啊！

（地：清水　唱：杨荣松）

金星山歌△（一）

1=D 2/4　　瑞金·汉

2 2 | i i i | 66 5 | 52 i i i | 66 5 | 2 2 26 i |
山歌　唱来哩　句句实　想起带妹哩　会讨食，生到　子女哩

66 55 | 2 2 i6 i | 65 5 ||
你哥分啊，反骚牛古哩　累死　力。

（地：金星　唱：胡道增）

金星山歌△（二）

1=D 2/4 3/4　　瑞金·汉

52 2 2 2 | i6 5 | 52 2 i i | i6 5 | 26 66 | 2 i i |
脚踏门斗　转江西，福过老妹哩　丢掉里，丢掉福过　老妹哩

i6 5 | 52 2 i | i6 5 ||
小哩可　回转江西　打单　身。

（地：金星，唱：胡道增）

金星山歌△（三）

1=D 2/4　　瑞金·汉

33 22 | 2 · i | i6 5 | 5i i2 | i6 5 | 22 55 |
狂风暴风　吹　落得多，那有洪水　不下河　那有　哥哥

i6i 2 | 5565 | 26i 6 | 5 — | 6 3 ||
不连　妹，那有妹子　不连　哥　喂　啊　喂！

注：连——嫁和娶的意思。（地：金星　唱：胡振福）

金星山歌△（四）

1=D 2/4　　瑞金·汉

i2 32 | 2 — | i2 2i | 5 — | 52 i2 | i2 i |
河下涨水　哟嗬　大半江　啊，总有流下　冒流上

5 — | 52 22 | i2 6i | 52 22 | i2 6i | 5 — ||
啊，总有哥哥　来娶妹哟，那有妹子　来娶郎　啊。

（地：金星　唱：胡德偕）

绵圹山歌△（一）

1=D 2/4 3/4　　瑞金·汉

665 | 56 2 · 3 | 223 26 | 665 | 56 i 2 | 26i 6 |
山歌越　唱呢　越心　开呀　泉水越　食　喽　越有　来

5 — | 22 55 | i6i i26 | 2i 26 i | 26 6 | 5 — ||
啾　总要哥哥　行如哩桃花运　越食越用喂　越发财　哟。

（地：绵圹　唱：刘先荣）

绵圹山歌△（二）

D调 3/4　　瑞金·汉

55 5 | 2 — | i2 32 | i2 25 | 25 6 | 5 — |
哥出高　山呢　妹出　窝　想来问你　人又多　喂，
过了一　窝呢　又一　窝　这窝竹笋　尾趣趣　喂，

22 555 | i2 i6 | i2 2i | 25 6 | 5 — | 6 3 ||
好得妹子介　主意好哇　眼睛一打　过别窝　喂。　啊　喂！
竹子低头介　食露水呀　妹子低头　哥使哥　喂。　啊　喂！

（地：绵圹　唱：王拾发）

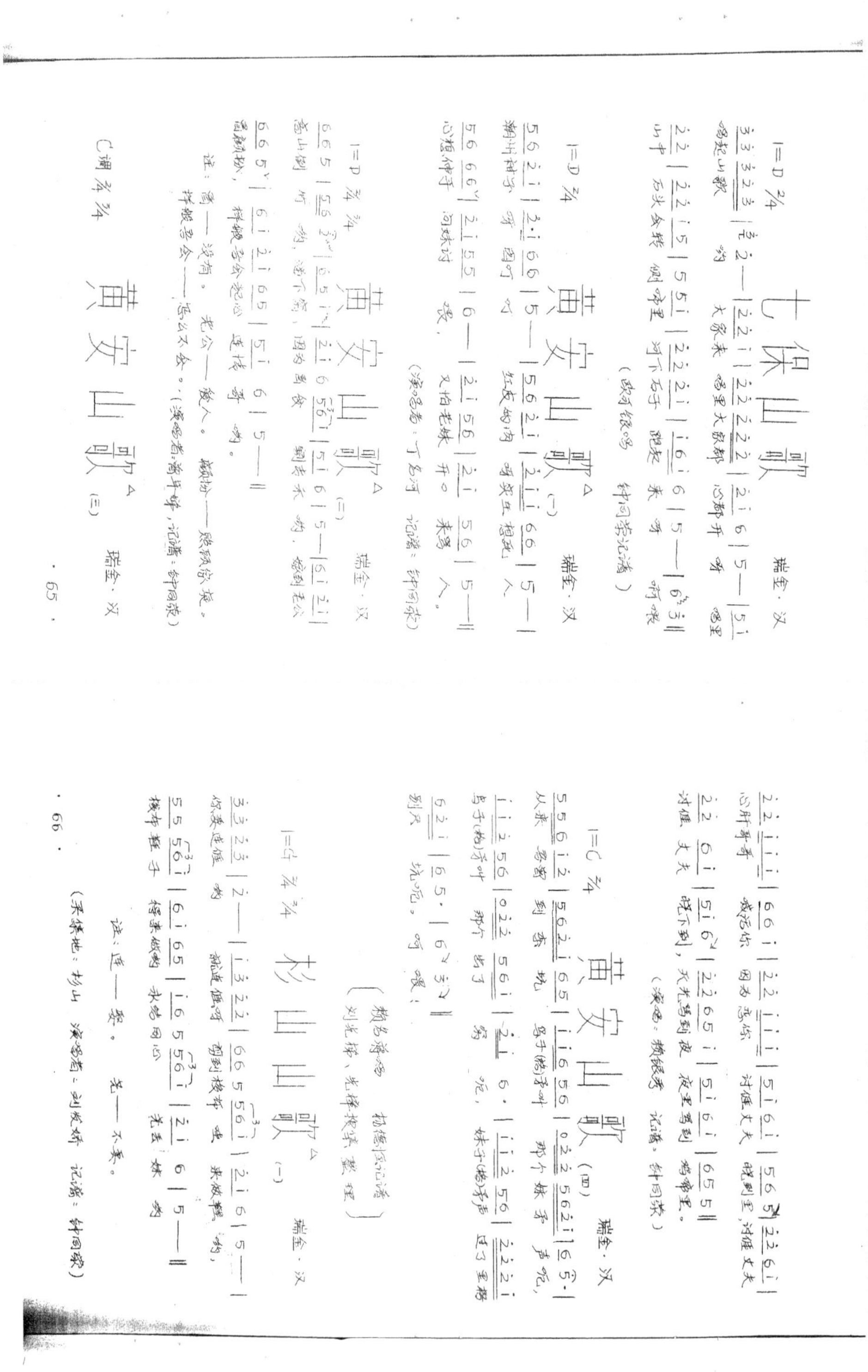

七保山歌

1=D 2/4　　瑞金·汉

3 3 3 2 3 | 3 2 — | 2 2 1 | 2 2 2 2 2 | 2 1 6 | 5 — | 5 1
唱起山歌　哟　大家来　唱里大家都　心都开　呀　唱里

2 2 | 2 2 1 5 | 5 5 1 | 2 2 2 1 | 1 6 1 6 | 5 — | 6 3 ‖
山中　石头会转　侧哗里　河下石子　跑起来　呀　啊喂

（欧阿银唱　钟同荣记谱）

黄安山歌△（一）

1=D 2/4　　瑞金·汉

5 6 2 1 | 2·1 6 6 | 5 — | 5 6 2 1 | 2 1 1 6 6 | 5 — |
潮州柑子　呀　圆叮　叮　红皮的肉　呀实生想死　人

5 6 6 6 | 2 1 5 5 | 6 — | 2 1 5 6 | 2 1 5 6 | 5 — ‖
心想伸手　问妹讨　喂，　又怕老妹　开口　来骂　人。

（演唱者：丁名河　记谱：钟同荣）

黄安山歌△（二）

1=D 2/4 3/4　　瑞金·汉

6 6 5 | 5 5 3 | 6 5 1 | 2 1 6 5 6 1 | 5 1 6 | 5 — | 6 1 2 1 |
高山倒　竹　哟，递下窝，因为当食　割去禾　哟，嫁到老公

6 6 5 | 6 1 2 1 6 5 | 5 1 6 | 5 — ‖
冒颇扮，　样般吾会起心　连情　哥　哟。

注：冒——没有。　老公——丈夫。　颇扮——照顾家庭。
样般吾会——怎么不会。（演唱者：肖年妹，记谱：钟同荣）

黄安山歌△（三）

C调 2/4 3/4　　瑞金·汉

2 2 1 1 1 | 6 6 1 | 2 2 1 1 1 | 5 1 6 1 | 5 6 5 | 2 2 6 1 |
心肝哥哥　　哦恋你　因为恋你　讨健丈夫　晚到里，讨健丈夫

2 2 6 1 | 5 1 6 | 2 2 6 5 1 | 5 1 6 1 | 6 5 5 ‖
讨健　丈夫　晚下到，天光骂到夜　夜里骂到　鸡啼里。

（演唱：赖银秀　记谱：钟同荣）

黄安山歌△（四）

1=C 2/4　　瑞金·汉

5 5 6 1 2 | 5 6 2 1 6 5 | 1 1 6 5 6 | 0 2 2 5 6 2 1 | 6 5· |
从来　寮窝　到　条　坑　鸟子(格)矛叶　那个　妹　矛　声　呃，

1 1 2 5 6 | 0 2 2 5 6 1 | 2 1 6· | 1 1 2 5 6 | 2 2 2 1
鸟子(格)矛叶　那个　出了　　窝　呃，妹子(格)矛声　过了里枵

6 2 1 | 6 5· | 6 3 ‖
到只　坑呃，　呵　喂！

（赖名薄唱　杨德恒记谱
刘光梯、光梯搜集　整理）

杉山山歌△（一）

1=G 2/4 3/4　　瑞金·汉

3 3 2 3 | 2 — | 1 3 2 2 | 6 6 5 5 6 1 | 2 1 6 | 5 — |
你要连健　哟　就连健呀　留到榜布　哩　来放鞋　哟，

5 5 5 6 1 | 6 1 6 5 | 1 6 5 5 6 1 | 2 1 6 | 5 — ‖
榜布鞋子　　得来做的　永结同心　　老去　妹　哟

注：连——娶。　无——不要。

（采集地：杉山　演唱者：刘发娇　记谱：钟同荣）

杉山山歌△（二）

1=D 2/4 3/4　瑞金·汉

你要 进堡哟， 进来坐 先你门前过 唱山歌 哟，
你的山歌 唱得 老妹到老 天下世间构难 讨老婆 哟。

注：无——不要。（演唱者：刘发轩，记谱：钟向荣）

杉山山歌△（三）

1=D 2/4 3/4　瑞金·汉

食烟 要 食哟 条子 烟 生揽 要 生牙 妹面前 哟，
哥哥食烟 妹中火哇 当得天上 和合仙 哟． 呵 喂！

注：中火——点火。
（采集地：杉山　演唱：方冬发　记谱：钟向荣）

清洒山歌

5=G 2/4　瑞金·汉

专竹子来 书 市 巴喂 先竹子来 ⋯开 花 喂，
八十三岁 争 劳 横 呵，全部 社员 笑哈 哈喂 笑哈哟．

（钟良志唱　杨裹锦记谱）

圳头山歌

1=F 2/4　瑞金·汉

锣鼓 打来 哟 （那个） 打咚卡卡哟 要 斗山歌

· 67 ·

噶怕 喂 你 哟， 你来 一只歌 我还你一 只
你留 山 歌 佢教（嗬哩） 你 哟。

（刘定炳唱　杨裹锦记谱）

万田山歌

1=♭A 2/4 3/4　瑞金·汉

山歌好 唱呢 难 起 头 喂 木匠 难造 纹
龙 喂 马 楼喂， 石匠 难雕 石狮子 哟， 铁匠 难
打 吧 钓鱼 钩喂。

（赖抚钟唱　杨德恒记谱　刘先梯搜集整理）

瑞林山歌

1=C 2/4　瑞金·汉

哎呀 咖 打大山歌 进了坑， 鹞子矛叫 妹矛
声 鹞子矛叫 出了 窝， 心 肝 妹， 妹子矛声 出了
坑。

（邱秉仁、林振发记谱
刘先梯、先梯搜集整理）

· 68 ·

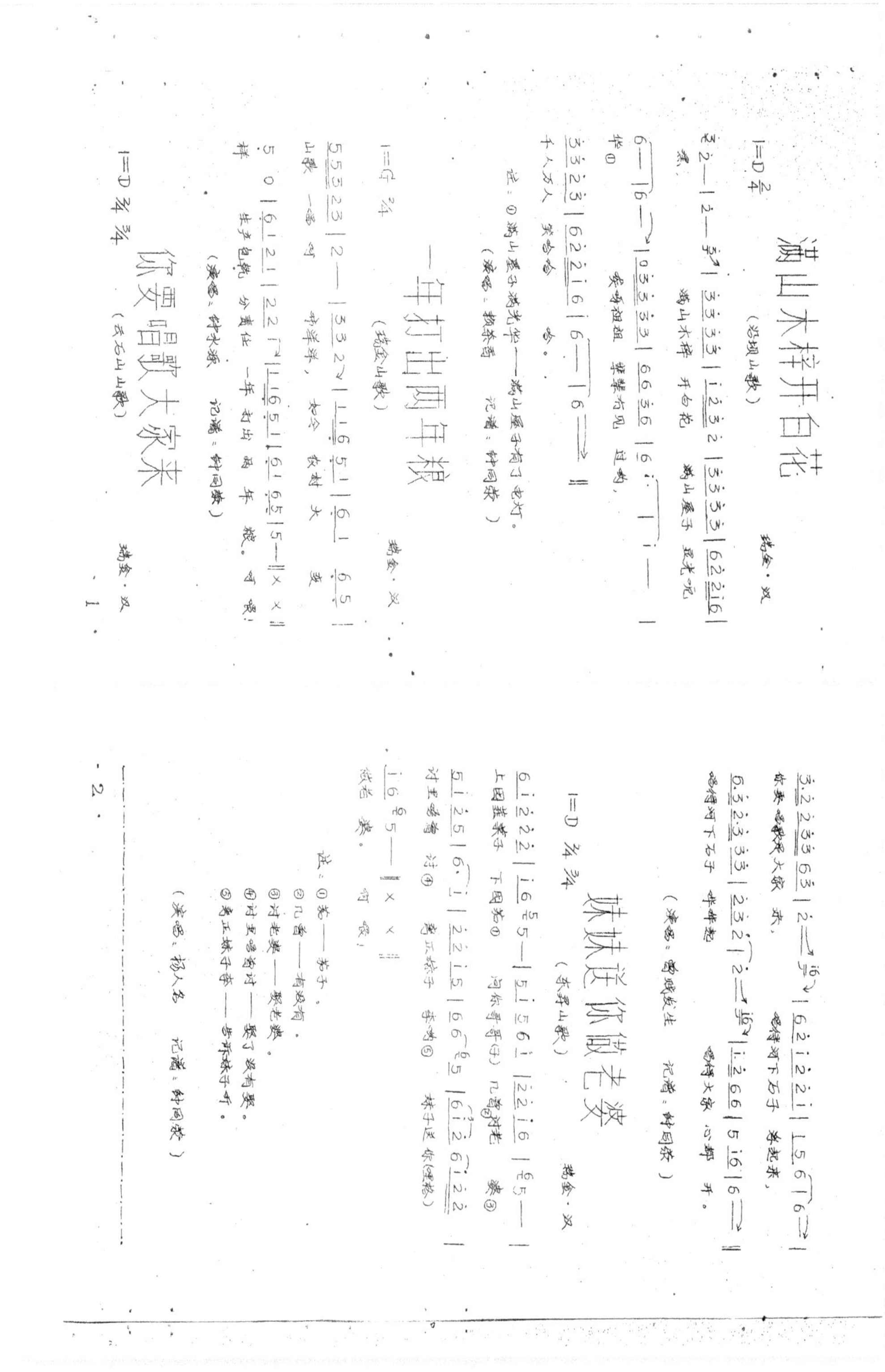

满山木梓开白花

1=D 2/4 （沿坝山歌） 瑞金·双

黑， 满山木梓 开白花 满山屋子 显光呢

华① 安哥祖祖 辈辈冇见 过哟，

千人万人 笑哈哈 哈。

注：①满山屋子满光华——满山屋子有了电灯。

（演唱：赖荼香 记谱：钟同荣）

一年打出两年粮

1=G 2/4 （瑞金山歌） 瑞金·双

山歌 一唱 呵 市洋洋， 如今 农村 大 变

样 生产包干 分责任 一年 打出 两 年 粮。 呵 喂！

（演唱：钟水源 记谱：钟同荣）

你要唱歌大家来

1=D 2/4 3/4 （云石山山歌） 瑞金·双

你要唱歌大家 来， 唱得河下石子 浮起来，

唱得河下石子 浮浮起 唱得大家 心都 开。

（演唱：曾贱发生 记谱：钟同荣）

妹妹送你做老婆

1=D 2/4 3/4 （东昇山歌） 瑞金·双

上园韭菜子 下园苋① 问你哥哥(子) 几曾②讨老 婆③

讨里唔曾 讨④ 养正妹子 李哟⑤ 妹子送 你(哩格)

做老 婆。 呵 喂！

注：①苋——苋子。
②几曾——有没有。
③讨老婆——娶老婆。
④讨里唔曾讨——娶了没有娶。
⑤养正妹子李——告诉妹子听。

（演唱：杨人名 记谱：钟同荣）

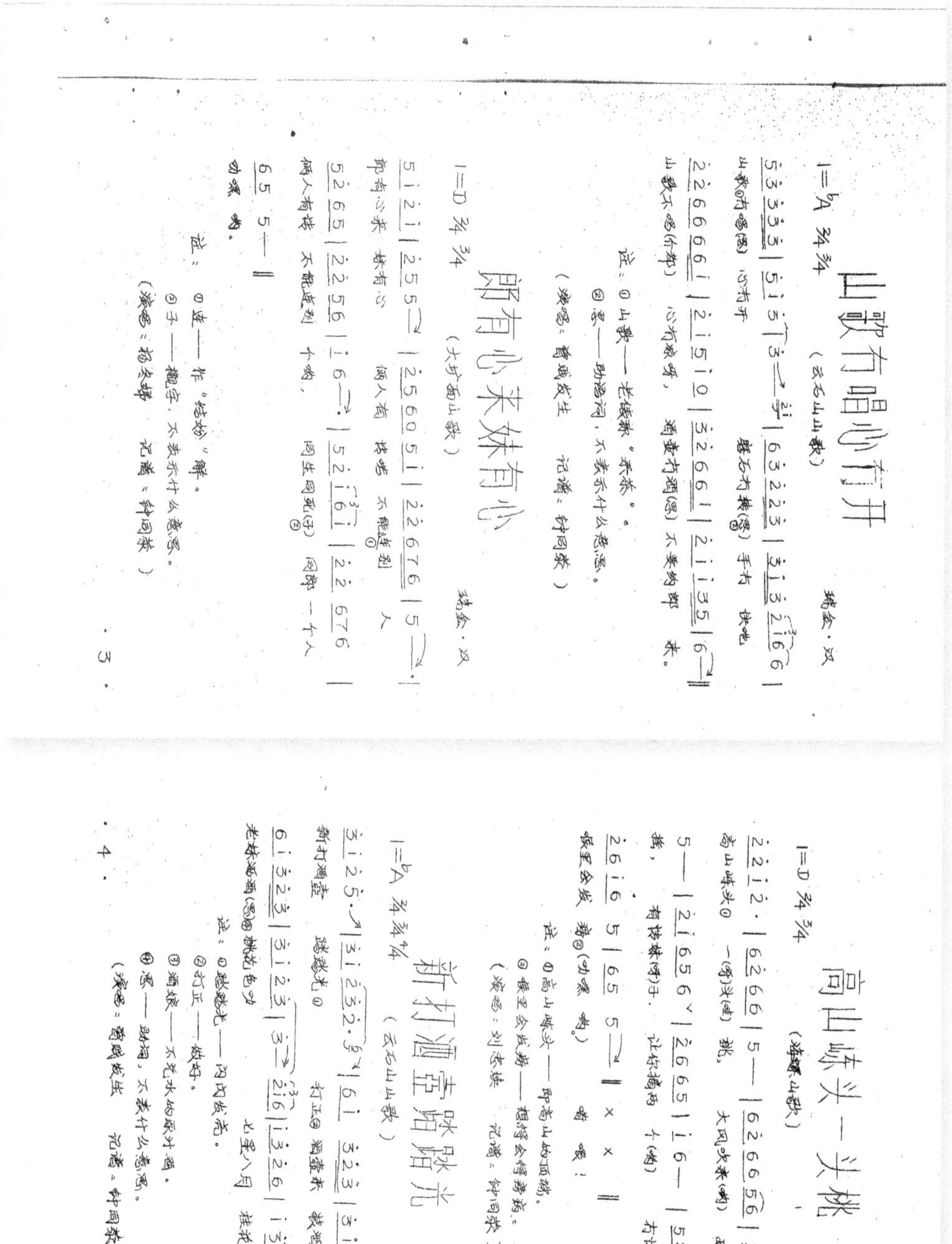

山歌冇唱心冇开

1=♭A 2/4 3/4　（云石山山歌）　瑞金·汉

山歌冇唱(思)心冇开　磨石冇转(思)手冇　快咃

山歌不唱(介郎)　心冇来呀，　酒壶冇酒(思)不要哟郎　来。

注：① 山歌——老俵称"乐茶"。
② 思——助语词，不表示什么意思。

（演唱：曾贱发生　记谱：钟同荣）

郎有心来妹有心

1=D 2/4 3/4　（大圹面山歌）　瑞金·汉

郎有心来　妹有心　俩人有　情咃　不能连①别　人

俩人有情　不能连别　个哟，　同生同死(子)②　同郎　一个人

叻嘿　哟。

注：① 连——作"结婚"解。
② 子——衬字，不表示什么意思。

（演唱：杨冬娣　记谱：钟同荣）

高山崃头一头桃

1=D 2/4 3/4　（壬田山歌）　瑞金·汉

高山崃头①　一(呀)头(哇)　桃，　大风吹来(哟)　两(呀)边(呀)

摇，　有情妹(呀)子，　让你摘两　个(哟)　有情妹(呀)子，

恨里会发　痨②(叻嘿　哟)　哟　喂！

注：① 高山崃头——即高山的顶端。
② 恨里会发痨——想得会得痨病。

（演唱：刘志姨　记谱：钟同荣）

新打酒壶踏踏光

1=♭A 2/4 3/4 4/4　（云石山山歌）　瑞金·汉

新打酒壶　踏踏光①　打正②　酒壶来　載酒娘③呀，

老妹冇酒(思)④桃花色哟　七星八月　桂花　香。

注：① 踏踏光——闪闪发亮。
② 打正——做好。
③ 酒娘——不兑水的原汁酒。
④ 思——助词，不表什么意思。

（演唱：曾贱发生　记谱：钟同荣）

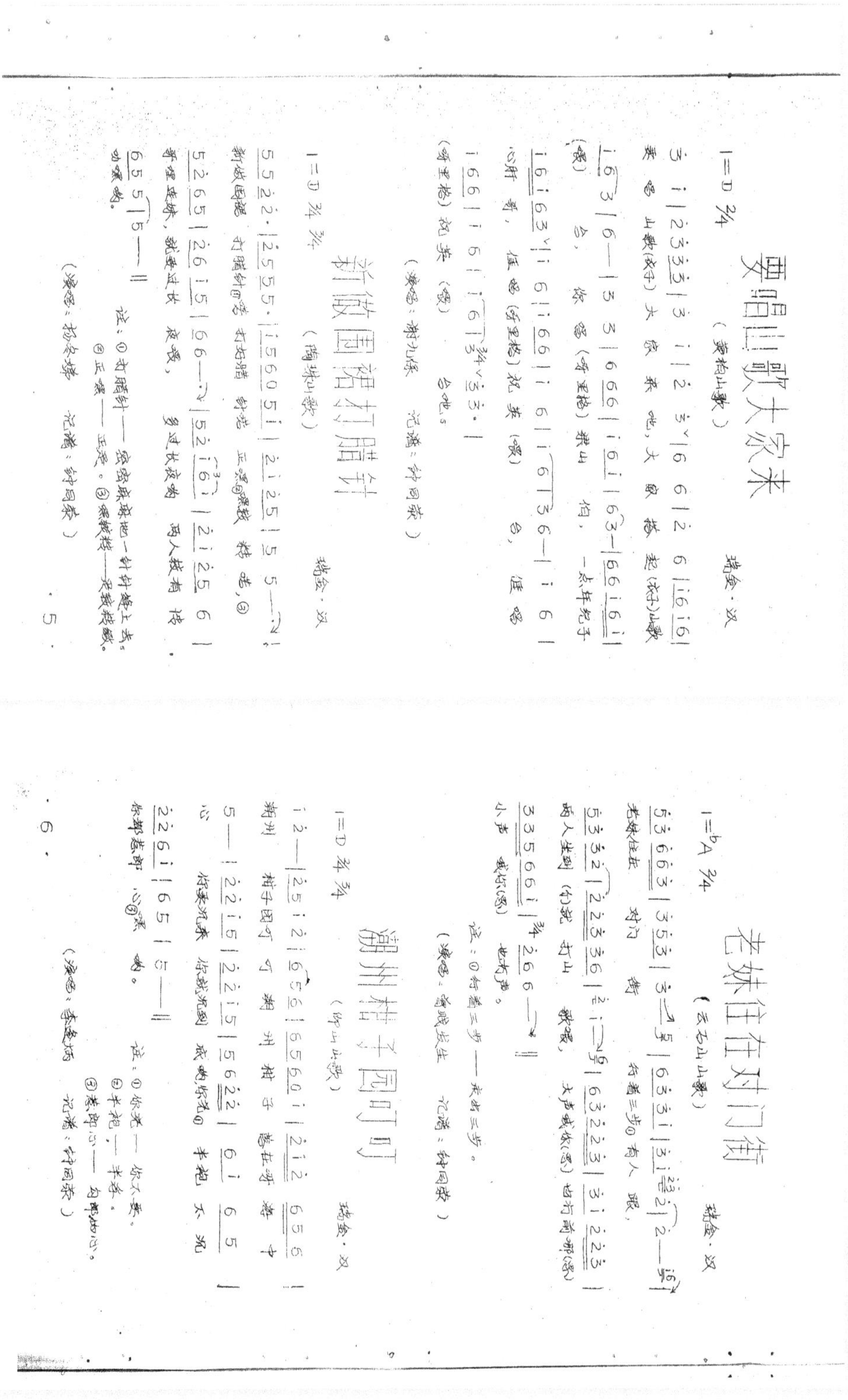

要唱山歌大家来

1=D 2/4 （黄柏山歌） 瑞金·汉

3 i | 2 3 3 3 | 3 i | 2 3 | 6 6 | 2 6 | i6 i6 |
要 唱 山歌(衣子) 大 家 来 吔，大 家 搭 起(衣子)山歌

i6 3 | 6 — | 3 3 | 6 66 | i 6 i | 6 3 — | 66 i 6 i |
(喂) 合， 你 唱 (呀里格) 来山 伯， 一点年纪子

i 6 i 6 3 | i 6 | i 66 | i 6 | i 6 | 3 6 — | i 6 |
心肝 哥， 连 唱 (呀里格) 祝 英 (喂) 合， 连 唱

i 66 | i 6 | i 6 | 3/4 3 3 3 · |
(呀里格) 祝 英 (喂) 合吔。

（演唱：谢九保 记谱：钟同荣）

新做围裙打腊针

1=D 2/4 3/4 （陶珠山歌） 瑞金·汉

5 5 2 2 · | 2 5 5 5 · | i 5 6 0 5 i | 2 i 2 5 | 5 5 — |
新做围裙 打腊针(1)哟 打好腊 针哟 正嘿(2)嘿钱 转 咗，(3)

5 2 6 5 | 2 6 i 5 | 6 6 — | 5 2 i 6 i | 2 i 2 5 6 |
哥哩连妹，就要过长 夜喂， 多过长夜哟 两人钱有 传

6 5 5 | 5 — ||
动嘿哟。

注：①打腊针——密密麻麻地一针针缝上去。
②正嘿——正是。③嘿钱转——是钱转钱。

（演唱：扬冬娣 记谱：钟同荣）

老妹住在对门街

1=♭A 2/4 （云石山山歌） 瑞金·汉

5 3 6 6 3 | 3 5 3 | 3 — 5 | 6 3 3 i | 3 i 2 | 2 — 5 |
老妹住在 对门 街 行着三步(1) 有人 跟，

5 3 3 2 | 2 2 3 3 6 | 2 i — 5 | 6 3 2 2 3 | 3 i 2 2 3 |
两人生到 (介)就 打山 歌喂， 大声喊你(恩) 也冇前哪(恩)

3 3 5 6 6 i | 3/4 2 6 6 — ||
小声 喊你(恩) 也冇声。

注：①行着三步——走出三步。

（演唱：曾贱发生 记谱：钟同荣）

潮州柑子园叮叮

1=D 2/4 3/4 （仰山山歌） 瑞金·汉

i 2 — | 2 5 i 2 | 6 5 6 | 6 5 6 0 i | 2 i 2 6 5 6 |
潮州 柑子园叮 叮 潮 州 柑 子 当在呀 海 中

5 — | 2 2 i 5 | 2 2 i 5 | 5 6 2 2 | 6 i 6 5 |
心 你要沉来 你就沉到 底哟，你莫(1) 半 袍 不 沉

2 2 6 i | 6 5 | 5 — ||
你都惹郎 心(3)嘿 哟。

注：①你莫——你不要。
②半袍——半浮。
③惹郎心——勾郎的心。

（演唱：李逢炳 记谱：钟同荣）

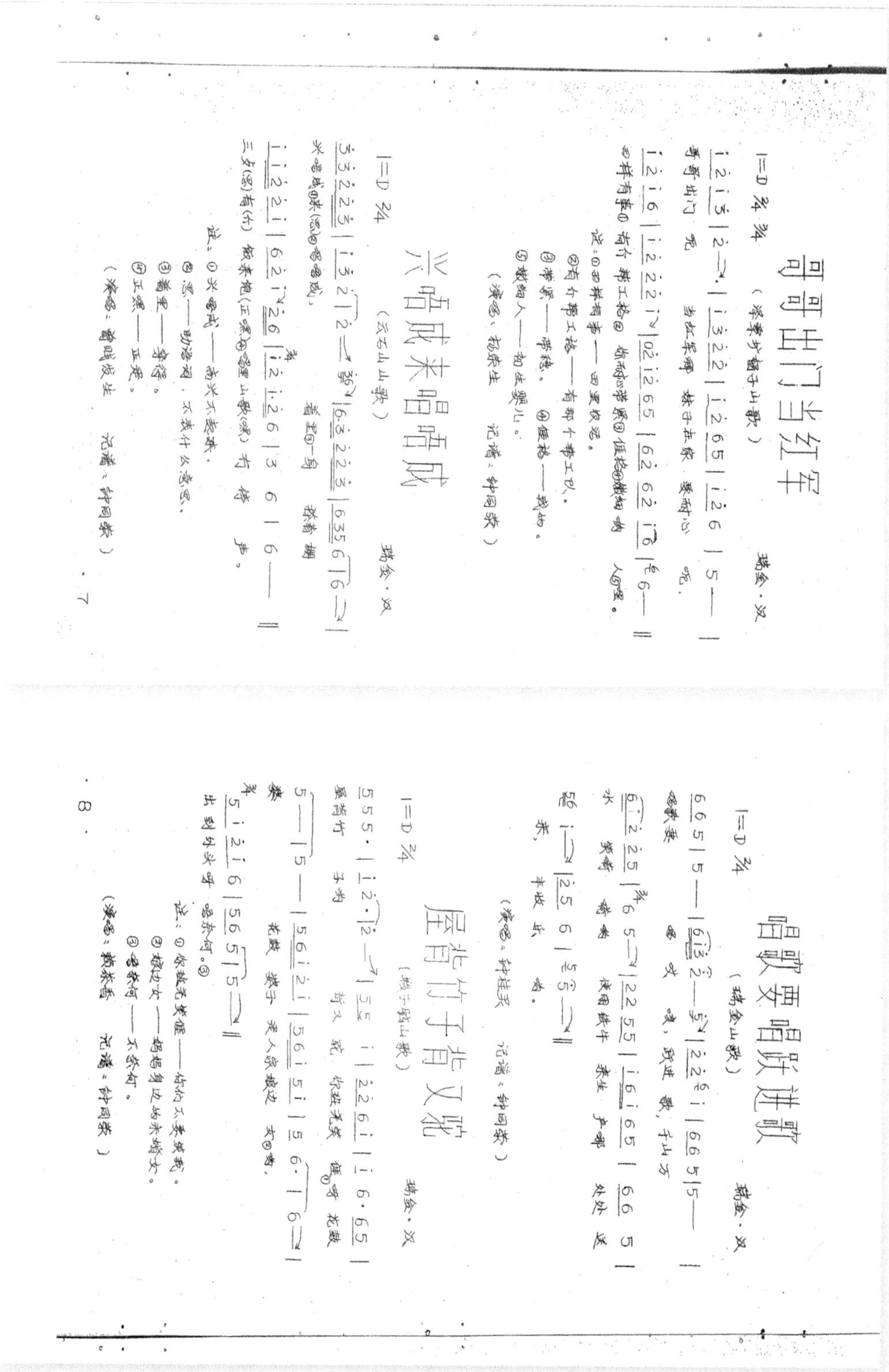

哥哥出门当红军

1=D 2/4 3/4　（泽覃乡韬子山歌）　瑞金·汉

1 2 1 3 | 2 — . | 1 3 2 2 | 1 2 6 5 | 1 2 6 | 5 — |
哥哥出门　呢　当红军哪　妹子在家　要耐心　呢。

1 2 1 6 | 1 2 2 2 1 | 02 12 65 | 62 62 16 | 6 — ‖
田样有事① 有介 帮工格② 你耐心带紧③ 侄格④嫩细 哟　人⑤哩。

注：①田样有事——田里农活。
②有介帮工格——有哪个帮工队。
③带紧——带稳。　④侄格——我的。
⑤嫩细人——初生婴儿。

（演唱：杨荣生　记谱：钟同荣）

兴唔成来唱唔成

1=D 2/4　（云石山山歌）　瑞金·汉

3 3 2 2 3 | 1 3 2 | 2 — 36 | 6.3 2 2 3 | 635 6 | 6 — |
兴唔成①来(思)②唱唔成，　着里③一身　搽着 棚

1 1 2 2 1 | 6 2 1 26 | 3/4 1 2 1.2 6 | 3 6 | 6 — ‖
三夕(思)有(介) 饭来饱(正嘿)④唱里山歌(嘿) 冇 侍　声。

注：①兴唔成——高兴不起来。
②思——助语词，不表什么意思。
③着里——穿得。
④正嘿——正是。

（演唱：曾贱发生　记谱：钟同荣）

· 7

唱歌要唱跃进歌

1=D 2/4　（瑞金山歌）　瑞金·汉

6 6 5 | 5 — | 613 2 — 5 | 2 2 1 | 6 6 5 | 5 — |
唱歌要　唱 哎　咳，跃进　歌，千山万

61 2 25 | 3/4 6 5 — | 22 55 | 161 65 | 66 5 |
水　笑荷　荷 哟　使用铁牛　来生　产哪　处处 送

56 1 — | 25 6 | 5 — ‖
来，　丰收 乐　哟。

（演唱：钟桂灵　记谱：钟同荣）

屋背竹子背又驼

1=D 2/4　（蛾子脑山歌）　瑞金·汉

5 5 5· | 1 2· | 2 — | 55 1 | 22 61 | 1 6· 65 |
屋背竹　子哟　背又 驼　你班无笑　倨①呀 花鼓

5 — | 5 — | 561 21 | 561 51 | 5 6· | 6 — |
婆　花鼓　婆子　是人家娘边　女②哟，

3/4 5 1 21 6 | 56 5 | 5 — ‖
出到外头呀　唔奈何。③

注：①你班无笑倨——你们不要笑我。
②娘边女——妈妈身边的未婚女。
③唔奈何——不奈何。

（演唱：赖荼香　记谱：钟同荣）

· 8 ·

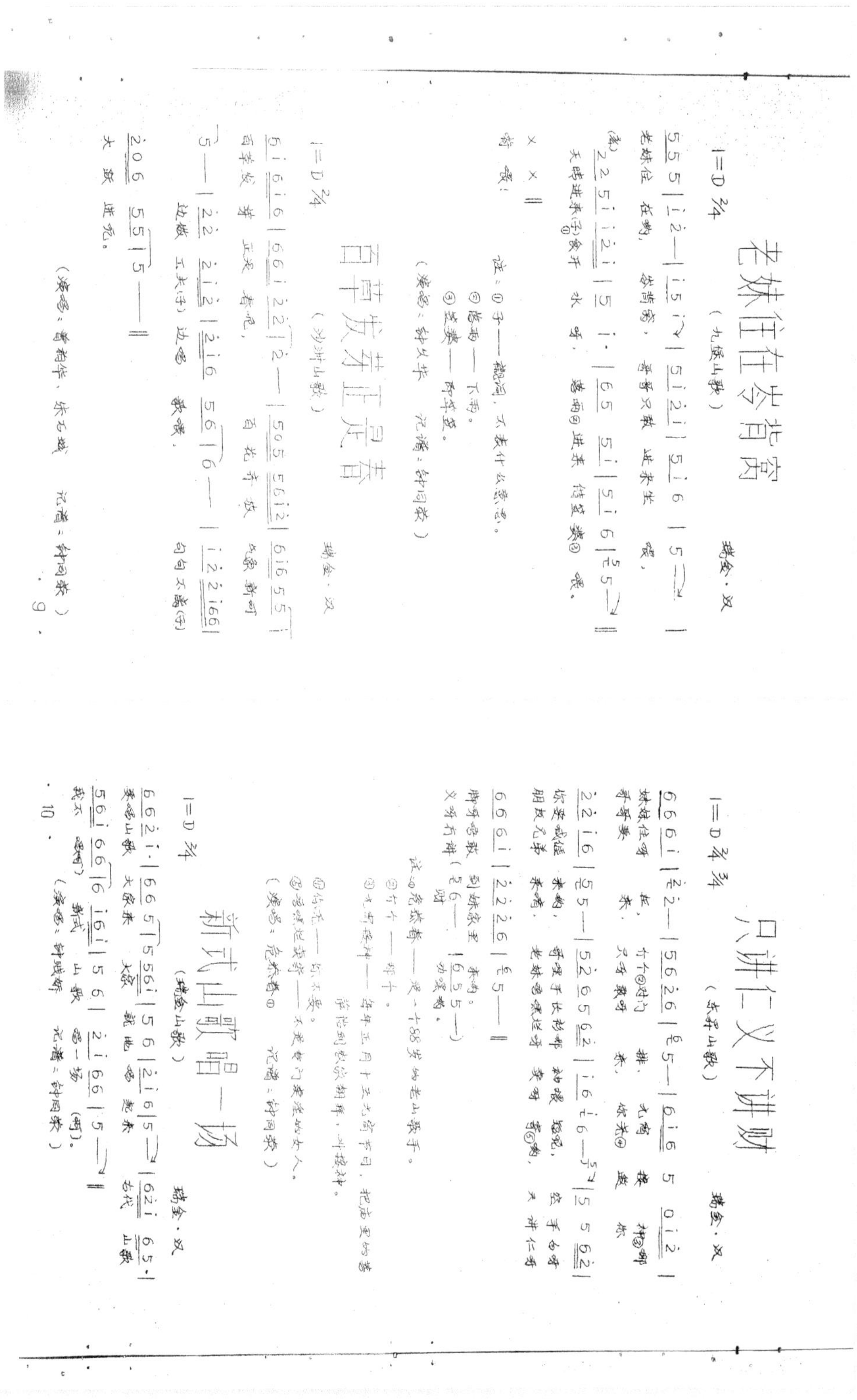

老妹住在岑背窝

1=D 2/4　　（九堡山歌）　　瑞金·汉

5 5 5 | 1 2 — | 1 5 1 | 5 1 2 1 | 5 1 6 | 5 — |

老妹住 在哟， 岑背窝， 哥哥只敢 进来坐 喂，

2 2 5 1 1 2 1 | 5 1· | 6 5 5 1 | 5 1 6 | 5 5 — ||

天晴进来(子)①食开 水 呀， 落雨②进来 倚笠 婆③ 喂。

× × ||

背 喂！

注：① 子——衬词，不表什么意思。

② 落雨——下雨。

③ 笠婆——即斗笠。

（演唱：钟久华　记谱：钟同荣）

百草发芽正是春

1=D 2/4　　（沙洲山歌）　　瑞金·汉

6 1 6 1 6 | 6 6 1 2 2 | 2 — | 5 0 5 5 6 1 2 | 6 1 6 5 5 |

百草发 芽 正是 春吧， 百 花齐 放 气象新呵

5 — | 2 2 2 1 2 | 2 1 6 5 6 | 6 — | 1 2 2 1 6 6 |

边做 工夫(子) 边唱 歌喂。 句句不离(子)

2 0 6 5 5 | 5 — ||

大 跃 进元。

（演唱：曾莉华、朱石城　记谱：钟同荣）

· 9 ·

只讲仁义不讲财

1=D 2/4 3/4　　（东升山歌）　　瑞金·汉

6 6 6 1 | 2 2 — | 5 6 2 6 | 5 — | 6 1 6 5 0 1 2 |

妹妹住呀 在， 个个②对门 排， 元宵 接 神③哪

哥哥要 来， 只子敢呀 来， 你若④ 邀 你

2 2 1 6 | 5 — | 5 2 6 5 6 2 | 1 6 6 — | 5 5 6 2 |

你要戒烟 来哟， 哥哩手长衫哪 袖喂 短呢， 空 手白呀

朋友兄弟 来唷， 老妹唱嘿烂呀 卖呀 货⑤哟， 只 讲仁呀

6 6 6 1 | 2 2 2 6 | 5 — ||

脚呀唱歌 到妹家里 来哟。

义呀冇讲（6 — | 6 5 5 —）

财　　功嘿哟。

注：① 危恭春——是一个88岁的老山歌手。

② 个个——那个。

③ 元宵接神——每年正月十五元宵节日，把庙里的菩萨抬到农家拜拜，叫接神。

④ 你若——你不要。

⑤ 唱嘿烂卖货——不是专门卖淫的女人。

（演唱：危恭春①　记谱：钟同荣）

新式山歌唱一场

1=D 2/4　　（瑞金山歌）　　瑞金·汉

6 6 2 1· | 6 6 5 | 5 5 6 1 | 5 6 | 2 1 6 | 5 — | 6 2 1 6 5· |

要唱山歌 大家来 大家 就也 唱 起来 古代 山歌

5 6 1 6 6 | 6 1 6 1 | 5 6 | 2 1 6 6 | 5 — ||

我不 唱呵） 新式 山 歌 唱一场 （呵）。

（演唱：钟贱娇　记谱：钟同荣）

· 10 ·

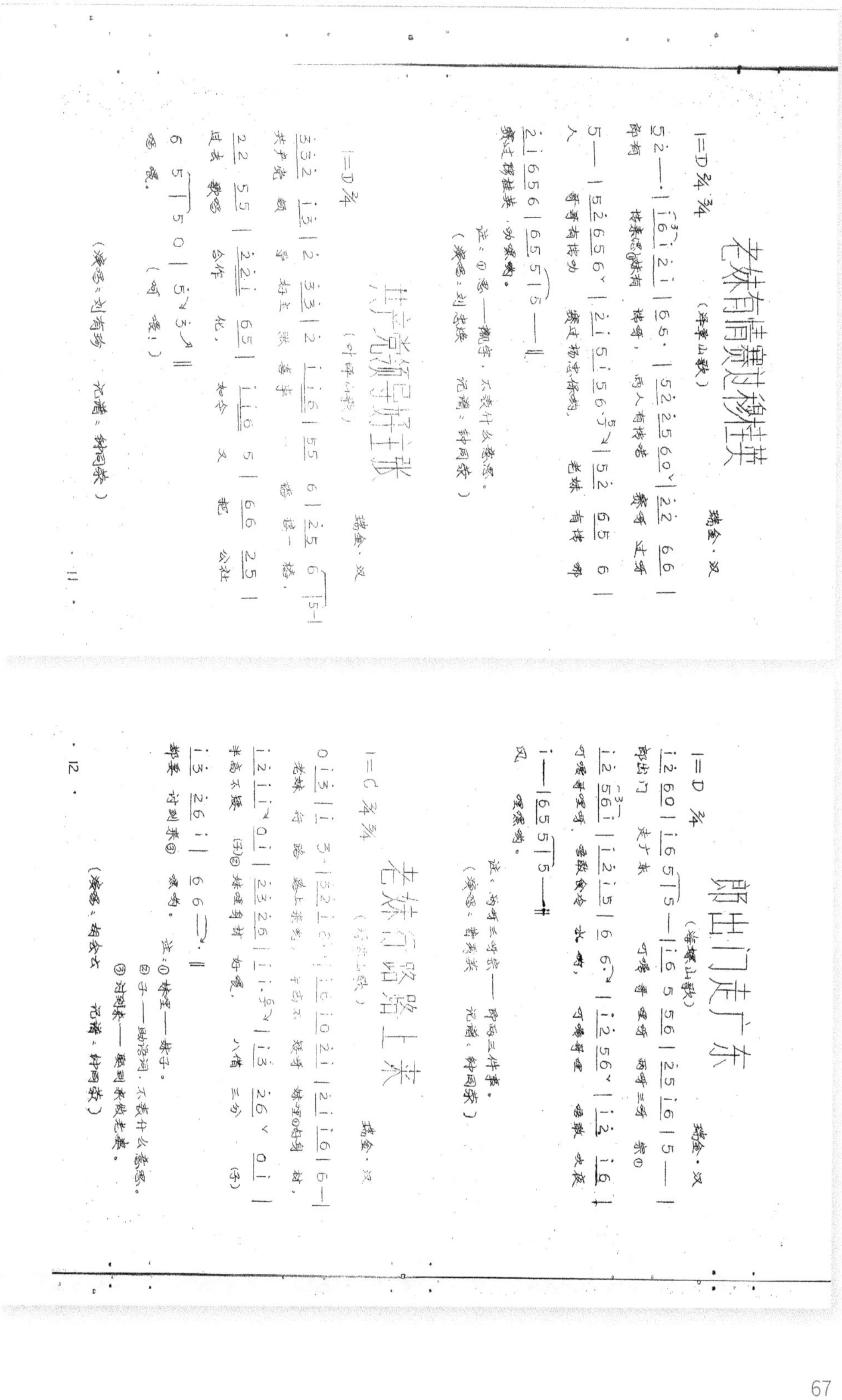

老妹有情赛过穆桂英

1=D 2/4 3/4　　（泽草山歌）　　瑞金·汉

52—·| 16 12 1 | 65· | 52 25 60 | 22 66 |
郎有　传表思①妹有　情呀，　两人有情啱　赛呀　过呀

5— | 52 65 6 | 21 51 56·5 | 52 65 6 |
人　哥哥有情动　赛过杨忠保哟，　老妹　有情　那

21 656 | 65 5 | 5—‖
赛过穆桂英·　动嘿哟。

注：① 思——衬字，不表什么意思。
（演唱：刘忠焕　　记谱：钟同荣）

共产党领导好主张

1=D 2/4　　（叶坪山歌）　　瑞金·汉

332 13 | 2 33 | 2 116 | 55 6 | 25 6 | 5— |
共产党　领　导　好主　张　善事　一　椿　接一　椿，

22 55 | 221 65 | 116 5 | 66 25 |
过去　歌唱　合作　化，　如今　又　把　公社

6 5 | 5 0 | 5 3 ‖
唱　喂。　（呵　喂！）

（演唱：刘有珍　　记谱：钟同荣）

郎出门走广东

1=D 2/4　　（海螺山歌）　　瑞金·汉

12 60 | 165 | 5— | 16 5 56 | 25 16 | 5— |
郎出门　走广东　　可嗳　哥　哩呀　两呀三呀　宗①

12 561 | 1215 | 6 6· | 12 56 | 12 16 |
可嗳哥哩呀，　唔敢食冷　水　哟，　可嗳哥哩　唔敢　吹夜

1— | 65 5 | 5—‖
风　哩嘿哟。

注：两呀三呀宗——即两三件事。
（演唱：曾秀英　　记谱：钟同荣）

老妹行路路上来

1=C 2/4 3/4　　（洋溪山歌）　　瑞金·汉

0 13 | 1 3· | 321 6· | 16 10 21 | 21 16 | 6— |
老妹　行　路　路上来哟，　半高不　矮呀　妹哩①好身　材，

121 1 01 | 23 26 | 1 1·5 | 13 26 01 |
半高不矮　（子）②妹哩身材　好嘿，　八借　三分　（子）

13 26 1 | 66 ‖
都要　讨到来③　嘿哟。

注：① 妹哩——妹子。
② 子——助语词，不表什么意思。
③ 讨到来——娶到来做老婆。

（演唱：胡会云　　记谱：钟同荣）

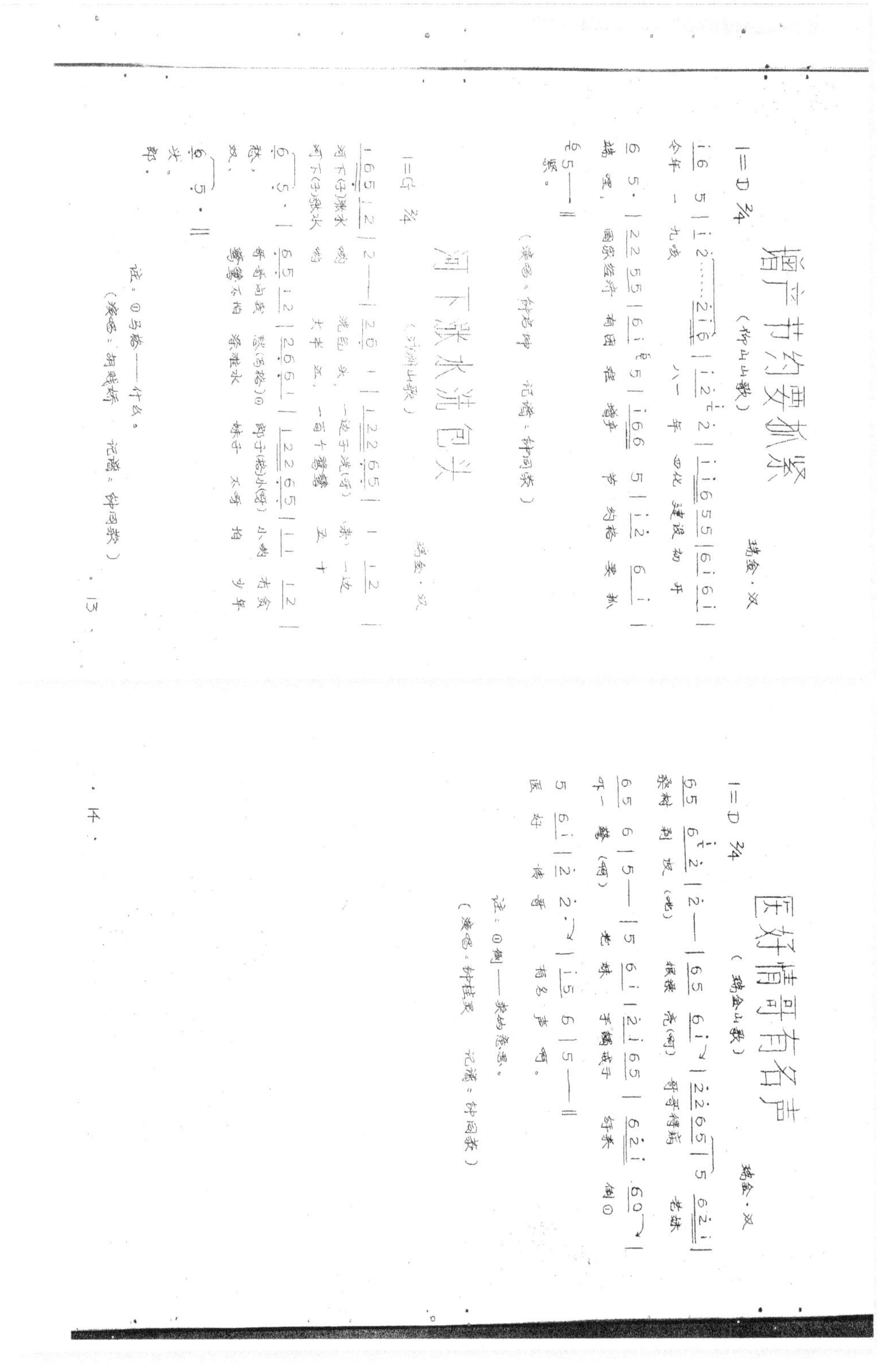

增产节约要抓紧

1=D 2/4　（仰山山歌）　瑞金·汉

i 6 5 | i 2……2 i 6 | i 2 2 | i i 6 5 5 | 6 i 6 i |
今年 一 九咳　八一 年 四化 建设 初 开

6 5· | 2 2 5 5 | 6 i 5 | i 6 6 5 | i 2 6 i |
端 呢，国家经济 有困 难 增产 节 约格 要 抓

5 — ‖
紧。

（演唱：钟岩坤　记谱：钟同荣）

河下涨水洗包头

1=G 2/4　（河洲山歌）　瑞金·汉

1 6 5 1 2 | 2 — | 2 6 1 | 1 2 2 6 5 | 1 1 2 |
河下(子)涨水 哟　洗包 头，一边子洗(牙) (索) 一边
河下(子)涨水 哟　大半 江，一百个鹭鸶 五 十

6 5· | 6 5 1 2 | 2 6 6 1 | 1 2 2 6 5 | 1 1 1 2 |
愁，　哥哥问我 愁(马格)① 郎子(格)小(呀) 小哟 有贪
双，　鹭鸶不怕 深潭水 妹子 不呀 怕 少年

6 5· ‖
头。
郎。

注：①马格——什么。

（演唱：胡贱娇　记谱：钟同荣）

医好情哥有名声

1=D 2/4　（瑞金山歌）　瑞金·汉

6 5 6 2 | 2 — | 6 5 6 i | 2 2 6 5 | 5 6 2 i |
棌村 刷 皮(哋)　很 亮(啊) 哥哥得病　老妹

6 5 6 | 5 — | 5 6 i | 2 i 6 5 | 6 2 i 6 0 |
吓一 惊(啊)　老 妹 手镯戒子 舒表 倒①

5 6 i | 2 2 | i 5 6 | 5 — ‖
医 好 情 哥 有名 声 啊。

注：①倒——卖的意思。

（演唱：钟桂灵　记谱：钟同荣）

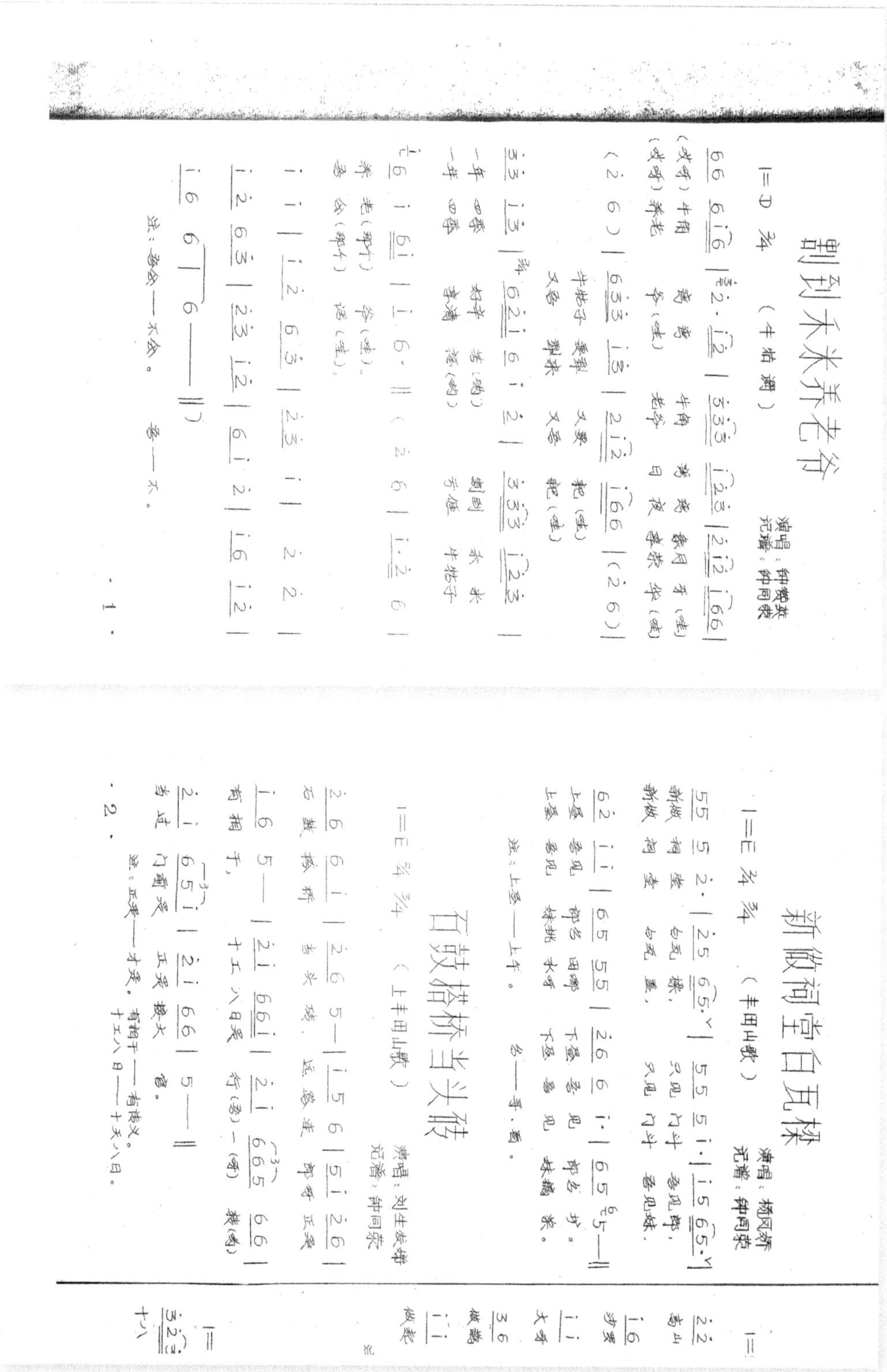

割到禾米养老爷

1=D 2/4　（牛牯调）

演唱：钟赞英
记谱：钟同荣

66 6i6 | 2· i2 | 333 i23 | 2i2 i66 |
（哎呀）牛角　　弯　弯　　牛角　　弯　弯　　象月　牙（哇）
（哎呀）养老　　爷（哇）　　老爷　　日　夜　　享荣　华（哇）

（2 6）| 633 i3 | 2i2 i66 |（2 6）|
牛牯子　要犁　　又要　　耙（哇）
又吾　　犁来　　又吾　　耙（哇）

33 i3 | 3/4 62i 6 i 2 | 333 i23 |
一年　四季　　好辛　苦（哟）　　割到　禾　米
一年　四季　　享清　福（哟）　　亏佳　牛牯子

6 i 6i | i 6· ‖（2 6 | i·2 6 |
养　老（那个）　爷（哇）。
吾　会（那个）　话（哇）。

i i | i2 63 | 23 i | 2 2 |
i2 63 | 23 i2 | 6i 2 | i6 i2 |
i6 6 | 6 —— ‖）

注：吾会——不会。　吾——不。

· 1 ·

新做祠堂白瓦梂

1=E 2/4 3/4　（丰田山歌）

演唱：杨凤娇
记谱：钟同荣

55 5 2· | 25 65· | 55 5 i· | i5 65· |
新做　祠　堂　　白瓦　梂，　　只见　门斗　　吾见郎，
新做　祠　堂　　白瓦　盖，　　只见　门斗　　吾见妹，

62 ii | 65 55 | 26 6 i· | 65 5 —— ‖
上昼　吾见　　郎乞　田啷　　下昼　吾　见　　郎乞　屵。
上昼　吾见　　妹挑　水呀　　下昼　吾　见　　妹摘　菜。

注：上昼——上午。　乞——弄、耍。

石鼓搭桥当头砖

1=E 2/4 3/4　（上丰田山歌）

演唱：刘生发娣
记谱：钟同荣

26 6i | 26 5 — | i5 6 | 5i 26 |
石鼓　搭桥　　当头　砖，　　远路　来　　郎呀　正是

i6 5 — | 2i 66i | 2i 665 66 |
有相　干，　　十工　八日是　　行（吾）一（呀）　转（哟）

2i 65i | 2i 66 | 5 —— ‖
当过　门甭是　　正是　接大　官。

注：正是——才是。有相干——有传义。
十工八日——十天八日。

· 2 ·

1=
22　高山
i6　步要
ii　大呀
36　做鹊
ii　做起

1=
323
十八

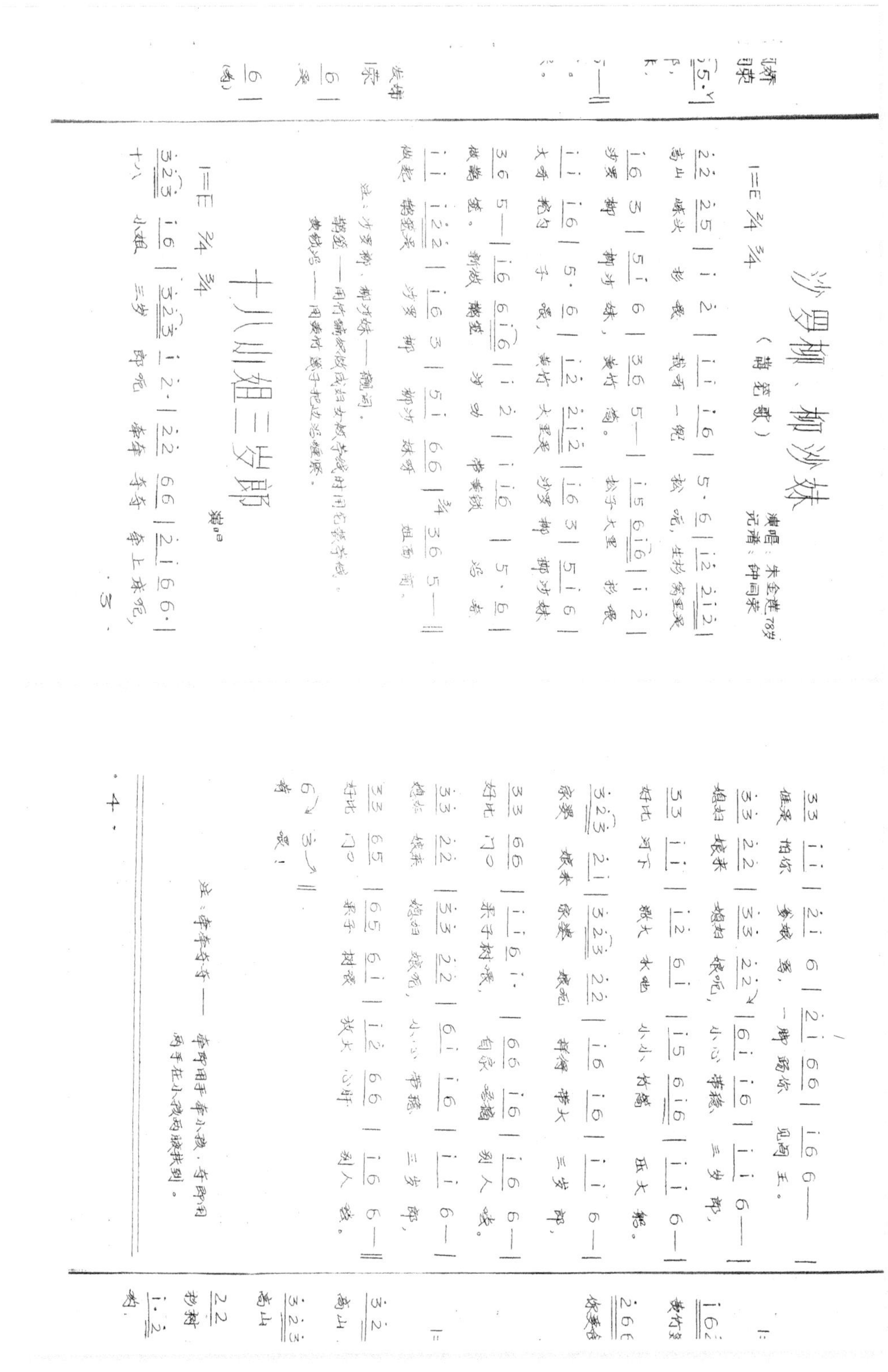

沙罗柳、柳沙妹

（蔺笼歌）

演唱：朱金莲 78岁
记谱：钟同荣

1=E 2/4 3/4

高山峰头杉哦栽呀一兜松呢，生杉窝里沙罗柳柳沙妹，黄竹篙。松子大里杉哦大呀抱勺子哦，黄竹大里来沙罗柳柳沙妹做蔺笼。新做蔺笼涉动带黄锁，冯奇做起蔺笼来沙罗柳柳沙妹呀姐面前。

注：沙罗柳、柳沙妹——衬词。
蔺笼——用竹编织做成妇女做苧线时用它装苧线。
黄锁冯——用黄竹篾子把边沿缠紧。

十八小姐三岁郎

演唱

1=E 2/4 3/4

十八小姐三岁郎呢，牵牵夺夺牵上床呢，

侄是怕你爹娘骂，一脚踢你见阎王。
媳妇娘来媳妇娘呢，小心带稳三岁郎，
好比河下撑大水咃小小竹篙压大船。
家婆娘来家婆娘呢，样得带大三岁郎，
好比门口果子树哦，自家唔摘别人啖。
媳妇娘来媳妇娘呢，小心带稳三岁郎，
好比门口果子树哦，放大心肝别人啖。
衰哦！

注：牵牵夺夺——牵即用手牵小孩，夺即用两手在小孩两腋扶到。

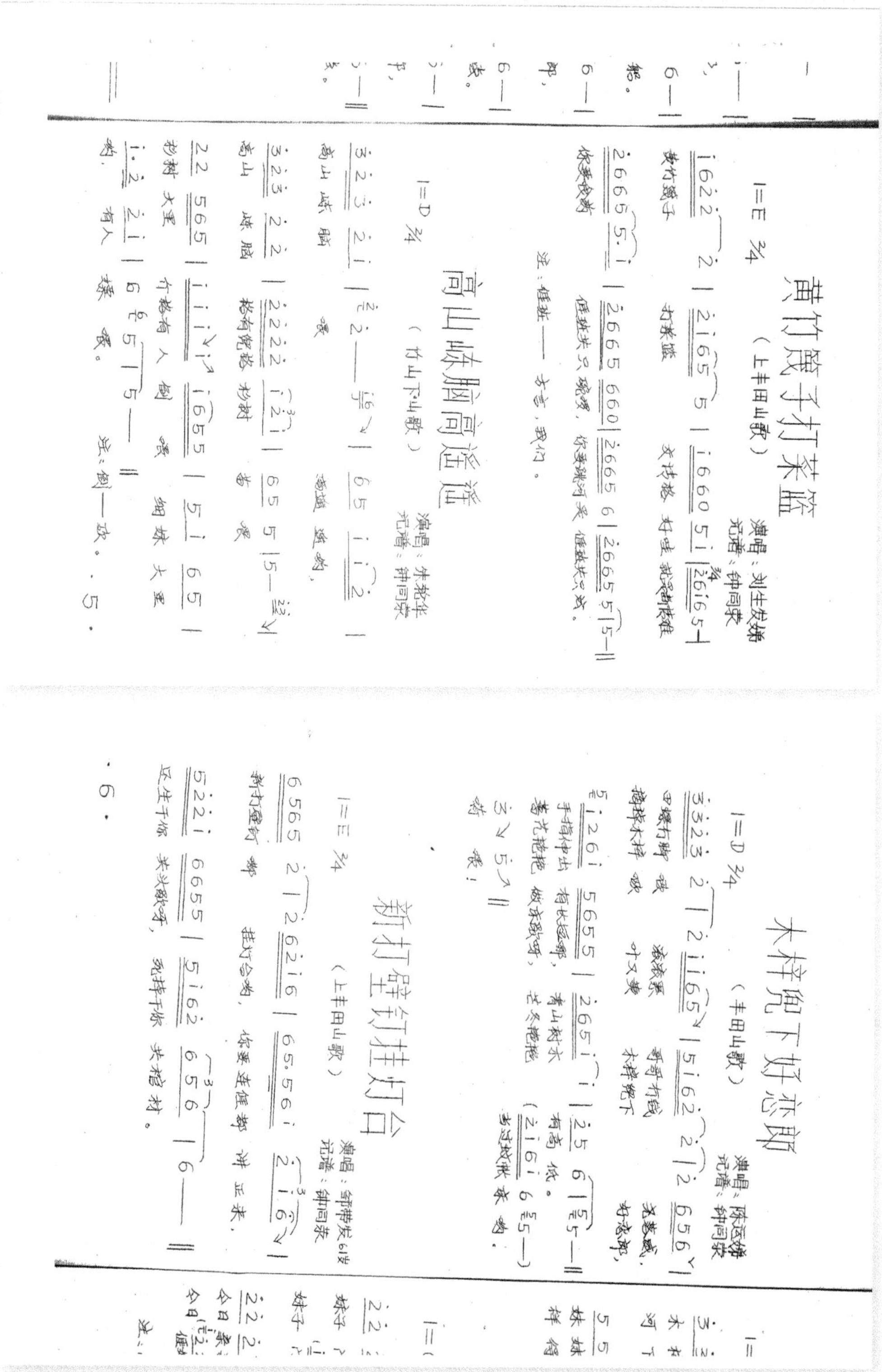

黄竹篾子打茶篮

（上丰田山歌）

1=E 2/4

演唱：刘生发娣
记谱：钟同荣

i622 2 | 2i65 5 | i660 5i | 2616 5— |

黄竹篾子 打茶篮 文诗格 好哇 就系有依难

2665 5.i | 2665 660 | 2665 6 | 2665 5 | 5— ‖

你要食药 偃班共只碗嘤，你要跳河吴 偃班共只坑。

注：偃班——方言，我们。

高山崃脑高遥遥

（竹山下山歌）

1=D 2/4

演唱：朱乾华
记谱：钟同荣

323 2i | 2— | 65 ii2 |

高山崃脑 喂 高遥 遥哟，

323 22 | 2222 i2i | 65 5 | 5— |

高山 崃脑 格有倪格 杉树 苗 喂

22 565 | iii i | i655 | 5i 65 |

杉树 大里 介格有人 倒 喂 细妹 大里

i.2 2i | 6 5 | 5— ‖

哟，有人 搽 喂。

注：倒——砍。

·5·

木梓兜下好恋郎

（丰田山歌）

1=D 2/4

演唱：陈运娣
记谱：钟同荣

3323 2 | 2 ii65 | 5i62 2 | 2 656 |

田螺冇脚 哦 滚滚累 哥哥冇钱 无喜感，
摘掉木梓 哦 叶又黄 木梓兜下 好恋郎，

i26i 5655 | 265i i | 25 6 | 5— ‖

手指伸出 有长短哪， 青山树木 有高 低。
蓄花艳艳 做床歌呀， 芒冬艳艳 （2i6i 6 5—）
当过城州 来 哟。

3 5 ‖

哟 喂！

新打壁钉挂灯台

（上丰田山歌）

1=E 2/4

演唱：邹带发61岁
记谱：钟同荣

6565 2 | 262i6 | 65.56i | 2i6 |

新打壁钉 哪 挂灯台哟， 你要连偃都 讲 正来。

522i 6655 | 5i62 656 | 6— ‖

还生干你 共头歌呀， 死掉干你 共棺 材。

·6·

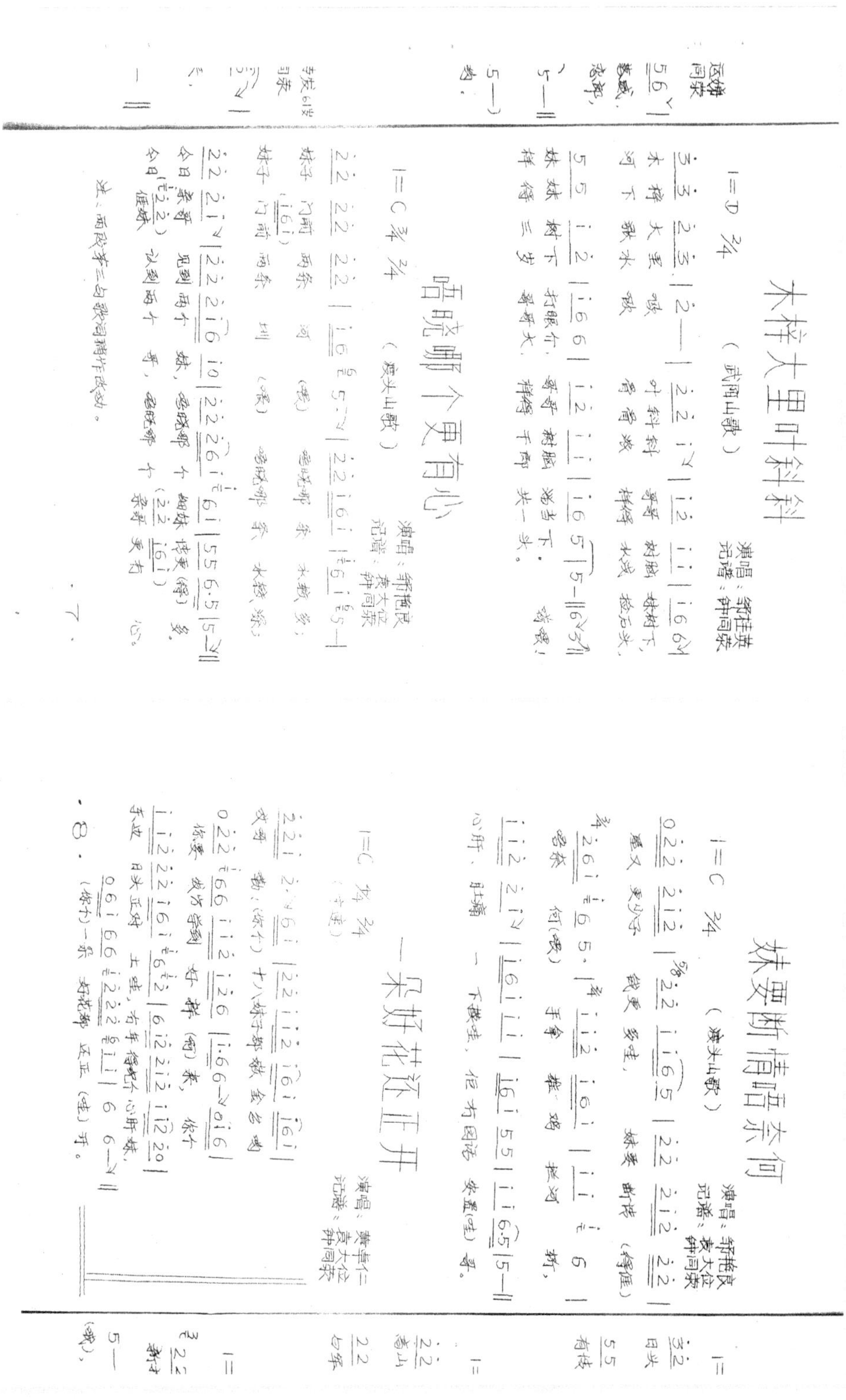

木梓大里叶斜斜

1=D 2/4 （武阳山歌）

演唱：邹桂英
记谱：钟同荣

木梓大里哎 叶斜斜 哥哥树脑 妹树下，
河下秋水哎 骨骨滚 样得水浅 捡石头，

妹妹树下 打眼介，哥哥树脑 猫当下。 嗬喂！
样得三岁 哥哥大，样得千郎 共一头。

唔晓哪个更有心

1=C 3/4 2/4 （寮头山歌）

演唱：邹艳良
记谱：袁大位 钟同荣

妹子 门前 两条 河（哎） 唔晓哪 条 水较 多；
妹子 门前 两条 圳（喂） 唔晓哪 条 水较 深；

今日 亲哥 见到 两个 妹，唔晓哪 个 细妹 情更（得） 多。
今日 侄妹 认到 两个 哥，唔晓哪 个 亲哥 更有 心。

注：两段第三句歌词稍作改动。

· 7 ·

妹要断情唔奈何

1=C 2/4 （寮头山歌）

演唱：邹艳良
记谱：袁大位 钟同荣

（唔）又 更少子 钱更 多哇， 妹要 断情 （得佢）
唔奈 何（哎） 手拿 雄 鸡 拦河 斩，
心肝、肚痛 一 下拔哇，佢 冇 回话 安置（哇） 哥。

一朵好花还正开

1=C 1/4 2/4 （中速）

演唱：黄卓仁
记谱：袁大位 钟同荣

（哎）哥 勤：（你个）十八妹子都 嫩 金 么 哟
你要 发方 学到 好 拚（呵） 来， 你个
东边 日头 正对 土 哇，有 年 得呢个 心肝 妹，
（你个）一朵 好花都 还正（哇） 开。

· 8 ·

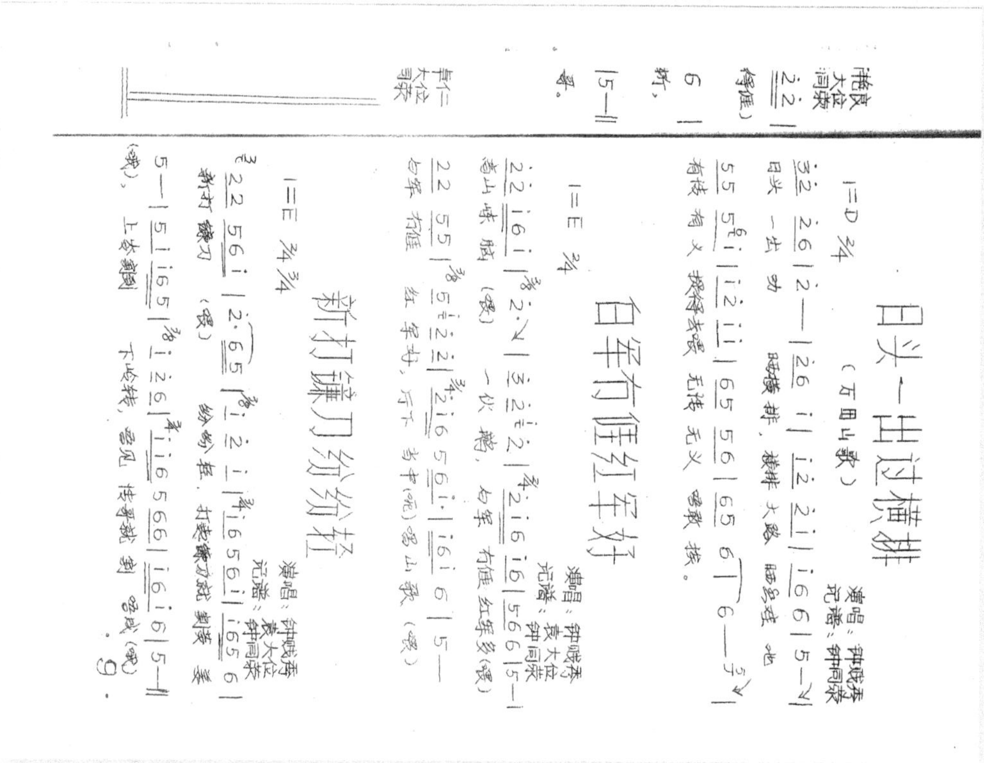

词：袁大位 钟同荣

22 |
得侄）

6 |
析，

|5—||
哥。

词：袁大位 钟同荣

日头一出过横排

1=D 2/4　（万田山歌）　演唱：钟贱秀　记谱：钟同荣

32 26 | 2 — | 26 1 | 12 21 | 166 | 5— |
日头 一出 功　晒横 排，横排 大路 晒乌娃 吔

55 5 1 | 12 11 | 65 56 | 65 6 | 6 — |
有情 有义 摸得去喂 无情 无义 唔敢 挨。

白军冇侄红军好

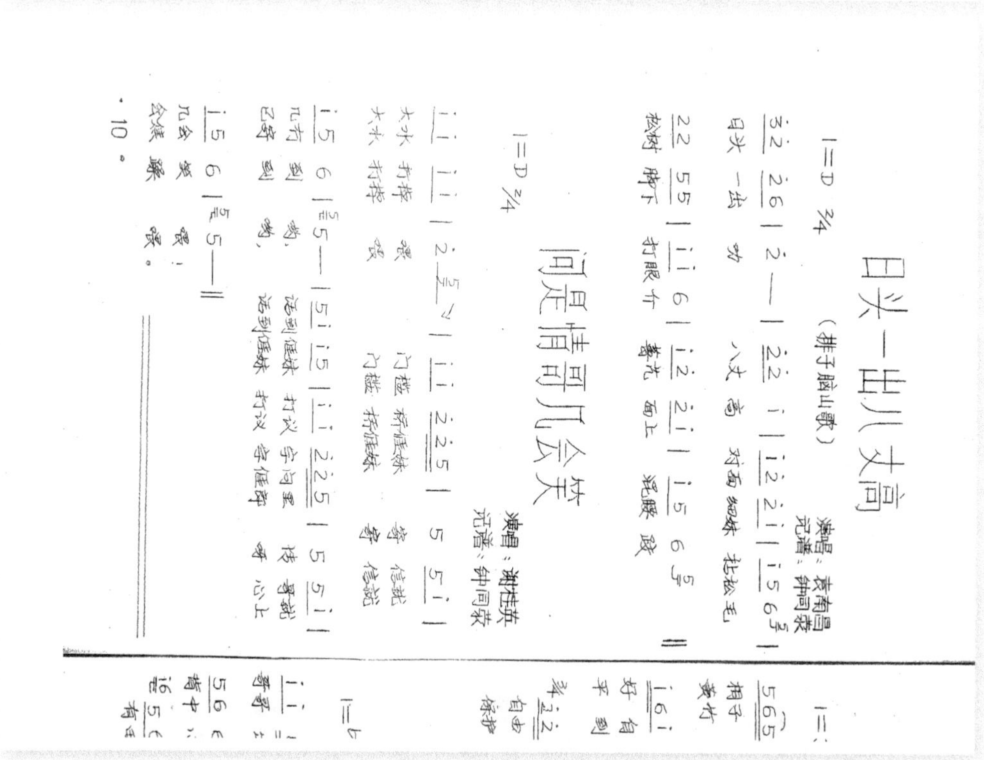

1=E 2/4　演唱：钟贱秀　记谱：袁大位 钟同荣

22 161 | 2· | 3 2 2 | 216 16 | 566 | 5— |
高山 岽脑 （喂） 一伙 鹅， 白军 有侄 红军多（喂）

22 55 | 5 22 | 216 561· | 161 6 | 5— |
白军 有侄 红 军好， 厅下 当中（呢）唱山歌（喂）

新打镰刀纷纷轻

1=E 2/4 3/4　演唱：钟贱秀　记谱：袁大位 钟同荣

22 561 | 2·65 | 1 2 1 | 16561 | 165 6 |
新打 镰刀 （喂）　纷纷 轻，打起镰刀就 割黄 姜

5— | 51 165 | 1 26 | 116 566 | 161 6 | 5— ||
（哦），上岭割到　下岭转，唔见 情哥就 到 唔成（哦）

·9·

日头一出八丈高

1=D 2/4　（排子脑山歌）　演唱：袁南昌　记谱：钟同荣

32 26 | 2 — | 22 1 | 12 21 | 156 |
日头 一出 功　八丈 高　对面 细妹 扯松毛

22 55 | 11 6 | 12 21 | 15 6 ||
松树 脚下 打眼介　薯花 面上 泥腰 跌

问是情哥几会笑

1=D 2/4　演唱：谢桂英　记谱：钟同荣

11 11 | 2 5 | 11 225 | 5 51 |
大水 打挎 喂　门槛 挢侄妹 寄 信就
大水 打挎 喂　门槛 挢侄妹 寄 信就

15 6 | 5— | 51 15 | 11 225 | 5 51 |
几冇 到 吻，话到侄妹 打议 字问里 传 哥就
已寄 到 吻，话到侄妹 打议 字侄部 呀 心上

15 6 | 5— ||
几会 笑 喂！
会… 躁 喂。

·10·

1=

565
相子
黄竹

161
好 自
平 到

3/4 12
自由
保护

1=

11
哥哥

56
背中

16 56
有

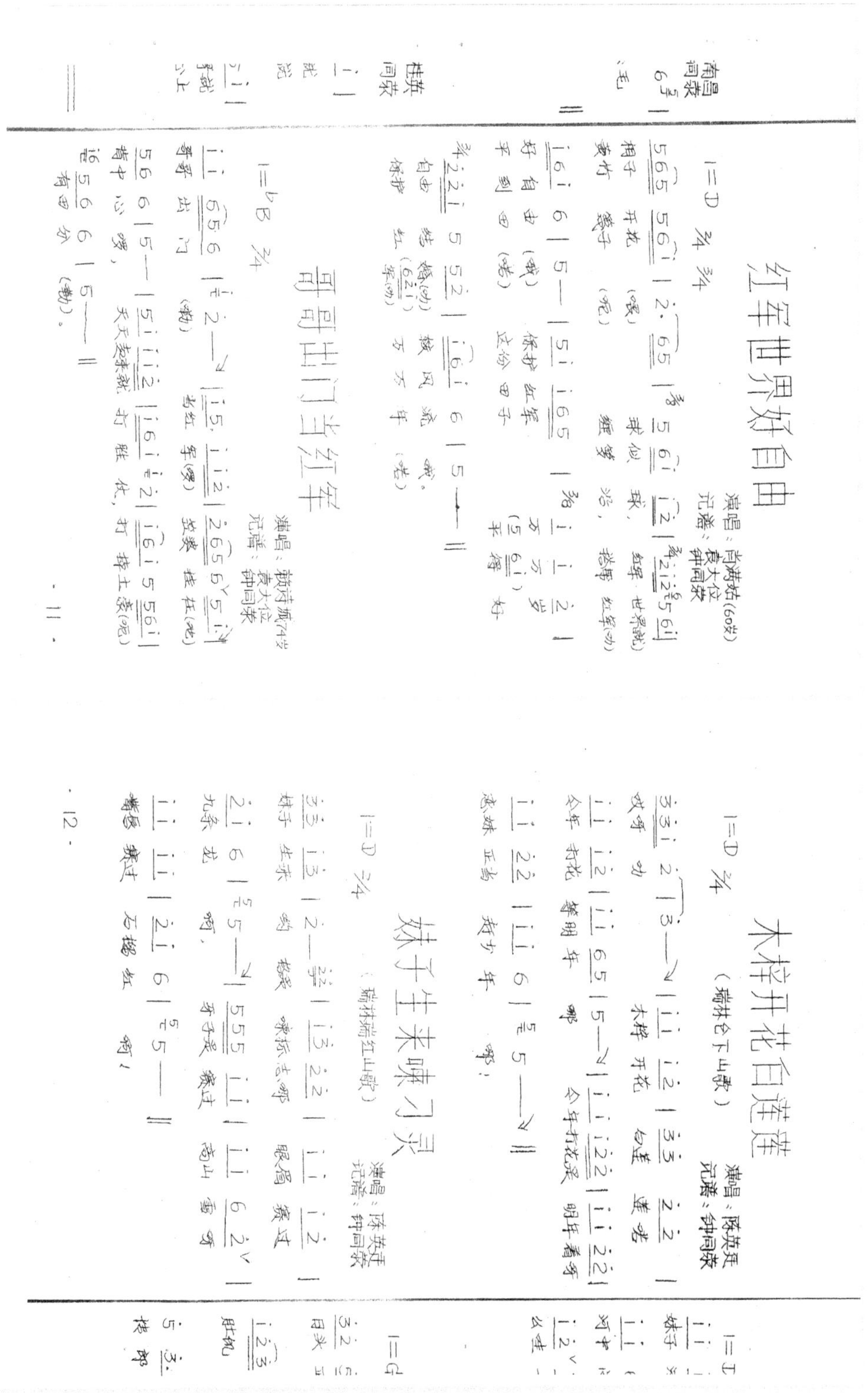

南昌
同荣

桂英
同荣

红军世界好自由

演唱：肖满姑（60岁）
记谱：袁大位 钟同荣

1=D 2/4 3/4

柑子开花（喂）球似球，红军世界就
黄竹篙子（呢）缠箩沿，搭帮红军（哟）

好自由（哦）保护红军 万万岁
平到田（喏）这份田子 平得好

自由结婚（哟）较风流哦。
保护红军（哟）万万年（喏）

哥哥出门当红军

演唱：赖诗城74岁
记谱：袁大位 钟同荣

1=♭B 2/4

哥哥出门（勒）当红军（啰）笠婆挂在（哇）
背中心啰，天天起来就打胜仗，打掉土豪（呢）
有田分（勒）。

木梓开花白莲莲

（瑞林仓下山歌）

演唱：陈英廷
记谱：钟同荣

1=D 2/4

哎呀哟 木梓开花白莲莲喏
今年打花等明年哪 今年打花哥 明年看呀
老妹正当青少年哪！

妹子生来啸刁灵

（瑞林瑞红山歌）

演唱：陈英廷
记谱：钟同荣

1=D 2/4

妹子生来哟格灵 啸标志哪 眼眉赛过
九条龙啊，牙子晃赛过 高山雪呀
嘴唇赛过石榴红啊！

1=D
妹子
河中
么哇

1=G
日头
肚饥
快郎

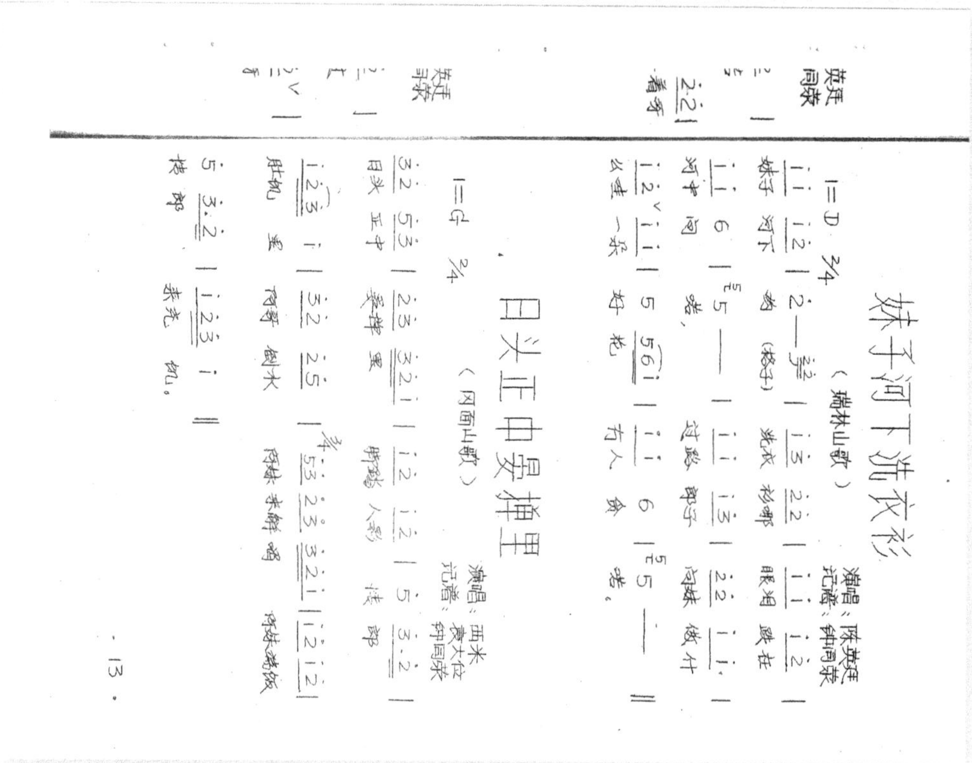

妹子河下洗衣衫

（瑞林山歌）

演唱：陈英廷
记谱：钟同荣

1=D 2/4

妹子 河下 哟（格子）洗衣 衫哪 眼泪 跌在
河中 间 喏， 过路 郎子 问妹 做什
么哇 一朵 好 花 冇人 贪 喏。

日头正中晏掸里

（冈面山歌）

演唱：西米
记谱：袁大位 钟同荣

1=G 2/4

日头 正中 晏掸 里 晒踏 人影 传 郎
肚饥 里 阿哥 倒水 阿妹 未解 喝 阿妹端饭
传 郎 未充 饥。

· 13 ·

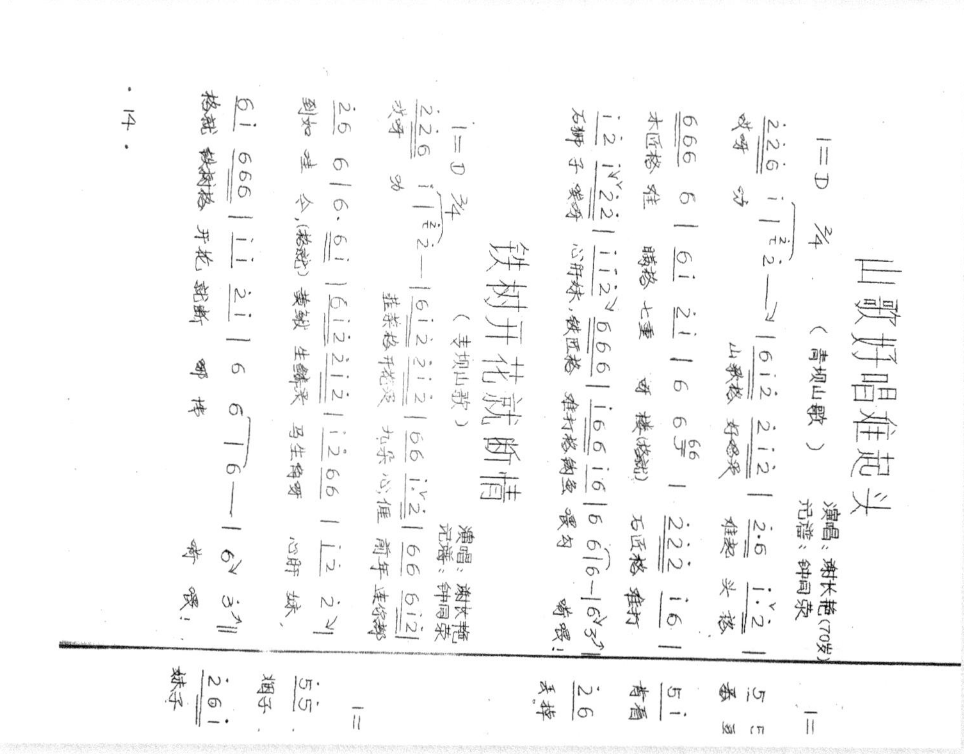

山歌好唱难起头

（青坝山歌）

演唱：谢长艳（70岁）
记谱：钟同荣

1=D 2/4

哎呀 动 山歌格 好唱哎 难起 头 格
木匠格 难 瞒格 七重 呀 楼（格就） 石匠格 难打
石狮 子 哎呀 心肝妹，铁匠格 难打格钩鱼 喂勾 嗬喂！

铁树开花就断情

（青坝山歌）

演唱：谢长艳
记谱：钟同荣

1=D 2/4

哎呀 动 挂菜格开花哎 九朵 心；催 前年 连你都
到如 哇 今，（格就） 黄鳅 生鳞哎 马生角呀 心肝 妹，
格就 铁树格 开花 就断 哪 传 嗬 喂！

· 14 ·

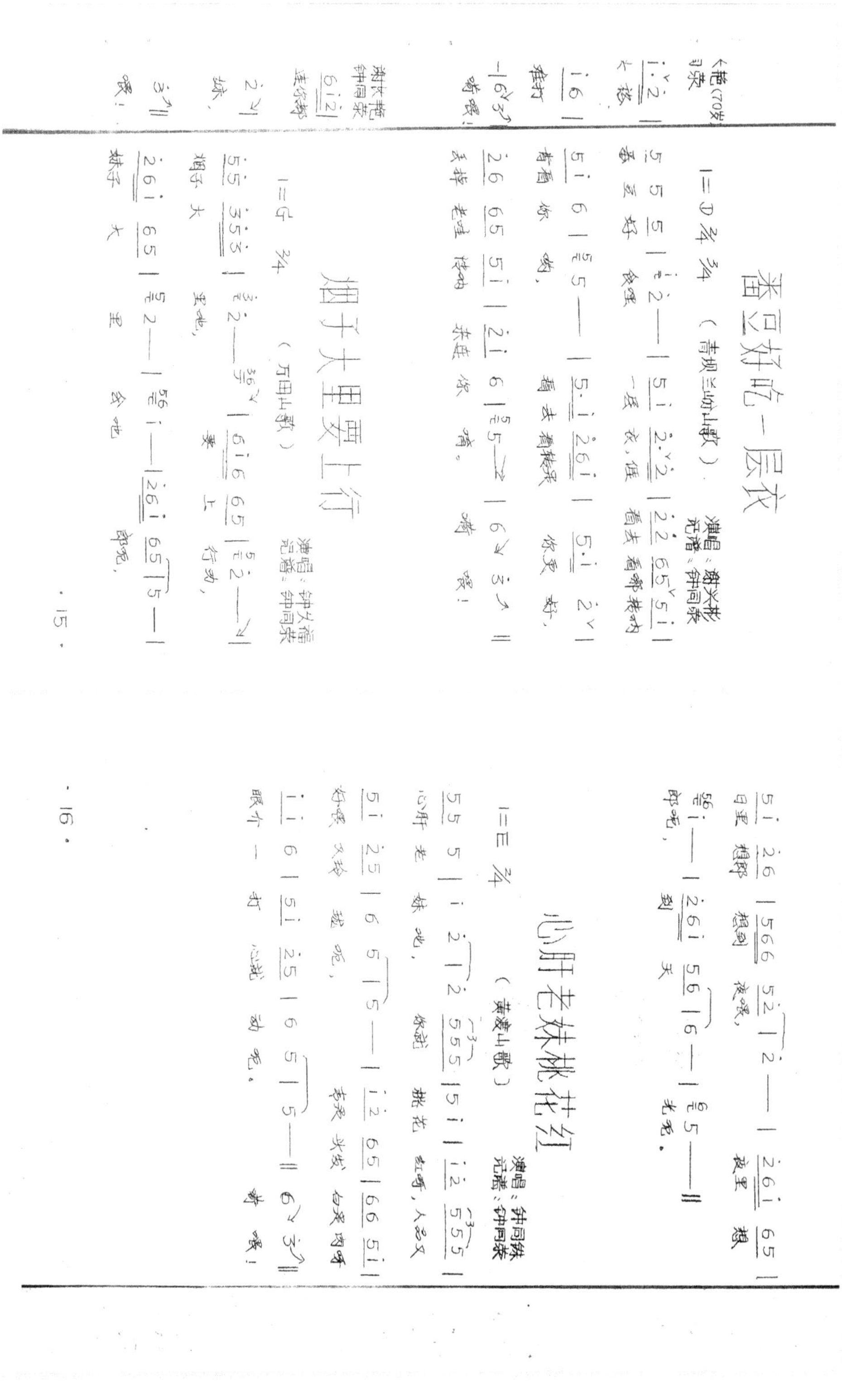

番豆好吃一层衣

1=D 2/4 3/4 （青坝兰岭山歌）

演唱：谢兴彬
记谱：钟同荣

番豆好食哩 一层衣，俚看去看哪转呐
肯看你哟， 看去看转来 你更好，
丢掉老娃俚呐 未连你 啃。 啃 喂！

烟子大里要上行

1=G 3/4 （万田山歌）

演唱：钟火福
记谱：钟同荣

烟子大 里吧， 要 上 行动，
妹子大 里 会吧 郎呢，

日里 想郎 想到 夜喂， 夜里 想
郎呢， 到 天 光呢。

心肝老妹桃花红

1=E 2/4 （黄凌山歌）

演唱：钟同铁
记谱：钟同荣

心肝 老 妹 吧， 你就 桃花 红呀，人品又
好喂 又玲 珑 呃， 青丝 头发 白里 肉呀
眼介 一 打 心就 动 呃。 啃 喂！

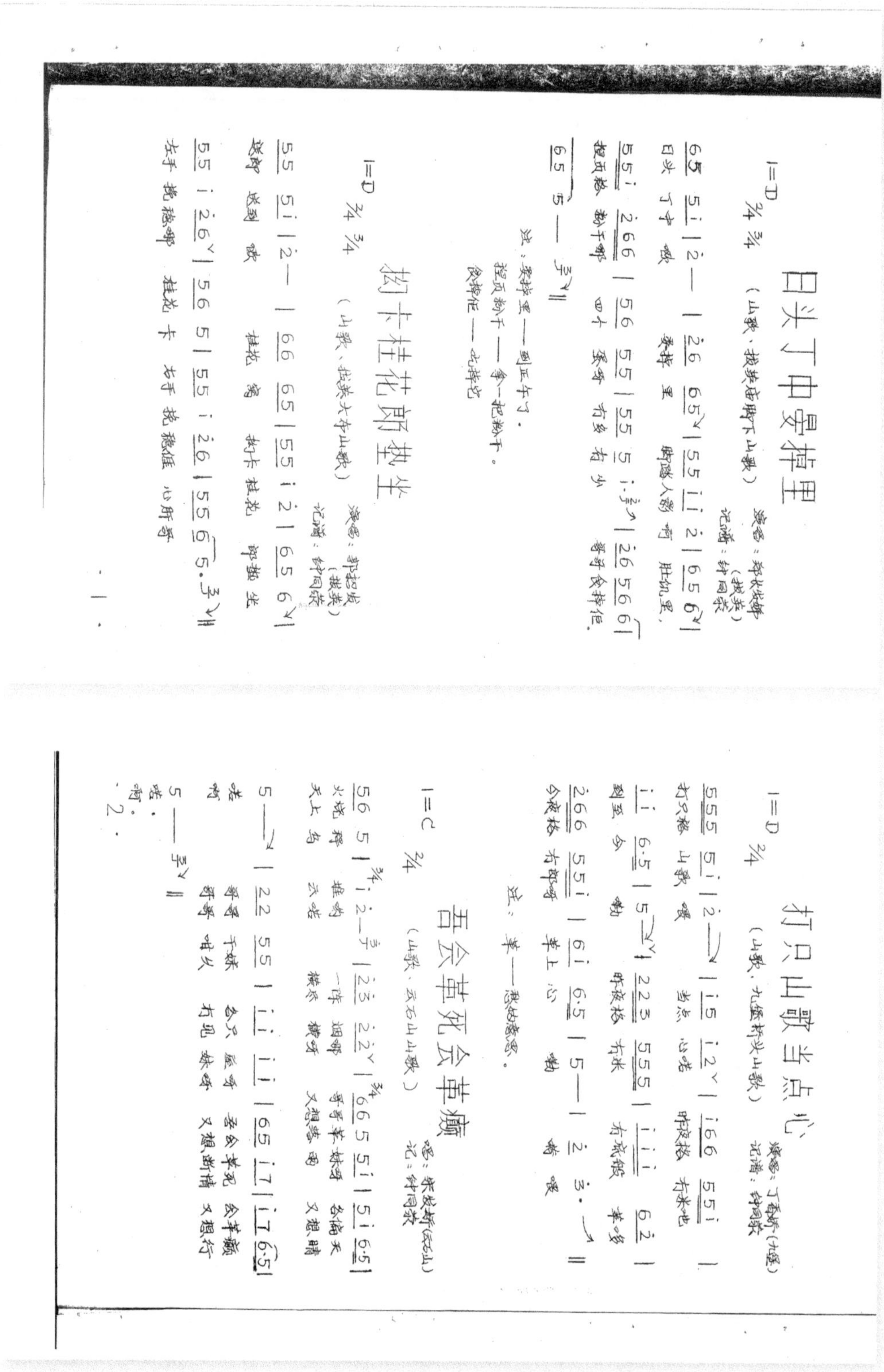

日头丁中晏掉里

1=D 2/4 3/4　（山歌、拔英庙脚下山歌）　演唱：郑长发娇（拔英）　记谱：钟同荣

65 5i | 2̇— | 2̇6 65 | 55 ii 2̇ | 65 6 |
日头 丁中 啾 晏掉 里 脚踏人影 啊 肚饥里，

55i 2̇66 | 56 55 | 55 5 i· | 2̇6 56 6 |
捏页格 粉干啊 四个 蛋呀 有多 有 少 哥哥食掉佢。

65 5 — ||

注：晏掉里——到正午了。
捏页粉干——拿一把粉干。
食掉佢——吃掉它

拗卡桂花郎垫坐

1=D 2/4 3/4　（山歌、拔英大布山歌）　演唱：郭招发（拔英）　记谱：钟同荣

55 5i | 2̇— | 66 65 | 55 i 2̇ | 65 6 |
送郎 送到 啾 桂花 窝 拗卡 桂花 郎垫 坐

55 i 2̇6 | 56 5 | 55 i 2̇6 | 55 6 5· ||
左手 挽稳啊 桂花 卡 右手 挽稳佢 心肝哥

· 1 ·

打只山歌当点心

1=D 2/4　（山歌、九堡桥头山歌）　演唱：丁香娇（九堡）　记谱：钟同荣

555 5i | 2̇— | i5 i2̇ | i66 55i |
打只格 山歌 喂 当点 心啫 昨夜格 冇米吔

ii 6·5 | 5— | 223 555 | iii 62̇ |
到至 今 呦 昨夜格 冇米 冇底般 革哆

266 55i | 6i 6·5 | 5— | 2̇ 3· ||
今夜格 冇郎呀 革上 心 呦 嵛 喂

注：革——愁的意思。

吾会革死会革癫

1=C 2/4　（山歌、云石山山歌）　唱：宋发娇（云石山）　记：钟同荣

56 5 | 3/4 i 2̇— | 2̇3 2̇2̇ | 3/4 665 5i | 5i 6·5 |
火烧 稈 堆哟 一阵 烟啊 哥哥革 妹呀 各偏 天
天上 乌 云啫 横尽 横呀 又想落 雨 又想 晴

5— | 22 55 | ii ii | 65 i7 | i7 6·5 |
啫 哥哥 干妹 各只 屋呀 吾会革死 会革癫
啊 哥哥 咁久 冇见 妹呀 又想断情 又想行

5 — ||
啫。
啊。

· 2 ·

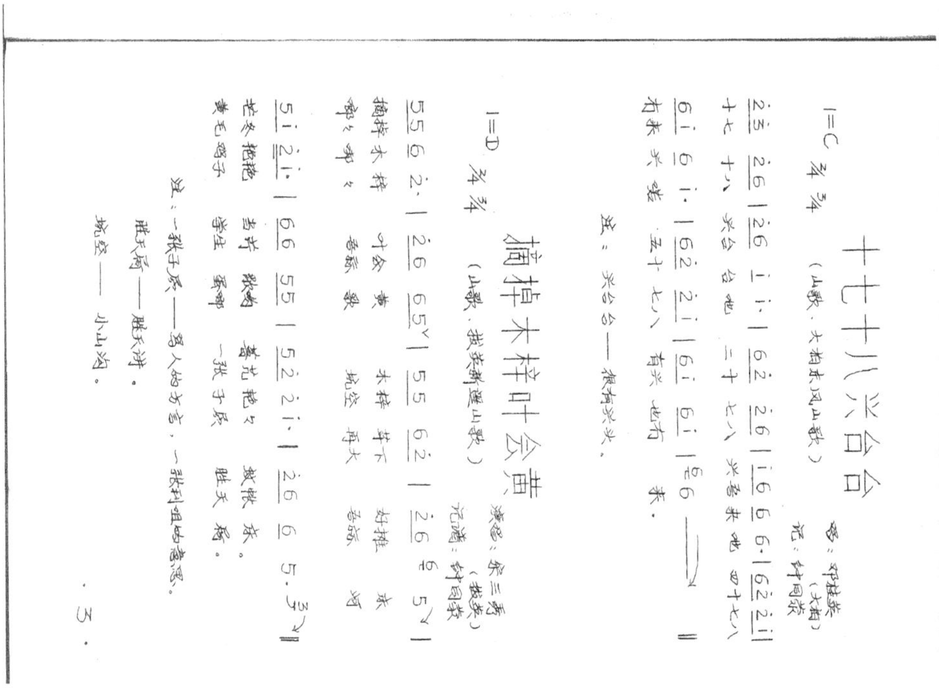

十七十八兴台台

1=C 2/4 3/4 （山歌、大柏东风山歌）

唱：邓桂英（大柏）
记：钟同荣

23 26 | 26 1 1· | 62 26 | 16 6 6· | 62 21 |
十七 十八 兴台 台吔 二十 七八 兴吾 来吔 四十七八

61 6 1· | 62 21 | 61 61 | 6 —— ‖
冇来 兴 啱 五十 七八 有兴 也冇 来。

注：兴台台——很有兴头。

摘掉木梓叶会黄

1=D 2/4 3/4 （山歌、拔英新迳山歌）

演唱：宋三秀（拔英）
记谱：钟同荣

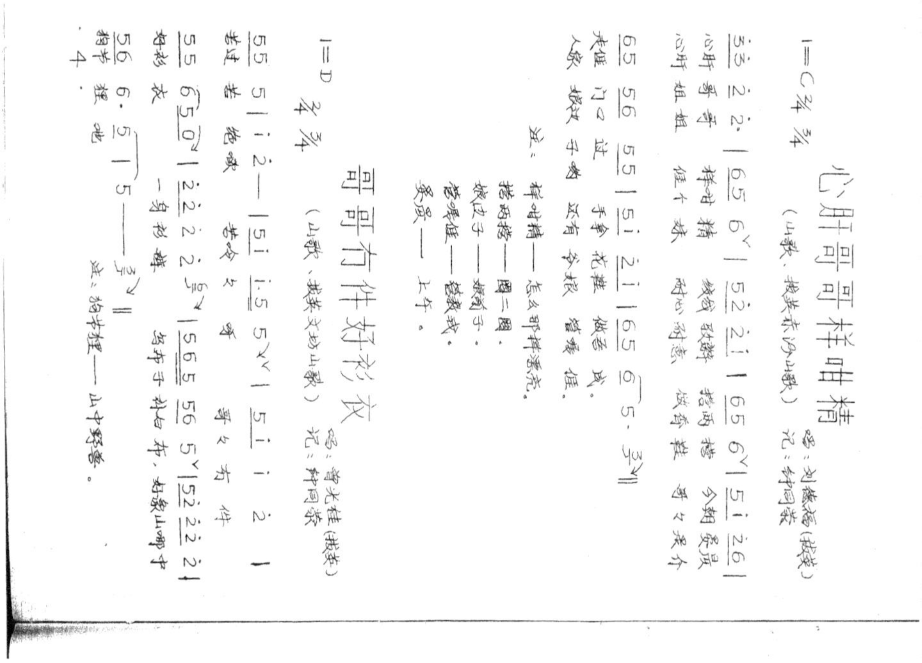

55 6 2· | 26 65 | 55 62 | 26 5 |
摘掉 木 梓 叶会 黄 木梓 苹下 好摊 东
哪々 哪 々 吾毓 歌 坑空 再大 吾毓 河

51 21· | 66 55 | 52 21· | 26 6 5· ‖
芒冬 艳艳 当打 歌哟 蕃芫 艳々 蚊帐 东。
黄毛 鸡子 学生 蛋哪 一张 子屄 胜天 屙。

注：一张子屄——骂人的方言，一张利咀的意思。
胜天屙——胜天讲。
坑空—— 小山沟。

· 3 ·

心肝哥哥样咁精

1=C 2/4 3/4 （山歌、拔英赤沙山歌）

唱：刘德福（拔英）
记：钟同荣

33 2 2· | 65 6 | 52 21 | 65 6 | 51 26 |
心肝 哥 哥 样咁 精 钱钱 致鲜 揩两 揩 今朝 晏昼
心肝 姐 姐 偓个 妹 耐心 耐意 做香 鞋 哥々 涊介

65 56 55 | 51 21 | 65 6 5· ‖
走偓 门口 过 手拿 花鞋 做吾 成。
人家 娘边 子哟 还有 爷娘 管教 偓。

注： 样咁精—— 怎么那样漂亮。
揩两揩—— 圈二圈。
娘边子—— 娘崽子。
管教偓—— 管教我。
晏昼—— 上午。

哥哥有件好衫衣

1=D 2/4 3/4 （山歌、拔英文坊山歌）

唱：曾光桂（拔英）
记：钟同荣

55 5 | 1 2 — | 51 1·5 5 | 51 1 2 |
苦过 苦 绝 啾 苦吟 々 呀 哥 々 有 件

55 6 50 | 22 2 2 | 565 56 5 | 52 22 2 |
好衫 衣 一身 衫 裤 乌布子 补白 布，好象山哪 中

56 6· 5 | 5 —— ‖
狗节 狸 吔

注：狗节狸—— 山中野兽。

· 4 ·

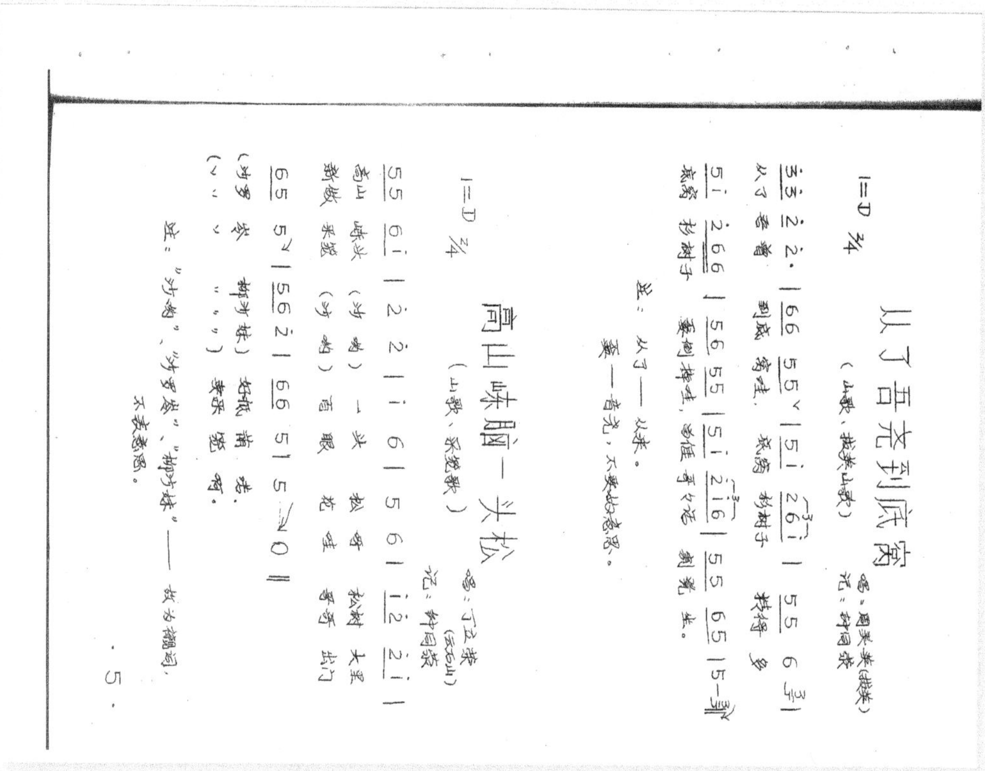

从了吾尧到底窝

1=D 2/4　（山歌、拔英山歌）　唱：周美英（拔英）　记：钟同荣

33 2 2· | 66 55 | 5i 26i | 55 6 3 |
从了吾曾　到底窝哇．氐窝　杉树子　拧得　多

5i 266 | 56 55 | 5i 2i6 | 55 65 | 5— ||
底窝　杉树子　蚕树挥哇，哟侄哥々还　刺光　生。

注：从了——从来。
蚕——音光，不要的意思。

高山岽脑一头松

1=D 2/4　（山歌、采笼歌）　唱：丁立荣（云石山）　记：钟同荣

55 6i | 2 2 | i 6 | 5 6 | i2 2i |
高山　岽头　（沙　哟）　一　头　松　呀　松树　大里
新做　采笼　（沙　哟）　百　眼　花　哇　哥哥　出门

65 5 | 56 2 | 66 5 | 5 0 ||
（沙罗　岑　柳沙妹）好抵　荫　凉．
（〃〃　〃　〃〃〃）妻采　笼　啊。

注：“沙哟”、“沙罗岑”、“柳沙妹”——故为衬词，不表意思。

· 5 ·

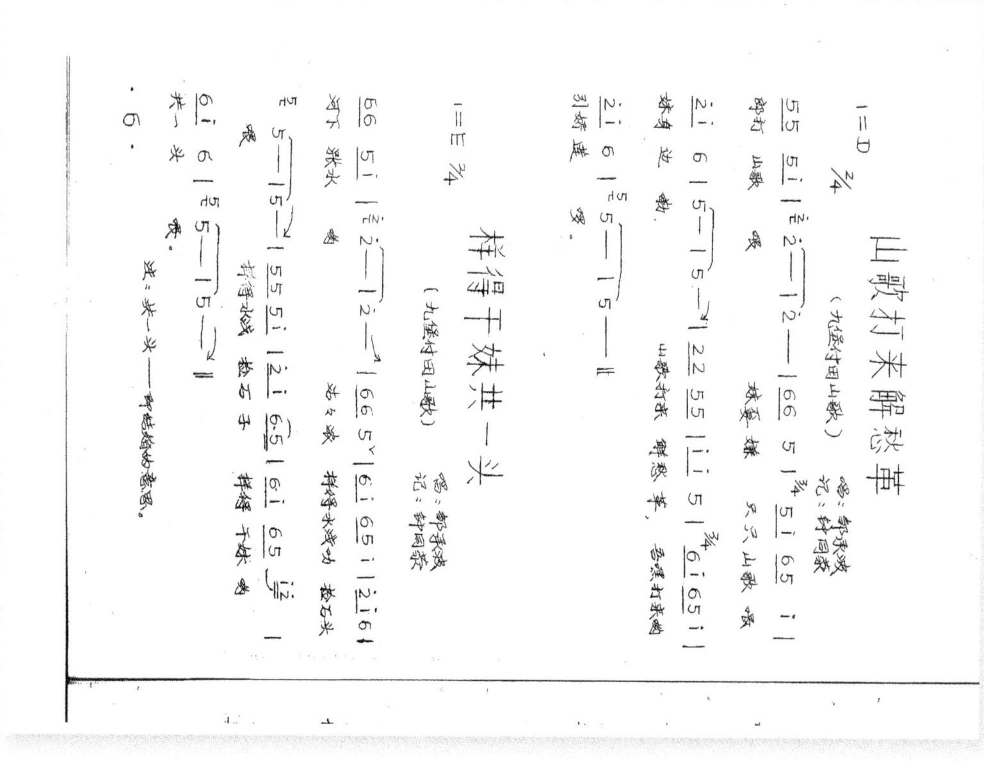

山歌打来解愁革

1=D 2/4　（九堡付田山歌）　唱：邹承波　记：钟同荣

55 5i | 2— | 2— | 66 5 | 3/4 5i 65 i |
郎打　山歌　哦　　妹要　妹　只只　山歌　哦

2i 6 | 5— | 5— | 22 55 | ii 5 | 3/4 6i 65 i |
妹身　边　勒．　山歌打来　解愁　革，吾嘿打来哟

2i 6 | 5— | 5— ||
引娇莲　啰。

样得干妹共一头

1=E 2/4　（九堡付田山歌）　唱：邹承波　记：钟同荣

66 5i | 2— | 2— | 66 5 | 6i 65 i | 2i6 |
河下　涨水　哟　　沾々浓　样得水哉呦　捡石头

5— | 5— | 55 5i | 2i 6·5 | 6i 65 i2 |
哦　　样得水哉　捡石　子　样得　干妹　哟

6i 6 | 5— | 5— ||
共一　头　哦。

注：共一头——即结婚的意思。

· 6 ·

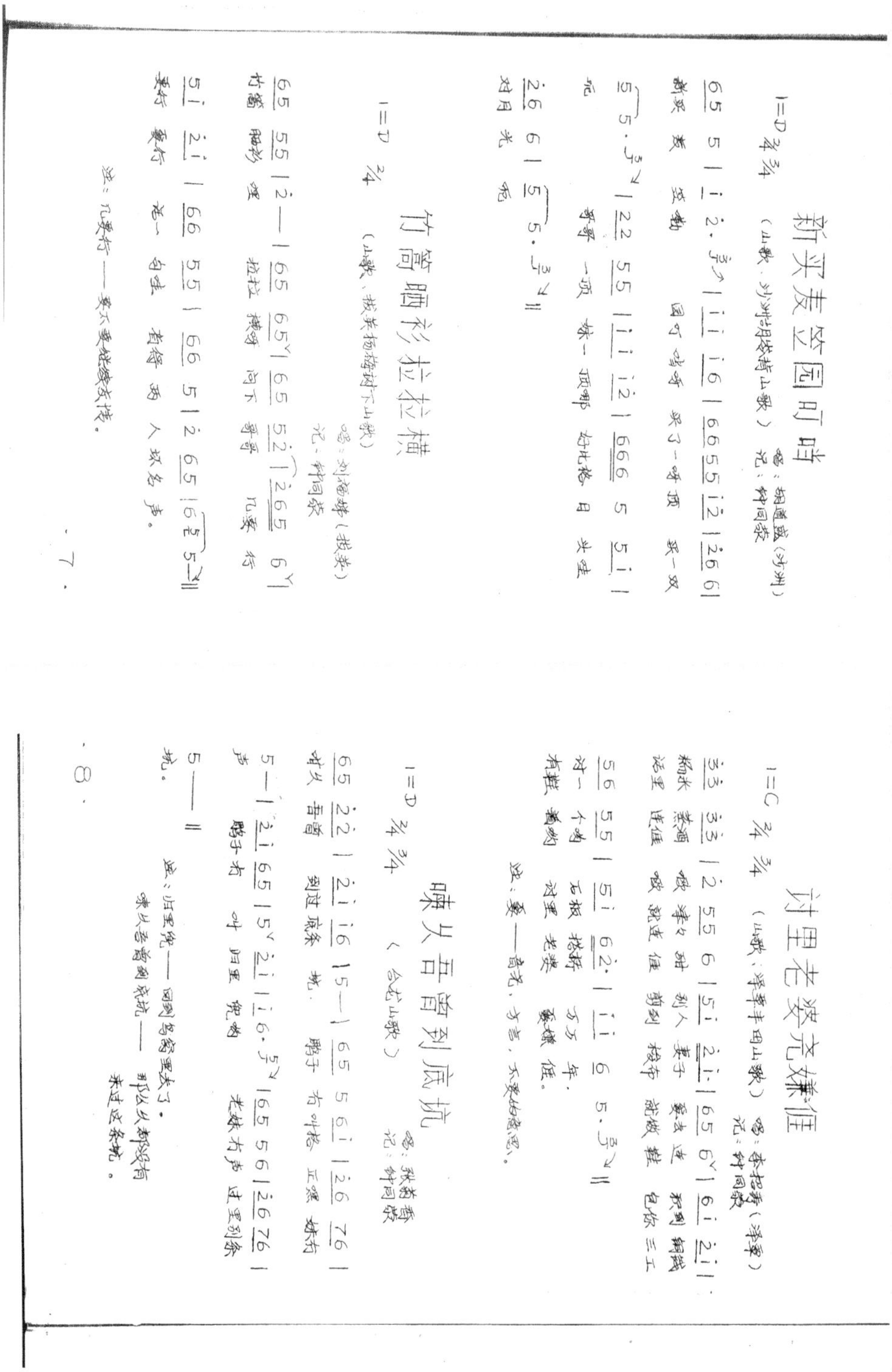

新买麦笠园叮哨

1=D 2/4 3/4 （山歌、沙洲胡岑持山歌） 唱：胡道盛（沙洲） 记：钟同荣

65 5 | 1 2. 3 | 11 16 | 6655 12 | 26 6 |
新买 麦 笠勒 园叮 哨呀 买了一呀 顶 买一双

5 5. 3 | 22 55 | 11 12 | 666 5 51 |
玩 哥哥 一顶 妹一 顶哪 好比格 日 头哇

26 6 | 5 5. 3 ||
对月 光 玩

竹篙晒衫拉拉横

1=D 2/4 （山歌、拔英杨梅树下山歌）
唱：刘福娣（拔英）
记：钟同荣

65 55 | 2 — | 65 65 | 65 52 | 265 6 |
竹篙 晒衫 哩 拉拉 横呀 问下 哥哥 几要 行

51 21 | 66 55 | 66 5 | 2 65 | 62 5 ||
要行 要行 话一 句哇 省得 两 人 坏名 声。

注：几要行——要不要继续交往。

· 7 ·

讨里老婆充嫌伍

1=C 2/4 3/4 （山歌：泽覃丰田山歌） 唱：李招秀（泽覃） 记：钟同荣

33 33 | 2 55 6 | 51 21 | 65 6 | 61 21 |
糯米 蒸酒 哦 津津 甜 别人 妻子 爱去 连 积到 铜钱
话里 连伍 哦 就连 伍 剪到 校布 就做 鞋 包你 三工

56 55 | 51 62 | 11 6 5. 3 ||
讨一 个哟 石板 搭桥 万万 年。
有鞋 着哟 讨里 老婆 爱嫌 伍。

注：爱——音无，方言，不要的意思。

嗦头吾曾到底坑

1=D 2/4 3/4 （合龙山歌） 唱：张菊香 记：钟同荣

65 22 | 21 16 | 5 — | 65 5 61 | 26 76 |
哪头 吾曾 到过 底条 坑。 鹏子 冇 叫格 正嘿 妹冇

5 — | 21 65 | 5 21 | 1 6. 5 | 65 56 | 26 76 |
声 鹏子冇 叫 归里 兜哟 老妹冇声 过里到条

5 — ||
坑。

注：归里兜——回到鸟窝里去了。
嗦头吾曾到底坑——那么头都没有来过这条坑。

· 8 ·

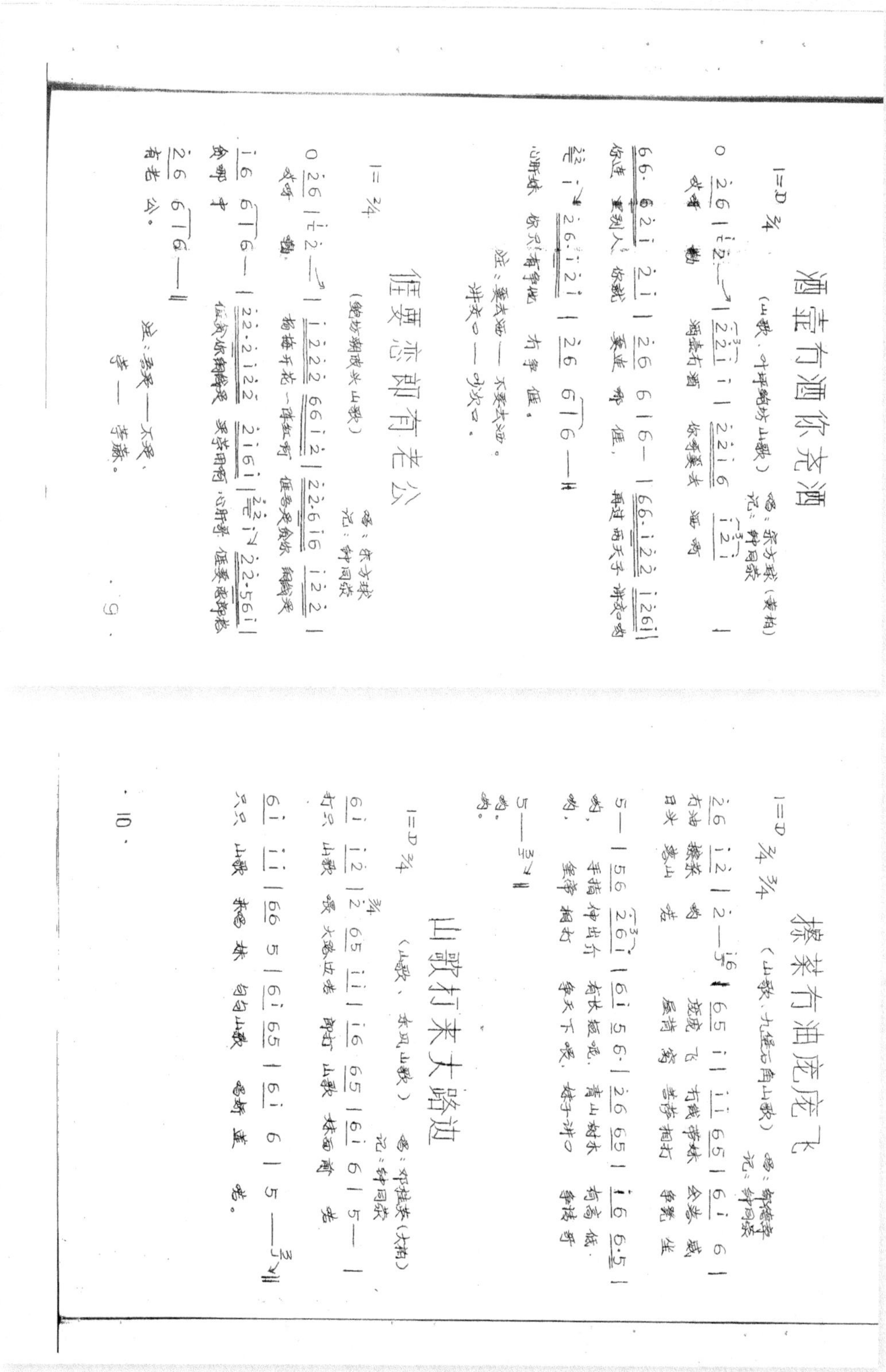

酒壶有酒你尧酒

1=D 2/4　（山歌、叶坪鲍坊山歌）　唱：东方球（黄柏）　记：钟同荣

0 2̇6 | i̇2̇— | 2̇2̇i̇ i̇ | 2̇2̇i̇6 i̇2̇i̇ |
哎呀 嘞　酒壶有酒　你哥要去　洒啊

66·6 2̇i̇ 2̇i̇ | 2̇6 6 | 6— | 66·i̇2̇2̇ i̇2̇6i̇ |
你连 重到人 你就　要连 哪 侄，　再过 两天子 讲交口哟

2̇2̇ i̇ 2̇6·i̇2̇i̇ | 2̇6 6 | 6 —‖
心肝妹 你只有争他 有争 侄。

注：要去洒——不要去洒。
讲交口——吵次口。

侄要恋郎有老公

1= 2/4　（鲍坊湖陂头山歌）　唱：东方球　记：钟同荣

0 2̇6 | i̇2̇— | i̇2̇2̇2̇ 66i̇2̇ | 2̇2̇·6i̇6 i̇2̇2̇ |
哎呀 嘞　杨梅开花一阵红啊　侄吾爱贪你　钢钱爱

i̇6 6 | 6— | 2̇2̇·2̇i̇2̇2̇ 2̇i̇6i̇ | 2̇2̇ i̇ 2̇2̇·56i̇ |
贪哪 中　侄贪你钢钱爱　爱苧甲啊　心肝哥　侄要恋郎格

2̇6 6 | 6 —‖
有老 公。

注：吾爱——不爱。
苧——苧麻。

· 9 ·

擦菜有油庞庞飞

1=D 2/4 3/4　（山歌、九堡石角山歌）　唱：邹德亭　记：钟同荣

2̇6 i̇2̇ | 2̇— | 65 i̇ | i̇i̇ 65 | 6i̇ 6 |
有油 擦菜 哟　庞庞 飞　有钱 带妹　会当 威
日头 落山 苦　屋背 窝　苦萨 相打　争凳 坐

5— | 56 2̇6i̇ | 6i̇ 5 6· | 2̇6 65 | i̇6 6·5 |
哟，　手指 伸出介　有长 短呢，　青山 树木　有高 低．
哟，　星帝 相打　争天下 喂，　妹子讲口　争情 哥

5 — ‖
哟。
哟。

山歌打来大路边

1=D 2/4　（山歌、东风山歌）　唱：邓桂英（大柏）　记：钟同荣

6i̇ i̇2̇ | 2̇ 65 i̇i̇ | i̇6 65 | 6i̇ 6 | 5— |
打只 山歌 喂 大路边苦　郎打 山歌　妹面 前　苦

6i̇ i̇i̇ | 66 5 | 6i̇ 65 | 6i̇ 6 | 5 —‖
只只 山歌 来唱 妹　句句山歌　唱妍 莲　苦。

· 10 ·

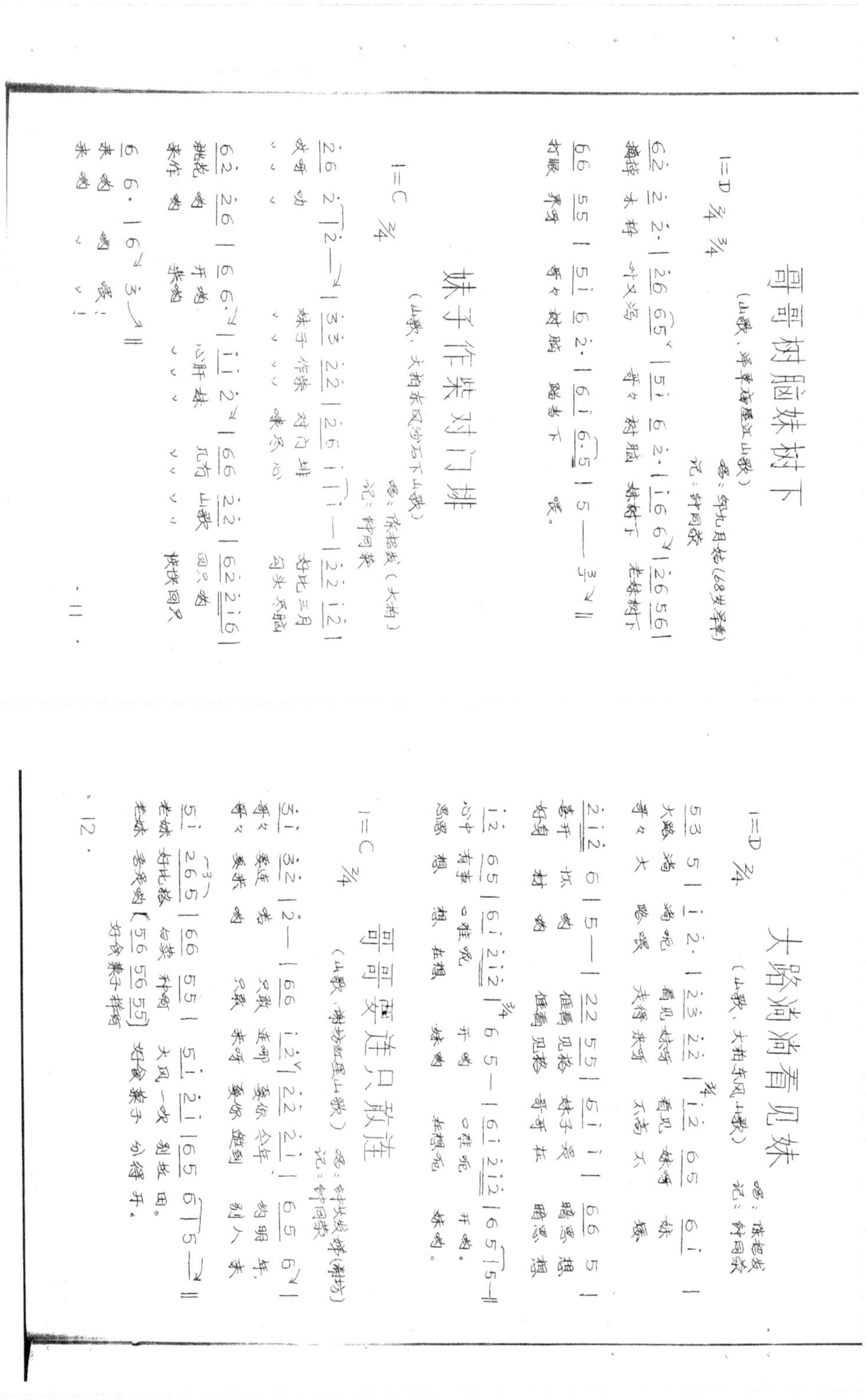

哥哥树脑妹树下

（山歌、泽覃庵屋江山歌）

1=D 2/4 3/4

唱：邹九月姑（68岁泽覃）
记：钟同荣

62 2 2· | 26 65 | 5i 6 2· | i6 6 | 26 56 |
摘掉 木 梓 叶又泻 哥々 树脑 妹树下 老妹树下

66 55 | 5i 6 2· | 6i 6·5 | 5 — 3 ‖
打眼 界呀 哥々 树脑 踏当下 喂。

妹子作柴对门排

（山歌、大柏东风沙石下山歌）

1=C 2/4

唱：陈超发（大柏）
记：钟同荣

26 2 | 2 — | 33 22 | 26 i | i — | 22 i2 |
哎呀 呦 妹子 作柴 对门 排 好比 三月
ˇ ˇ ˇ ˇ ˇ ˇˇ 嗦尽 心 勾头 尽脑

62 26 | 6 6· | ii 2 | 66 22 | 62 2i6 |
桃花 哟 开 哟 心肝 妹 几有 山歌 回只 哟
来作 哟 柴哟 ˇ ˇ ˇ ˇˇ ˇˇ 快快回只

6 6· | 6 3 ‖
来 哟 哟 喂！
来 哟 ˇ ˇ！

· 11 ·

大路淌淌看见妹

1=D 2/4

（山歌、大柏东风山歌）

唱：陈超发
记：钟同荣

53 5 | i 2· | 23 22 | 3/4 i2 65 6i |
大路 淌 淌 呢 看见 妹呀 看见 妹呀 妹
哥々 大 路 喂 走得 来呀 不高 不 矮

2i2 6 | 5 — | 22 55 | 6i i | 66 5 |
喜开 怀 哟 佴看 见格 妹子 哭 暗思 想
好身 材 哟 佴看 见格 哥哥 在 暗思 想

i2 65 | 6i 2i2 | 3/4 6 5 — | 6i 2i2 | 65 | 5 — ‖
心中 有事 口难 呢 开 哟 口难 呢 开 哟。
思思 想 想 在想 妹 哟 在想 呢 妹 哟。

哥哥要连只敢连

1=C 2/4

（山歌、谢坊红星山歌）

唱：钟长发妹（谢坊）
记：钟同荣

3i 32 | 2 — | 66 i2 | 22 2i | 65 6 |
哥々 要连 若 只敢 连哪 要你 今年 约 明 年，
哥々 要来 哟 只敢 来呀 要你 邀到 别 人 来

5i 265 | 66 55 | 5i 2i | 65 6 | 5 — ‖
老妹 好比格 白菜 种哟 大风 一吹 别 丘 田。
老妹 丢哭哟 [56 56 55] 好食 菜子 分 得 开。
好食菜子样哟

· 12 ·

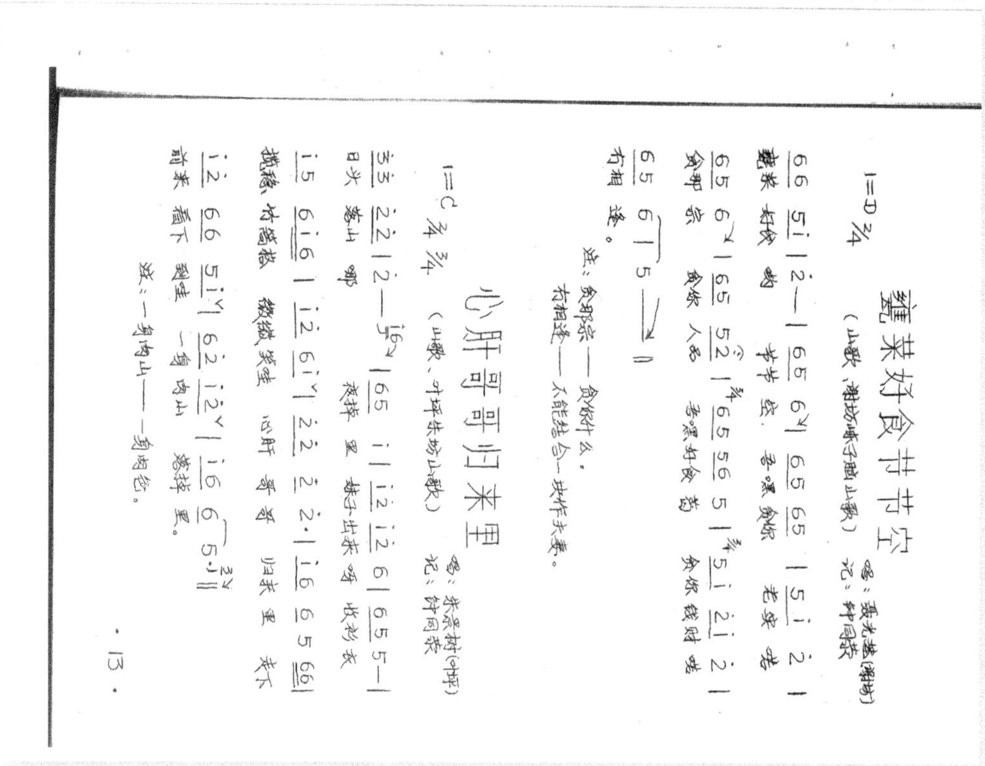

甕菜好食节节空

1=D 2/4　（山歌、谢坊嵊子脑山歌）　唱：聂光楚（谢坊）　记：钟同荣

66 5i | 2— | 65 6 | 65 65 | 5i 2 |
甕菜 好食 哟　节节 空，吾嘿 贪你　老实 啰

65 6 | 65 52 | 6556 5 | 5i 2i 2 |
贪那 宗　贪你 人呢　吾嘿好食 药　贪你 钱财 啰

65 6 | 5 — ‖
冇相 逢。

注：贪那宗——贪你什么。
冇相逢——不能结合一块作夫妻。

心肝哥哥归来里

1=C 2/4 3/4　（山歌、叶坪朱坊山歌）　唱：朱景树（叶坪）　记：钟同荣

33 22 | 2 — | 65 i | i2 i2 6 | 65 5— |
日头 落山 哪　夜掉 里　妹子出来 呀　收衫 衣

i5 6i6 | i2 6i | 22 2 2· | i6 6 5 66 |
搅稳 竹篙格　微微 笑哇　心肝 哥 哥　归来 里　走下

i2 66 5i | 62 i2 | i6 6 5· ‖
前来 看下 到哇　一身 肉山　落掉 里。

注：一身肉山——一身肉包。

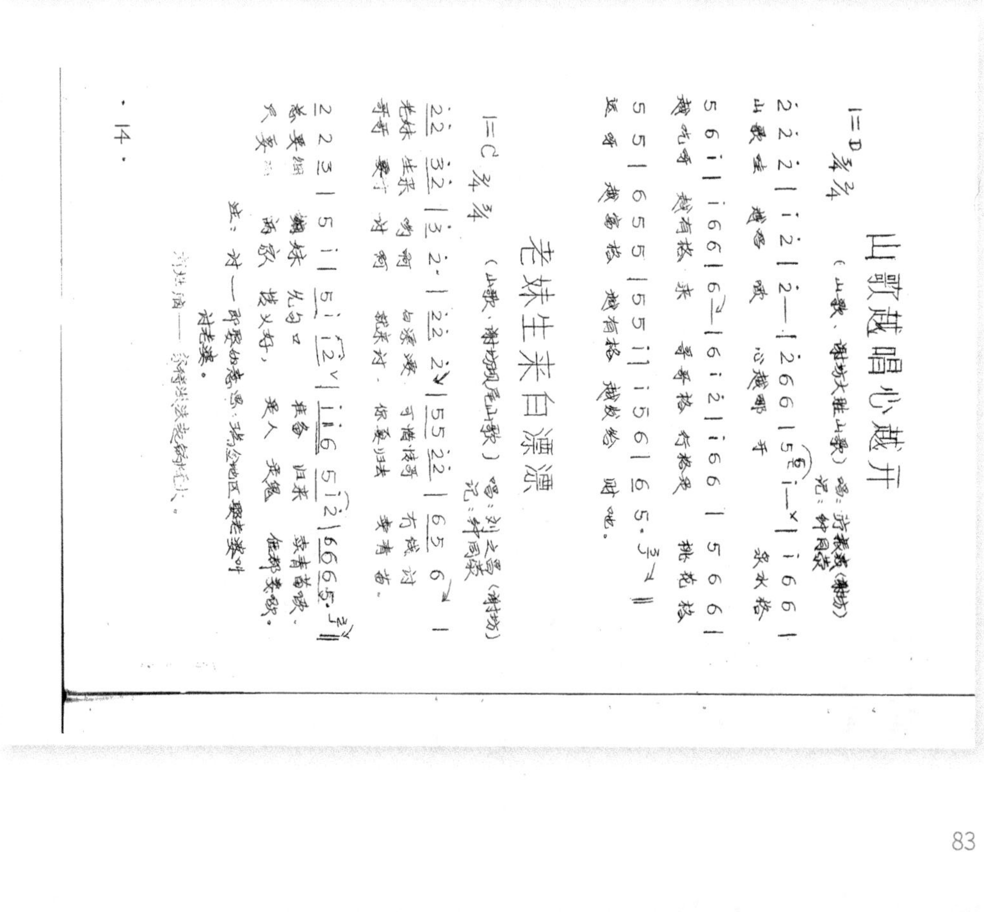

山歌越唱心越开

1=D 3/4 2/4　（山歌、谢坊大胜山歌）　唱：古振森（谢坊）　记：钟同荣

2 2 2 | i 2 | 2 — | 2 6 6 | 5 i — | i 6 6 |
山 歌 哇　越 唱　哦　心 越 哪　开　　泉 水 格

5 6 i | i 6 6 | 6 — | 6 i 2 | i 6 6 | 5 6 6 |
越 吮 呀　越 有 格　来　哥 哥 格　行 格 兜　桃 花 格

5 5 | 6 5 5 | 5 5 i | i 5 6 | 6 5· ‖
运 呀　越 富 格　越 有 格　越 发 给　财 哋。

老妹生来白漂漂

1=C 2/4 3/4　（山歌、谢坊坝尾山歌）　唱：刘之昌（谢坊）　记：钟同荣

22 32 | 3 2· | 22 2 | 55 22 | 65 6 |
老妹 生来　哟 呵　白漂 漂　可惜 怯哥　冇钱 讨
哥哥 要丁　讨 呵　就来 讨、　你 要 归去　卖青 苗。

2 2 3 | 5 i | 5i i2 | ii6 5i2 | 666 5· ‖
总 要 细　老 妹　允句 口　准备　归来　卖青苗哎。
只 要　两 家　讲 义 好，　爱人　爱鬼　催都 要哎。

注：讨——即娶的意思，瑞金地区娶老婆叫讨老婆。

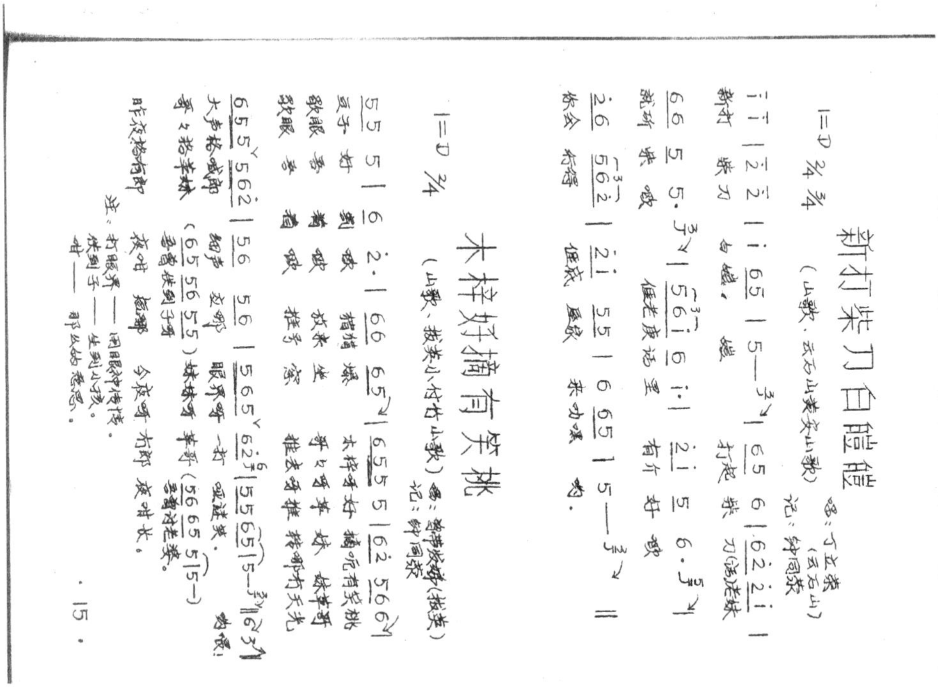

新打柴刀白皑皑

1=D 2/4 3/4　（山歌．云石山黄安山歌）　唱：丁立荣（云石山）　记：钟同荣

1 1 | 2 2 | 1 65 | 5— | 65 6 | 62 21 |
新打 柴刀 白皑， 皑 打起 柴 刀(话)老妹

66 5 5· | 561 6 1· | 21 5 6· |
就斫 柴 哦 佢老庚话里 有介 好 哦

26 562 | 21 55 | 6 65 | 5— ||
你会 行得 佢底 屋家 来动嘿 哟。

木梓好摘有笑桃

1=D 2/4　（山歌、拔英小付竹山歌）　唱：曾带发娣（拔英）　记：钟同荣

55 5 | 6 2· | 66 65 | 655 5 | 62 566 |
豆子 好 割 哦 猜猜 嫖 木梓呀好 摘呢有笑桃
歌眠 吾 着 哦 放来 坐 哥々呀 革 妹 妹革哥
歌眠 吾 看 哦 推子 窗 推去呀推 转哪有天光

655 562 | 56 56 | 565 62 | 55 65 | 5— || 63 |
大声格喊郎 细声 齐哪 眼界呀 一打 哑谜笑． 哟喂！
哥々格革妹 （65 56 55）妹妹呀 革哥（56 65 5 | 5—）
吾会伏到子呀 吾会讨老婆。

昨夜格有郎 夜咁 短哪 今夜呀 冇郎 夜咁长。

注：打眼界——用眼神传情。
伏到子——生到小孩。
咁——那么的意思。

· 15 ·

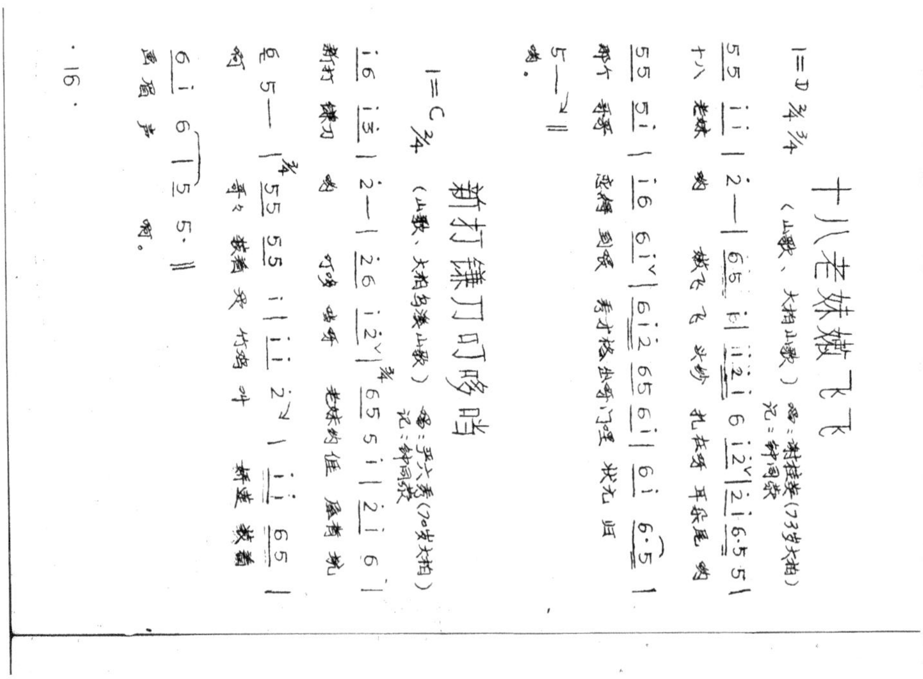

十八老妹嫩飞飞

1=D 2/4 3/4　（山歌、大柏山歌）　唱：谢桂英（73岁大柏）　记：钟同荣

55 11 | 2— | 65 1 | 121 6 12 | 21 6·5 5 |
十八 老妹 哟 嫩飞 飞 头纱 扎在呀 耳朵尾 哟

55 51 | 16 61 | 612 65 61 | 61 6·5 |
那个 哥哥 恋得 到哦 秀才格出呀门哩 状元 归

5— ||
哟。

新打镰刀叮哆哨

1=C 2/4　（山歌、大柏乌溪山歌）　唱：严六秀（70岁大柏）　记：钟同荣

16 13 | 2— | 26 12 | 3/4 65 5 1 | 21 6 |
新打 镰刀 哟 叮哆 哨呀 老妹的佢 屋背 坑

5 5— | 2/4 55 55 1 | 11 2 | 11 65 |
啊 哥々 拔着 天 竹鸡 叫 娇莲 拔着

61 6 | 5 5· ||
画眉 声 啊。

· 16 ·

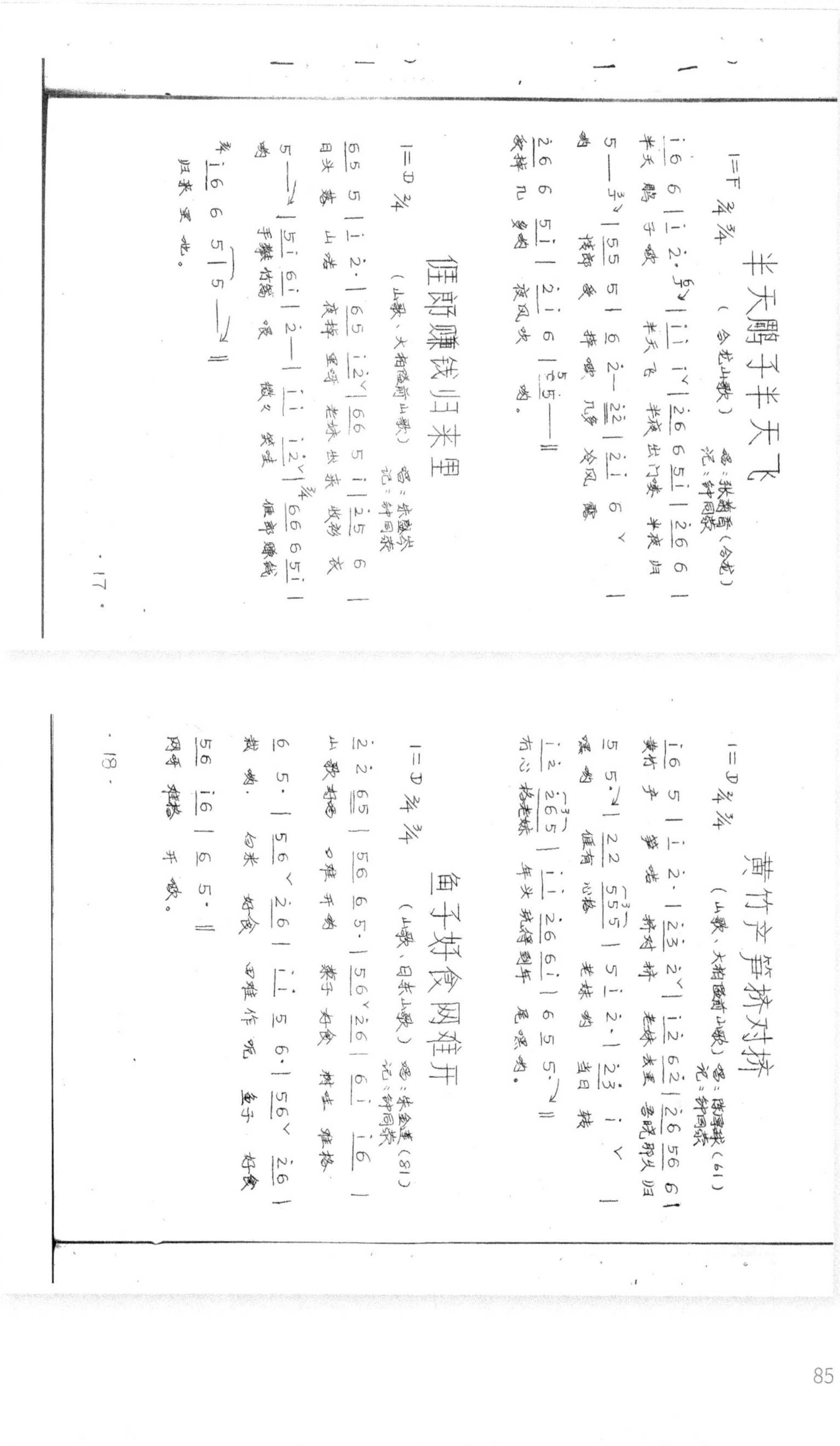

半天鹏子半天飞

1=F 2/4 3/4 （合龙山歌） 唱：张菊香（合龙） 记：钟同荣

半天鹏子哟 半天飞 半夜出门娄 半夜归

哟 做郎爱 掉哟、几多 冷风 露

爱掉几多哟 夜风吹 哟。

俚郎赚钱归来里

1=D 2/4 （山歌、大柏隘前山歌） 唱：朱盛岑 记：钟同荣

日头落 山啰 夜掉里呀 老妹出来 收衫衣

哟 手攀竹篙 哏 微々笑哇 俚郎赚钱

归来里哋。

黄竹产笋挤对挤

1=D 2/4 3/4 （山歌、大柏隘前山歌） 唱：陈厚球（61） 记：钟同荣

黄竹产笋啰 挤对挤 老妹去里 冒晓那头归

嘿哟 俚有心格 老妹哟 当日转

有心格老妹 年头玩得到年 尾嘿哟。

鱼子好食网难开

1=D 2/4 3/4 （山歌、日东山歌） 唱：朱金莲（81） 记：钟同荣

山歌好唱 口难开哟 菜子好食 树哇难格

栽哟。 白米好食 田难作呢 鱼子好食

网呀难格开哟。

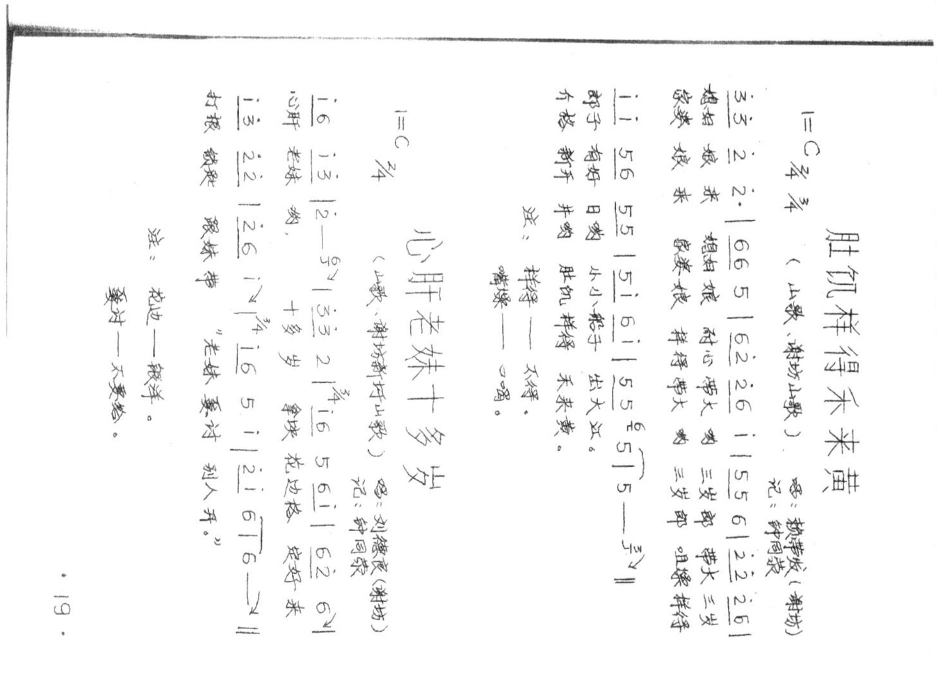

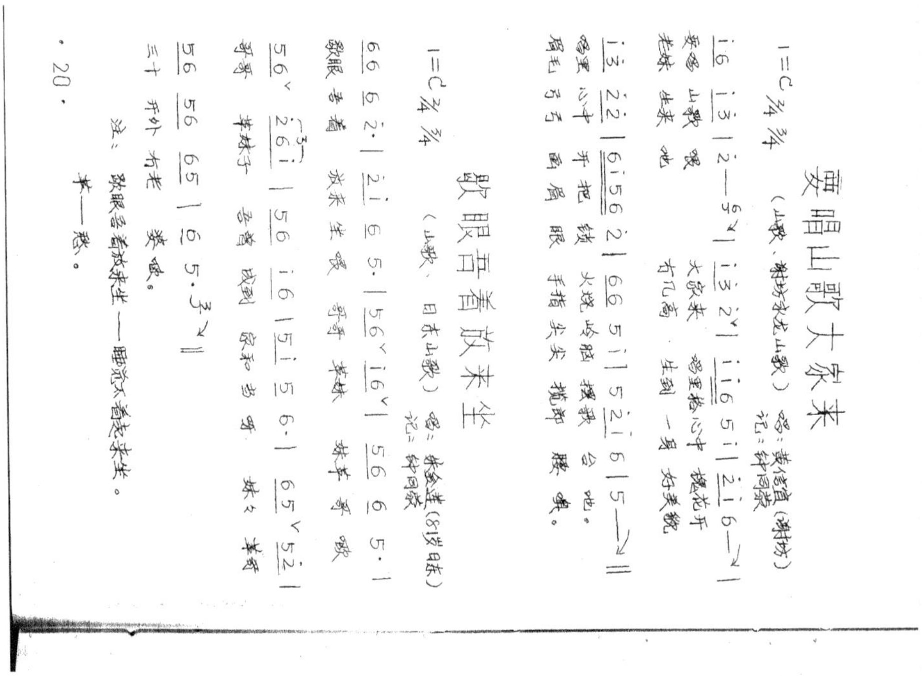

肚饥样得禾来黄

1=C 2/4 3/4 （山歌、谢坊山歌） 唱：赖带妏（谢坊）
记：钟同荣

媳妇 娘 来 媳妇娘 耐心 带大 哟 三岁郎 带大 三岁
家婆 娘 来 家婆娘 样得 带大 哟 三岁郎 咀燥 样得

郎子 有好 日哟 小小船子 出大江。
介格 新开 井哟 肚饥 样得 禾来黄。

注：样得——不得。
嘴燥——口渴。

心肝老妹十多岁

1=C 2/4 （山歌、谢坊新圩山歌） 唱：刘德良（谢坊）
记：钟同荣

心肝 老妹 哟， 十多 岁 拿块 花边格 定好 来
打根 銊匙 跟妹 带 "老妹 委讨 别人 开。"

注：花边——银洋。
委讨——不要给。

• 19 •

要唱山歌大家来

1=C 2/4 3/4 （山歌、谢坊永龙山歌） 唱：黄信宜（谢坊）
记：钟同荣

要唱 山歌 喂 大家来 唱里格心中 桃花开
老妹 生来 哋 冇几高 生到 一身 好美貌

唱里 心中 开 把 锁 火烧 岭脑 摆歌 台 哋。
眉毛 弓弓 画 眉 眼 手指 尖尖 揽郎 腰 哦。

歇眼吾着放来坐

1=C 2/4 3/4 （山歌、日东山歌） 唱：朱金莲（81岁日东）
记：钟同荣

歇眼 吾 着 放来 坐 喂 哥哥 苹妹 妹苹 哥 哦
哥哥 苹妹子 吾曾 成到 家和 当 呀 妹々 苹哥
三十 开外 冇老 婆 哦。

注：歇眼吾着放来坐——睡觉不着起来坐。
苹——愁。

• 20 •

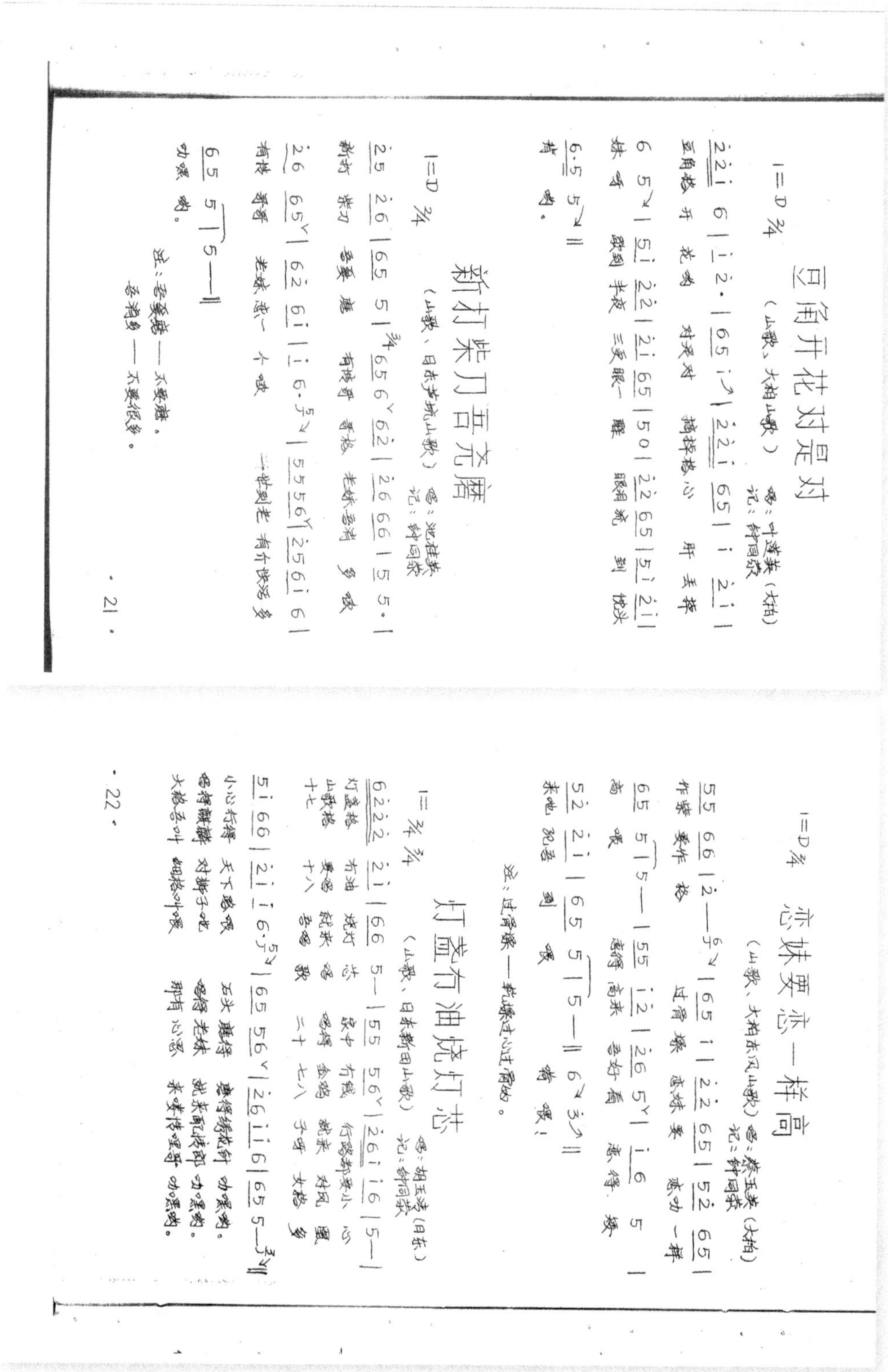

豆角开花对是对

1=D 2/4　（山歌、大柏山歌）　唱：叶莲英（大柏）
记：钟同荣

22i 6 | i 2· | 65 i | 22i 65 | i 2i |
豆角格 开 花 哟 对是对 摘掉格心 肝 丢掉

6 5 | 5i 22 | 2i 65 | 5 0 | 22 65 | 5i 2i |
妹 呀 歌到 半夜 三更眼一 醒 眼泪 流 到 枕头

6·5 5 ||
背 哟。

新打柴刀吾尧磨

1=D 2/4　（山歌、日东芦坑山歌）　唱：池桂英
记：钟同荣

25 26 | 65 5 | 3/4 656 62 | 26 66 | 5 5· |
新打 柴刀 吾要 磨 有情哥 哥格 老妹吾消 多 哎

26 65 | 62 6i | i 6· 5 | 5556 | 256i 6 |
有情 哥哥 老妹 恋一 个 哎 一世到老 有介快活 多

65 5 | 5 — ||
动嘿 哟。

注：吾要磨——不要磨。
吾消多——不要很多。

恋妹要恋一样高

1=D 2/4　（山歌、大柏东风山歌）　唱：蔡玉英（大柏）
记：钟同荣

55 66 | 2 — 5 | 65 i | 22 65 | 52 65 |
作崇 要作 格 过骨 燥 恋妹 要 恋an 一样

65 5 | 5 — | 55 i2 | 26 5 | i 6 5 |
高 喂 恋得 高来 吾好 看 恋 得 矮

52 2i | 65 5 | 5 — || 6 3 ||
来吔 死吾 到 喂 背 喂！

注：过骨燥——乾燥过心过骨的。

灯盏冇油烧灯芯

1= 2/4 3/4　（山歌、日东新田山歌）　唱：胡玉凌（日东）
记：钟同荣

6222 2i | 66 5— | 55 56 | 26i i6 | 5— |
灯盏格 冇油 烧灯 芯 家中 冇钱 行路都要小 心
山歌格 要唱 就来 唱 唱得 金鸡 就来 对凤 凰
十七 十八 吾唱 歌 二十 七八 子呀 女格 多

5i 66 | 2i i 6· 5 | 65 56 | 26i i6 | 65 5— 3 ||
小心行得 天下路喂 石头 磨得 磨得绣花针 动嘿哟。
唱得麒麟 对狮子吔 唱得 老妹 就来配情郎 动嘿哟。
大格吾叫 细格叫喂 那有 心思 来嘹情哩哥 动嘿哟。

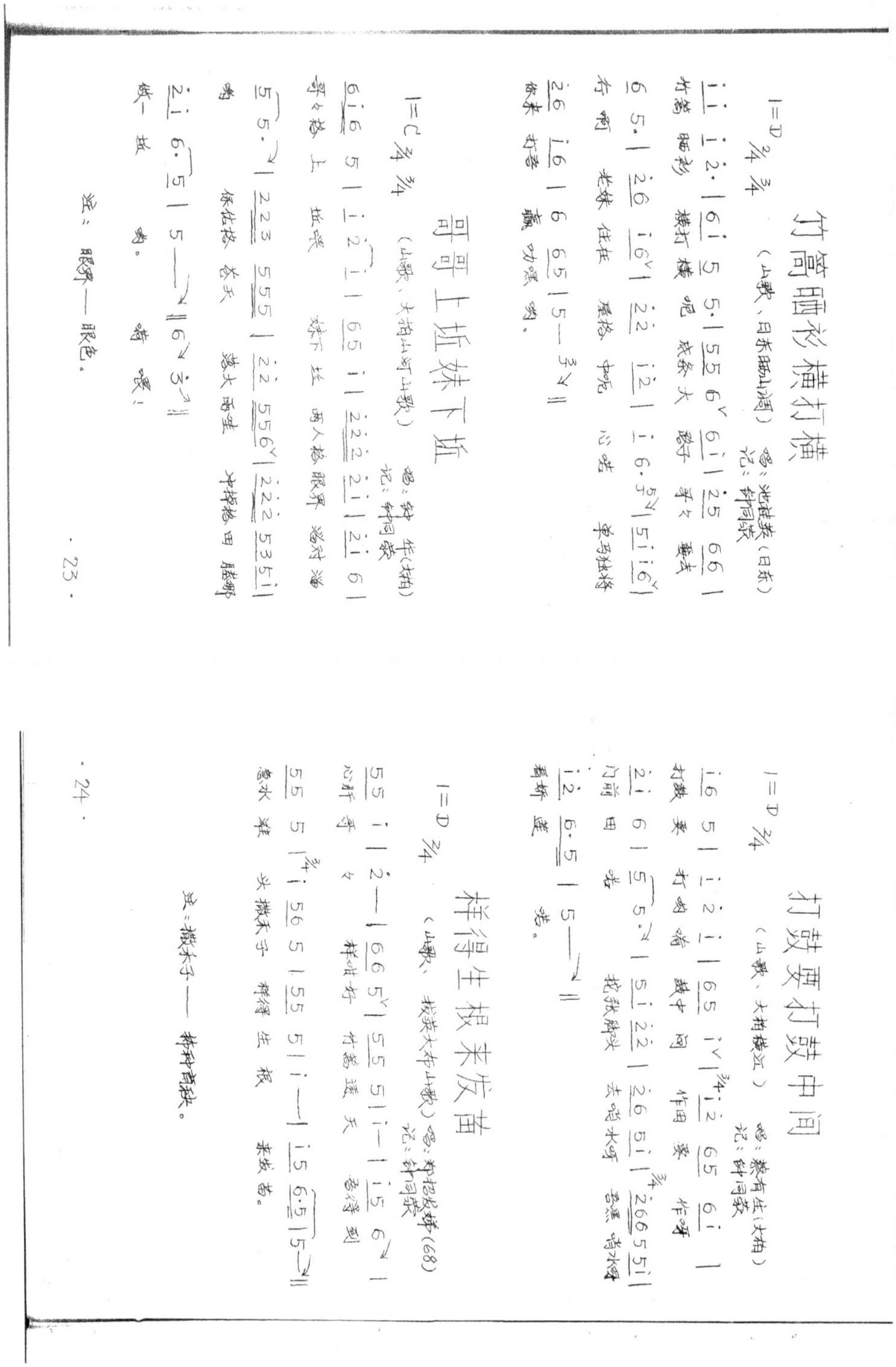

竹篙晒衫横打横

1=D 2/4 3/4 （山歌、日东畈山调） 唱：池桂英（日东）
记：钟同荣

i i i 2· | 6 i 5 5· | 5 5 6 6 i | 2 5 6 6 |
竹篙 晒衫 横打 横 呢 成条 大 路子 哥々 要去

6 5· | 2 6 i 6 | 2 2 i 2 | i 6· 5 | 5 i i 6 |
行 啊 老妹 住在 屋格 中呢 心 啱 单马独将

2 6 i 6 | 6 6 5 | 5 — 3 ||
你来 打苍 赢 叻嘿 哟。

哥哥上坵妹下坵

1=C 2/4 3/4 （山歌、大柏山对山歌） 唱：钟 华（大柏）
记：钟同荣

6 i 6 5 | i 2 i | 6 5 i | 2 2 2 2 i | 2 i 6 |
哥々格 上 坵喂 妹下 坵 两人格 眼界 溜对 溜

5 5· | 2 2 3 5 5 5 | 2 2 5 5 6 | 2 2 2 5 3 5 i |
哟 係佐格 苍天 落大 雨哇 冲掉格田 塍那

2 i 6· 5 | 5 — ‖ 6 3 ||
做一 坵 哟。 嗬 喂！

注：眼界——眼色。

· 23 ·

打鼓要打鼓中间

1=D 2/4 （山歌、大柏横江） 唱：蔡有生（大柏）
记：钟同荣

i 6 5 | i 2 i | 6 5 i | 3/4 i 2 6 5 6 i |
打鼓 要 打 哟 啃 鼓中 间 作田 要 作呀

2 i 6 | 5 5· | 5 i 2 2 | 2 6 5 i | 3/4 2 6 6 5 5 i |
门前 田 啱 抢秋脚头 去哨 水呀 吾黑 哨水呀

i 2 6· 5 | 5 — ||
看娇 莲 啱。

样得生根来发苗

1=D 2/4 （山歌、拔英大布山歌） 唱：郑招发娣（68）
记：钟同荣

5 5 i | 2 — | 6 6 5 | 5 5 5 | i — | i 5 6 |
心肝 哥 々 样咁好 竹篙 透 天 吾得 到

5 5 5 | 3/4 i 5 6 5 | 5 5 5 | i — | i 5 6· 5 | 5 — ||
急水 滩 头 撒禾子 样得 生 根 来发 苗。

注：撒禾子——播种育秧。

· 24 ·

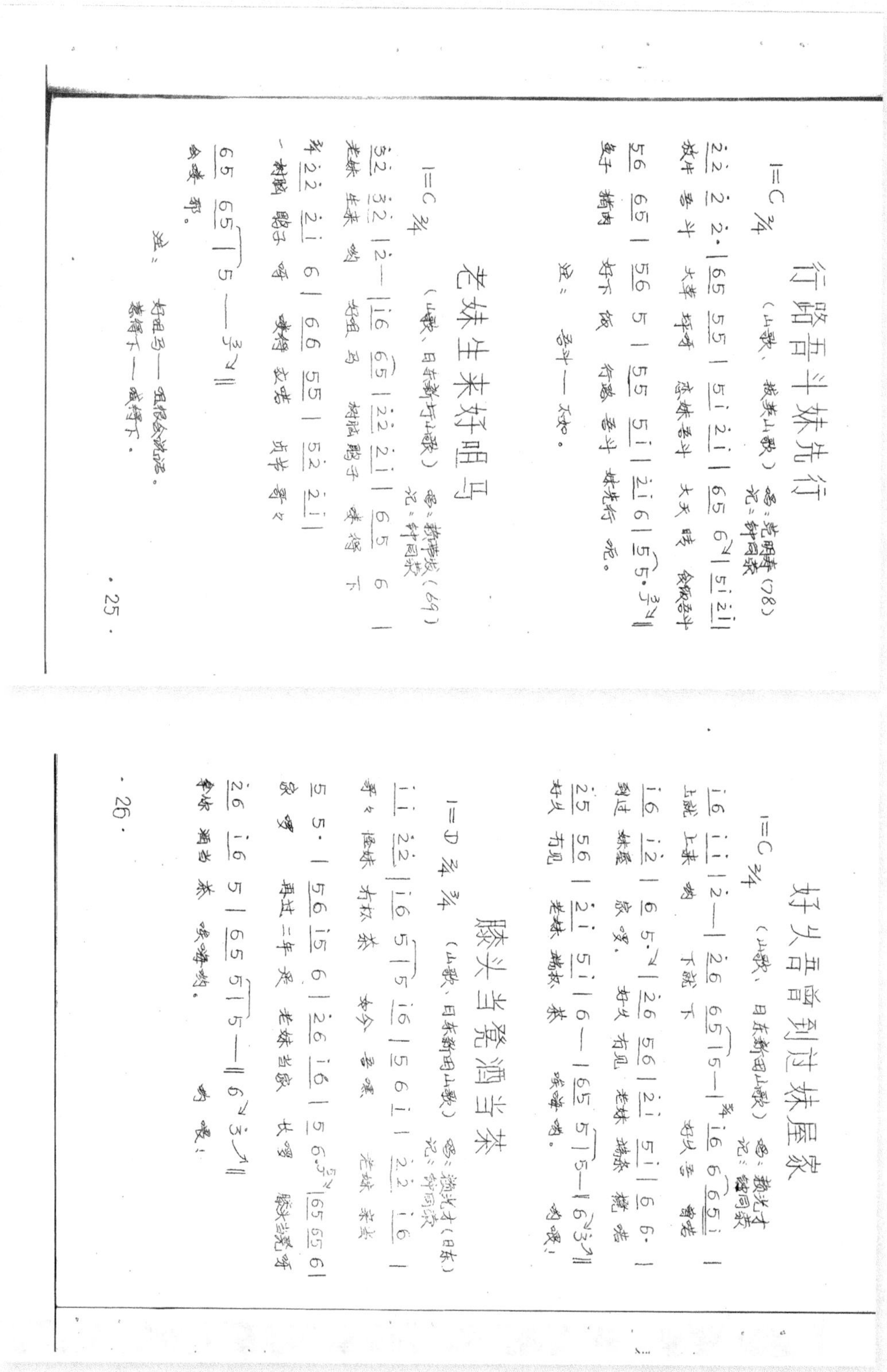

行路吾斗妹先行

1=C 2/4　（山歌、拔英山歌）　唱：范明寿（78）
记：钟同荣

2 2　2　2·｜65　55｜5 i　2 i｜65　6｜5 i　2 i｜
放牛　吾斗　大草　坪呀　恋妹吾斗　大天　晓　食饭吾斗

56　65｜56　5｜55　5 i｜2 i 6｜5 5·3‖
鱼子　猪肉　好下　饭　行路　吾斗　妹先行　呢。

注：吾斗——不如。

老妹生来好咀马

1=C 2/4　（山歌、日东新圩山歌）　唱：赖带发（69）
记：钟同荣

32　32｜2—｜i6　65｜22　2 i｜65　6｜
老妹　生来　哟　好咀　马　树脑　鹧子　嘆得　下

2 2　2 i　6｜66　55｜52　2 i｜
一树脑　鹧子　呀　嘆得　么啱　贞节　哥々

65　65｜5 —3‖
会嘆　耶。

注：好咀马——咀很会说话。
嘆得下——哄得下。

好头吾曾到过妹屋家

1=C 2/4　（山歌、日东新田山歌）　唱：赖光才
记：钟同荣

i6　i i｜2—｜26　65｜5—｜3/4 i6　6　65 i｜
上就　上来　哟　下就　下　好头　吾　曾啱

i6　i2｜6　5·｜26　56｜2 i　5 i｜6　6·｜
到过　妹屋　家　啰。　好头　有见　老妹　端条　凳　啱

25　56｜2 i　5 i｜6—｜65　5｜5—‖6 3‖
好头　有见　老妹　端杯　茶　　唉嗨　哟。　哟　喂！

膝头当凳酒当茶

1=D 2/4 3/4　（山歌、日东新田山歌）　唱：赖光才（日东）
记：钟同荣

i i　22｜i6　5｜5　i6｜5　6　i｜22　i6｜
哥々　怪妹　冇杯　茶　如今　吾　嘿　老妹　亲当

5　5·｜56　i5　6｜26　i6｜5　6·5｜65　65　6｜
家　啰　再过　二年　无　老妹　当家　长　啰　膝头当凳　呀

26　i6　5｜65　5｜5—‖6 3‖
拿你　酒当　茶　唉嗨　哟。　哟　喂！

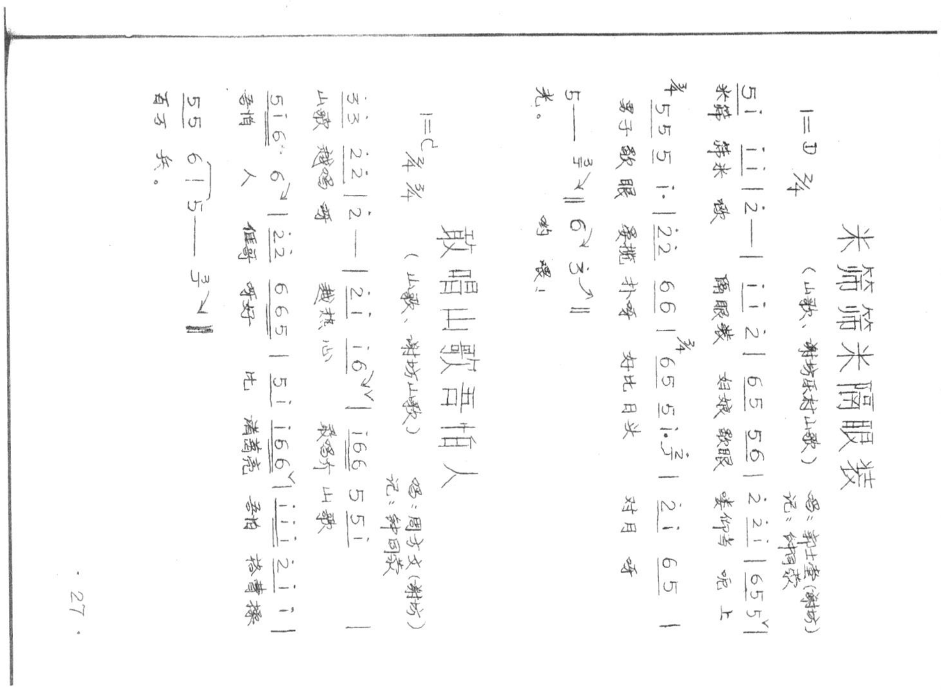

米筛筛米隔眼装

1=D 2/4　（山歌、谢坊乐村山歌）　唱：郭士堂（谢坊）　记：钟同荣

5i ii | 2— | ii 2 | 65 56 | 2 2i | 655 |
米筛 筛米 啵　隔眼装　妇娘 歌眼　嗳仰当 呃上

3/4 555 i· | 22 66 | 3/4 65 5i· 3 | 2i 65 |
男子歌眼 要揽 扑呀　好比日头　对月 呀

5— 3 ‖ 6 3 ‖
光。　哟 喂！

敢唱山歌吾怕人

1=C 2/4 3/4　（山歌、谢坊山歌）　唱：周方文（谢坊）　记：钟同荣

33 22 | 2— | 2i i6 | i66 5 5i |
山歌 越唱 呀　越热 心　最唱介 山歌

5i6 6 | 22 665 | 5i i66 | iii 2i i |
吾怕 人　佴哥 呀好　比 满茜亮 吾怕 格茜搡

55 6 | 5— 3 ‖
百万 兵。

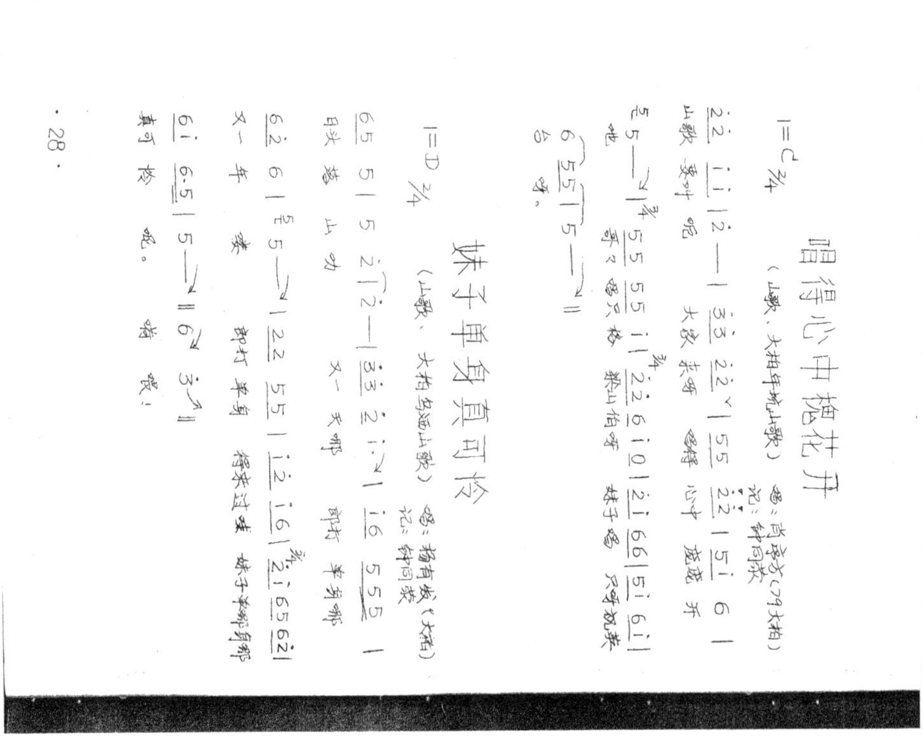

唱得心中槐花开

1=C 2/4　（山歌、大柏年坑山歌）　唱：肖序方（79大柏）　记：钟同荣

22 ii | 2— | 33 22 | 55 22 | 5i 6 |
山歌 要叶 呃　大家 来呀　唱得 心中 庞庞 开

5 5— | 3/4 55 55 i | 3/4 22 6 i 0 | 2i 66 | 5i 6i |
吔　哥々 唱只 格　梁山伯呀　妹子唱 只呀祝英

6 55 | 5— ‖
台 呀。

妹子单身真可怜

1=D 2/4　（山歌、大柏乌涵山歌）　唱：杨有发（大柏）　记：钟同荣

65 5 | 5 2 | 2— | 33 2 i· | i6 555 |
日头 落 山 叻　又一 天哪　郎打 单身哪

62 6 | 5 5— | 22 55 | i2 i6 | 3/4 2i 65 62 |
又一 年　凄　郎打 单身　得来过 味　妹子单身那

6i 6·5 | 5— ‖ 6 3 ‖
真可 怜 呢。　嗬 喂！

02 第二类 · 民歌

CATEGORY II ·FOLK SONGS

导读

“民歌”是民众在日常生活中自发创作、口耳相传的歌唱形式，具有强烈的地方性与即兴性。赣南地区的民歌往往旋律自由、质朴真挚，多见于田间劳动、山野对唱和节庆场合。其歌词内容广泛，既有描绘自然与乡村风貌的抒情曲调，也有青年男女即兴唱和的爱情歌谣。这些作品不仅是日常生活的艺术再现，也是研究地方社会文化与集体记忆的重要资料。

Introduction

Folk Songs are spontaneously created and orally transmitted forms of singing rooted in everyday life, characterized by strong regional features and improvisation. In southern Jiangxi, folk songs are known for their free-flowing melodies and sincerity, often performed during agricultural work, antiphonal singing in the mountains, or festive gatherings. Their lyrics range from lyrical depictions of natural scenery and rural life to improvised love duets between young men and women. These songs serve as both artistic reflections of daily experience and valuable sources for understanding local culture and collective memory.

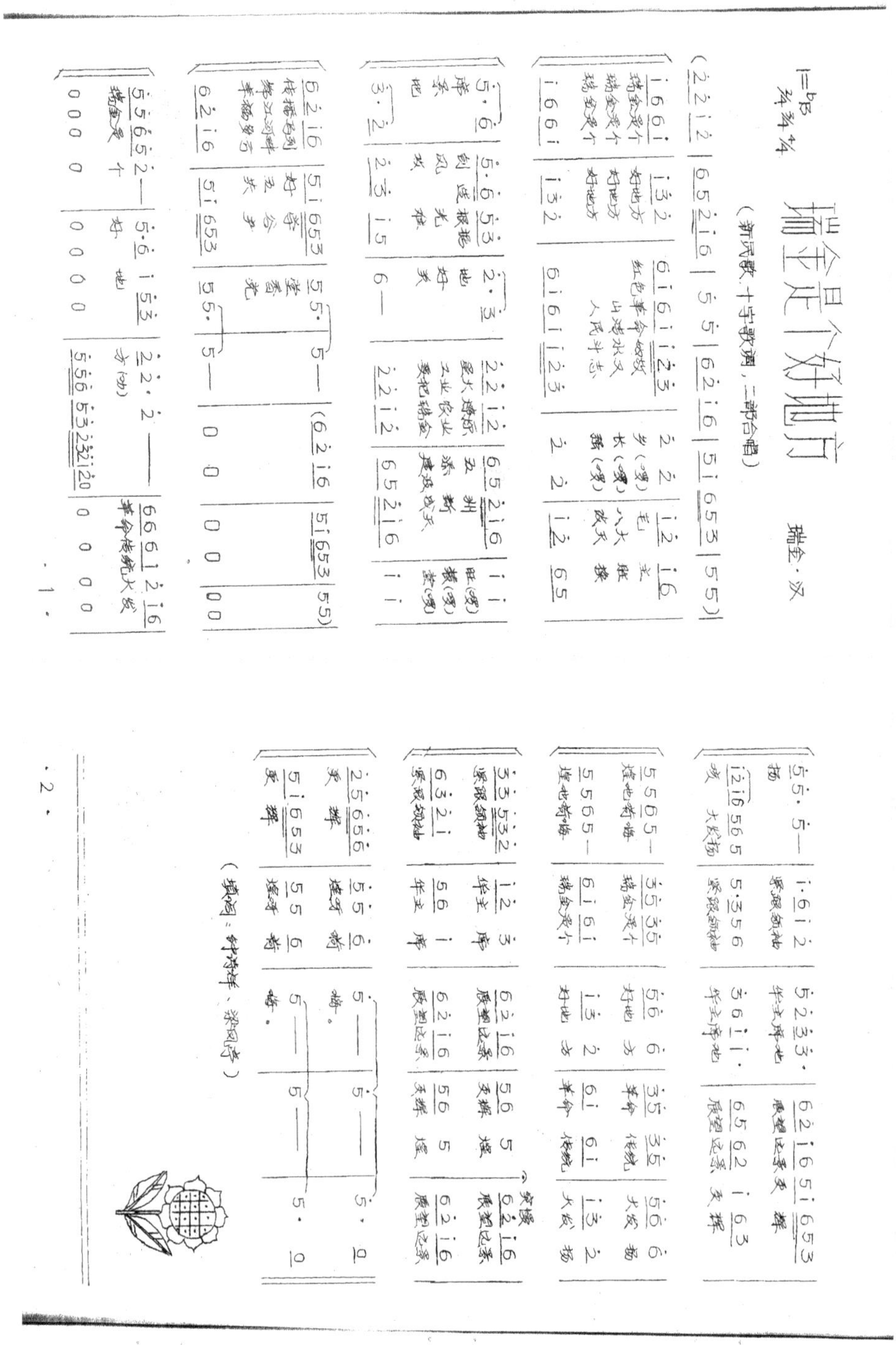

瑞金是个好地方

1=bB 2/4 3/4 4/4

瑞金·汉

（新民歌.十字歌调，二部合唱）

瑞金是个 好地方 红色革命好战 乡（啰） 毛 主 席 创 造 根据 地 星火燎原 五 洲 旺（啰）

瑞金是个 好地方 山清水又 长（啰） 八大 胜 景 风 光 好 工业农业 添 新 装（啰）

瑞金是个 好地方 人民斗志 强（啰） 改天 换 地 斗 志 昂 要把瑞金 建设成天 堂（啰）

传播四列 好 字 堂 / 锦江河畔 五 谷 香 / 幸福万方 丰 产 光

瑞金是 个 好 地 方（呦） 革命传统大发 扬

紧跟领袖 华主席也 展望远景更 辉 / 大发扬 紧跟领袖 华主席也 展望远景 更辉

煌也前 嗨 瑞金是个 好地 方 革命 传统 大发 扬

紧跟领袖 华主 席 展望远景 更辉 煌 突慢 展望远景

更 辉 煌呀 前 嗨。

（填词：钟诗祥、梁凤亭）

· 1 ·

· 2 ·

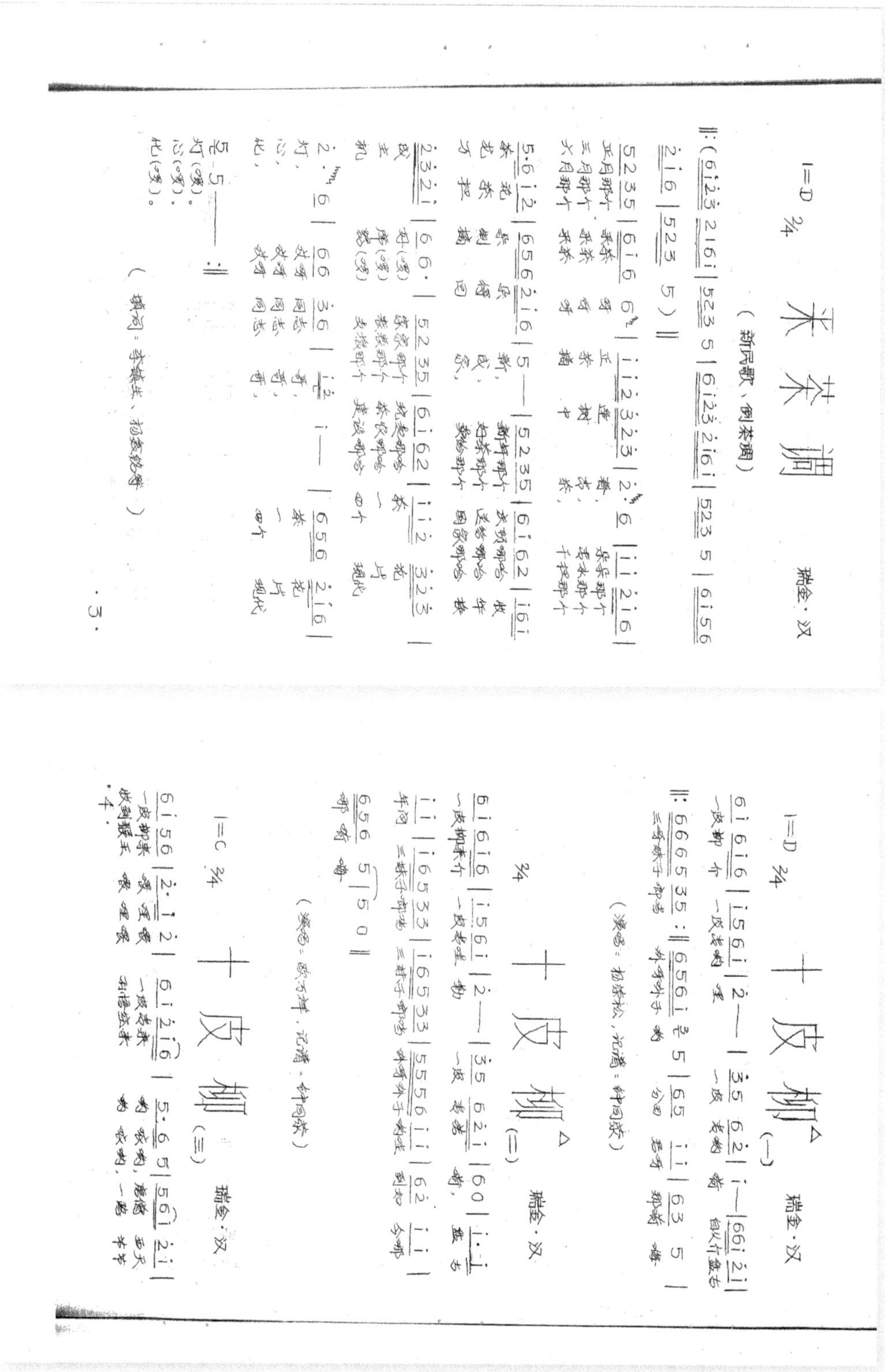

1=D 2/4

釆茶调

瑞金·汉

（新民歌、倒茶调）

‖:(6i2̇3̇ 2̇16i | 523 5 | 6i2̇3̇ 2̇16i | 523 5 | 6i56
2̇i6 | 523 5)‖

5235 | 6i6 6 | ii2̇ 3̇2̇3̇ | 2̇· 6 | ii 2̇i6 |
正月那个 采茶 呀 正 逢 春， 朵朵那个
三月那个 采茶 呀 茶 树 青， 青水那个
六月那个 采茶 呀 摘 中 茶， 千担那个

5·6 i2̇ | 656 2̇i6 | 5 — | 5235 | 6i62 | i6i
茶 花 朵 朵 新， 新鲜那个 头顶哪哈 收
龙 茶 制 得 成， 妇茶那个 送给哪哈 年
万 担 摘 回 家， 卖给那个 国家哪哈 换

2̇3̇2̇i | 66· | 5235 | 6i62 | ii2̇ 3̇2̇3̇ |
战 好(嘿) 家家那个 玩起哪哈 茶 花
主 席(嘿) 表表那个 茶农哪哈 一 片
机 器(嘿) 支援那个 建设哪哈 四个 现代

2̇· 6 | 66 36 | i2̇ i — | 656 2̇i6 |
灯， 哎呀 同志 哥， 茶 花
心， 哎呀 同志 哥， 一 片
化， 哎呀 同志 哥， 四个 现代

5 5 — :‖
灯(嘿)。
心(嘿)。
化(嘿)。

（填词：李镇生、杨鑫铭等）

·3·

1=D 2/4

十皮柳△（一）

瑞金·汉

6i 6i6 | i56i | 2̇ — | 3̇5 62̇ | i — | 66i 2̇i |
一皮柳 个 一皮老哟 哩 一皮 老哟 荷 自从竹盘古

‖: 666535 :‖ 656i 2̇5 | 65 ii | 63 5 |
三哥妹子部当 外呀外子 哟 分田 老呀 那荷 嗨

（演唱：杨崇松，记谱：钟同荣）

2/4

十皮柳△（二）

瑞金·汉

6i6i6 | i56i | 2̇ — | 3̇5 62̇i | 60 | i·i |
一皮柳来个 一皮老哩 勒 一皮 老弟 荷， 盘古

ii | i6533 | i6533 | 5556 ii | 62̇ ii |
年间 三妹子部当 三妹子部当 外呀外子哟哩 到如 今哪

656 5 | 50 ‖
哪 荷 嗨

（演唱：欧万祥，记谱：钟同荣）

1=C 2/4

十皮柳（三）

瑞金·汉

6i56 | 2̇·i 2̇ | 6i 2̇i6 | 5·6 5 | 56i 2̇i |
一皮柳来 喂 哩 喂 一皮老来 哟 依哟， 唐僧 西天
收到猴王 喂 哩 喂 孙悟空来 哟 依哟， 一路 节节

·4·

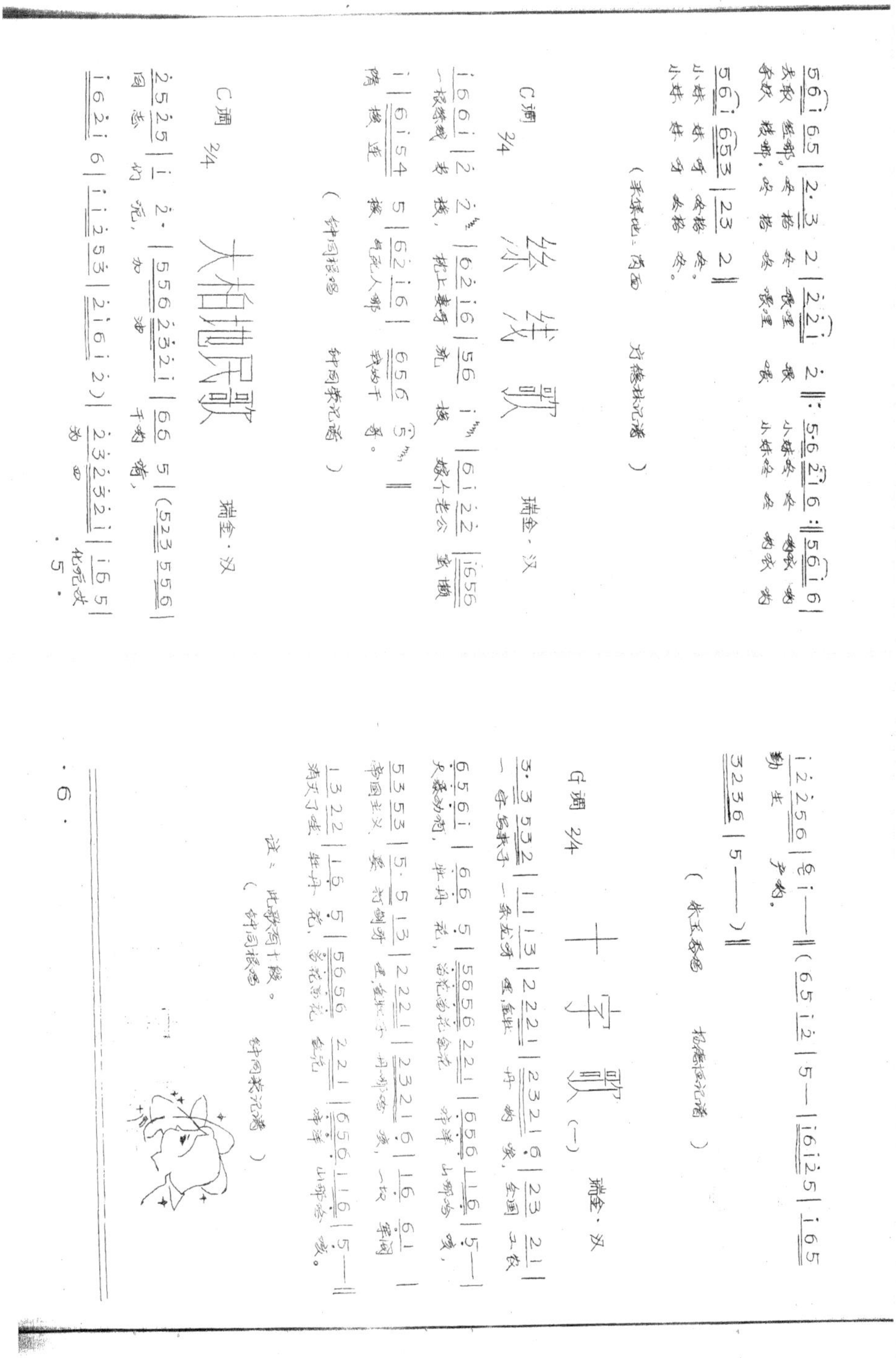

56i 65 | 2·3 2 | 22i 2 ‖: 5·6 2i 6 :‖ 56i 6 |
去取 经哪。哎 格 哎 哏哩 哏 小妹哎 哎 哟依 哟
杀妖 精哪。哎 格 哎 喂哩 喂 小妹哎 哎 哟依 哟

56i 653 | 23 2 ‖
小妹 妹 呀 哎格 哎。
小妹 妹 呀 哎格 哎。

（采集地：岗面　刘德林记谱）

丝线歌

C调 2/4　瑞金·汉

i 6 6i | 2 2 | 62 i6 | 56 i | 6i 22 | i656 |
一根丝线 考 毯， 枕上妻呀 梳 梭 嫁个老公 实懒

i | 6i54 5 | 62 i6 | 656 5 ‖
惰 梭 连 梭 气死人哪 我的干 哥。

（钟同根唱　钟同荣记谱）

大柏地民歌

C调 2/4　瑞金·汉

2525 | i 2· | 556 232i | 66 5 | (523 556 |
同 志 们 呢， 加 油 干啊 啃，

i62i 6 | ii253 | 2i6i 2) | 232 32i | i6 5 |
为 四 化死 攻

i2256 | 6i — ‖ (65 i2 | 5 — | i6i25 | i65
勤 生 产的。

3236 | 5 —) ‖

（朱玉香唱　杨德恒记谱）

十字歌（一）

G调 2/4　瑞金·汉

3·3 532 | 11 13 | 2 221 | 2321 6 | 23 21 |
一 字写来子 一条龙呀 哩，金牡 丹 的 咳， 全国 工农

656i | 66 5 | 5556 221 | 656 116 | 5 — |
大暴动啊， 牡丹 花， 当花当花 金花 荷洋 山那哈 咳，

5353 | 5·5 13 | 2 221 | 2321 6 | 16 61 |
帝国主义 要 打倒呀 哩，金牡子 丹那哈 咳， 一切 军阀

1322 | 15 5 | 5656 221 | 656 116 | 5 — ‖
消灭了哇， 牡丹 花， 当花当花 金花 荷洋 山那哈 咳。

注：此歌有十段。
（钟同根唱　钟同荣记谱）

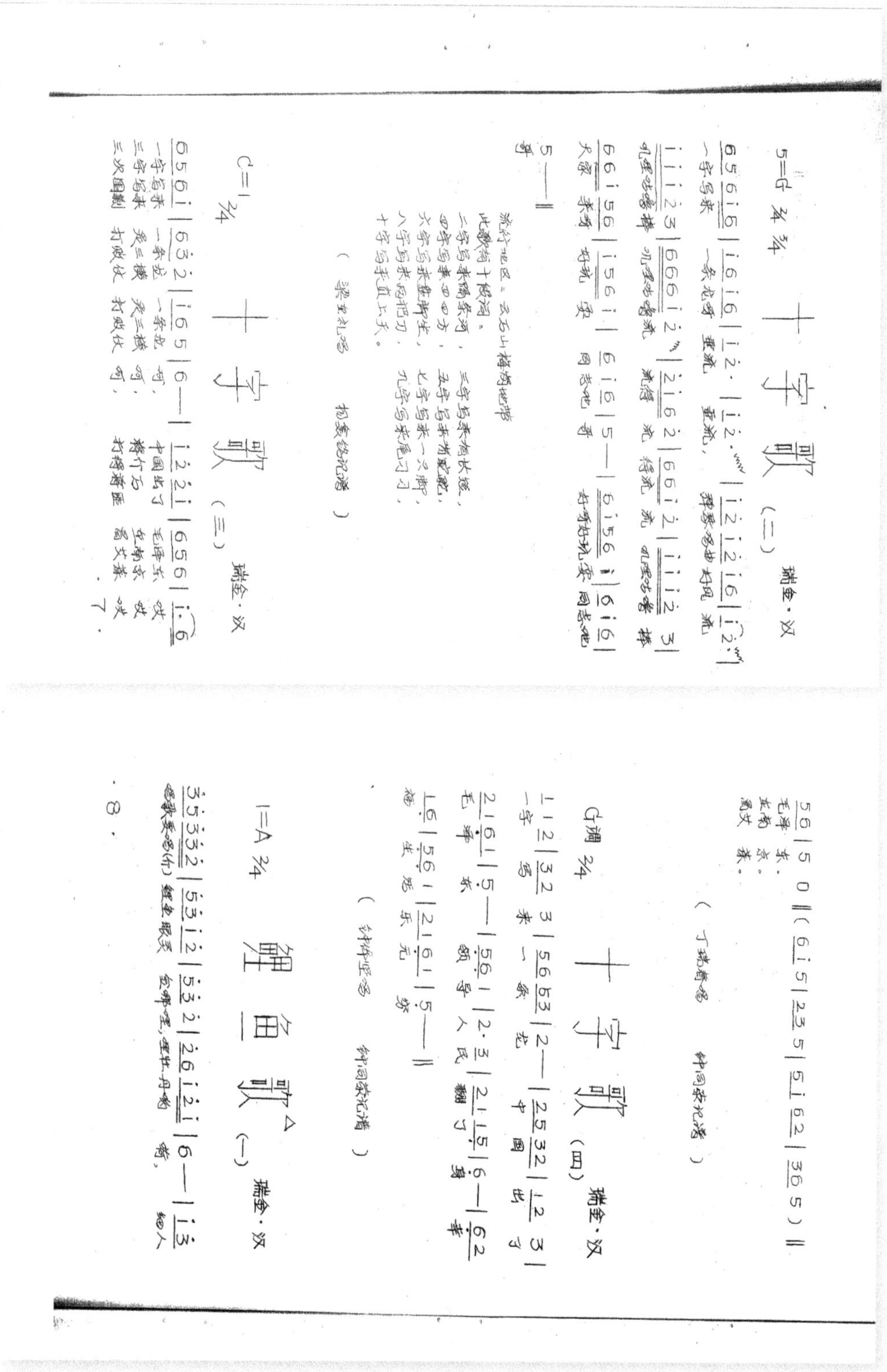

十字歌（二）

5=G 2/4 3/4　　瑞金·汉

65 6i6 | i6 i6 | i 2· | i 2· | i2 i2 i6 | i 2· |
一字写来　一条龙呀　垂流　垂流，　弹琴唱曲好风　流

iii 2 3 | 666i 2 | 2i6 2 | 66i 2 | iii 2 3 |
叽哩咕噜捧　叽哩咕噜流　流得　流　得流　流　叽哩咕噜　捧

66i 56 | i56 i | 6 i6 | 5 — | 6i56 i | 6 i6 |
大家　来呀　好玩　耍　同志吔　哥　好呀好玩耍　同志吔

5 — ‖
哥

流行地区：云石山梅岗地带
此歌有十段词：
二字写来隔条河，　三字写来有长短，
四字写来四四方，　五字写来背驼驼，
六字写来盘脚坐，　七字写来一只脚，
八字写来两把刀，　九字写来尾刁刁，
十字写来直上天。

（梁宜礼唱　杨衰铭记谱）

十字歌（三）

C=1 2/4　　瑞金·汉

656i | 63 2 | i65 | 6 — | i2 2i | 656 | i· 6
一字写来　一条龙　一条龙　呵，　中国出了　毛泽东　哎
三字写来　是三横　是三横　呵，　蒋介石　在南京　哎
三次围剿　打败仗　打败仗　呵，　打得蒋匪　蜀艾苏　哎

· 7 ·

56 | 5 0 ‖（6i 5 | 23 5 | 5i 62 | 36 5）‖
毛泽　东。
在南　京。
蜀艾　苏。

（丁瑞香唱　钟司荣记谱）

十字歌（四）

G调 2/4　　瑞金·汉

1 1 2 | 32 3 | 56 53 | 2 — | 25 32 | 12 3 |
一字　写　来　一　条　龙　中　国　出　了

21 61 | 5 — | 56 1 | 2· 3 | 21 15 | 6 — | 62
毛　泽　东　领　导　人　民　翻　了　身　幸

16 | 56 1 | 21 61 | 5 — ‖
福　生　活　乐　元　穷

（钟倖坚唱　钟司荣记谱）

鲤鱼歌△（一）

1=A 2/4　　瑞金·汉

35 332 | 53 i2 | 53 2 | 26 i2i | 6 — | i3
唱歌要唱(介)鲤鱼眼灵　全哪哩，哩牡丹哟　荷，　细人

· 8 ·

相打 大人老顶 真 哪哗哩 哗 荷花斗水 开哟 嗬
各人 牵开(介) 各人妫呀 哩， 哩牡丹哟 嗬， 否敢
起手(介) 打 到 人哪 哗哩 哗，荷花斗水 开哟 嗬。
否敢 起手(介) 打人家子贱 孙子子呀 哩， 哩牡丹哟
嗬， 开啱 否敢 另介八十 婆婆老大 人 哪 哗哩哗
荷花 斗水 开 哟 嗬。

（ 演唱：方行佐 记谱：钟同荣 ）

鲤鱼歌（二）

瑞金·汉

1=A 3/4

(领)人民公社 兴旺 花哟 哩(合)乡会 错哟 嗳(领)共产 主义
幸福 家 (合)哎当真哟 哗 哩 哗。

（ 杨振华唱 钟同荣记谱 ）

·9·

鲤鱼歌（三）

瑞金·汉

G调 3/4

工人哪个 大 哥 呀， 费 尽 心 哪 移 动
我 们 哗 革 新 哪 技 术 革 新 用 机
器 瘦 土 也 能 出 黄 金 技 术
花 朵 遍地开 依 旧 思 想 一 扫 光

（ 谢香兰唱 方德林记谱 ）

鲤鱼歌（四）

瑞金·汉

1=A 2/4

唱歌要唱 鲤鱼眼真 真哟哩 哩牡子丹嘤 咳， 细人 相打
大人莫去 信， 哗哩子哗 各人牵开 各人 妫哟 哩，
哩牡子丹嘤 咳， 免得言语 话至伤人 心哟哗哩子 哗，
牡哗金金 哗良山哟 咳。

（ 曾光焰唱 钟同荣记谱 ）

·10·

扫龙歌

1=G 2/4　　瑞金·汉

1.6 1.6 | 1·2 2 | 1·6 5 | 6 0 | 612 2 | 3216 |
修 好 水 库 开 好 圹 战 胜 水灾呀

5· 0 | 612 1 | 1·6 5 | (16 16 | 1·2 2 | 1·6 5 |
嗨 有 力 量 哟，

6· 0) | 66 16 | 1232 | 1·6 5 | 6 0 | 6123 |
不怕老 天 呀 不 下 雨， 气

12 | 16 5 | 621 | 16 5 | 6·(61 | 1·6 5) ||
死 龙 王 和 那 玉 皇

（谢香兰唱　钟同荣记谱）

体育歌

1=G 2/4　　瑞金·汉

231 | 2— | 1·216 | 5— | 6161 | 235 | 556 |
先立 正， 向右看 齐， 向 前 看，大家 振 数
向右 转， 四路纵 队， 齐 步 走，步伐 要整齐
向左 转， 四路纵 队， 一 二 一，步调 一 致

161 | 5·653 | 2— ||
一二三 一二三 四。
一二一 一二三 四。
来来来 武装起 来。

（钟同铁唱　钟盛辉记谱）

·11·

封建婚姻

1=D 2/4　　瑞金·汉

i i i65 | 5 3 | i23 | 2 2 | i i i6 | 56 i |
封建那个 婚 姻 苦 根 当 呀，一生那个 一 世
家婆那个 打 呀 老 公 骂 呵，眼泪那个 直 流

35 i6 | 5 0 ||
做 牛 马。
肚 里 去。

（钟同铁唱　钟盛辉记谱）

革命故乡沙洲坝

1=G 2/4　　瑞金·汉

22532 | 12532 | 556 2321 | 5621 6 |
革命故乡 沙 洲 坝 书记 挂 帅 干 劲 大
革命故乡 沙 洲 坝 小土 高 炉 开 红 花

135656 | 232 161 | 255 2321 | 6516 5 ||
钢铁 土 炉 遍地 起呀， 铁水 奔 流 开红 花。
罗有 书 记 干劲 大呀 全民 不 把 火线 下。

（谢香兰唱　钟同荣记谱）

太阳出来

1=D 2/4　　瑞金·汉

2236i | 2·32 | 5562i | 656 | 6656i | 223 |
太阳 出来 放金光 百鸟 欢唱 新时样 公社 条件 所有

5 | 66565 | 62i ||
制 美满 幸福 富又强

（谢香兰唱　钟同荣记谱）

·12·

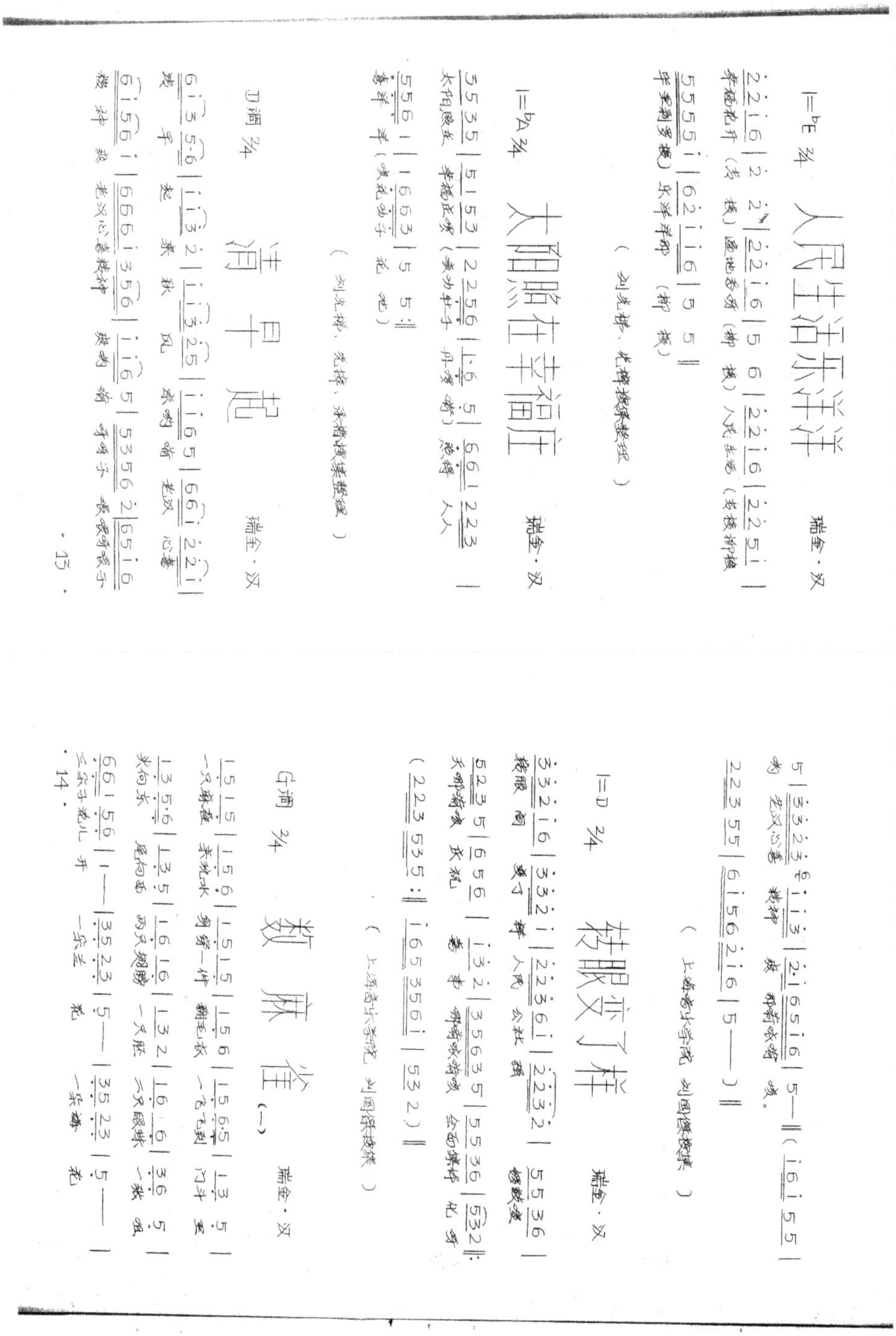

1=♭E 2/4 **人民生活乐洋洋** 瑞金·汉

2 2 i 6 | 2 2 | 2 2 i 6 | 5 6 | 2 2 i 6 | 2 2 5 i |
幸福花开（吉 梭）遍地香呀（柳 梭）人民生活（吉梭柳梭

5 5 5 5 i | 6 2 i i 6 | 5 5 ‖
半里剩罗梭）乐洋洋那 （柳 梭）

（ 刘光梯、光梓搜集整理 ）

1=♭A 2/4 **太阳照在幸福庄** 瑞金·汉

5 5 3 5 | 5 1 5 3 | 2 2 5 6 | 1 6 5 | 5 6 1 2 2 3 |
太阳照在 幸福庄哎（夜办轩子 丹梗 啃）照得 人人

5 5 6 1 | 1 6 6 3 | 5 5 :‖
喜洋 洋（哎花动子 花 池）

（ 刘光梯、光梓、承楷搜集整理 ）

D调 2/4 **清早起** 瑞金·汉

6 i 3 5·6 | i i 3 2 | i i 3 2 5 | i i 6 5 | 6 6 i 2 2 i |
清 早 起 来 秋 风 亦哟 喃 老汉 心喜

6 i 5 6 i | 6 6 6 i 3 5 6 | i i 6 5 | 5 3 5 6 2 | 6 5 i 6
精 神 爽 老汉心喜精神 爽哟 喃 呀呀子 喂喂呀喂子

·15·

5 | 3 3 2 3 i i 3 | 2·i 6 5 i 6 | 5 — ‖（ i 6 i 5 5 |
哟 老汉心喜 精神 爽 那莉咏喃 咳。

2 2 3 5 5 | 6 i 5 6 2 i 6 | 5 — ）‖

（ 上海音乐学院 刘国傑搜集 ）

1=D 2/4 **转眼变了样** 瑞金·汉

3 3 2 i 6 | 3 3 2 i | 2 2 3 6 i | 2 2 3 2 | 5 5 3 6 |
转眼 间 变了 样 人民 公社 强 锣鼓喧

5 2 3 5 | 6 5 6 | i 3 2 | 3 5 6 3 5 | 5 5 3 6 | 5 3 2 :‖
天哪荷咳 庆祝 喜 事 那荷咳荷咳 全面跃进 化 呀

（ 2 2 3 5 3 5 :‖ i 6 5 3 5 6 i | 5 3 2 ）‖

（ 上海音乐学院 刘国傑搜集 ）

G调 2/4 **数麻雀（一）** 瑞金·汉

1 5 1 5 | 1 5 6 | 1 5 1 5 | 1 5 6 | 1 5 6·5 | 1 3 5 |
一只麻雀 来玩水 身穿一件 翻毛衣 一飞飞到 门斗 里

1 3 5·6 | 1 3 5 | 1 6 1 6 | 1 3 2 | 1 6 6 | 3 6 5 |
头向东 尾向西 两只翅膀 一只脏 二只眼珠 一张 嘴

6 6 1 5 6 | 1 — | 3 5 2 3 | 5 — | 3 5 2 3 | 5 — |
三朵子花儿 开 一朵兰 花 一朵梅 花

·14·

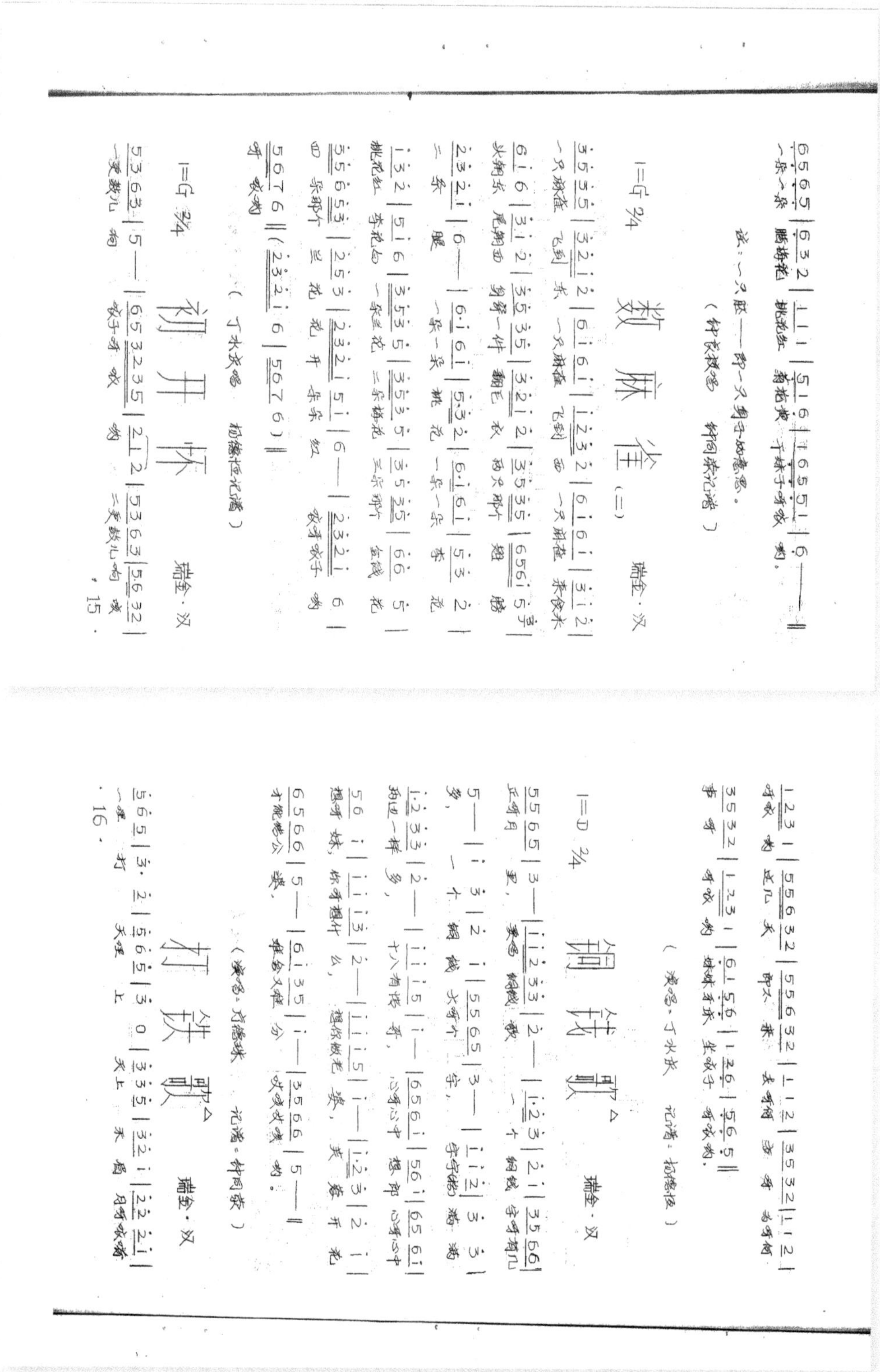

6565 | 632 | 111 | 516 | 16551 | 6 — ‖
一朵一朵 腊梅花 桃花红 菊花黄 干妹子呀依 哟。

注：一只胚——即一只翅子的意思。

（钟良棋唱　钟同荣记谱）

数麻雀（二）

1=G 2/4　瑞金·汉

3535 | 3212 | 6161 | 1232 | 6161 | 312 |
一只麻雀 飞到 东 一只麻雀 飞到 西 一只麻雀 来食米

616 | 312 | 3535 | 3212 | 3535 | 65615 |
头翎东 尾翎西 身穿一件 翻毛 衣 两只那个 翅 膀

2321 | 6 — | 6161 | 532 | 6161 | 53 2 |
二 朵 腿 一朵一朵 桃 花 一朵一朵 李 花

132 | 516 | 3535 | 3535 | 3535 | 66 5 |
桃花红 李花白 一朵兰花 二朵梅花 三朵那个 金钱 花

556553 | 253 | 23215 1 | 6 — | 2321 6 |
四 朵那个 兰 花 花 开 朵朵 红 依呀依子 哟

5676 ‖ (23216 | 5676) ‖
呀 依哟

（丁水庆唱　杨德恒记谱）

初开怀

1=G 2/4　瑞金·汉

5363 | 5 — | 653235 | 212 | 5363 | 5632 |
一更鼓儿 响 依子呀 依 哟 二更鼓儿响 依

· 15 ·

1231 | 55632 | 55632 | 112 | 3532 | 112 |
呀依 哟 这几 天 郎不 来 去呀何 方 呀 为呀何

3532 | 1231 | 6156 | 126 | 565 ‖
事 呀 呀依 哟 妹妹牙床 坐依子 呀依哟。

（演唱：丁水庆　记谱：杨德恒）

铜钱歌△

1=D 2/4　瑞金·汉

5565 | 3 — | 11233 | 2 — | 123 | 21 | 3566 |
正呀月 里， 要唱 铜钱 歌 一 个 铜钱 字呀有几

5 — | 13 | 21 | 5565 | 3 — | 112 | 33 |
多， 一 个 铜 钱 大呀个 字， 字字(的) 满 满

1233 | 2 — | 1115 | 1 — | 6561 | 561 | 6561 |
两边一样 多， 十八有楼 哥， 心呀心中 想 郎 心呀心中

56 1 | 1113 | 2 — | 1115 | 1 — | 123 | 21 |
想呀 妹， 你呀想什 么， 想你做老 婆， 芙 蓉 开 花

6566 | 5 — | 6135 | 1 — | 3566 | 5 — ‖
才能结公 婆， 难舍又难 分 哎哎哎哎 哟。

（演唱：刘德珠　记谱：钟同荣）

打铁歌△

瑞金·汉

565 | 3·2 | 565 | 30 | 335 | 321 | 2221 |
一哩 打 天哩 上 天上 禾 眉 月呀依嘀

· 16 ·

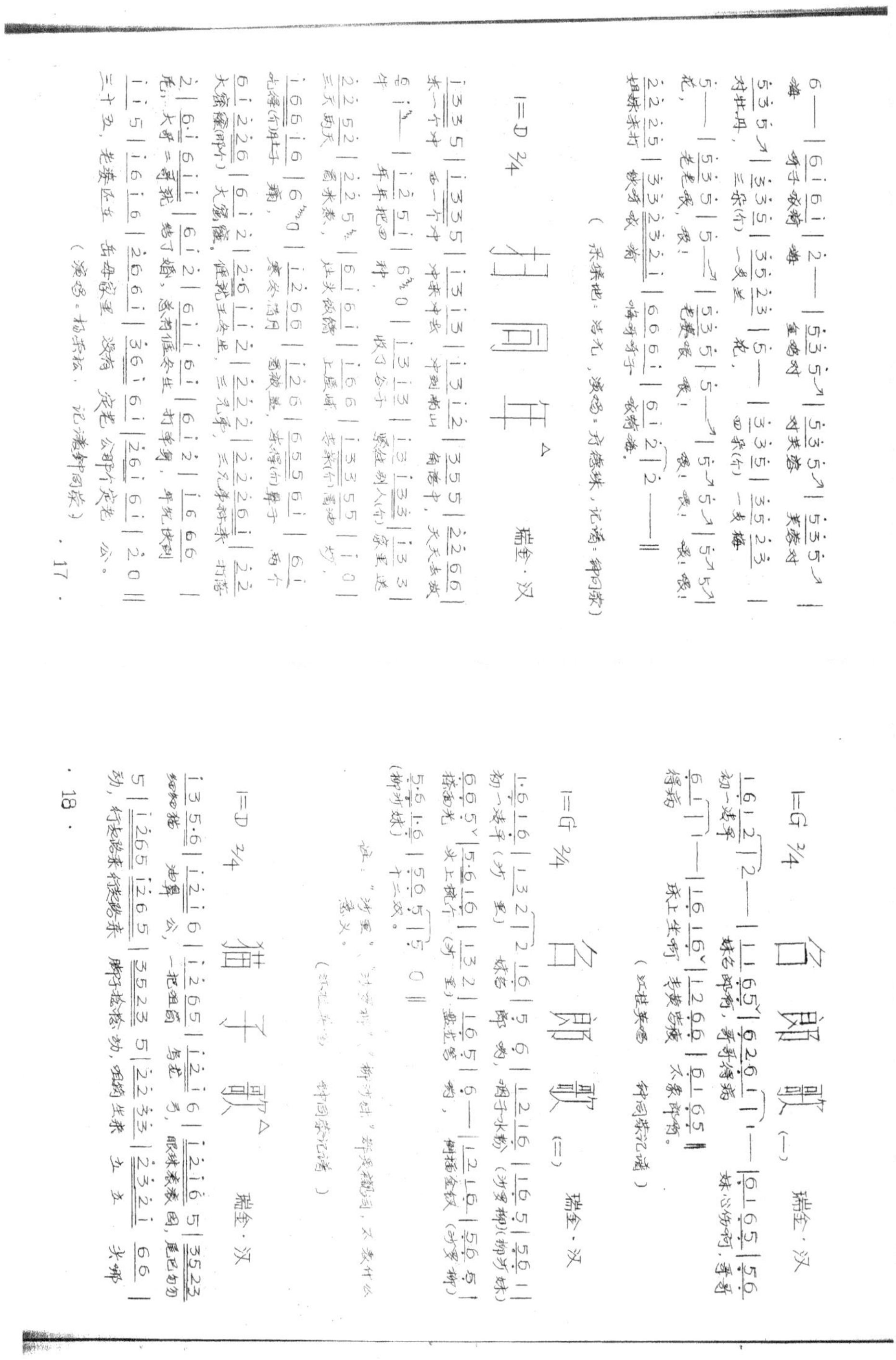

6 — | 6 i 6 i | 2 — | 5 3 5 ↗ | 5 3 5 ↗ | 5 3 5 ↗ |
嗨　　呀子依莳嗨　　金鸡对　对芙蓉　芙蓉对

5 3 5 ↗ | 3 3 5 | 3 5 2 3 | 5 — | 3 3 5 | 3 5 2 3 |
对牡丹，　三朵(个)　一支兰　花，　四朵(个)　一支梅

5 — | 5 3 5 | 5 — ↗ | 5 3 5 | 5 — ↗ | 5 ↗ 5 ↗ | 5 ↗ 5 ↗ |
花，　老老哦，哦！　老妻哦　哦！　哦！哦！　哦！哦！

2 2 2 5 | 3 3 2 3 2 i | 6 6 6 i | 6 i 2 | 2 — ||
姐妹来打　铁呀依　莳　嗨呀呀子　依莳嗨。

（采集地：洁元，演唱：方德珠，记谱：钟同荣）

打同年△

1=D 2/4　　瑞金·汉

i 3 3 5 | i 3 3 5 | i 3 i 3 | i 3 i 2 | 3 5 5 | 2 2 6 6 |
东一个冲　西一个冲　冲东冲去　冲到南山　角落中，天天去放

6 i — | i 2 5 i | 6 0 | i 3 i 3 | i 3 i 3 3 | i 3 3 |
牛　　年年把田　种，　收了谷子　紧丝别人(个)家里送

2 2 5 2 | 2 2 5 | 6 i 6 i | i 6 6 | i 3 3 5 5 | i 0 |
三天两天　看米煮，　灶头饭馈　上屋咪　壶茶(个)菜油　炒，

i 6 6 i 6 | 6 0 | i 2 6 6 | i 2 6 | 6 5 5 6 i | 6 i |
冷得(个)用杠子　痛，　寒冬腊月　看被盖，　冻得(个)鼻子　两个

6 i 2 2 6 | 6 i 2 | 2·6 i i 2 | 2 2 2 | 2 2 2 6 i | 2 2 |
大窟窿(哪个)　大窟窿。　健就王冬生，　三兄弟，　三兄弟林来　打落

2 | 6·i 6 i i | 6 i 2 | 6 i i 6 i | 6 i 2 | i 6 6 6 |
屉，大哥二哥就　结了婚，　总有侄冬生　打单身，　年纪快到

i i 5 | i 6 i 6 | 2 6 6 i | 3 6 i 6 i | 2 6 i 6 i | 2 0 ||
三十五，老婆还在　岳母家里　没有　定老公那个定老　公。

（演唱：杨荣根，记谱：钟同荣）

· 17 ·

名郎歌（一）

1=G 2/4　　瑞金·汉

1 6 1 2 | 2 — | 1 1 6 5 | 6 2 6 1 | 1 — | 6 1 6 5 | 5 6 |
初一送早　　妹名郎啊，哥哥得病　　妹心伤啊，哥哥

6 1 | 1 — | 1 6 1 6 | 1 2 6 6 | 6 1 6 5 ||
得病　　床上生啊　书黄肖瘦　不象郎啊。

（江桂英唱　钟同荣记谱）

名郎歌（二）

1=G 2/4　　瑞金·汉

1·6 1 6 | 1 3 2 | 2 1 6 | 5 6 | 1 2 1 6 | 1 6 5 | 5 6 1 |
初一送早（沙　里）　妹名　郎　哟，咽子水粉（沙罗柳）(柳沙妹)

6 6 5 | 5·6 1 6 | 1 3 2 | 1 6 5 | 6 — | 1 2 1 6 | 5 6 5 |
搽面光　头上梳个（沙　里）盘龙髻　哟，　侧插金钗（沙罗柳）

5·6 1·6 | 5 6 5 | 5 0 ||
（柳沙妹）　十二双。

注："沙里"、"沙罗柳"、"柳沙妹"都是衬词，不表什么意义。

（江桂英唱　钟同荣记谱）

猫子歌△

1=D 2/4　　瑞金·汉

i 3 5·6 | i 2 i 6 | i 2 6 5 | i 2 i 6 | i 2 i 6 5 | 3 5 2 3 |
细细猫　油鼻　公，一把粗筒　白花　弓，眼珠滚滚圆，尾巴勿勿

5 | i 2 6 5 i 2 6 5 | 3 5 2 3 5 | 2 2 3 3 | 2 3 2 i 6 6 |
动，行起路来行起路来　脚子捻捻动，坐稍坐来　立　立　尖哪

· 18 ·

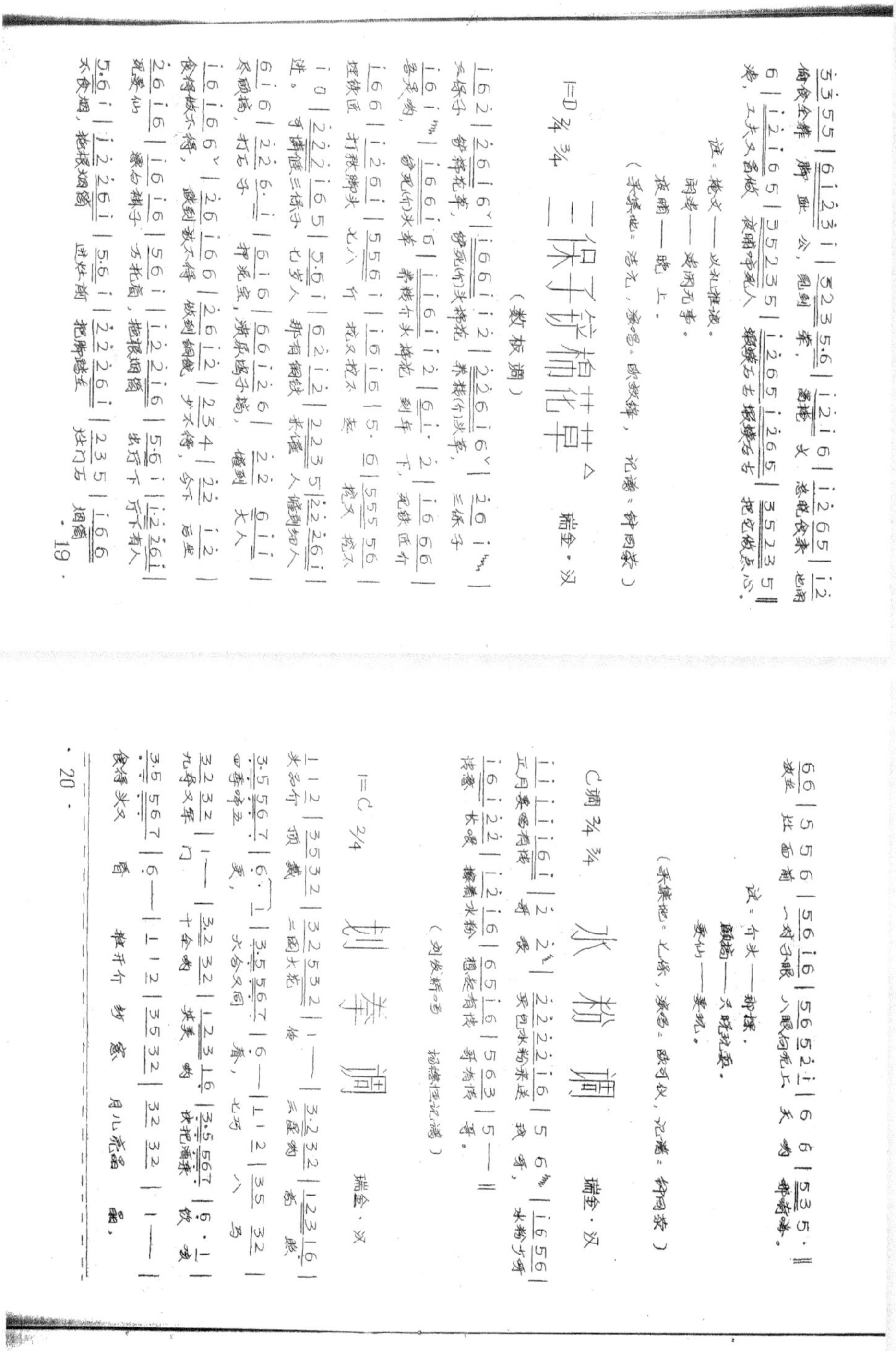

3 3 5 5 | 6 i 2 3 i | 5 2 3 5.6 | i 2 i 6 | i 2 6 5 | i 2
偷食金犁 脚 盆 公，見到 菜， 掩文 总眠食来 也闲

6 | i 2 i 6 5 | 3 5 2 3 5 | i 2 6 5 i 2 6 5 | 3 5 2 3 5 ‖
游，工夫又呂做 夜晡哼死人 蝦蟆石古蝦蟆石古 把它做点心。

注：掩文——以礼推诿。
闲游——游闲无事。
夜晡——晚上。

（采集地：浩元，演唱：欧效锋， 记谱：钟同荣）

三保子铲棉花草△

1=D 2/4 3/4　　瑞金·汉

（数板调）

i 6 2 | 2 6 i 6 | i 6 6 i i 2 | 2 2 6 i 6 | 2 6 i |
三保子 铲棉花草， 铲死(个)头棉花 养转(个)头草， 三保子

i 6 i | i 6 6 i 6 | i i 6 i i 2 | 6 i · 2 | i 6 6 6 |
吾灵哟， 铲死(个)头草 养转个头棉花 到年 下， 死铁匠个

i 6 6 | i 2 6 i | 5 5 6 i | i 6 i 6 | 5 · 6 | 5 5 5 5 6 |
埋铁匠 打秋脚头 七八 个 挖又挖不 起 挖又 挖不

i 0 | 2 2 2 i 6 5 | 5.6 i | 6 2 i 2 | 2 2 3 5 | 2 2 2 6 i |
进。 可怜谁三保子 七岁人 那有铜铁 来偃 人偃到细人

6 i 6 | 2 2 6 · i | 6 i 6 | 6 6 i 2 6 | 2 2 6 i i |
尽顾搞，打石 子 押泥宝，演床鸡子搞， 偃到 大人

i 6 i 6 6 | 2 6 i 6 6 | 2 6 i 2 | 2 3 4 | 2 2 i 2 |
食得做不得， 做到衣不得 做到铜钱 少不得，今下 后生

2 6 i 6 | i 6 i 6 | 5 6 i | i 2 2 i 6 | 5.6 i | i 2 2 6 i |
死爱仙 擦台桃子 方托盾，抱根烟筒 出厅下 厅下有人

5.6 i | i 2 2 6 i | 5.6 i | 2 2 2 6 i | 2 3 5 | i 6 6
不食烟，抱根烟筒 进灶前 把脚踏在 灶门石 烟筒

· 19 ·

6 6 | 5 5 6 | 5 6 i 6 | 5 6 5 2 i | 6 6 | 5 3 5 · ‖
放在 灶 面 前 一对子眼 八眼向死上 天 哟 那嗬嗨。

注：个头——那棵。
顾搞——只晓玩耍。
要仙——要玩。

（采集地：七保，演唱：欧可仪，记谱：钟同荣）

水粉调

C调 2/4 3/4　　瑞金·汉

i i i i i 6 i | 2 2 | 2 2 2 2 i 6 | 5 6 | i 6 5 6 |
正月要唱有传 哥 哎 买包水粉来送 我 哥， 水粉少呀

i 6 i 2 2 | i 2 i 6 | 6 5 i 6 | 5 6 3 | 5 — ‖
情意 长喂 擦着水粉 想起有传 哥有传 哥。

（刘发娇唱　杨德恒记谱）

划拳调

1=C 2/4　　瑞金·汉

1 1 2 | 3 5 3 2 | 3 2 5 3 2 | 1 — | 3.2 3 2 | 1 2 3 1 6 |
头名个 顶 戴 三国大花 传 三星哟 高 照

3.5 5 6 7 | 6 · 1 | 3.5 5 6 7 | 6 — | 1 1 2 | 3 5 3 2 |
四季喷五 更， 六合又同 春， 七巧 八 马

3 2 3 2 | 1 — | 3.2 3 2 | 1 2 3 1 6 | 3.5 5 6 7 | 6 · 1 |
九寿又年 门 十全哟 共美 哟 我把酒来 饮 哎

3.5 5 6 7 | 6 — | 1 1 2 | 3 5 3 2 | 3 2 3 2 | 1 — |
食得头又 昏 推开个 纱 窗 月儿亮晶 晶，

· 20 ·

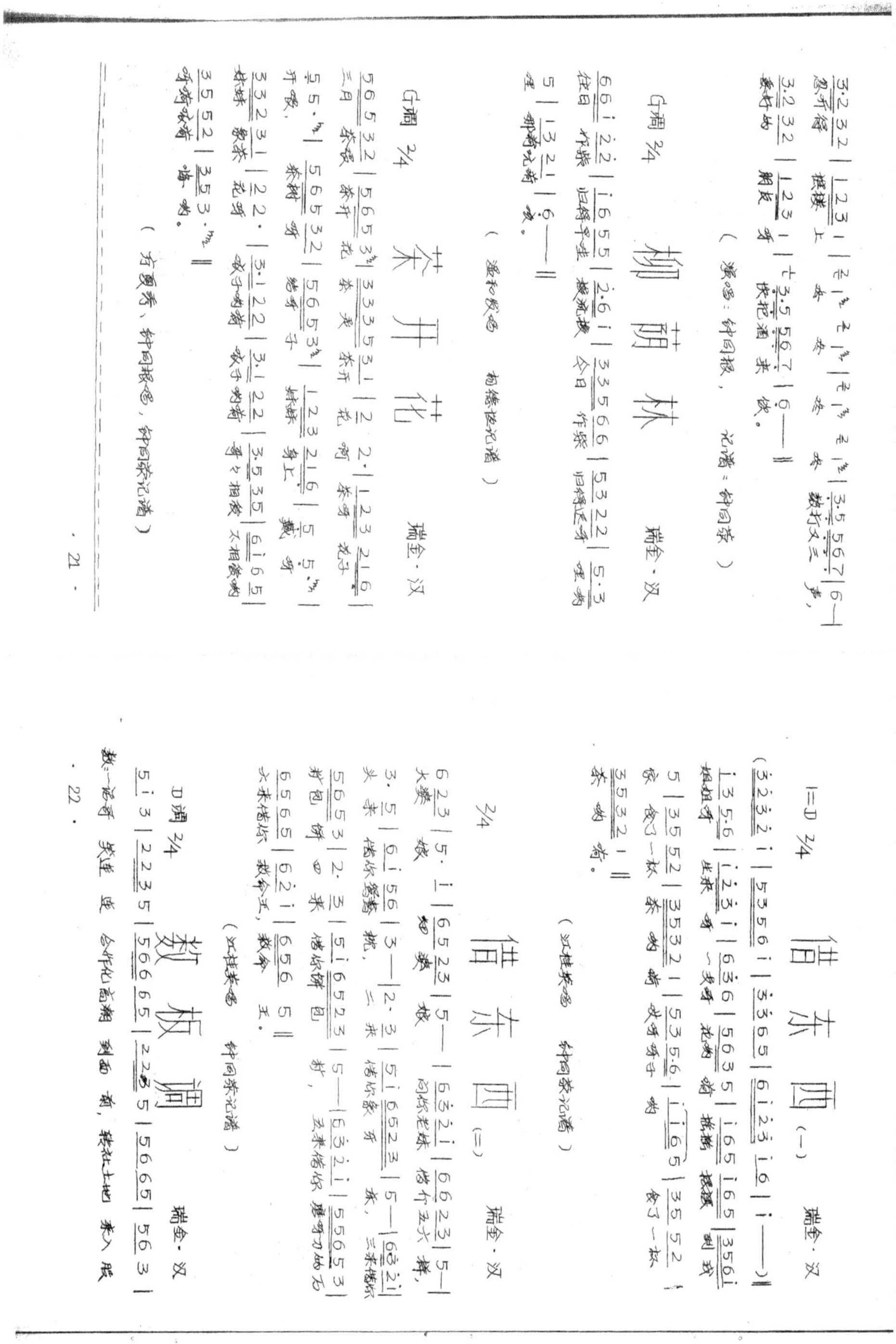

3·2 3 2 | 1 2 3 1 | ... | 3·5 5 6 7 | 6 — |
忽开得 捱搂 上 安 安 哙 安 敖打又三 声，

3·2 3 2 | 1 2 3 1 | 3·5 5 6 7 | 6 —— ‖
爱好的 朋友 呀 快把酒 来 饮。

（演唱：钟同根， 记谱：钟同荣）

柳荫林

G调 2/4　　　瑞金·汉

6 6 i 2 2 | i 6 5 5 | 2·6 i | 3 3 5 6 6 | 5 3 2 2 | 5·3
往日 作柴 归得早些 换梳换 今日 作柴 归得迟呀 哩哟

5 | 1 3 2 1 | 6 —— ‖
哩 那样吃莳 夜。

（温和椒唱　杨德俊记谱）

茶开花

G调 2/4　　　瑞金·汉

5 6 5 3 2 | 5 6 5 3 | 3 3 3 5 3 1 | 2 2· | 1 2 3 2 1 6 |
三月 茶哎 茶开 花 茶 哎 茶开 花 呵 茶呀 花子

5 5· | 5 6 5 3 2 | 5 6 5 3 | 1 2 3 2 1 6 | 5 5· |
开哎， 茶树 呀 结呀 子 妹妹 身上 戴 呀

3 3 2 3 1 | 2 2· | 3·1 2 2 | 3·1 2 2 | 3·5 3 5 | 6 i 6 5 |
妹妹 象茶 花呀 哎子哟荷 哎子哟荷 哥々相救 不相救哟

3 5 5 2 | 3 5 3· ‖
呀荷哎荷 嗨 哟。

（方夏秀、钟同根唱，钟同荣记谱）

借东西（一）

1=D 2/4　　　瑞金·汉

（3 2 3 2 i | 5 3 5 6 i | 3 3 6 5 | 6 i 2 3 i 6 | i —— ）‖

i 3 5·6 | i 2 3 i | 6 3 6 | 5 6 3 5 | i 6 5 i 6 5 | 3 5 6 i
姐姐呀 生来 呀 一支呀 花哟 荷 摇摇 摆摆 到我

5 | 3 5 5 2 | 3 5 3 2 1 | 5 3 5·6 | i i 6 5 | 3 5 5 2 |
家 食了一杯 茶 哟 荷 哎呀呀子 哟 食了一杯

3 5 3 2 1 ‖
茶 哟 荷。

（江桂英唱　钟同荣记谱）

借东西（二）

2/4　　　瑞金·汉

6 2 3 | 5· i | 6 5 2 3 | 5 — | 6 3 2 i | 6 6 2 3 | 5 — |
大婆 娘 细 婆 娘 问你老妹 借个五六 样，

3· 5 | 6 i 5 6 | 3 — | 2· 3 | 5 i 6 5 2 3 | 5 — | 6 3 2 i |
头 来 借你鸳鸯 枕， 二 来 借你象 牙 床， 三来借你

5 6 5 3 | 2· 3 | 5 i 6 5 2 3 | 5 — | 6 3 2 i | 5 5 6 5 3 |
打包 饼 四 来 借你饼 包 打， 五来借你 磨呀刀的石

6 5 6 5 | 6 2 i | 6 5 6 5 ‖
六来借你 救命王，救命 王。

（江桂英唱　钟同荣记谱）

数板调

D调 2/4　　　瑞金·汉

5 i 3 | 2 2 3 5 | 5 6 6 6 5 | 2 2 3 5 | 5 6 6 5 | 5 6 3 |
数一语哥 笑连 连 合作化高潮 到面 前，转社土地 来入 股

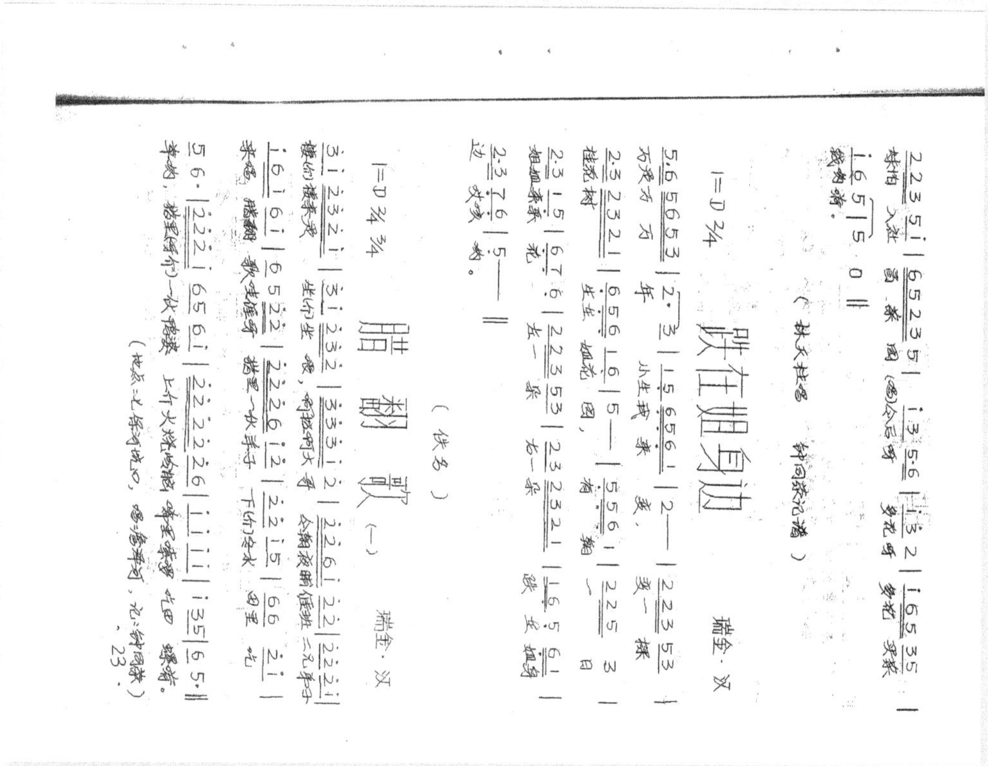

2 2 3 5 i | 6 5 2 3 5 | i 3 5·6 | i 3 2 | i 6 5 3 5 |
妹怕 入社 留 家 园（唱）今后呀 多花呀 多花 买来
i 6 5 | 5 0 ||
钱勿猜。

（林天柱唱 钟同荣记谱）

跌在姐身边

瑞金·汉

1=D 2/4

5.6 5 6 5 3 | 2· 3 | 1 5 6 5 6 1 | 2 — | 2 2 3 5 3 |
万变万 万 年 小生我 来 变， 变一 棵
2·3 2 3 2 1 | 6 5 6 1 6 | 5 — | 5 5 6 1 | 2 2 5 3 |
桂花树 生生 姐花 园， 有 朝 一 日
2·3 1 5 | 6 7 6 | 2 2 3 5 3 | 2 3 2 3 2 1 | 1 6 5 6 1 |
姐姐来采 花 左一 朵 右一朵 跌 在 姐身
2·3 7 6 | 5 — ||
边 哎哎 哟。

（佚名）

腊翻歌（一）

瑞金·汉

1=D 2/4 3/4

3 i 2 3 2 i | 3 i 2 3 2 | 3 3 3 i 2 | 2 2 6 i 2 2 | 2 2 2 i |
捜（介）捜来来 生（介）生 哦，阿拉阿大哥 今朝夜晡侄班 二九羊子
i 6 i 6 i | 6 5 2 2 | 2 2 2 6 i 2 | 2 2 i 5 | 6 6 2 i |
来唱 腊翻 歌哇侄呀 搭里一伙羊子 下（介）冬水 田里 吃
5 6· | 2 2 2 i 6 5 6 i | 2 2 2 2 2 6 | i i i i | i 3 5 | 6 5· ||
草哟， 猪里（牙介）一伙猪婆 上介火烧岭脑 嘴里嗦啰 吃田 螺呀。

（地点：七保河坑口，唱：詹萍河，记：钟同荣）

· 23 ·

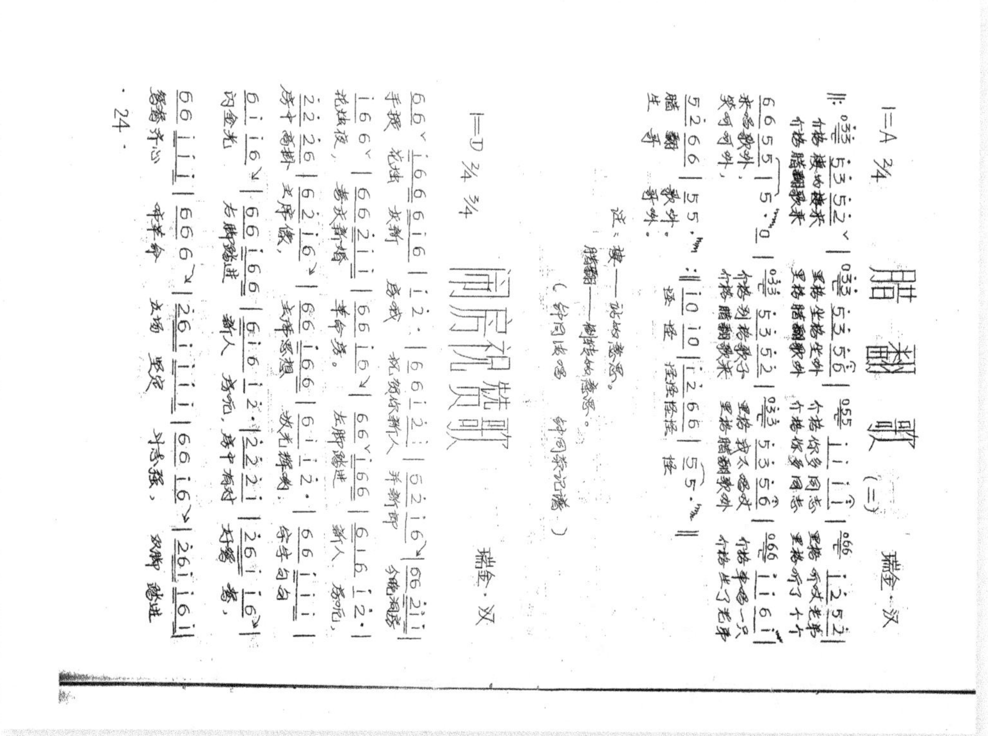

腊翻歌（二）

瑞金·汉

1=A 2/4

||: 0 3 3 5 3 5 2 | 0 3 3 5 3 5 6 | 0 5 5 i i i i | 0 6 6 i 2 5 2 |
介格 捜的捜来 里格 生格生外 介格 你多同志 里格 听哎老弟
介格 腊翻歌来 里格 腊翻歌外 介格 你多同志 里格 听了个个
6 6 5 5 | 5 · 0 | 0 3 3 5 3 5 2 | 0 3 3 5 3 5 6 | 0 6 6 i i 6 i |
来唱歌外， 介格 到格歌子 里格 我不唱哎 介格 半唱一只
笑呵呵外， 介格 腊翻歌来 里格 腊翻歌外 介格 生了老弟
5 2 6 6 | 5 5· :|| i 0 i 0 | i 2 6 6 | 5 5· ||
腊 翻 歌外。 怪 怪 怪怪怪怪 怪
生 哥 哥外。

注：捜——站的意思。
腊翻——倒转的意思。

（钟同浓唱 钟同荣记谱）

闹房祝赞歌

瑞金·汉

1=D 2/4 3/4

6 6 i 6 6 6 i 6 | i 2· | 6 6 i 2 | 5 2 i 6 | 6 6 2 i i |
手提 花烛 龙新 房哦 祝贺你新人 并新郎 今晚洞房
i 6 6 | 6 6 2 i i | 6 6 i 6 | 6 6 i 6 6 | 6 i 6 i 2· |
花烛夜， 革命新婚 革命房。 左脚踏进 新人 房呢，
2 2 2 6 | 6 2 i 6 | 6 6 i 6 6 | 6 i i 2· | 6 6 i i i |
房中高挂 主席像， 主席思想 放光辉哟， 字字句句
6 i i 6 | 6 6 i 6 6 | 6 i 6 i 2· | 2 2 2 i | 2 6 i i 6 |
闪金光 右脚踏进 新人 房呢，房中有对 好鸳 鸯，
6 6 i i i | 6 6 6 | 2 6 i i i i | 6 6 i 6 | 2 6 i i 6 i |
鸳鸯齐心 闹革命 立场 坚定 斗志强， 双脚 踏进

· 24 ·

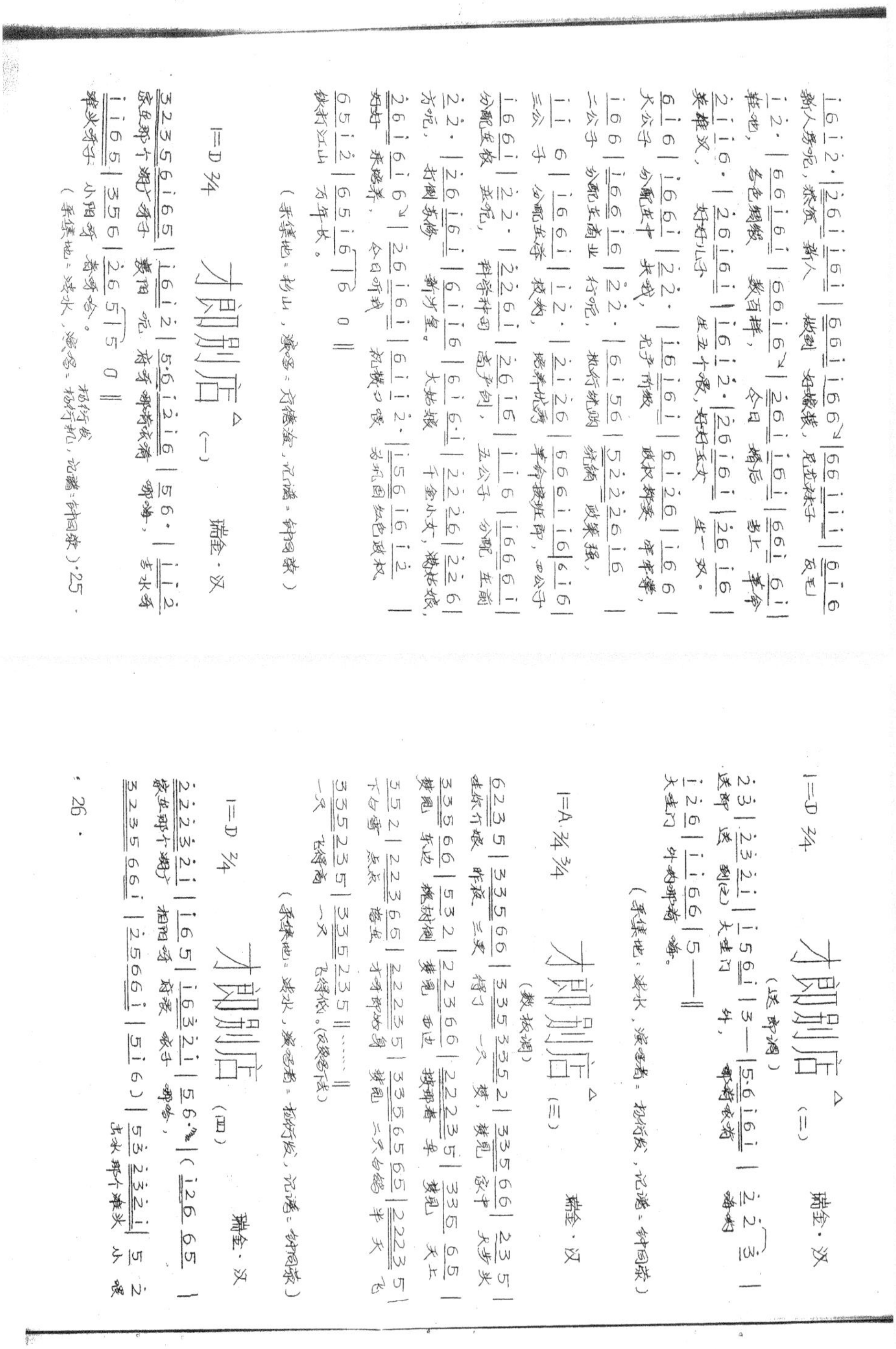

新人劳呢，恭贺 新人 做到 好嫁装，尼龙袜子 灰毛 鞋也，各色绸缎 数百样，今日 婚后 当上 革命 英雄汉，好好儿子 生五个喂，好好玉女 生一双。大公子 分配在中 央戏，无产阶级 政权都要 牢牢掌，二公子 分配在商业 行呢，执行统购 统销 政策强，三公 子 分配在洋 枝构，培养优秀 革命接班郎，四公子 分配在农 丢呢，科学种田 高产创，五公子 分配 在前 方呢，打倒苏修 新沙皇。大姑娘 千金小女，满姑娘，好好 来培养，今日听我 祝福口喂 为巩固红色政权 铁打江山 万年长。

（采集地：杉山，演唱：刘德滏，记谱：钟同荣）

才郎别店△（一）

瑞金·汉

1=D 2/4

家在那个湖广呀子 襄阳 呢 府呀哪啊依啊 哪嗨，吉水呀 滩头呀子 小阳呀 着呀哈。

（采集地：浓水，演唱：杨行发，记谱：钟同荣）

·25·

才郎别店△（二）

瑞金·汉

1=D 2/4

（送郎调）

送郎 送 到(之) 大旗门 外，哪嗬依嗬 嗨哟 大旗门 外哟哪嗬 嗨。

（采集地：浓水，演唱者：杨行发，记谱：钟同荣）

才郎别店△（三）

瑞金·汉

1=A 2/4 3/4

（数板调）

昨你个娘 昨夜 三更 得了 一只 梦，梦见 家中 大步头 梦见 东边 槐树倒 梦见 西边 揪那着 牟 梦见 天上 下白雪 点点 落在 才呀郎的身 梦见 二只白鸽 半 天 飞 一只 飞得高 一只 飞得低。（反复多下去）

（采集地：浓水，演唱者：杨行发，记谱：钟同荣）

才郎别店△（四）

瑞金·汉

1=D 2/4

家在那个湖广 相阳呀 府哀 依子 哪哈，吉水那个滩头 小 喂

·26·

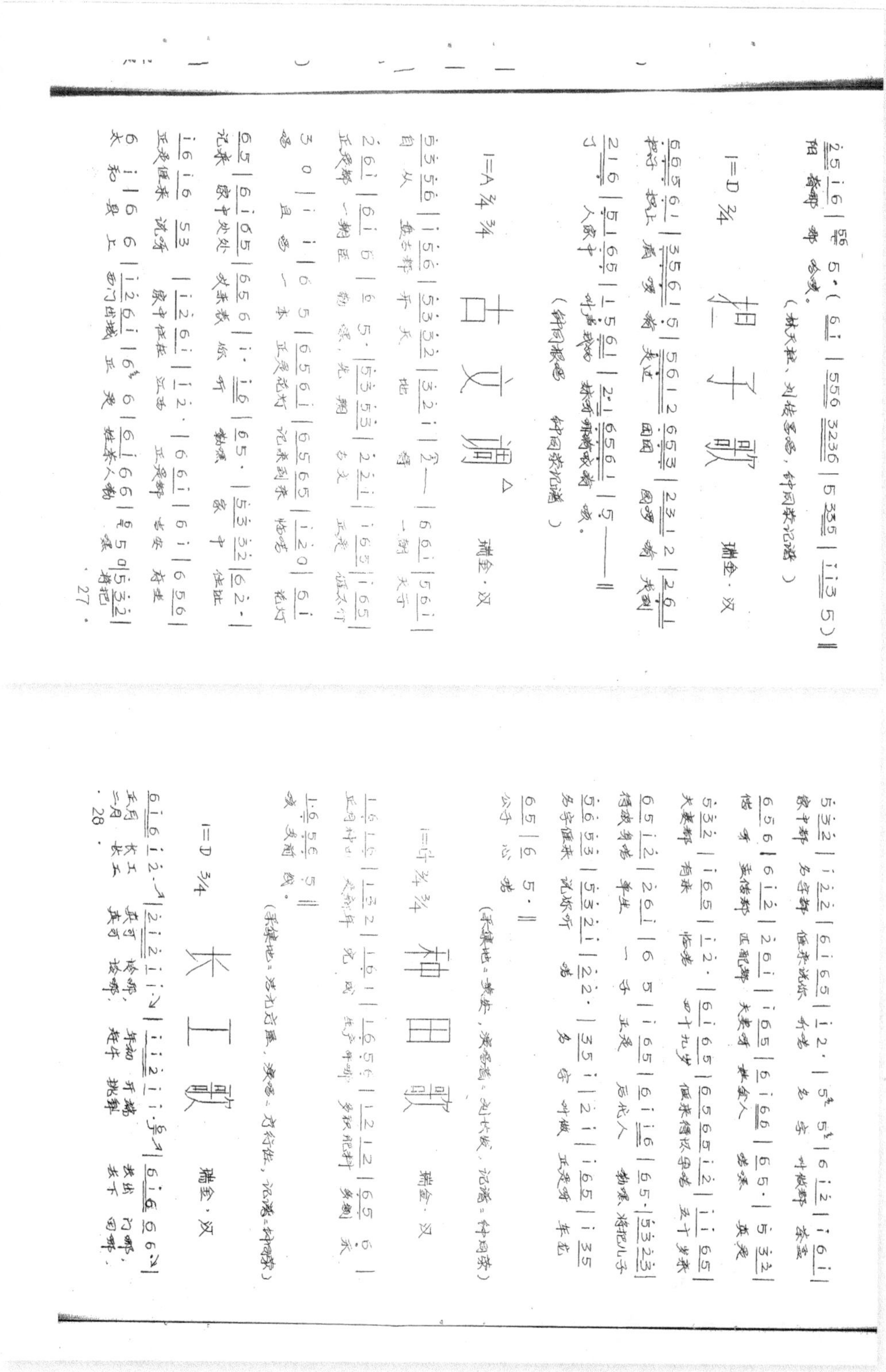

2 5 i 6 | 5 5· (6 i | 5 5 6 3 2 3 6 | 5 3 3 5 | i i 3 5) ‖
阳 荷 都 哪 哈 哎。

（林天柱、刘佳昌唱，钟同荣记谱）

担子歌

1=D 2/4　　瑞金·汉

6 6 5 6 i | 3 5 6 1 5 | 5 6 1 2 6 5 3 | 2 3 1 2 | 2 6 1 |
担子 担上 肩 哟 嗬 走过 团团 团哟 嗬 走到

2 1 6 | 5 1 6 5 | 1 5 6 1 | 2·1 6 5 6 1 | 5 — ‖
了 人家中 叫声我的 妹呀哪嗬哎嗬 哎。

（钟同根唱　钟同荣记谱）

古文调△

1=A 2/4 3/4　　瑞金·汉

5 3 5 6 | i 5 6 | 5 3 3 2 | 3 2 i | 2 — | 6 6 i | 5 6 i |
自 从 盘古帮 开 天 地 哦 一朝 天子

2 6 i | 6 i 6 | 6 5· | 5 3 5 3 | 2 2 i | i 6 5 | i 6 5 |
正是都 一朝臣 勒 喂，先 朝 古 文 正是 说不尽

3 0 | i i | 6 5 | 6 5 6 i | 6 5 6 5 | i 2 0 | 6 i |
唱 且 唱 一 本 正是花灯 记来到来 唱呢 花灯

6 5 | 6 i 6 5 | 6 5 6 | i· i 6 | 6 5· | 5 3 3 2 | 6 2· |
记来 家中处处 丈夫表 你 听 勒喂 家 中 住址

i 6 i 6 5 3 | i 2 6 i | i 2· | 6 6 i | 6 i | 6 5 6 |
正是住来 说呀 家中住在 江西 正是都 吉安 府里

6 i | 6 6 | i 2 6 i | 6 6 | 6 i 6 6 | 5 0 | 5 3 2 |
太 和 县 上 西门出城 正 是 姓苏人勒 喂 将把

· 27 ·

5 3 2 | i 2 2 | 6 i 6 5 | i 2· | 5 5 | 6 i 2 | i 6 i |
家中都 名字都 但来说你 听呀 名 字 叫做都 苏孟

6 5 6 | 6 i 2 | 2 6 i | i 6 5 | 6 i 6 6 | 6 5· | 5 3 2 |
做 呀 孟信都 匹配都 夫妻呀 林金人 勒喂 英是

5 3 2 | i 6 5 | i 2· | 6 i 6 5 | 6 5 6 5 i 2 | i i 6 5 |
夫妻都 有来 忙呀 四十九岁 但来得仔来呀 五十岁来

6 5 i 2 | 2 6 i | 6 5 | i 6 5 | 6 i i 6 | 6 5· | 5 3 2 3 |
得被身呀 单生 一 子 正是 后代人 勒喂 将把儿子

5 6 5 3 | 5 3 2 i | 2 2· | 3 5 i | 2 i | i 6 5 | i 3 5 |
名字但来 说你听 呀 名 字 叫做 正是呀 车龙

6 5 | 6 5· ‖
公子 心 呀

（采集地：黄安，演唱者：刘长发，记谱：钟同荣）

种田歌

1=G 2/4 3/4　　瑞金·汉

1 6 1 5 | 1 3 2 | 1 6 1 | 1 6 5 6 | 1 2 1 2 | 6 5 6 |
正月种田 是新年 完 成 生产计划 多积肥料 多制 禾

1·6 5 6 5 ‖
哎 支前 线。

（采集地：黄元庭，演唱：刘行佐，记谱：钟同荣）

长工歌

1=D 3/4　　瑞金·汉

6 i 6 i 2· | 2 i 2 i i· | i i 2 i i· | 6 i 6 6 6· |
正月 长工 真可 怜哪， 年初 开端 我出 门哪，
二月 长工 真可 怜哪， 赶牛 挑粪 去下 田哪，

· 28 ·

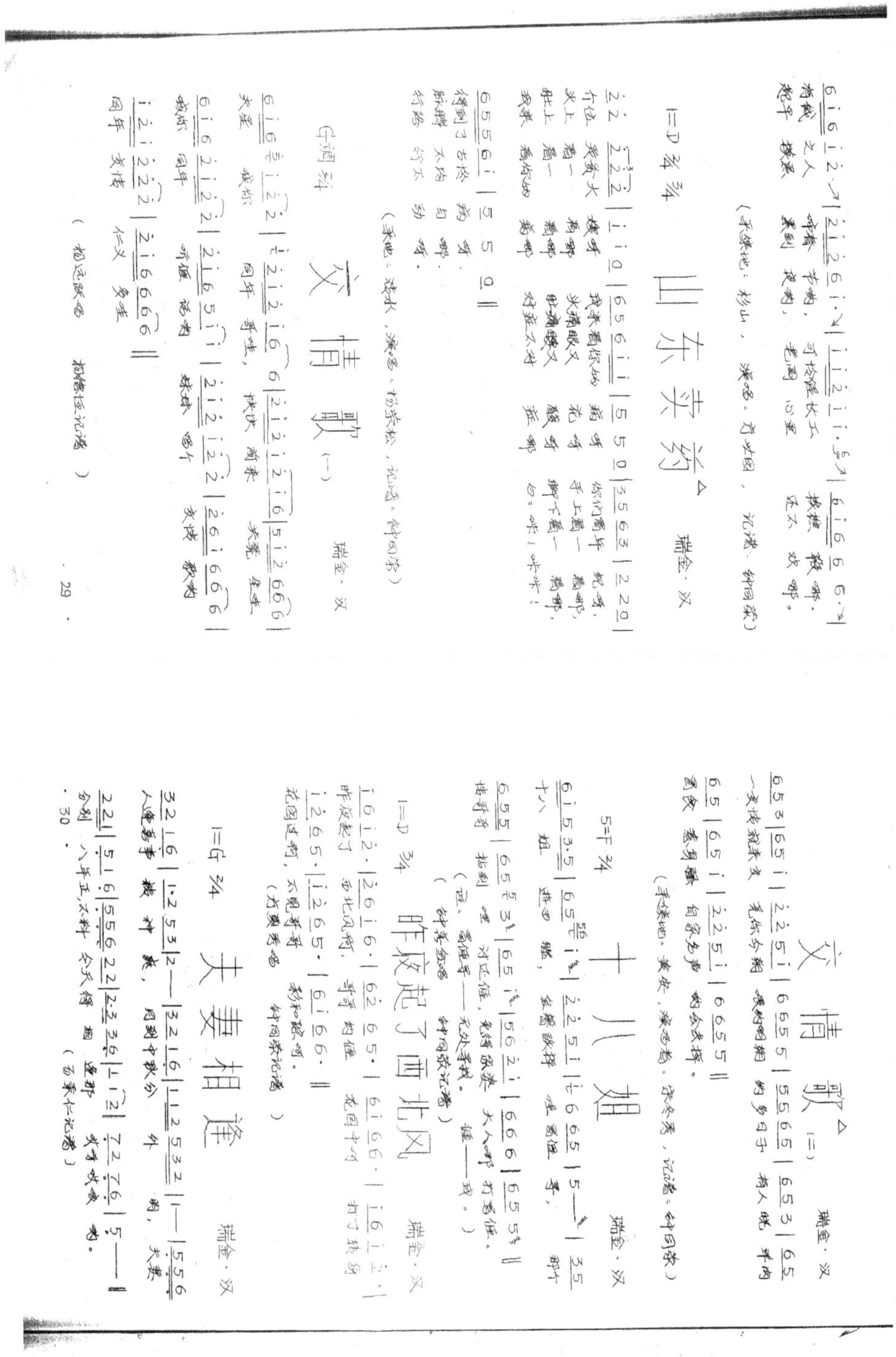

6 1 6 1 2· | 2 1 2 6 1· | 1 1 2 1 1· | 6 1 6 6 6· |
有钱 之人 啼春 节哟， 可怜佳长工 挨燕 裤哪。
起早 摸黑 累到 夜哟， 老阔 心里 还不 欢哪。

（采集地：杉山， 演唱：齐世国， 记谱：钟同荣）

山东卖药△

1=D 2/4 3/4　　瑞金·汉

2 2 2 2 2 | 1 1 0 | 6 5 6 1 1 | 5 5 0 | 3 5 6 3 | 2 2 0 |
介位 老爹大 嫂呀 我来看你的 病 呀 你们看年 纪呀，
头上 看一 看哪 头痛眼又 花 呀 手上看一 看哪，
肚上 看一 看哪 肚痛腰又 酸 呀 脚下看一 看哪，
我来 看你的 病哪 对症不对 症 哪 白：咔！咔咔！

6 5 5 6 1 | 5 5 0 ||
得到了古怪 病 呀．
脉膊 不均 匀 哪．
行路 行不 动 呀．

（采地：壬水，演唱：杨荣松，记谱：钟同荣）

交情歌（一）

G调 2/4　　瑞金·汉

6 1 6 1 2 2 | 2 1 2 1 6 6 | 2 1 2 1 2 1 6 | 5 1 2 6 6 6 |
大星 戒你 同年 哥哇， 快快 前来 央觉 生哇

6 1 6 2 1 2 2 | 2 1 6 5 1 1 | 2 1 2 1 2 2 | 2 6 1 6 6 6 |
戒你 同年 听侄 话哟 妹妹 唱个 交情 歌哟

1 2 1 2 2 2 | 2 1 6 6 6 6 ||
同年 交情 仁义 多哇

（杨远跃唱　杨德恒记谱）

交情歌（二）△

瑞金·汉

6 5 3 | 6 5 1 | 2 2 5 1 | 6 6 5 5 | 5 5 6 5 | 6 5 3 | 6 5
一交情就来交 冇你分翔 喂哟明翔 哟多日子 有人晓 半肉

6 5 | 6 5 1 | 2 2 5 1 | 6 6 5 5 ||
面食 惹身骚 自家名声 哟会丢掉。

（采集地：黄安，演唱者：宋冬秀，记谱：钟同荣）

十八姐

5=F 2/4　　瑞金·汉

6 1 5 3·5 | 6 5 1 | 2 2 5 1 | 6 6 5 | 5 — | 3 5
十八 姐 游田 塍， 自讐跌挥 哩冒佢 寻， 那个

6 5 5 | 6 5 3 | 6 5 1 | 5 6 2 1 | 6 6 6 | 6 5 5 ||
情哥哥 拈到 哩 讨还佢， 免得家婆 大人哪 打骂佢。

（注：冒佢寻——无处寻找。 佢——我。）
（钟善金唱　钟同荣记谱）

昨夜起了西北风

1=D 3/4　　瑞金·汉

1 6 1 2· | 2 6 1 6· | 6 2 6 5· | 6 1 6 6· | 1 6 1 2· |
昨夜起了 西北风啊， 哥哥 约佢 花园中啊 打了转身

1 2 6 5· | 1 2 6 5· | 6 1 6 6· ||
花园过啊， 不见哥哥 影和踪啊。

（方颈秀唱　钟同荣记谱）

夫妻相逢

1=G 2/4　　瑞金·汉

3 2 1 6 | 1·2 5 3 | 2 — | 3 2 1 6 | 1 1 2 5 3 2 | 1 — | 5 5 6
人逢喜事 精 神 爽， 月到中秋分 外 明， 夫妻

2 2 1 | 5 1 6 | 5 5 6 2 2 | 2·3 3 6 | 1 1 2 | 7 2 7 6 | 5 — ||
分别 八年正，不料 今天得 相 逢那 哎呀 哎哎 哟。

（石秉仁记谱）

03 第三类 · 小调

CATEGORY III · MINOR TUNES /OR POPULAR TUNES

导读

“小调”是一类旋律相对固定、节奏规整的歌谣，通常源于市井、乡村娱乐活动或家庭场景。与山歌的自由抒情相比，小调更注重音乐性和叙事性，歌词题材涵盖爱情、家庭、生活趣事等。赣南小调往往在婚嫁、节庆或休闲聚会时演唱，具有较强的娱乐性和流行性。它们反映了民众的日常生活节奏与审美趣味，是区域性音乐文化的重要组成部分。

比如婚嫁歌贯穿于婚礼的各个环节：迎亲、送嫁、哭嫁、婚宴对唱等。其歌词既表现对新人的祝福与喜悦，也包含离别的哀伤、对家庭关系的隐喻，折射出婚姻制度下女性情感的复杂面向。哭嫁歌尤为独特，常以泣声吟唱，表达新娘对父母的依恋与对未来的忧虑。婚嫁歌在旋律上多有起伏，兼具热烈与哀婉的双重色彩，成为理解赣南地区婚俗文化的重要窗口。

Introduction

Minor Tunes(or Popular Tunes) are folk songs with relatively fixed melodies and regular rhythms, often originating from urban marketplaces, village entertainment, or domestic settings. Compared to the freer lyrical form of mountain songs, minor tunes place greater emphasis on musicality and narrative. Their lyrics typically focus on themes such as love, family, and everyday humor. In southern Jiangxi, minor tunes were commonly performed during weddings, festivals, or leisure gatherings, embodying entertainment value and popular taste while forming an integral part of regional musical culture.

For example, Wedding Songs accompany every stage of the marriage ritual—welcoming the groom, sending off the bride, weeping songs, and antiphonal singing at the banquet. The lyrics convey both blessings and joy for the couple, as well as sorrowful tones of departure and nuanced reflections on family ties, revealing the complex emotions of women within the institution of marriage. The *crying songs* are especially distinctive, often performed with sob-like intonation, expressing the bride’s attachment to her parents and apprehension about the future. Musically, wedding songs are marked by rising and falling contours, blending festivity with melancholy, offering valuable insight into the marriage customs of southern Jiangxi.

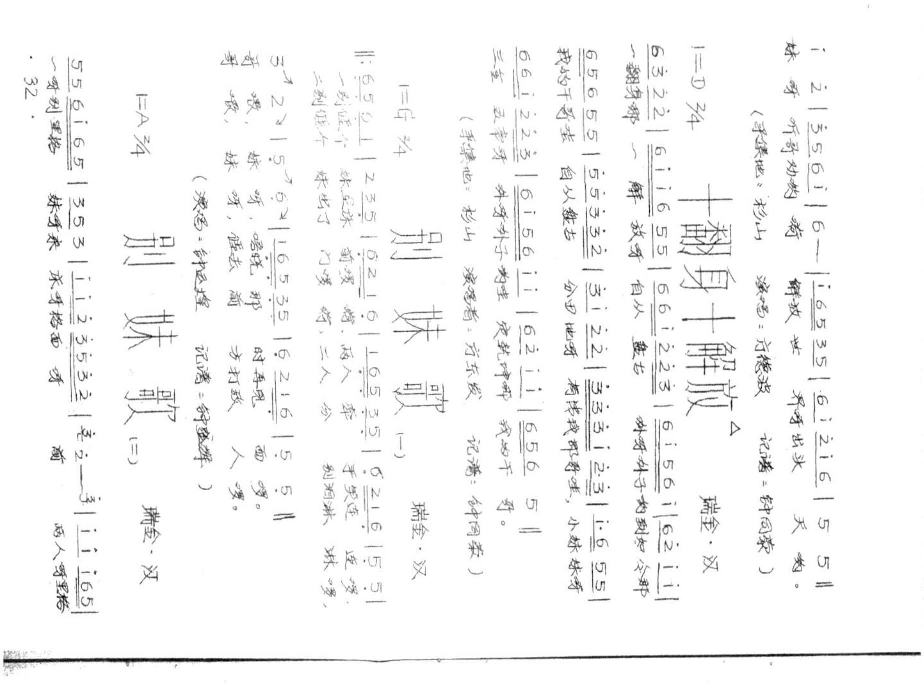

妹 呀 听哥劝哟 嗬 解放 世 界呀出头 天 哟。

（采集地：杉山 演唱：方德波 记谱：钟同荣）

十翻身十解放△

1=D 3/4 瑞金·汉

一翻身那 一 解 放呀 自从 盘古 外呀外子哟到如今那
我的干哥哥 自从盘古 分田地呀 有情我那哥哥哇，小妹妹呀
三全 五帝呀 外呀外子哟哇 定乾坤那 我的干 哥。

（采集地：杉山 演唱者：方东发 记谱：钟同荣）

别妹歌（一）

1=G 3/4 瑞金·汉

一别哥个 妹呈珠 前嘞 嗬，两人 牵 手笑连 连嘞，
二别哥个 妹出了 门嘞 嗬，二人 分 别泪淋 淋嘞，
哥 喂， 妹 呀，嗬晓 那 时再见 面 嘞。
哥 喂， 妹 呀，嗬去 前 方打敌 人 嘞。

（演唱：钟远煌 记谱：钟盛辉）

别妹歌（二）

1=A 3/4 瑞金·汉

一呀别里格 妹呀来 床呀格面 呀 前 两人呀里格
笑哥手 笑 连 连 今天那个 和呀里格哥 来呀格
分 呀 面， 弯晓呀里格 那时呀 再 见 面。

（采集地：叶坪 钟同荣记谱）

坐牢歌

1=D 2/4 3/4 瑞金·汉

一坐(个)牢 是新坪 做到犯人 苦真可怜 住背手里 猴古 样
井察鬼子 满街牵 吓里魂魄 呀上西天。

（演唱：欧可仪 记谱：钟同荣）

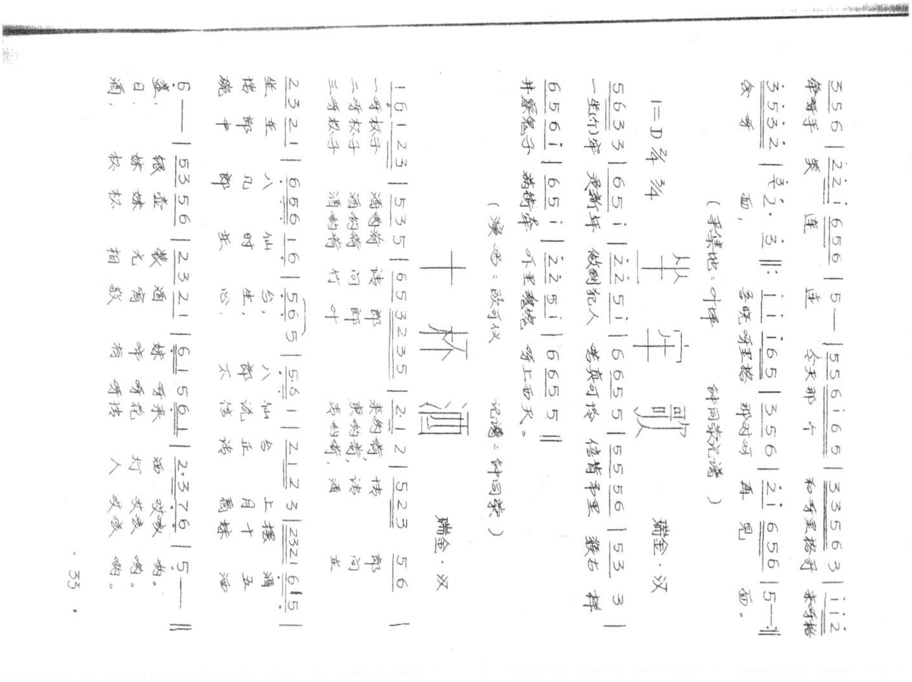

十杯酒

瑞金·汉

一呀杯子 酒哟嗬 请 郎 来哟嗬，请 郎
二呀杯子 酒哟嗬 问 郎 来哟嗬，请 问
三呀杯子 酒哟嗬 竹 叶 青哟嗬，酒 在
坐 在 八 仙 台， 八 仙 台 上 摆 酒
情 郎 几 时 生， 郎 说 正 月 十 五
碗 中 郎 在 心， 不 信 请 看 妹 酒
盏， 银 壶 装 酒 妹 呀来 酒 哎哎 哟。
日， 妹 妹 元 宵 市 呀花 灯 哎哎 哟。
酒， 杯 杯 相 敬 有 呀情 人 哎哎 哟。

· 32 ·

· 33 ·

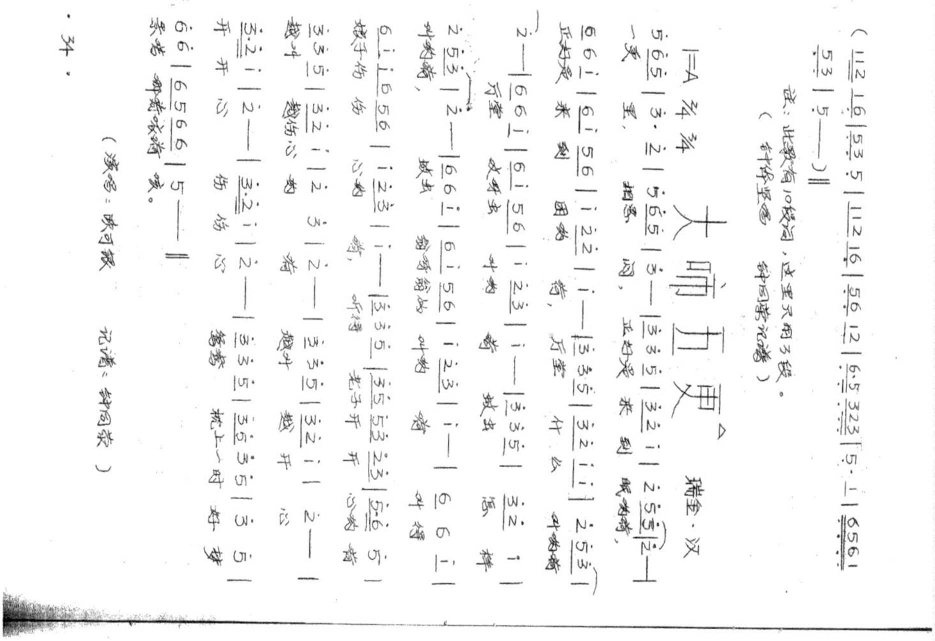

注：此歌有10段词，这里只用3段。
（钟侨坚唱　钟同荣记谱）

大吶五更△

1=A 2/4 3/4　瑞金·汉

一更 里， 相思 闷， 正好是 来 到 眠的荷，
正好是 来 到 困的 荷， 厅堂 什 么 叫的荷
厅堂 蚊子虫 叫的 荷 蚊虫 怎 样
叫的荷， 蚊虫 翁呀翁的 叫的 荷 叫 得
娘子伤 伤 心的 荷， 听得 老子开 开 心的 荷
越叫 越伤心 的 荷 越叫 越 开 心
开 开 心 伤 伤 心 鸳鸯 枕上一时 好 梦
景光 哪荷咳荷 咳。

（演唱：欧可银　记谱：钟同荣）

瓜子仁（一）

G调 2/4　瑞金·汉

小妹那格 住 在 大 桂 路 边的 荷 一 爱 的
一盘那格 瓜 子 三那 十 双的 荷 手巾 的
一面那格 镜 子 四 四 方的 荷 外面 的

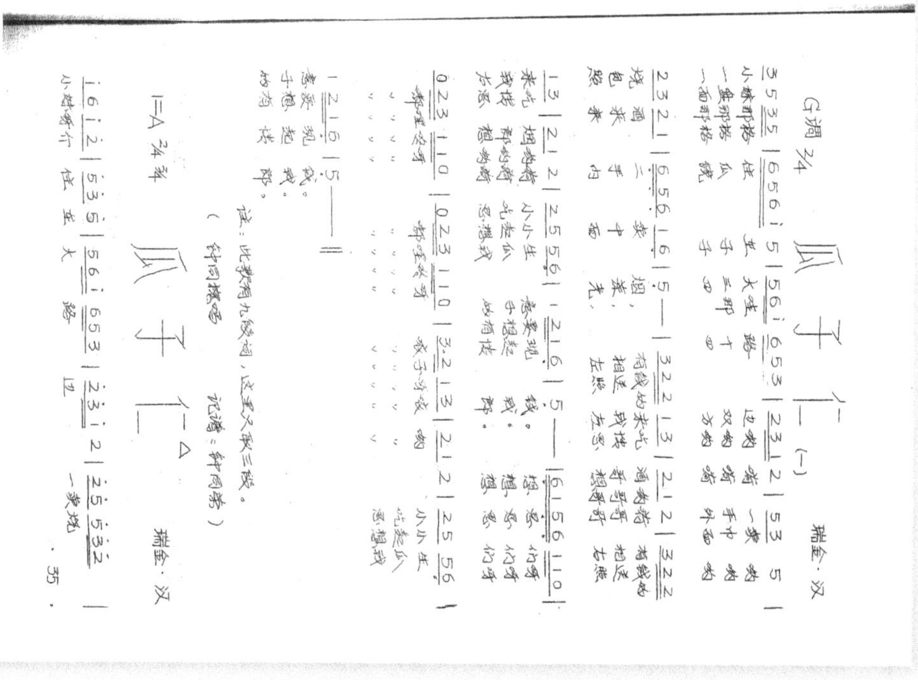

烧 酒 二 斤 烟， 有钱的来吃 酒的荷 有钱的
包 袱 手 巾 菜， 相送 我 情 哥哥哥 相送
照 来 内 面 光， 左照 左思 想哥哥 右照

来吃 烟的荷 小小生 意要现 钱。 想 思 仍呀
我情 郎的荷 吃起瓜 子想起 我。 想 思 仍呀
右思 想的荷 思想我 的有 情 郎。 想 思 仍呀

都哩 仍呀 都哩 仍呀 夜子呀 夜 哟 小小 生
吃起瓜
思想我

意要 现 钱。
子想 起 我。
的有 情 郎。

注：此歌有九段词，这里只取三段。
（钟同荣唱　记谱：钟同荣）

瓜子仁△

1=A 2/4 3/4　瑞金·汉

小妹呀介 住 在 大 路 边 一爱 烧

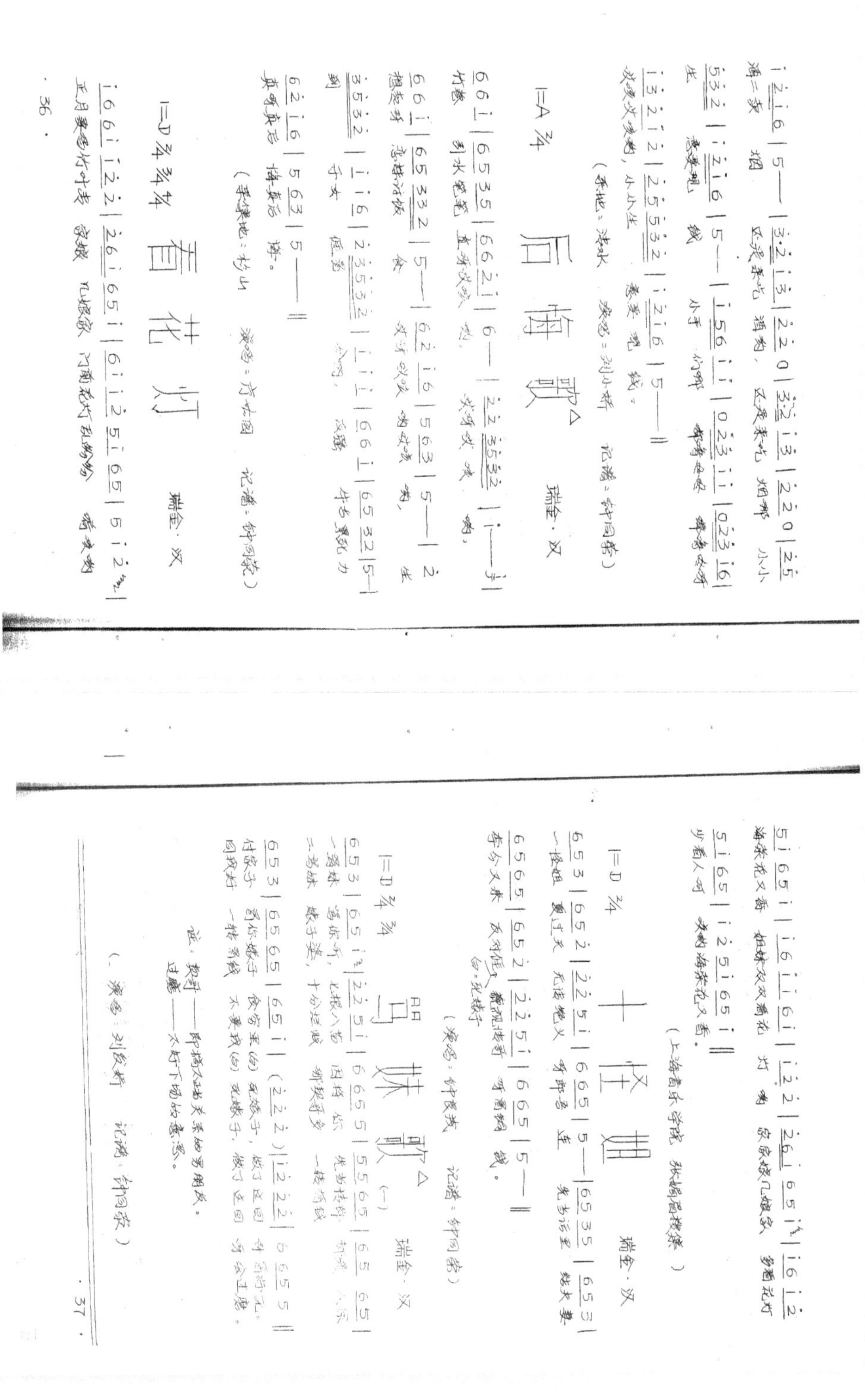

i 2̇i6 | 5— | 3̇·2̇ i3̇ | 2̇2̇0 | 3̇2̇ i3̇ | 2̇2̇0 | 2̇5
酒二壶　烟　还是来吃　酒哟，还是来吃　烟那　小小

532 | i2̇i6 | 5— | i56 ii | 02̇3̇ ii | 02̇3̇ i6 |
生　意要现　钱　小手　们那　都寿要呀　呀寿要呀

i3̇ 2̇i2̇ | 2̇5 532 | i2̇i6 | 5— ‖
哎哎哎哎哟，小小生　意要现　钱。

（采地：清水　演唱：刘小娇　记谱：钟同荣）

后悔歌△

1=A 2/4　瑞金·汉

66i | 6535 | 662i | 6— | 2̇2̇ 3̇5̇3̇2̇ | i— i |
竹卷　剥水笔笔　直呀哎哎　哟，　哎呀哎　哎　哟，

66i | 65 332 | 5— | 62̇ i6 | 563 | 5— | 2̇
想起呀　恋妹讨饭　食　哎呀哎哎　哟哎哎　哟，　生

3̇5̇3̇2̇ | i i6 | 2̇3̇5̇3̇2̇ | i i i | 66i | 65 32 | 5— |
到　子女　便弟　公呀，　反踢　牛书累死力

62̇ i6 | 563 | 5— ‖
真呀真后　悔真后　悔。

（采集地：杉山　演唱：方太园　记谱：钟同荣）

看花灯

1=D 2/4 3/4 4/4　瑞金·汉

i6 6i i2̇2̇ | 2̇6i 65i | 6i i2̇ 5i 65 | 5 i 2̇ |
正月要唱竹叶青　家娘　几娘家　门前花灯乱纷纷　嗬哎哟

· 36 ·

5i 65i | i6 ii 6i | i2̇2̇ | 2̇6i 65 i | i6 i2̇
海棠花又香　姐妹双双看花　灯　哟　家家娘几娘家　多看花灯

5i 65 | i2̇ 5i 65 i ‖
少看人呀　哎哟海棠花又香。

（上海音乐学院　张娟眉搜集）

十怪姐

1=D 2/4　瑞金·汉

653 | 652̇ | 2̇2̇ 5i | 665 | 5— | 65 35 | 653 |
一怪姐　夏过天　无话艳火　呀郎吾　连　先当话里　结夫妻

6565 | 652̇ | 2̇2̇ 5i | 665 | 5— ‖
李今又来　反对侄　藏视传哥　呀看钢　钱。
白：死婊子

（演唱：钟良我　记谱：钟同荣）

骂妹歌△（一）

1=D 2/4 3/4　瑞金·汉

653 | 65 i | 2̇2̇ 5i | 6655 | 5565 | 65 65 |
一骂妹　骂你呀，七根八节　困将你　先当恃宠
二骂妹　婊子婆，十分烂贱　哪契哥多　一转骂钱

653 | 6565 | 65 i | (2̇2̇2̇) | i2̇ 2̇2̇ | 6655 ‖
付家子　骂你婊子　食穷鬼(白)死婊子，做了这回　呀骂你完。
回我好　一转骂钱　不要我(白)死婊子，做了这回　呀会过磨。

注：契哥——即搞不正当关系的男朋友。
过磨——不好下场的意思。

（演唱：刘发娇　记谱：钟同荣）

· 37 ·

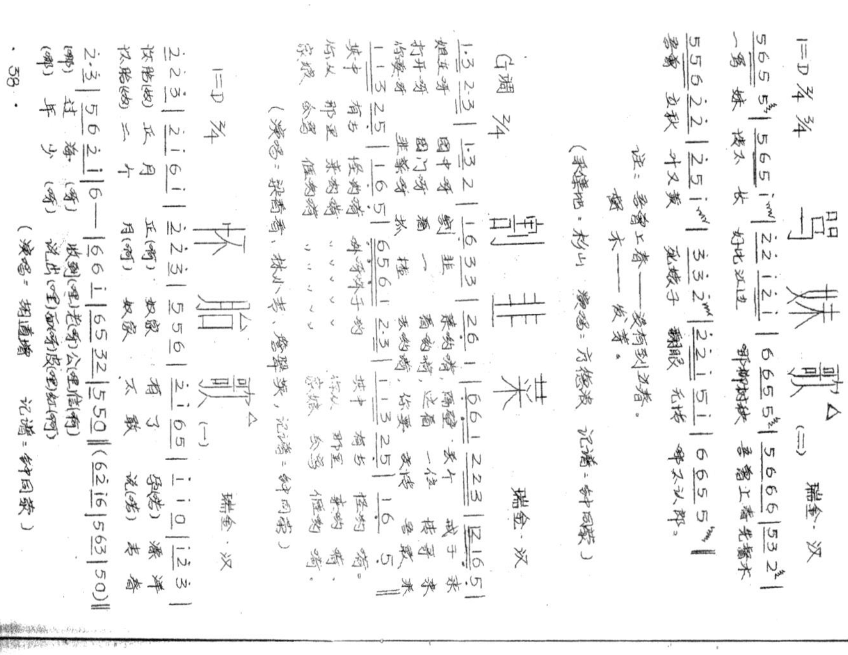

骂妹歌△（二）　瑞金·汉

1=D 2/4 3/4

一蔓妹　摸不长　好比江边　哪柳树秧　吾曾上春先督木

吾曾立秋　寸又黄　死娘子　翻眼　无传　郎不认郎。

注：吾曾上春——没有到立春。督木——发芽。

（采集地：杉山　演唱：方德波　记谱：钟同荣）

割韭菜　瑞金·汉

G调 3/4

姐在呀　园中呀　割韭　菜哟嗬，隔壁　去个　戒子来
打开呀　园门呀　看一　看哟嗬，这看　一位　请哥来
你要呀　韭菜呀　拣一　担　去哟嗬，你要　文传　吾蔽来

其中　有去　佳哟嗬　咿呀呀子哟　其中　有去　佳哟嗬。
你从　那里　来哟嗬　……　你从　那里　来哟嗬。
家娘　会骂　佳哟嗬　……　家娘　会骂　佳哟嗬。

（演唱：梁香香、林小书、詹翠英，记谱：钟同荣）

怀胎歌△（一）　瑞金·汉

1=D 3/4

怀胎(哟)　正月　正(呀)　奴家　有了　孕(呀)　漂洋
怀胎(哟)　二个　月(呀)　奴家　不敢　说(呀)　去春

(哪)　过　海　(呀)　收到(哩)老(呀)公(哩)信(呵)
(哪)　年　少　(呀)　说出(哩)面(呀)皮(哩)红(呵)

（演唱：胡道增　记谱：钟同荣）

· 58 ·

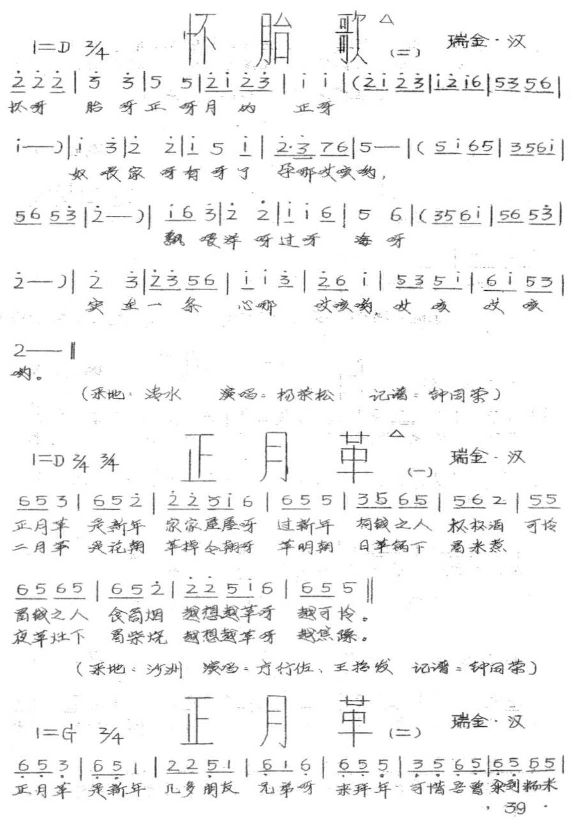

怀胎歌△（二）　瑞金·汉

1=D 3/4

怀呀　胎　呀　正　呀月　的　正呀

奴　我　家　呀　有　呀　了　孕哪哎哎哟，

飘　漾洋　呀　过　呀　海　呀

实　是　一　条　心哪　哎哎哟　哎　哎　哎　哎

哟。

（采地：壬水　演唱：杨荣松　记谱：钟同荣）

正月革△（一）　瑞金·汉

1=D 2/4 3/4

正月革　贺新年　家家庭屋呀　过新年　有钱之人　杯杯酒　可怜
二月革　贺花朝　革担会朝呀　革明朝　日革锅下　莫米煮

莫钱之人　食莫烟　越想越革呀　越可怜。
夜革灶下　莫柴烧　越想越革呀　越烦躁。

（采地：沙洲　演唱：方行位、王格发　记谱：钟同荣）

正月革（二）　瑞金·汉

1=G 3/4

正月革　贺新年　几多朋友　兄弟呀　来拜年　可惜吾曾　象到粘米

· 39 ·

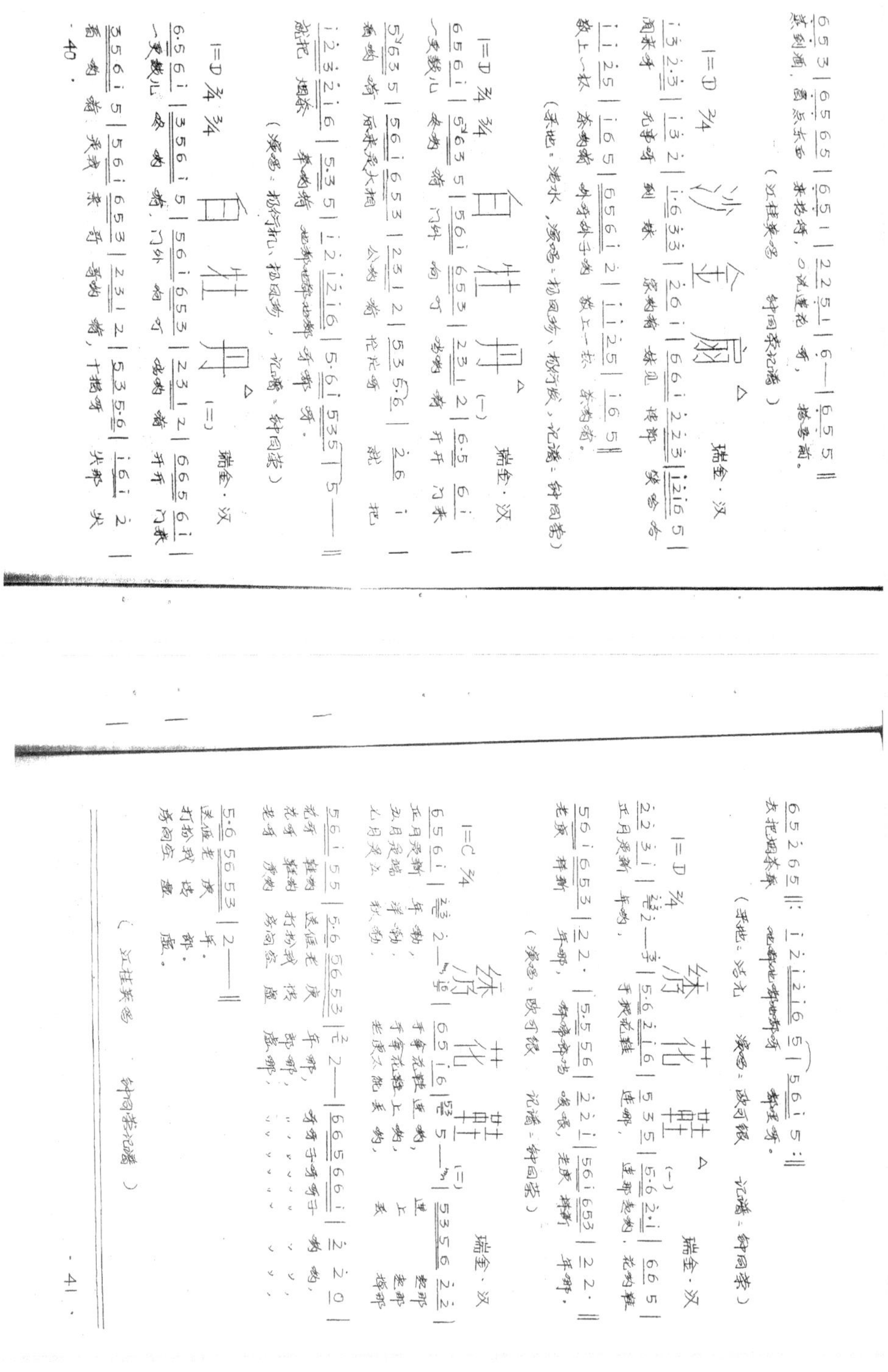

6 5 3 | 6 5 6 5 | 6 5 1 | 2 2 5 1 | 6 — | 6 5 5 ‖
蒸到酒，画点东西 来招待，口说莲花 呀， 指多前。

（江桂英唱　钟同荣记谱）

沙金扇△

瑞金·汉

1=D 3/4

1 3 2·3 | 1 3 2 | 1·6 3 3 | 2 6 1 | 6 6 1 2 2 3 | 1 2 1 6 5 |
阔来呀 　兄事呀 到 妹 　家的箱 妹见 将郎 　笑哈哈

1 1 2 5 | 1 6 5 | 6 5 6 1 2 | 1 1 2 5 | 1 6 5 ‖
敬上一杯 　茶的箱 　外呀外子的 　敬上一杯 　茶的箱。

（采地：湾水，演唱：杨凤珍、杨衍发，记谱：钟同荣）

白牡丹△（一）

瑞金·汉

1=D 2/4 3/4

6 5 6 1 | 5 6 3 5 | 5 6 1 6 5 3 | 2 3 1 2 | 6·5 6 1 |
一更鼓儿 　冬的 　将 门外 　响 叮 　当的 将 　开开 　门来

5 6 3 5 | 5 6 1 6 5 3 | 2 3 1 2 | 5 3 5·6 | 2 6 1 |
看的 将 　原来是大相 　公的 将 　忙忙呀 　就 把

1 2 3 2 1 6 | 5·3 5 | 1 2 1 2 1 6 | 5·6 1 5 3 5 | 5 — ‖
就把 　烟茶 　举的将 　也都也都也都 　呀哪 　呀。

（演唱：杨衍机、杨凤珍，　记谱：钟同荣）

白牡丹△（二）

瑞金·汉

1=D 2/4 3/4

6·5 6 1 | 3 5 6 1 5 | 5 6 1 6 5 3 | 2 3 1 2 | 6 6 5 6 1 |
一更鼓儿 　咚 的 　将，门外 　响 叮 　当的 将 　开开 　门来

3 5 6 1 5 | 5 6 1 6 5 3 | 2 3 1 2 | 5 3 5·6 | 1 6 1 2 |
看 的 将 　来我 亲 哥 　哥的 将，十指呀 　尖那 尖

6 5 2 6 5 ‖: 1 2 1 2 1 6 5 | 5 6 1 5 :‖
去把烟茶奉 　也都也都也都呀 　都呀呀。

（采地：培元　演唱：欧可银　记谱：钟同荣）

绣花鞋△（一）

瑞金·汉

1=D 2/4

2 2 3 1 | 2 — | 5·6 2 1 6 | 5 3 5 | 5·6 2·1 | 6 6 5 |
正月是新 　年哟， 　手拿花鞋 　连哪， 　连那起哟，花的鞋

5 6 1 6 5 3 | 2 2· | 5·5 5 6 | 2 2 1 | 5 6 1 6 5 3 | 2 2· ‖
老庚 　拜新 　年哪， 　哪嘚哪吔 　喂喂， 　老庚 　拜新 　年哪。

（演唱：欧可银　记谱：钟同荣）

绣花鞋△（二）

瑞金·汉

1=C 3/4

6 5 6 1 | 2 — | 6 5 1 6 | 5 — | 5 3 5 6 2 2 |
正月是新 　年 嘞， 　手拿花鞋 　连 哟， 　连 　起那
五月是端 　阳 嘞， 　手拿花鞋 　上 哟， 　上 　起那
七月是立 　秋 嘞， 　老庚不能 　丢 哟， 　丢 　撑那

5 6 1 5 5 | 5·6 5 6 5 3 | 2 — | 6 6 5 6 6 1 | 2 2 0 |
花呀 　鞋哟 　送低老 　庚 　年哪， 　呀呀子呀呀子 　哟 哟，
花呀 　鞋哟 　打扮我 　传 　郎哪， 　〃〃〃〃〃〃 　〃 〃，
老呀 　庚哟 　房间空 　虚 　虚哪， 　〃〃〃〃〃〃 　〃 〃，

5·6 5 6 5 3 | 2 — ‖
送低老 　庚 　年。
打扮我 　传 　郎。
房间空 　虚 　虚。

（江桂英唱　钟同荣记谱）

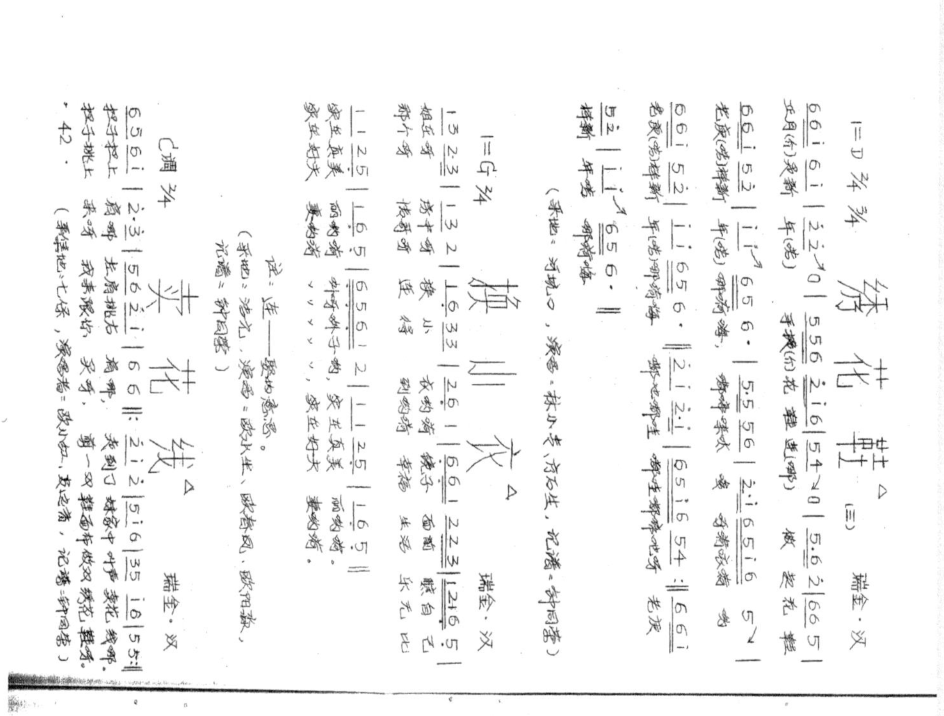

绣花鞋△（三）

1=D 2/4 3/4　　瑞金·汉

66i 6i | 22 0 | 556 2i6 | 54 0 | 5.6 2 | 665 |
正月(介)是新　年(嘞)　手拿(介)花　鞋　起(哪)　做　起花　鞋

66i 52 | ii 656· | 5.5 56 | 2.i 65i6 | 5 |
老庚(嘞)样新　年(嘞)哪荷嗨，　哪呀咪来　哟　哥荷哎荷　哟

66i 52 | ii 656· ‖ 2i 2i | 65i6 54 :‖ 66i
老庚(嘞)样新　年(嘞)哪荷嗨　哪也哪生　哪生哪咿也呀　老庚

52 | ii 656· ‖
样新　年嘞　哪荷嗨

（采地：河坑口，演唱：林小秀、方石生，记谱：钟同荣）

换小衣△

1=G 3/4　　瑞金·汉

13 23 | 13 2 | 16 33 | 26 1 | 661 223 | 1216 5 |
姐在呀　房中呀　换　小　衣哟荷　镜子　面前　瞧自　己
那个呀　情哥呀　连　得　到哟荷　幸福　生活　乐无　比

11 25 | 16 5 | 6561 2 | 11 25 | 16 5 ‖
实在真美　丽哟荷　妹呀妹子哟，实在真美　丽哟荷。
实在好夫　妻哟荷　ヽヽヽヽヽ，实在好夫　妻哟荷。

注：连——娶的意思。
（采地：沙元，演唱：欧火生、欧春凤、欧阳淼，记谱：钟同荣）

卖花线△

C调 2/4　　瑞金·汉

656i | 2.3 | 562i | 66 ‖: 2i 2 | 5i6 | 35 i6 | 55 :‖
担子担上　肩哪　左肩挑右　肩哪，　走到了　妹家中　叫声　卖花　线哪。
担子挑上　来呀　我来跟你　买呀，　剪一双　鞋面布做双　绣花　鞋呀。

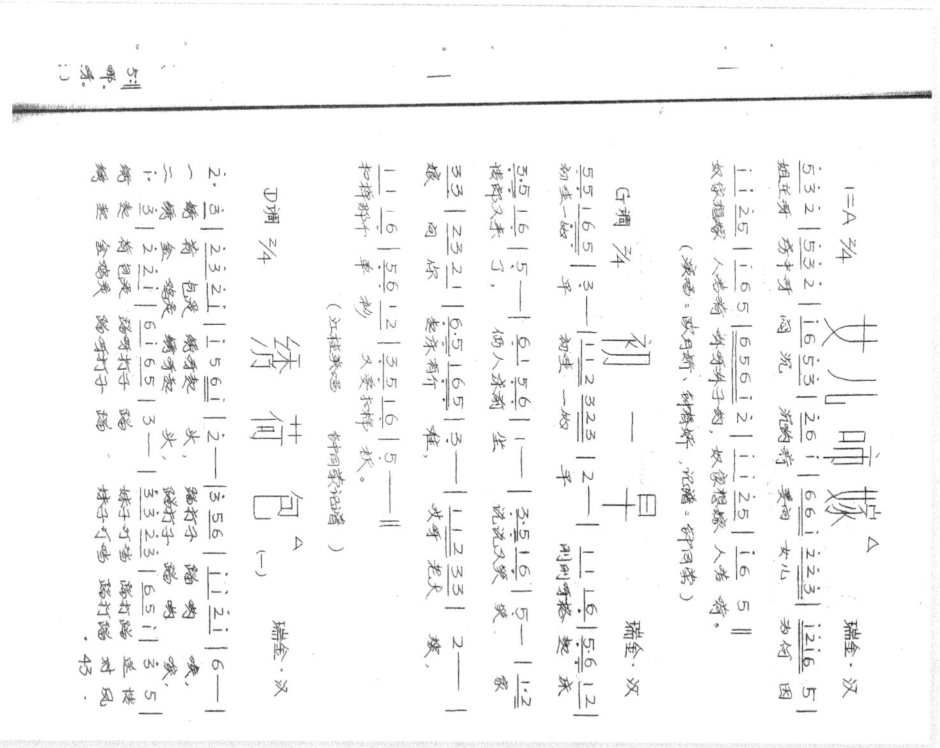

· 42 ·　（采集地：七保，演唱者：欧小红、黄之清，记谱：钟同荣）

女儿啼嫁△

1=A 2/4　　瑞金·汉

532 | 532 | i653 | 26 i | 66i 223 | i2i6 5 |
姐在呀　房中呀　闷　沉　沉哟荷　要问　女儿　为何　因

ii 25 | i65 | 656i 2 | ii 25 | i6 5 ‖
奴家想嫁　人老荷　妹呀妹子哟，奴家想嫁　人老　荷。

（演唱：欧月娇、钟桂娇，记谱：钟同荣）

初一早

G调 2/4　　瑞金·汉

55 165 | 3— | 112 323 | 2— | 11 16 | 56 12 |
初生一日　早　初生　一日　早　刚刚呀格　起　床

35 16 | 5— | 61 56 | 1— | 35 16 | 5— | 12
情郎又来　了，　俩人床前　坐　说说又哭　哭　家

33 | 2321 | 65 165 | 3— | 112 33 | 2— |
娘　问　你　起床有个　难，　丈呀　老丈　嫂，

11 16 | 56 12 | 35 16 | 5— ‖
扣拌那个　羊　衫　又要扣拌　衩。

（江桂英唱　钟同荣记谱）

绣荷包△（一）

D调 2/4　　瑞金·汉

2· 3 | 232i | i56i | 2— | 356 | ii 2i | 6— |
一　绣　荷　包是　绣呀起　头，　踏打子　踏　哟　喂，
二　绣　金　鸡是　绣呀起　头，　踏打子　踏　哟　喂，

i· 3 | 22i | 6i65 | 3— | 3323 | 65i | 35 |
绣　起　荷包是　踏呀打子　踏　妹子叮当　踏打踏　送　情
绣　起　金鸡是　踏呀打子　踏　妹子叮当　踏打踏　对　凤

· 43 ·

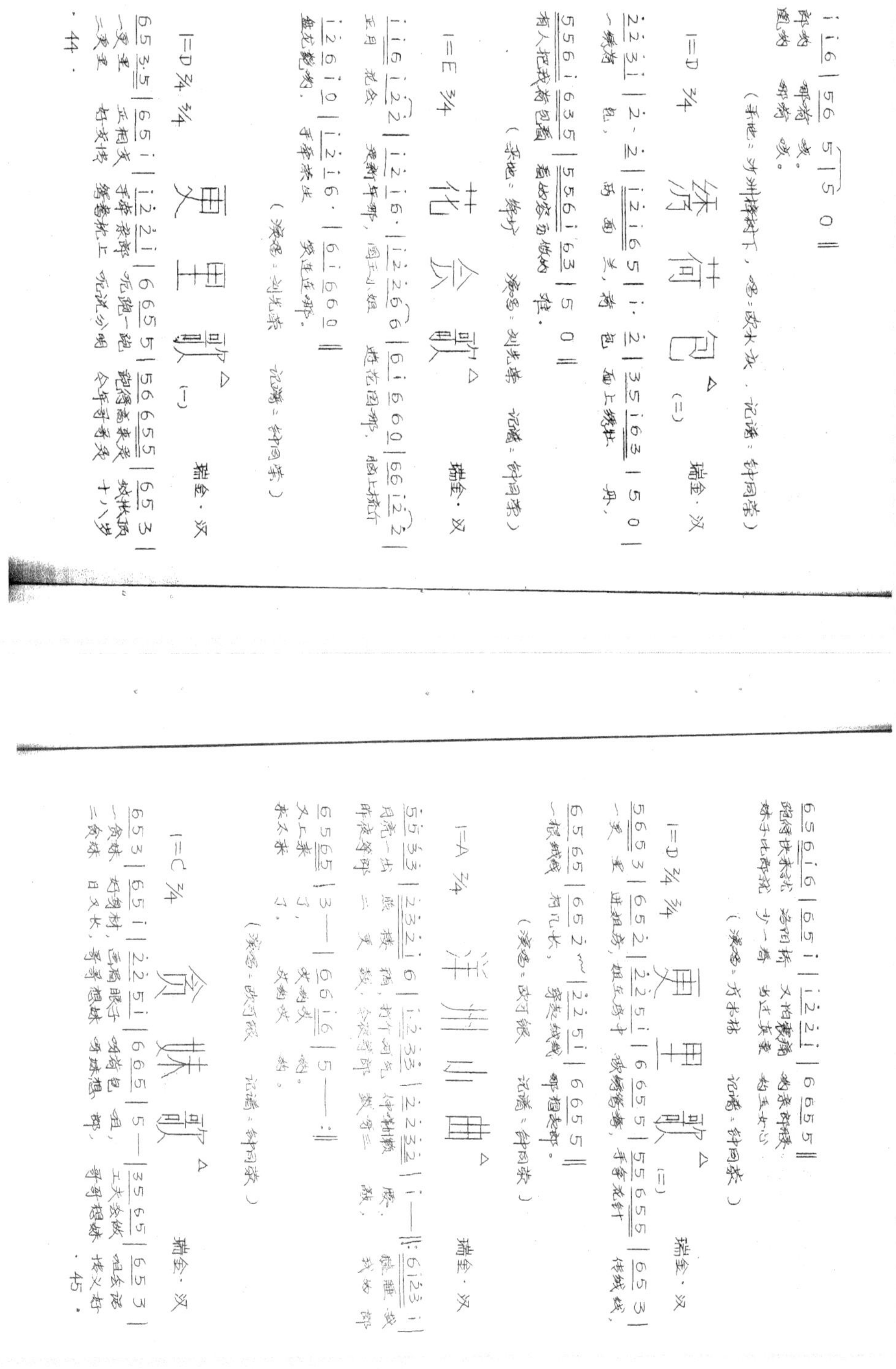

i i6 | 56 5 | 5 0 ‖
郎哟 哪荷 唉。
阎哟 哪荷 唉。

（采地：沙洲梓树下，唱：欧水灰，记谱：钟同荣）

绣荷包△（二）

1=D 3/4 瑞金·汉

22 3i | 2· 2 | i2i6 5 | i· 2 | 35 i63 | 5 0 |
一绣荷 包， 西 面 兰，荷 包 面上绣牡 丹，

556i 635 | 556i 63 | 5 0 ‖
有人把我荷包看 看妹容易做的 难。

（采地：绛坊 演唱：刘先荣 记谱：钟同荣）

花会歌△

1=E 3/4 瑞金·汉

ii6 i22 | i2 i6· | i22 6 6 | 6i 660 | 66 i22 |
正月 花会 是新年哪，国王小姐 游花园哪，脑上梳介

i26 i0 | i2 i6· | 6i 660 ‖
盘龙髻哟， 手牵茶生 笑连连哪。

（演唱：刘先荣 记谱：钟同荣）

更里歌△（一）

1=D 2/4 3/4 瑞金·汉

65 3·5 | 65 i | i2 2i | 6 65 5 | 56 655 | 65 3 |
一更里 正相交 手牵亲郎 呃跑一跑 跑得高来恶 蚊帐顶
二更里 好交情 鸳鸯枕上 呃说分明 今年哥哥是 十八岁

·44·

65 6i6 | 65 i | i2 2i | 6 655 ‖
跑得快来就 洛阳桥 又怕震痛 妹亲郎腰
妹子比郎就 少一番 当过真意 妹玉女心

（演唱：方书林 记谱：钟同荣）

更里歌△（二）

1=D 2/4 3/4 瑞金·汉

5653 | 65 2 | 22 5i | 6 655 | 55 655 | 65 3 |
一更 里 进姐房，姐在房中 欲绣鸳鸯，手拿花针 传绒线，

65 65 | 65 2~ | 22 5i | 6 655 ‖
一根绒线 有几长， 穿起绒线 哪想起郎。

（演唱：欧阿银 记谱：钟同荣）

洋州小曲△

1=A 3/4 瑞金·汉

55 33 | 232i 6 | i2 33 | 22 32 | i — ‖: 6i23 i |
月亮一出 照 楼 角，打个阿欠 伸懒腰 腰。 晓睡 我
昨夜等郎 二 更 鼓，今夜等郎 鼓打三 鼓， 我 妹 郎

65 65 | 3 — | 66 i6 | 5 — :‖
又上来 了， 哎哟哎 哟。
来不来 了， 哎哟哎 哟。

（演唱：欧阿银 记谱：钟同荣）

贪妹歌△

1=C 2/4 瑞金·汉

65 3 | 65 i | 22 5i | 6 65 | 5 — | 35 65 | 65 3 |
一贪妹 好身材，画眉眼子 哪荷包 姐， 工夫会做 姐会话
二贪妹 日又长，哥哥想妹 哪妹想 郎， 哥哥想妹 情义好

·45·

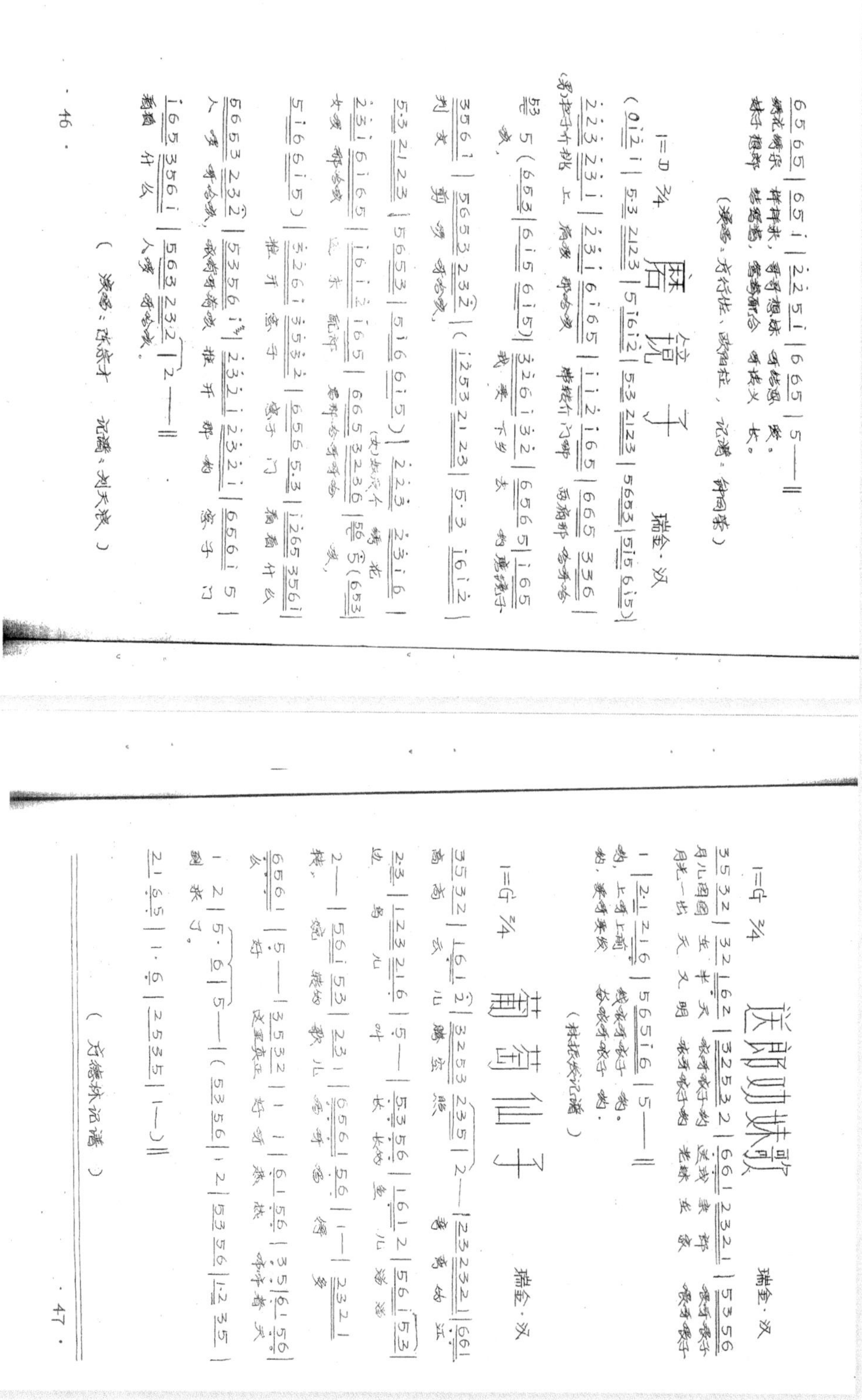

6565 | 65i | 225i | 665 | 5 — ‖
绣花绣朵 样样来，哥哥想妹 呀结恩 爱。
妹子想郎 结鸳鸯，鸳鸯配合 呀结义 长。

（演唱：方行佐、欧阳柱，记谱：钟国荣）

磨镜子

1=D 2/4　　瑞金·汉

(0i2i | 5·3 2123 | 5i6i2 | 5·3 2123 | 5653 | 5i5 6i5) |
223 23i | 23i 6i65 | ii2 i65 | 665 336 |
(男)担子介挑 上 肩啰 那哈哎 带转介门哪 西南那 哈呀哈
53 5 (653 | 6i5 6i5) | 326i 32 | 6565 | i65 |
哎， 我 要 下乡 去 哟磨镜子
356i | 5653 232 | (i253 2123 | 5·3 i6i2 |
判 文 剪 啰 呀哈哎，
5·3 2123 | 5653 | 5i6 6i5) | 223 23i6 |
(女)妹妹介 绣 花
23i 6i65 | i6i2 i65 | 665 3236 | 56 5 (653 |
女啰 那哈哎 进 来 配那 磨那哈呀呀哈 哎，
5i6 6i5) | 326i 3532 | 656 5·3 | i265 356i |
推 开 窗 子 窗子 门 看看 什么
5653 232 | 5356 i | 232i 232i | 656i 5 |
人 啰 呀哈哎， 哎哟呀哟哎 推 开 那 哟 窗 子 门
i65 356i | 563 232 | 2 — ‖
看看 什么 人啰 呀哈哎。

（演唱：陈宗才　记谱：刘天宸）

送郎劝妹歌

1=G 3/4　　瑞金·汉

3532 | 32 162 | 32532 | 661 2321 | 5356
月儿团团 生 半 天 哝呀哝子哟 送我 亲 郎 喂呀喂子
月光一出 天 又 明 哝呀哝子哟 老妹 在 家 喂呀喂子
1 | 2·1 216 | 565i6 | 5 — ‖
哟，上呀上前 哉哝呀哝子 哟。
哟，要呀要发 奋哝呀哝子 哟。

（林振发记谱）

葡萄仙子

1=G 2/4　　瑞金·汉

3532 | 161 2 | 3253 235 | 2 — | 23232i | 661
高 高 云 儿 腾 空 照 青 青 的 江
23 | 123 216 | 5 — | 5356 | 1612 | 56i 53 |
边 鸟 儿 叶 长 长的 鱼 儿 游 游
2 — | 56i 53 | 231 | 6561 56 | 1 — | 2321 |
转， 婉 转的 歌 儿 唱 呀 唱 得 多
6561 | 5 — | 3532 | 1 1 | 61 56 | 35 61 56 |
么 好 这里真正 好 呀 热 热 咪咪着 天
1 2 | 5·6 | 5 — | (5356 | 12 | 5356 | 12 35 |
到 来 了。
21 65 | 1·6 | 2535 | 1 —) ‖

（方德林记谱）

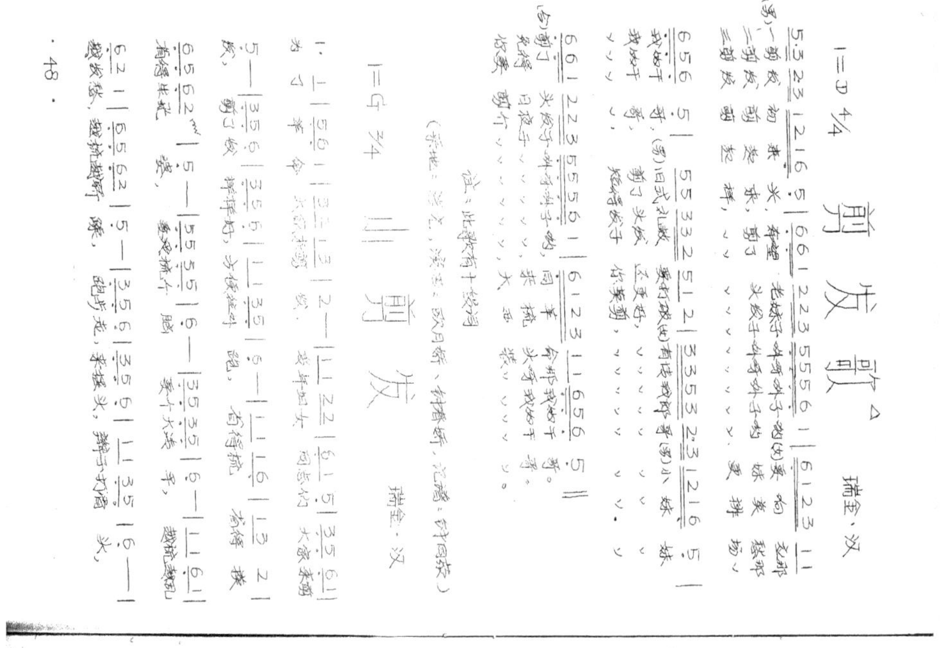

剪发歌△

1=D 4/4　　　　瑞金 · 汉

5·3 2·3 1216 5 | 661 223 5556 1 | 6123 11
(男)一剪发 初 来 头，希望 老妹子哟呀哟子哟(女)要 响 应那
二剪发 剪 起 来，剪了 头发子哟呀哟子哟 妹 莫 愁那
三剪发 剪 起 样，∨∨ ∨∨∨∨∨∨∨∨∨ 更 排 场∨

656 5 | 55 332 512 | 3353 2·3 1216 5 |
我的干 哥，(男)旧式礼教 要打破(女)有传我郎 哥(男)小 妹 妹
我的干 哥， 剪了头发 还更好，∨∨∨∨∨ ∨∨ ∨
∨∨∨ ∨， 短得发子 你莫剪，∨∨∨∨∨ ∨∨。∨

661 223 5556 1 | 6123 11 656 5 ‖
(合)剪了 头发子哟呀哟子哟，同 革 命那我的干 哥。
免得 日夜子∨∨∨∨∨∨，来 梳 头呀我的干 哥。
你要 剪个∨∨∨∨∨∨∨，大 西 装∨ ∨∨∨ ∨。

注：此歌有十段词

（采地：潭头，演唱：欧月娇、钟春娇，记谱：钟同荣）

小剪发

1=G 3/4　　　　瑞金 · 汉

1· 1 | 56 1 | 3213 | 2 — | 11 22 | 61 5 | 35 61 |
为 了 革 命 大家来剪 发， 青年妇女 同志们 大家来剪

5 — | 35 6 | 35 6 | 11 35 | 6 — | 11 16 | 13 2 |
发， 剪了发 样样好，方便往外 跑， 省得梳 省得 挨

65 62 | 5 — | 55 55 | 6 — | 35 35 | 6 — | 11 61 |
省得生虱 婆， 要想梳个 脑 要个大海 平， 越梳越乱

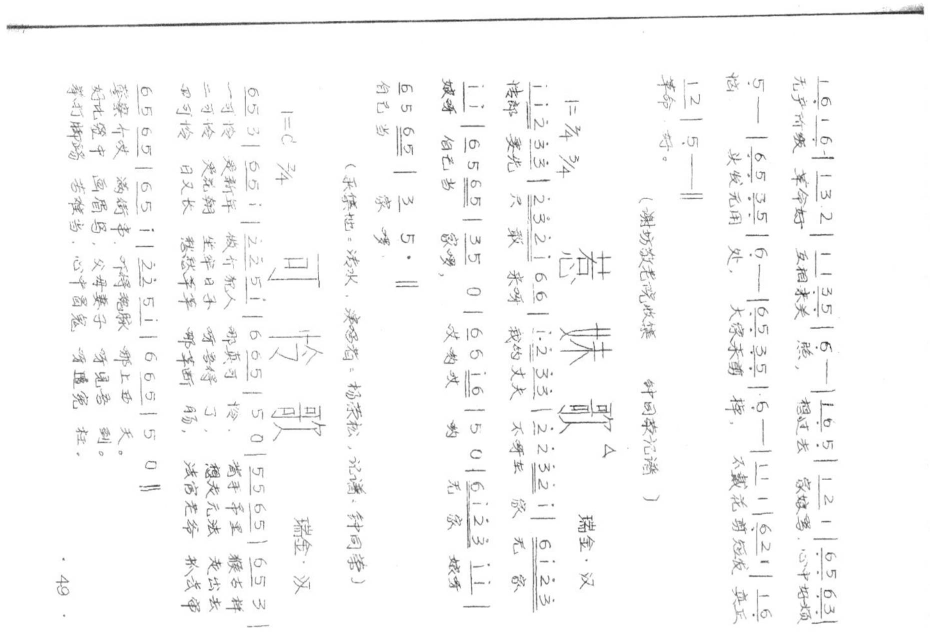

62 1 | 55 62 | 5 — | 35 6 | 35 6 | 11 35 | 6 — |
越发愁，越梳越斩 躁， 跑步走，来摇头，辫子打背 头，

16 16 | 13 2 | 11 35 | 6 — | 16 5 | 12 1 | 65 63 |
无产阶级 革命好 互相来关 照， 想过去 家娘骂，心中好烦

5 — | 65 35 | 6 — | 65 35 | 6 — | 11 1 | 621 | 16
恼 头发无用 处， 大家来剪 掉， 不戴花剪短发 真正

12 | 5 — ‖
革命 好。

（谢坊敬老院收集　　钟同荣记谱）

惹妹歌△

1=2/4 3/4　　　　瑞金 · 汉

11 2 33 | 2321 66 | 1·2 33 | 2 2 32 1 | 6123
情郎 要先 只 敢 来呀 我的丈夫 不呀在 家 无 家

11 | 65 65 | 35 0 | 66 16 | 5 0 | 6123 11 |
娘呀 自己当 家啰， 哎哟哎 哟 无 家 娘呀

65 65 | 3 5· ‖
自己当 家 啰

（采集地：沙洲，演唱者：杨荣松，记谱：钟同荣）

可怜歌

1=C 2/4　　　　瑞金 · 汉

653 | 65 1 | 2251 | 665 | 5 0 | 5565 | 653 |
一可怜 是新年 做个犯人 那真可 怜， 当手吊里 猴古样
二可怜 是花朝 坐牢日子 呀苦得 了， 想走无法 走出去
四可怜 日又长 愁愁苦苦 那苦断 肠， 法官老爷 抓我审

6565 | 65 1 | 2251 | 665 | 5 0 ‖
警察个哎 满街串，吓得魂脉 那上西 天。
好比笼中 画眉鸟，父母妻子 呀见吾 到。
拳打脚踢 苦难当，心中含冤 呀遭冤 枉。

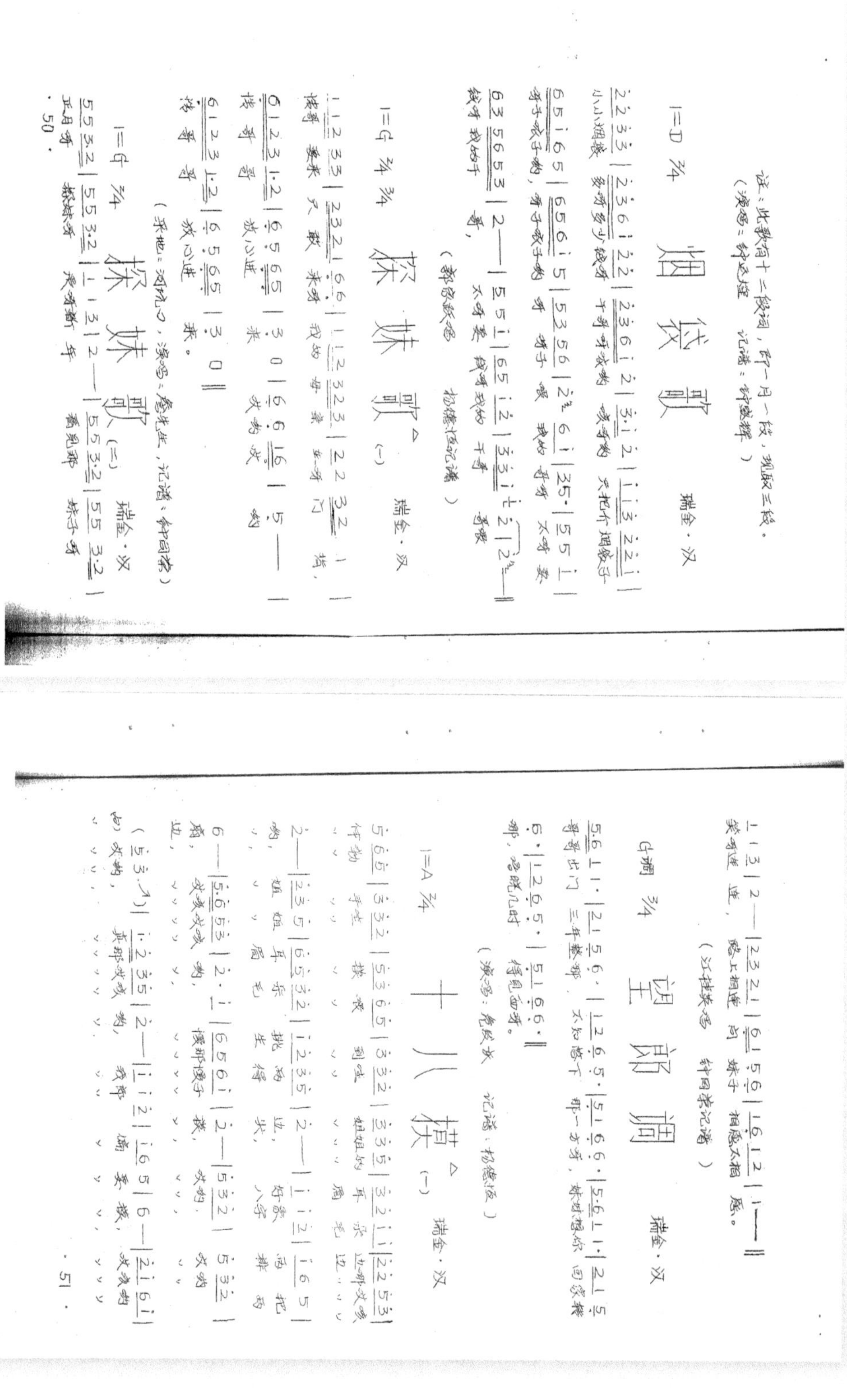

注：此歌有十二段词，即一月一段，现取三段。
（演唱：钟达煌　记谱：钟盛辉）

烟袋歌

1=D 2/4　　瑞金·汉

2233 | 236i 22 | 236i 2 | 3·i 2 | i i3 22i |
小小烟袋　多呀多少钱呀　干哥呀衣哟　哎呀哟　只把个烟袋子

65i65 | 656i 5 | 5356 | 2 6i | 35· | 55 i |
呀子衣子哟，呀子衣子哟　呀　呀子　喂　我的　哥呀　不呀要

63 5653 | 2 — | 55i | 65 i2 | 33i 2 | 2 — ‖
钱呀　我的干　哥，　不呀要　钱呀我的　干哥　哥哎

（郭家跃唱　杨德恒记谱）

探妹歌（一）

1=G 2/4 3/4　　瑞金·汉

1123 33 | 2321 66 | 112 323 | 22 32 1 |
情哥　要来　只　敢　来呀　我的　母　亲　在呀　门　背，

61231·2 | 6565 | 3 0 | 66 16 | 5 — |
情　哥　哥　放心进　来　哎哟　哎　哟

61231·2 | 6565 | 3 0 ‖
情　哥　哥　放心进　来。

（采地：河坑口，演唱：詹先生，记谱：钟同荣）

探妹歌（二）

1=G 2/4　　瑞金·汉

55 3·2 | 55 3·2 | 1 13 | 2 — | 55 3·2 | 55 3·2 |
正月呀　探妹呀　过呀新　年　看见那　妹子呀

1 13 | 2 — | 2321 | 61 56 | 16 12 | 1 — ‖
笑呀连　连，　路上相逢　问　妹子　相愿不相　愿。

（江桂英唱　钟同荣记谱）

望郎调

G调 3/4　　瑞金·汉

5·6 1 1· | 21 56· | 126 5· | 51 66· | 5·61 1· | 21 5
哥哥出门　三年整那，不知落下　那一方呀，妹妹想你　回家转

6· | 126 5· | 51 66· ‖
哪，哈晓几时　得见面呀。

（演唱：詹联长　记谱：杨德恒）

十八摸（一）

1=A 2/4　　瑞金·汉

5 65 | 3 32 | 53 65 | 3 32 | 335 | 32 ii | 22 53 |
伸　手　摸　喂　到　哇　姐姐的　耳　朵　边哪哎哟
（眉　毛　边）

2 — | 23 5 | 65 32 | i 235 | 2 — | i i2 | i6 5 |
哟，　姐　姐　耳　朵　挑　两　边，　好象　两　把
（眉　毛　生　得　尖，　八字　排　两）

6 — | 5·6 53 | 2· i | 656i | 2 — | 532 | 532 |
扇，　哎哎哎哎　哟，　摸那摸子　摸，　哎哟，　哎哟
（边，）

(53 ·↗) | 1·2 35 | 2 — | i i2 | i6 5 | 6 — | 2i 6i |
（白）哎哟，　真那哎哎　哟，　我那　偏　要　摸，　哎哎哟

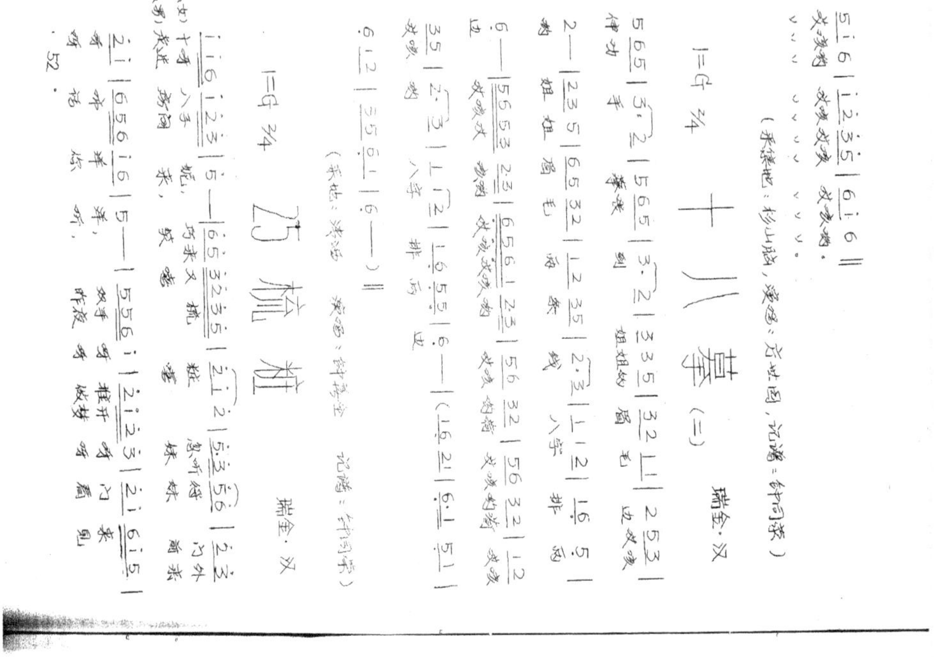

5 1 6 | 1 2 3 5 | 6 1 6 ‖
哎咳哟 哎咳哎咳 哎哎哟。

（采集地：杉山脑，演唱：方世因，记谱：钟同荣）

十八摹（二）

1=G 2/4　　瑞金·汉

5 6 5 | 3· 2 | 5 6 5 | 3· 2 | 3 3 5 | 3 2 1 1 | 2 5 3 |
伸 动 手 摹 我 到 姐姐的 眉 毛 边 哎咳

2 — | 2 3 5 | 6 5 3 2 | 1 2 3 5 | 2· 3 | 1 1 2 | 1 6 5 |
哟 姐 姐 眉 毛 两 条 线 八字 排 两

6 — | 5 5 5 3 2 3 | 6 5 6 1 2 3 | 5 6 3 2 | 5 6 3 2 | 1 2 |
边 哎咳哎 咳哟 哎咳哎咳哟 哎咳 哟嗬 哎咳哟嗬 哎咳

3 5 | 2· 3 | 1 1 2 | 1 6 5 5 | 6 — | (1 6 2 1 | 6· 1 5 1 |
哎咳 哟 八字 排 两 边

6 1 2 | 5 5 6 1 | 6 —) ‖

（采地：涛源　演唱：钟芳金　记谱：钟同荣）

巧梳粧

1=G 2/4　　瑞金·汉

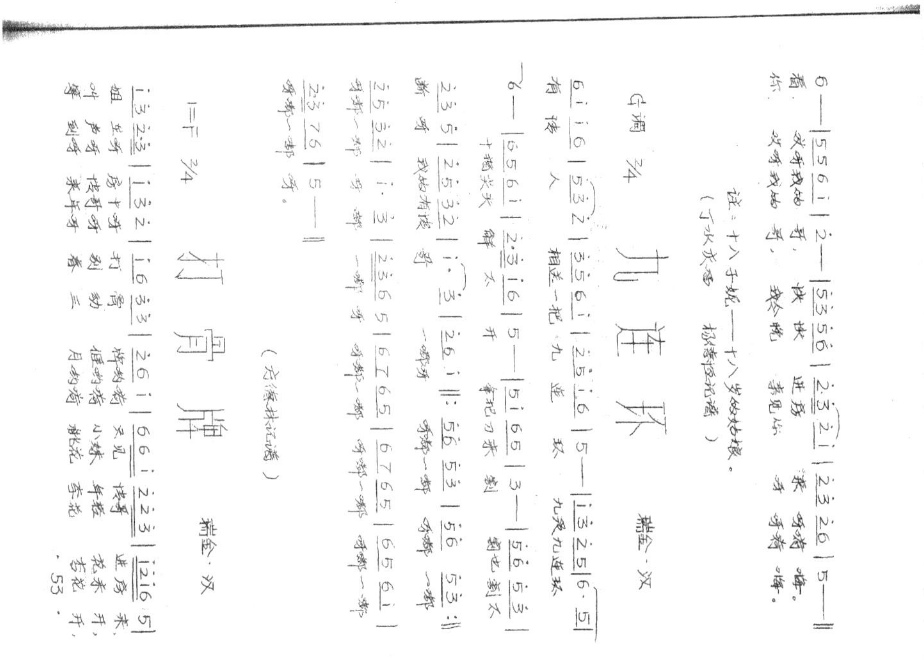

1 1 6 1 2 3 | 5 — | 6 5 3 2 3 5 | 2 1 2 | 5 3 5 6 | 2 3 |
（女）十呀 八子 妮， 巧来又 梳 粧 忽听得 门外
（男）老进 房间 来， 笑 嘻 嘻 妹 妹 前来

2 1 | 6 5 6 1 6 | 5 — | 5 5 6 1 | 2 1 2 3 | 2 1 6 1 5 |
呀 叩 洋 洋， 奴手 呀 推开 呀 门 来
呀 话 你 听， 昨夜 呀 做梦 呀 看 见

6 — | 5 5 6 1 | 2 — | 5 3 5 6 | 2 3 2 1 | 2 3 2 6 | 5 — ‖
看， 哎呀我的 哥， 快 快 进 房 来 呀嗬 嗨。
你， 哎呀我的 哥， 我今晚 亲见你 呀 呀嗬 嗨。

注：十八子妮——十八岁的姑娘。
（丁水庆唱　杨德经记谱）

九连环

G调 2/4　　瑞金·汉

6 1 1 6 | 5 3 2 | 3 5 6 1 | 2 5 1 6 | 5 — | 1 3 2 5 | 6· 5 |
有 传 人 相送一把 九 连 环 九晃九连环

6 — | 6 5 6 1 | 2·3 1 6 | 5 — | 5 1 6 5 | 3 — | 5 6 5 3 |
十指尖尖 解 不 开 拿把刀来 割 割也割不

2 3 5 | 2 5 3 2 | 1· 3 | 2 6 1 ‖: 5 6 5 3 | 5 6 5 3 :‖
断 呀 我的有情 哥 一哪呀 呀哪一哪 呀哪 一哪

2 5 3 2 | 1· 3 | 2 3 6 5 | 6 7 6 5 | 6 7 6 5 | 6 5 6 1 |
呀哪一哪 呀 哪 一哪 呀 呀哪一哪 呀哪一哪 呀哪一哪

2 3 7 6 | 5 — ‖
呀哪一哪 呀。

（方德林记谱）

打骨牌

1=F 2/4　　瑞金·汉

1 3 2 3 | 1 3 2 | 1 6 3 3 | 2 6 1 | 6 6 1 2 2 3 | 1 2 1 6 5 |
姐 在呀 房中呀 打 骨 哗的嗬 只见 情哥 进房 来，
叫 声呀 情哥呀 剁 动 佢的嗬 小妹 年轻 花未 开，
等 到呀 来年呀 春 三 月的嗬 桃花 李花 杏花 开，

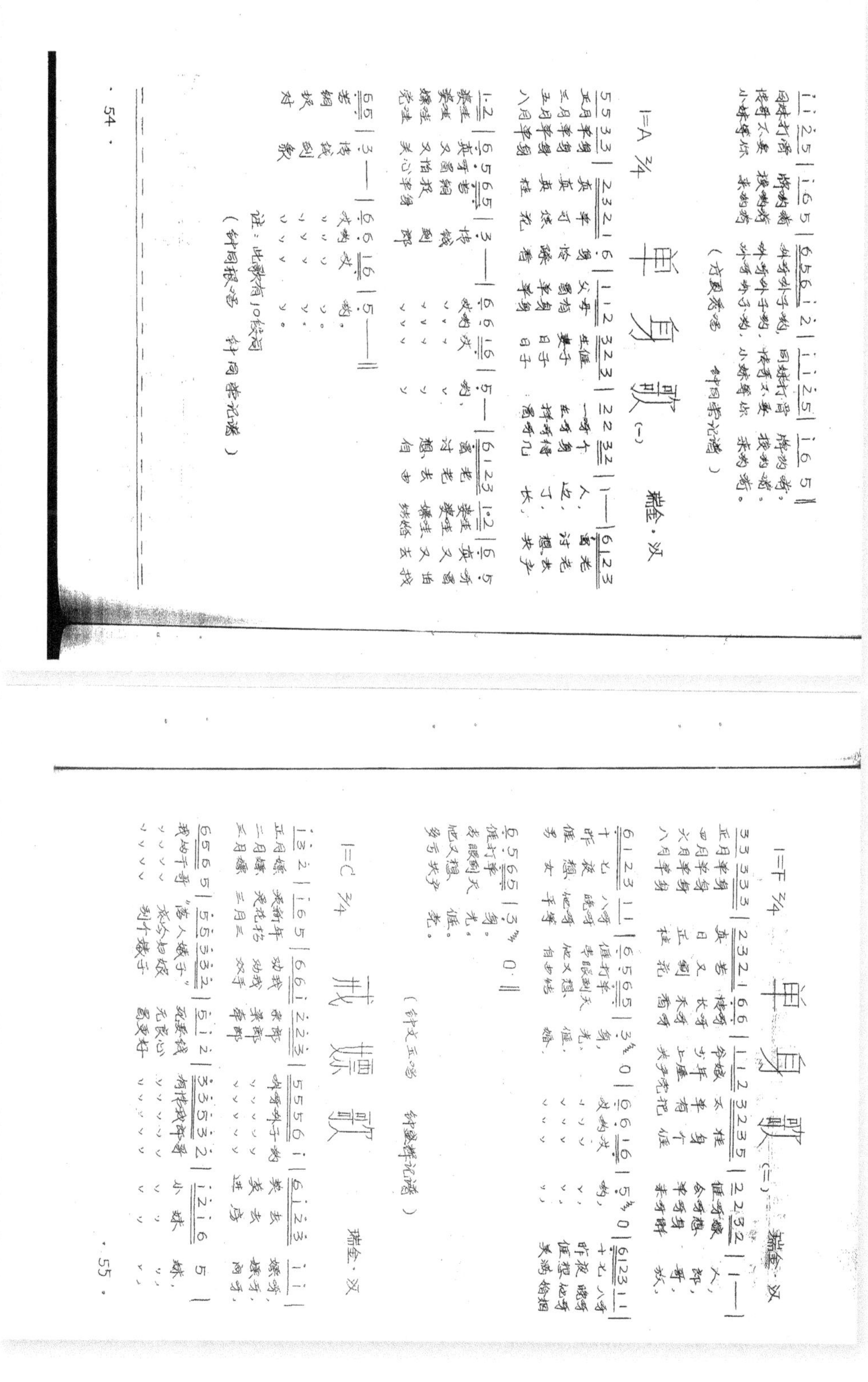

i i 2 5 | i 6 5 | 6 5 6 i 2 | i i 2 5 | i 6 5 ‖

同妹打胥　脟哟嗬　咻呀咻子哟，同妹打胥　脟哟嗬。
传哥不要　挨哟嗬　咻呀咻子哟，传哥不要　挨哟嗬。
小妹等你　来哟嗬　咻呀咻子哟，小妹等你　来哟嗬。

（方夏秀唱　钟同荣记谱）

单身歌（一）

1=A 3/4　　瑞金·汉

5 5 3 3 | 2 3 2 1 6 | 1 1 2 3 2 3 | 2 2 3 2 | 1 — | 6 1 2 3

正月单身　真单身　父母生涯　一呀个　人，　留老
三月单身　真可怜　留有妻子　在呀身　边，　讨老
五月单身　真殊珠　单身日子　拌呀得　了，　想去
八月单身　桂花香　单身日子　留呀几　长，　共产

1·2 | 6 5 6 5 | 3 — | 6 6 1 6 | 5 — | 6 1 2 3 1·2 | 6 5

婆娃　真呀苦　传　哎哟哎　哟，　留老　婆娃　真呀
婆娃　又留铜　钱　ッッッ　ッ，　讨老　婆娃　又留
嫖娃　又怕找　到　ッッッ　ッ，　想去　嫖娃　又怕
党娃　关心单身　郎　ッッッ　ッ，　自由　结婚　去找

6 5 | 3 — | 6 6 1 6 | 5 — ‖

苦　传　哎哟哎　哟。
铜　钱　ッッッ　ッ。
找　到　ッッッ　ッ。
对　象　ッッッ　ッ。

注：此歌有10段词

（钟同根唱　钟同荣记谱）

· 54 ·

单身歌（二）

1=F 3/4　　瑞金·汉

3 3 3 3 3 | 2 3 2 1 6 6 | 1 1 2 3 2 3 5 | 2 2 3 2 | 1 — |

正月单身　真苦　情呀　爷娘不　挂　涯呀嫖　人，
四月单身　日又　长呀　少年单　身　会呀想　郎，
六月单身　正割　禾呀　上屋有　个　单呀身　哥，
八月单身　桂花　香呀　共产党把　涯　来呀解　放。

6 1 2 3 1 1 | 6 5 6 5 | 3 0 | 6 6 1 6 | 5 0 | 6 1 2 3 1 1 |

十七　八呀　涯打单　身，　哎哟哎　哟，　十七　八呀
昨夜　晚呀　老眼到天　光，　ッッッ　ッ，　昨夜　晚呀
涯想　他呀　他又想　涯，　ッッッ　ッ，　涯想　他呀
男女　平等　自由结　婚，　ッッッ　ッ，　美满　婚姻

6 5 6 5 | 3 0 ‖

涯打单　身。
老眼到天　光。
他又想　涯。
多亏共产　党。

（钟文玉唱　钟盛辉记谱）

戒嫖歌

1=C 3/4　　瑞金·汉

i 3 2 | i 6 5 | 6 6 i 2 2 3 | 5 5 5 6 i | 6 i 2 3 | i i |

正月嫖　过新年　劝我　家郎　咻呀咻子哟　莫去　嫖呀，
二月嫖　过花朝　劝我　家郎　ッッッッッ　莫去　嫖呀，
三月嫖　三月三　叔手　牵郎　ッッッッッ　进房　间呀，

6 5 6 5 | 5 5 3 3 2 | 5 i 2 | 3 3 5 3 2 | i 2 i 6 | 5 |

我妈干哥　"落人嫫子"　死要钱　有钱我郎哥　小妹　妹，
ッッッッ　东今妇娘　无良心　ッッッッッ　ッッ　ッ，
ッッッッ　到个嫫子　哥更好　ッッッッッ　ッッ　ッ，

· 55 ·

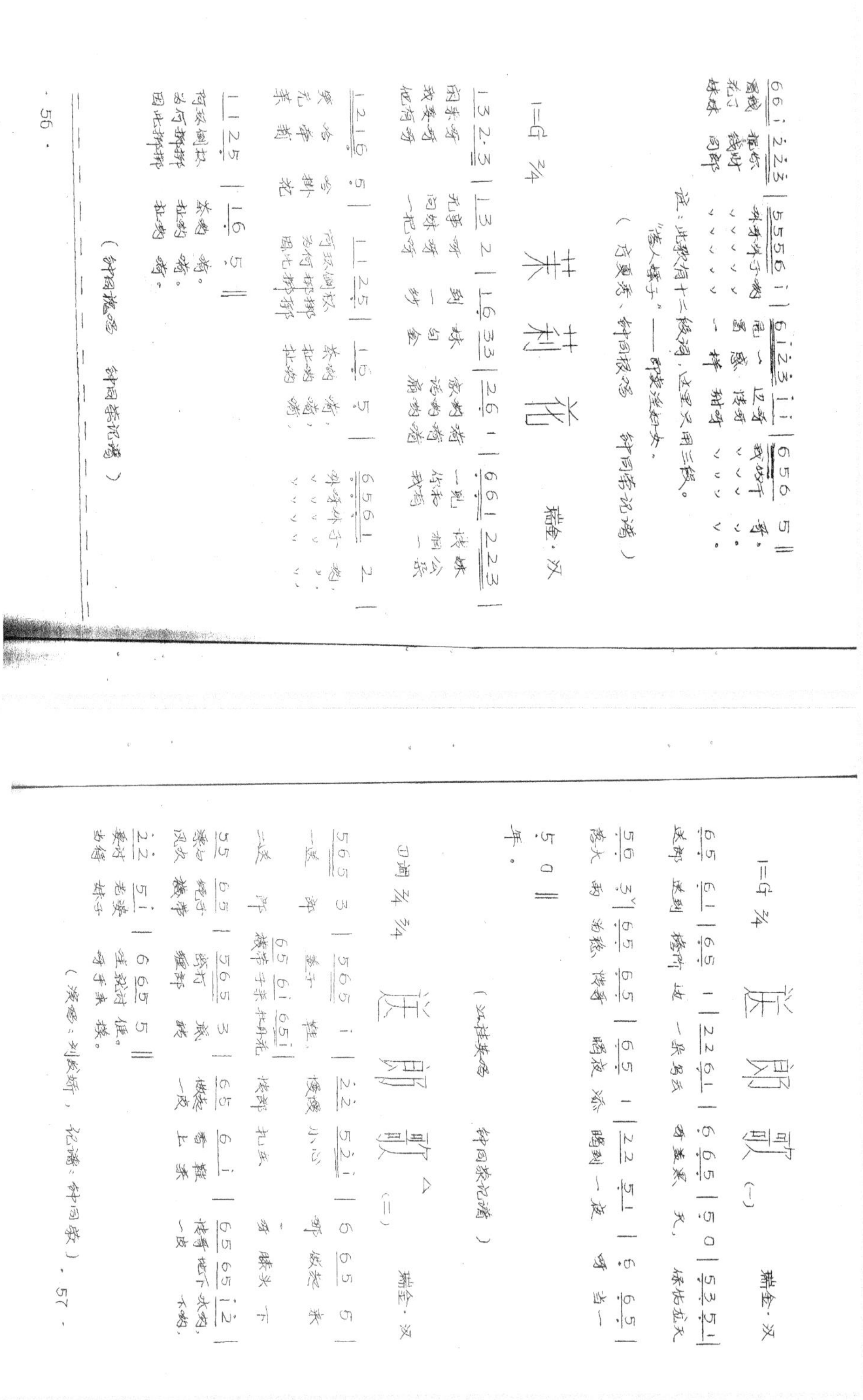

66 i 223 | 5556 i | 6 i23 i i | 656 5 ‖

眉钱 探你 外呀外子哟 甩一 边呀 我的干 哥。
花了 钱财 ∨∨∨∨∨ 冒 感 情呀 ∨∨∨ ∨。
妹妹 同郎 ∨∨∨∨∨ 一 样 甜呀 ∨∨∨ ∨。

注：此歌有十二段词，这里只用三段。
"客人嫁子"——即卖淫妇女。
（方夏秀、钟同根唱　钟同第记谱）

茉莉花

1=G 2/4　瑞金·汉

13 2·3 | 13 2 | 16 33 | 26 1 | 661 223 |

闲来呀 无事呀 到 妹 家哟 嗬 一见 情妹
我来呀 问妹呀 一 句 话哟 嗬 你和 相公
他有呀 一把呀 纱 金 扇哟 嗬 我有 一朵

1216 5 | 1125 | 16 5 | 6561 2 |

笑 哈 哈 阿坛倒杈 茶哟 嗬， 外呀外子 哟，
无 牵 挂 为何挪挪 扯哟 嗬， ∨∨∨∨ ∨，
茉 莉 花 因此挪挪 扯哟 嗬， ∨∨∨∨ ∨，

1125 | 16 5 ‖

阿坛倒杈 茶哟 嗬。
为何挪挪 扯哟 嗬。
因此挪挪 扯哟 嗬。

（钟同槐唱　钟同第记谱）

送郎歌（一）

1=G 2/4　瑞金·汉

65 61 | 65 1 | 2261 | 6 65 | 5 0 | 5351 |

送郎 送到 檐阶 边 一朵乌云 呀盖黑 天， 保佑龙天

56 3 | 65 65 | 65 1 | 22 51 | 6 65 |

落大 雨 汤稳、情哥 暗夜 添 暗到一夜 呀 当一

5 0 ‖

年。

（江桂英唱　钟同荣记谱）

送郎歌（二）

卫调 2/4 3/4　瑞金·汉

565 3 | 565 i | 22 52i | 6 65 5 |

一送 郎 盖子 鞋， 慢慢 小心 郎 做起 来

65 6i 65i |

二送 郎 襟带 子来 牡丹花 情郎 扎丢 呀 膝头 下

55 65 | 565 3 | 65 6 i | 65 65 i2 |

漂白 绳子 密打 底 做起 香 鞋 情哥 地下 水哟，
风吹 襟带 缠郎 转 一皮 上 来 一皮 下哟，

22 5i | 6 65 5 ‖

要讨 老婆 莲就讨 佢。
当得 妹子 呀手 来 挨。

（演唱：刘发娇，记谱：钟同荣）

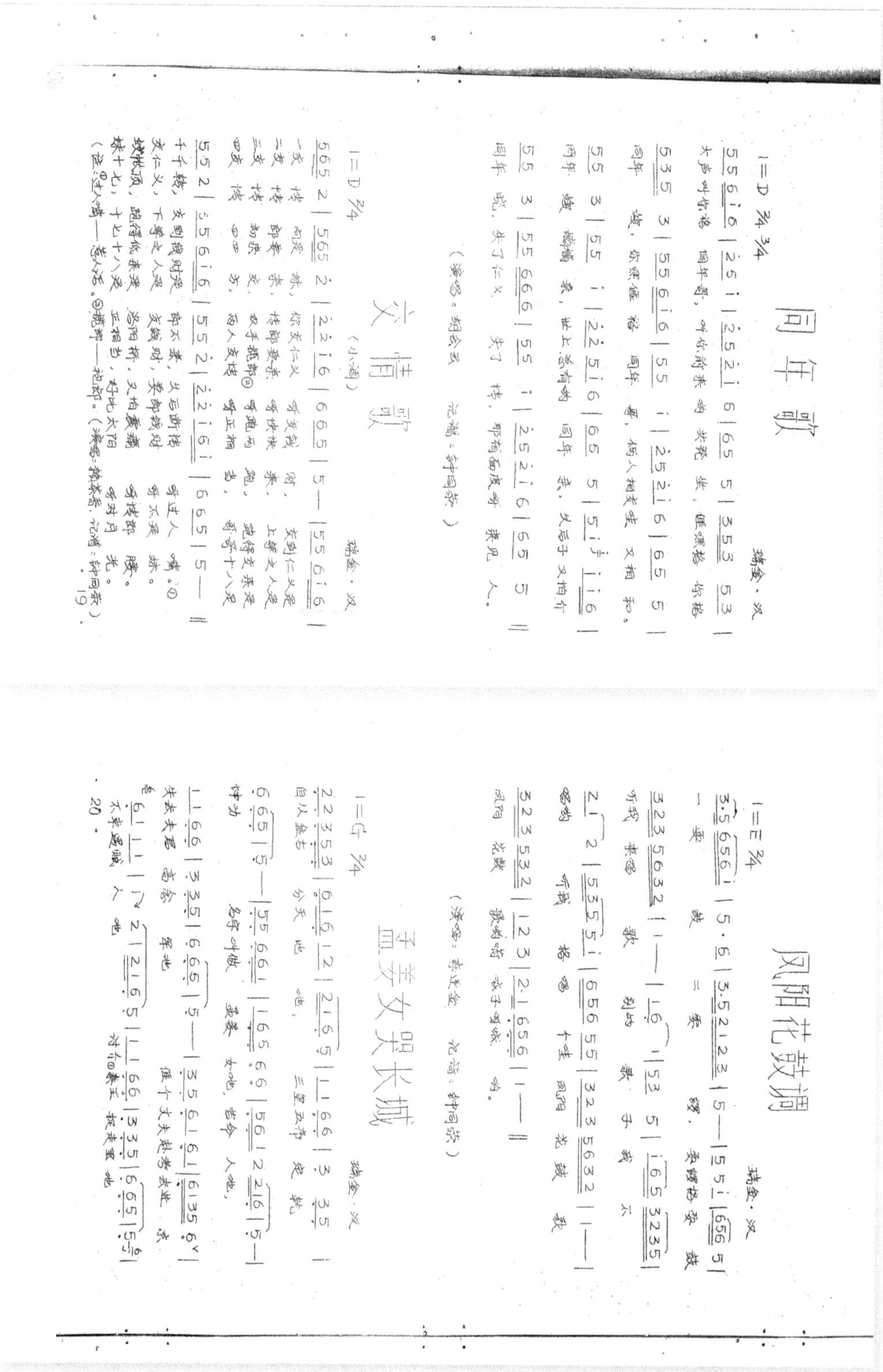

同年歌

1=D 3/4 3/4　　　瑞金・汉

55 61̇6 | 2̇5 1̇ | 2̇5 2̇1̇ 6 | 65 5 | 353 53 |
大声叫你诶 同年哥，叫你前来哟 共凳 坐，俚嘿格 你格

535 3 | 55 61̇6 | 55 1̇ | 2̇5 2̇1̇ 6 | 65 5 |
同年 嫂，你嘿俚 格 同年 哥，俩人相交哇 又相 和。

55 3 | 55 1̇ | 2̇2̇ 51̇ 6 | 65 5 | 51̇ 1̇1̇6 |
同年 嫂 嫡嫡 亲，世上总有哟 同年 亲，久后子 又怕介

55 3 | 55 666 | 55 1̇ | 2̇5 2̇1̇ 6 | 65 5 ‖
同年 呢，失了仁义 失了 情，那有面皮呀 来见 人。

（演唱：胡会云　记谱：钟同荣）

交情歌

1=D 2/4　（小调）　瑞金・汉

565 2 | 565 2̇ | 2̇2̇ 1̇6 | 6 65 | 5 — | 55 61̇6 |
一交 情 问晓 妹，你交仁义 呀交钱 财， 交到仁义是
二交 情 郎要 来，情郎要来 呀快快 来， 上等之人是
三交 情 初恋 交，双手揽郎② 呀跑两 跑， 跑得交来是
四交 情 四四 方，两人交情 呀正相 当， 哥哥十八是

55 2 | 55 61̇6 | 55 2̇ | 2̇2̇ 1̇61̇ | 6 65 | 5 — ‖
千千转，交到钱财是 郎不来，久后断情 呀过人 嘴。①
交仁义，下等之人是 交钱财，要郎钱财 呀不是 妹。
蚊帐顶，跑得低来是 洛阳桥，又怕震痛 呀情郎 腰。
妹十七，十七十八是 正相当，好比太阳 呀对月 光。

（注：①过人嘴——惹人话。②揽郎——抱郎。（演唱：赖茶香，记谱：钟同荣）

· 19 ·

凤阳花鼓调

1=E 2/4　瑞金・汉

3·5 6561̇ | 5·6 | 3·5 2123 | 5 — | 5 51̇ | 656 5 |
一 要 鼓 二 要 锣，要锣格 要 鼓

323 5632 | 1 — | 16 1 | 53 5 | 1̇65 3235 |
听我 来唱 歌 别的 歌 子 我 不

21̇ 2 | 535 51̇ | 656 55 | 323 5632 | 1 — |
唱哟 听我 格 唱 个哇 凤阳 花 鼓 歌

323 532 | 12 3 | 2·1 656 | 1 — ‖
凤阳 花鼓 歌哟嗬 依子呀依 哟。

（演唱：李逆金　记谱：钟同荣）

孟姜女哭长城

1=G 2/4　瑞金・汉

22 353 | 616 12 | 216 5 | 11 66 | 3 35 |
自从盘古 分天 地 地， 三皇五帝 定 乾

6 65 | 5 — | 55 661 | 165 66 | 561 2 216 | 5 — |
坤功 名字叫做 孟姜 女哇，苦命 人哇，

11 66 | 3 35 | 6 65 | 5 — | 35 61 61 | 6135 6 |
失去夫君 高念 军哇 俚个丈夫赴考去进 京

是 61 11 | 1 2 | 216 5 | 11 66 | 3 35 | 6 65 | 5 6 |
不幸遇贼 人 哇 讨个秦王 捉走里 哇

· 20 ·

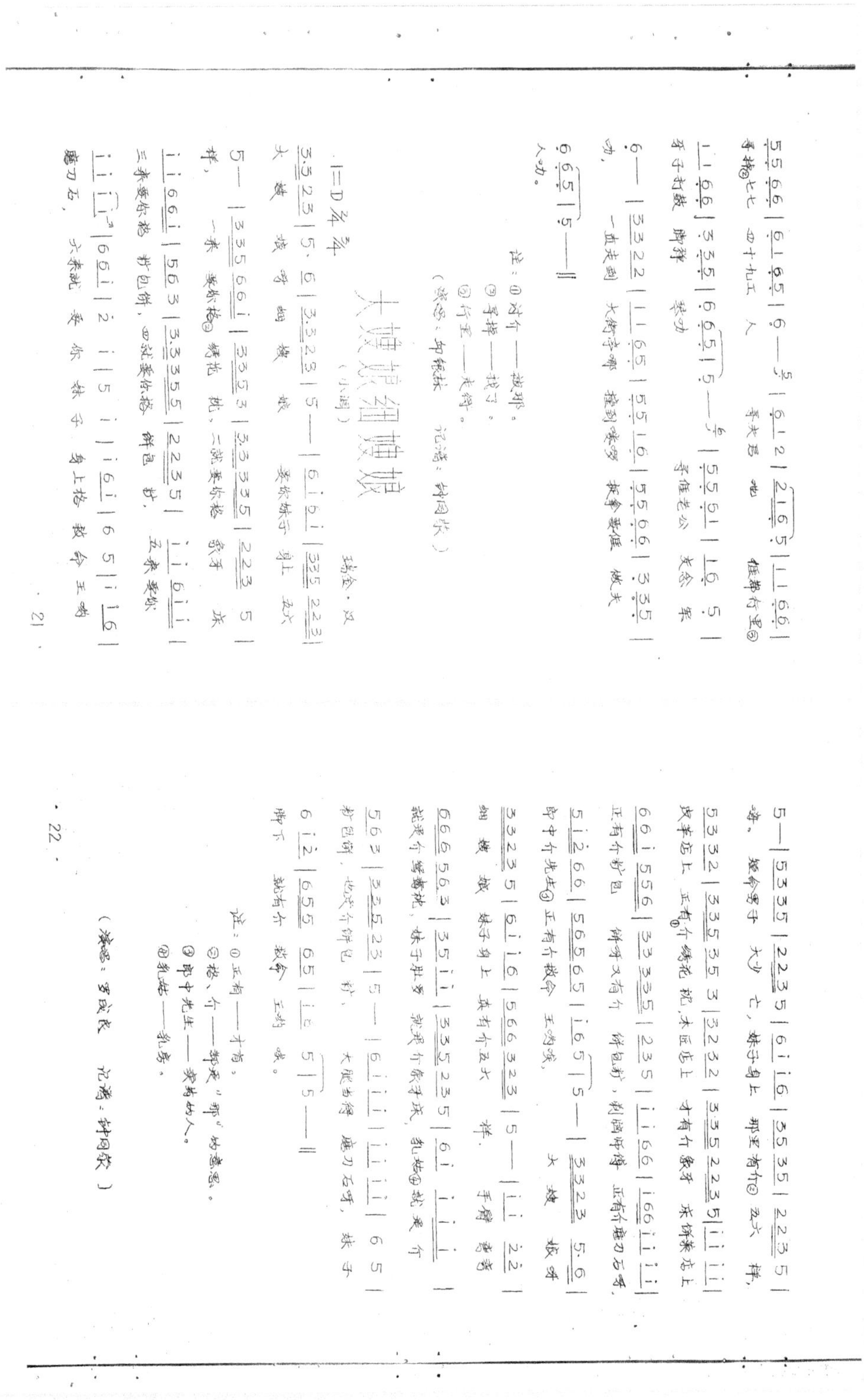

5 5 6 6 | 6 1 6 5 | 6 — | 6 1 2 | 2 1 6 5 | 1 1 6 6 |
寻摔②七七 四十九工 人 哥夫君 哋 佢都行里③

1 1 6 6 | 3 3 5 | 6 6 5 | 5 — | 5 5 6 1 | 1 6 5 |
牙子打鼓 脚摔 琴动 寻佢老公 丈念 牢

6 — | 3 3 2 2 | 1 1 6 5 | 5 5 1 6 | 5 5 6 6 | 3 3 5 |
动， 一直走到 大街亭哪 撞到喽啰 捉拿要佢 做夫

6 6 5 | 5 — ‖
人动。

注：①讨介——被那。
②寻摔——找了。
③行里——走得。
（演唱：印银林 记谱：钟同荣）

大嫂娘细嫂娘

（小调） 瑞金·汉

1=D 2/4 3/4

3.5 2 3 | 5· 6 | 3.3 2 3 | 5 — | 6 i 6 i | 3 3 5 2 2 3 |
大 嫂 娘 呀 细 嫂 娘 要你妹子 身上 五六

5 — | 3 3 5 6 6 i | 3 3 5 3 | 3.3 3 3 5 | 2 2 3 5 |
样， 一来 要你格② 绣花 枕，二就要你格 象牙 床

i i 6 6 i | 5 6 3 | 3.3 3 5 5 | 2 2 3 5 | i i 6 i i |
三来要你格 粉包饼，四就要你格 饼包 钉， 五来要你

i i i i | 6 5 i | 2 i | 5 i | i 6 i | 6 5 | i 1 6 |
磨刀石， 六来就 要 你 妹 子 身上格 救 命 王 哟

· 21 ·

5 — | 5 3 3 5 | 2 2 3 5 | 6 i i 6 | 3 5 3 5 | 2 2 3 5 |
嗨。 短命男子 大少 亡，妹子身上 那里有介② 五六 样，

5 3 3 2 | 3 3 5 3 5 3 | 3 2 3 2 | 3 3 5 2 2 3 5 | i i i i |
皮革店上 正有①介绣花 枕，木匠店上 才有介象牙 床饼条店上

6 6 i 5 5 6 | 3 3 3 3 5 | 2 3 5 | i i 6 6 | i 6 6 i i i i |
正有介粉包 饼呀又有介 饼包钉，剃脑师傅 正有介磨刀石呀，

5 i 2 6 6 | 5 6 5 6 5 | i 6 5 | 5 — | 3 3 2 3 5· 6 |
郎中介先生③ 正有介救命 王哟嗨， 大 嫂 娘 呀

3 3 2 3 5 | 6 i i 6 | 5 6 6 3 2 3 | 5 — | i i 2 2 |
细 嫂 娘 妹子身上 真有介五六 样． 手臂 弯弯

6 6 6 5 6 3 | 3 5 i i | 3 3 5 2 3 5 | 6 i i i i |
就是介绣花枕，妹子肚罗 就是介象牙床，乳姑④就 是 介

5 6 3 | 3 3 5 2 3 | 5 — | 6 i i i | i i i i | 6 5 |
粉包饼，也就介饼包 钉， 大腿当得 磨刀石呀， 妹 子

6 i 2 | 6 5 5 6 5 | i 6 5 | 5 — ‖
脚下 就有介 救命 王哟 嗨。

注：①正有——才有。
②格、介——都是"那"的意思。
③郎中先生——实药的人。
④乳姑——乳房。

（演唱：罗成良 记谱：钟同荣）

· 22 ·

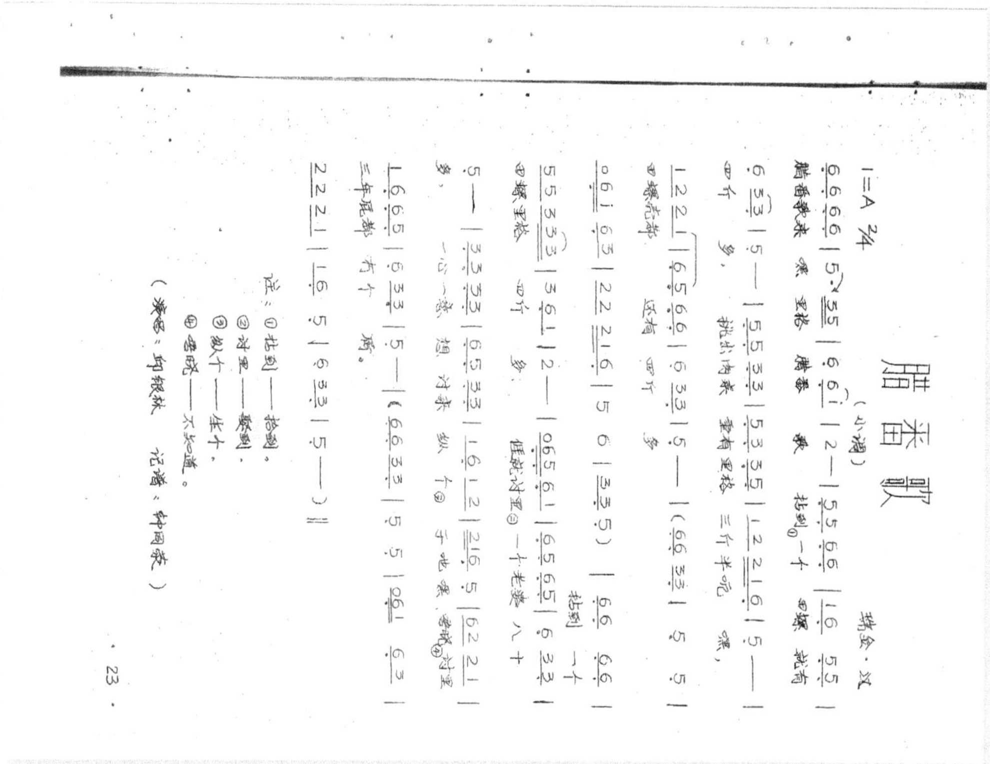

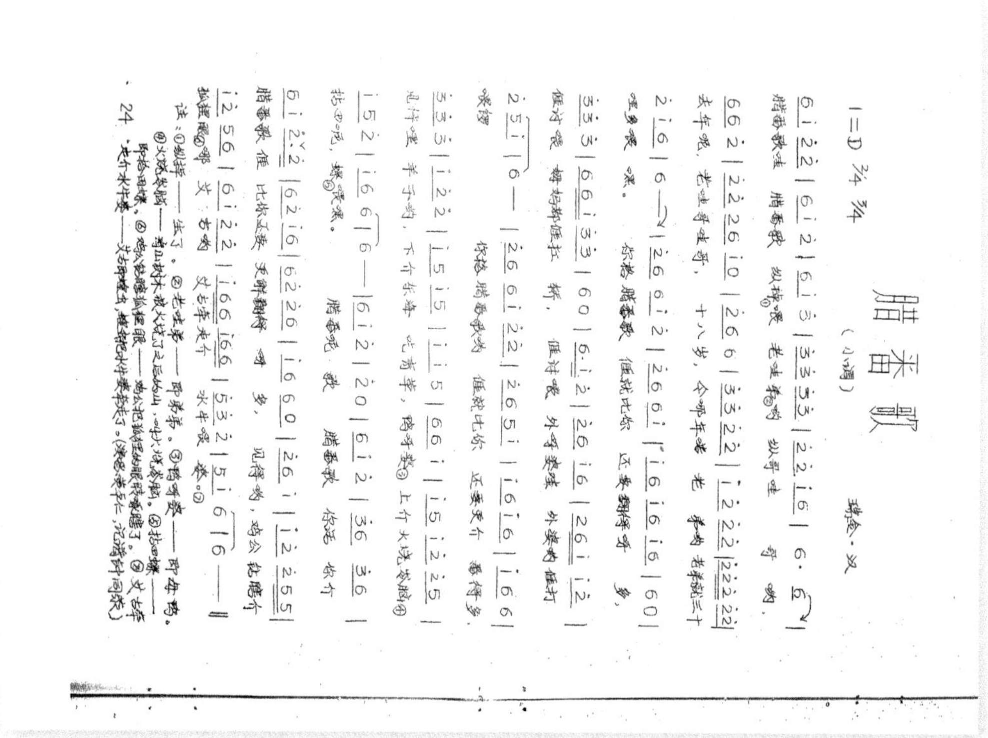

腊番歌

（小调）

1=A 2/4　　　　瑞金·汉

6666 | 5 55 | 6 6i | 2 — | 55 66 | 16 55 |
腊番歌来 嘿 里格 腊番 歌 拈到①一个 田螺 就有

6 33 | 5 — | 55 33 | 53 35 | 12 216 | 5 — |
四个 多， 挑出肉来 重有里格 三个半吒 嘿，

1221 | 6566 | 6 33 | 5 — | (66 33 | 5 5 |
田螺壳都 还有 四个 多

06i 63 | 22 216 | 5 6 | 335) | 66 66 |
拈到 一个

55 333 | 3 61 | 2 — | 065 61 | 6565 | 6 33 |
田螺里格 四个 多， 佢就讨里②一个老婆 八十

5 — | 33 33 | 65 33 | 16 12 | 216 5 | 62 21 |
多， 一心一意 想 讨来 纵 个③ 子吔 噢，晏晓④讨里

1665 | 6 33 | 5 — | (6633 | 5 5 | 061 63 |
三年屁都 冇个 屙。

2221 | 16 5 | 6 33 | 5 —) ||

注：①拈到——拾到。
②讨里——娶到。
③纵个——生个。
④晏晓——不知道。

（演唱：邱银林　记谱：钟同荣）

· 23 ·

腊番歌

（小调）

1=D 2/4 3/4　　　　瑞金·汉

6i 22 | 6i 2 | 6i 3 | 33 33 | 22 i6 | 6· 6 |
腊番歌哇 腊番歌 纵摔①喂 老哇弟②哟 纵哥哇 哥 哟，

66 2 | 22 26 i0 | 26 6 | 33 22 | i2 22 | 222 22 |
去年吒，老哇哥哇哥， 十八岁，今哪年嗒 老 弟哟 老弟就三十

2 i6 | 6 — | 26 6i 2 | 26 6i | i6 i6 i6 | 6 0 |
哩多喂 嘿。 你格腊番歌 佢就比你 还要翻得呀 多，

33 3 | 66i 33 | 6 0 | 6.i 2 | 26 i6 | 26i i2 |
佢讨喂 姆妈都佢扛 轿， 佢讨喂 外呀婆哇 外婆哟佢打

2 5i | 6 — | 26 6i 22 | 26 5i | i6 i6 | i6 6 |
喂锣 你格腊番歌哟 佢就比你 还要更个 番得多。

33 3 | i2 2 | i5 i5 | ii 5 | 66 i | i5 i2 25 |
见得哩 羊子哟，下个东海 吃青草，鸦呀婆③ 上个火烧岽脑④

i5 2 | i6 6 | 6 — | 6i 2 | 2 0 | 6i 2 | 36 36 |
拈田吒，螺⑤喂嘿。 腊番吒 歌 腊番歌 你还 你个

6i 22 | 62 i6 | 62 26 | i6 60 | 26 i | i2 255 |
腊番歌 佢 比你还要 更解翻得 呀 多， 见得哟，鸡公钻瞎个

i2 56 | 6i 22 | i66 i66 | 53 2 | 5i 6 | 6 — ||
狐狸眼⑥哪 艾 古哟 艾古牵走个 水牛喂 婆。⑦

注：①纵摔——生了。②老哇弟——即弟弟。③鸦呀婆——即母鸡。④火烧岽脑——为山树木被火烧了之后的山，叫火烧岽脑。⑤拈田螺——即拾田螺。⑥鸡公钻瞎狐狸眼——鸡公把狐狸的眼睛啄瞎了。⑦艾古牵走个水牛婆——艾古即蝗虫，蝗虫把水牛婆牵走了。（演唱：黄平仁，记谱：钟同荣）

· 24

别郎歌

1=D 2/4 3/4 瑞金·汉

i66 i 2· | i656 | i265 | 6566 | i6 i 2· |
昨夜格老天 吹北风呀，老妹的郎 花园中呀，进去 打开

i656 | i265· | 6655 | i6 i 2· | i6 56 |
花园看呀，一场欢喜 一场空呢，心肝哥哥 哥哥心哪，

i22 65· | 6555 | i66 i 2· | i256 | i26 5· |
十分格家娘 错得黑哪 地下 撒了 石灰粉哪 四向起 角，

6655 ||
按嗡铃呢。

（演唱：胡会太 记谱：钟同荣）

鸦片歌

1=G 2/4 3/4 （小调） 瑞金·汉

3532 | 3122 | 2 — | 022 25 | 21 21 | 165 16 |
老婆一讨 会发癫唉①， 佢个 老婆 喊佢爱学食介格鸦片

55· | 035 161 | 261 21 | 21 26· | 225 36 |
烟唉， 介格鸦片 斗子 往你咀上刁呀， 阿欠 一打

1561 | 135 135 | 65 (61 | 55 1612 | 5 5·) |
冷水一食 蛮象 生神 仙唉 唉……

5353 | 3122 | 2 — | 261 5121 | 161 66 |
食到鸦片 害死人唉， 佢呀介两穴风水② 卸佢就卖到③

55· | 22261 | 51 26· | 22261 | 31 16 |
里唉， 粜④掉谷来格 量米⑤食唉， 腊掉⑥瓦来格 真正盖衫

55 (61 | 55 1612 | 55·) | 5353 | 3122 |
皮唉，唉…… 食到鸦片 煤蛮穷 哎，

2 — | 022 61 661 | 1655 | 5· 35 | 555 161 |
介格 夜晡睛眼格 盖竹筒唉， 介格 你问佢竹筒格

161 66· | 135 135 | 15 135 | 65 5 (61 |
样般 盖唉， 两头 一擗⑦ 中间 爱打 风 唉。唉

55 1612 | 5 5·) ||
唉……。

注：①发癫——发疯。 ②风水——祖坟。
③卖到里——卖掉里。 ④粜——卖出。
⑤量米——买米。 ⑥腊掉——下掉。
⑦擗——塞。

（演唱：邱银林 记谱：钟同荣）

长工歌

1=D 2/4 3/4 瑞金·汉

i6 i 2· | 2 i 6 i | i265· | 6655 | i6 i 2· |
正月长工 真可怜呀 挖张脚头① 扫秧田②呀 上般扫来
二月长工 真可怜呀 牵只牛子 去下田呀 牛绳扮在④

265 i | i265 | 56 55 ||
下般转呀， 吆晓佢址③ 做秧 田呀。
牛背转呀， 捐脚⑤再痛 要下 田呀。

注：①挖张脚头——扛把锄头。②扫秧田——耙秧田。③吆晓佢址——不知道哪些田。④牛绳扮在——牛绳挂在。捐脚——裂了缝的脚，老俵叫"捐脚"。（演唱：杨冬娣 记谱：钟同荣）

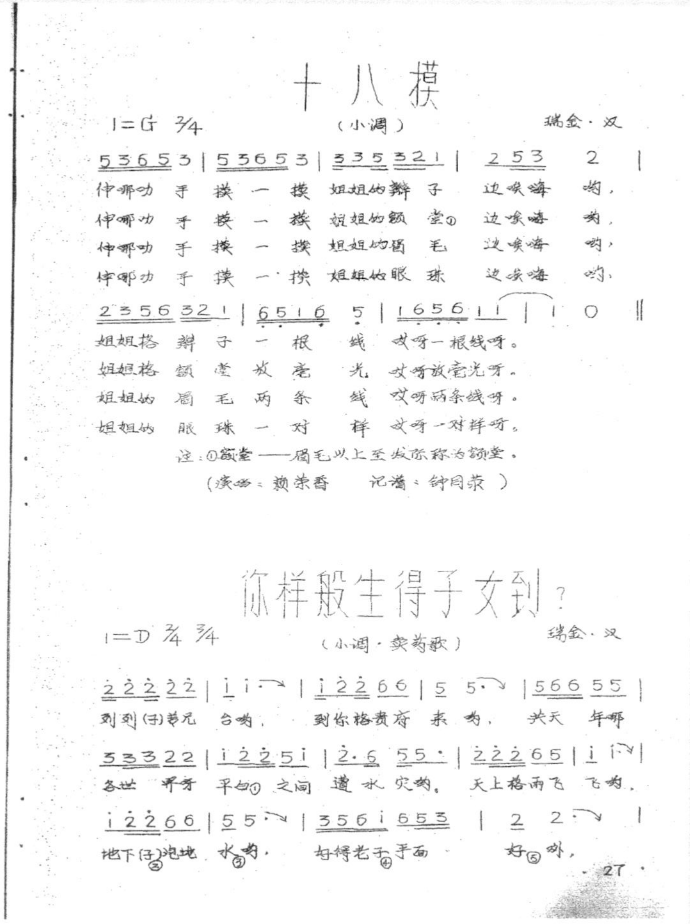

十八摸

（小调）

瑞金·汉

1=G 3/4

伸哪呦 手 摸 一 摸 姐姐的辫 子 边唉嗨 哟，姐姐格 辫 子 一 根 线 哎呀一根线呀。

伸哪呦 手 摸 一 摸 姐姐的额 堂① 边唉嗨 哟，姐姐格 额 堂 放 亮 光 哎呀放亮光呀。

伸哪呦 手 摸 一 摸 姐姐的眉 毛 边唉嗨 哟，姐姐的 眉 毛 两 条 线 哎呀两条线呀。

伸哪呦 手 摸 一 摸 姐姐的眼 珠 边唉嗨 哟，姐姐的 眼 珠 一 对 样 哎呀一对样呀。

注：①额堂——眉毛以上至发际称为额堂。

（演唱：赖荣香　记谱：钟同荣）

· 27 ·

你样般生得子文到？

（小调·卖药歌）

瑞金·汉

1=D 2/4 3/4

刘到(子)弟兄 台哟，到你格贵府 来 哟，共天 年哪

各世 弄牙 平句① 之间 遭 水 灾哟，天上格雨飞 飞哟，

地下(子)②泡地 水③哟，好得老子④手面 好⑤咧，

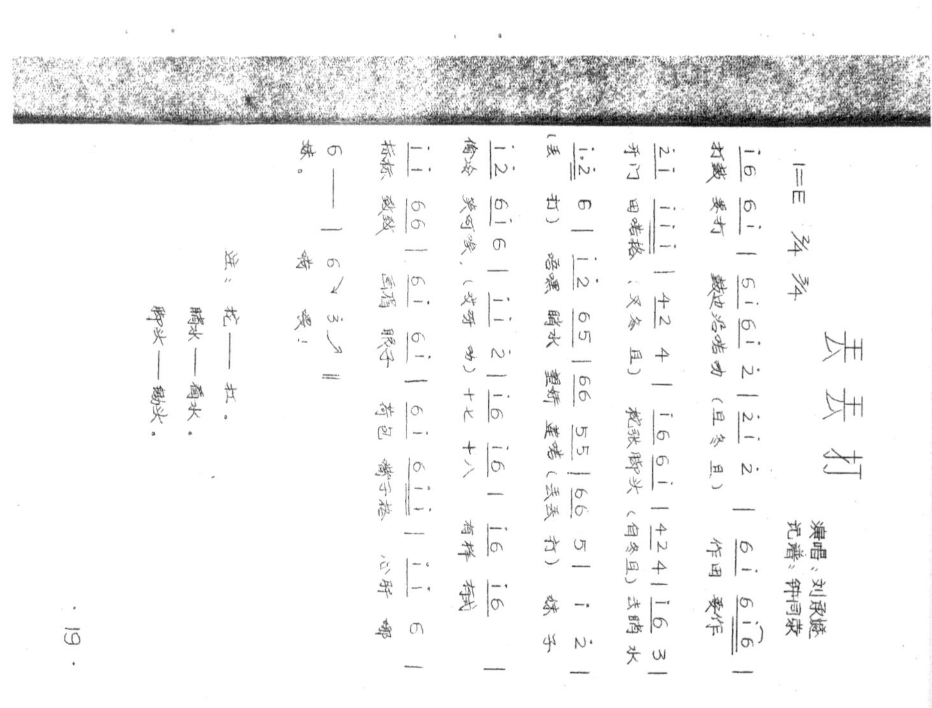

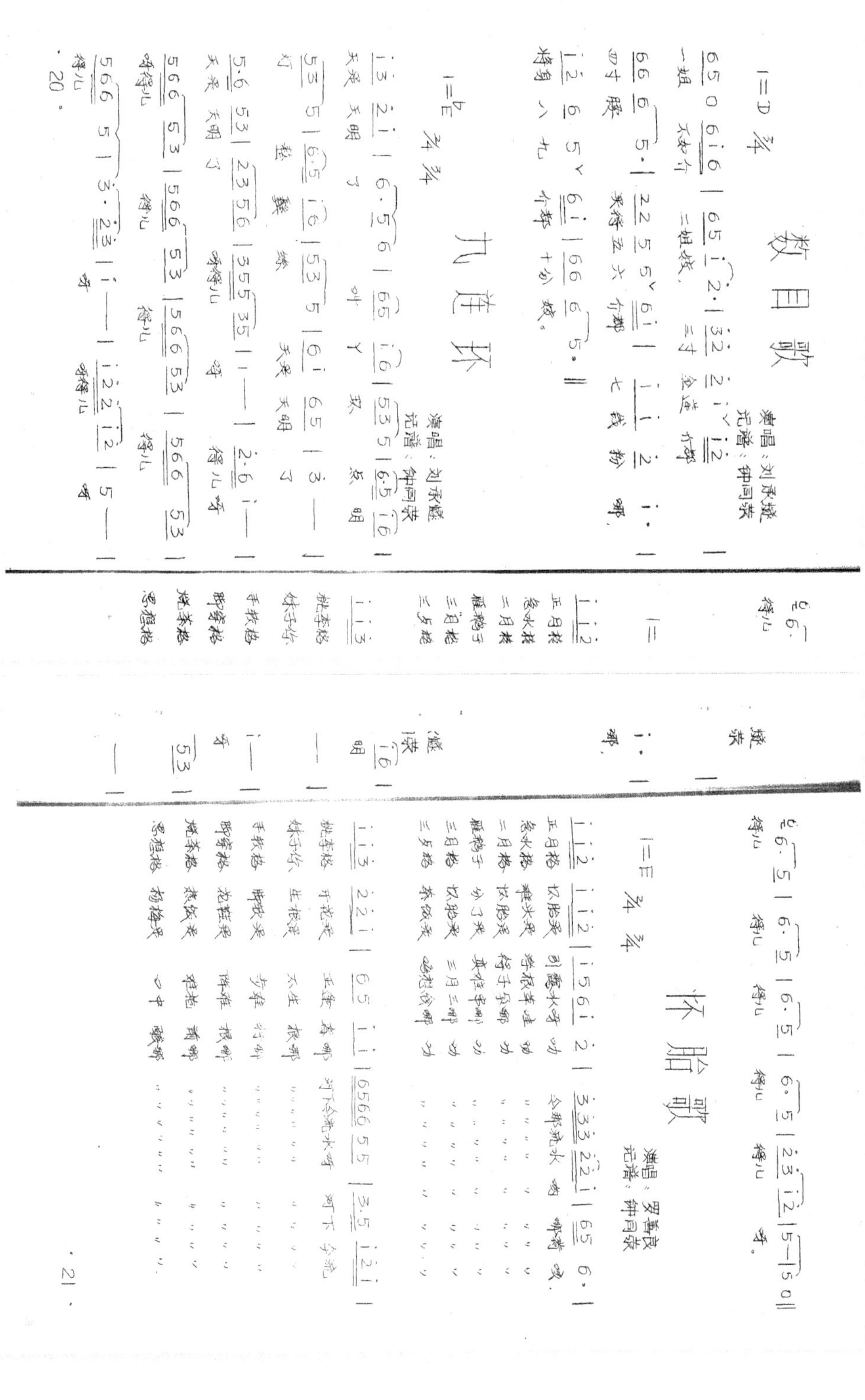

数目歌

1=D 3/4

演唱：刘承燧
记谱：钟同荣

65 0 6i6 | 65 i 2· | 32 2 i i2 |
一姐 不如介 二姐娇， 三寸 金莲 介哪

66 6 5· | 22 5 5 6i | i i 2 i· |
四寸 腰 哭得五 六 介哪 七 钱 粉 哪，

i2 6 5 6i | 66 6 5· ||
将身 八 九 介哪 十分 娇。

九连环

1=♭E 2/4 3/4

演唱：刘承燧
记谱：钟同荣

i3 2i | 6·5 6 | 65 i6 | 535 | 6·5 i6 |
天呆 天明 了 叫 丫 环 点 明

53 5 | 6·5 i6 | 53 5 | 6i 65 | 3 — |
灯 梳 妆 梳 天呆 天明 了

5·6 53 | 2356 | 355 35 | i — | 2·6 i — |
天呆 天明 了 呀得儿 呀 得儿呀

566 53 | 566 53 | 566 53 | 566 53 |
呀得儿 得儿 得儿 得儿

566 5 | 3·23 | i — | i22 i2 | 5 — |
得儿 呀 呀得儿 呀

· 20 ·

燧
荣

1=

i i2
正月格
急水格
二月格
雁鹅子
三月格
三月格

i·
哪，

燧
荣

i6
明

i i3
桃李格
妹子你
手软格
脚穿格
烧茶格
思想格

—

i —
呀

53

—

6 6·5 | 6·5 | 6·5 | 6·5 | 23 i2 | 5— | 5 0 ||
得儿 得儿 得儿 得儿 得儿 呀。

怀胎歌

1=E 2/4 3/4

演唱：罗善良
记谱：钟同荣

i i2 i i2 | i56i 2 | 333 22i | 65 6· |
正月格 怀胎哭 引露水呀 叻 今那流水 哟 哪哟 哎．
急水格 难头哭 浮根革连 叻 〃 〃 〃 〃 〃 〃 〃 〃
二月格 怀胎哭 得子孕哪 叻 〃 〃 〃 〃 〃 〃 〃 〃
雁鹅子 分了哭 真难串哪 叻 〃 〃 〃 〃 〃 〃 〃 〃
三月格 怀胎哭 三月三哪 叻 〃 〃 〃 〃 〃 〃 〃 〃
三月格 茶饭哭 吃想食哪 叻 〃 〃 〃 〃 〃 〃 〃 〃

i i3 22i | 65 i i | 6566 55 | 3·5 i2i |
桃李格 开花哭 正逢 春哪 河下今流水呀 河下 今流
妹子你 生根哭 不生 根哪 〃 〃 〃 〃 〃 〃 〃 〃 〃 〃
手软格 脚软哭 步难 行哪 〃 〃 〃 〃 〃 〃 〃 〃 〃 〃
脚穿格 花鞋哭 阵难 根哪 〃 〃 〃 〃 〃 〃 〃 〃 〃 〃
烧茶格 煮饭哭 难抱 锅哪 〃 〃 〃 〃 〃 〃 〃 〃 〃 〃
思想格 杨梅哭 口中 酸哪 〃 〃 〃 〃 〃 〃 〃 〃 〃 〃

· 21 ·

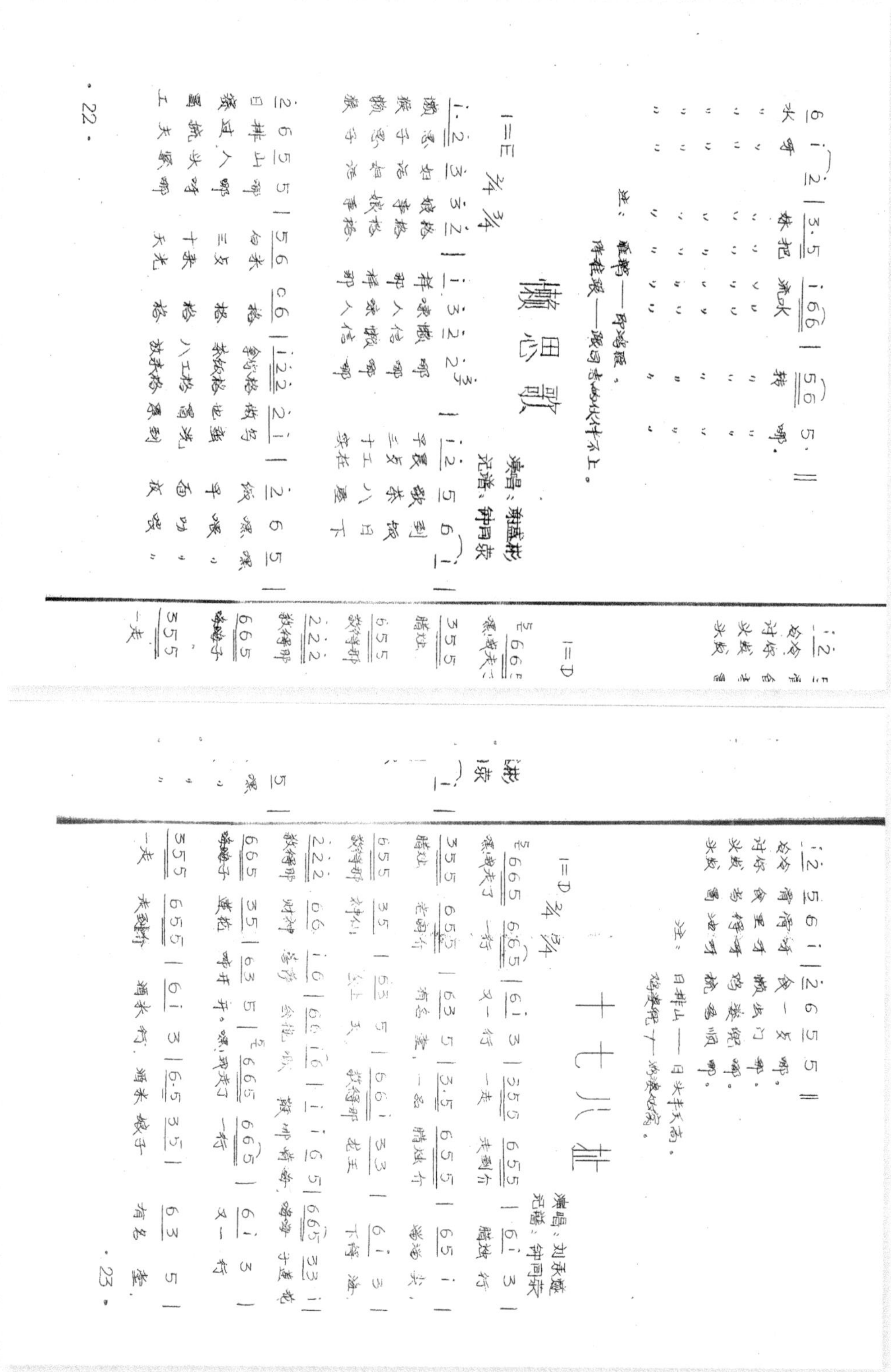

6 i 2 | 3·5 i 66 | 56 5· ||
水 呀 妹把 流水 转 哪。
〃 〃 〃 〃 〃 〃 〃 〃
〃 〃 〃 〃 〃 〃 〃 〃
〃 〃 〃 〃 〃 〃 〃 〃
〃 〃 〃 〃 〃 〃 〃 〃
〃 〃 〃 〃 〃 〃 〃 〃

注：雁鹅——即鸿雁。
跟往跟——跟同志的伙伴不上。

懒思歌

演唱：谢盛彬
记谱：钟同荣

1=E 2/4 3/4

i·2 3 3 2 | i 3 2 2 | i2 5 6 i |
懒 思 妇 娘格 样嘞懒 哪 早晨 歌 到
猴 子 话 事格 那人信 哪 三乡 茶 饭
懒 思 妇 娘格 样嘞懒 哪 十工 八 日
猴 子 话 事格 那人信 哪 实在 塑 下

2 6 5 5 | 56 06 | i22 2i | 2 6 5 |
日 排 山 哪 白米 格 拿你格 做乡 饭 嘿 嘿
食 过 人 哪 三乡 格 茶饭格 也蛮 早 喂 〃
冒 梳 头 呀 十来 格 八工格 冒洗 面 呦 〃
工 夫 紧 哪 天光 格 放米格 原到 夜 哦 〃

i2 5
冷冷 胃
讨你 食
头发 当
头发 冒
1=D
5 665
嘿,我走了
355
腊烛
655
数得那
222
数得那
665
嗨嗨子
355
一走

i2 5 6 i | 2 6 5 5 ||
冷冷 胃胃呀 食一乡 哪。
讨你 食里呀 懒出门 哪。
头发 当得呀 鸡婆窝 哪。
头发 冒油呀 梳唔顺 哪。

注：日排山——日头丰天高。
鸡婆窝——鸡婆的窝。

十七八扯

演唱：刘承燧
记谱：钟同荣

1=D 2/4 3/4

5 665 665 | 6i 3 | 355 655 | 6i 3 |
嘿,我走了 一行 又一行 一走 走到介 腊烛 行

355 655 | 63 5 | 3·5 655 | 65 i |
腊烛 老哥介 有名 堂, 一名 腊烛介 尖尖 尖,

655 35 | 63 5 | 66i 33 | 6i 3 |
数得那 神仙: 上 天, 数得那 龙王 下得 海,

222 66 i6 | 66 i6 | i i 6 5 | 665 33 i |
数得那 财神 菩萨 会拖 钱, 鲢鲤 鲭鱼, 嗨嗨 子莲 花

665 35 | 63 5 | 5 665 665 | 6i 3 |
嗨嗨子 莲花 呼开 开。嘿,我走了 一行 又一 行

355 655 | 6i 3 | 6·5 35 | 63 5 |
一走 走到介 酒米 行, 酒米 娘子 有名 堂,

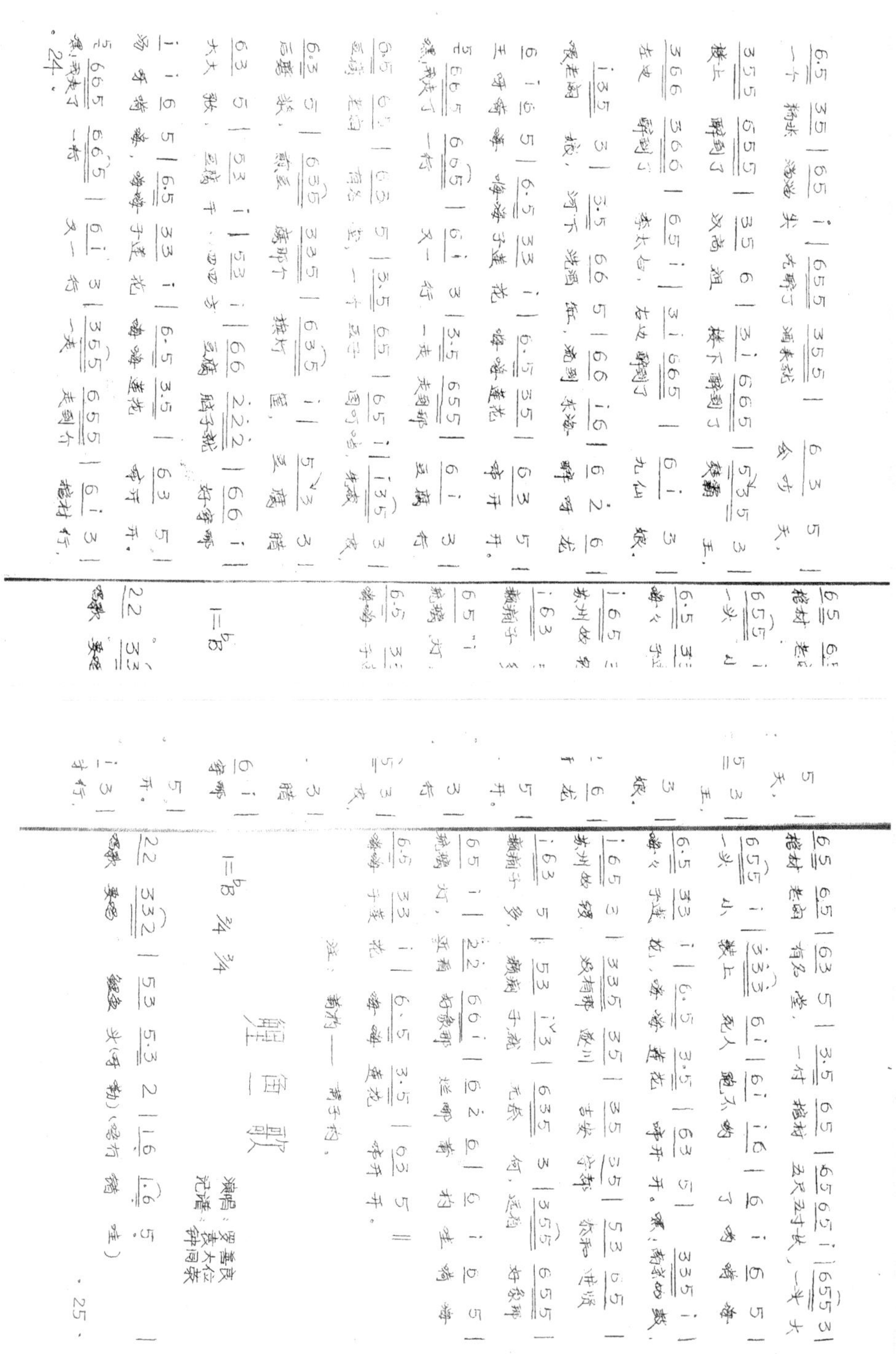

6.5 35 | 65 i | 655 355 | 6 3 5 |
一个 稍迷 滔滔 尖 吃醉了 酒来就 会 吁 天，

355 655 | 35 6 | 3i 665 | 535 3 |
楼上 醉到了 双尚 祖 楼下 醉到了 楚霸 王，

366 366 | 65 i | 3i 665 | 6i 3 |
左边 醉到了 李太白，右边 醉到了 九仙 娘。

i35 3 | 3.5 66 5 | 66 i6 | 6 2 6 |
喂老阔 娘，河下 洗酒 缸，流到 东海 醉 呀 龙

6 i 6 5 | 6.5 33 i | 6.5 35 | 6 3 5 |
王 呀 嗬 嗨 嗨嗨 子莲 花 嗨嗨 莲花 啼 开 开。

5 665 665 | 6i 3 | 3.5 655 | 6i 3 |
嘿，我走了 一行 又一 行 一走 走到那 豆腐 行

6.5 65 | 63 5 | 3.5 65 | 65 i | i35 3 |
豆腐 老阔 有名 堂，一个 豆子 圆叮咚，朱夜 夜，

6.3 5 | 635 335 | 635 i | 53 3 |
石磨 浆，煎豆 腐那个 旗灯 笼，豆腐 睛

63 5 | 53 i | 53 i | 66 222 | 66 i |
大大 敌，豆腐 干，四四 方 豆腐 脑子就 好穿 哪

i i 6 5 | 6.5 33 i | 6.5 3.5 | 63 5 |
汤 呀 嗬 嗨，嗨嗨 子莲 花 嗨嗨 莲花 啼开 开。

5 665 665 | 6i 3 | 355 655 | 6i 3 |
嘿，我走了 一行 又一 行 一走 走到个 棺材 行，

·24·

65 65
棺材 老…
655 i
一头 小
6.5 33
嗨々 子…
i65 3
苏州 的 …
i63 5
癞痢子 …
65 i
琉璃 灯
6.5 33
嗨嗨 子…
1=♭B
22 33
唱歌 要…

5 天，
5 3 王，
3 娘。
6 龙
5 开。
3 行
5 3 夜，
3 睛
6 i 穿哪
5 开。
i 3 才行，

65 65 | 63 5 | 3.5 65 | 6565 i | 6553 |
棺材 老阔 有名 堂，一付 棺材 五尺五寸长，一头 大

655 i | 333 6i | 6i i6 | 6 i 6 5 |
一头 小 装上 死人 跑不 的 了 哟 嗬 嗨

6.5 33 i | 6.5 3.5 | 63 5 | 335 i |
嗨々 子莲 花，嗨嗨 莲花 啼开 开。嘿，南京的 载，

i65 3 | 335 35 | 35 35 | 53 65 |
苏州 的 锅 双桐那 遂川 吉安 宁都 尔和 世贤

i63 5 | 53 i3 | 635 3 | 355 655 |
癞痢子 多，癞痢 子就 无奈 何，远看 好象那

65 i | 22 66i | 6 2 6 | 6 i 6 5 |
琉璃 灯，近看 好象那 烂哪 葡 杓 哇 嗬 嗨

6.5 33 i | 6.5 3.5 | 63 5 ||
嗨嗨 子莲 花 嗨嗨 莲花 啼开 开。

注：葡杓——葫子杓。

鲤鱼歌

1=♭B 2/4 3/4

演唱：罗善良
记谱：袁大位 钟同荣

22 332 | 53 5.3 2 | 16 1.6 5 |
唱歌 要唱 鲤鱼 头(呀 勒)(唱冇 错 哇)

·25·

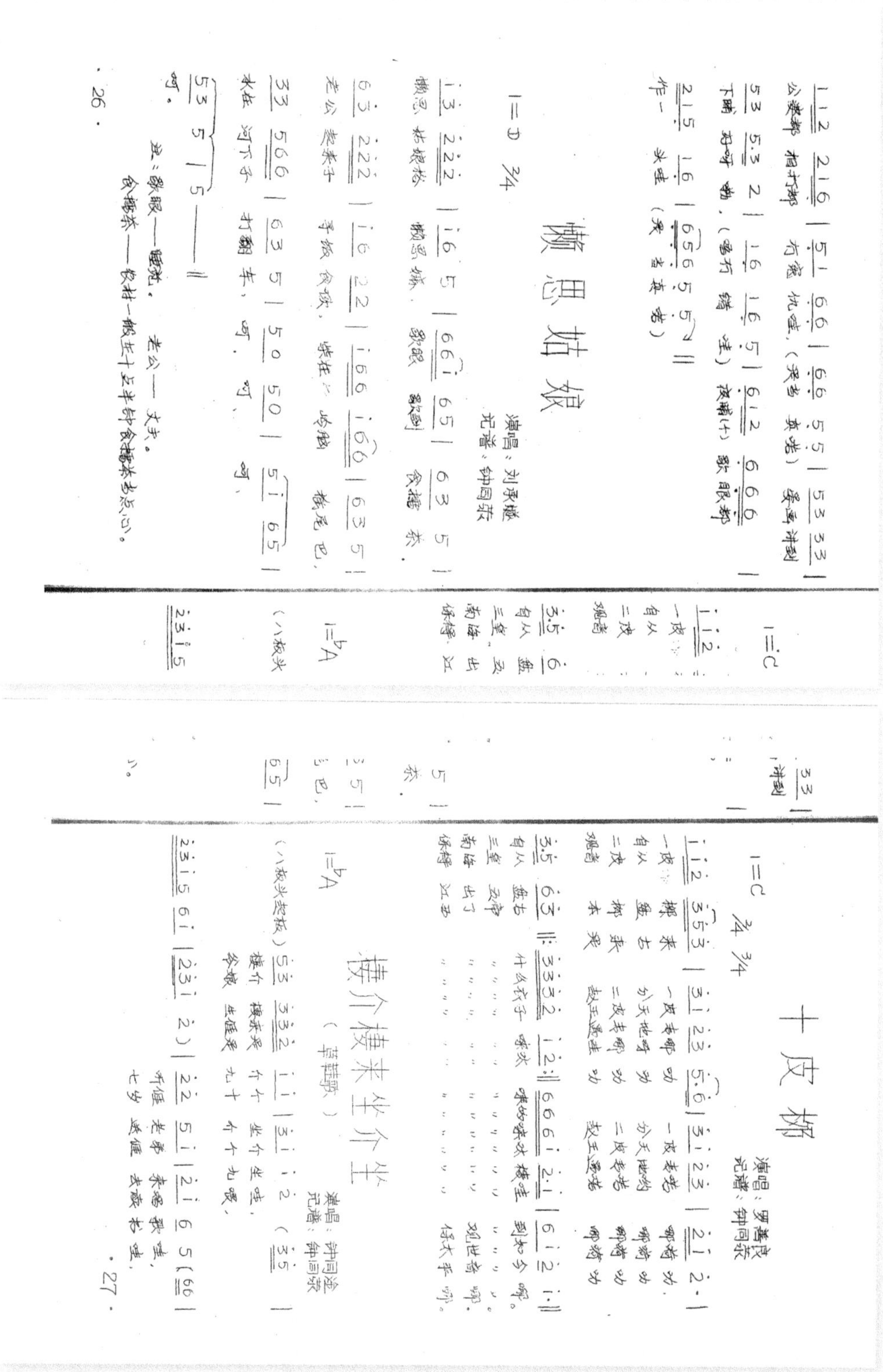

112 216 | 51 66 | 66 55 | 53 33 |
公婆都 相打都 有冤 仇哇,（我当 真诺） 晏画 讲到

53 5.3 2 | 16 16 5 | 612 666 |
下晡 好呀 嘞,（唔冇 错 哇） 夜晡(十) 歌眼都

215 16 | 656 5 5 ||
作一 头哇 （我 当 真 诺）

懒思姑娘

1=D 3/4

演唱：刘承巘
记谱：钟同荥

13 222 | 16 5 | 661 65 | 63 5 |
懒思 姑娘格 懒思嫲, 歌眼 歌到 食擂 茶。

63 222 | 16 22 | 166 166 | 63 5 |
老公 起来子 寻饭 食该, 紫在 岭脑 株尾 巴,

33 566 | 63 5 | 50 50 | 51 65 |
水在 河下子 打翻 车, 呵, 呵, 呵,

53 5 | 5 — ||
呵。

注：歌眼——睡觉。　老公——丈夫。
食擂茶——农村一般在十点半钟食擂茶当点心。

· 26 ·

十皮椰

1=C 2/4 3/4

演唱：罗善良
记谱：钟同荥

112 353 | 31 23 5.6 | 31 23 | 21 2· |
一皮 椰 来 一皮去哪 叻 一皮去诺 哪荷 叻,
自从 盘 古 分天地呀 叻 分天地哟 哪荷 叻
二皮 椰 来 二皮去哪 叻 二皮去诺 哪荷 叻
观音 本 是 赵王遇哇 叻 赵王遇诺 哪荷 叻

3.5 63 |: 3332 12 :| 6661 2.1 | 612 1· ||
自从 盘古 什么衣子 咪欢 咪的咪欢 楼哇 到如今 啊。
三皇 五帝 〃〃〃〃 〃〃 〃〃〃〃 〃〃 〃〃〃 〃。
南海 出了 〃〃〃〃 〃〃 〃〃〃〃 〃〃 观世音 啊。
保存 江西 〃〃〃〃 〃〃 〃〃〃〃 〃〃 保太平 啊。

楼介楼来坐介坐

（草鞋歌）

1=♭A

演唱：钟同淦
记谱：钟同荥

（八板头起板）53 332 11 | 31 12 （35 |
楼介 楼来是 介个 坐介坐哇,
爷娘 生涯是 九十 介个九喂,

2315 61 | 231 2) | 22 51 | 21 6 5 (66 |
听哩 老弟 来唱歌哇,
七岁 送哩 去读书哇,

· 27 ·

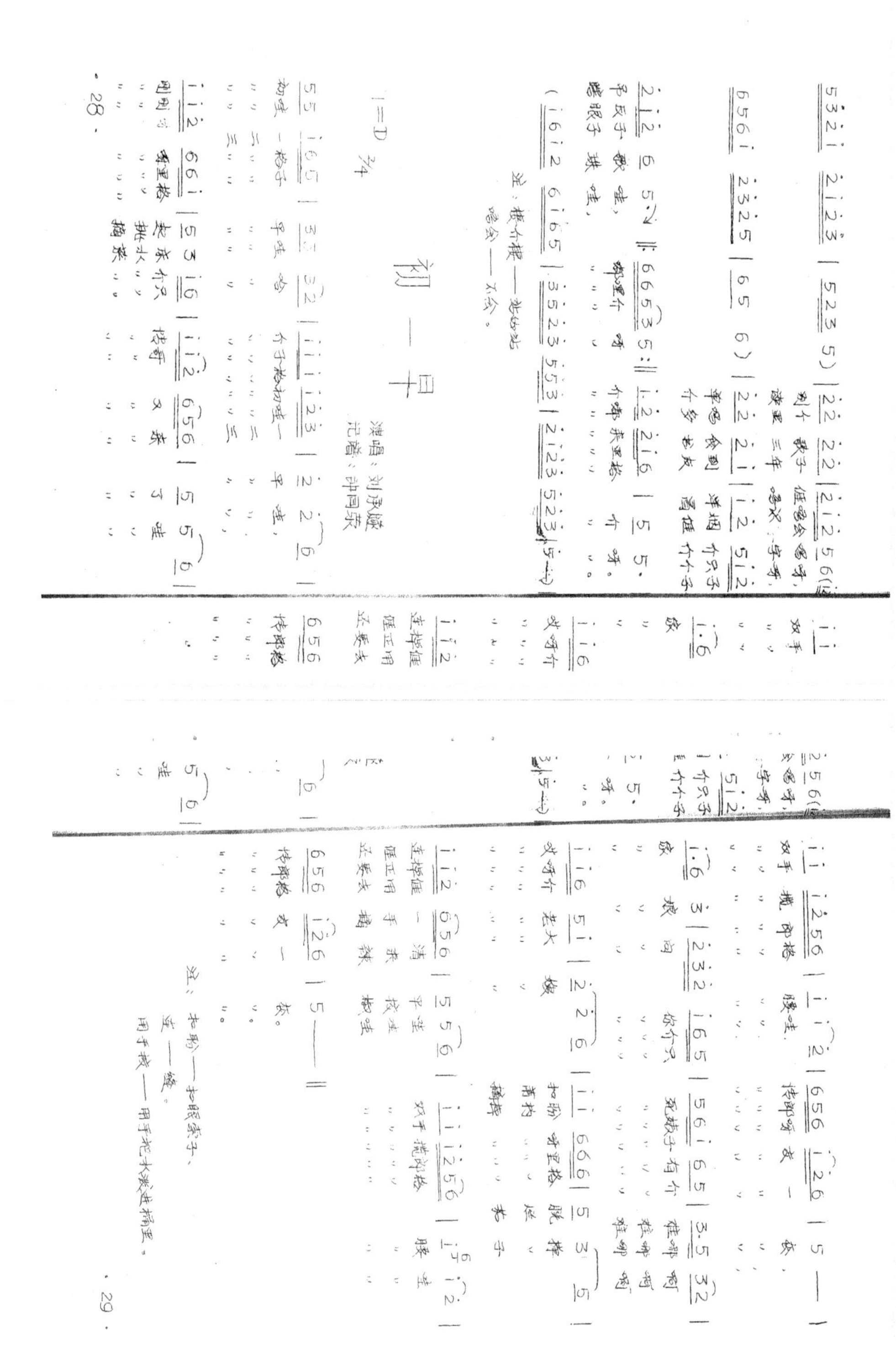

5̇3̇2̇i̇ 2̇i̇2̇3̇ | 5̇2̇3̇ 5̇) | 2̇2̇ 2̇2̇ | 2̇i̇2̇ 5 6(| i̇ i̇

刘个 歌子 係喝会喝呀，双手
读里 三年 喝识 一字呀，

656i̇ 2̇3̇2̇5̇ | 65 6) | 2̇2̇ 2̇i̇ | i̇2̇ 5i̇2̇ | i̇·6

辛吧 食到 洋烟 介只子 家
介多 老友 涌涯 介个子

2̇i̇2̇ 6 5 | 66535 :‖ i̇·2̇ 2̇i̇6 | 5 5· | i̇i̇6

吊反子 歌 哇， 都哩介 呀 介哪来里格 介 呀。 艾呀介
瞎眼子 珠 哇，

(i̇6i̇2̇ 6i̇65 | 3̇5̇2̇3̇ 5̇5̇3̇ | 2̇i̇2̇3̇ 5̇2̇3̇ | 5 —)

注：梗介梗——地处地
哈会——不会。

初一早

1=D 2/4

演唱：刘承嫙
记谱：钟同荣

55 i̇65 | 33 32 | i̇i̇i̇ i̇2̇3̇ | 2 2 6 | 656

初哇 一格子 早哇 哈 介子格初哇一 早 哇， 传郎格
〃〃 二〃〃 〃〃〃〃〃二
〃〃 三〃〃 〃〃〃〃〃三

i̇i̇2̇ 66i̇ | 5 3 i̇6 | i̇i̇2̇ 656 | 5 5 6 | i̇i̇2̇

刚刚 哪里格 起床 介只 传哥 又 来 了 哇 连埗涯
挑水〃〃
摘菜〃〃

i̇i̇ i̇2̇56 | i̇ i̇ 2̇ | 656 i̇26 | 5 — |

双手 揽 郎格 腰哇， 传郎呀 衣 一 衣，

i̇·6 3 | 2̇3̇2̇ i̇65 | 56i̇ 65 | 3·5 32 |

家 娘 问 你介只 死嫁子 有介 难哪 呵
难哪 呵
难哪 呵

i̇i̇6 5i̇ | 2 2 6 | i̇i̇ 666 | 5 3 5 |

艾呀介 老大 嫂 扣盼 呀里格 脱 掉
甫杓 〃〃〃 烂 〃
搞搽 〃〃〃 老 子

i̇i̇2̇ 656 | 5 5 6 | i̇i̇ i̇2̇56 | i̇ i̇2̇ |

连埗涯 一 清 早 哇 双手 揽郎格 腰 哇
涯正甬 手 来 拢 哇
还要去 摘 辣 椒哇

656 i̇26 | 5 — ‖

传郎格 衣 一 衣。

注：扣盼——扣眼索子。
连——缝。
甬手拢——用手把水泼进桶里。

· 28 ·　　· 29 ·

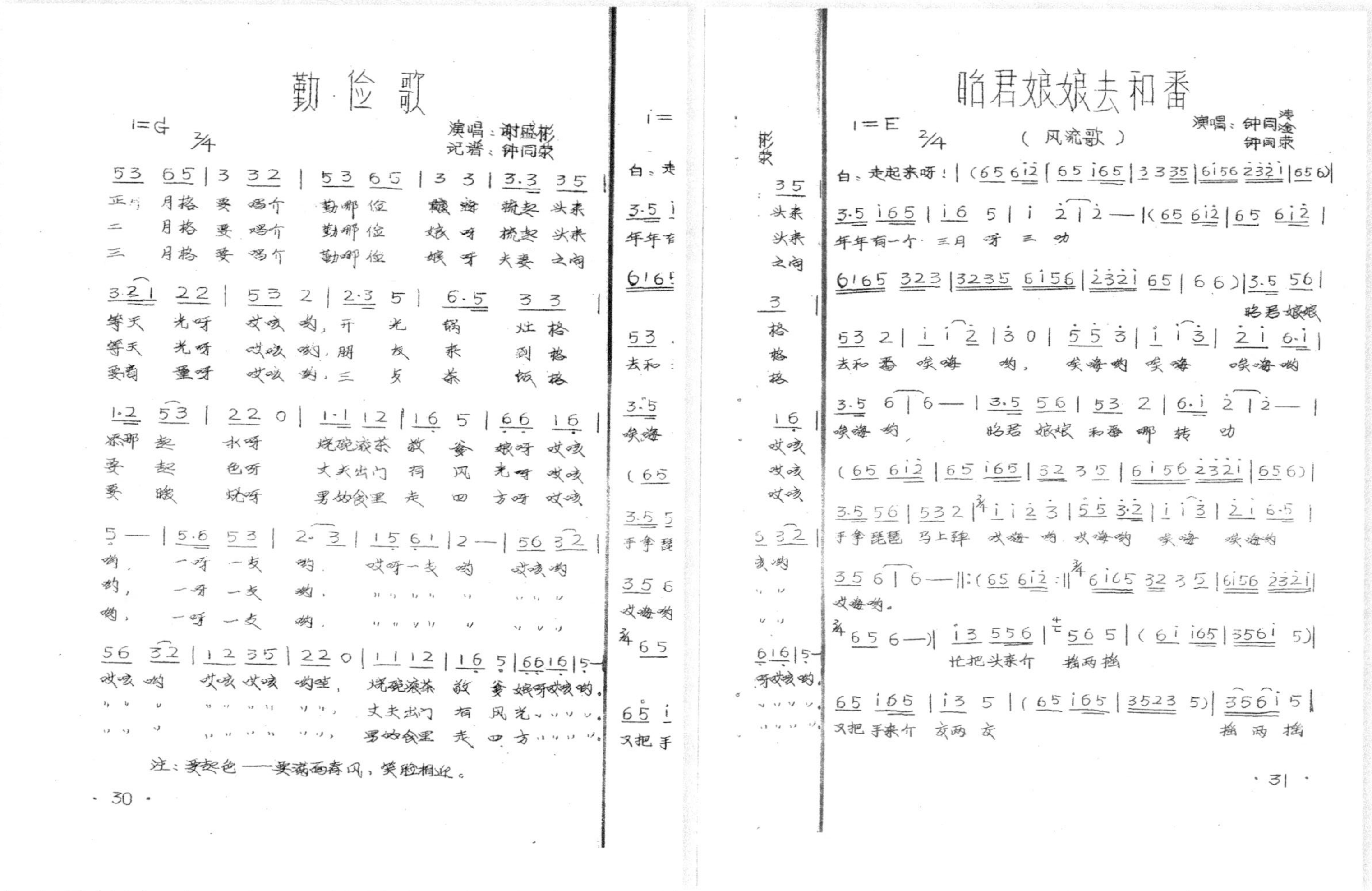
勤俭歌
1=G 2/4
演唱：谢盛彬
记谱：钟同荣
注：要起色——要满面春风，笑脸相迎。
· 30 ·
昭君娘娘去和番
1=E 2/4
（风流歌）
演唱：钟同涛
钟同荣
白：走起来呀！
· 31 ·

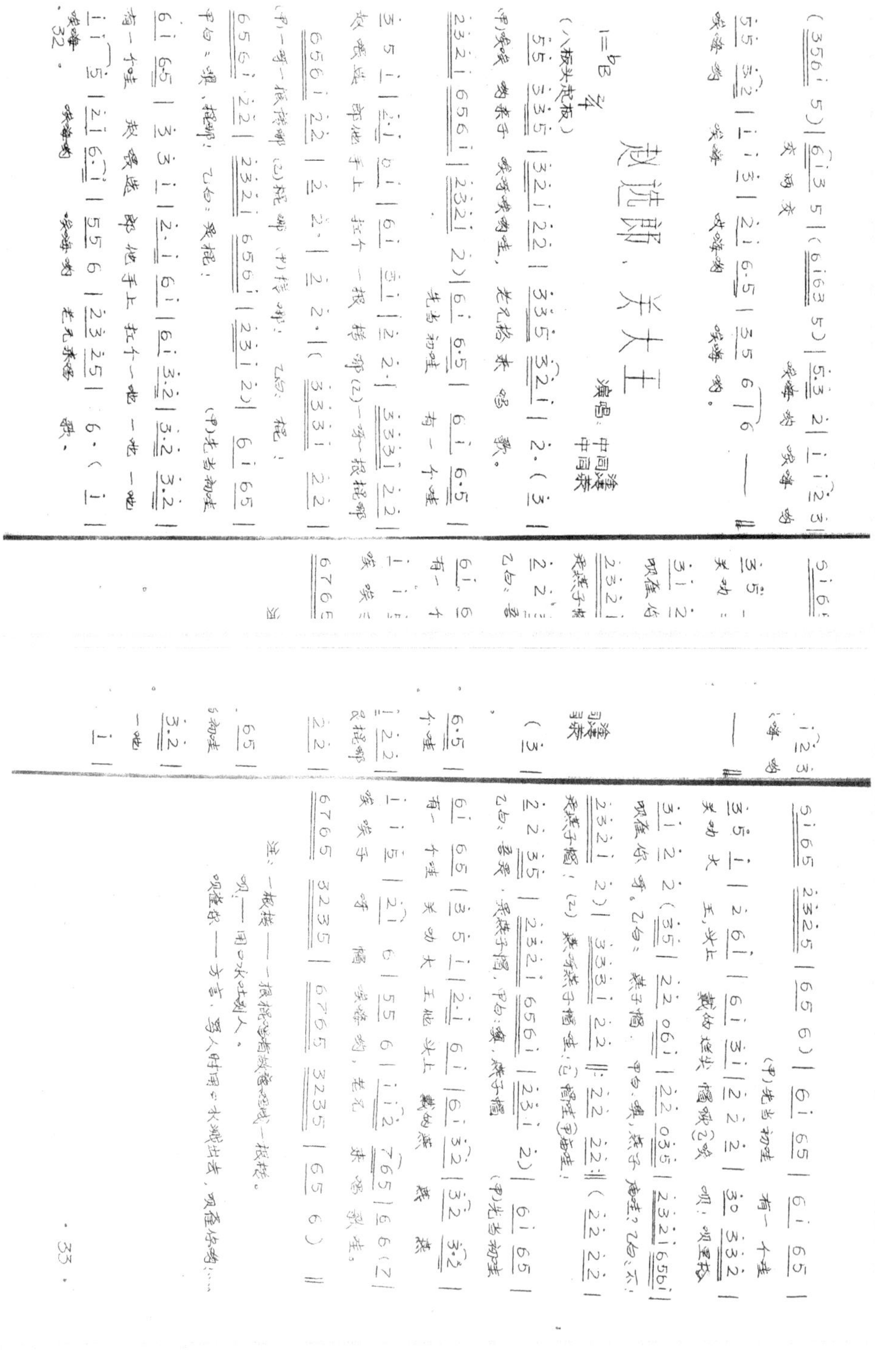

交 两 交 　 唉嗨哟 唉嗨 哟

唉嗨 哟 　 唉嗨 　 哎嗨哟 　 唉嗨 哟。

赵选郎、关大王

1=♭B 2/4

演唱：中同淦 中同荥

（八板头起板）

(甲)唉唉 哟朵子 唉呀唉哟哇，老兄格 来 唱 歌。

先当 初哇 　 有一 个哇

赵 喉选 郎他 手上 扛个 一根 楞 哪(乙)一呀一根棍哪

(甲)一呀一根楞哪 (乙)棍 哪 (甲)楞 哪！ 乙白：棍！

甲白：呗，棍哪！ 乙白：是棍！ 　 (甲)先当初哇

有一 个哇 　 赵 喉选 郎 他手上 扛个一吔 一吔 一吔

唉嗨 　 唉嗨哟 　 唉嗨哟 　 老兄来唱 　 歌。

·32·

(甲)先当 初哇 　 有一 个哇

关 叻 大 　 王，头上 　 戴的 烂尖 帽唉(乙)唉 　 呗！呗里格

呗霍 你 呀。乙白： 燕子帽。 甲白：呗，燕子 庙哇？乙白：不！

是燕子帽！ (乙) 燕呀燕子帽 哇！(乙)帽哇(甲)庙哇！

乙白：吾是，是燕子帽，甲白：噢，燕子帽 　 (甲)先当初哇

有一 个哇 　 关 叻 大 王他 头上 戴的燕 　 燕 燕

唉 唉子 　 呀 　 帽 　 唉嗨 哟，老兄 　 来 唱 歌哇。

注：一根楼——一根棍子者故意说成一根楼。

呗——用口水吐别人。

呗霍你——方言，骂人时用口水溅出去，呗霍你哟！……

·33·

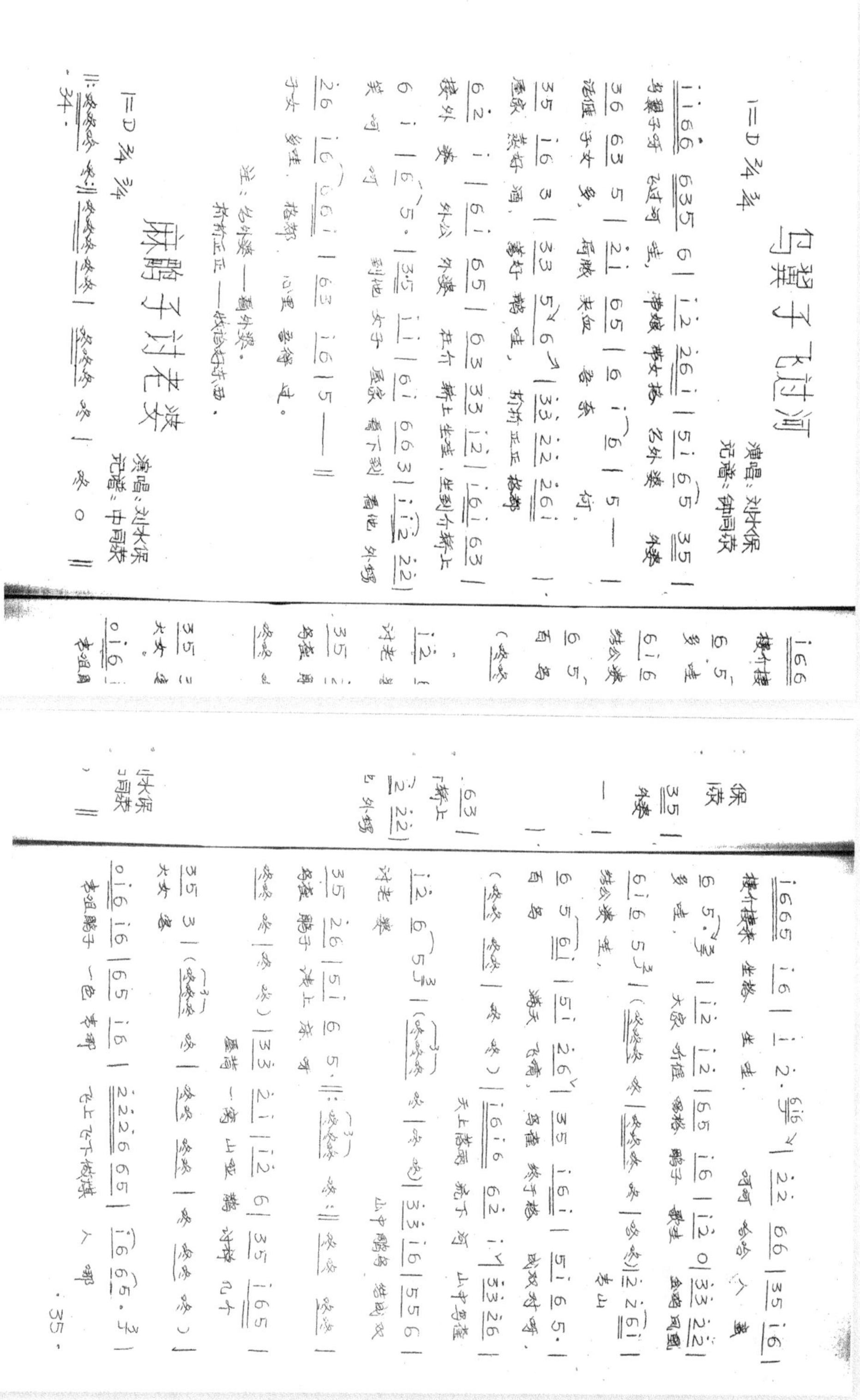

乌翼子飞过河

1=D 2/4 3/4

演唱：刘水保
记谱：钟同荥

乌翼子呀 飞过河 哇，带娘 带女 格 名外婆 外婆
话涯 子女 多，舅舅 夹血 吞 东 何。
屋家 蒸好 酒，蓄好 鹅 哇，扐扐正正 格都
接外 婆 外公 外婆 在介 奔上 生哇，坐到介 奔上
笑 呵 呵 到他 女子 屋家 看下到 看他 外甥
子女 多哇，格都 心里 吾得 过。

注：名外婆——看外婆。
扐扐正正——收拾好东西。

麻鹊子讨老婆

1=D 2/4 3/4

演唱：刘水保
记谱：中同荥

· 34 ·

楼介楼来 生格 生 哇， 呵呵 哈哈 八 哥
多 哇， 大家 听但 哪格 鹊子 歌唱 金鸡 凤凰
结公婆 哇， 青山
百 鸟 满天 飞， 鸟雀 终于格 成双对 呀，
天上落雨 流下 河 山中鸟雀
讨老 婆 山中鹊鸟 结成双
鸟雀 鹊子 凑上 床 呀
屋背 一窝 山鸦 鹊 讨得 几个
大女 客
书姐鹊子 一色 书哪 飞上飞下做媒 人 哪

· 35 ·

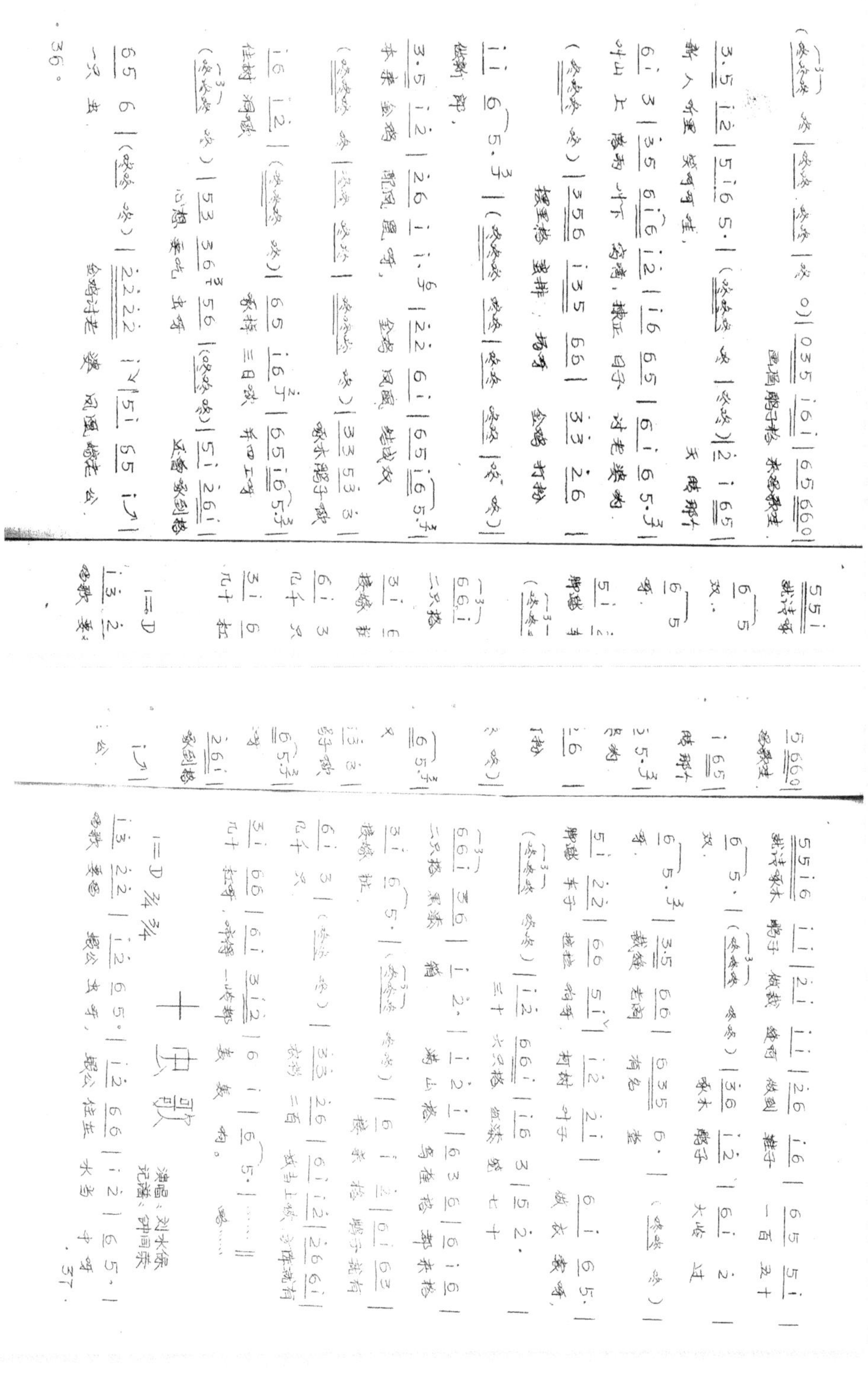

画眉鹞子格 来唱歌生.
新人听里 笑呵呵哇， 天晓那个
叫山上 落雨 叫下 窝窝，揀正 日子 讨老婆哟.
摆里格 蛮排，场呀 金鸡 打扮
做新 郎，
本来 金鸡 配凤凰呀， 金鸡 凤凰 结成双
啄木鹞子啾
住树 洞啾 啄梓 三日啾 开四工呀
心想 要吃 虫呀 还曾啄到格
一只 虫. 金鸡讨老 婆 凤凰嫁老 公.

·36·

就诗啄木 鹞子 做裁 缝呵 做到 鞋子 一百 五十
双. 啄木 鹞子 大岭 过
呀. 裁缝 老阔 有名 声
脚踏 车子 扯扯 向呀， 打树 叶子 做衣 裳呀，
三十 六只格 油漆 笼 七十
二只格 黑漆 箱 满山格 乌桂格 都来格
接嫁 妆. 接亲 格 鹞子就有
几千 只 放的 二百 或者上啾 子阵就有
几十 杠呀，啼得 一岭都 轰 轰 响。 咯……

十虫歌

1=D 3/4 3/4

演唱：刘水保
记谱：钟同荣

唱歌 要唱 虾公 虫呀， 虾公 住在 水当 中呀

·37·

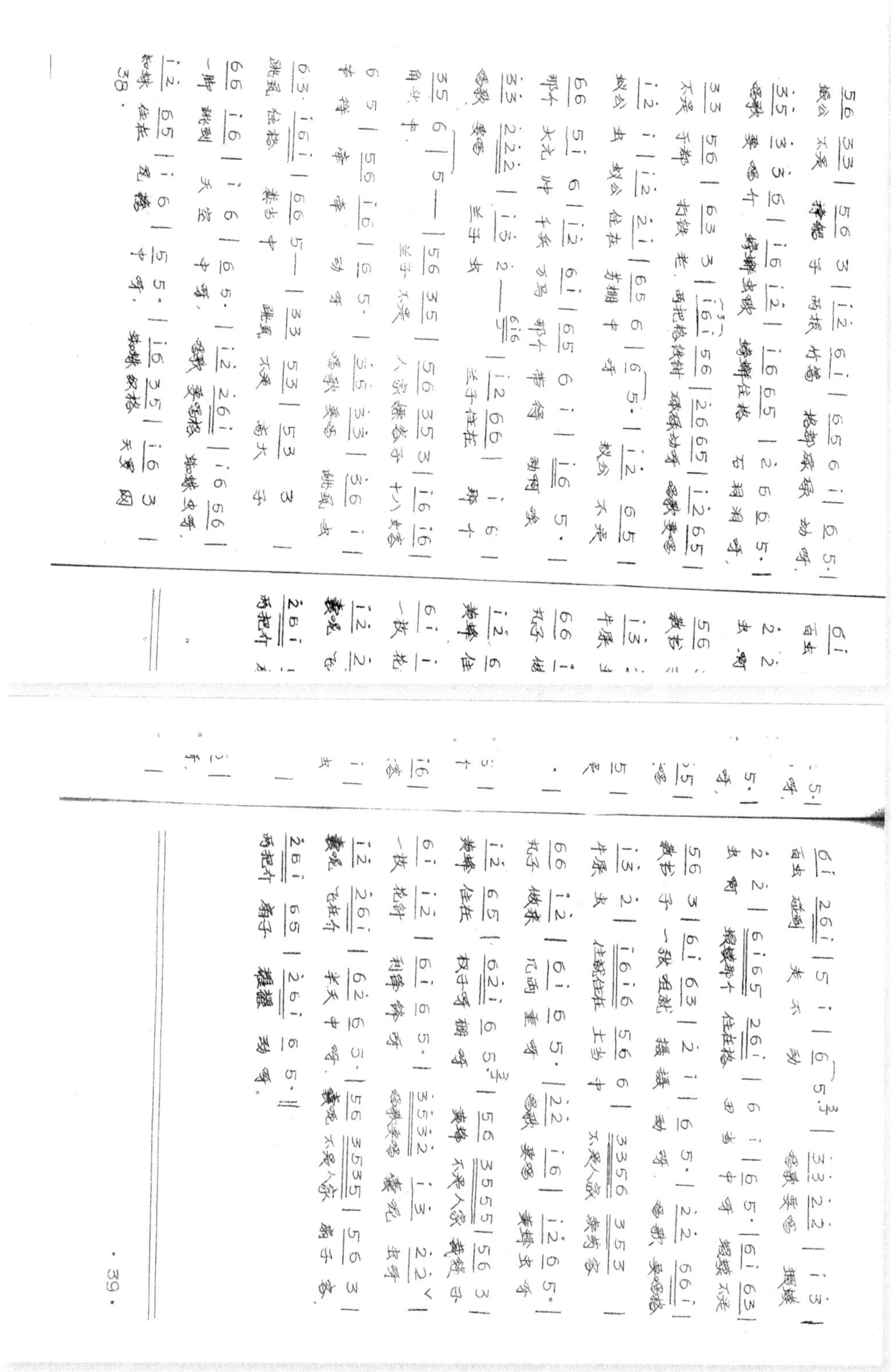
38.
39.

童养媳

1=D 2/4

演唱：钟晓秀
记谱：钟同荣

一岁娘生我哥，二岁娘面前动，三岁童养媳，孩人欺她，四岁学挑水，五岁学扫地地，六岁放牛割薯，花地天老爷地还话准有用的东西她。

老鼠歌

（儿歌）

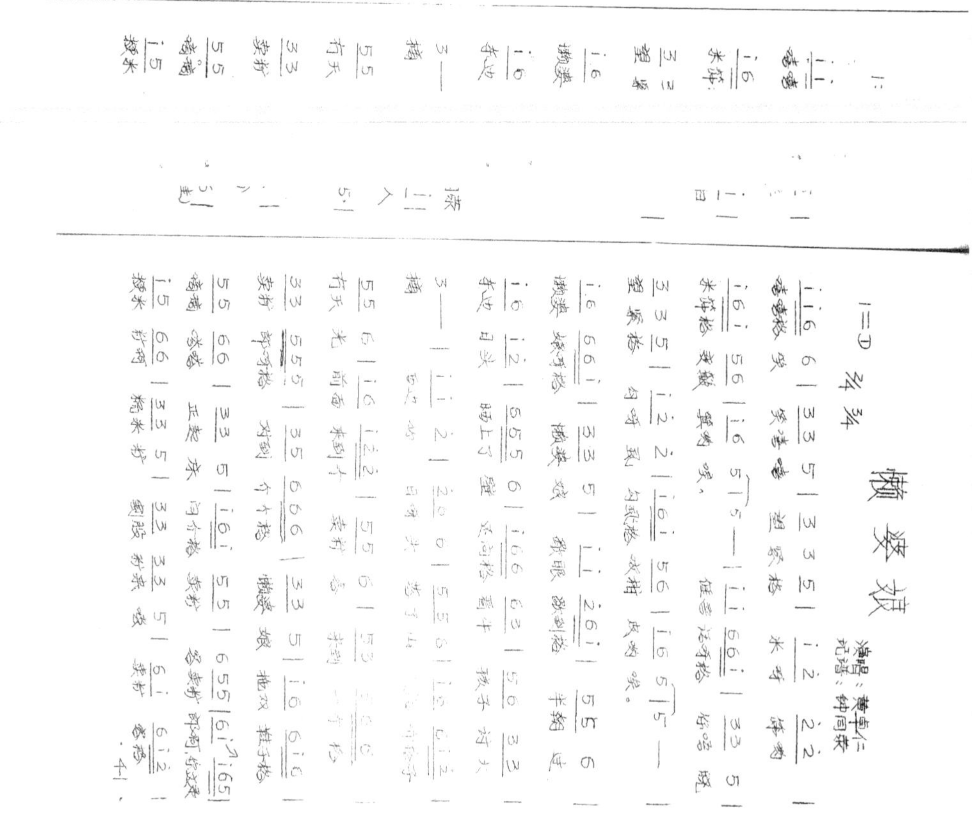

1=♭B 2/4 3/4

演唱：刘水保
记谱：袁大应、钟同荣

老鼠子哇 吖吖□□ 打开轿门 看新人 看到新人脑哇，百朵花子带满脑，看到新人耳呀 金子银饰带满耳，看到新人面哪，胭脂水粉搽乡面哪，看到新人手，金子戒子带满手(哇)，看到新人脚哇，绣花鞋子蛮有看(哟)。

·40·

懒婆娘

1=D 2/4 3/4

演唱：黄卓仁
记谱：钟同荣

嘻嘻格笑 笑嘻嘻 望紧格 水呀 饰哟 米筛格 □□ 箕哟 唉。 □□ □□格 你晤 晓 望紧格 日呀 风 日风格 □□ 皮哟 唉。 懒婆 娘呀格 懒婆 娘 □眼 □□格 半□ 过 东边 日头 晒上了 壁 还□格 看牛 孩子 讨 大 摘 □□ □□ 日□ 头 落了 山 □□ □□子 有天 光 前面 来到个 卖粉 嘉 来到 一个 格 卖粉 郎呀格 对到 个个格 懒婆 娘 拖双 鞋子格 嘀嘀 嗒嗒 正起 床 问个格 卖粉 □卖粉 郎呀 你这 粳米 粉呀 糯米 粉 剁股 粉来 哎 卖粉 □□

·41·

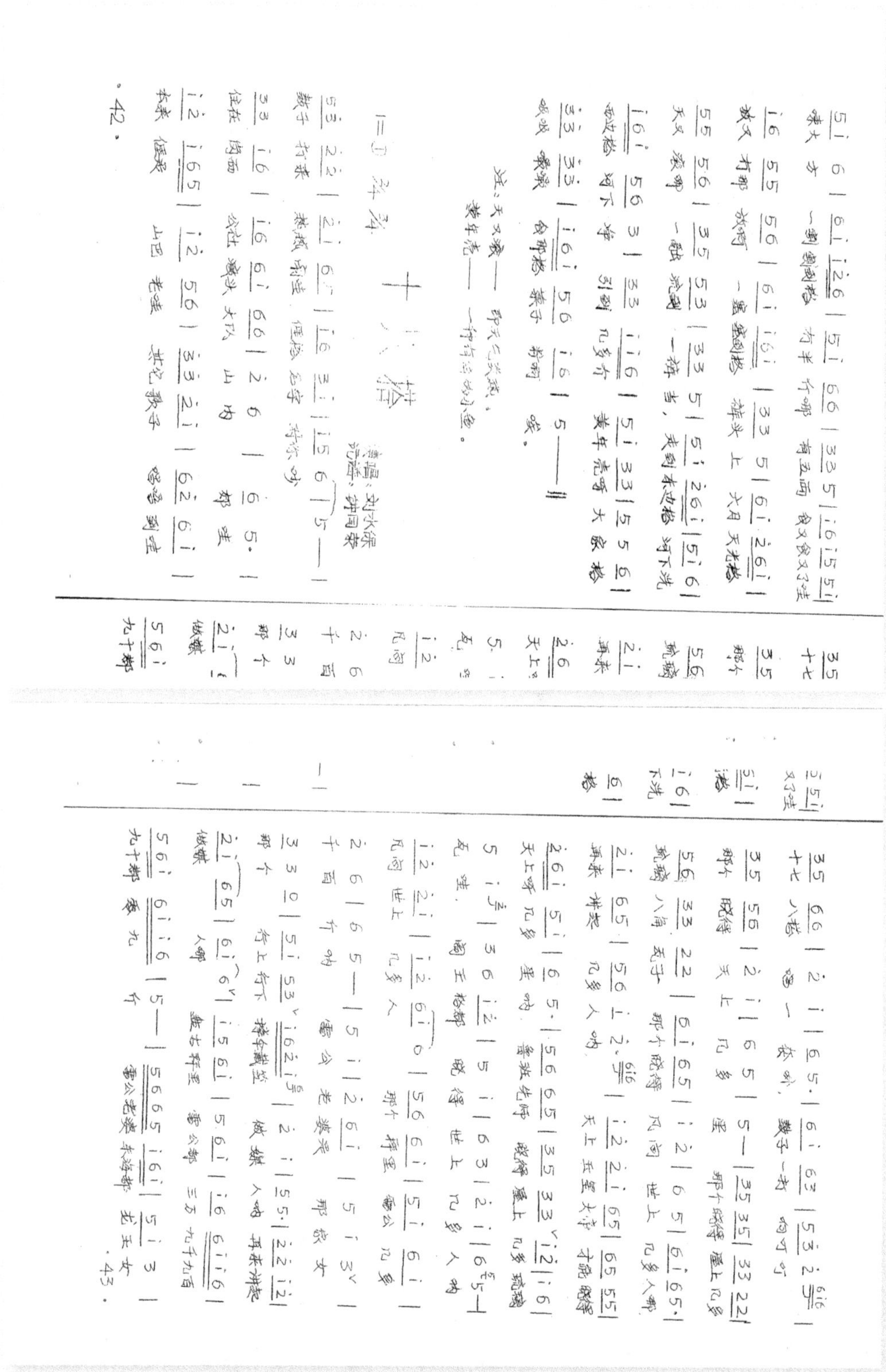

5 i 6 | 6 i i 2 6 | 5 i 6 6 | 3 3 5 | i 6 i 5 5 i |
崃大方　一到到到格　有半个哪　有五两　食又食又了哇

i 6 5 5 5 6 | 6 i i 6 i | 3 3 5 | 6 i 2 6 i |
放又打都　放啊　一塞塞到格　旗头上　六月天光格

5 5 5 6 | 3 5 5 3 | 3 3 5 | 5 i 2 6 i | 5 i 6 |
天又滚啊　一融流到　一旗当，走到东边格　河下洗

i 6 i 5 6 3 | 3 3 i i 6 | 5 i 3 3 | 5 5 6 |
西边格　河下净　引到几多介　黄年壳呀　大家格

3 3 3 3 | i 6 i 5 6 i 6 | 5 —— ‖
哦哦哦哦　食那格　菜子　好啊　唉。

注：天又滚——即天气炎热。
　　黄年壳——一种有壳的小鱼。

十八格

1=D 2/4 3/4

演唱：刘水保
记谱：钟同荣

5 3 2 2 | 2 i 6 5 | i 6 3 i | i 5 6 | 5 — |
鼓子　打来　热热闹闹哇　侄格名字　叫你吵

3 3 i 6 | i 6 6 i 6 6 | 2 6 | 6 5· |
住在　闵西　公社　藏头大队　山内　那哇

i 2 i 6 5 | i 2 5 6 | 3 3 2 i | 6 2 6 i |
本来　侄来　山巴　老哇　其它歌子　唱唱到哇

·42·

5 5 i | 3 5 6 6 | 2 i | 6 5· | 6 i 6 3 | 5 3 2 6i6 |
又了哇　十七　八格　唱一　套咧，数子一打　响可叮

5 i | 3 5 5 6 | 2 i | 6 5 | 5 — | 3 5 3 5 | 3 3 2 2 |
格　那个　晓得　天上　几多　星　那个晓得　屋上几多

i 6 | 5 6 3 3 2 2 | 6 i 6 5 | i 2 | 6 5 | 6 i 6 5· |
下洗　琉璃　八角　瓦子　那个晓得　凡间　世上　几多人哪

6 | 2 i 6 5 | 5 6 i 2· 6i6 | i 2 2 i 6 5 | 6 5 5 5 |
格　再来　讲起　几多人呐　天上　玉皇大帝　才能晓得

2 6 i 5 i | 6 5· | 5 6 6 5 | 3 5 3 3 i 2 | i 6 |
天上呀　几多　星呐　鲁班先师　晓得　屋上　几多琉璃

5 i | 3 6 i 2 | 5 i | 6 3 | 2 i | 6 5 — |
瓦哇，阎王格都　晓得　世上　几多　人呐

i 2 2 i | i 2 6 i 6 | 5 6 6 i | 5 i 6 i |
凡间　世上　几多人　那个　秤里　雷公　几多

2 6 | 6 5 — | 5 i | 2 6 i | 5 i 3 |
千百　介呐　雷公　老婆来　那家女

3 3 0 | 5 i 5 3 i 6 2 i | 2 i | 5 5· | 2 2 i 2 |
那个　行上行下　撑伞戴笠　做媒　人呐　再来讲起

2 i 6 5 | 6 i 6 | i 5 6 i | 5 6 i | i 6 6 i i 6 |
做媒　人哪　盘古秤里　雷公都　三万　九千九百

5 6 i 6 i i 6 | 5 — | 5 6 6 5 i 6 i | 5 i 3 |
九十都　零九　介　雷公老婆　东海都　龙王女

·43·

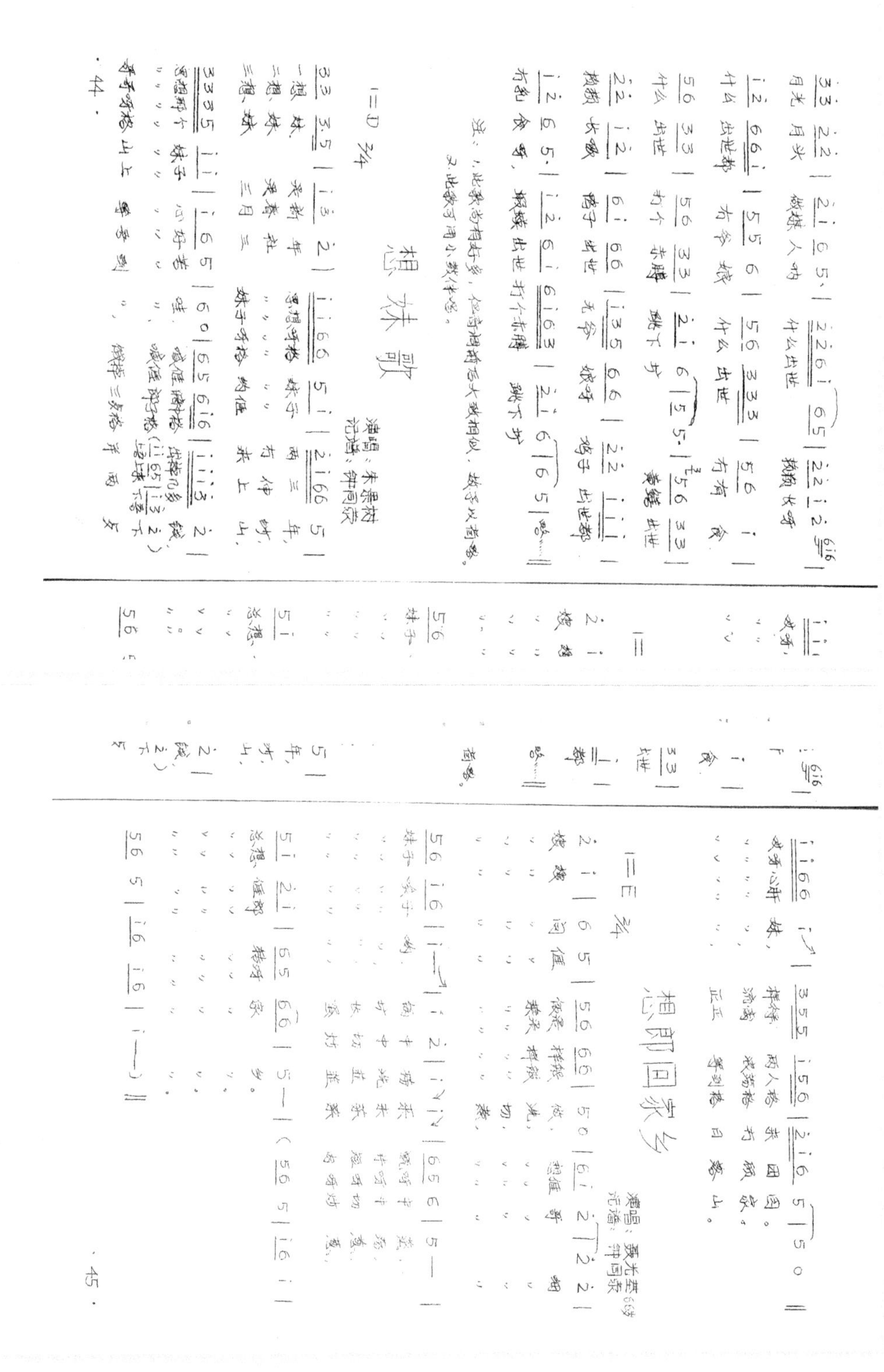

月光月头 做妹人呐 什么出世 赖赖长呀
什么出世都 有爷娘 什么出世 有有食
什么出世 打个赤膊 跳下圹 黄鳝出世
赖赖长哦 鸡子出世 无爷娘呀 鸡子出世都
有乱食呀，虾蟆出世 打个赤膊 跳下圹

注：1.此歌尚有好多，但奇特前后大致相似，故予以省略。
2.此歌可用小数伴唱。

想妹歌

1=D 2/4

演唱：朱景树
记谱：钟同荣

一想妹，关新年 思想呀格 妹子 两三年，
二想、妹 关春社 有伸坳，
三想、妹 三月三 妹子呀格 约佢 来上山。
思想那个 妹子 心好苦 哇，喊佢嚼呷格 出摔几多 钱，
喊佢卸子格（上坐上来下去下）
哥哥呀格 山上 等要到，钱摔三夜格 岸两 歹

哎呀心肝 妹，拌拌 两人格 来 团 圆。
流离 衣若格 冇 额 家。
正正 等到格 日 落 山。

想郎回家乡

1=E 2/4

演唱：聂光荃
记谱：钟同荣

嫂嫂 问佢 饭吃 样般 做，想佢 哥 细
菜不 样般 洗，
切，
煮，
妹子 嫂子 呐，锅 中 煮 汞 就呀 中 菜，
总想 佢郎 转呀 家 乡。

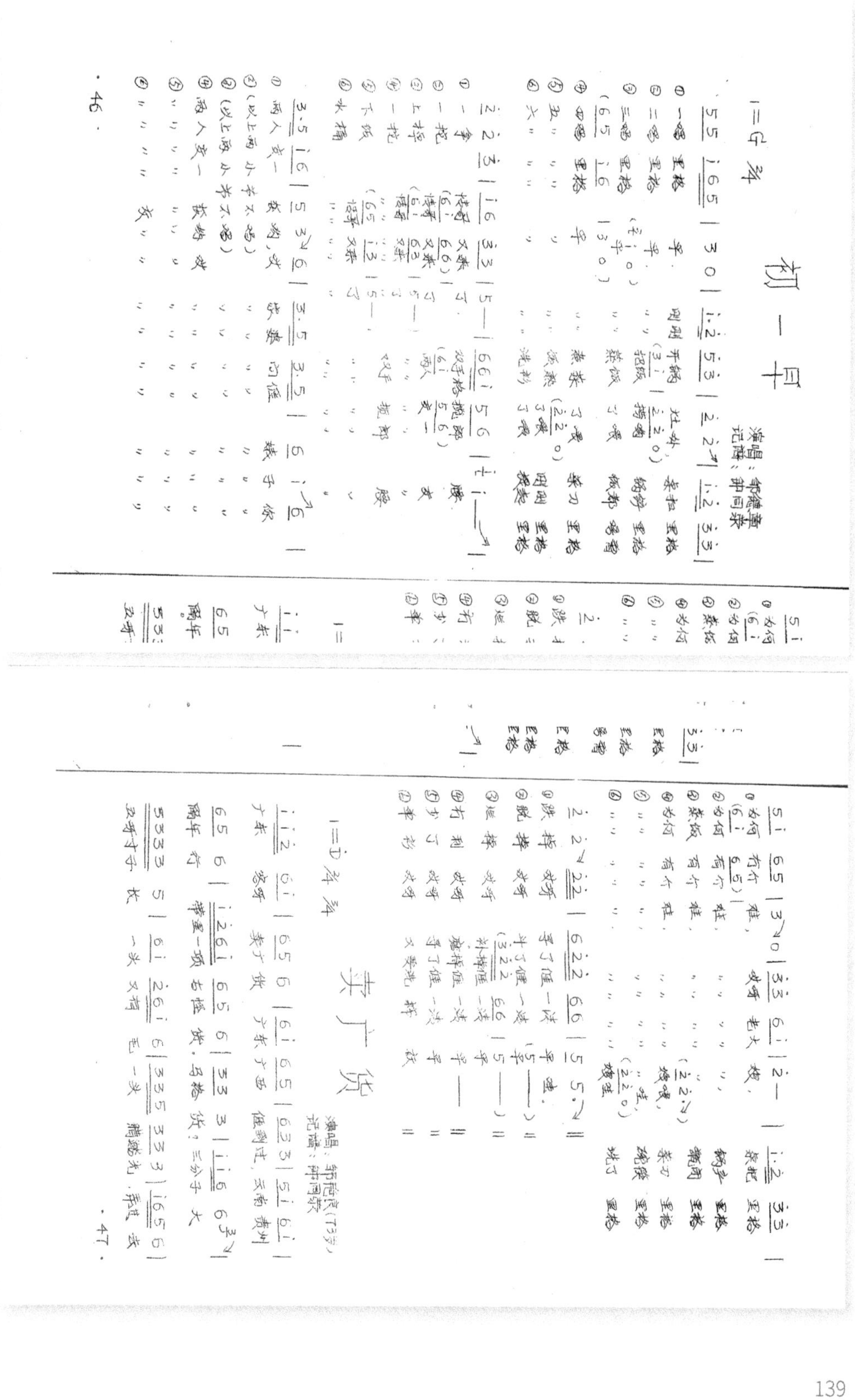

初一早

1=G 2/4

演唱：郜德章
记谱：郜同荣

· 46 ·

卖广货

1=D 2/4 3/4

演唱：郜尨良（73岁）
记谱：郜同荣

· 47 ·

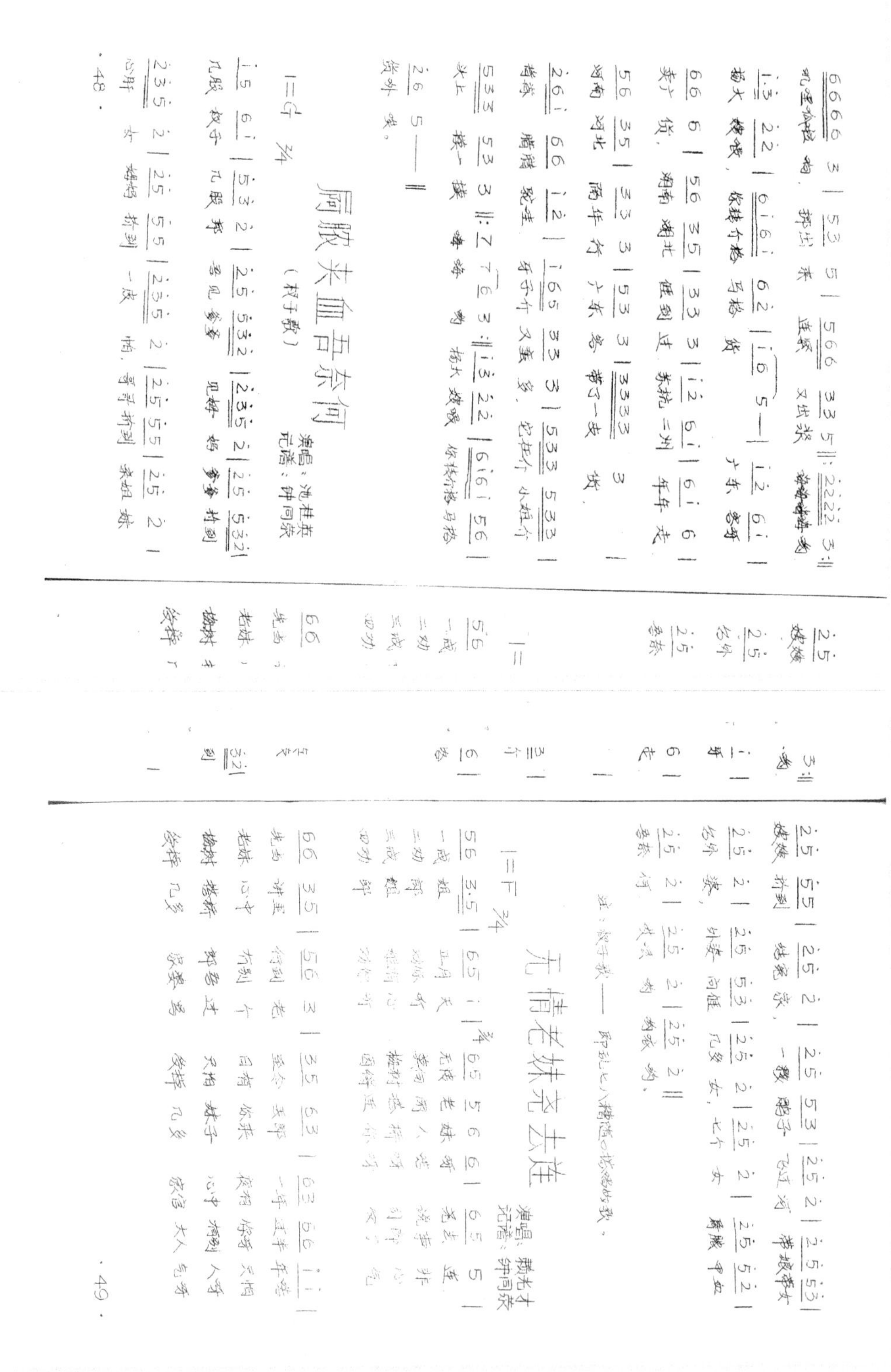

6666 3 | 53 5 | 566 33 5 ‖: 2222 3 :‖
巩哩喻啦 哟， 挪出 来 连紧 又出浆 嗨嗨嗨嗨 哟

1.3 22 | 6161 62 | 16 5 — | 12 61 |
扬大 嫂哦， 你转介格 马格 货 广东 客呀

66 6 | 56 35 | 33 3 | 12 61 | 61 6 |
卖广 货， 湖南 湖北 佢到 过 苏杭 二州 年年 走

56 35 | 33 3 | 53 3 | 3333 3 |
河南 河北 隔年 行 广东 客 带了一支 货，

261 66 12 | 165 33 3 | 533 533 |
背篼 腊腊 驼哇 牙子介 又重 多， 它在介 小姐介

533 53 3 ‖: 7 76 3 :‖ 13 22 | 6161 56 |
头上 摸一 摸 嗨嗨 哟 杨大 嫂哦 你转介格 马格

26 5 — ‖
货外 唉。

屙胺夹血吾奈何

（杈子歌）

演唱：池桂英
记谱：钟同荣

1=G 3/4

15 61 | 53 2 | 25 532 | 235 2 | 25 532 |
几股 杈子 几股 邦 吾见 爹爹 见姆 妈 爹爹 折到

235 2 | 25 55 | 235 2 | 25 55 | 25 2 |
心肝 女 姆妈 折到 一皮 怕， 哥哥 折到 亲姐 妹

25 55 | 25 2 | 25 53 | 25 2 | 25 53 |
嫂嫂 折到 姑宪 家， 一栽 鸭子 飞过 河 带娘带女

25 2 | 25 53 | 25 2 | 25 2 | 25 52 |
分外 婆， 外婆 问佢 几多 女， 七个 女 屙胺 甲血

25 2 | 25 2 | 25 2 ‖
吾奈 何 哎哎 哟 哟依 哟。

注：杈子歌—— 即乱七八糟随口搭唱的歌。

无情老妹尧去连

演唱：赖光才
记谱：钟同荣

1=F 2/4

56 3.5 | 65 1 | 3/4 65 5 6 6 | 65 5 |
一劝 姐 正月 天 无情 老 妹 呀 尧去 连
二劝 郎 劝你 听 莫问 闲 人 话 说事 非
三劝 姐 姐有 心 梅树 搭 桥 呀 引郎 心
四劝 郎 劝你 听 因得 连 你 呀 受了 气

66 35 | 56 3 | 35 63 | 63 66 11 |
先当 讲到 行到 老 至今 丢郎 一年 过半 年哩
老妹 心中 有别 个 自有 你来 夜相 惊呀 只怕
梅树 搭桥 郎吾 过 只怕 妹子 心中 有别 人呀
受抨 几多 家婆 骂 受抨 几多 家信 大人 气呀

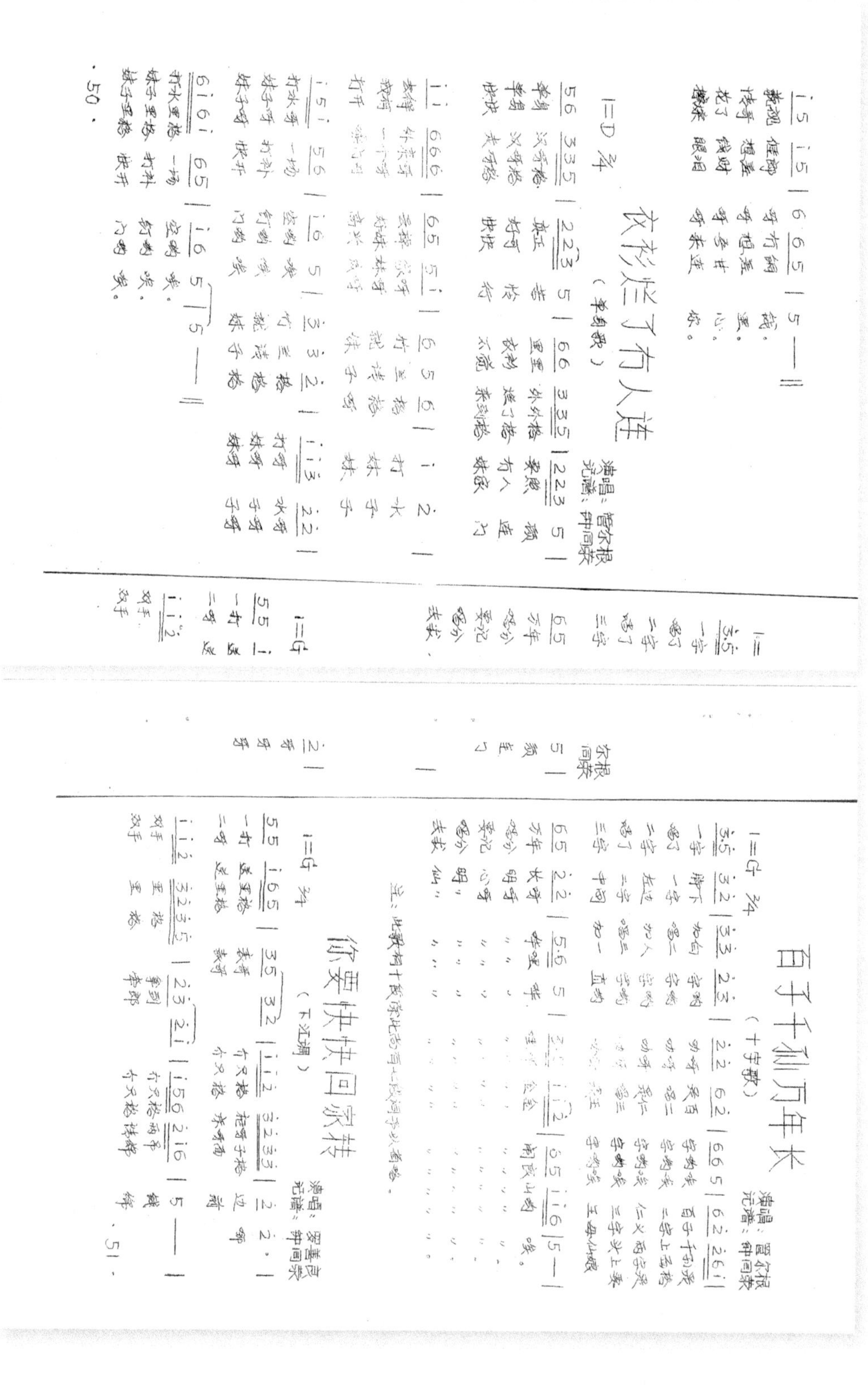

i5 i5 | 6 65 | 5 — ‖
敢视 侄郎 呀有铜 钱。
传哥 想丢 呀想丢 里。
花了 钱财 呀吾甘 心。
擦球 眼泪 呀来连 你。

衣衫烂了有人连

1=D 2/4　（单身歌）

演唱：管尔根
记谱：钟同荣

56 335 | 223 5 | 66 335 | 223 5 |
单身 汉呀格 真正 苦 里里 外外格 要照 顾
单身 汉呀格 好可 怜 衣衫 烂了格 有人 连
快快 走呀格 快快 行 不觉 来到格 妹家 门

i i 666 | 65 5i | 6 5 6 | i 2 |
去得 外家呀 去掉 家呀 竹 兰 格 打 水
我有 一个呀 好妹 妹呀 就 诗 格 妹 子
打开 嗦门呀 高兴 成呀 妹 子 呀 妹 子

i5i 56 | i6 5 | 3 3 2 | ii3 22 |
打水呀 一场 空哟 唉 竹 兰 格 打呀 水呀
妹子呀 打补 钉哟 唉 就 诗 格 妹呀 子呀
妹子呀 快开 门哟 唉 妹 子 格 妹呀 子呀

6i6i 65 | i6 5 | 5 — ‖
打水里格 一场 空哟 唉。
妹子里格 打补 钉哟 唉。
妹子里格 快开 门哟 唉。

百子千孙万年长

1=G 3/4　（十字歌）

演唱：管尔根
记谱：钟同荣

3·5 32 | 33 23 | 22 62 | 665 | 62 26i |
一字 脚下 加白 字哟 叻呀 是百 字哟唉 百子千孙是
唱了 一字 唱二 字哟 叻呀 唱二 字哟唉 二字上面格
二字 左边 加人 字哟 叻呀 是仁 字哟唉 仁义两字是
唱了 二字 唱三 字哟 叻呀 唱三 字哟唉 三字头上要
三字 中间 加一 直哟 叻呀 是王 字哟唉 王母仙娘

65 22 | 5·6 5 | 3·3 ii2 | 65 ii6 | 5 — |
万年 长呀 哗哩 哗 哩哗 金金 闹喧山哟 唉。
唱分 明呀 〃 〃 〃 〃 〃 〃 〃 〃 〃 〃。
要记 心呀 〃 〃 〃 〃 〃 〃 〃 〃 〃 〃。
唱分 明〃 〃 〃 〃 〃 〃 〃 〃 〃 〃 〃。
去装 仙〃 〃 〃 〃 〃 〃 〃 〃 〃 〃 〃。

注：此歌词十段，除此而有七段词予以省略。

你要快快回家转

1=G 2/4　（下江调）

演唱：罗善良
记谱：钟同荣

55 i65 | 35 32 | ii2 3233 | 2 2· |
一打 送里格 表哥 个只格 花呀子格 边 哪
二呀 送里格 表哥 个只格 来呀面 前

ii2 3235 | 23 2i | i56 2i6 | 5 — |
双手 里 格 拿到 个只格两吊 钱
双手 里 格 拿郎 个只格铜钱

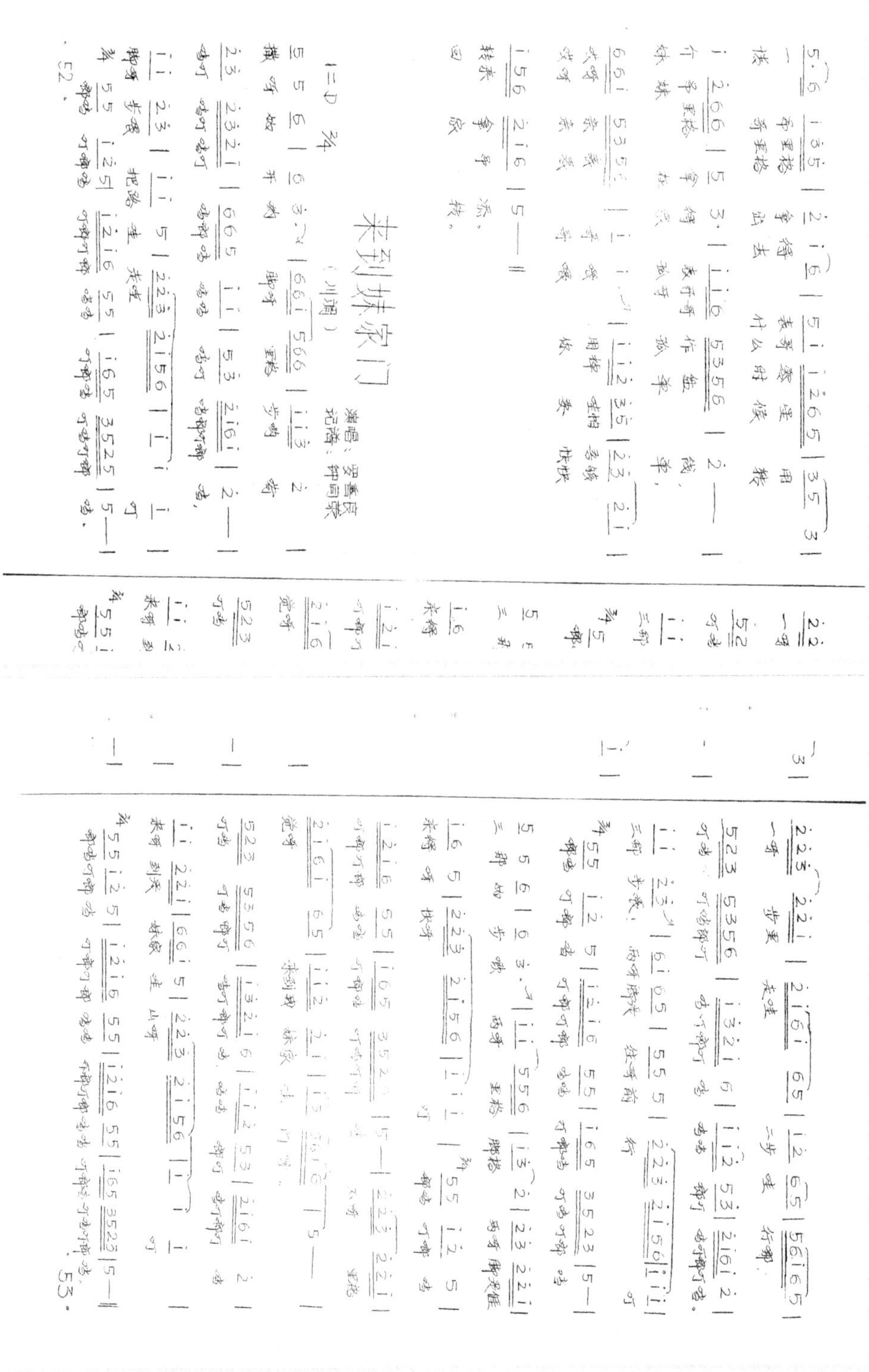

一 吊里格 拿得 表哥零星 用
愀 哥里格 出去 什么时候 转
个吊里格 拿得 表哥哥作盘 钱，
妹妹 在家 孤守 孤单 单，
哎呀 亲表 哥喂 用锌 里怕 吾够
哎呀 亲表 哥喂 你 要 快快
转来 拿吊 添。
回 家 转。

来到妹家门

（川调）

演唱：罗善良
记谱：钟同荣

1=D 2/4

撒呀 妙 开 哟 脚呀 里格 步哟 踏
哟可 哟可哟可 哟啷哟 哟哟 哟可 哟啷可啷 哟，
脚呀 步喂 把路 生 走哇 可
啷哟 可啷哟 可啷可啷 哟哟 可啷哟 可哟可啷 哟。

一呀 步里 走哇 二步 哇 行啷，
可哟 可哟啷可 哟可啷可 哟 哟哟 啷可 哟可啷可哟。
三啷 步哦，两呀脚呀 往呀前 行 可
啷哟 可啷 哟 可啷可啷 哟哟 可啷哟 可哟可啷 哟
三 啷 妙 步 哦 两呀 里格 脚格 两呀 脚畀
亲得 呀 快呀 可 啷哟 可啷 哟
可啷可啷 哟哟 可啷哟 可哟可啷 哟 里格
觉呀 来到我 妹家 门呀。
可哟 可哟啷可 哟可啷可哟 哟哟 啷可 哟可啷可 哟
来呀 到哎 妹家 生 山呀 可
啷哟可啷 哟 可啷可啷 哟哟 可啷可啷哟哟 可啷哟可哟可啷 哟。

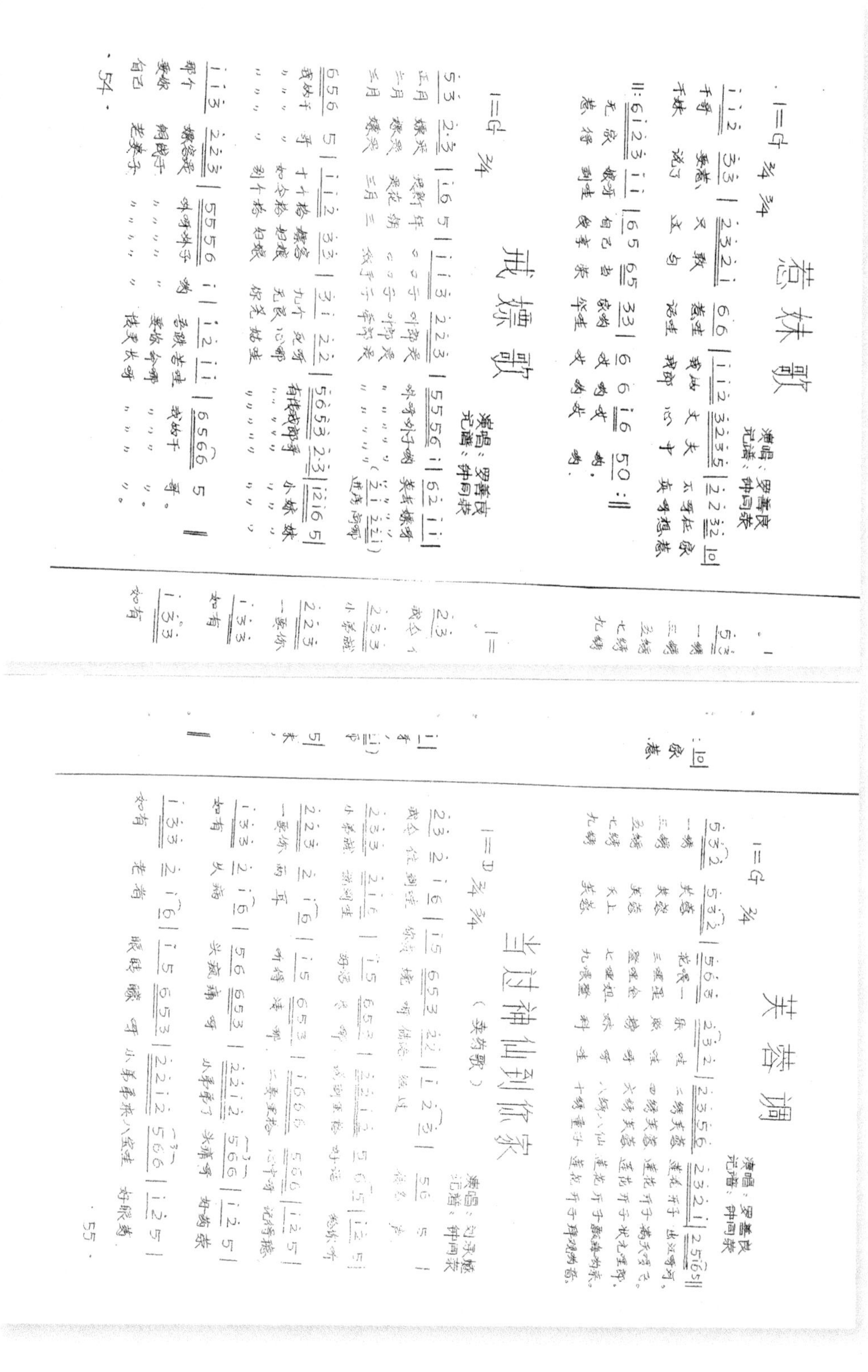

惹妹歌

1=G 3/4 3/4

演唱：罗善良
记谱：钟同荣

戒嫖歌

1=G 3/4

演唱：罗善良
记谱：钟同荣

· 54 ·

芙蓉调

1=G 3/4

演唱：罗善良
记谱：钟同荣

当过神仙到你家

（卖药歌）

1=D 2/4 3/4

演唱：刘承矮
记谱：钟同荣

· 55 ·

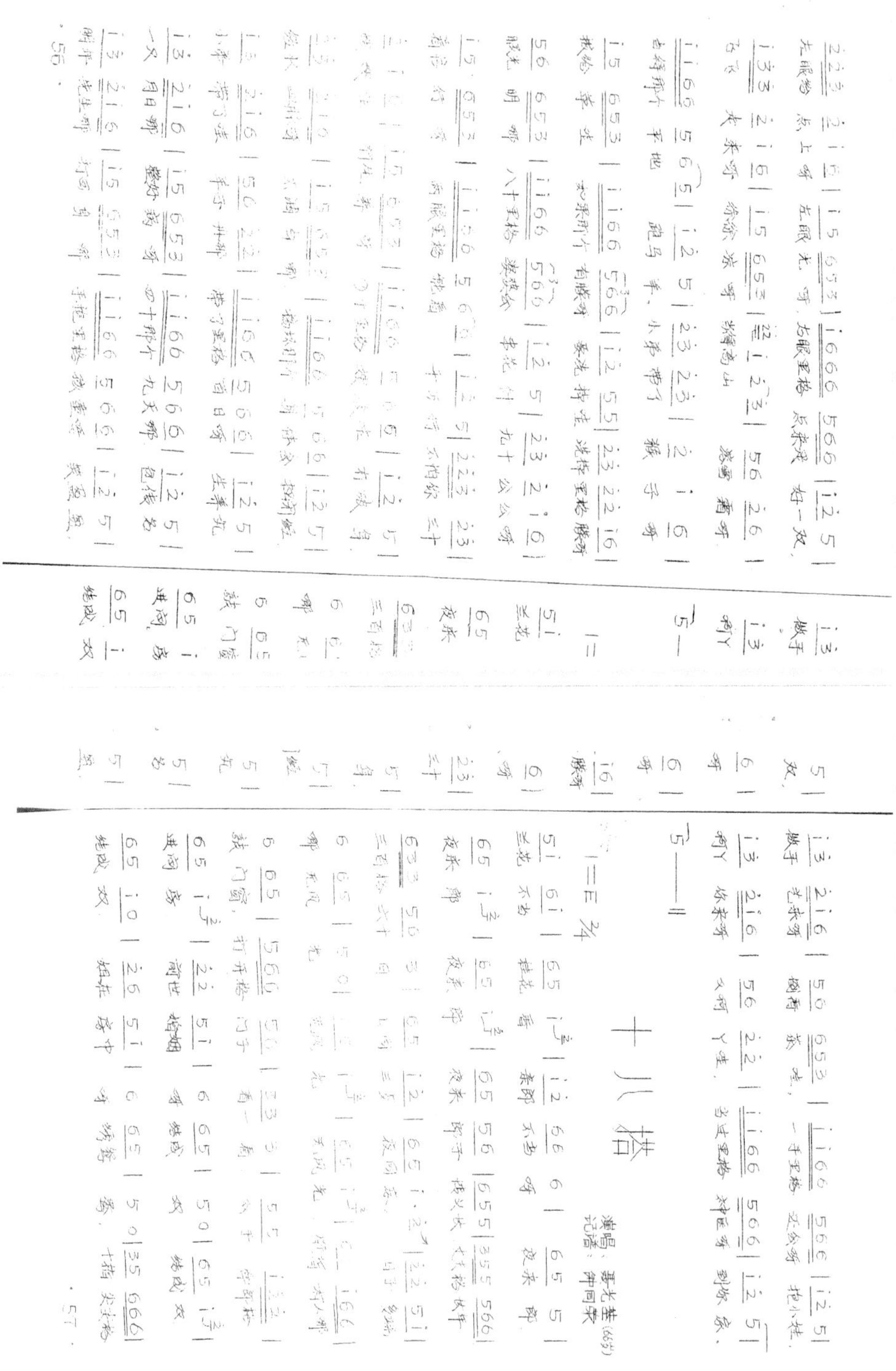

223 2 i 6 | i 5 653 | i666 566 | i2 5 |
左眼给 点上 呀 左眼光 呀 右眼里格 点来采 好一双，

i33 2 i 6 | i5 653 | 22 i 23 | 56 26 |
飞飞 走来呀 徐徐 宗 呀 嵴嶂高山 着呀

ii66 565 | i2 5 | 23 23 | 2 i 6 |
古得那个 平地 跑马 羊，小弟带了 猴 子 呀

i5 653 | ii66 566 | i2 55 | 23 22 i6 |
抵给 第 生 如果那个 有朕呀 要洗 搒 生 洗搒里格 朕呀

56 653 | ii66 566 | i2 5 | 23 2 i 6 |
朕光 明 哪 八十里格 婆婆会 串花 付 九十 公 公呀

i5 653 | ii56 56i | i2 5 | 223 23 |
着总 付 呀 两眼里格 眺着 十 不怕你 三十

· 56 ·

i3 2i6 | 56 653 | ii66 566 | i2 5 |
做手 艺来呀 倒荷 茶 哇， 一手里格 还会呀 抱小娃，

i3 2i6 | 56 22 | ii66 566 | i2 5 |
呵Y 你来呀 又呵 Y生， 当过里格 神匠呀 到你 家。

5 —— ‖

十八搭

演唱：聂光莹（66岁）
记谱：钟同荣

1=E 2/4

5i 6i | 65 i3 | i2 56 6 | 65 5 |
兰花 不当 桂花 香 亲郎 不当 呀 夜来 郎

65 i3 | 65 i3 | 65 56 | 655 | 355 566 |
夜来 郎 夜来 郎 夜来 郎子

· 57 ·

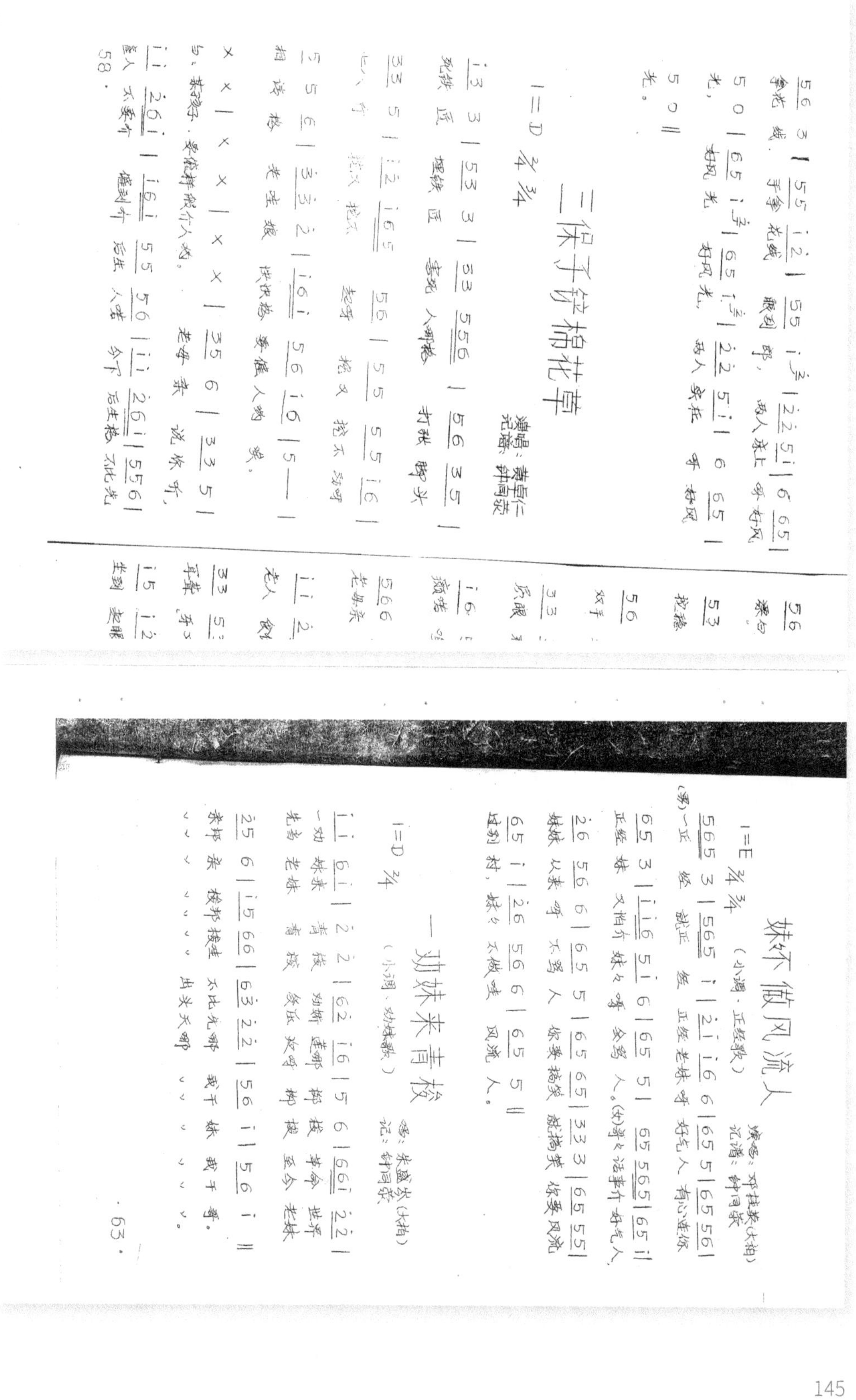

56 3 | 55 1̇2̇ | 55 1̇ 2̇ | 2̇2̇ 51̇ | 6 65 |
拿花 线， 手拿 花线 眼到 郎， 两人 床上 呀 好风

5 0 | 65 1̇ 2̇ | 65 1̇ 2̇ | 2̇2̇ 51̇ | 6 65 |
光， 好风 光 好风光， 两人 实在 呀 好风

5 0 ||
光。

三保子铲棉花草

1＝D 2/4 3/4

演唱：黄卓仁
记谱：钟同荣

1̇3 3 | 53 3 | 53 556 | 56 35 |
死铁 匠 埋铁 匠 害死 人哪格 打拱 脚头

33 5 | 1̇2 1̇65 | 56 | 55 55 1̇6 |
七八 个 挖又 挖不 起呀 挖又 挖不 动呀

5 5 6 | 3 3 2 | 1̇61̇ 56 1̇6 | 5 — |
扫 诗 格 老 生 娘 快快格 要催 人哟 哎。

x x | x x | x x | 35 6 | 33 5 |
与：某孩子，要依样般个人哟， 老母 亲 说 你 听，

1̇1̇ 26 1̇ | 1̇61̇ 55 56 | 1̇1̇ 261̇ | 556 |
盖人 不要个 催到个 后生 人嗒 今下 后生格 不比光

58 ·

56 …
嘿句

53 …
挖稳

56 …
双手

33 …
尻眼

1̇6 …
癫嗒

566
老母亲

1̇1̇ 2̇…
老人 食…

33 5…
耳聋 牙…

1̇5 1̇2…
生到 起眼

妹㸦做风流人

1＝E 2/4 3/4　（小调·正经歌）

演唱：邓桂英（大柏）
记谱：钟同荣

565 3 | 565 1̇ | 2̇1̇ 1̇6 6 | 65 5 | 65 56 |
（男）一正 经 就正 经 正经 老妹 呀 好乞人 有心连你

65 3 | 1̇1̇6 51̇ 6 | 65 5 | 65 565 | 65 1̇ |
正经 妹 又怕介 妹々 呀 会骂 人。（女）哥々 话事介 好乞人，

26 56 6 | 65 5 | 65 65 | 33 3 | 65 55 |
妹妹 从来 呀 不骂 人 你要 搞笑 就搞笑 你要 风流

65 1̇ | 26 56 6 | 65 5 ||
过别 村， 妹々 不做 哇 风流 人。

一劝妹来青梭

1＝D 2/4　（小调、劝妹歌）

唱：朱盛尧（大柏）
记：钟同荣

1̇1̇ 61̇ | 2 2 | 62 1̇6 | 5 6 | 661̇ 2̇2̇ |
一劝 妹来 青 梭 劝娇 莲哪 柳 梭 革命 世界
先当 老妹 青 梭 参加 农呀 柳 梭 至今 老妹

25 6 | 1̇5 66 | 63 2̇2̇ | 56 1̇ | 56 1̇ ||
亲邦 亲 梭邦 梭哇 不比 先哪 我干 妹 我 干 哥。
〃〃 〃 〃〃〃〃 出头 天哪 〃〃 〃 〃 〃 〃。

· 63 ·

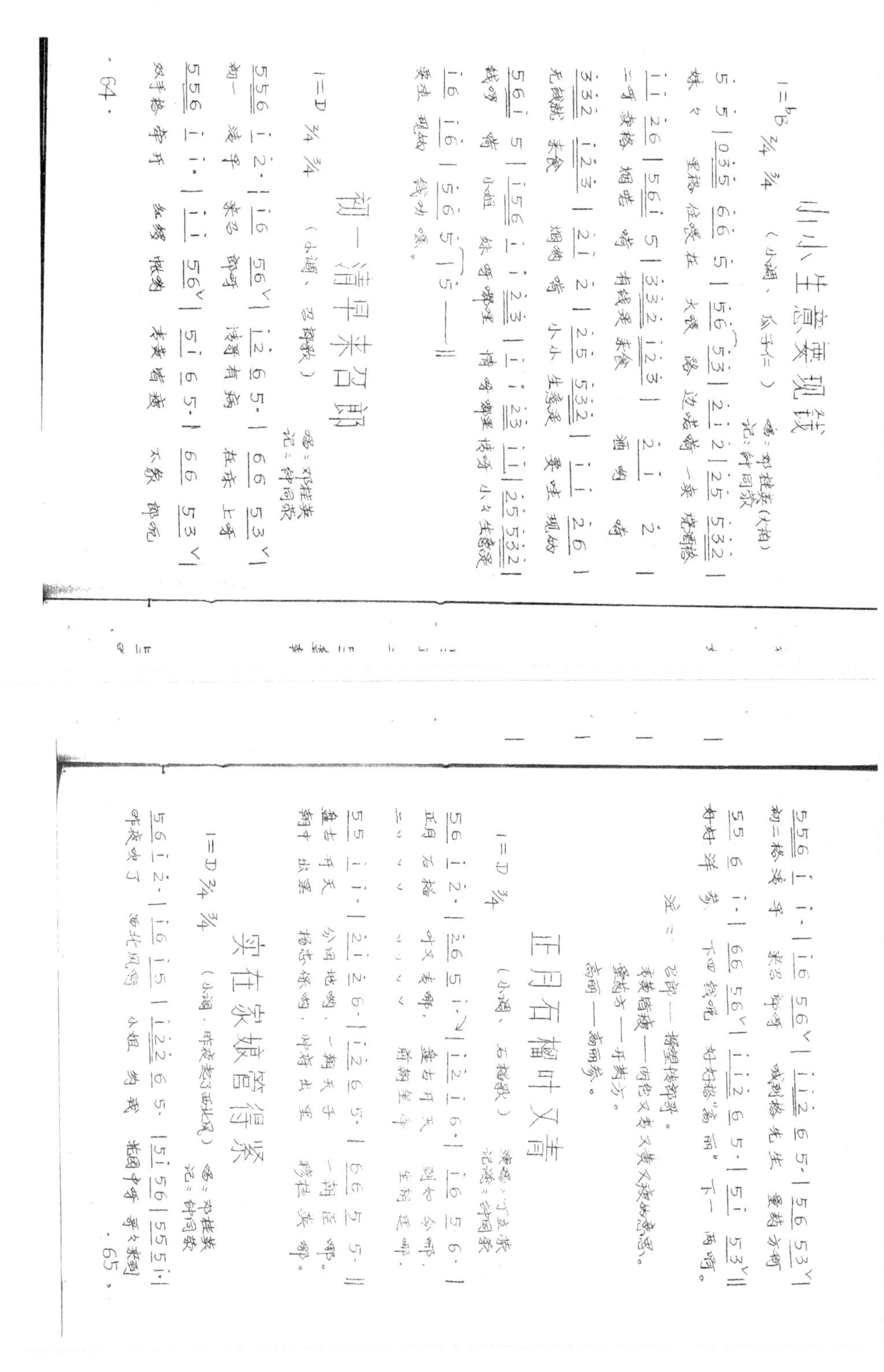

小小生意要现钱

1=bB 2/4 3/4 （小调、瓜子仁） 唱：邓桂英（大柏）
记：钟同荣

5 5 | 0 3 5 6 6 5 | 5 6 5 3 | 2 1 2 | 2 5 5 3 2 |
妹 々 里格 住喂 在 大喂 路 边啰 嗬 一卖 烧酒格

1 1 2 6 | 5 6 1 5 | 3 3 2 1 2 3 | 2 1 2 |
二呀 卖格 烟啰 嗬 有钱是 来食 酒 哟 嗬

3 3 2 1 2 3 | 2 1 2 | 2 5 5 3 2 | 1 1 2 6 |
无钱就 来食 烟哟 嗬 小小 生意是 要哇 现的

5 6 1 5 | 1 5 6 1 1 2 3 | 1 1 2 3 1 1 | 2 5 5 3 2 |
钱呀 嗬 小姐 妹 呀 哪哩 情 呀 哪哩 情呀 小々 生意是

1 6 1 6 | 5 6 5 | 5 —— ||
要生 现的 钱 咖 嘿。

· 64 ·

初一清早来召郎

1=D 2/4 3/4 （小调、召郎歌） 唱：邓桂英
记：钟同荣

5 5 6 1 2 · | 1 6 5 6ᵛ | 1 2 6 5 · | 6 6 5 3ᵛ |
初一 清 早 来召 郎呀 情哥 有 病 在床 上呀

5 5 6 1 1 · | 1 1 5 6ᵛ | 5 1 6 5 · | 6 6 5 3ᵛ |
双手格 牵 开 红绣 帐哟 青黄 面 瘦 不象 郎呢

5 5 6 1 1 · | 1 6 5 6ᵛ | 1 1 2 6 5 · | 5 6 5 3ᵛ |
初二格 清 早 来召 郎呀 喊到格 先 生 量药 方呵

5 5 6 1 · | 6 6 5 6ᵛ | 1 1 2 6 5 · | 5 1 5 3ᵛ ||
好好 洋 参 下四 钱呢 好好格"高 丽" 下一 两呵。

注：召郎——探望情郎哥。
青黄面瘦——肉色又青又黄又瘦的意思。
量药方——开药方。
高丽——高丽参。

正月石榴叶又青

1=D 3/4 （小调、石榴歌） 演唱：丁立荣
记谱：钟同荣

5 6 1 2 · | 2 6 5 1 · | 1 2 1 6 · | 1 6 5 6 · |
正月 石 榴 叶又 青哪， 盘古 开 天 到如 今哪。
二 〃 〃 〃 〃 〃 〃 〃 前朝 皇 帝 生朝 廷哪。

5 5 1 1 · | 2 1 2 6 · | 1 2 6 5 · | 6 6 5 5 · ||
盘古 开 天 分田 地哟， 一朝 天 子 一朝 臣 哪。
朝中 出 異 杨忠 保哟， 冲存 出 里 穆桂 英 哪。

· 65 ·

实在家娘管得紧

1=D 2/4 3/4 （小调、昨夜起了西北风） 唱：邓桂英
记：钟同荣

5 6 1 2 · | 1 6 1 5 | 1 2 2 6 5 · | 5 1 5 6 | 5 5 5 1 · |
昨夜 吹了 西北 风哟 小姐 约 我 花园中呀 哥々 来到

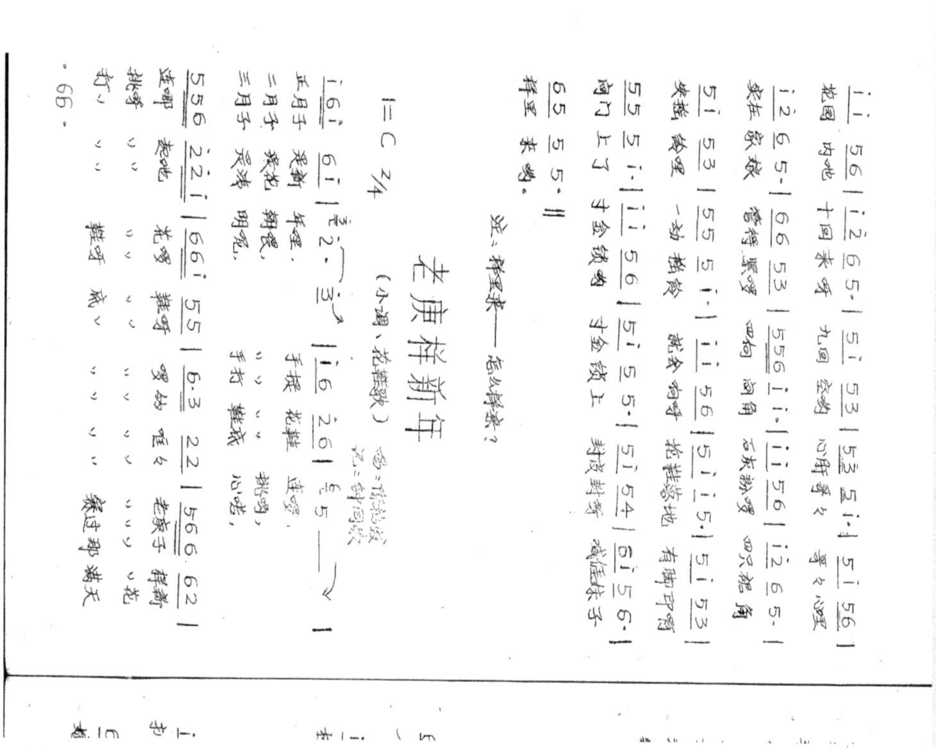

i i 56 | i 2 6 5· | 5 i 53 | 53 5 i· | 5 i 56 |
花园 内吔 十回 来呀 九回 空哟 心肝哥々 哥々心哩

i 2 6 5· | 66 53 | 556 i i· | i i 56 | i 2 6 5· |
实在 家娘 管得 紧啰 四向 间角 石灰粉啰 四只裙 角

5 i 53 | 55 5 i· | i i 56 | 5 i i 5· | 5 i 53 |
类摇 铃哩 一动 摇铃 就会 响呀 花鞋落地 有脚印哨

55 5 i· | i i 56 | 5 i 5 5· | 5 i 54 | 6 i 5 6· |
向门 上了 寸金 锁哟 寸金 锁上 封皮 封好 戒怪 妹子

65 5 5· ‖
样里 来哟。

注：样里来——怎么样来？

老庚样新年

1=C 2/4　（小调、花鞋歌）　唱：陈拾发　记：钟同荣

i 6 i 6 i | 2· 3 | i 6 2 6 | 5 —— |
正月子 是新 年哩， 手提 花鞋 连啰，
二月子 桃花 翻喂， 〃〃 〃〃 挑哟，
三月子 是清 明呢， 手打 鞋底 心嗒，

556 22 i | 66 i 55 | 6·3 22 | 566 62 |
连哪 起吔 花啰 鞋呀 啰呦 哐々 老庚子 样新
挑呀 〃〃 〃〃 〃〃 〃〃 〃〃 〃〃 〃花
打〃 〃〃 鞋呀 底〃 〃〃 〃〃 赛过那满天

5 5 55 | 5 i 22 | 6 i 55 | 6·3 22 |
年 喏 哪呦 咪吹 梭哟 呀嘀 哎呀 啰呦 哐々
翔 哟 〃〃 〃〃 〃〃 〃〃 〃〃 〃〃 〃〃
星 哟 〃〃 〃〃 〃〃 〃〃 〃〃 〃〃 〃〃

566 62 | 5 5· ‖
老庚子 样新 年 哩。
老庚子 样花 翔 喂。
赛过那 满天 星 喏。

注：此歌有12段，每月一段，这里记将一至三月记入谱内。

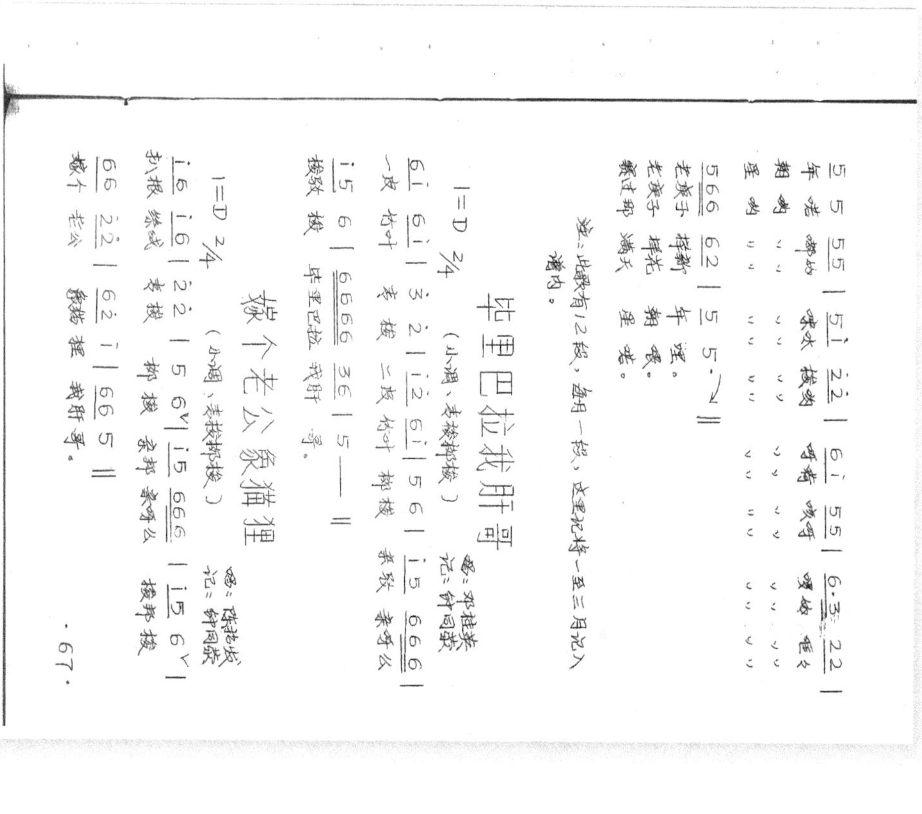

毕里巴拉我肝哥

1=D 2/4　（小调、专梭椰梭）　唱：邓桂英　记：钟同荣

6 i 6 i | 3 2 | i 2 6 i | 5 6 | i 5 666 |
一皮 竹叶 专 梭 二皮 竹叶 椰 梭 来致 亲呀么

i 5 6 | 6666 36 | 5 —— ‖
梭致 梭 毕里巴拉 我肝 哥。

嫁个老公象猫狸

1=D 2/4　（小调、专梭椰梭）　唱：陈拾发　记：钟同荣

i 6 i 6 | 2 2 | 5 6 | i 5 666 | i 5 6 |
扒根 丝线 专 梭 椰 梭 亲邦 亲呀么 梭邦 梭

66 22 | 62 i | 66 5 ‖
嫁个 老公 象猫 狸 我肝 哥。

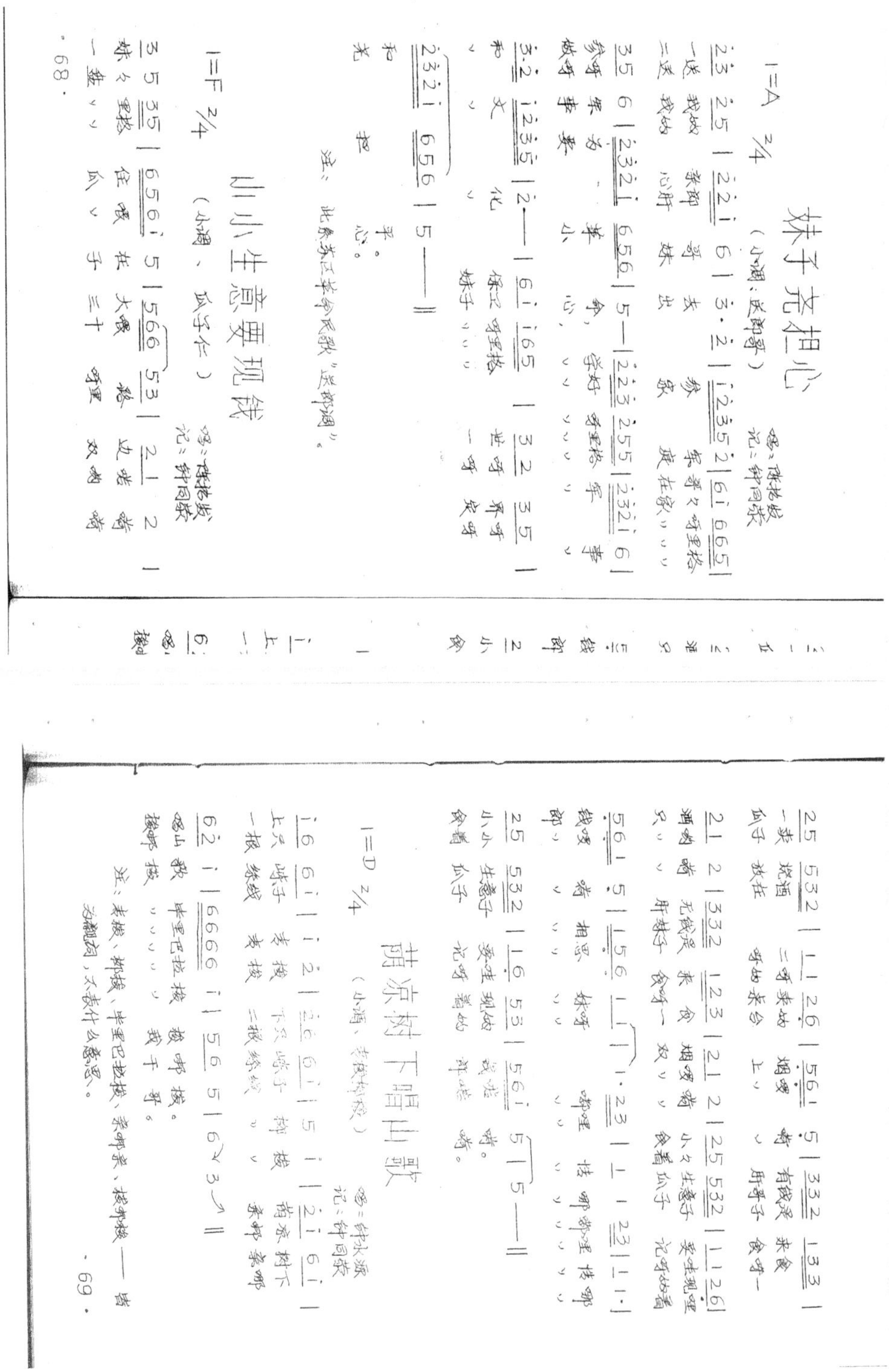

妹子莫担心

1=A 2/4　（小调：送郎哥）　唱：陈拾发　记：钟同荣

23 25 | 22i 6 | 3·2 | i235 2 | 6i 665 |
一送 我的 亲郎 哥 去 参 军哥々呀里格
二送 我的 心肝 妹 出 家 庭在家ソソソ

35 6 | 232i 656 | 5— | 223 255 | 232i 6 |
参呀 军 为 革 命， 学好 呀里格 军 事
做呀 事 要 小 心， ソソ ソソソ ソ ソ

3·2 i235 | 2— | 6i i65 | 32 35 |
和 文 化 保卫 呀里格 世呀 界呀
ソ ソ ソ 妹子ソソソ 一呀 定呀

232i 656 | 5— ||
和 平。
莫 担 心。

注：此系苏区革命民歌“送郎调”。

小小生意要现钱

1=F 2/4　（小调、瓜子仁）　唱：陈拾发　记：钟同荣

3 5 35 | 656i 5 | 566 53 | 21 2 |
妹々 里格 住 哦 在 大哦 路 边 哟 嗬
一盘ソソ 瓜ソ 子 三十 呀里 双 哟 嗬

25 532 | 11 26 | 561 5 | 332 133 |
一卖 烧酒 二呀 卖哟 烟 哦 嗬 有钱 的 来食
瓜子 放在 呀哟 桌台 上ソ ソ 厅哥子 食呀一

21 2 | 332 123 | 21 2 | 25 532 | 1126 |
酒哟 嗬 无钱 的 来 食 烟 哦 嗬 小々 生意子 要哇 现哩
只ソ ソ 厅妹子 食呀一 双ソ ソ 食着 瓜子 记呀 的着

561 5 | 156 11 | 1·23 | 1 | 23 | 11· |
钱哦 嗬 相思 妹呀 哪哩 情 哪 哪哩 情 哪
郎ソ ソ ソソ ソソ ソソ ソ ソソソ ソ ソ

25 532 | 16 53 | 56i 5 | 5— ||
小小 生意子 要哇 现的 钱 哦 嗬。
食着 瓜子 记呀 着的 郎 哦 嗬。

荫凉树下唱山歌

1=D 2/4　（小调、[illegible]）　唱：钟水源　记：钟同荣

i6 6i | i 2 | 26 6i | 5 i | 2i 6i |
上只 峡子 专 接 下只 峡子 柳 接 荫凉 树下
一根 丝线 专 接 二根 丝线 ソ ソ 亲哪 亲哪

62 i | 6666 i | 56 5 | 6 3 ||
唱山 歌 半里巴拉 接 接 哪 接。
接哪 接 ソソソソ ソ 我 干 哥。

注：专接、柳接、半里巴拉接、亲哪亲、接哪接——皆为衬词，不表什么意思。

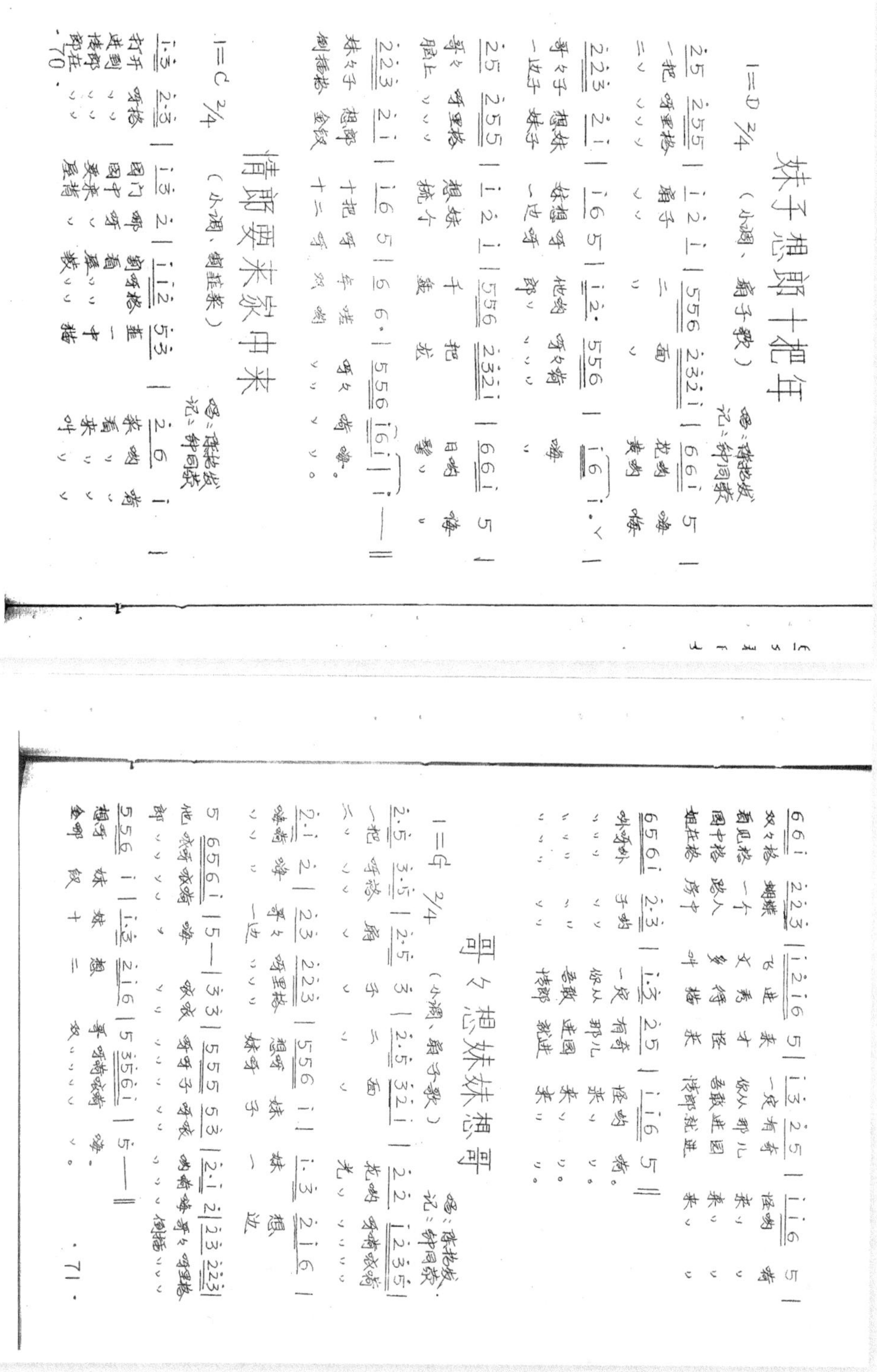

妹子想郎十把年

1=D 2/4　（小调、扇子歌）　唱：陈拾发　记：钟同荣

25 255 | 121 | 556 2321 | 661 5 |
一把 呀里格　扇子　二　面　花哟　嗨
二〃 〃〃〃　〃〃　〃　〃　黄哟　嗨

223 21 | 165 | 12· 556 | 16 1·Y |
哥々子 想妹　妹想呀　他哟 呀々嗬　嗨
一边子 妹子　一边呀　郎〃 〃〃〃　〃

25 255 | 121 | 556 2321 | 661 5 |
哥々 呀里格　想妹　千　把　日哟　嗨
脑上 〃〃〃　梳个　金　龙　髻〃　〃

223 21 | 165 | 6 6· | 556 161 | 1 — ||
妹々子 想郎　十把呀　年 嗟　呀々　嗬　嗨。
倒插格 金钗　十二呀　双 哟　〃〃　〃　〃。

情郎要来家中来

1=C 2/4　（小调、剪韭菜）　唱：陈拾发　记：钟同荣

13 23 | 13 2 | 112 53 | 26 1 |
打开 呀格　园门 哪　割呀格 韭　菜 哟 嗬
进到 〃〃　园中 呀　看　一　看 〃 〃
情郎 〃〃　要来 〃　屋〃〃 中　来 〃 〃
郎在 〃〃　屋背 〃　装〃〃 猫　叫 〃 〃

· 70 ·

66i 223 | 1216 5 | 13 25 | 116 5 |
双々格 蝴蝶　飞 进 来　一定 有奇　怪哟 嗬
看见格 一个　文 秀 才　你从 那儿　来〃 〃
园中格 路人　多 得 怪　吾敢 进园　来〃 〃
姐在格 房中　叫 猫 来　情郎 就进　来〃 〃

6561 23 | 13 25 | 116 5 ||
咧呀咧 子哟　一定 有奇　怪哟 嗬。
〃〃〃 〃〃　你从 那儿　来〃 〃。
〃〃〃 〃〃　吾敢 进园　来〃 〃。
〃〃〃 〃〃　情郎 就进　来〃 〃。

哥々想妹妹想哥

1=G 2/4　（小调、扇子歌）　唱：陈拾发　记：钟同荣

25 35 | 25 3 | 25 321 | 22 1235 |
一把 呀格　扇　子　二　面　花哟 呀嗬咳嗬
二〃 〃〃　〃　〃　〃　〃　光〃 〃〃〃〃

21 2 | 23 223 | 556 1 | 13 216 |
嗨嗬 嗨　哥々 呀里格　想呀 妹　妹 想
〃〃 〃　一边 〃〃〃　妹呀 子　一 边

5 6561 | 5 — | 33 | 555 53 | 21 2 | 23 223 |
他 咳呀咳嗬　嗨　咳咳　呀呀子 呀咳　哟嗬 嗨　哥々 呀里格
郎 〃〃〃〃　〃　〃〃　〃〃〃 〃〃　〃〃 〃　倒插 〃〃〃

556 1 | 13 216 | 5 3561 | 5 — ||
想呀 妹　妹 想　哥 呀嗬咳嗬　嗨。
金哪 钗　十 二　双 〃〃〃〃　〃。

· 71 ·

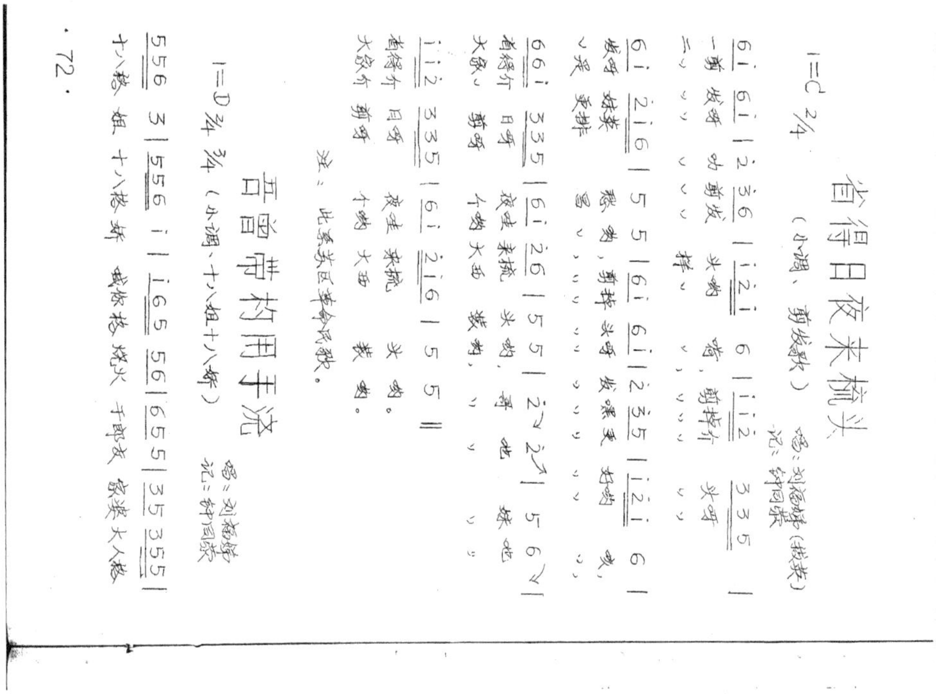

省得日夜来梳头

1=C 2/4

（小调、剪发歌）

唱：刘福娣（拔英）
记：钟同荣

6i 6i | 2 36 | i2i 6 | ii2 335 |
一剪 发呀 功剪发 头哟 嗬，剪掉介 头呀
二〃 〃〃 〃〃〃 样〃 〃，〃〃〃 〃〃

6i 2i6 | 5 5 | 6i 6i | 2 35 | i2i 6 |
发呀 妹英 愁哟，剪掉 头呀 发嘿更 好哟 哎，
〃采 更排 图〃，〃〃 〃〃 〃〃〃 〃〃 〃，

66i 335 | 6i 26 | 5 5 | 2 2 | 5 6 |
省得介 日呀 夜哇 来梳 头哟，哥 也 妹 也
大家〃 剪呀 个哟 大西 装哟，〃 〃 〃 〃

ii2 335 | 6i 2i6 | 5 5 ‖
省得介 日呀 夜哇 来梳 头 哟。
大家介 剪呀 个哟 大西 装 哟。

注：此系苏区革命民歌。

吾曾带村用手浇

1=D 2/4 3/4（小调、十八姐十八娇）

唱：刘福娣
记：钟同荣

556 3 | 556 i | i65 56 | 655 | 35 355 |
十八格 姐 十八格 娇 喊你格 烧火 干郎友 家婆大人格

· 72 ·

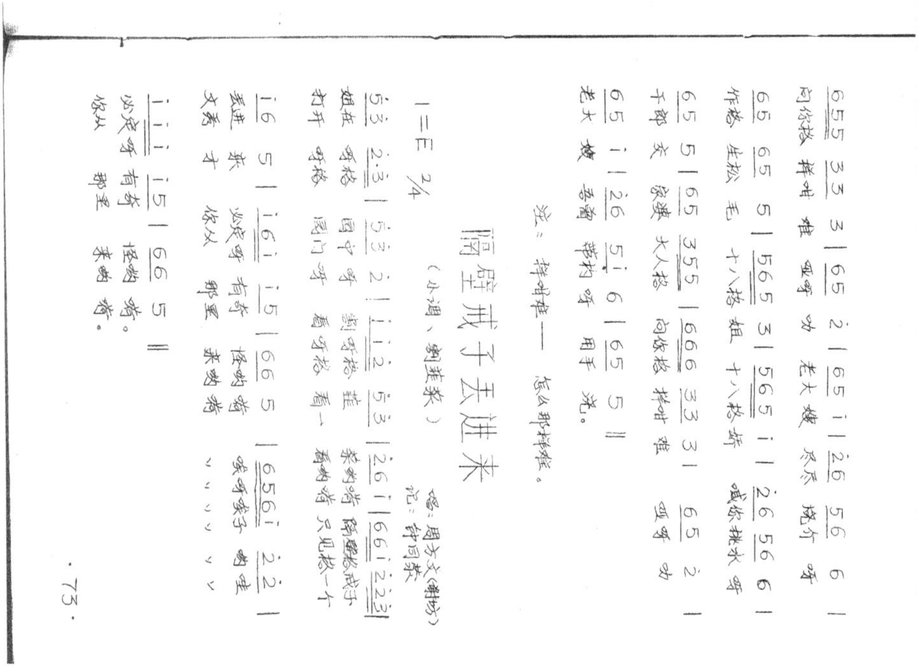

655 33 3 | 65 2 | 65 i | 26 56 6 |
问你格 样咁 难 哑呀 叻 老大 嫂 尽尽 烧介 呀

65 65 5 | 565 3 | 565 i | 26 56 6 |
作格 生松 毛 十八格 姐 十八格 娇 喊你 挑水 呀

65 5 | 65 355 | 666 33 3 | 65 2 |
干郎 友 家婆 大人格 问你格 样咁 难 哑呀 叻

65 i | 26 5i 6 | 65 5 ‖
老大 嫂 吾曾 带村 呀 用手 浇。

注：样咁难——怎么那样难。

隔壁戒子丢进来

1=E 2/4

（小调、剿莲菜）

唱：周方文（谢坊）
记：钟同荣

53 2·3 | 53 2 | ii2 53 | 26 i | 66i 223 |
姐在 呀格 园中 呀 剿呀格 莲 菜哟嗬 隔壁格戒子
打开 呀格 园门 呀 看呀格 看一 看哟嗬 只见格一个

i6 5 | i6i i5 | 66 5 | 656i 22 |
丢进 来 必定呀 有奇 怪哟 嗬 咲呀嗳子 哟哇
文秀 才 你从 那里 来哟 嗬 〃〃〃〃 〃〃

iii i5 | 66 5 ‖
必定呀 有奇 怪哟 嗬。
你从 那里 来哟 嗬。

· 73 ·

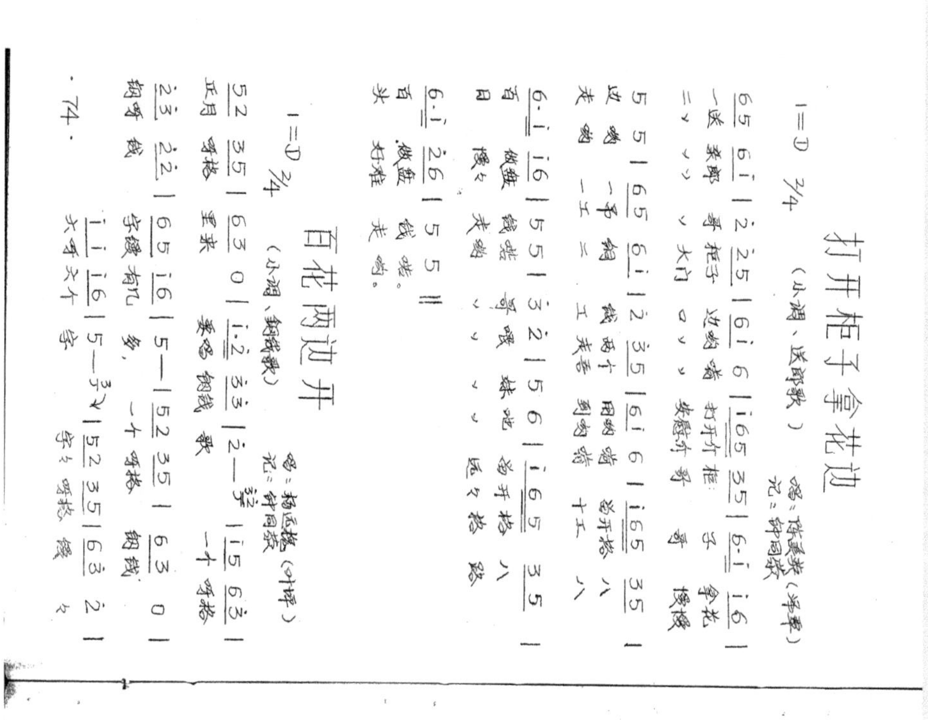

打开柜子拿花边

1=D 2/4　（小调、送郎歌）　唱：陈勇英（深岸）　记：钟同荣

65 6i | 2 25 | 6i 6 | i65 35 | 6·i i6 |
一送 亲郎 哥 柜子 边哟 啃 打开介 柜 子 拿花
二〃 〃〃 〃 大门 口〃 〃 安慰介 哥 哥 慢慢

5 5 | 65 6i | 2 35 | 6i 6 | i65 35 |
边 哟 一吊 铜 钱 两个 用哟 啃 当开格 八
走 哟 一工 二 工 夫吾 到哟 啃 十工 八

6·i i6 | 5 5 | 3 2 | 5 6 | i65 35 |
百 做盘 钱 啦 哥 喂 妹 吔 当 开 格 八
日 慢々 走 哟 〃 〃 〃 〃 远々 格 路

6·i 26 | 5 5 ||
百 做盘 钱 啦。
头 好难 走 哟。

百花两边开

1=D 2/4　（小调、铜钱歌）　唱：杨远格（叶坪）　记：钟同荣

52 35 | 63 0 | i·2 33 | 2— | i5 63 |
正月 呀格 里来 要唱 铜钱 歌 一个 呀格

23 22 | 65 i6 | 5— | 52 35 | 63 0 |
铜呀 钱 字镘 有几 多， 一个 呀格 铜钱

ii i6 | 5— | 52 35 | 63 2 |
六呀 六个 字 字々 呀格 镘 々

65 i6 | 5— | 33 65 | i— | 65 66 |
二边一样 多 十八 有情 妹 十八 有情

5— | 53 566 | 223 5 | 53 566 | 223 5 |
哥 心呀 心中格 想呀格 郎 心呀心中格 想呀格 妹

ii i3 | 2 3· | ii 656 | i i· | ii2 333 |
想妹 做什 么 喂 想妹 做老 婆喂 芙蓉 里格

23 2 | 65 i6 | 5— | 33 66 | i i 2 |
开花 连我 情郎 哥 烂衫 得来 丢 吔，

35 i6 | 5 5· | 3 6 | 335 i65 | 33 i6 i |
妹子 蛮难 舍 哟 喂，打！ 连妹 有介 久哇 千哥々

i 335 | 23 53 | i6 i | i 66i | 556 i6 |
喂 哥哥呀 想妹 妹呀 千妹子 喂 妹子格 想哥 哥呀

i6 i6 | i6 i6 | 2 23 | 556 | 2 2 3 |
想呀 想呀 想呀 想呀 想、呀 想、呀 想、呢

65 i6 | 5— | 65 0 | 35 0 | 355 i6i |
想佴 有情 哥 唉哟 呀哟 呀子 哦嗬

2·3 | 556 232i | 6—
嗨 百花 两边 开。

注：字镘——古铜钱分两面，一面是四个字，一面是二条龙，龙叫镘。

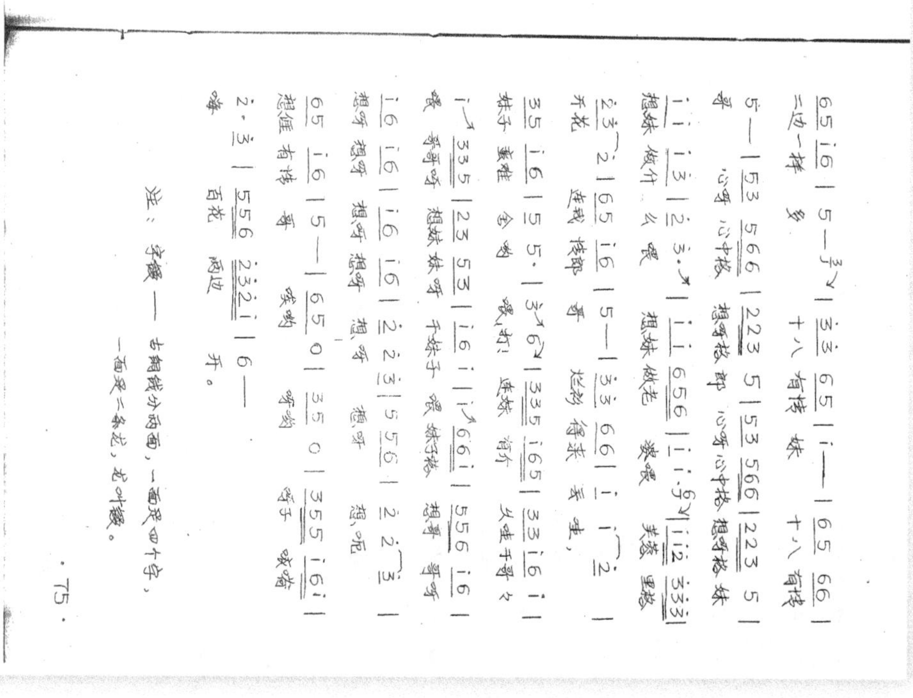

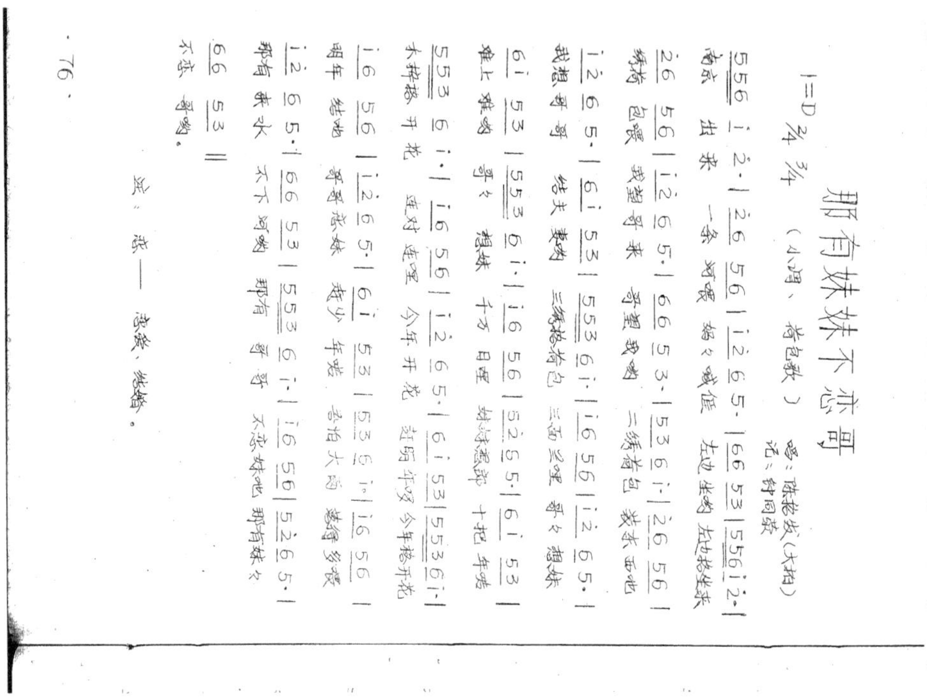

那有妹妹不恋哥

1=D 2/4 3/4 （小调、荷包歌）

唱：陈拾发（大拍）
记：钟同荥

556 1̇ 2̇· | 2̇6 56 | 1̇2̇ 6 5· | 66 53 | 556 1̇ 2̇· |
南京 出 来 一条 河喂 妈々 喊侄 左边 坐哟 左边拾坐来

2̇6 56 | 1̇2̇ 6 5· | 66 5 3· | 53 6 1̇· | 2̇6 56 |
绣荷 包喂 我望 哥 来 哥望 我哟 二绣荷 包 装东 西吧

1̇2̇ 6 5· | 6 1̇ 53 | 553 6 1̇· | 1̇6 56 | 1̇2̇ 6 5· |
我想 哥 哥 结夫 妻哟 三绣拾荷包 三面 兰哩 哥々 想妹

6 1̇ 53 | 553 6 1̇· | 1̇6 56 | 52̇5 5· | 6 1̇ 53 |
难上 难哟 哥々 想妹 千万 日哩 妹々想郎 十把 年哟

553 6 1̇· | 1̇6 56 | 1̇2̇ 6 5· | 6 1̇ 53 | 553 6 1̇· |
木梓拾 开 花 连对 连哩 今年 开 花 赶丙 年呀 今年拾开花

1̇6 56 | 1̇2̇ 6 5· | 6 1̇ 53 | 53 5 1̇· | 1̇6 56 |
明年 结吔 哥哥 恋妹 走少 年呫 吾怕 大肉 落得 多喂

1̇2̇ 6 5· | 66 53 | 553 6 1̇· | 1̇6 56 | 52̇6 5· |
那有 来 水 不下 河哟 那有 哥 哥 不恋 妹吧 那有妹々

66 53 ‖
不恋 哥哟。

注：恋—— 恋爱、结婚。

· 76 ·

正 月 离

1=D 2/4 （小调、离歌）

唱：陈拾发
记：钟同荥

1̇3̇ 2̇ | 2̇6 1̇ | 2̇1̇2̇ 65 | 3/4 65 65 5 | 5·6 1̇6 |
正月 离 离掉 里 家家 屋屋 透明 做掉 里 个个 透明

1̇6 1̇3̇ | 2̇ — | 2̇6 1̇ | 1̇6 5 | 66 1̇ | 65 1̇ |
等到 郎来 归 丁挨 郎 年纪 小 万记 郎 筑城 墙

1̇6 5 | 3/4 1̇66 63 5 ‖
找义 妹 眼泪 呀 落上 床。

医好倨哥有风光

1=D 2/4 3/4 （小调、召郎歌）

唱：陈拾发
记：钟同荥

53 5 1̇· | 1̇6 5 6· | 52̇ 6 5· | 6 1̇ 53 |
初一 透 早 来召 郎呢 手拿 锁匙 开笼 箱啊

53 5 1̇· | 1̇6 5 6· | 5 1̇ 6 5· | 6 1̇ 53 |
好々 荷 包 挑一 只呢 转々 托 难 挑一 双啊

5 1̇ 6 5· | 66 53 | 533 5 1̇· | 1̇6 5 6· |
打扮 倨 郎 转家 乡啊 初二拾 透 早 来召 郎 呢

52̇ 6 5· | 6 1̇ 53 | 53 5 1̇· | 1̇6 5 6· |
喊到 先 生 开药 方啊 拌々 好 药 要下 齐 吧

5 1̇ 6 5· | 6 1̇ 53 ‖
送好 倨 哥 有风 光啊。

· 77 ·

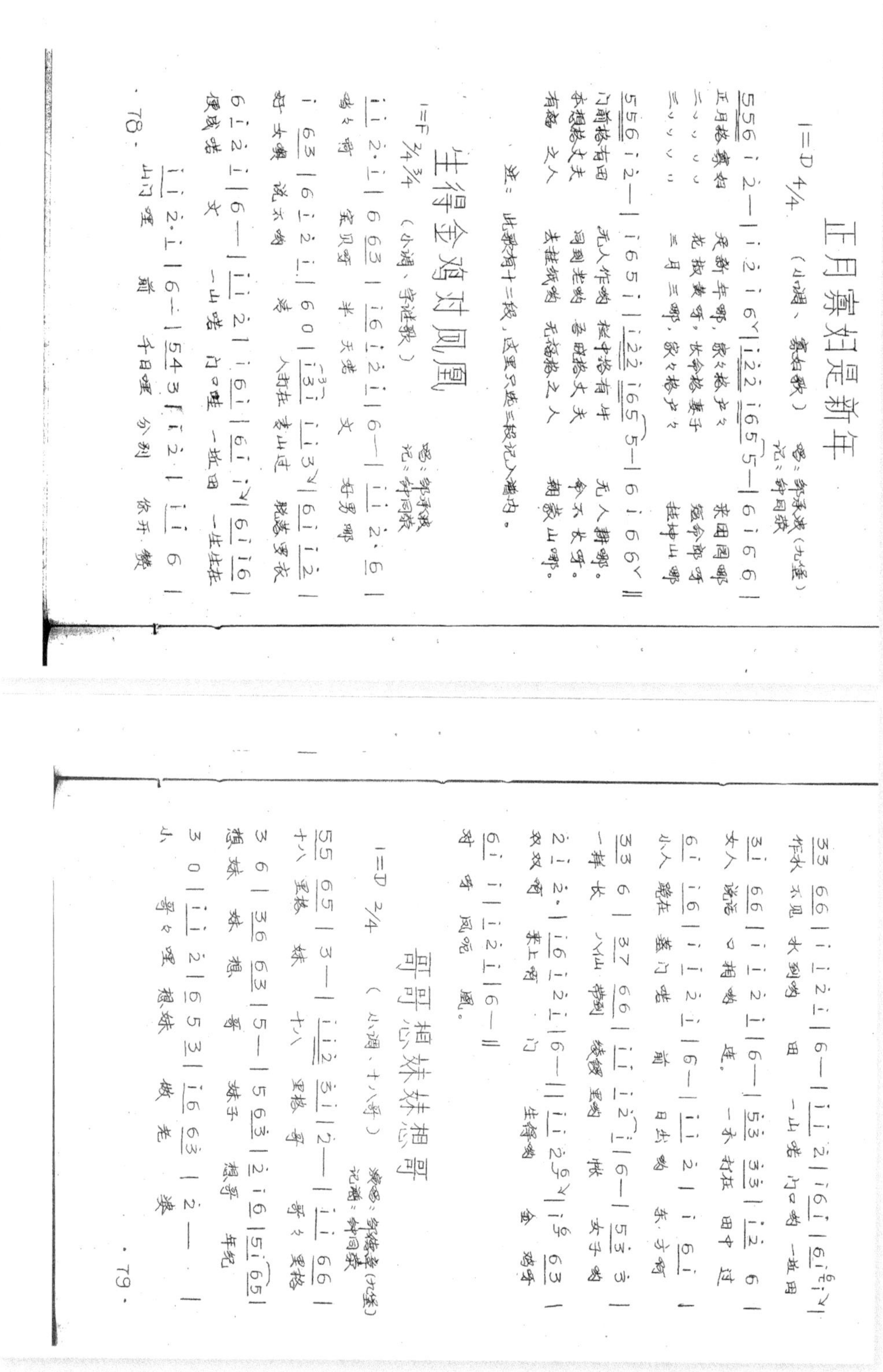

正月寡妇是新年

1=D 4/4 （小调、寡妇歌） 唱：邹承波（九堡） 记：钟同荣

556 1̇ 2̇— | 1̇ 2̇ 1̇ 6ˇ | 1̇2̇2̇ 1̇65 5— | 6 1̇ 6 6 |
正月格寡妇 是新年哪，家家格户户 来团圆哪
二…… 花椒黄呀，长命格妻子 短命郎呀
三…… 三月三哪，家家格户户 挂坤山哪

556 1̇ 2̇— | 1̇ 6 5 1̇ | 1̇2̇2̇ 1̇65 5— | 6 1̇ 6 6ˇ ‖
门前格有田 无人作哟 栏中格有牛 无人耕哪。
本想格丈夫 同到老哟 吾晓格丈夫 命不长呀。
有福 之人 去挂纸哟 无福格之人 翻蔡山哪。

注：此歌有十二段，这里只选三段记入谱内。

生得金鸡对凤凰

1=F 2/4 3/4 （小调、字谜歌） 唱：邹承波 记：钟同荣

1̇1̇ 2̇·1̇ | 6 63 | 1̇6 1̇2̇1̇ | 6— | 1̇1̇ 2̇·6 |
哥哥 呵 宝贝呀 半 天光 文 好男哪

1̇ 63 | 6 1̇ 2̇ 1̇ | 6 0 | 1̇3̇1̇ 1̇1̇3ˇ | 6 1̇ 1̇ 2̇ |
好 女嘛 说不哟 转 人打在 枣山过 脱落罗衣

6 1̇ 2̇ 1̇ | 6— | 1̇1̇ 2̇ | 1̇ 6 1̇ | 6 1̇ 1̇ˇ | 6 1̇ 1̇6 |
便成啰 文 一山啰 门口哇 一垃田 一生生在

1̇1̇ 2̇·1̇ | 6— | 543 | 1̇ 2̇ | 1̇1̇ 6 |
山门哩 前 千日哩 分别 你开赞

·78·

33 66 | 1̇ 1̇ 2̇ 1̇ | 6— | 1̇1̇ 2̇ | 1̇6 1̇ | 6 1̇ 1̇ˇ |
作水 不见 水到哟 田 一山啰 门口哟 一垃田

3 1̇ 66 | 1̇ 1̇ 2̇ 1̇ | 6— | 53 33 | 1̇2̇ 6 |
女人 说话 口相哟 连。 一禾 打在 田中 过

6 1̇ 1̇6 | 1̇ 1̇ 2̇ 1̇ | 6— | 1̇1̇ 2̇ | 1̇ 6 1̇ |
小人 跪在 墓门啰 前 日出哟 东方呵

33 6 | 37 66 | 1̇1̇ 1̇2̇1̇ | 6— | 53 3 |
一样 长 八仙 带到 绫锣 里哟 帐 女子哟

2̇ 1̇ 2̇· | 1̇6 1̇2̇1̇ | 6— ‖ 1̇1̇ 2̇ | 1̇ 63 |
双双 呵 来上呵 门 生得哟 金 鸡呀

6 1̇ 1̇ | 1̇2̇1̇ | 6— ‖
对 呀 凤呃 凰。

哥哥想妹妹想哥

1=D 2/4 （小调、十八哥） 演唱：邹德章（九堡） 记谱：钟同荣

55 65 | 3— | 1̇1̇2̇ 3̇1̇ | 2̇— | 1̇1̇ 66 |
十八 里格 妹 十八 里格 哥 哥哥 里格

3 6 | 36 63 | 5— | 5 63 | 2 1 6 | 5 1̇ 65 |
想 妹 妹 想 哥 妹子 想哥 年纪

3 0 | 1̇1̇ 2̇ | 6 5 3 | 1̇6 63 | 2̇— |
小 哥哥哩 想妹 做 老 婆

·79·

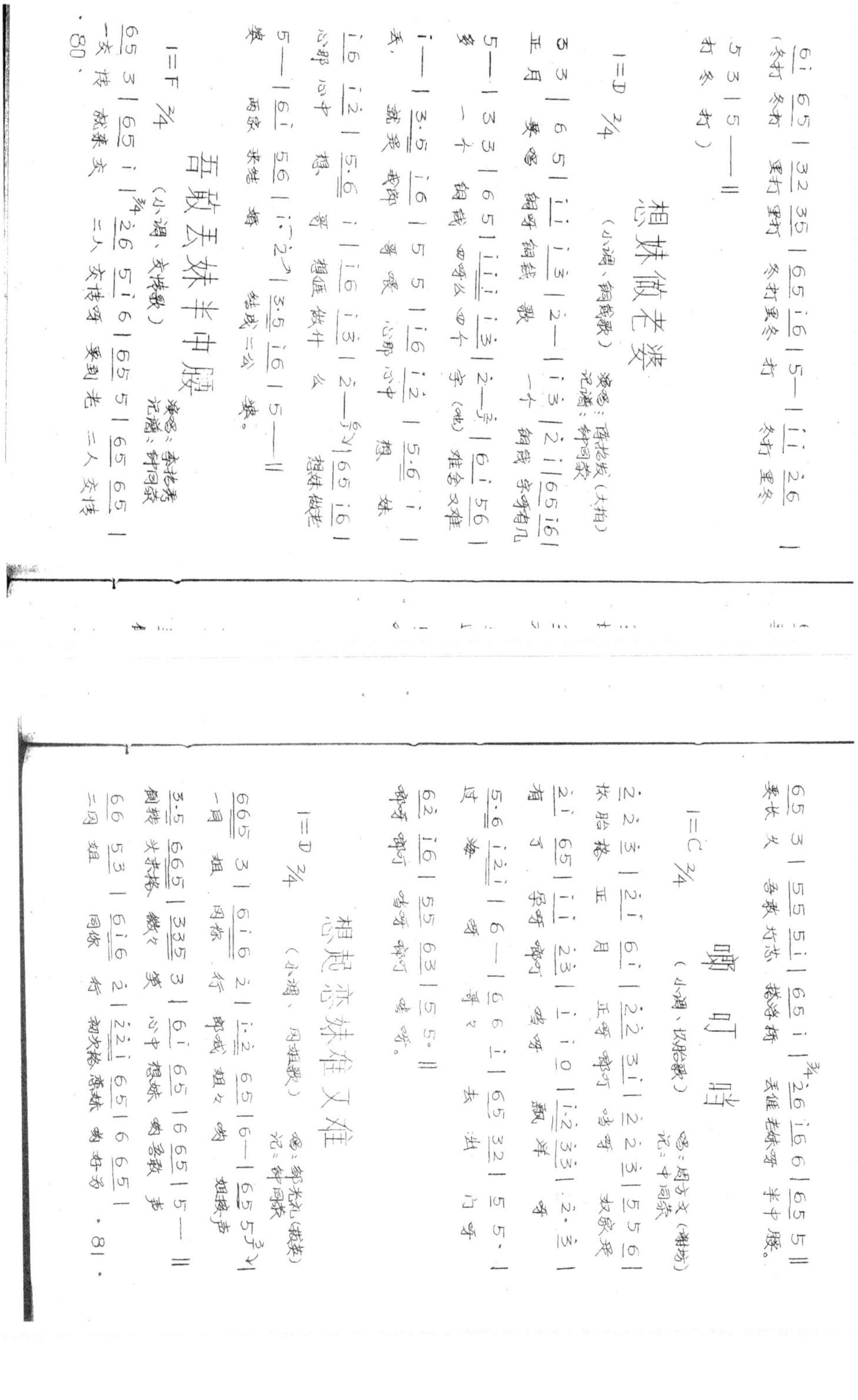

6i 65 | 32 35 | 65 i6 | 5— | ii 26 |
（冬打 冬打 里打 里打 冬打里冬 打 冬打 里冬

53 | 5 —— ||
打冬 打）

想妹做老婆

1=D 2/4 （小调、铜钱歌） 演唱：陈艳发（大柏） 记谱：钟同荣

33 | 65 | ii i3 | 2— | i3 | 2i | 65 i6 |
正月 要唱 铜呀铜钱 歌 一个 铜钱 字呀有几

5— | 33 | 65 | iii i3 | 2—2 | 6i 56 |
多 一个 铜钱 四呀么四个 字（哋） 难舍又难

i— | 3·5 i6 | 55 | i6 i2 | 5·6 i |
丢， 就是 我郎 哥喂 心那心中 想 妹

i6 i2 | 5·6 i | i6 i3 | 2— | 65 i6 |
心那心中 想 哥 想涯做什 么 想妹做老

5— | 6i 56 | i2 | 3·5 i6 | 5 — ||
婆 两家 来结 婚 结成二公 婆。

吾敢丢妹半中腰

1=F 2/4 （小调、交情歌） 演唱：李艳秀 记谱：钟同荣

65 3 | 65 i | 3/4 26 5i 6 | 65 5 | 65 65 |
一交 情 就来 交 二人 交情呀 要到 老 二人 交情

65 3 | 55 5i | 65 i | 3/4 26 i6 6 | 65 5 ||
要长 久 吾敢 灯芯 搭浮 桥 丢涯 老妹呀 半中 腰。

嘟叮哨

1=C 2/4 （小调、怀胎歌） 唱：周方文（谢坊） 记：中同荣

223 | 2i 6i | 22 3i | 223 | 556 |
怀胎格 正 月 正呀 嘟叮 哨呀 奴家是

2i 65 | ii 23 | i i 0 | i·2 33 | 2·3 |
有 了 孕呀 嘟叮 哨呀 飘 洋 呀

5·6 i2i | 6— | 66 i | 65 32 | 55· |
过 海 呀 哥々 去 出 门呀

62 i6 | 55 63 | 55· ||
嘟呀 嘟叮 哨呀 嘟叮 哨呀。

想起恋妹准又难

1=D 2/4 （小调、问姐歌） 唱：邹光礼（拔英） 记：钟同荣

665 3 | 6i6 2 | i·2 65 | 6— | 65 5 |
一月 姐 问你 行 郎戒 姐々 哟 姐接声

3·5 665 | 335 3 | 6i 65 | 665 | 5— ||
倒转 头来格 微々 笑 心中 想妹 哟吾敢 声

66 53 | 6i6 2 | 22i 65 | 665 |
二冈 姐 问你 行 初次格 恋妹 哟好 多

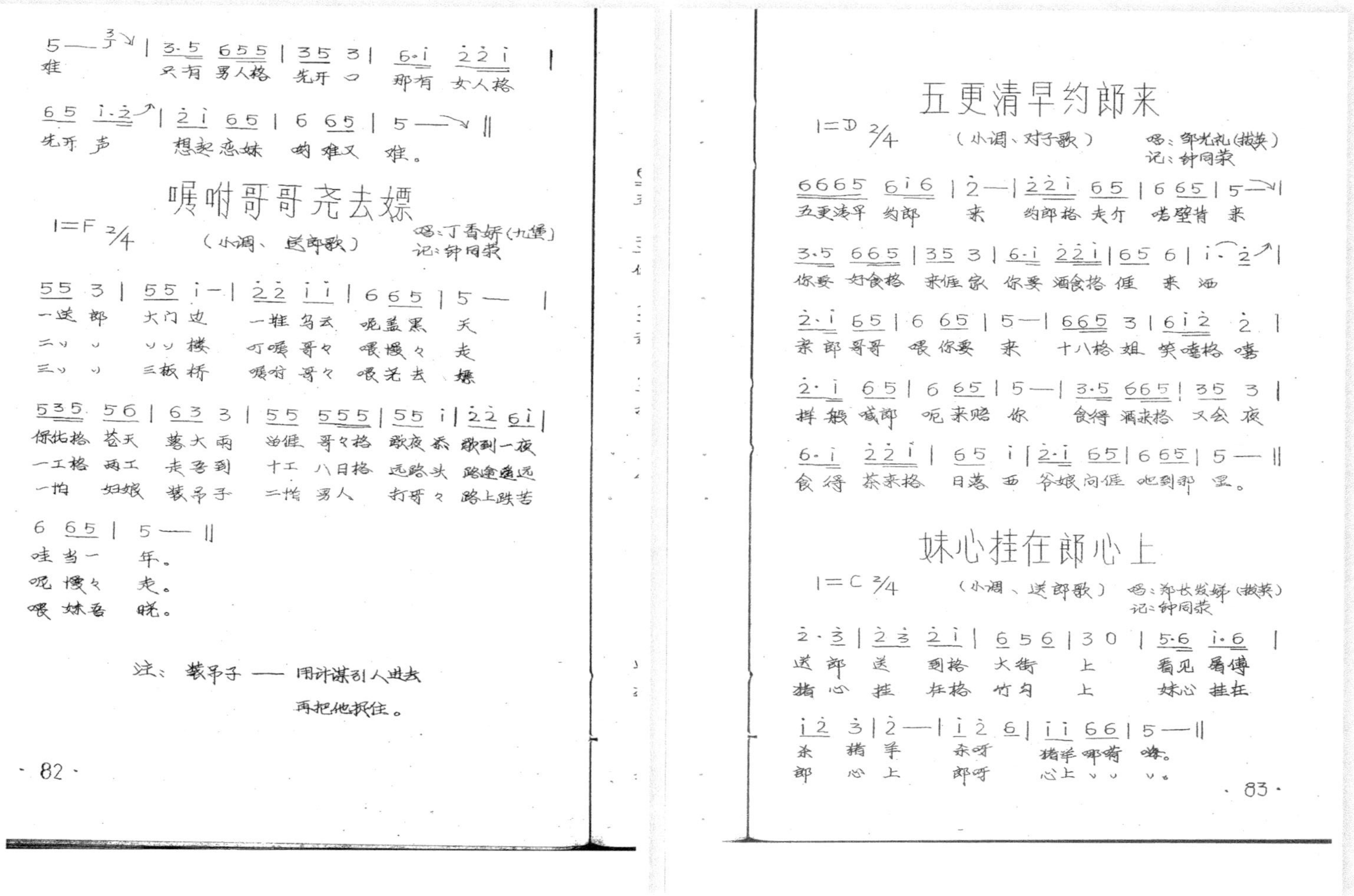

5 — | 3·5 6 5 5 | 3 5 3 | 6·i 2 2 i |
难 只有 男人格 先开 口 那有 女人格

6 5 i·2 | 2 i 6 5 | 6 6 5 | 5 — ||
先开 声 想起恋妹 哟 难又 难。

唲哨哥哥充去嫖

1=F 2/4 （小调、送郎歌） 唱：丁香娇（九堡） 记：钟同荣

5 5 3 | 5 5 i — | 2 2 i i | 6 6 5 | 5 — |
一送 郎 大门 边 一驻 乌云 呢盖 黑 天
二〃 〃 〃〃 楼 叮嘱 哥々 喂慢々 走
三〃 〃 三板 桥 嘱咐 哥々 喂充 去 嫖

5 3 5 5 6 | 6 3 3 | 5 5 5 5 5 | 5 5 i | 2 2 6 i |
保佑格 苍天 落大 雨 留捱 哥々格 歌夜 亦 歌到一夜
一工格 两工 走 总到 十工 八日格 远路头 路途遥远
一怕 妇娘 装吊子 二怕 男人 打哥々 路上跌苦

6 6 5 | 5 — ||
哇 当一 年。
呢 慢々 走。
喂 妹吾 晓。

注：装吊子 —— 用计谋引人进去
再把他抓住。

五更清早约郎来

1=D 2/4 （小调、对子歌） 唱：邹光礼（拔英） 记：钟同荣

6 6 6 5 6 i 6 | 2 — | 2 2 i 6 5 | 6 6 5 | 5 — |
五更清早 约郎 来 约郎格 夫介 喏壁背 来

3·5 6 6 5 | 3 5 3 | 6·i 2 2 i | 6 5 6 | i· 2 |
你要 好食格 来偓 家 你要 酒食格 偓 来 ⿰

2·i 6 5 | 6 6 5 | 5 — | 6 6 5 3 | 6 i 2 2 |
亲 郎 哥哥 喂 你要 来 十八格 姐 笑嘻格 嘻

2·i 6 5 | 6 6 5 | 5 — | 3·5 6 6 5 | 3 5 3 |
挥 般 喊郎 呢 来赔 你 食得 酒来格 又会 夜

6·i 2 2 i | 6 5 i | 2·i 6 5 | 6 6 5 | 5 — ||
食 得 茶来格 日落 西 爷娘 向偓 吔到郎 里。

妹心挂在郎心上

1=C 2/4 （小调、送郎歌） 唱：郑长发娇（拔英） 记：钟同荣

2·3 | 2 3 2 i | 6 5 6 | 3 0 | 5·6 i·6 |
送 郎 送 到格 大街 上 看见 屠傅
指 心 挂 在格 竹勺 上 妹心 挂在

i 2 3 | 2 — | i 2 6 | i i 6 6 | 5 — ||
杀 猪 羊 杀呀 猪羊 哪哟 嗨。
郎 心 上 郎呀 心上 〃 〃 〃。

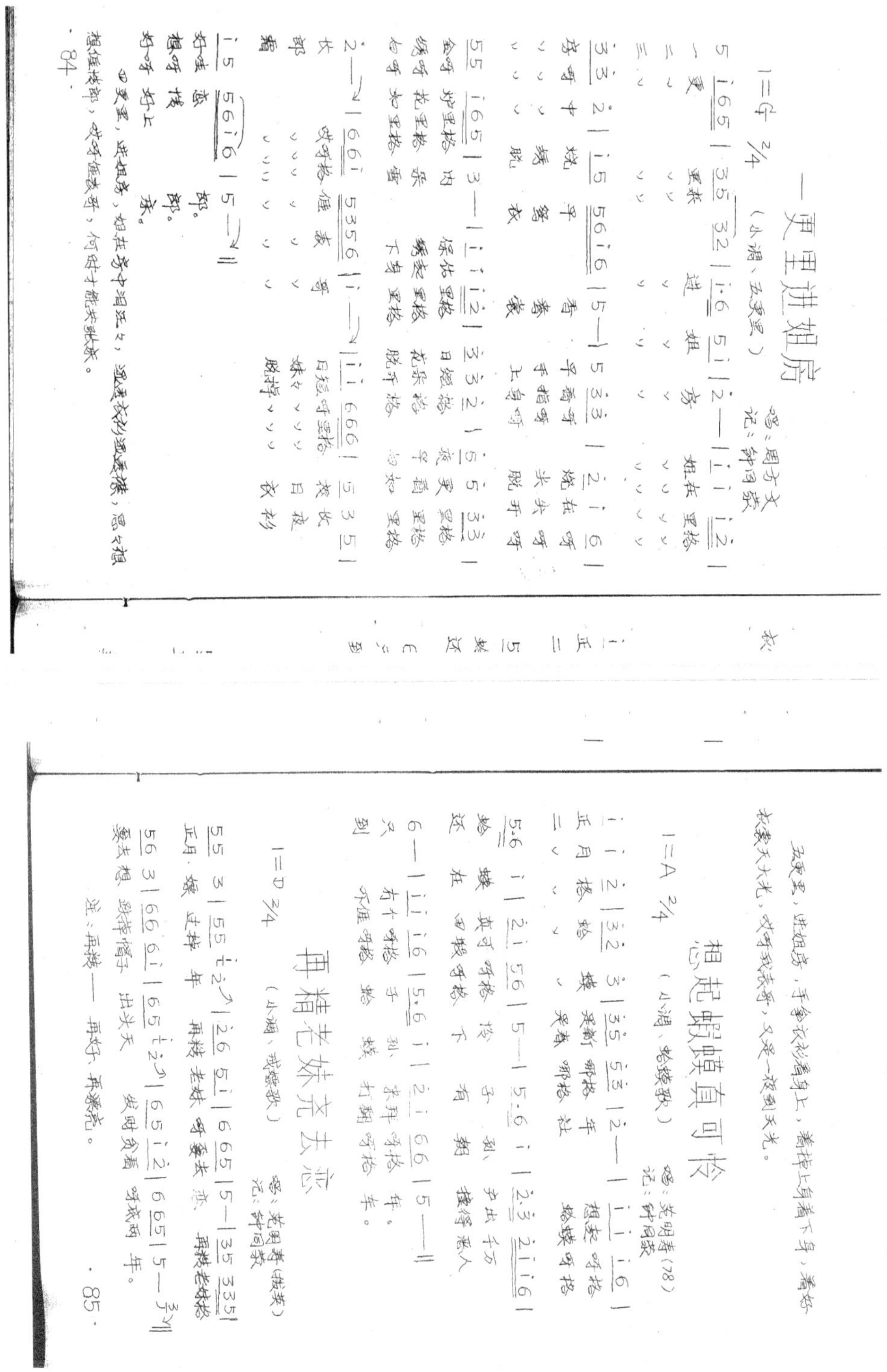

一更里进姐房

1=G 2/4 （小调、五更里） 唱：周方文 记：钟同荣

5 i65 | 35 32 | i·6 5i | 2 — | ii i2 |
一更 里来 进 姐 房 姐在 里格
二 ～ ～～ ～ ～ ～ ～～ ～～
三 ～ ～～ ～ ～ ～ ～～ ～～

33 2 | i5 56i6 | 5 — | 5 33 | 2 i 6 |
房呀 中 烧 平 香 平香呀 烧 在 呀
～～ ～ 绣 鸳 鸯 手指呀 尖 尖 呀
～～ ～ 脱 衣 裳 上身呀 脱 开 呀

55 i65 | 3 — | ii i2 | 332 | 65 33 |
金呀 炉里格 内 保佑 里格 日短 格 夜 更 里格
绣呀 花里格 朵 绣起 里格 花朵 格 平 看 里格
白呀 如里格 雪 下身 里格 脱开 格 如 如 里格

2 — | 66i 5356 | i — | ii 666 | 535 |
长 哎呀格 佢 表 哥 日短呀里格 夜 长
郎 ～～～ ～ ～ ～ 妹々 ～～～ 日 夜
霜 ～～～ ～ ～ ～ 脱掉 ～～～ 衣 衫

i5 56i6 | 5 — ||
好哇 恋 郎。
想呀 情 郎。
好呀 好上 床。

四更里，进姐房，姐在房中泪汪々，泪透衣衫泪透裤，思々想想佢情郎，哎呀佢表哥，何时才能共眠床。

· 84 ·

五更里，进姐房，手拿衣衫着身上，着掉上身着下身，着好衣裳天大光，哎呀我表哥，又是一夜到天光。

想起蛤蟆真可怜

1=A 2/4 （小调、蛤蟆歌） 唱：范明寿（78） 记：钟同荣

i i 2 | 32 3 | 35 53 | 2 — | ii i6 |
正 月 格 蛤 蟆 是新 哪格 年 想起 呀格
二 ～ ～ ～ ～ 是春 哪格 社 蛤蟆 呀格

5·6 i | 2i 56 | 5 — | 5·6 i | 2·3 2ii6 |
蛤 蟆 真可 呀格 怜 子 孙 产出 千万
还 在 田坝 呀格 下 有 翻 撞得 恶人

6 — | ii i6 | 5·6 i | 2i 66 | 5 — ||
只 有个 呀格 子 孙 来拜 呀格 年。
到 吓佢 呀格 蛤 蟆 打翻 呀格 车。

再精老妹亮去恋

1=D 2/4 （小调、戒嫖歌） 唱：范明寿（拔英） 记：钟同荣

55 3 | 55 i2 | 26 5i | 6 65 | 5 — | 35 335 |
正月·嫖 过掉 年 再精 老妹 呀 要去 恋 再精老妹格

56 3 | 66 6i | 65 i2 | 65 i2 | 6 65 | 5 — ||
要去 想 跌掉 帽子 出头天 发财 贪看 呀 花 两 年。

注：再精—— 再好、再漂亮。

· 85 ·

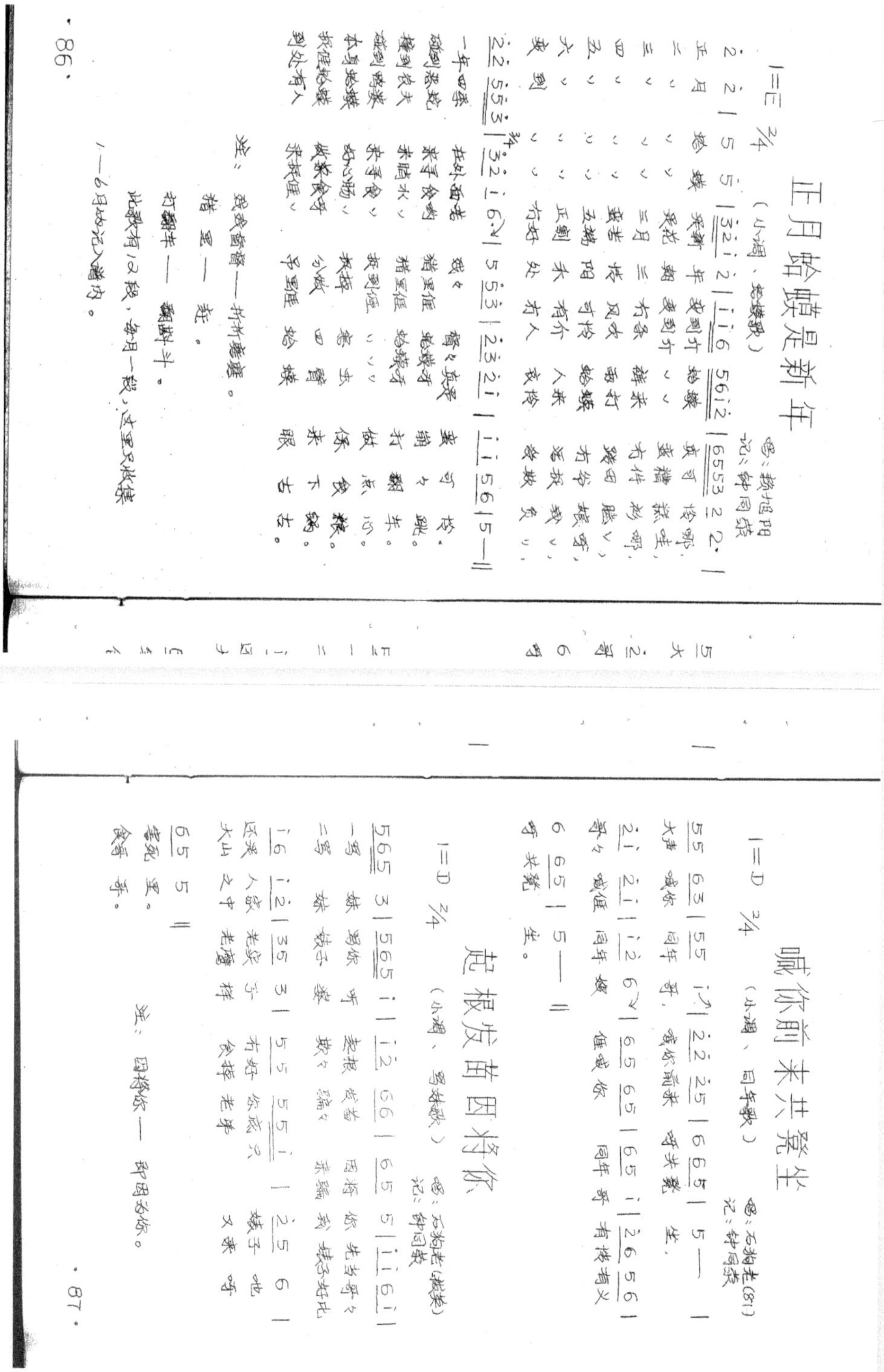

正月蛤蟆是新年

1=E 2/4　（小调、蛤蟆歌）　唱：赖旭阳　记：钟同崇

2 2 | 5 5 | 32i 2 | ii6 56i2 | 6553 2 2· |

正月　蛤蟆　采新年　变到介　蛤蟆　真可怜哪，
二〃　〃〃　采花翻　变到介　〃〃　蛮糟糕哇，
三〃　〃〃　三月三　冇条　薛来　冇件衫哪，
四〃　〃〃　蛮苦　怜风吹　雨打　踏田塍〃，
五〃　〃〃　五端阳　可怜　蛤蟆　冇爷娘呀，
六〃　〃〃　正割禾　有介　人来　活捉我〃，
变到　〃〃　冇好处　有人　哀怜　叁欺负〃，

22 553 | 3/4 32 i 6 | 5 53 | 2321 | ii 56 | 5— ||

一年四季　在外面苦　戏〃　瞢〃真吾　蛮可怜。
碰到恶蛇　来寻食哟　猪里偃　蛤蟆牙　蹦〃跳。
撞到农夫　来睛水〃　猪里偃　蛤蟆牙　打翻年。
碰到鸭婆　来寻食〃　捉到偃　〃〃〃　做点心。
本身蛤蟆　好心肠〃　扒掉　害虫　保食粮。
抓偃蛤蟆　做菜食呀　分做　四背　来下锅。
到处有人　来抓偃〃　吊黑偃　蛤蟆　眼古古。

注：戏戏瞢瞢——折折磨磨。
猪里——赶。
打翻年——翻斛斗。
此歌有12段，每月一段，这里只收集1—6月的记入谱内。

·86·

喊你前来共凳坐

1=D 2/4　（小调、同年歌）　唱：石狗老(81)　记：钟同崇

55 63 | 55 i | 22 25 | 665 | 5— |
大声喊你　同年哥，喊你前来　呀共凳　坐。

2i 2i | i2 6 | 65 65 | 65 i | 26 56 |
哥〃喊偃　同年嫂　偃喊你　同年哥　有情有义

6 65 | 5— ||
呀共凳　坐。

起根发苗因将你

1=D 2/4　（小调、骂妹歌）　唱：石狗老(搬笑)　记：钟同崇

565 3 | 565 i | i2 66 | 65 5 | ii6i |
一骂　妹骂你　听　起根发苗　因将　你　先当哥〃
二骂　妹婊子　婆　欺〃骗〃　来骗　我　婊子好比

i6 i2 | 35 3 | 55 55i | 25 6 |
还米　人家　老实　子　有好　你底只　婊子　吔
大山　之中　老鹰　样　食掉　老弟　又来　呀

65 5 ||
害死　里。
食哥　哥。

注：因将你——即因为你。

·87·

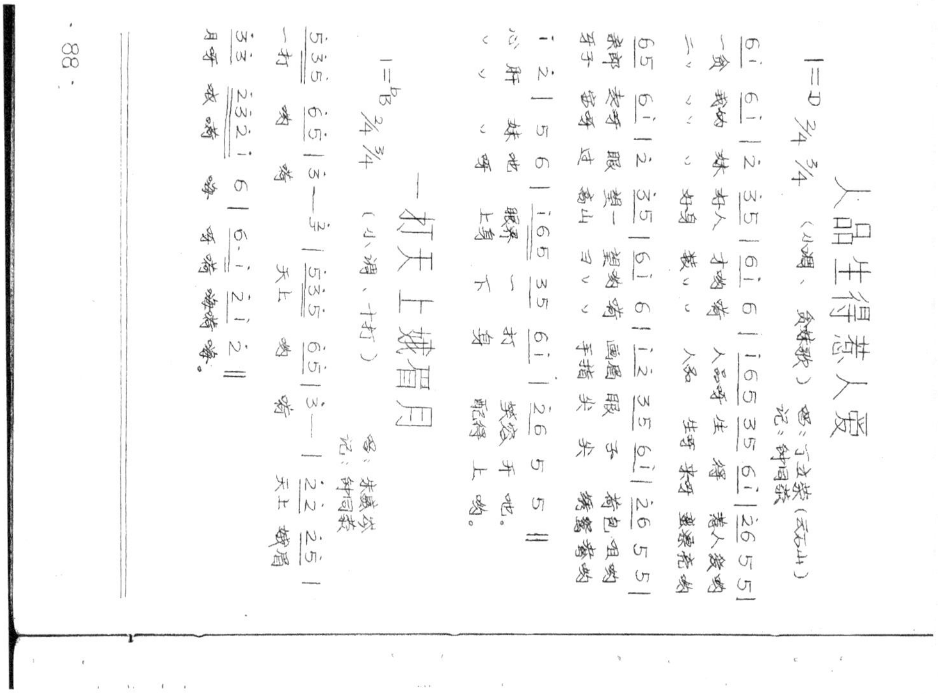

人品生得惹人爱

1=D 2/4 3/4 （小调、贪妹歌） 唱：丁立荣（云石山）
记：钟同荣

61 61 | 2 35 | 61 6 | 165 35 61 | 26 5 5 |
一贪 我的 妹 好人 才哟 嗬 人品呀 生 得 惹人爱哟
二〃 〃〃 〃 好身 装〃〃 人品 生呀 来呀 蛮漂亮哟

65 61 | 2 35 | 61 6 | 12 35 61 | 26 5 5 |
亲郎 老呀 眼 望一 望哟 嗬 画眉 眼 子 荷包 咀哟
牙子 密呀 过 高山 马〃〃 手指 尖 尖 绣鸳鸯哟

1 2 | 5 6 | 165 35 61 | 26 5 5 ||
心 肝 妹 哋 眼界 一 打 笑容 开 哋。
〃 〃 〃 呀 上身 下 身 配得 上 哟。

一打天上娥眉月

1=♭B 2/4 3/4 （小调、十打） 唱：朱盛岑
记：钟同荣

535 65 | 3— 3 | 535 65 | 3— | 22 25 |
一打 哟 嗬 天上 哟 嗬 天上 娥眉

33 2321 6 | 6·1 21 2 ||
月呀 哎 嗬 嗨 呀 嗬 嗨嗬 嗨。

· 88 ·

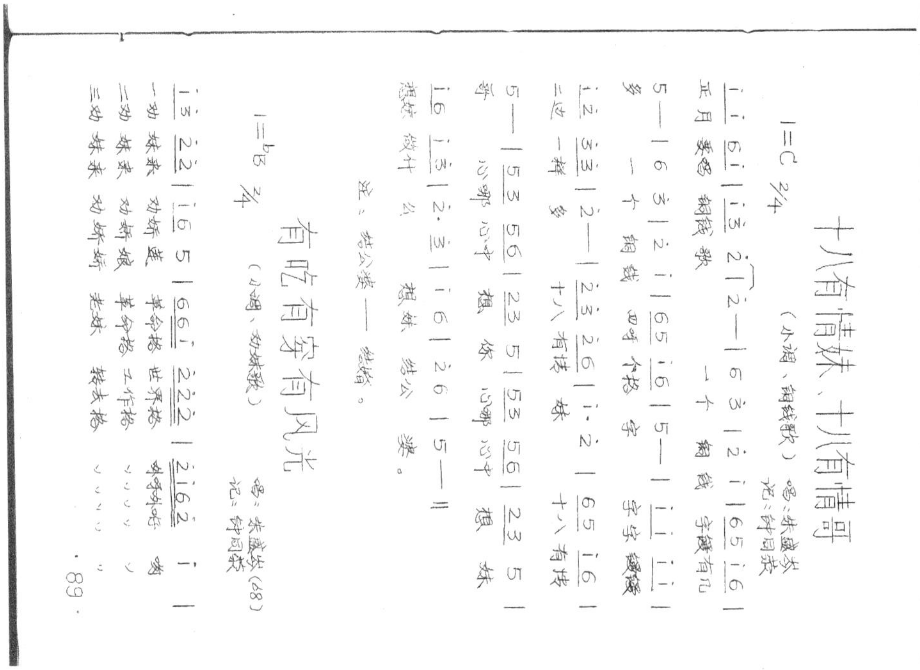

十八有情妹、十八有情哥

1=C 2/4 （小调、铜钱歌） 唱：朱盛岑
记：钟同荣

11 61 | 13 2 | 2— | 6 3 | 2 1 | 65 16 |
正月 要唱 铜钱 歌 一 个 铜 钱 字镶有几

5— | 6 3 | 2 1 | 65 16 | 5— | 11 11 |
多 一 个 铜 钱 四呀 个格 字 字字 镶镶

12 33 | 2— | 23 26 | 1·2 | 65 16 |
二边 一样 多 十八 有情 妹 十八 有情

5— | 53 56 | 23 5 | 53 56 | 23 5 |
哥 心哪 心中 想 你 心哪 心中 想 妹

16 13 | 2·3 | 1 6 | 26 | 5— ||
想妹 做什 么 想 妹 结公 婆。

注：结公婆——结婚。

有吃有穿有风光

1=♭B 2/4 （小调、劝妹歌） 唱：朱盛岑（68）
记：钟同荣

13 22 | 16 5 | 661 222 | 2162 1 |
一劝 妹来 劝娇 莲 革命格 世界格 哟呀哟呀 哟
二劝 妹来 劝娇 娘 革命格 工作格 〃〃〃〃 〃
三劝 妹来 劝娇 娇 老妹 转去格 〃〃〃〃 〃

· 89 ·

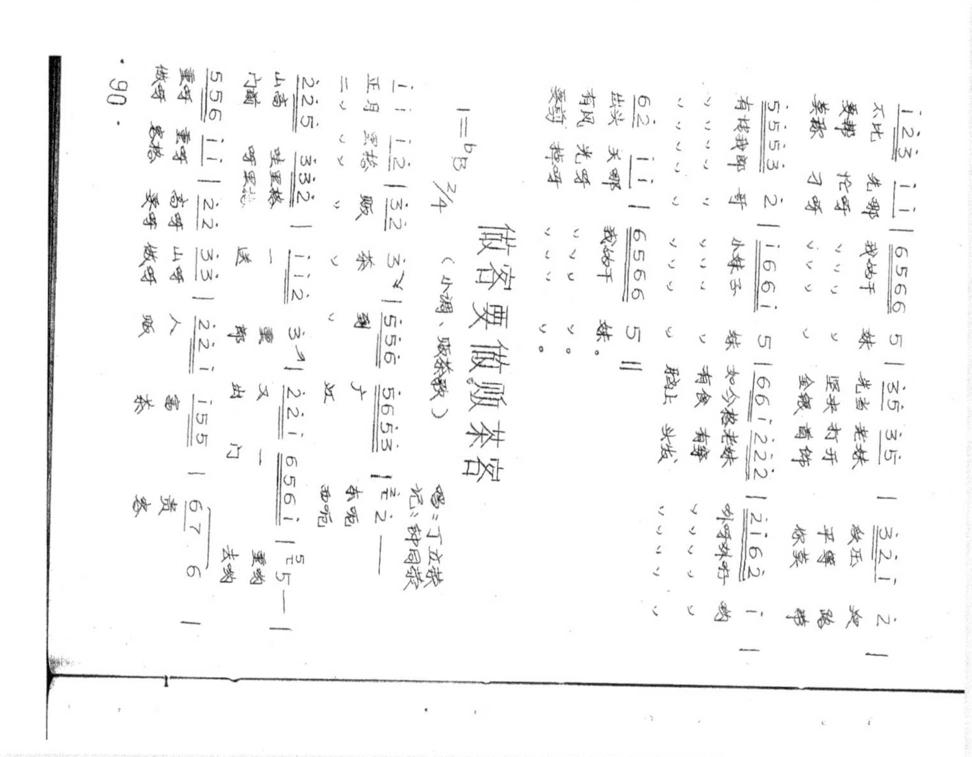

123 11 | 6566 5 | 35 35 | 321 2 |
不比 先哪 我的干 妹 先当 老妹 敌压 处
要帮 忙呀 〃〃〃 〃 坚决 打开 平等 路
莫称 刁呀 〃〃〃 〃 金银 首饰 你莫 带

5553 2 | 1661 5 | 661 222 | 2162 1 |
有传我郎 哥 小妹子 妹 如今格老妹 外呀外呀 哟
〃〃〃〃 〃 〃〃〃 〃 有食 有穿 〃〃〃〃 〃
〃〃〃〃 〃 〃〃〃 〃 脑上 头发 〃〃〃〃 〃

62 11 | 6566 5 ||
出头 天哪 我的干 妹。
有风 光呀 〃〃〃 〃。
要剪 掉呀 〃〃〃 〃。

做客要做贩茶客

1=^bB 2/4　（小调、贩茶歌）　唱：丁立荣　记：钟同荣

11 12 | 32 3 | 556 5653 | 2 2 —
正月 里格 贩 茶 到 广 东呢
二〃 〃〃 〃 〃 〃 江 西呢

225 332 | 112 3 | 221 6561 | 5 — |
山高 哇里格 一 要 又 一 重哟
门前 呀里格 送 郎 出 门 去哟

556 11 | 22 33 | 221 155 | 67 6 |
重呀 重呀 高呀 山呀 人 富 贵
做呀 客格 要呀 做呀 贩 茶 客

112 16 | 5.6 11 | 221 6561 | 5 — 3 ||
如今呀 里格 天 下呀 一呀 般 同呢。
出到呀 里格 门 外呀 天呀 下 知呢。

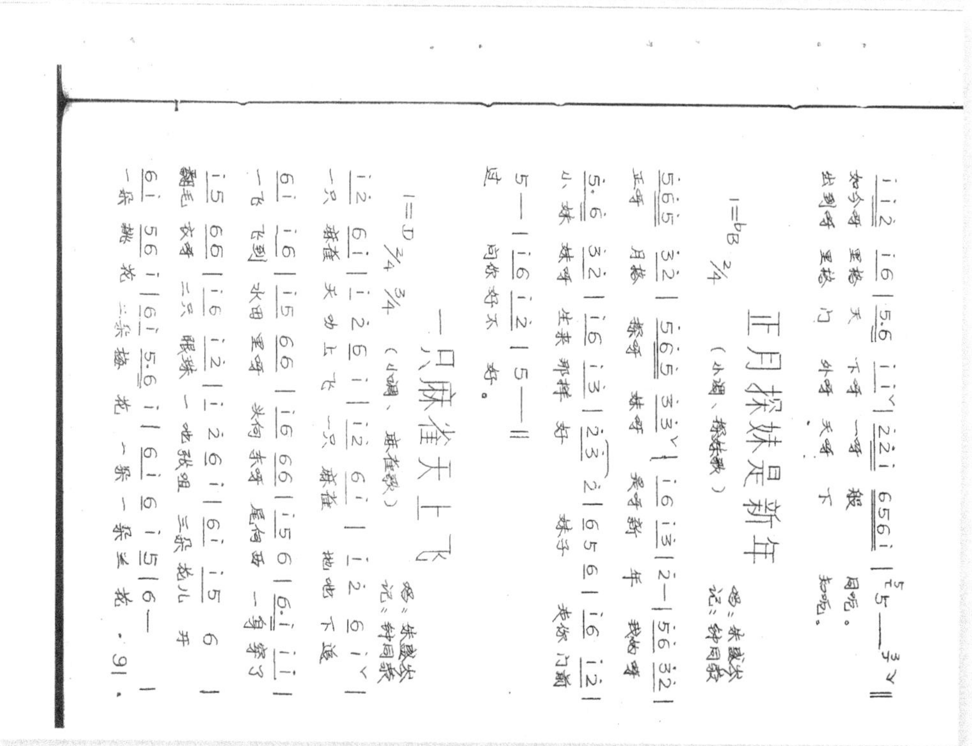

正月探妹是新年

1=^bB 2/4　（小调、探妹歌）　唱：朱盛发　记：钟同荣

565 32 | 565 33 | 16 13 | 2 — | 56 32 |
正呀 月格 探呀 妹呀 是呀 新 年 我的 呀
5.6 32 | 16 13 | 23 2 | 656 | 16 12 |
小 妹 妹呀 生来 那样 好 妹子 走你 门前
5 — | 16 12 | 5 — ||
过 问你 好不 好。

一只麻雀天上飞

1=D 2/4 3/4　（小调、麻雀歌）　唱：朱盛发　记：钟同荣

12 61 | 1 2 6 1 | 12 61 | 1 2 6 1 |
一只 麻雀 天 动 上 飞 一只 麻雀 地 也 下 追
61 16 | 15 66 | 16 66 | 15 6 | 6.1 11 |
一飞 飞到 水田 里呀 头向 东呀 尾向 西 一身 穿了
15 66 | 16 12 | 1 2 6 1 | 61 15 6 |
翻毛 衣呀 二只 眼珠 一 也 张 咀 三朵 花儿 开
61 56 1 | 61 5.6 1 | 61 6 1 5 | 6 — |
一朵 桃 花 二朵 梅 花 一朵 一 朵 兰 花

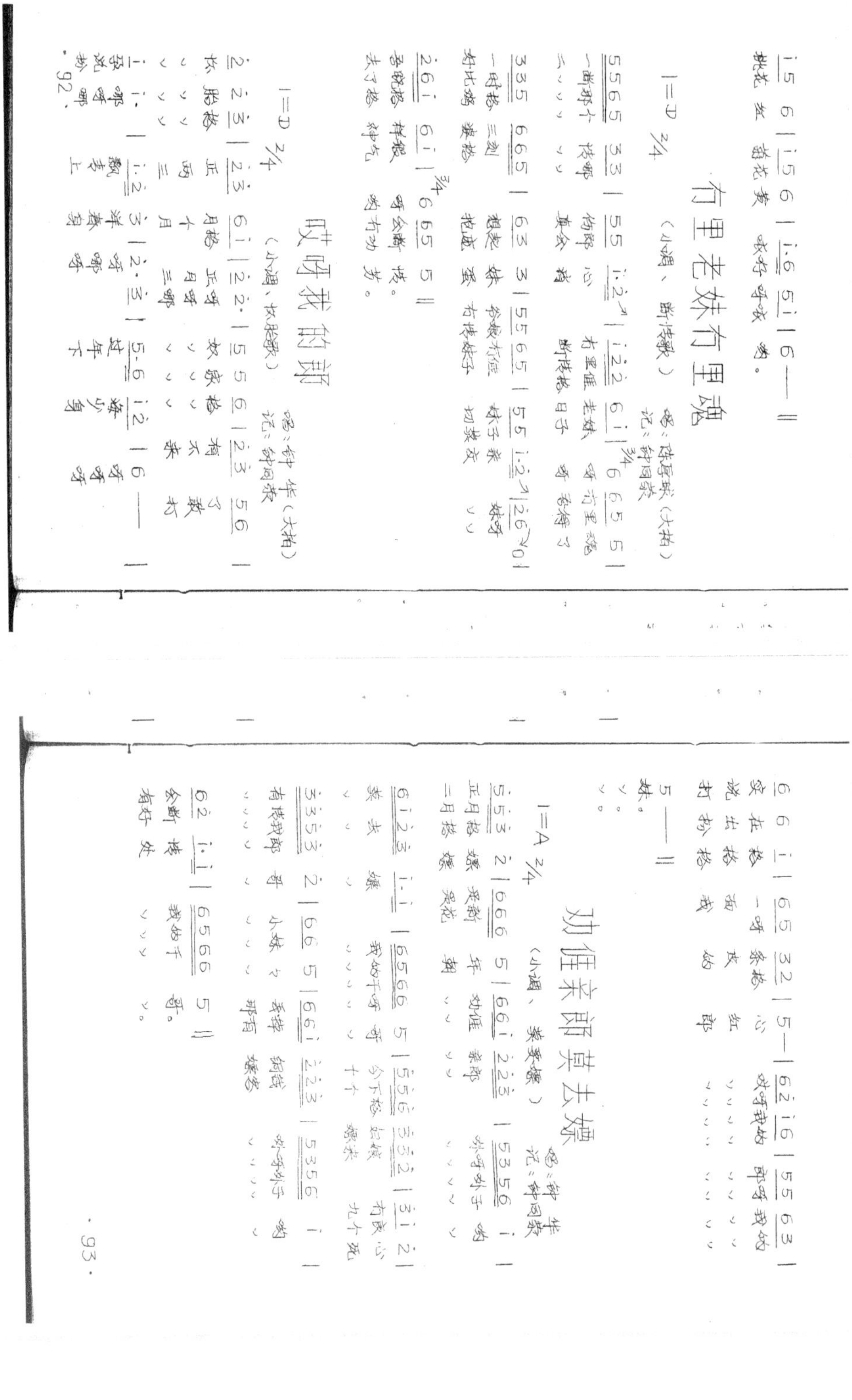

1̇5 6 | 1̇5 6 | 1̇·6 51̇ | 6 — ‖
桃花 红 菊花 黄 咳好 呀咳 哟。

有里老妹有里魂

1=D 2/4　（小调、断传歌）　唱：陈厚球（大拍）
记：钟同荣

5565 33 | 55 1̇·2̇ | 1̇2̇2 61̇ | 3/4 6 65 5 |
一断那个 传哪 伤郎 心 有里佴 老妹 呀 有里魂
二 ∨∨∨ ∨∨ 真会 绡 断传格 日子 呀 晤得了

335 665 | 63 3 | 5565 | 55 1̇·2̇ | 26 0 |
一时格 三刻 想起 妹 爷娘冇佂 妹子亲 妹呀
好比鸡 婆格 抱庞 蛋 冇传妹子 切莫交 ∨∨

2̇61̇ 61̇ | 3/4 6 65 5 ‖
吾晓格 样般 呀会断 传。
去了格 神气 哟冇劝 劳。

哎呀我的郎

1=D 2/4　（小调、怀胎歌）　唱：钟 华（大拍）
记：钟同荣

2̇ 2̇3̇ | 2̇3̇ 61̇ | 2̇ 2̇· | 5 5 6 | 2̇3̇ 56 |
怀 胎格 正 月格 正呀 奴 家格 有 了
∨ ∨∨ 两 个 月呀 ∨ ∨∨ 不 敢
∨ ∨∨ 三 月 三哪 ∨ ∨∨ 亲 打

1̇ 1̇· | 1̇·2̇ 3̇ | 2̇·3̇ | 5·6 1̇2̇ | 6 — |
孕 哪 飘 洋 呀 过 海 呀
说 呀 专 春 哪 年 少 呀
扮 哪 上 穿 呀 下 身 呀

·92·

6 6 1̇ | 65 32 | 5 — | 62̇ 1̇6 | 55 63 |
实 在 格 一呀 条格 心 哎呀我的 郎呀 我的
说 出 格 面 皮 红 ∨∨∨∨ ∨∨∨∨
打 扮 格 我 的 郎 ∨∨∨∨ ∨∨∨∨

5 — ‖
妹。
∨。
∨。

劝佴亲郎莫去嫖

1=A 2/4　（小调、莫要嫖）　唱：钟 华
记：钟同荣

553 2 | 666 5 | 661̇ 2̇2̇3̇ | 5356 1̇ |
正月格 嫖 买新 年 劝佴 亲郎 哟呀妹子 哟
二月格 嫖 买花 朝 ∨∨ ∨∨ ∨∨∨∨ ∨

61̇2̇3̇ 1̇·1̇ | 6566 5 | 556 3̇3̇2̇ | 3̇1̇ 2̇ |
莫 去 嫖 我的千呀 哥 今下格 妇娘 有良 心
∨ ∨ ∨ ∨∨∨∨ ∨ 十个 嫖杂 九个 死

3353 2 | 66 5 | 661̇ 2̇2̇3̇ | 5356 1̇ |
有传我郎 哥 小妹 々 吾拌 铜钱 哟呀妹子 哟
∨∨∨∨ ∨ ∨∨ ∨ 那有 嫖客 ∨∨∨∨ ∨

62̇ 1̇·1̇ | 6566 5 ‖
会断 传 我的千 哥。
有好 处 ∨∨∨ ∨。

·93·

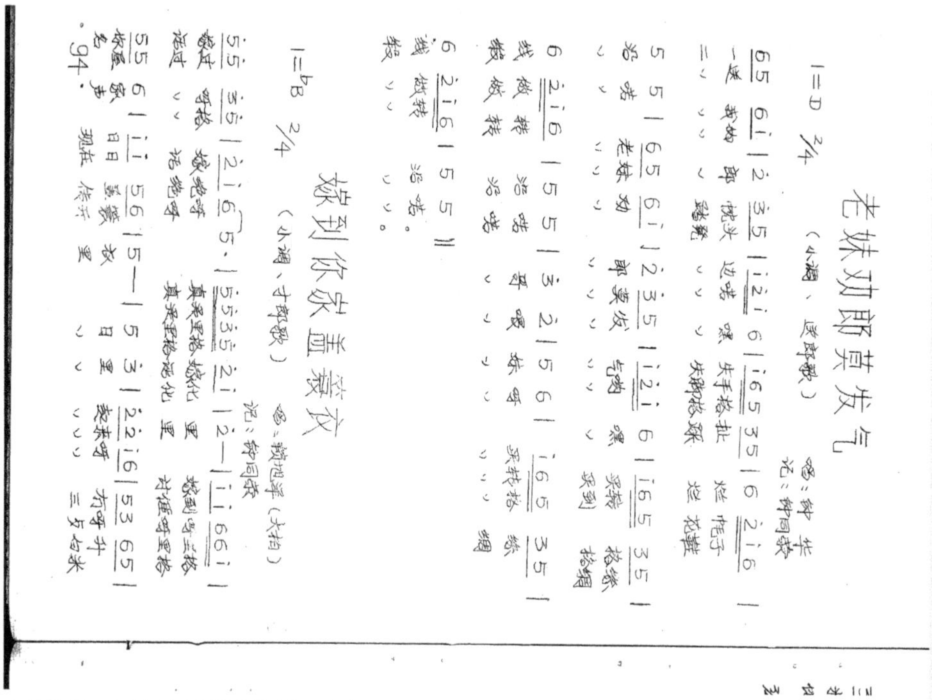

老妹劝郎莫发气

1=D 2/4　（小调、送郎歌）　唱：钟华　记：钟同荣

一送我哟郎　枕头边唠嘿　失手格扯烂帐子
二～～～～　踏凳～～～　失脚格踩烂花鞋

沿唠　老妹劝郎莫发气哟嘿　买转格丝
～～　～～～～～～～～　买到格绸

线做转沿唠　哥喂妹呀　买转格丝
缎做转沿唠　～～～～　～～～绸

线做转沿唠。
缎～～　～～。

嫁到你家盖蓑衣

1=♭B 2/4　（小调、寸郎歌）　唱：赖旭泽（大柏）　记：钟同荣

嫁过呀格嫁绝呀　真是里格嫁化里　嫁到呀三格
话过～～话绝呀　真是里格话化里　讨尴呀里格

你屋家　日日蓑衣　日里　起来呀　冇呀升
名声　现在　传开里　～～　～～～　三夕白米

·94·

米哟　夜晡呀格　歇眼呀哈　屋家冇床被呀
饭唠　～～　～～　～～～～　屋家绣花被呀

实在嫁绝里哟　今生呀格　今世
实在话绝里哟　取得呀格　气来

真是对凿里。
两拳打死你。

注：嫁过嫁绝——原意是嫁到丈夫冇生冇养，绝了子孙，这里是用来骂人的词。
话过话绝——用来骂人的词。
嫁化里——嫁差了。
对凿里——碰着了。

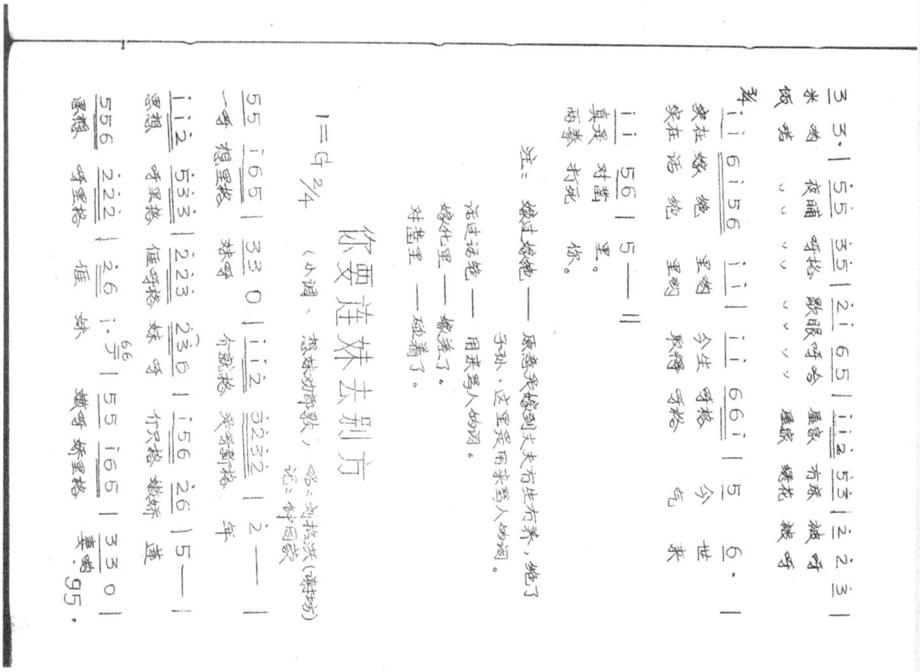

你要连妹去别方

1=G 2/4　（小调、想妹劝郎歌）　唱：刘抢洪（谢坊）　记：钟同荣

一呀想里格妹呀　介就格采呀到格年
思想呀里格尴呀格妹呀　介只格嫩娇莲
思想呀里格尴妹　嫩呀娇里格妻哟

·95·

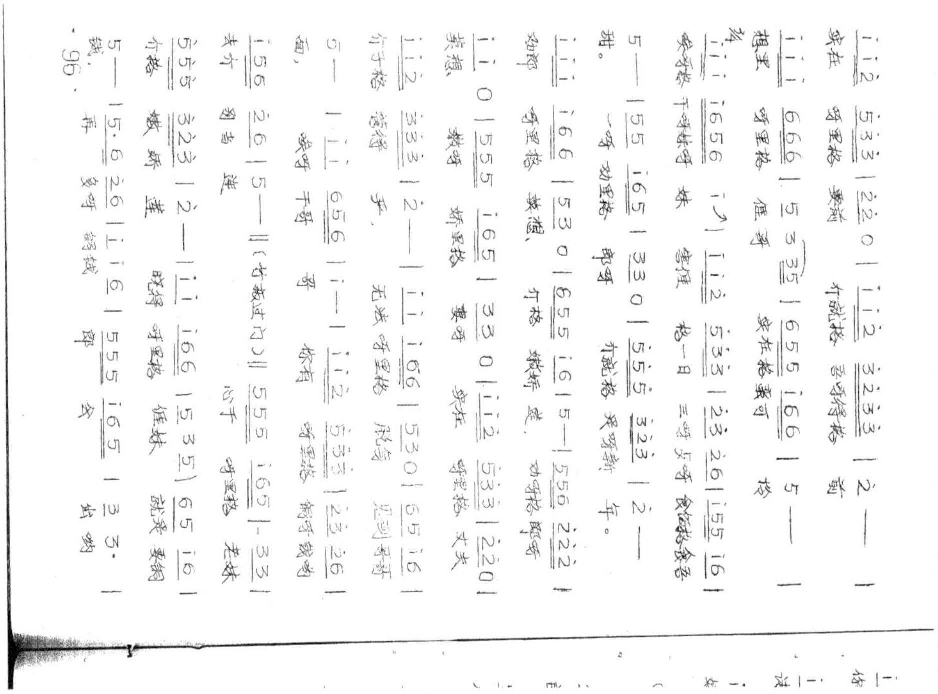

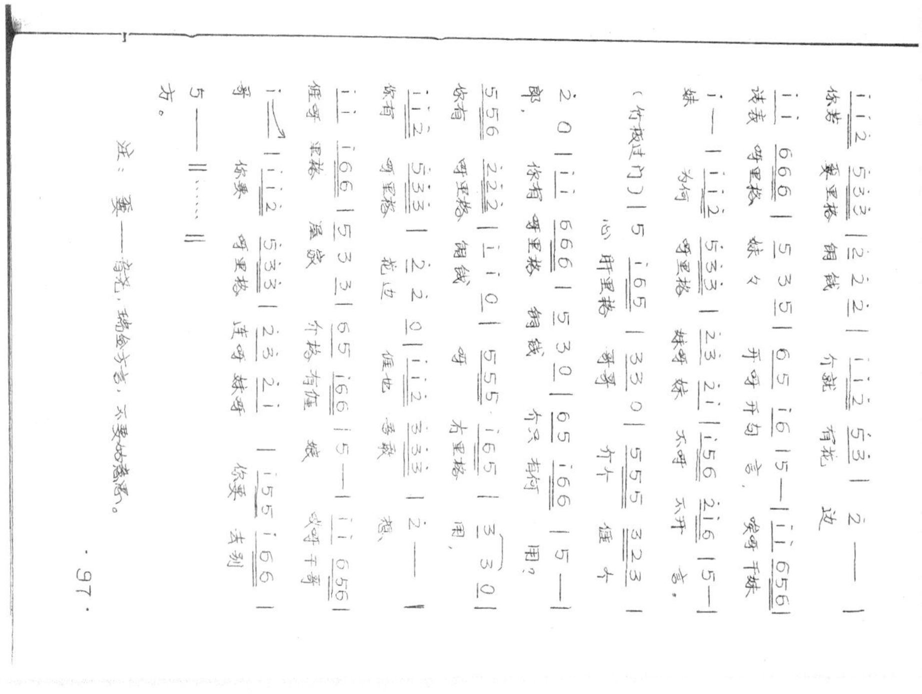

1 1 2 5 3 3 | 2 2 0 | 1 1 2 3 2 3 3 | 2 — |
实在 呀里格 要前 个就格 吾呀得格 前

1 1 1 6 6 6 | 5 3 3 5 | 6 5 5 1 6 6 | 5 — |
想里 呀里格 涯哥 实在格 宴可 怜

1 1 1 1 6 5 6 1 | 1 1 2 5 3 3 | 2 3 2 6 | 1 5 5 1 6 |
唉呀格 干呀妹呀 妹 害涯 格一日 三呀 与呀 食饭格食吾

5 — | 5 5 1 6 5 | 3 3 0 | 5 5 5 3 2 3 | 2 — |
甜。 一呀 劝里格 郎呀 个就格 哭呀新 年。

1 1 1 1 6 6 | 5 3 0 | 6 5 5 1 6 | 5 — | 5 5 6 2 2 2 |
劝郎 呀里格 莫想、 个格 嫩娇 莲， 劝呀格 郎呀

1 1 0 | 5 5 5 1 6 5 | 3 3 0 | 1 1 2 5 3 3 | 2 2 0 |
莫想、 嫩呀 娇里格 要呀 实在 呀里格 丈夫

1 1 2 3 3 3 | 2 — | 1 1 1 6 6 | 5 3 0 | 6 5 1 6 |
个子格 舍得 乎， 无法 呀里格 脱身 见到哥哥

5 — | 1 1 6 5 6 | 1 — | 1 1 2 5 3 3 | 2 3 2 6 |
面， 唉呀 干哥 哥 你有 呀里格 铜呀钱呦

1 5 6 2 6 | 5 — ‖（竹板过门）‖ 5 5 5 1 6 5 | - 3 3 |
去个 别古 连 心干 呀里格 老妹

5 5 5 3 2 3 | 2 — | 1 1 1 6 6 | 5 3 5 | 6 5 1 6 |
个格 嫩 娇 莲 晓得 呀里格 涯妹 就是 要铜

5 — | 5·6 2 6 | 1 1 6 | 5 5 5 1 6 5 | 3 3· |
钱， 再 多呀 铜钱 郎 会 出 哟

·96·

1 1 2 5 3 3 | 2 2 2 | 1 1 2 5 3 | 2 — |
你若 要里格 铜 钱 个就 有花 边

1 1 6 6 6 | 5 3 5 | 6 5 1 6 | 5 — | 1 1 6 5 6 |
诗表 呀里格 妹 么 开呀 开句 言， 唉呀 干妹

1 — | 1 1 2 5 3 3 | 2 3 2 1 | 1 5 6 2 1 6 | 5 — |
妹 为何 呀里格 妹呀 妹 不呀 不开 言。

（竹板过门）| 5 1 6 5 | 3 3 0 | 5 5 5 3 2 3 |
心 肝里格 哥哥 个个 涯 个

2 0 | 1 1 6 6 6 | 5 3 0 | 6 5 1 6 6 | 5 — |
郎， 你有 呀里格 铜 钱 个只 有何 用？

5 5 6 2 2 2 | 1 1 0 | 5 5 5 1 6 5 | 3 3 0 |
你有 呀里格 铜钱 呀 有里格 用，

1 1 2 5 3 3 | 2 2 0 | 1 1 2 3 3 3 | 2 — |
你有 呀里格 花边 涯也 吾敢 想、

1 1 1 6 6 | 5 3 3 | 6 5 1 6 6 | 5 — | 1 1 6 5 6 |
涯呀 里格 屋家 个格 有涯 娘 哎呀 干哥

1 — | 1 1 2 5 3 3 | 2 3 2 1 | 1 5 5 1 6 6 |
哥 你要 呀里格 连呀 妹呀 你要 去别

5 — ‖……‖
方。

注：要——意思，瑞金方言，不要的意思。

·97·

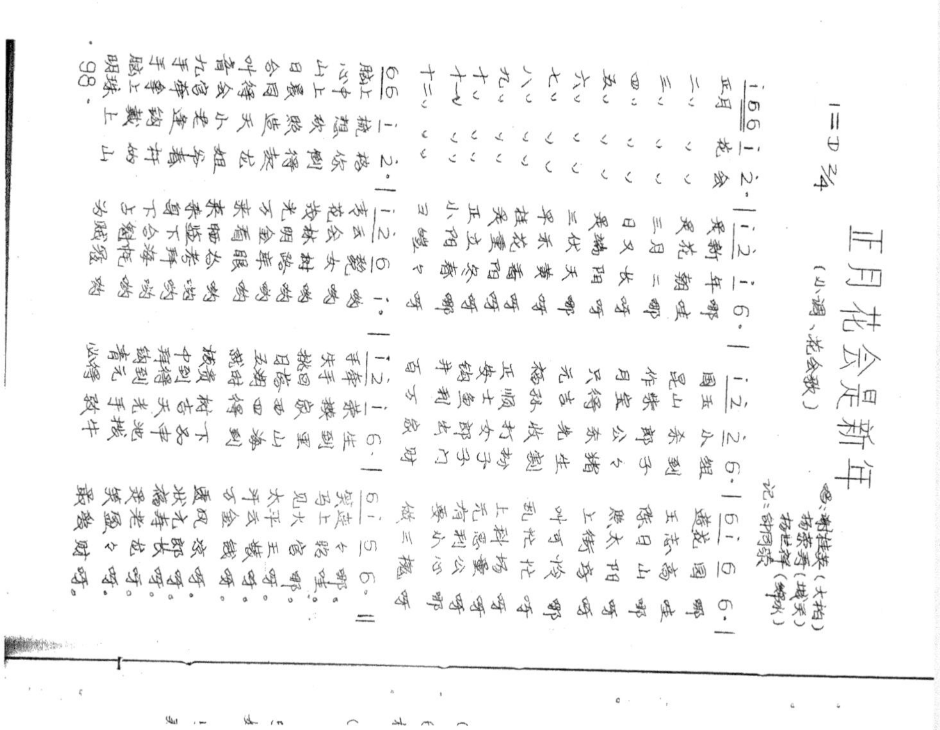

正月花会是新年

1=D 2/4　（小调、花会歌）

唱：谢桂英（大柏）
杨荣秀（坳头）
杨世祥（蟀水）
记：钟同荣

i66 i 2· | i2 i 6· | i2 2 6· | 6i 6 6· |

正月花会 是新年哪 国玉小组 游花园哪
二〃〃〃 是花朝哇 昆山杀到 王志高哇
三〃〃〃 三月二哪 作柴郎子 陈日山哪
四〃〃〃 日又长呀 月宝公公 照太阳呀
五〃〃〃 是端阳呀 只得杀猪 上街卖呀
六〃〃〃 三伏天哪 元吉先生 叫可怜哪
七〃〃〃 早禾黄呀 福孙收割 乱忙忙呀
八〃〃〃 桂花香呀 正顺打扮 上科场呀
九〃〃〃 是重阳呀 安士女子 元思量呀
十〃〃〃 正立冬呀 钩鱼郎子 有利公呀
十一〃〃〃 小阳春哪 井利出门 要小心哪
十二〃〃〃 习嗑嗑呀 百万家财 做三槐呀

66 i 2· | i2 6 i· | i2 i 6· | 6i 5 6· ||

脑上梳格 青云貌哟 手牵荣生 笑迹迹哪。
心中想你 花会女哟 失手摸到 马上骆哇。
山上砍倒 茂林树哟 挑回家里 见大官哪。
日晨照得 光明路哟 日落西山 太平王呀。
合同造契 万金库哟 五湖四海 汗云装呀。
叫得天龙 来看眼哟 就时得到 万金钱呀。
音会小姐 来晒谷哟 板贵树下 透风凉呀。
九官老爷 来监考哟 中到吉名 状元郎呀。
手牵逢春 身下拜哟 拜得天申 福寿长呀。
手拿钩杆 下合海哟 钩到光池 是老龙呀。
脑上戴的 占魁帽哟 青元手拢 笑盈盈呀。
明珠上山 为贼寇哟 必得致牛 最发财呀。

·98·

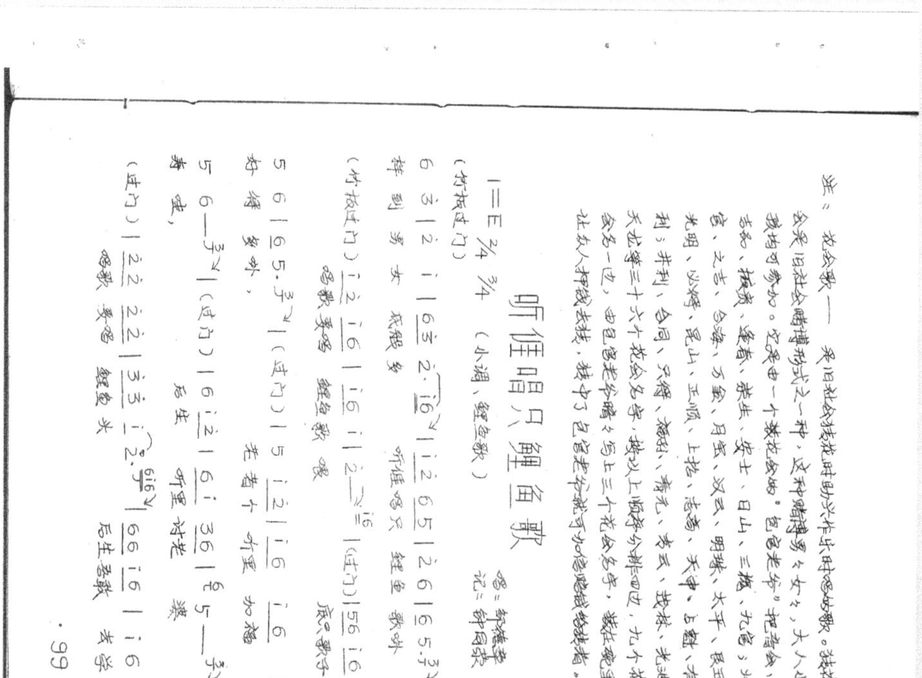

注：花会歌—— 是旧社会猜花时助兴作乐时唱的歌。猜花会是旧社会赌博形式之一种，这种赌博男々女々，大人小孩均可参加。它是由一个装花会的"包官老爷"把青会、吉品、板贵、逢春、荣生、安士、日山、三槐、九官；火官、之吉、合海、万金、月宝、汉云、明珠、太平、良玉；光明、必得、昆山、正顺、上招、志高、天申、占魁、有利；井利、合同、只得、福孙、青元、青云、茂林、光池、天龙等三十六个花会名字，按以上顺序分排四边，九个花会名一边，由包官老爷暗々写上三个花会名字，装在碗里，让众人押钱去猜，猜中了包官老爷就可加倍赔钱给猜者。

听佢唱只鲤鱼歌

1=E 2/4 3/4　（小调、鲤鱼歌）

唱：邹德莘
记：钟同荣

（竹板过门）

6 3 | 2 i | 63 2· i6 | i2 65 | 26 | 6 5·3 |
拌到男女 花般多 听佢唱只 鲤鱼 歌咻

（竹板过门）i2 i6 | i6 i | 2— | （过门）| 56 i6 |
唱歌要唱 鲤鱼歌 喂 底只歌子

5 6 | 6 5·3 | （过门）| 5 i2 | i6 i6 |
好得 多咻， 老者个 听里 加福

5 6— | （过门）| 6 i2 | 6i 36 | 5— |
寿 哇， 后生 听里 讨老 婆

（过门）| 22 22 | 33 i 2·616 | 66 i6 | i 6 |
唱歌 要唱 鲤鱼 头 后生吾敢 去学

·99·

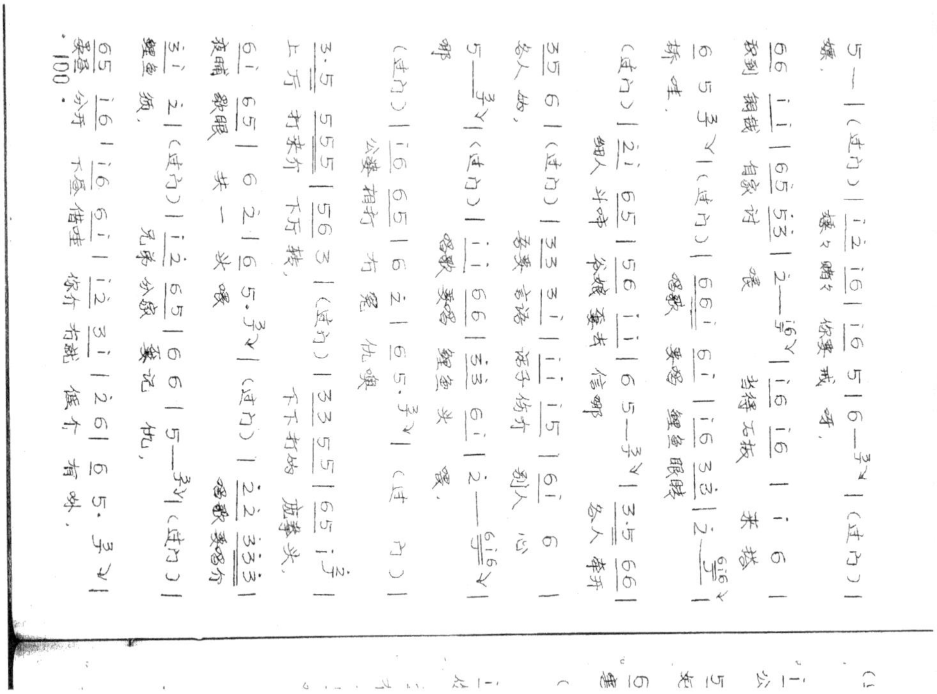

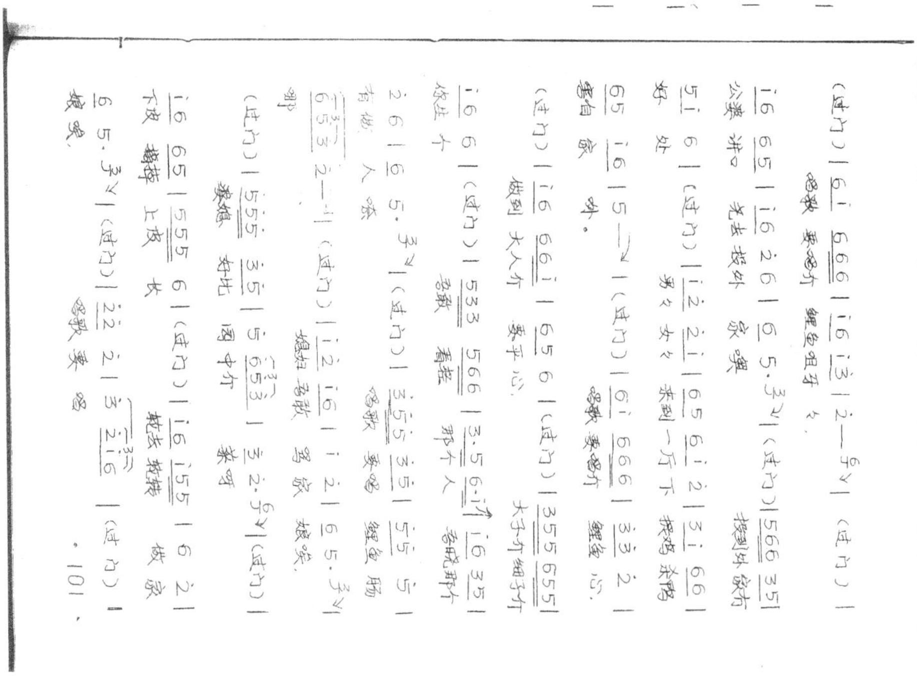

5 — | (过门) | 1̇2̇ 1̇6 | 1̇6 5 | 6 — | (过门) |
嫖． 嫖々赌々 你要戒 呀，

66 1̇1̇ | 65 53̇ | 2̇ — | 1̇6 1̇6 | 1̇ 6 |
积到 铜钱 自家讨 喂 当得石板 来 搭

6 5 | (过门) | 66 1̇ 6 1̇ | 1̇6 3 3̇ | 2̇ — |
桥 哇． 唱歌 要唱 鲤鱼眼睛

(过门) | 2̇1̇ 65 | 56 1̇1̇ | 6 5 — | 3·5 66 |
细人斗伴 爷娘 要去 信哪 各人牵开

35 6 | (过门) | 33 31̇ | 1̇1̇ 1̇5 | 61̇ 6 |
各人 做， 吾要 言语 流子 伤个 别人 心

5 — | (过门) | 1̇1̇ 66 | 33̇ 61̇ | 2̇ — |
哪 唱歌 要唱 鲤鱼 头 喂．

(过门) | 1̇6 65 | 6 2̇ | 6 5· | (过 门) |
公婆相打 冇 冤 仇噢

3·5 555 | 56 3 | (过门) | 33 55 | 65 1̇ |
上 厅 打来个 下厅 转， 下下打的 庞拳头，

61̇ 65 | 6 2̇ | 6 5· | (过门) | 2̇2̇ 3̇3̇3̇ |
夜晡 歇眼 共 一 头 喂 唱歌 要唱个

31̇ 2̇ | (过门) | 1̇2̇ 65 | 6 6 | 5 — | (过门) |
鲤鱼 须， 兄弟 分家 要记 仇，

65 1̇6 | 1̇6 61̇ | 1̇2̇ 31̇ | 2̇6 | 6 5· |
晏昼 分开 下昼 借哇 你个 冇就 佢个 有 咧，

·100·

(过门) | 61̇ 666 | 1̇6 1̇3̇ | 2̇ — | (过门) |
唱歌 要唱个 鲤鱼咀牙 々．

1̇6 65 | 1̇6 2̇6 | 6 5· | (过门) | 566 35 |
公婆 讲口 先去 投外 家 噢 投到外家冇

51̇ 6 | (过门) | 1̇2̇ 2̇1̇ | 65 61̇ 2̇ | 31̇ 66 |
好 处 男々 女々 来到一厅 下 捉鸡 杀鸭

65 1̇6 | 5 — | (过门) | 61̇ 666 | 3̇3̇ 2̇ |
害自 家 咧。 唱歌 要唱个 鲤鱼 心．

(过门) | 1̇6 661̇ | 65 6 | (过门) | 355 655 |
做到 大人个 要平 心， 大子个细子个

1̇6 6 | (过门) | 533 566 | 3·5 6·1̇ | 1̇6 35 |
你生 个 吾敢 看轻 那个 人 吾晓那个

2̇6 | 6 5· | (过门) | 355 35 | 55 5 |
有做 人 啥 唱歌 要唱 鲤鱼 肠

653 2̇ — | (过门) | 1̇2̇ 1̇6 | 1̇ 2̇ | 6 5· |
哪 媳妇 吾敢 骂 家 娘唉，

(过门) | 555 35 | 5 653 | 3 2̇· | (过门) |
婆媳 好比 同中个 亲呀

1̇6 65 | 555 6 | (过门) | 1̇6 1̇55 | 6 2̇ |
下皮 搞碎 上皮 长 转去 转转 做 家

6 5· | (过门) | 2̇2̇ 2̇ | 3 2̇1̇6 | (过门) |
娘 唉， 唱歌 要 唱

·101·

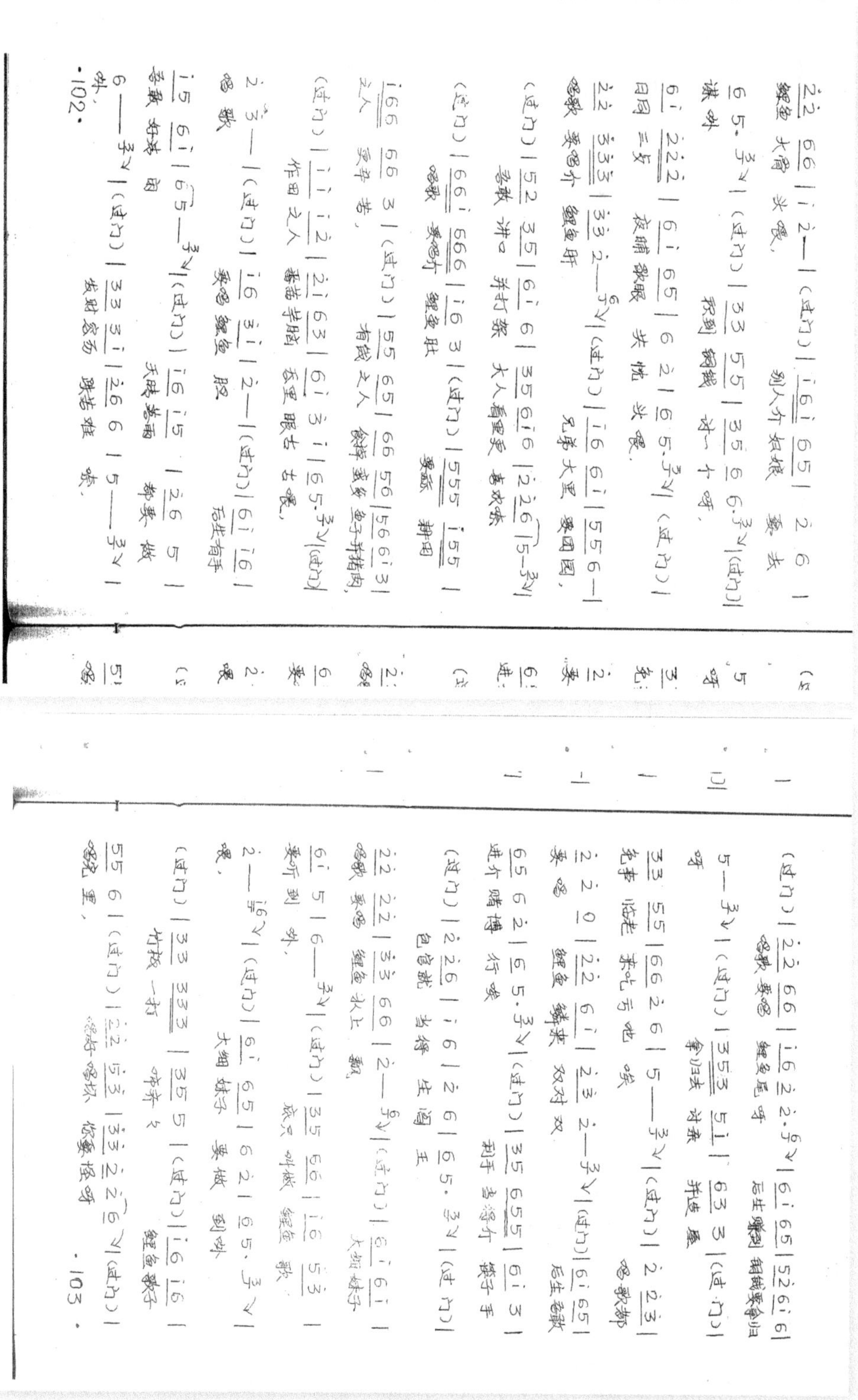

22 66 | 1 2— | (过门) | 161 65 | 2 6 |
鲤鱼 大骨 头喂，　别人介 妇娘 要 去

6 5· 3 | (过门) | 33 55 | 35 6 6· 3 | (过门) |
谋 咧　积到 铜钱 讨一 个 呀，

61 222 | 61 65 | 6 2 | 6 5· 3 | (过门) |
日间 三支　夜晡 歌眼 失 忱 头 喂，

22 333 | 33 2— 6 3 | (过门) | 16 61 | 556 — |
唱歌 要唱介 鲤鱼 肝　兄弟 大里 要团 园，

(过门) | 52 35 | 61 6 | 35 616 | 226 | 5— 3 |
吾敢 讲口 并打 架 大人看里更 喜欢佬

(过门) | 661 666 | 16 3 | (过门) | 555 155 |
唱歌 要唱介 鲤鱼 肚　要添 耕田

166 66 3 | (过门) | 55 65 | 66 56 | 5661 3 |
之人 受辛 苦，　有钱 之人 食撑 蚕乡 鱼子并猪肉，

(过门) | 11 12 | 21 63 | 61 3 1 | 6 5· 3 | (过门) |
作田 之人 番茄 芋脑 吞里 眼古 古喂，

2 3— | (过门) | 16 31 | 2— | (过门) | 61 16 |
唱 歌　要唱 鲤鱼 胶　后生 有手

15 61 | 65— 3 | (过门) | 16 15 | 26 5 |
吾敢 好汤 由　天晴 落雨 都要 做

6—— 3 | (过门) | 33 31 | 26 6 | 5—— 3 |
咧，　发财 容易 赚若 难 呢，

·102·

(过门) | 22 66 | 16 2 2· 6 3 | 61 65 | 5261 6 |
唱歌 要唱 鲤鱼尾 呀　后生 赚到 铜钱要拿归

5— 3 | (过门) | 353 51 | 63 3 | (过门) |
呀　拿归去 讨亲 并支 屋

33 55 | 66 2 6 | 5—— 3 | (过门) | 2 23 |
免事 临老 来吃 亏 也 唉　唱歌都

2 2 0 | 22 61 | 23 2— 3 | (过门) | 61 65 |
要 唱　鲤鱼 鳞来 双对 双　后生 老嵌

65 6 2 | 6 5· 3 | (过门) | 35 655 | 61 3 |
进介 赌博 行 唉　利手 当得介 筷子 手

(过门) | 2 26 | 1 6 | 2 6 | 6 5· 3 | (过门) |
包官就 当得 生 阎 王

22 22 | 33 66 | 2— 6 3 | (过门) | 61 61 |
唱歌 要唱 鲤鱼 水上 飘　大细 妹子

61 5 | 6— 3 | (过门) | 35 66 | 16 53 |
要听 到 咧，　底只 咐做 鲤鱼 歌

2— 16 | (过门) | 61 65 | 6 2 | 6 5· 3 |
喂，　大细 妹子 要做 到咧

(过门) | 33 333 | 35 5 | (过门) | 16 16 |
竹板 一打　咐齐 々　鲤鱼 歌子

55 6 | (过门) | 22 53 | 33 2 26 | (过门) |
唱完 里，　唱好 唱坏 你要怪 呀

·103·

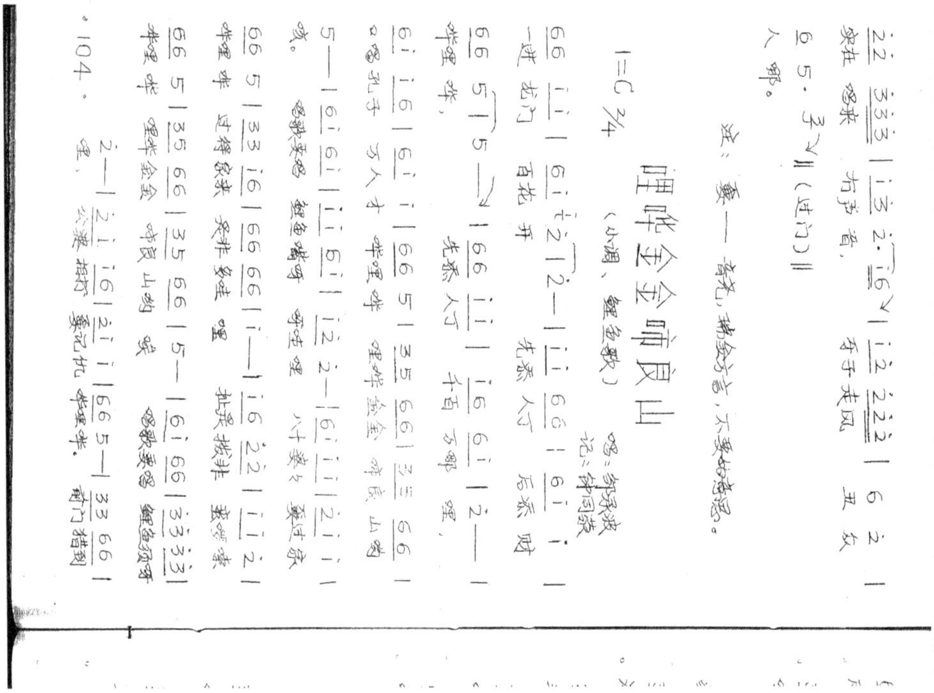

22 333 | 13 2· 16 | 12 222 | 6 2 |
实在 唱来 冇声 音， 牙子 走风 丑 众

6 5· 3 ‖（过门）‖
人 哪。

注：嫑——音尧，瑞金方言，不要的意思。

哩哗金金咿良山

1=C 2/4 （小调、鲤鱼歌） 唱：邹承波 记：钟同荣

66 11 | 61 2 | 2— | 11 66 | 61 1 |
一进 龙门 百花 开 先添 人丁 后添 财

66 5 | 5— | 66 11 | 16 61 | 2— |
哗哩 哗， 先添 人丁 千百 万哪 哩，

61 16 | 61 1 | 66 5 | 35 66 | 35 66 |
口唱 孔子 万人 才 哗哩 哗 哩哗 金金 咿良 山哟

5— | 61 61 | 11 61 | 12 2— | 61 11 | 21 1 |
唛。 唱歌 要唱 鲤鱼 嘴呀 呀生 哩 八十 婆婆 要过 家

66 5 | 33 16 | 66 66 | 1— | 16 22 | 11 2 |
哗哩 哗 过得 家来 吴非 多娃 哩 扯吴 拨非 蛮嘞 凄

66 5 | 35 66 | 35 66 | 5— | 61 66 | 3333 |
哗哩 哗 哩哗 金金 咿良 山哟 唛 唱歌 要唱 鲤鱼 须呀

2— | 21 16 | 21 1 | 66 5— | 33 66 |
哩， 公婆 相打 嫑记 仇 哗哩 哗。 前门 猎到

·104·

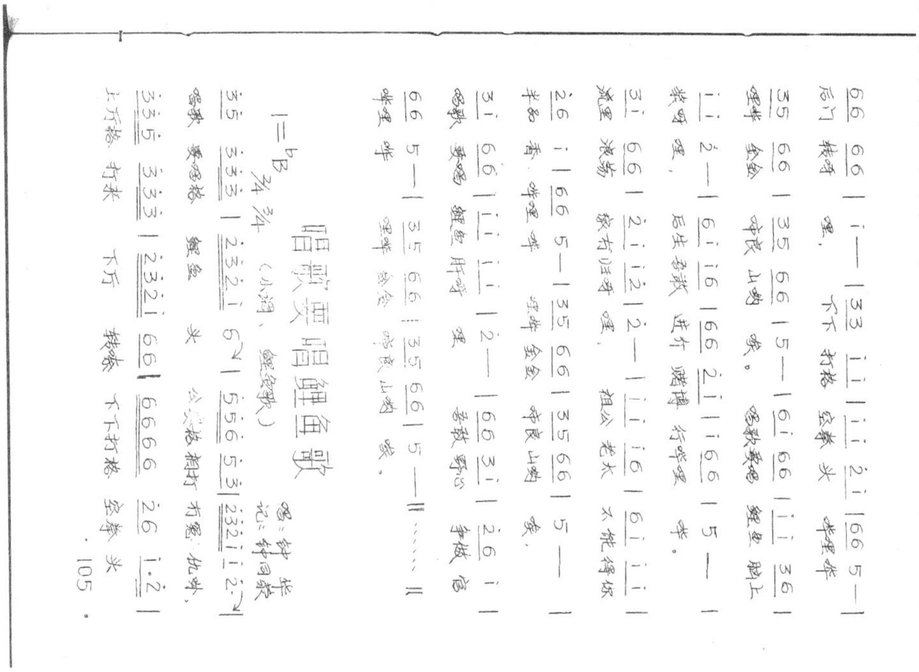

66 66 | 1— | 33 11 | 11 21 | 66 5— |
后门 转呀 哩， 下下 打格 空拳 头 哗哩 哗

35 66 | 35 66 | 5— | 61 66 | 11 36 |
哩哗 金金 咿良 山哟 唛。 唱歌 要唱 鲤鱼 脑上

11 2— | 61 16 | 66 21 | 166 | 5— |
紫呀 哩， 后生 子孙 莫介 赌博 行哗哩 哗。

31 66 | 21 12 | 2— | 11 16 | 61 11 |
流里 浪荡 家有 归呀 哩， 祖公 老太 不能 得你

26 1 | 66 5— | 35 66 | 35 66 | 5— |
半句 香， 哗哩 哗 哩哗 金金 咿良 山哟 唛，

31 66 | 11 11 | 2— | 66 31 | 26 1 |
唱歌 要唱 鲤鱼 肝呀 哩 吾敢 野心 争做 官

66 5— | 35 66 | 35 66 | 5— ‖ …… ‖
哗哩 哗 哩哗 金金 咿良 山哟 唛。

唱歌要唱鲤鱼歌

1=♭B 2/4 3/4 （小调、鲤鱼歌） 唱：钟华 记：钟同荣

35 333 | 2321 6 | 556 53 | 2321 12· |
唱歌 要唱格 鲤鱼 头 公婆格 相打 冇冤 仇哟，

335 333 | 2321 66 | 6666 26 12 |
上厅格 打来 下厅 转嘛 下下打格 空拳 头

·105·

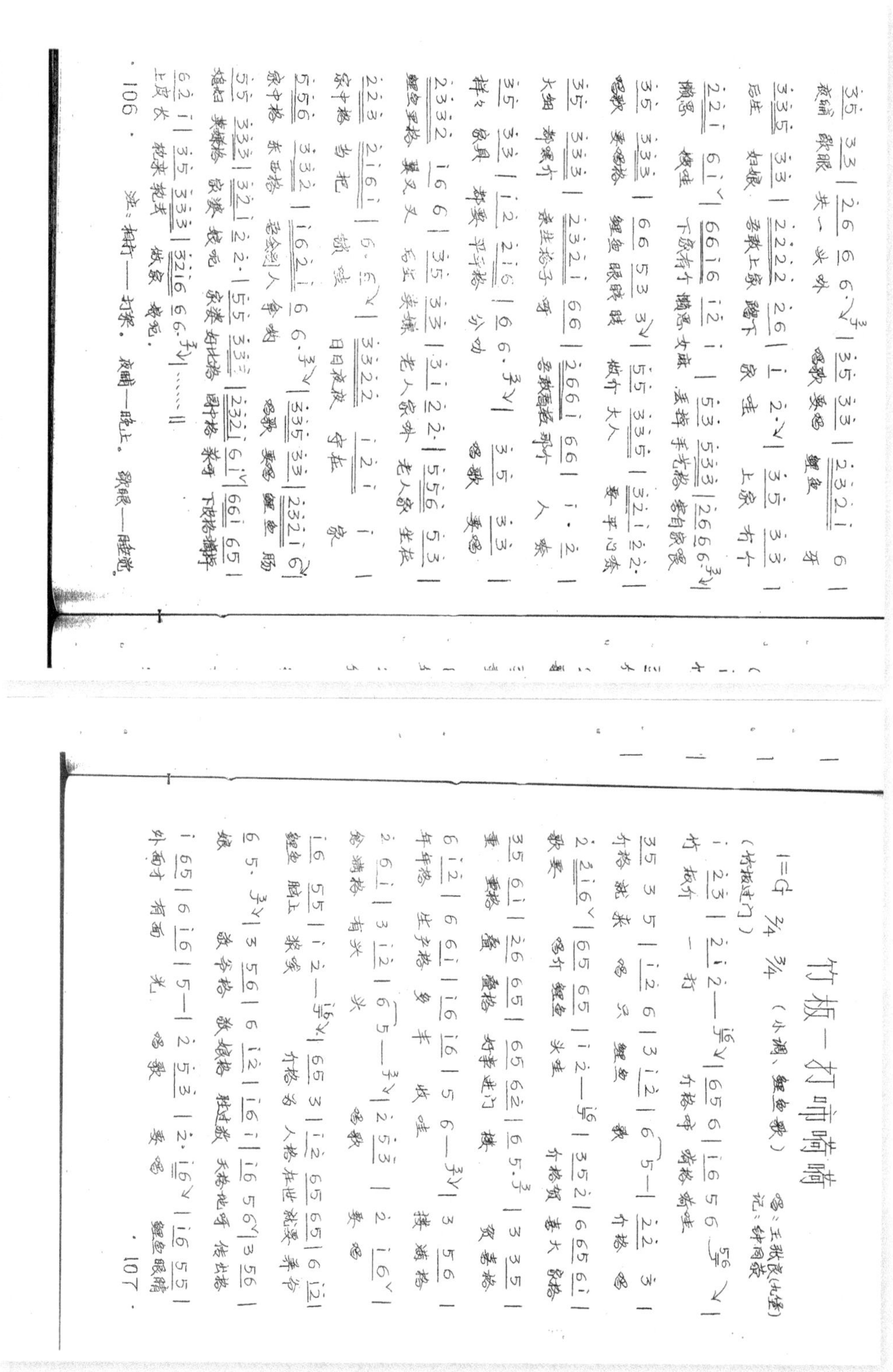

夜晡 歌眼 共一头吶 唱歌 要唱 鲤鱼 牙

后生 妇娘 吾歌上家 蹬下 家 哇 上家 有个

懒思 嫂哇 下家有个 懒思女麻 丢掉 手艺格 害自家喂

唱歌 要唱格 鲤鱼 眼睛 睛 做个 大人 要 平心索

大细 都喂介 亲生格子 呀 吾敢看着 那个 人 嗦

样々 家具 都要 平平格 分 动 唱歌 要唱

鲤鱼里格 莫又又 后生 夹嫁 老人家吶 老人家 生在

家中格 当把 锁 哇 日日夜夜 守在 家

家中格 东西格 吾会到人 争 呐 唱歌 要唱 鲤鱼 肠

媳妇 莫嫌格 家婆 较呃 家婆 好比格 园中格 菜呀 下皮格 摘掉

上皮 长 枕来 轮来 做家 婆呃.

· 106 ·

注：相打——打架。夜晡——晚上。歌眼——睡觉。

竹板一打响嘀嘀

1=G 2/4 3/4 （小调、鲤鱼歌）

唱：王张良(九堡)
记：钟同荣

（竹板过门）

竹 板介 一 打 介格呼 嘀格 嘀哇

介格 就 来 唱 只 鲤鱼 歌 介格 唱

歌要 唱介 鲤鱼 头哇 介格贺 喜大 家格

重 重格 叠 叠格 好事进门 楼 贺 喜格

年年格 生产格 多 丰 收 哇 搂 满格

仓满格 有头 头 唱歌 要 唱

鲤鱼 脑上 浆 唉 介格 为 人格 在世 就要 养爷

娘 敬爷格 敬娘格 胜过敬 天格他呀 传出格

外面才 有面 光 唱歌 要唱 鲤鱼眼睛

· 107 ·

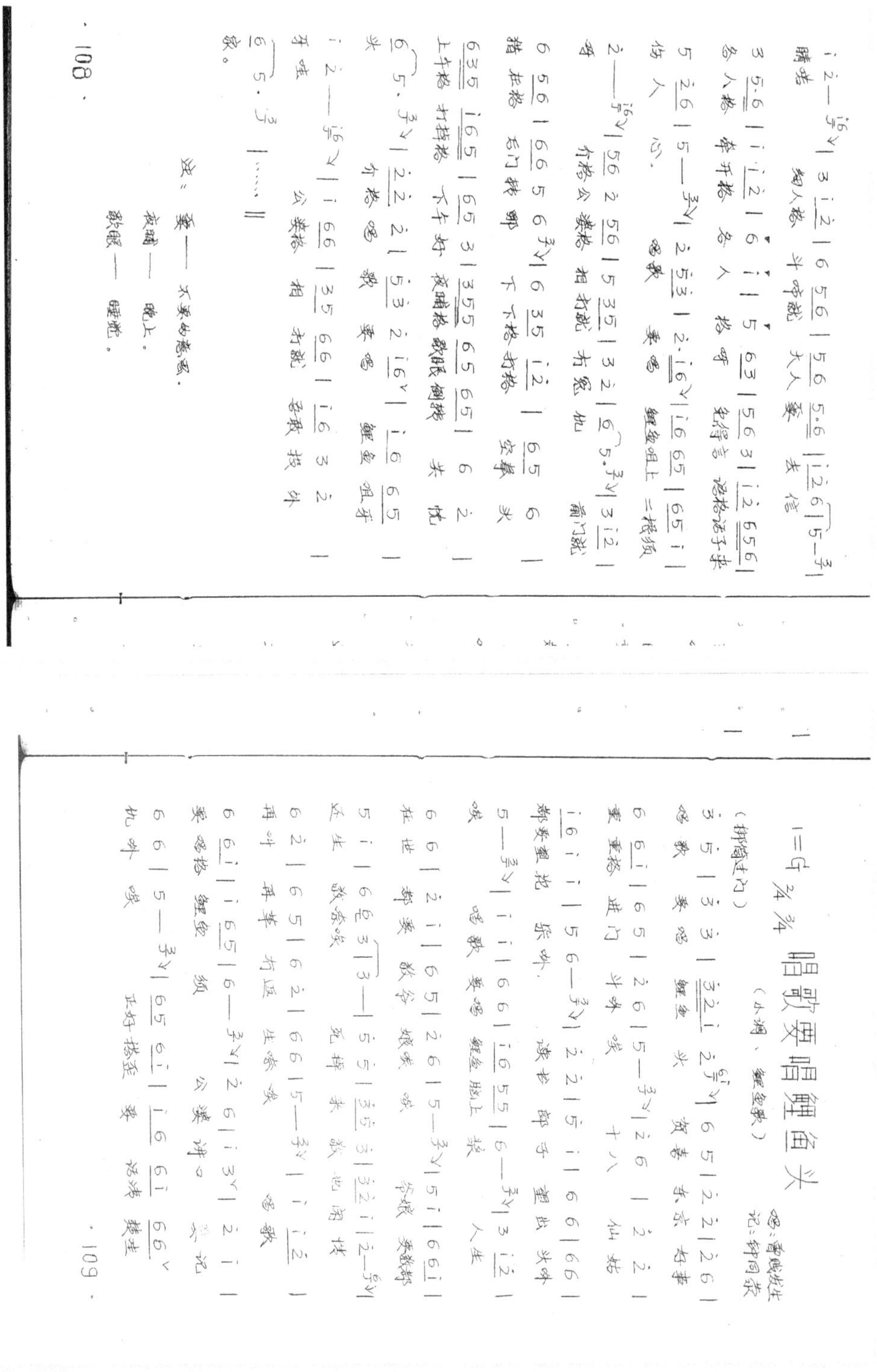

睛咾　　细人格　斗吵就　大人要　去信

各人格　牵开格　各人　格呀　免得言　语格话子来

伤人心。　　唱歌　要唱　鲤鱼咀上　二根须

呀　　介格公婆格　相打就　冇冤仇　　前门就

猎在格　后门转哪　下下格打格　空拳头

上午格　打拧格　下午好　夜晡格歇眠倒转　失忧

头　　介格唱歌　要唱　鲤鱼咀牙

牙哇　　公婆格　相　打就　吾歌投外

家。

注：要——不要的意思。

夜晡——晚上。

歇眠——睡觉。

· 108 ·

唱歌要唱鲤鱼头

1=G 2/4 3/4

（小调、鲤鱼歌）

唱：曾贱发生
记：钟同荣

（掷筒过门）

唱歌　要唱　鲤鱼　头　贺喜　东京　好事

重重格　进门　斗哟　唉　　十八　仙姑

都要望　祝　乐哟。　读书　郎子　望出　头哟

唉　　唱歌　要唱　鲤鱼脑上　操　　人生

在世　都要　敬爷　娘唉　唉　　爷娘　要敬都

还生　敬奈唉　　死掉　来　敬　也闲　情

再哟　再革　冇返　生嗦　唉　　唱歌

要唱格　鲤鱼　须　　公婆　讲口　要记

仇哟　唉　　正好搭歪　要　话诗　楚生

· 109 ·

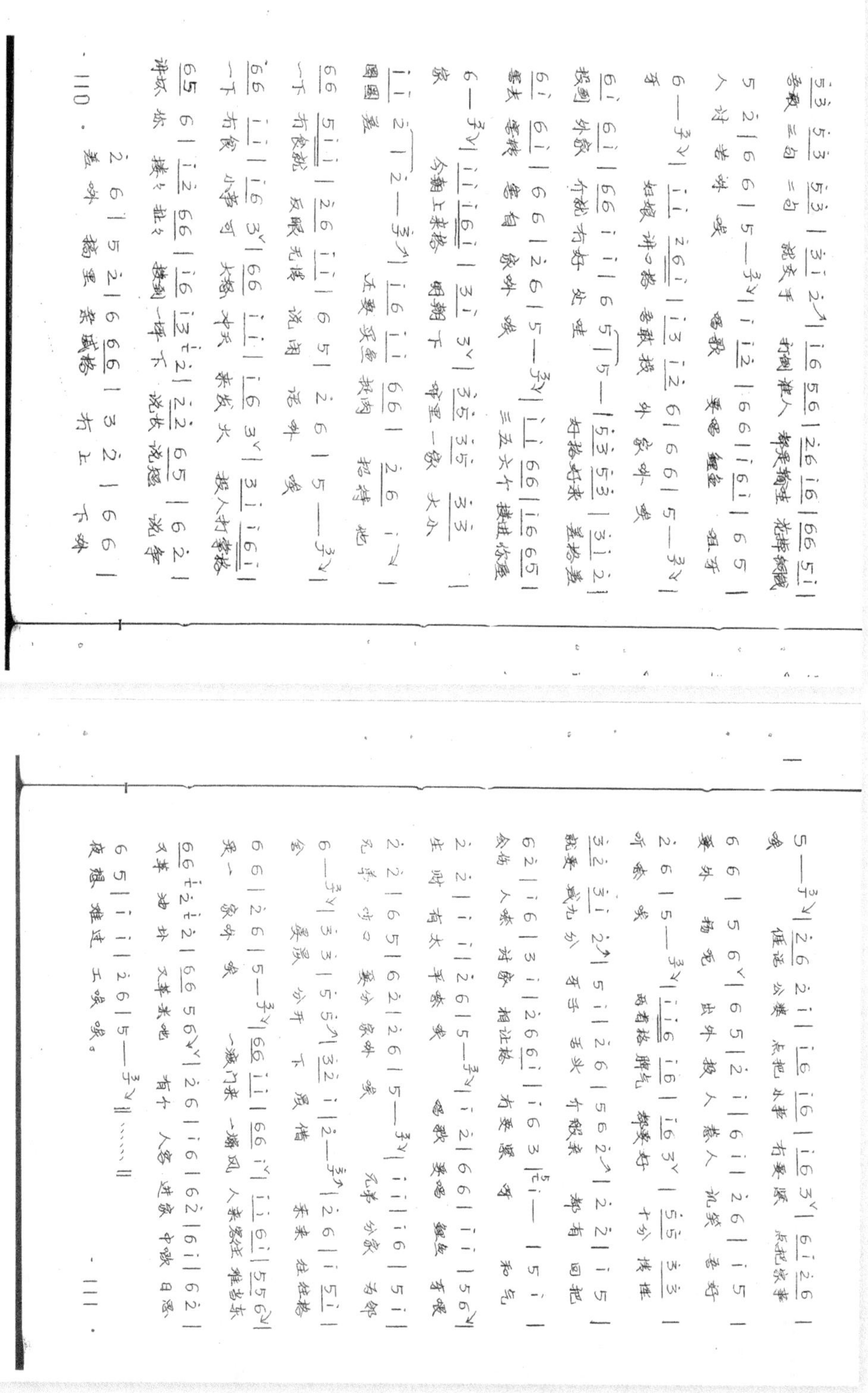

5 3 5 3 5 3 | 3 1 2 | 1 6 5 6 | 2 6 1 6 | 6 6 5 1 |
吾敢三句二句 就交手 打倒碓人 都是输哇 花掉铜钱

5 2 | 6 6 | 5 — 3 | 1 1 2 | 6 6 | 1 6 1 | 6 5 |
人讨 苦呀 唉 唱歌 要唱 鲤鱼 姐牙

6 — 3 | 1 1 2 6 1 | 1 3 1 2 6 | 6 6 | 5 — 3 |
牙 妇娘 讲口格 吾敢投 外家 呀 唉

6 1 6 1 | 6 6 1 1 | 6 5 | 5 — | 5 3 5 3 | 3 1 2 |
投到 外家 介就 有好 处哇 好格好来 差格差

6 1 6 1 | 6 6 | 2 6 | 5 — 3 | 1 1 6 6 | 1 6 6 5 |
害去 害转 害自 家呀 唉 三五六个 搂进你屋

6 — 3 | 1 1 1 6 1 | 3 1 3 | 3 5 3 5 3 3 |
家 今朝上来格 明朝下 呀里一家 大小

1 1 2 | 2 — 3 | 1 6 1 1 6 6 | 2 6 1 |
团团 差 还要买鱼 买肉 招待 他

6 6 5 1 1 | 2 6 1 1 | 6 5 | 2 6 | 5 — 3 |
一下 有食就 反眼无情 说闲 话呀 唉

6 6 1 1 | 1 6 3 | 6 6 1 1 | 1 6 3 | 3 1 1 6 1 |
一下 有食 小事可 大格 冲天 来发火 投人打掌格

6 5 6 | 1 2 6 6 | 1 6 1 3 1 2 | 2 2 6 5 | 6 2 |
讲坏 你 搂々 扯々 搂到一坪 下 说长 说短 说争

2 6 | 5 2 | 6 6 6 | 3 2 | 6 6 |
差呀 搞里 亲戚格 有上 下呀

· 110 ·

5 — 3 | 2 6 2 1 | 1 6 1 6 | 1 6 3 | 6 1 2 6 |
唉 佢话 公婆 点把 小事 有要紧 点把家事

6 6 | 5 6 | 6 5 | 2 1 | 6 1 | 2 6 | 1 5 |
要外 扬咤 出外 投人 惹人 讥笑 吾好

2 6 | 5 — 3 | 1 1 6 1 6 | 1 6 3 | 5 5 3 3 |
听紧 唉 两着格 脾气 都要好 十分 携挂

3 2 3 1 2 | 5 1 | 2 6 | 5 6 2 | 2 2 | 1 5 |
就要 减九分 牙子 舌头 介般亲 都有 回把

6 2 | 1 6 | 3 1 | 2 6 6 1 | 1 6 3 | 1 — | 5 1 |
会伤 人嗦 讨家 相让格 有要紧 呀 和气

2 2 | 1 1 | 2 6 | 5 — 3 | 1 2 | 6 6 | 1 1 | 5 6 |
生财 有太 平索 唉 唱歌 要唱 鲤鱼 牙喂

2 2 | 6 5 | 6 2 | 2 6 | 5 — 3 | 1 1 | 1 6 | 5 1 |
兄弟 吵口 要分 家呀 唉 兄弟 分家 为邻

6 — 3 | 3 3 | 5 5 | 3 2 1 | 2 — 3 | 2 6 | 1 5 1 |
舍 晏晨 分开 下 晨借 来来 往往格

6 6 | 2 6 | 5 — 3 | 6 6 1 1 | 6 6 1 | 1 1 6 1 | 5 5 6 |
晃一 家呀 唉 一派门来 一瑞风 人亲客往 难当东

6 6 1 2 1 2 | 6 6 5 6 | 2 6 | 1 6 | 6 2 | 6 1 | 6 2 |
又革 油卦 又革米吔 有个 人客 进家 中欧 日思

6 5 | 1 1 | 2 6 | 5 — 3 ‖……‖
夜想 难过 工唉 唉。

· 111 ·

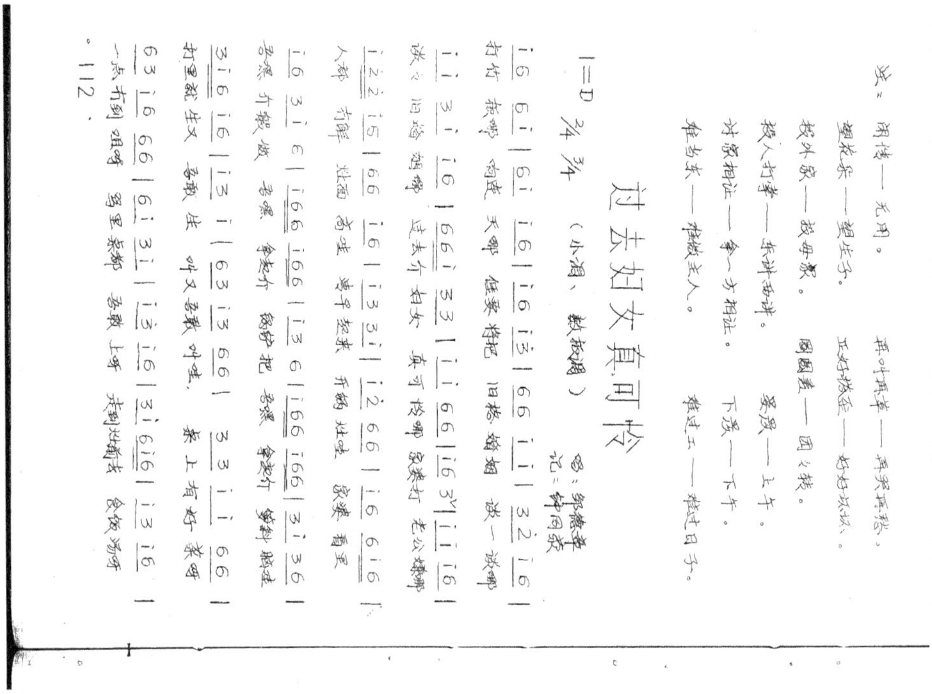

注：闲传——无用。　　再叫再革——再哭再愁。
望花朵——望生子。　　正好揿歪——好好坏坏。
转外家——投母家。　　团团转——团々转。
投人打掌——东讲西讲。　　晏昼——上午。
讨家相让——争一方相让。　　下昼——下午。
难当东——难做主人。　　难过工——难过日子。

过去妇女真可怜

1=D 2/4 3/4　（小调、鼓板调）　　唱：邹德章
　　　　　　　　　　　　　　　　记：钟同荣

1̇6 61̇ | 61̇ 1̇6 | 1̇6 1̇3̇ | 66 1̇1̇ | 3̇2̇ 1̇6 |
打竹 板哪 响连 天哪 任要 将把 旧格 婚姻 谈一 谈哪

1̇1̇ 31̇ 1̇6 | 661̇ 33 | 1̇1̇ 66 | 1̇6 3ᵛ | 1̇1̇ 1̇6 |
谈々 旧格 婚姻 过去介 妇女 真可 怜哪 家婆打 老公嫌哪

1̇2̇2̇ 1̇5 | 66 1̇6 | 1̇3 31̇ | 1̇2̇ 66 | 1̇6 61̇6 |
人都 有鲜 灶面 高哇 透早 起来 开锅 灶哇 家婆 看里

1̇6 31̇ 6 | 1̇66 1̇66 | 1̇3 6 | 1̇66 1̇66 | 31̇ 36 |
吾嘿 介锅 做 吾嘿 拿起介 锅铲 把 吾嘿 拿起介 箩料 脑哇

31̇6 1̇6 | 1̇3 1̇ | 63 1̇3 66 | 33 1̇1̇ 66 |
打里就 生又 吾敢 生 叫又吾敢 叫哇， 桌上 有好 菜呀

63 1̇6 66 | 61̇ 31̇ | 1̇3 1̇6 | 31̇ 61̇6 | 1̇3 1̇6 |
一点 冇到 咀呀 筠里 桌都 吾敢 上呀 走到灶前去 食饭 汤呀

· 112 ·

61̇ 63 66 | 1̇6 1̇1̇ 3ᵛ | 1̇6 1̇1̇ 66 |
芋头 并芋 脑哇 三岁 还冇 饱 三年 冇衣 做哇

61̇ 1̇6 36 | 1̇6 1̇1̇ 1̇6 | 1̇6 33 1̇6 | 61̇ 33 1̇6 |
四年 冇布 剪哪 穿得 都叫 叮哪 活象豆角 藤哪 大家 想下子呀

1̇6 61̇ 6 | 61̇ 1̇6 | 1̇6 1̇6 | 1̇6 1̇1̇ | 66 1̇6 |
可怜 不可 怜 细媳 妇哇 真吃 亏呀 长时 猎得 庞々 飞呀

33 1̇1̇ | 1̇6 3 | 33 1̇1̇ | 1̇6 1̇6 | 33 1̇1̇ |
食掉 几多 家婆 打 吃了 几多 老大 亏呀 食掉 几多

1̇1̇ 1̇3 66 | 33 1̇1̇ | 1̇6 1̇ | 1̇6 1̇1̇ |
蚊子 狗虱 咬哇 睡掉 几多 草皮 堆 长时 猎得

66 1̇ | 1̇1̇ 31̇ | 1̇3 1̇6 | 31̇ 1̇6 | 1̇6 6 |
庞々 飞， 猎得 蚤都 吾敢 归呀 鱼子 猪肉 冇到 咀

1̇2̇ 1̇2̇ 1̇2̇ | 1̇2̇· 5ᵛ | 5·6 1̇ 1̇ ||
芋荷 擦菜 困々 垒池

1̇61̇ 61̇ 1̇6 | 1̇6 1̇6 | 31̇ 61̇5 | 66 1̇6 |
谈起介 旧婚 姻哪 真气 人哪 有几大子就 我嫁 人哪

31̇ 363 | 1̇1̇ 56 | 66 1̇6 | 1̇6 66 | 36 1̇6 1̇6 |
女人 好象介 鸡毛 子呀 过去 封建 开八 字呀 操个好日子呀

1̇1̇ 1̇61̇ | 61̇ 3 | 33 333 | 1̇6 1̇6 3 | 1̇6 1̇1̇ |
嘀々 嗒々都 就来 讨 七手 八脚 扭进花轿脑 花轿门中

66 3 | 1̇61̇ 1̇1̇ 3 | 61̇ 31̇1̇ | 61̇ 1̇ |
一把 锁 除里你 走进 土 轿夫 把她就 带回 家。

· 113 ·

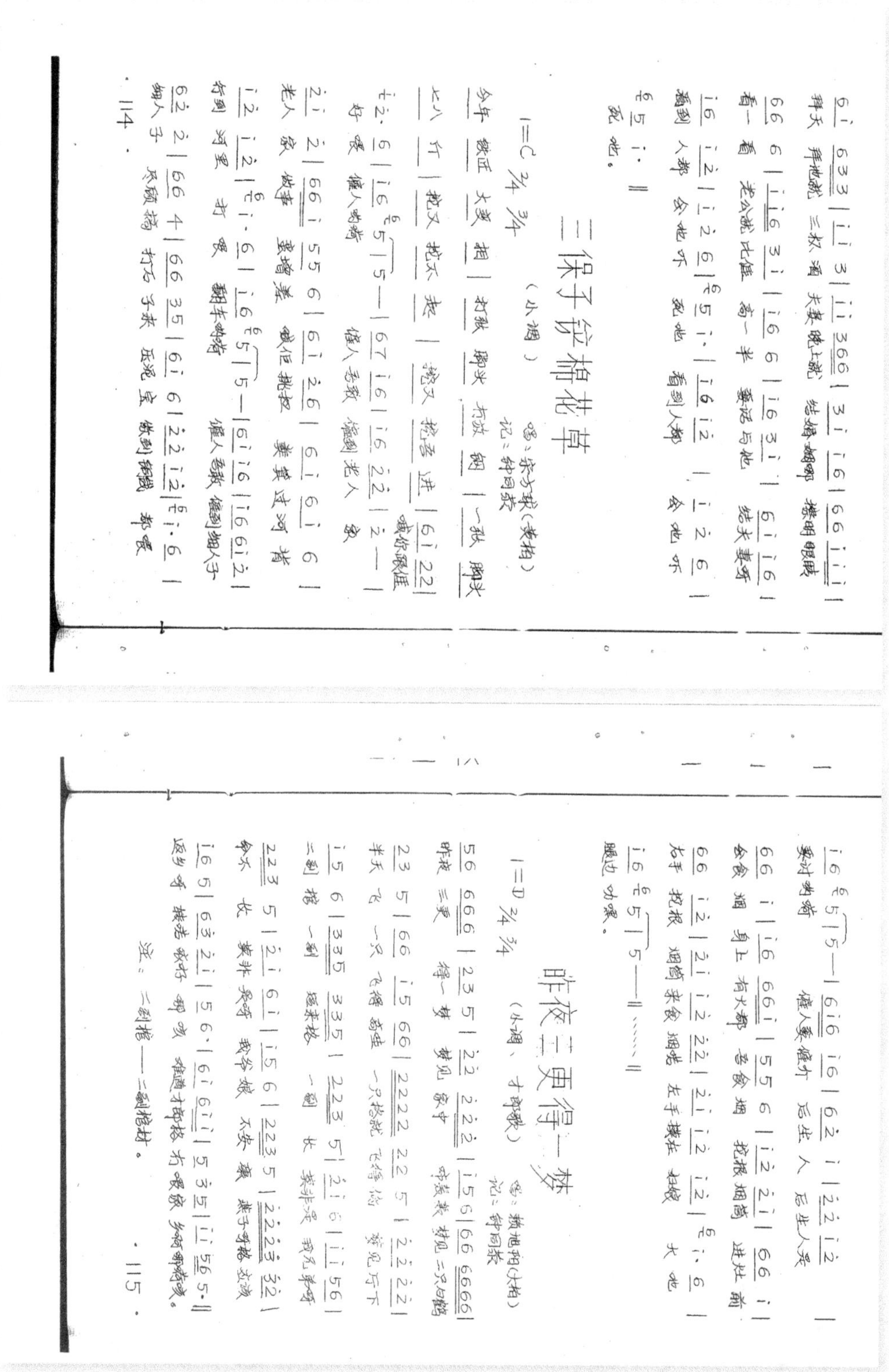

6 1 633 | 1 1 3 | 1 1 366 | 3 1 16 | 66 111 |
拜天　拜地就　三杯　酒　夫妻晚上就　结婚姻哪　擦明眼睛

66 6 | 116 31 | 16 6 | 16 31 | 61 16 |
看一　看　老公就比偃　高一　半　要话与他　结夫妻呀

16 12 | 1 2 6 | 5 1· | 16 12 | 1 2 6 |
看到　人都　会他吓　死他　看到人都　会他吓

5 1· ‖
死他。

三保子铲棉花草

（小调）

1=C 2/4 3/4

唱：宗方球（黄柏）
记：钟同荪

今年　铁匠　大爹　掴 | 打铁　脚头　打放　铜 | 一铁　脚头
七八　斤 | 挖又　挖不　起 | 挖又　挖吾　进 | 61 22 |
喊你跟偃

2· 6 | 16 5 | 5 — | 67 16 | 16 22 | 2 — |
好　喂　偃人哟嗬　偃人乞敢　偃到老人　家

21 2 | 66 1 55 6 | 61 26 | 61 61 6 |
老人　家　做事　蛮增差　喊佢挑担　卖　箕过河　背

12 12 | 1· 6 | 16 5 | 5 — | 61 16 | 16 61 2 |
行到　河里　打　喂　翻车哟嗬　偃人乞敢　偃到细人子

62 2 | 66 4 | 66 35 | 61 6 | 22 12 | 1· 6 |
细人子　尽硕　搞　打石　子来　压泥　宝　做到铜钱　都喂

16 5 | 5 — | 616 16 | 62 1 | 22 12 |
要讨哟嗬　偃人要偃介　后生　人　后生人吴

66 1 | 16 661 | 55 6 | 12 21 | 66 1 |
会食　烟　身上　有火都　吾食　烟　挖根　烟筒　进灶　前

66 12 | 21 12 22 | 21 12 | 12 | 1· 6 |
右手　挖根　烟筒　来食　烟呢　左手　摸在　妇娘　大　他

16 5 | 5 — ‖ …… ‖
眼边　叻喂。

昨夜三更得一梦

（小调、才郎歌）

1=D 2/4 3/4

唱：赖旭翔（大柏）
记：钟同荪

56 666 | 23 5 | 22 222 | 15 6 | 66 6666 |
昨夜　三更　得一　梦　梦见　家中　咁羞羞　梦见二只白鹤

23 5 | 66 15 66 | 2222 22 5 | 22 22 |
半天　飞　一只　飞得　高些　一只格就　飞得低　梦见厅下

15 6 | 335 335 | 223 5 | 21 6 | 11 56 |
二副　棺　一副　短来格　一副　长　莫非是　我兄弟呀

223 5 | 21 61 | 15 6 | 223 5 | 2223 32 |
命不　长　莫非　是呀　我爷娘　不安　康　燕子呀格　立孩

16 5 | 63 21 | 5 6· | 61 611 | 5 35 | 11 56 5· ‖
返乡　呀　转去　敬好　哪　咳　难道才郎格　冇喂家　乡阿哪嗬咳。

注：二副棺——二副棺材。

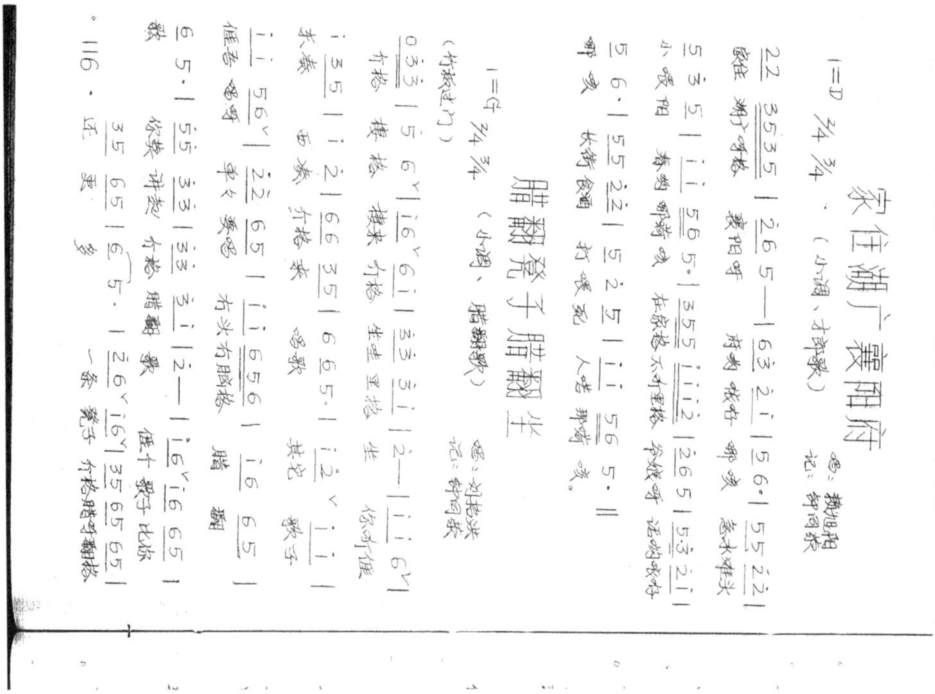

家住湖广襄阳府

1=D 2/4 3/4 ·（小调、才郎歌）

唱：赖旭阳
记：钟同茯

22 3535 | 2̇6 5— | 63̇ 2̇i̇ | 5 6· | 55 2̇2̇ |
家住 湖广呀格 襄阳呀 府哟 依好 哪 咳 急水滩头

5 3̇ 5 | i̇i̇ 56 5· | 355 i̇i̇i̇2̇ | 2̇6 5 | 5·3̇ 2̇i̇ |
小 喂 阳 春哟 哪 莳 咳 在家格不行里格 爷娘呀 话哟依好

5 6· | 55 2̇2̇ | 5 2̇ 5 | i̇i̇ 56 5· ‖
哪 咳 长街食酒 打 喂 死 人嗜 那 莳 咳。

腊翻凳子腊翻生

1=G 2/4 3/4（小调、腊翻歌）

唱：刘振洪
记：钟同茯

（竹板过门）

0 3̇3̇ | 5 6 | i̇6 6i̇ | 3̇3̇ 3̇i̇ | 2̇— | i̇i̇ 6 |
介格 楼 格 楼来 介格 生哇 里格 生 你听倨

i̇ 3̇5 | i̇ 2̇ | 66 35 | 6 65· | i̇2̇ | i̇i̇ |
东奏 西奏 介格 来 唱歌 其它 歌子

i̇i̇ 56 | 2̇2̇ 65 | i̇i̇ 656 | i̇6 65 |
倨吾 唱呀 单々 要唱 有头有脑格 腊 翻

6 5· | 55 3̇3̇ | 3̇3̇ 3̇i̇ | 2̇— | i̇6 i̇6 65 |
歌 你莫 讲起 介格 腊翻 歌 倨个 歌子 比你

35 65 | 6 5· | 2̇6 i̇6 | 35 65 65 |
· 116 · 还 更 多 一条 凳子 介格腊呀翻格

6 6 | 2̇2̇ 65 66 | i̇5 65 | 6 5· | 5 56 |
合 呀 腊翻 合来 介就 腊 翻 生 你莫格

3̇3̇ 6i̇ | 3̇3̇ 3̇i̇ | 2̇— | i̇6 i̇i̇ 56 |
讲起 介就 腊呀 翻格 生 倨格 歌子 比你

3·5 65 | 6 5· | 56 65 65 | i̇i̇ 5 | 6— |
还 更格 多。 屋背 种里 一蔸 蜜尾竹 呀

65 65 65 | 65 65 | i̇6 65 | 3·5 65 |
做里 十块 夹板 要来 千你 比歌 一起 和 一格

6 5· | 55 3̇3̇ | 6i̇ 3̇5 | 3̇i̇ 2̇ |
和 你莫 讲起 介就 要和 就来 和

i̇6 i̇i̇ i̇6 | i̇6 3·5 | 65 65· | i̇6 i̇6 |
倨唱 歌子 比你 还更 翻 得 多 爷娘生倨

i̇6 i̇6 | 5 6— | 63 35 | i̇i̇ 65 | 65 65· |
二呀 兄呀 弟 呀 生掉 老 弟 就出生 哥 哥

55 33 | 3̇3̇ 6i̇ | 3̇3̇ 3̇i̇ | 2̇— | i̇6 i̇6 |
你莫 讲起 生掉 老弟 生呀哥 哥 倨唱 歌子

65 35 | 65 65 | 5— | i̇2̇ i̇6 | i̇i̇ i̇i̇ |
还更 比你 屁 得格 多 讨倨 母妈 介格倨扛

5 6— | i̇6 i̇5 | i̇i̇ i̇5 | i̇5 65 | 6 5· |
轿 喹 讨倨 奶々 倨就 在介 打 铜 锣

55 33 | 6i̇ 333i̇ | 2̇— | i̇6 i̇6 |
你莫 讲起 介格 打呀铜格 锣 倨唱歌子 · 117 ·

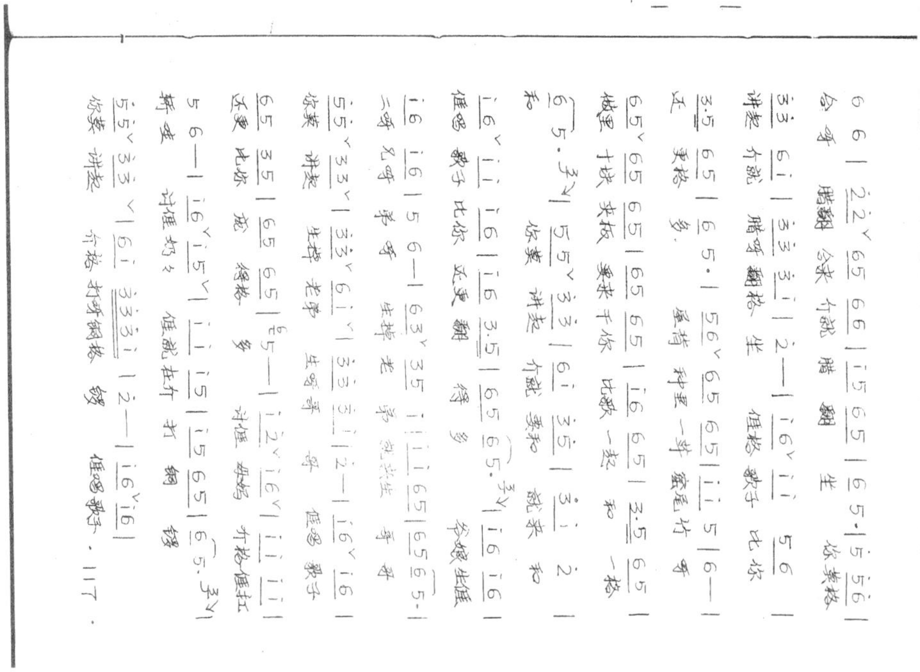

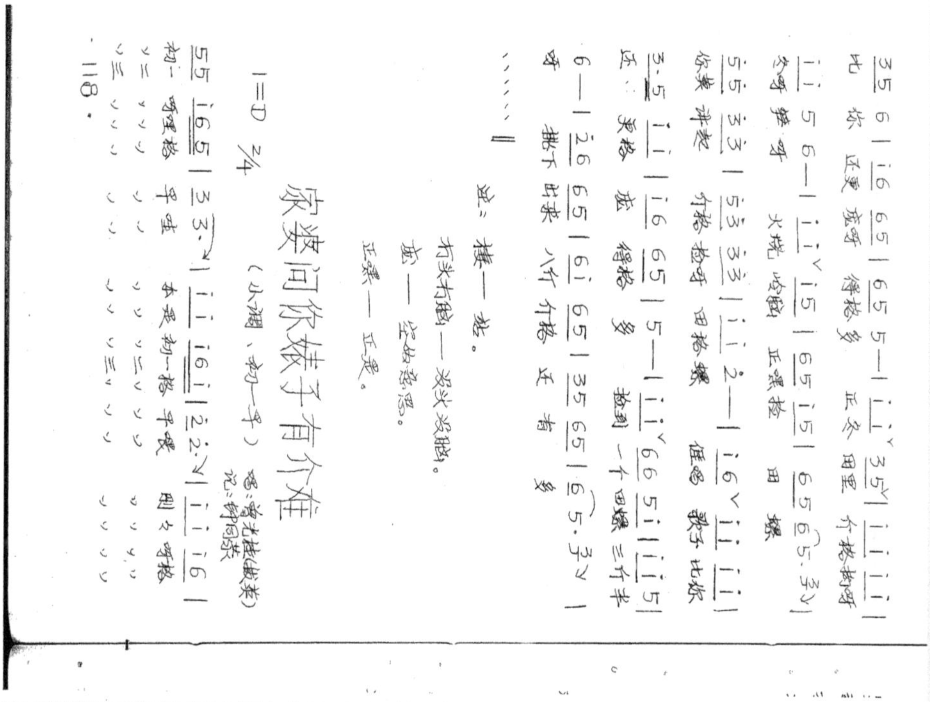

35 6 | i6 65 | 65 5— | ii 35 | ii ii |
比 你 还更 庞呀 得格 多 正冬 田里 介格 捡呀

ii 5 6— | ii i5 | 65 i5 | 65 65.3 |
冬呀 箩 呀 火烧 岭脑 正嘿 捡 田 螺

55 33 | 53 33 | ii 2— | i6 ii ii |
你莫 讲起 介格 捡呀 田格 螺 低吗 歌子 比你

3.5 ii | i6 65 | 5— | ii 66 5i | ii 5 |
还 更格 庞 得格 多 捡到 一个 田螺 三斤 半

6— | 26 65 | 6i 65 | 35 65 | 65.3 |
呀 挑下 出来 八斤 介格 还 有 多

、、、、、、 ‖

注：接— 站。

有头有脑— 没头没脑。

庞— 空的意思。

正嘿— 正是。

家婆问你婊子有介难

1=D 2/4（小调、初一乎） 唱：曾光桂(散英)
记：钟同荣

55 i65 | 3 3. | ii i6i | 22. | ii i6 |
初一 呀哩格 乎 唓 本是 初一格 乎喂 刚々 呀格
ソ二 ソソソ ソ ソ ソソ ソ二ソソソ ソソソソ
ソ三 ソソソ ソ ソ ソソ ソ三ソソソ ソソソソ

5 5 6 | 32 66 | 5— | ii 6i | 2. 3 |
起 床 亲郎 又来 了。 伸手 揽郎 腰
挑 水 ソソ ソソ ソ。 ソソ ソソ ソ
烧 火 ソソ ソソ ソ ソソ ソソ ソ

5.6 2i | 6— | ii 66 | 5 3. | 56 55 |
同郎 交一 交， 家婆 哇格 问 你 婊子 有介
ソソ ソソ ソ ソソ ソソ ソソ ソソソソ
ソソ ソソ ソ ソソ ソソ ソソ ソソソソ

3— | ii i6i | 2— | ii i6 | 5 i 2 |
难 丈呀 老大 嫂 刚々 呀格 下 床
ソ ソソソソ ソ 莆枘 ソソ 冇 带
ソ ソソソソ ソ 生柴 ソソ 冇 燥

65 56 | 5— ‖
细人 又来 叫。
用呀 用手 洗。
烧掉 一浅 乎。

注：交一交— 玩耍一交。

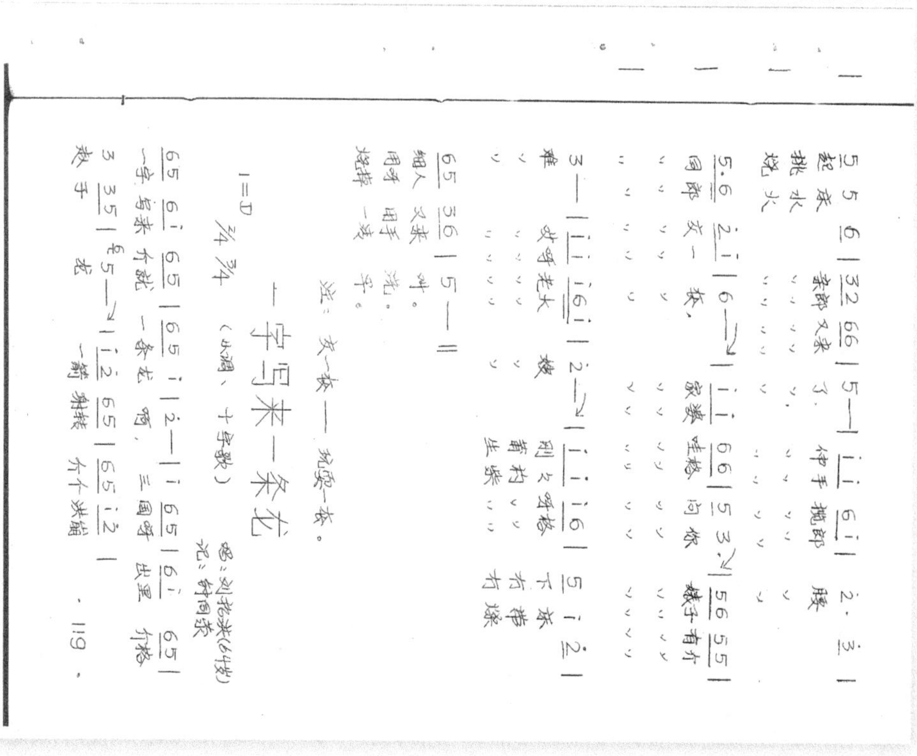

一字写来一条龙

1=D 2/4 3/4（小调、十字歌） 唱：刘松洪(64岁)
记：钟同荣

65 6i 65 | 65 i | 2— | i 65 | 6i 65 |
一字 写来 介就 一条 龙 啊， 三国呀 出里 介格

3 35 | 5— | i2 65 | 65 i2 |
赵 子 龙 一箭 射转 介个 洪脑

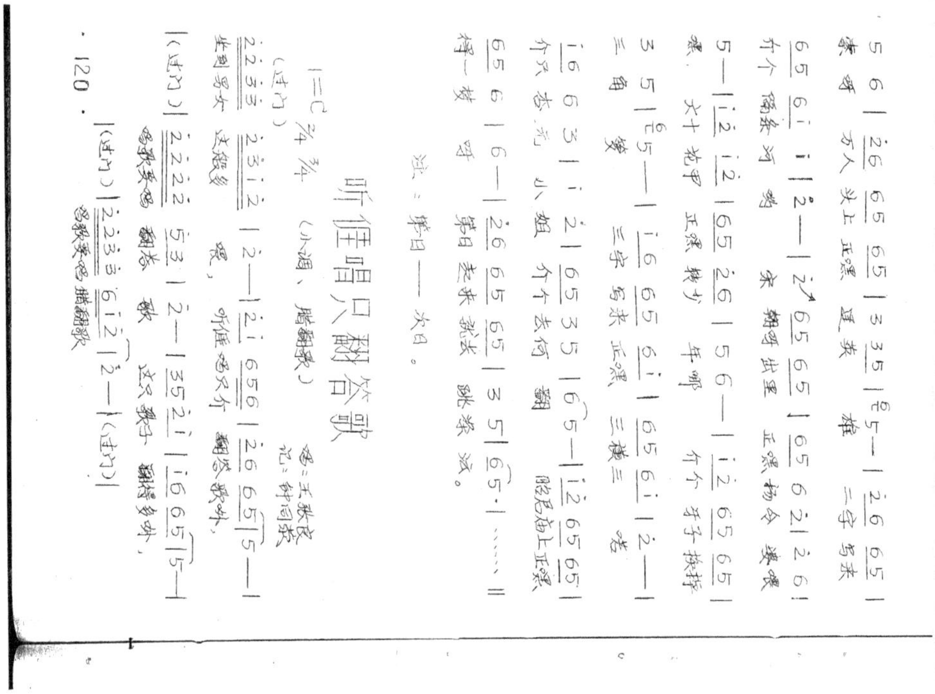

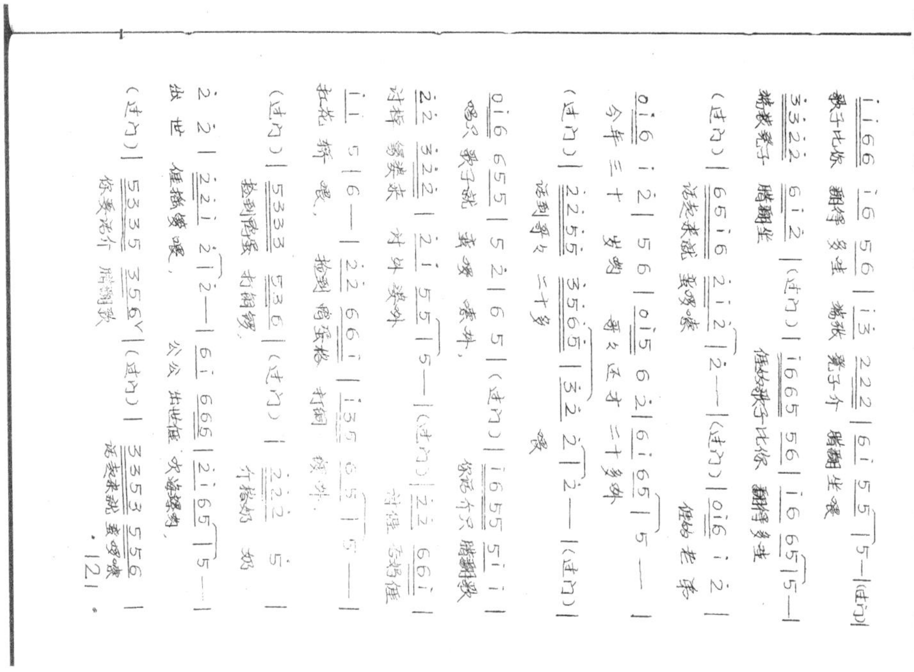

索 呀 万人 头上 正嘿 迁 英 雄 二字 写来

介个 隔条 河 哟 来 翻呀 出里 正嘿 杨令 婆喂

嘿。大十 花甲 正嘿 转步 年 哪 介个 牙子 挨捋

三 角 箩 三字 写来 正嘿 三横三 啫

介只 杏 元 小 姐 介个 去何 翻 脑瓜庙上 正嘿

捋一 枝 呀 第日 起来 就去 跳 涂 泳。

注：第日——次日。

听𠊎唱只翻答歌

1=C 2/4 3/4 （小调、腊翻歌） 唱：王张良 记：钟同荣

（过门）

坐到男女 这般多 喂，听𠊎唱只介 翻答 歌外，

（过门） 唱歌要唱 翻答 歌 这只歌子 翻得多外，

（过门） 唱歌要唱 腊翻歌 （过门）

·120·

歌子比你 翻得 多生 端张 凳子介 腊翻 生喂 （过门）

端张凳子 腊翻生 （过门） 佢好歌子比你 翻得多生

（过门） 话起来就 蛮啰嗦 （过门） 佢的 老 弟

今年 三十 岁哟 哥哥 还才 二十多外

（过门） 话到哥哥 二十多 喂 （过门）

唱只 歌子就 蛮啰 嗦外， 你话介只 腊翻歌

讨样 舅婆来 对 外 婆外 背侄 老奶佢

扛花 轿 喂， 捡到 鸭蛋格 打铜 锣外。

（过门） 捡到鸭蛋 打铜锣 （过门） 介捡奶 奶

出 世 佢摇篮 喂， 公公 出世佢 吹海螺哟，

（过门） 你要话介 腊翻歌 （过门） 话起来就 蛮啰嗦

·121·

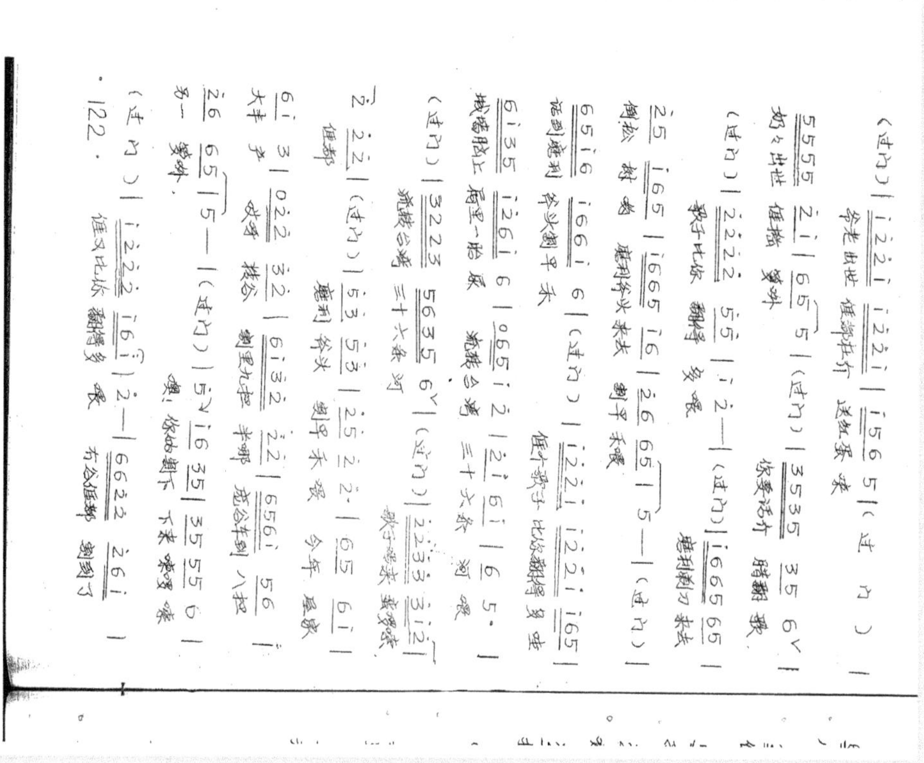

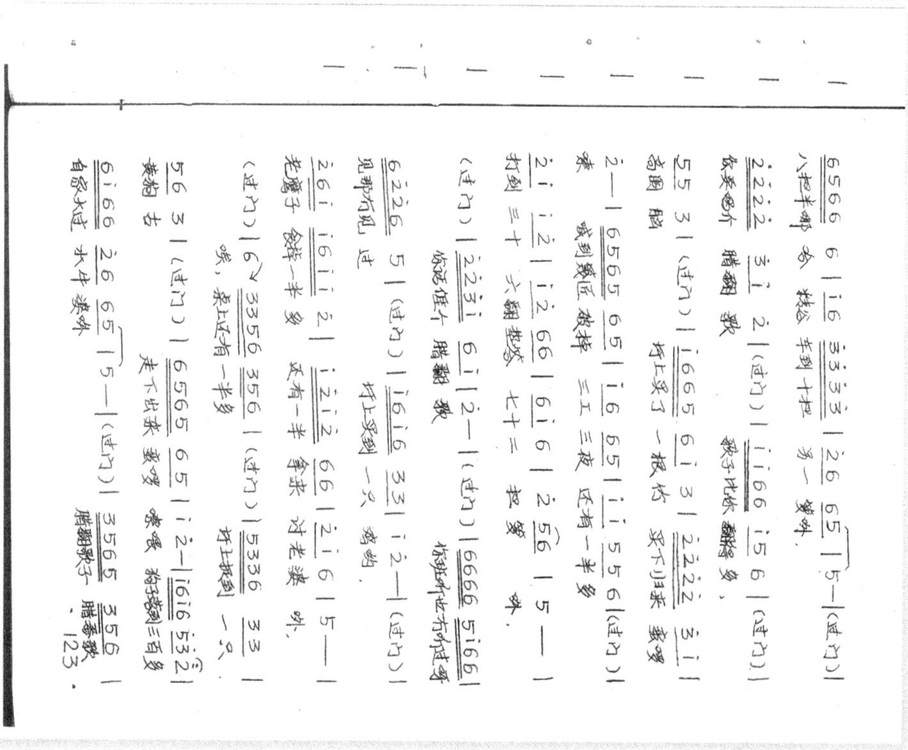

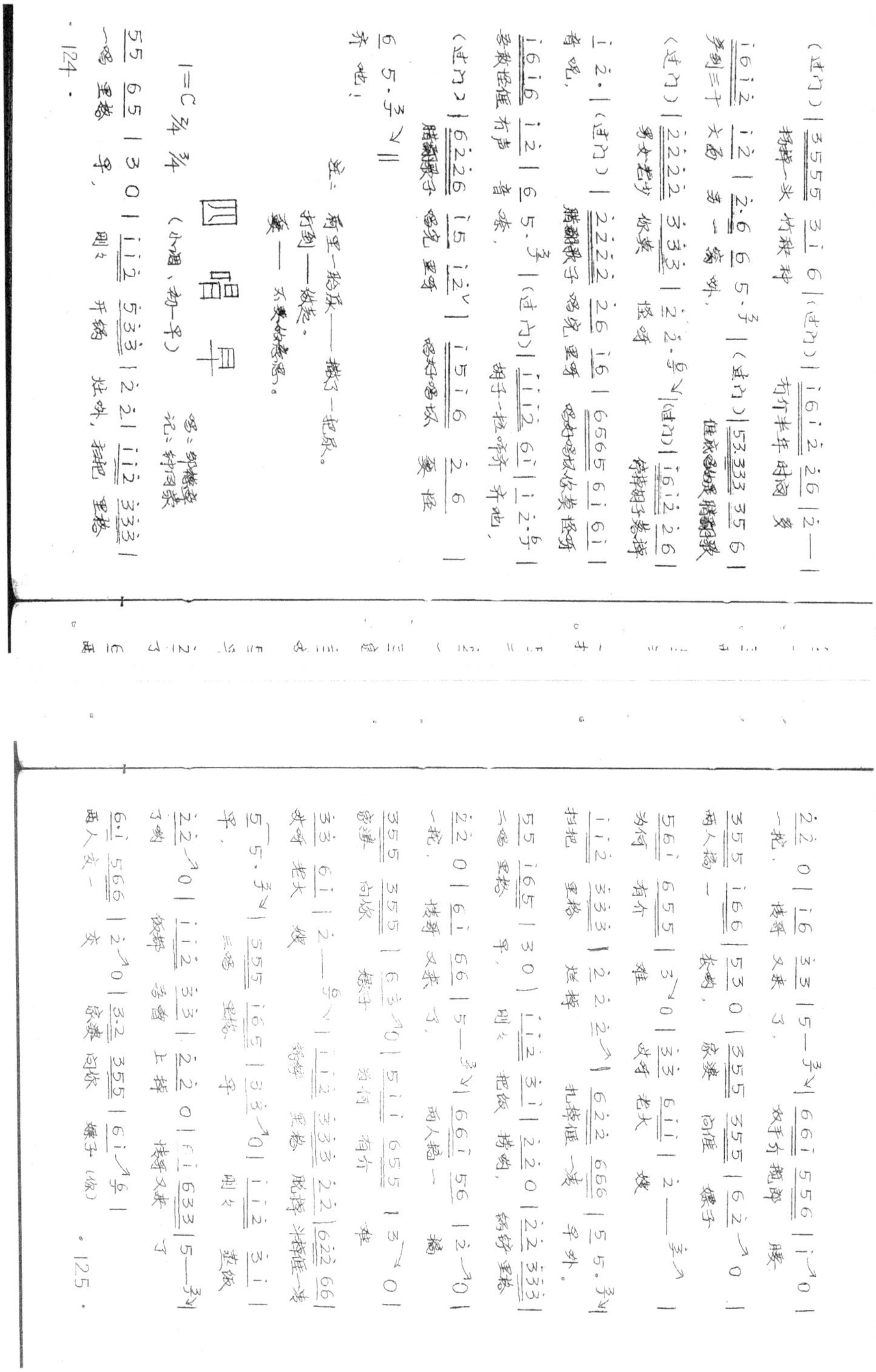

(过门) | 3555 3 1 6 | (过门) | 1612 26 | 2 — |
扬掉一头 竹秧种　　有介半年 时间 多

1612 12 | 2·6 6 5· | (过门) | 53333 35 6 |
争到三十 大面 另一 窝 咻，　佢底唱的是 腊翻歌

(过门) | 2222 333 | 2 2· | (过门) | 1612 26 |
男女老少 你莫 怪呀　　锣掉胡子蒸掉

1 2· | (过门) | 2222 26 16 | 6565 61 61 |
有 呢，　腊翻歌子 唱完 里呀　唱好唱坏你莫 怪呀

1616 12 | 6 5· | (过门) | 1112 61 | 1 2· |
要敢捱捱 有声 音 嗦，　胡子一拉 呼齐 齐 吔，

(过门) | 6226 15 12 | 1516 2 6 |
腊翻歌子 唱完 里呀　唱好唱坏 耍 怪

6 5· ||
齐 吔！

注：肩里一胎尿——撒了一把尿。
打到——做起。
耍——不要好意思。

四 唱 早

1=C 2/4 3/4　（小调、初一早）　唱：邹楼凌　记：钟同荣

55 65 | 3 0 | 112 533 | 2 21 | 112 333 |
一唱 里格 早，　刚刚 开锅 灶咻，扫把 里格

· 124 ·

22 0 | 16 33 | 5 — | 661 556 | 1 0 |
一把，　佬哥 又来 了，　双手介 抱郎 腰

355 166 | 53 0 | 355 355 | 62 0 |
两人搞一 　套哟，　家婆 向佢 嫖子

561 655 | 3 0 | 33 611 | 2 — |
为何 有介 难　　哎呀 老大 嫂

112 333 | 2 2 2 | 622 666 | 5 5· |
扫把 里格 烂掉　　扎掉佢 一边 早 咻。

55 165 | 3 0 | 112 31 | 22 0 | 22 333 |
二唱 里格 早，　刚刚 把饭 捞哟，锅铲 里格

22 0 | 61 56 | 5 — | 661 56 | 2 0 |
一把，　佬哥 又来 了，　两人搞一 搞

355 355 | 63 0 | 511 655 | 3 0 |
家婆 向你 嫖子　　为何 有介 难

33 61 | 2 — | 112 333 22 | 622 66 |
哎呀 老大 嫂　　锅铲 里格 脱掉 斗掉佢一边

5 5· | 555 165 | 33 0 | 112 31 |
早，　三唱 里格 早，　刚刚 蒸饭

22 0 | 112 33 | 22 0 | 61 633 | 5 — |
了哟　饭都 香香 上 掉　佬哥又来 了

61 566 | 2 0 | 32 355 | 61 |
两人交一 交　家婆 向你 嫖子（你）

· 125 ·

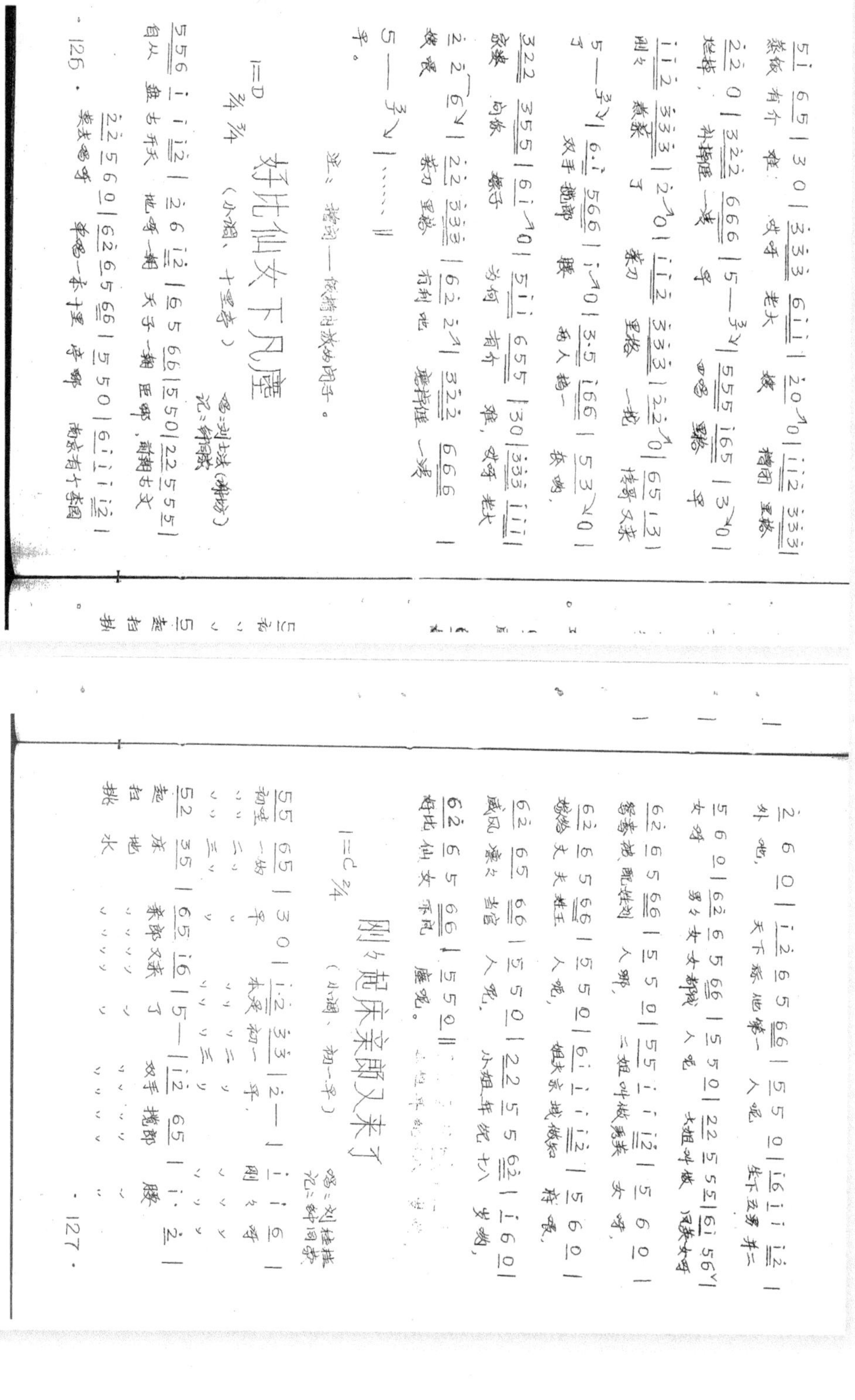

5i 65 | 3 0 | 333 6ii | 20 0 | ii2 333 |
蒸饭 有介 难， 哎呀 老大 嫂 樯闲 里格

22 0 | 322 666 | 5 — 3 | 555 i65 | 3 0 |
烂掉， 补掉哩 一遍 乎 四吆 里格 乎

ii2 333 | 2 0 | ii2 333 | 22 0 | 65 13 |
刚々 煮菜 了 菜刀 里格 一抛 情哥 又来

5 — 3 | 6.i 566 | i 0 | 3.5 i66 | 53 0 |
了 双手 搅郎 腰 两人 搞一 夜哟，

322 355 | 6i 0 | 5ii 655 | 30 | 333 iii |
家婆 向你 嫂子 为何 有介 难，哎呀 老大

22 6 | 22 333 | 62 2 | 322 666 |
嫂 喂 菜刀 里格 冇利 吧 磨掉哩 一遍

5 — 3 | …… ||
乎。

注：樯闲——饭樯内放的闲子。

好比仙女下凡尘

1=D 2/4 3/4　（小调、十里亭）

唱：刘士法（游坊）
记：钟同荣

556 i i i2 | 2 6 i2 | 6 5 66 | 5 5 0 | 22 5 5 5 |
自从 盘古 开天 地呀 一朝 天子 一朝 臣哪，前朝古文

22 5 6 0 | 62 6 5 66 | 5 5 0 | 6i i i i2 |
英太 吆呀 单吆 一本 十里 亭哪 南京有个李国

2 6 0 | i2 6 5 66 | 5 5 0 | i6 i i i2 |
外 吧， 天下 称他 第一 人呢 生下五男并二

5 6 0 | 62 6 5 66 | 5 5 0 | 22 5 55 | 6i 56 |
女呀 男々 女 女都成 人呢 大姐 叫做 凤英女呀

62 6 5 66 | 5 5 0 | 55 i i i2 | 5 6 0 |
鸳鸯 被、配姓刘 人哪， 二姐 叫做 秀英 女呀，

62 6 5 66 | 5 5 0 | 6i i i i2 | 5 6 0 |
嫁给 丈 夫 姓王 人呢， 姐夫 京城 做知 府 喂，

62 65 66 | 5 5 0 | 22 5 5 62 | i 6 0 |
威风 凛々 当官 人呢， 小姐 年 纪 十八 岁 哟，

62 6 5 66 | 5 5 0 ||
好比 仙 女 下凡 尘呢。

刚々起床亲郎又来了

1=C 2/4　（小调、初一早）

唱：刘桂桂
记：钟同荣

55 65 | 3 0 | i.2 33 | 2 — | i i 6 |
初一 一的 早 本是 初一 早， 刚 々 呀
〃〃 二〃 〃 〃〃 〃二 〃 〃 〃 〃
〃〃 三〃 〃 〃〃 〃三 〃 〃 〃 〃

52 35 | 65 i6 | 5 — | i2 65 | i. 2 |
起 床 亲郎 又来 了 双手 搅郎 腰
扫 地 〃〃〃〃 〃 〃〃 〃〃 〃
挑 水 〃〃〃〃 〃 〃〃 〃〃 〃

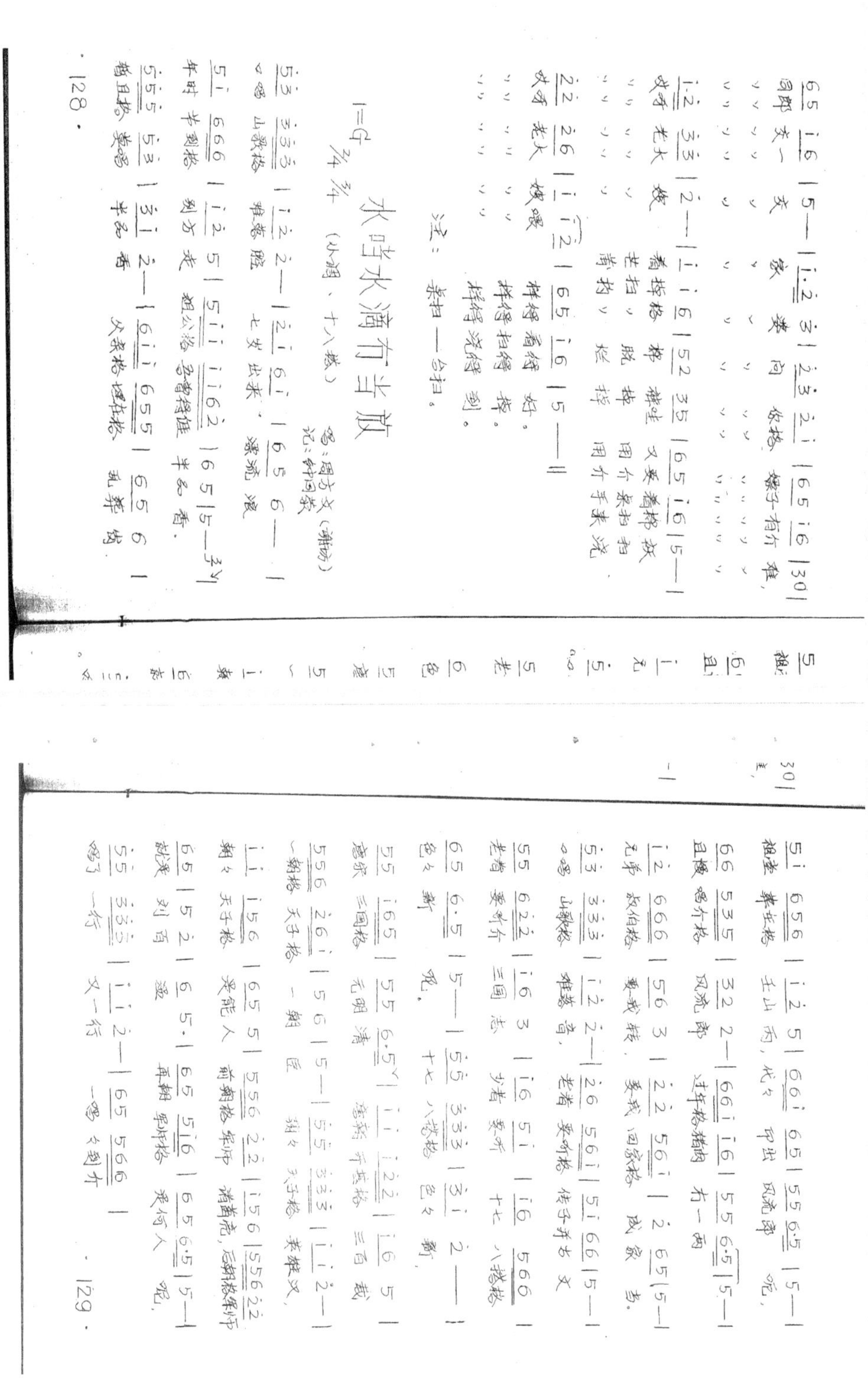

65 i6 | 5— | i·2 3 | 23 2i | 65 i6 | 30 |
同郎 交一 交 家 娄 向 你格 嫂子 有介 难，

i·2 33 | 2— | i i 6 | 52 35 | 65 i6 | 5— |
哎呀 老大 嫂 着掉格 棉 襟哇 又要 着棉 袄
芒扫 脱 掉 用介 桌扫 扫
箭杓 烂 掉 用介 手来 浇

22 26 | i i2 | 65 i6 | 5— ||
哎呀 老大 嫂喂 样得 着得 好。
样得 扫得 掉。
样得 浇得 到。

注：桌扫——台扫。

水唔水滴冇当放

1=G 2/4 3/4 （小调、十八格）

唱：周方文（谢坊）
记：钟同荣

53 333 | i2 2— | 2i 6i | 65 6— |
口唱 山歌格 难落 腔 七岁 出来 漂流 浪

5i 666 | i2 5 | 5ii ii62 | 65 | 5— |
年时 节到格 列方 走 祖公格 吾曾得佳 半 加 香。

555 53 | 3i 2— | 6ii 655 | 65 6 |
酱且格 莫唱 半 加 香 父亲格 埋在格 乱葬 岗

· 128 ·

5i 656 | i2 5 | 66i 65 | 55 6·5 | 5— |
祖堂 葬在格 壬山 丙，代々 甲出 风流郎 呢，

66 535 | 32 2— | 66i i6 | 55 6·5 | 5— |
且慢 唱介格 风流 郎 过年格 猪肉 有一 两

i2 666 | 56 3 | 22 56i | 2 65 | 5— |
兄弟 叔伯格 要我 转， 要我 回家格 成 家 当。

53 333 | i2 2— | 26 56i | 5i 66 | 5— |
口唱 山歌格 难落 音， 老者 要听格 传子 开古 文

55 622 | i6 3 | i6 5i | i6 566 |
老者 要听介 三国 志 少者 要听 十七 八搭格

65 6·5 | 5— | 55 333 | 3i 2— |
色々 新 呢。 十七 八搭格 色 々 新，

55 i65 | 55 6·5 | ii i22 | i6 5 |
唐宋 三国格 元明 清 唐朝 开基格 三百 载

556 26i | 56 | 5— | 55 333 | ii 2— |
一朝格 天子格 一 朝 臣 朝々 天子格 英雄 汉，

ii i56 | 65 5 | 556 22 | i56 | 556 22 |
朝々 天子格 是能 人 前朝格 军师 诸葛亮，后朝格 军师

65 | 52 | 6 5· | 65 5i6 | 65 6·5 | 5— |
就是 刘 百 温 再朝 军师格 是何人 呢，

55 333 | ii 2— | 65 566 |
唱了 一行 又一 行 一唱 々到 介

· 129 ·

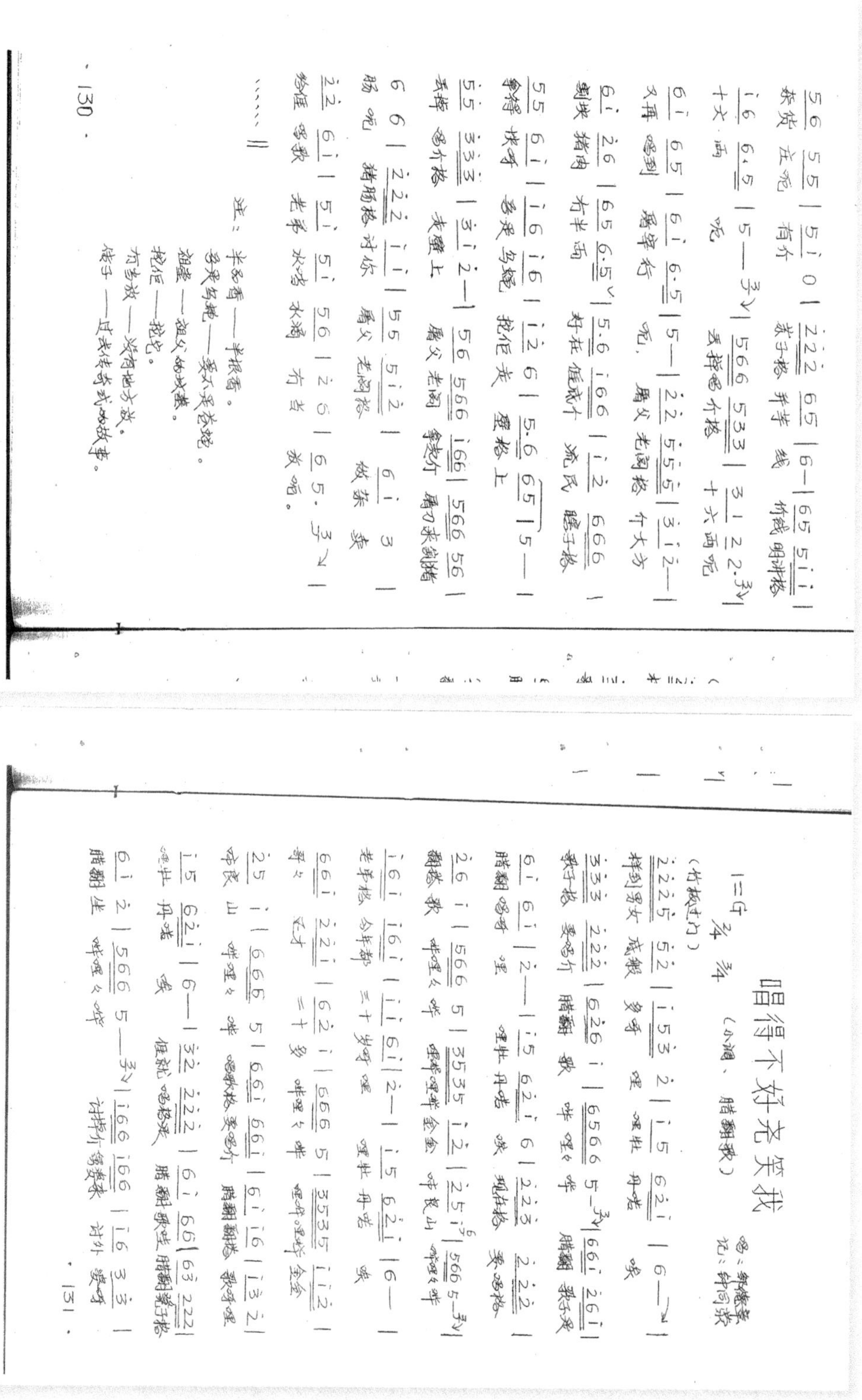

56 55 | 51 0 | 222 65 | 6— | 65 511 |
杂货 庄呃 有介 茶子格 并芋 线 竹线 明讲格

16 6.5 | 5— 3↘ | 566 533 | 31 2 2.3↘ |
十文 两 呃 丢掉吧介格 十六两呃

61 65 | 61 6.5 | 5— | 22 555 | 31 2— |
又再 喝到 屠宰行 呃， 屠父老阔格 介大方

61 26 | 65 6.5ˇ | 5.6 166 | 12 666 |
割块 猪肉 冇半 两 好在 佢底个 流氏 瞎子格

55 61 | 16 16 | 12 6 | 5.6 65 | 5— |
争得 快呀 系是乌蝇 挖佢走 壁格上

55 333 | 31 2— | 56 566 166 | 566 56 |
丢掉 喝介格 走壁上 屠父 老阔 拿起介 屠刀来剁猪

6 6 | 222 11 | 55 512 | 61 3 |
肠 呃 猪肠格 讨你 屠父 老阔格 做东 卖

22 61 | 51 51 56 | 2 6 | 6 5. 3↘ |
给侄 唱歌 老弟 水嗒 水渴 冇当 放呃。

...... ||

注：半名香——半根香。
系是乌蝇——要不是苍蝇。
祖壶——祖父的故事。
挖佢——挖它。
冇当放——没有地方放。
传子——过去传奇式的故事。

· 130 ·

唱得不好充笑我

1=G 2/4 3/4 （小调、腊翻歌）

唱：郭德章
记：钟同荣

（竹板过门）

2225 52 | 153 2 | 15 621 | 6— |
样到男女 底般 多呀 哩 哩牡 丹嗒 唉

333 222 | 626 1 | 6566 5—3↘ | 661 261 |
歌子格 要唱介 腊翻 歌 哗 哩々 哗 腊翻 歌子是

61 61 | 2— | 15 621 6 | 223 222 |
腊翻 唱呀 哩 哩牡 丹嗒 唉 现在格 要唱格

26 1 | 566 5 | 3535 12 | 25 1 | 566 5—3↘ |
翻搭 歌 哗哩々 哗 哗哗哩哗 金金 呤良山 哗哩々哗

161 161 | 11 61 | 2— | 15 621 | 6— |
老弟格 今年都 三十 岁呀 哩 哩牡 丹嗒 唉

661 221 | 62 1 | 666 5 | 3535 112 |
哥々 还才 二十 多 哗哩々 哗 哗哗哩哗 金金

25 1 | 666 5 | 661 661 | 61 16 | 132 |
呤良 山 哗哩々 哗 唱歌格 要唱介 腊翻 翻搭 歌呀哩

15 621 | 6— | 32 222 | 61 66 | 63 222 |
哩牡 丹嗒 唉 佢就 唱格是 腊翻 歌哇 腊翻歌子格

61 2 | 566 5—3↘ | 166 166 | 16 33 |
腊翻 坐 哗哩々 哗 讨掉介 舅婆来 讨外 婆呀

· 131 ·

2̇ — | i3̇ 6i6 | 5 — | 2̇2̇ i6 | 2̇6 i | 566 5 3∨ |
哩 有点 错哟 唉 俚个 名叫 翻搭秋 哗哩々哗

i3̇ 3ii | 66i 63̇ | 2̇ — | i5 62̇i | 6 — |
爷老 出世俚 发红 蛋呀 哩 哩牡 丹呰 唉

66i 2̇2̇2̇ | 2̇6 i | i3̇ 5 | 66 5 | 2̇2̇2̇ i6i |
奶々 出世格 俚摇篮 有点错 哗哩哗 冬水 田里格

ii 6i | 2̇ — | 3̇i 66 | 5 — | ii 2̇6i |
挖冬 笋呀 哩 有点 错哟 唉 烧火 岭上格

56 i | 666 5 3∨ | 5i6 ii6 | ii 6i | 2̇ — |
捡田 螺 哗哩 哗 捡个格 田螺有 三斤 半哪 哩

2̇5 66 | 5 — | i6 6i6 | i2̇ i | 666 5 3∨ |
吾会 错哟 唉 批到 肉来有 九斤 多 哗哩々哗

i6 6i6 | ii 63̇ | 2̇ — | i6 66 | 5 — |
磨利 剃刀来 刨松 树呀 哩 吾会 错哟 唉

i2̇ 2̇6i | 62̇ i | 666 5 3∨ | 6i 36 |
磨利 斧头来 割早禾 哗哩々 哗 城墙 脑上

iii 6i | 2̇ — | i5 i66 3∨ | i6 62̇ |
扁把 尿呀 哩 哩牡 丹呰 唉 印得 大江

2̇2̇ 66 i | 666 5 3∨ | i6 6i6 | ii i3̇ 2̇∨ |
三十 六条河 哗哩々 哗 你话 讲煞俚 腊翻秋哇 哩

i5 62̇i 6∨ | i2̇ 226i | 66 i |
哩牡 丹呰 唉 俚个 歌子比你 旋得 多

·132·

666 5 | 666 i6 | i2̇ 6i 3∨ | i6 3̇2̇ |
哗哩々 哗 昨日 圩上 买了 一头 竹 喊到 篾匠

i6 2̇2̇ 2̇6 | 6i 66 i∨ | i6 i2̇ | 6i 66 |
破掉 三工 三夜 还有 一半 多 打到 三十 六翻 篾箩

6i 66 i2̇ i | 6i 63̇ | 2̇6 66 | 5 — 3∨ |
七十 二担 箩 竹子 剩到 一半 多哟 唉

i6 i66 | i6 3̇3̇ | 2̇ —∨ | i5 62̇i | 6 — |
你话 你哟 翻搭 秋呀 哩 哩牡 丹呰 唉

3̇i 2̇6 i66 | 6i i | 66 5 3 | i6 i6i |
还有 俚又 来思格 腊翻 秋 哗哩 哗 圩上 买到格

66 3̇3̇ 2̇ | i5 62̇i | 6 — | 2̇6 i6i | 62̇ i |
一只 鸡呀 哩 哩牡 丹呰 唉 买下 归来格 蛮好啖

66 5 3∨ | i6i 66i | 6i 6i 2̇ | i5 62̇i |
哗哩 哗 几大格 重量俚 话多 到去哩 哩牡 丹呰

6 — | 3̇3̇ 2̇6i | 56 i | 666 i | 62̇ i |
唉 崖鹰 吊走格 一半 多 一半 用来 讨老 婆

66 5 | 3535 i2̇ | 2̇5 i | 666 5 3∨ |
哗哩 哗 哩哗哩哗 金金 哼良山 哗哩 哗

6i i6i | 66 6i | 2̇ i5 | 6i 6 | 3̇3̇ 2̇6i |
腊翻 歌子格 唱到 底呀 哩 哩牡 丹呰 唉 底个 叫做格

66 i | 66 5 | 3535 i2̇ | 2̇5 i | 666 5 3∨ |
腊翻 歌 哗哩 哗 哩哗哩哗 金金 哼良山 哗哩 哗

·133·

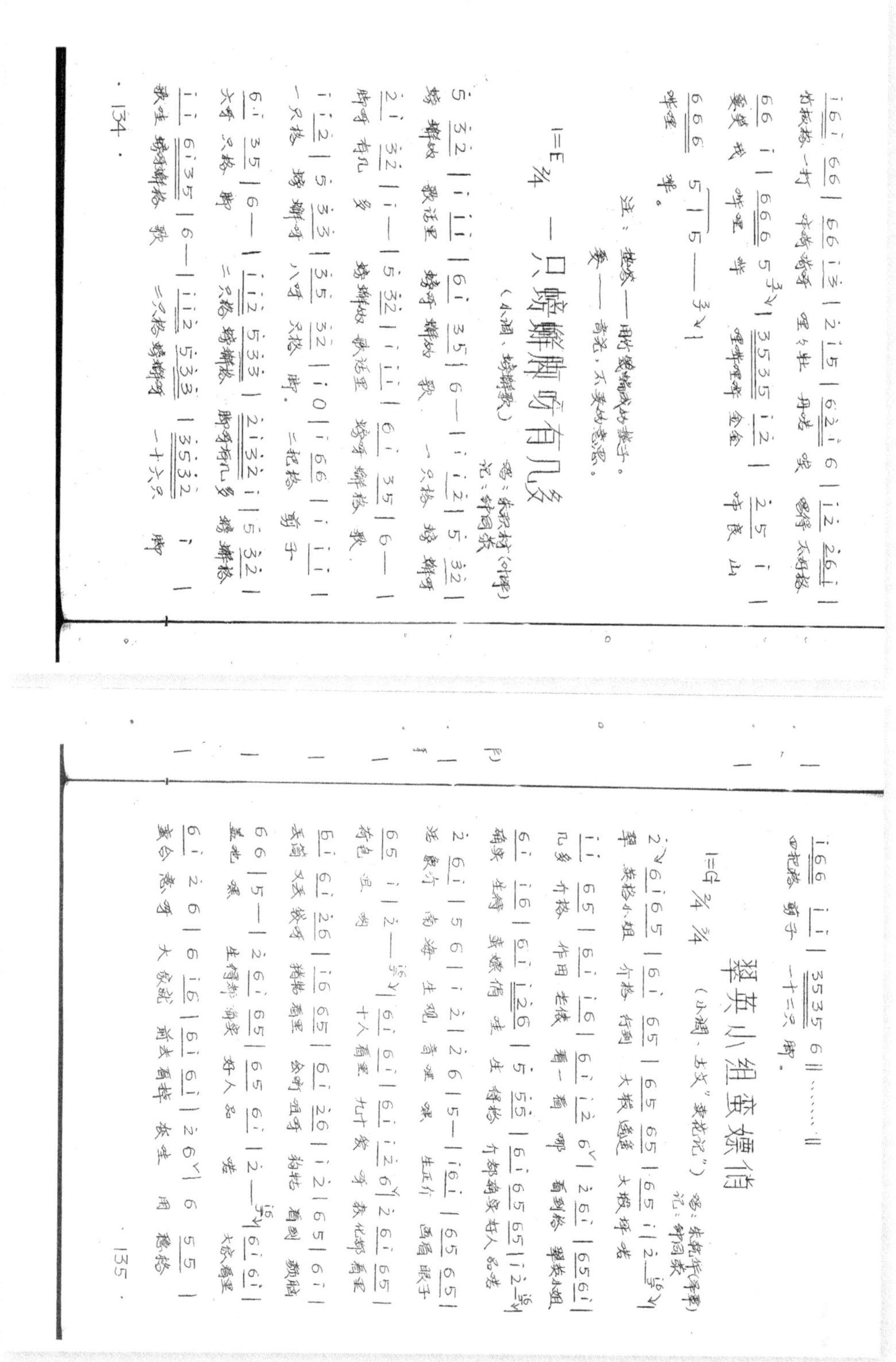

竹板格一打 呀嘀嘀呀 哩々壮 丹咾 唉 嘿得 不好格
耍笑 我 哗哩 哗 哩哗哩哗 金金 咘 良 山
哗哩 哗。

注：丝篓——用竹篾编成的篓子。
耍——高兴，不要的意思。

一只螃蟹脚呀有几多

1=E 2/4

（小调、螃蟹歌）　唱：朱积村（叶坪）　记：钟同荣

螃 蟹奴 歌话里 螃呀 蟹的 歌 一只格 螃 蟹呀
脚呀 有几 多 螃蟹奴 歌话里 螃呀 蟹格 歌
一只格 螃 蟹呀 八呀 只格 脚。 二把格 剪 子
大呀 只格 脚 二只格 螃蟹格 脚呀有几多 螃 蟹格
歌哇 螃蟹蟹格 歌 二只格 螃蟹呀 一十六只 脚

·134·

四把格 剪子 一十二只 脚。

翠英小组蛮嫖俏

1=G 2/4 3/4

（小调、古文"卖花记"）　唱：朱乾华（泽覃）　记：钟同荣

翠 英格小姐 个格 行到 大转 迤逶 大般坪 咾
几多 个格 作用 老俵 看一 看 哪 看到格 翠英小姐
确实 生得 蛮嫖 俏 哇 生 得格 个都确实 好人 品 咾
活 象个 南 海 生 观 音 哩 嘿 生正个 画眉 眼子
荷色 咀 哟 十八 看里 九十 发 呀 教化都 看里
丢简 又丢 袋呀 猪牯 看里 会啼 阻呀 狗牯 看到 颈脑
盖地 嘿 生得都 确实 好人 品 咾 大家看里
蛮合 意呀 大家就 前去 看捧 衣哇 用 稳格

·135·

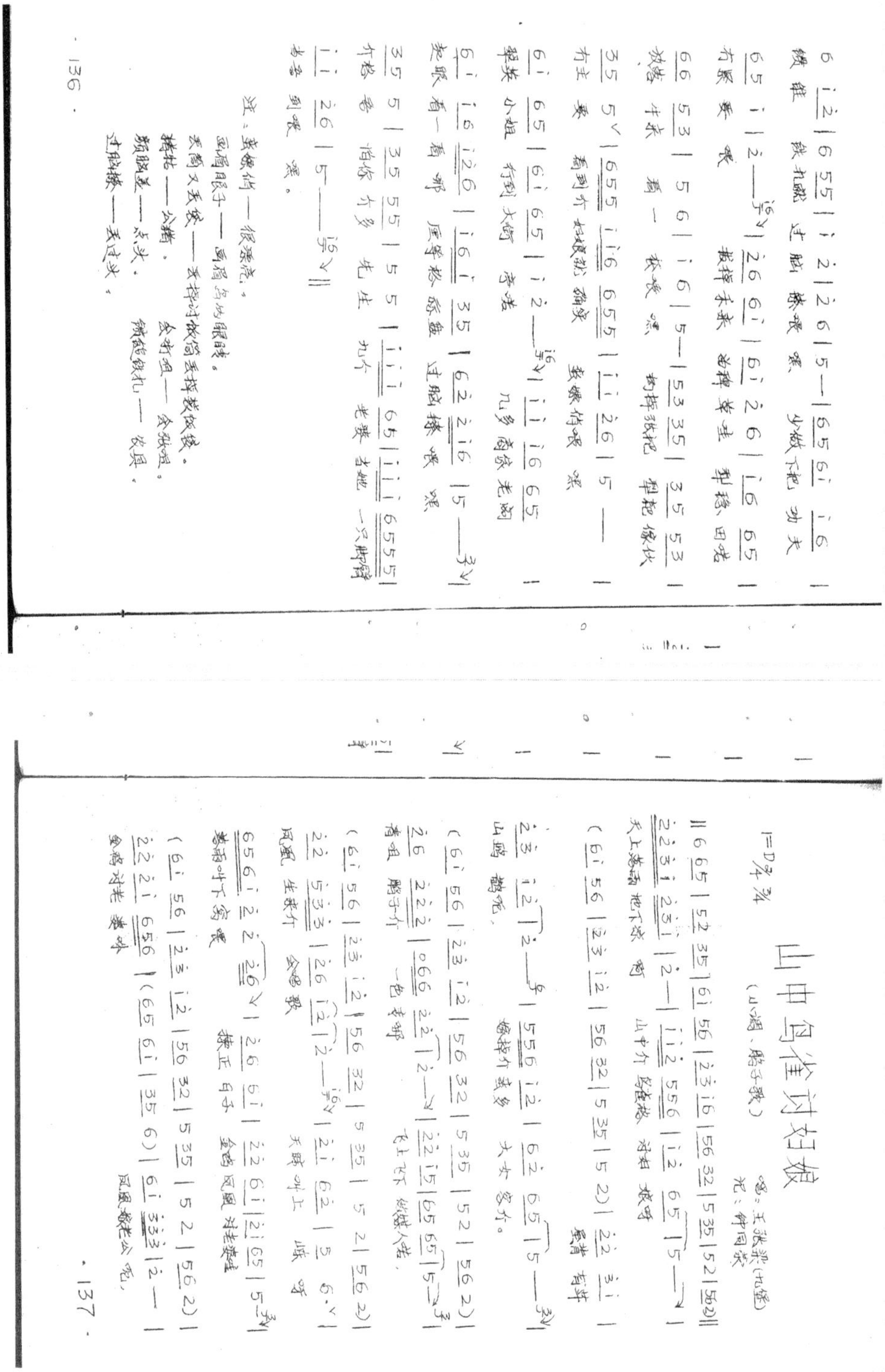

6 i 2 | 6 55 | i 2 | 2 6 | 5 — | 65 6i i 6 |
锁 难 铁扎毗 过 脑 搽喂 嘿， 少做下把 功 夫

65 i | 2 — | 26 6i | 6i 2 6 | i6 65 |
冇累 要 喂 拔择禾来 当牌 草 哇 犁移、田佬

66 53 | 5 6 | i 6 | 5 — | 53 35 | 35 53 |
放落 牛来 看 一 夜喂 嘿 钩择张耙 犁耙 像伙

35 5 | 655 ii6 655 | ii 26 | 5 — |
冇主 要 看到介 妇娘就 确实 蛮嫽俏喂 嘿

6i 65 | 6i 65 | i 2 — | ii i6 65 |
翠英 小姐 行到 大街 亭 港 几多 商家 老阔

6i i6 i26 | i6i 35 | 62 2i6 | 5 — |
虹眼 看一 看 哪 厘等 格 称盘 过 脑 搽 喂 嘿

35 5 | 35 55 | 5 5 | iii 65 | iii 6555 |
介格 老 怕你 介多 先 生 九介 老婆 者她 一只脚臂

ii 26 | 5 — ||
书音 到 喂 嘿。

注：蛮嫽俏——很漂亮。
画眉眼子——画眉鸟的眼睛。
丢脑又丢袋——丢掉讨饭篮丢掉装饭袋。
猪牯——公猪。 贪吥但——贪张但。
颔脑盖——点头。 锁难铁扎——农具。
过脑搽——丢过头。

山中鸟雀讨妇娘

1=D 2/4 3/4

（小调、船子歌）

唱：王张梁（九堡）
记：钟同荣

|| 6 65 | 52 35 | 6i 56 | 23 i6 | 56 32 | 5 35 | 5 2 | 5 6 2) ||

223i 23i | 2 — | ii2 556 | i2 65 | 5 — |
天上落雨 地下凉 啊 山中介 鸟雀格 讨妇 娘呀

(6i 56 | 23 i2 | 56 32 | 5 35 | 5 2) | 22 3i |
蛋背 有芽

23 i2 | 2 — | 556 i2 | 62 65 | 5 — |
山鸥 鹊呢， 嫁掉介 蛮多 大女 客介。

(6i 56 | 23 i2 | 56 32 | 5 35 | 5 2 | 56 2) |

26 222 | 066 22 | 2 — | 22 i5 | 65 65 | 5 — |
青姐 船子介 一色 专哪 飞上飞下 做媒人佬，

(6i 56 | 23 i2 | 56 32 | 5 35 | 5 2 | 56 2) |

22 533 | 26 i2 | 2 — | 2i 62 | 5 6 |
凤凰 生来介 会唱 歌 天眼 叫上 咏 呀

656i 2 2 26 | 26 6i | 22 6i | 2i 65 | 5 — |
落雨叫下 窝 喂 拣正 日子 金鸡 凤凰 讨老婆哇

(6i 56 | 23 i2 | 56 32 | 5 35 | 5 2 | 56 2) |

22 2i 656 | (65 6i | 35 6) | 6i 333 | 2 — |
金鸡讨老 婆 咏 凤凰嫁老公 呢，

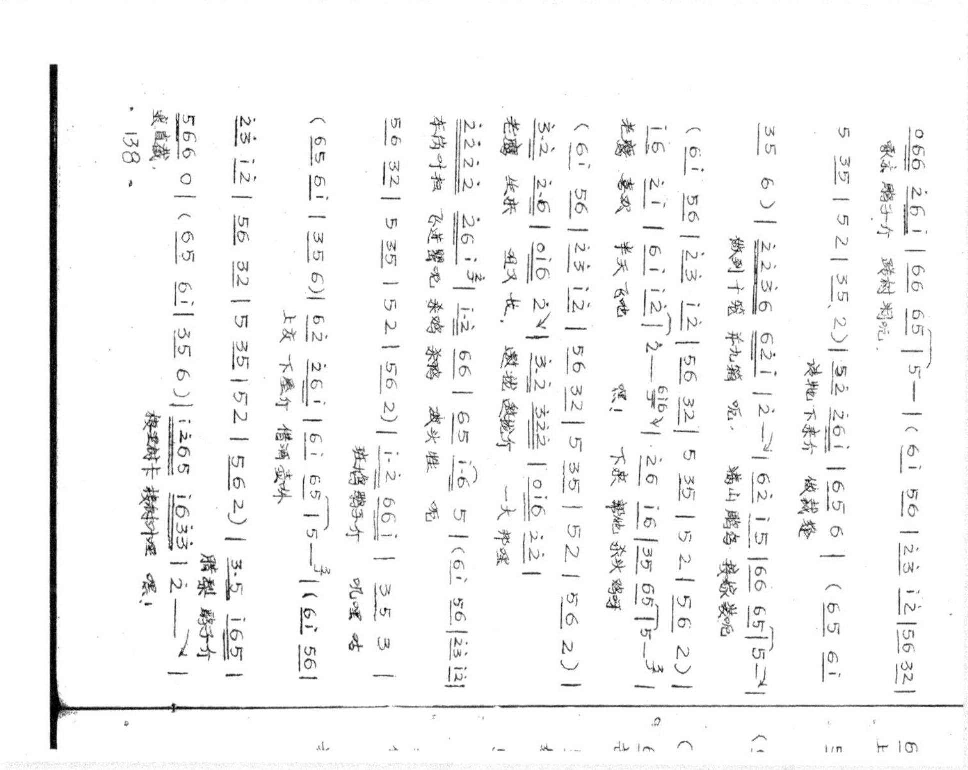

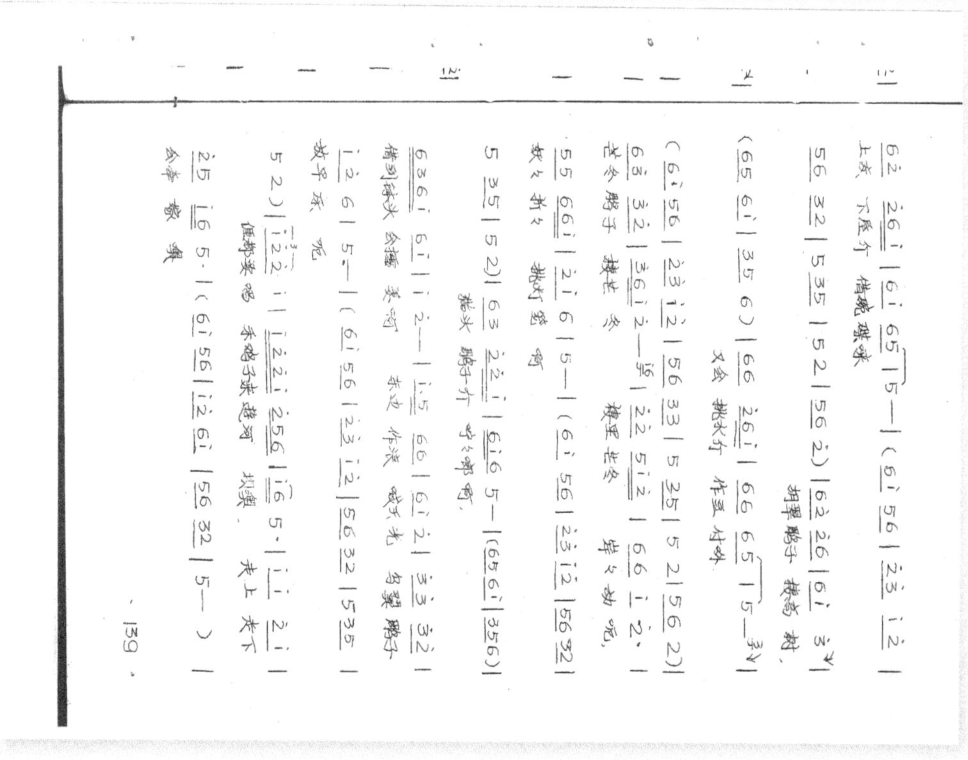

歌哥 鹏子介 踏树 枒呢，

诗牝下来介 做鼓篷

做到十篾 弟九箱 呢， 满山鹏鸟 接嫁装呢

老鹰 喜欢 半天飞吔 嘿！ 下来 帮他 杀头鸡呀

老鹰 生来 丑又长， 邀拢 邀拢介 一大 帮哩

车仿吁扫 飞进翳呢 杀鸡 杀鸭 戏头牲 呃

班鸠鹏子介 吼哩咕

上友 下屋介 借酒壶咻

腊梨 鹏子介

桌直截， 楼里村卡 楼树外哩 嘿！

·138·

上友 下屋介 借碗碟咻

胡翠鹏子 楼高 树，

又会 挑水介 作豆 付咻

芒冬鹏子 楼芒 冬 楼里芒冬 岸々劫 呢，

妖々 折々 挑灯笼 呵

猫头 鹏子介 吁々啷呵，

借到禄头 会摇 姜呵 东边 作浪 喊天光 乌鸦 鹏子

放早 床 呢

便都要唱 禾鸡子来 趁河 坝窦， 走上 走下

会奉 嫁 嫂

·139·

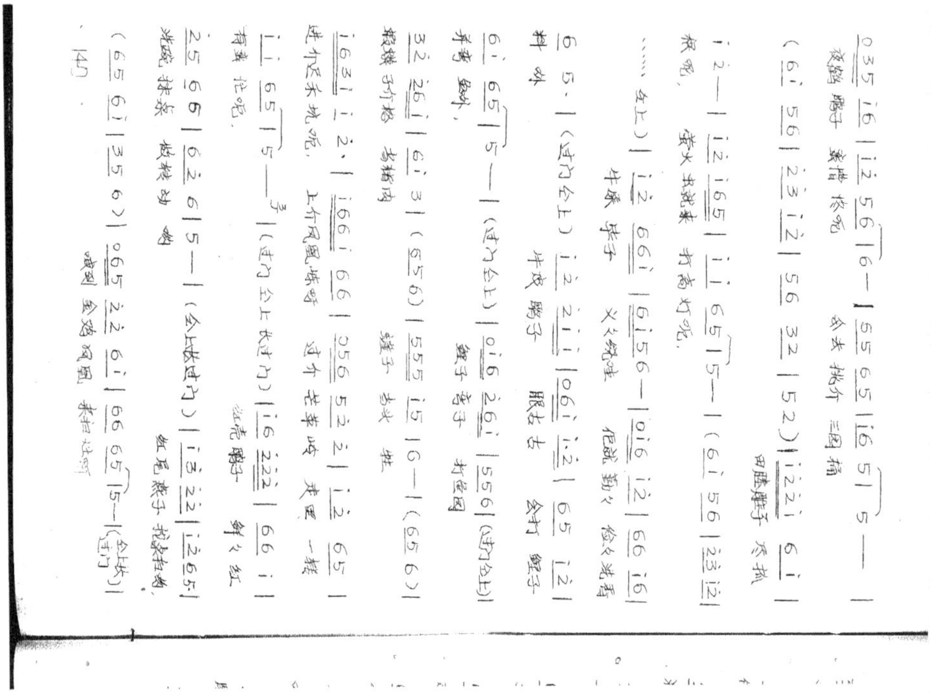

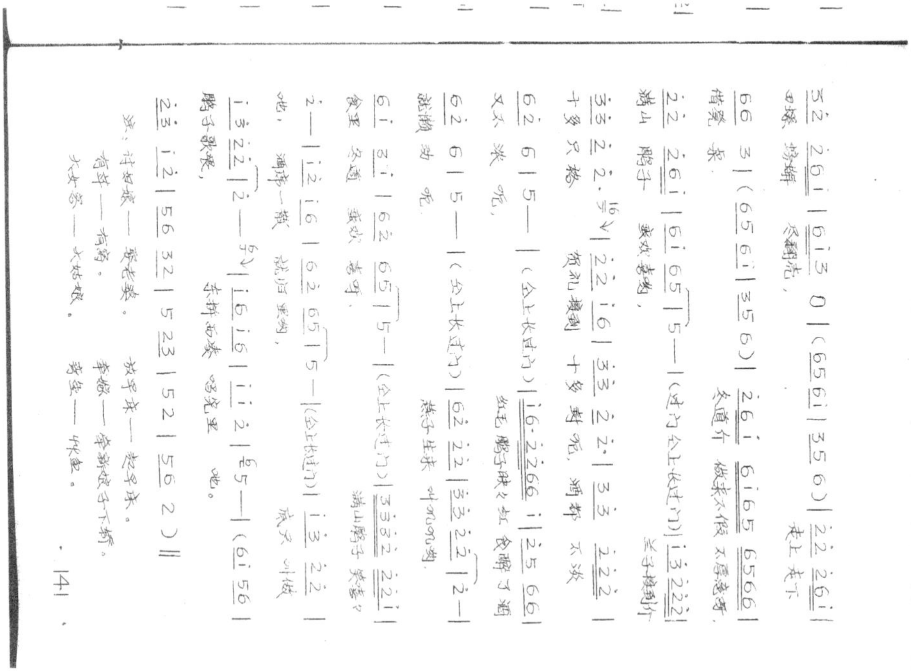

夜鹞鹏子 衰憎咯呢 会去挑介 三四桶

田膝雕子 尽抓

枫呢， 萤火虫就来 打高灯呢，

······仝上） 牛冻 学子 又々绕嗟 佢就 勤々 捡々洗看

料 咻 牛皮鹏子 眼古古 会打 鲤子

弄弯 鱼咻， 鲤子 宫子 打鱼网

蝦蟆子介格 书猪肉 罐子 书头 牲

进介泥禾坑呢， 上介凤凰蛛呀 过介茫革岭 走里 一辗

有面 伦呢， 红壳鹏子 解々红

光碗 抹桌 做粄劝 哟 红尾燕子 扰桌扫哟，

哦到 金鸡凤凰 来扫灶呀

· 140 ·

田螺 螃蟹 尽翻壳， 走上 走下

借凳 桌 冬道介 做来不假 不厚意呀，

满山 鹏子 欢欢喜哟， 兰子接到介

十多只格 贺礼接到 十多封呢， 酒都 不淡

又不 淡 呢， 红毛鹏子映々红 食嘚了酒

就懒 劝 呢 燕子生来 叫叽叽哟，

食里 冬道 欢欢 喜呀， 满山鹏子 笑嘻々

吔， 酒席一散 就归 里哟， 底只 叫做

鹏子歌哦， 东拼西凑 唱完里 吔。

注：讨姆嫁——娶老婆。 放早床——起早床。
有苹——有剩。 牵姆——牵新娘子下轿。
大女客——大姑娘。 畜生——牲畜。

· 141 ·

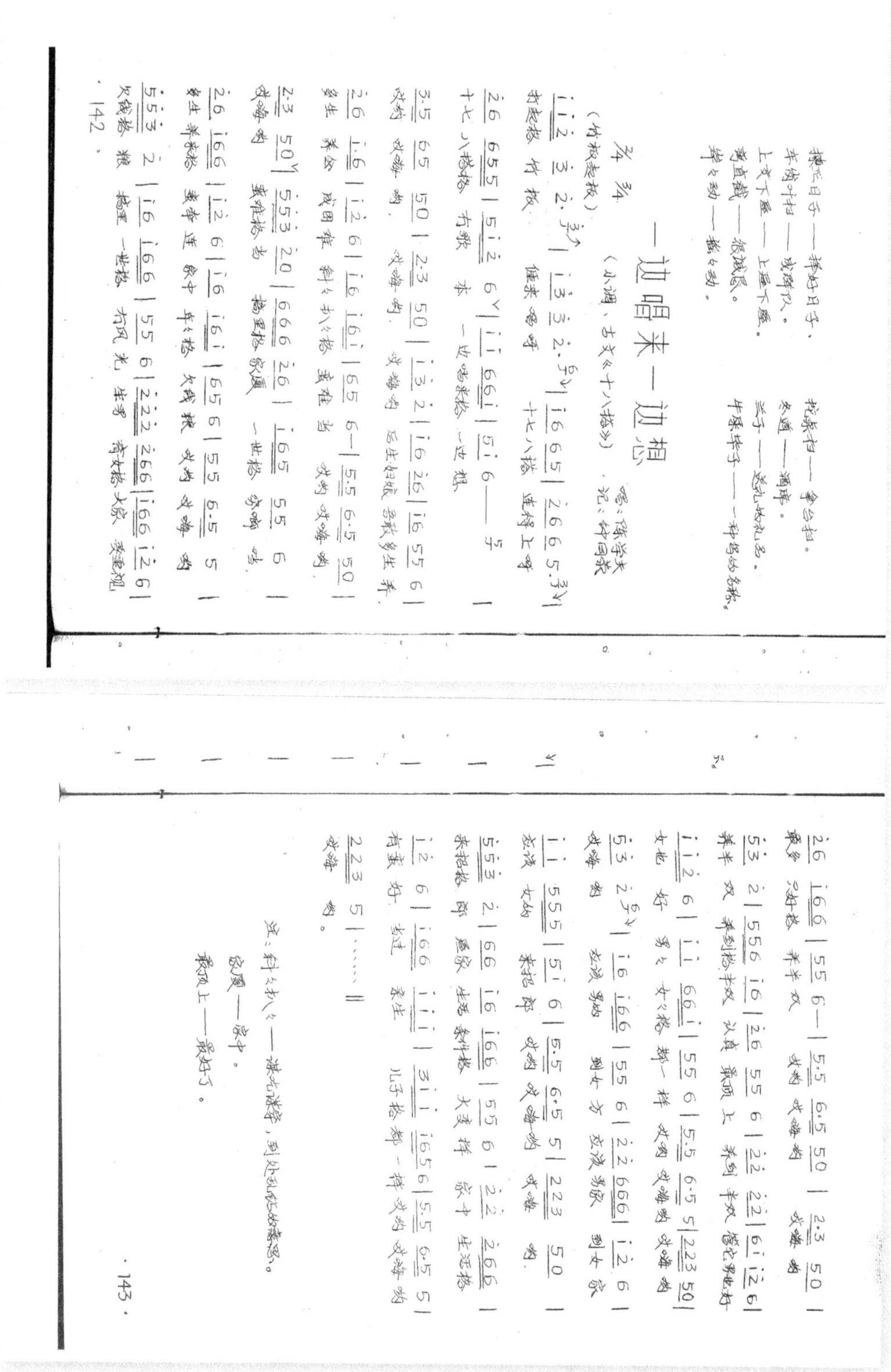

揀正日子——择好日子，
车俏叶扫——成群队。
上文下壓——上座下座。
骛直截——很诚恳。
岸々动——摇々动。

托桌扫——拿台扫。
冬道——酒席。
兰子——送礼的礼品。
牛屎华子——一种鸟的名称。

一边唱来一边想

2/4 3/4（小调、古文《十八搭》）　唱：陈学夫　记：钟同荣

（竹板起板）

i i 2 3 2· | i 3 3 2· | i 6 6 5 | 2 6 6 5· |
打起格 竹 板　　佢来 唱 呀　十七八搭　连得上呀

2 6 6 5 5 | 5 i 2 6 | i i 6 6 i | 5 i 6—— |
十七 八搭格 有歌 本 一边唱来格 一边 想

3·5 6 5 5 0 | 2·3 5 0 | i 3 2 | i 6 2 6 | i 6 5 5 6 |
哎哟 哎嗨 哟，哎嗨 哟，哎嗨哟 后生妇娘 吾敢多生 养，

2 6 i·6 | i 2 6 | i 6 i 6 i | 6 5 6— | 5·5 6·5 5 0 |
多生 养会 成困难 斜々扒々格 畫难 当 哎哟 哎嗨 哟，

2·3 5 0 | 5 5 3 2 0 | 6 6 6 2 6 | i 6 5 5 5 6 |
哎嗨 哟 畫难格 当 搞里格 家厦 一世格 穷唧 哟，

2 6 i 6 6 | i 2 6 | i 6 i 6 i | 6 5 6 | 5 5 6·5 5 |
多生 养来格 畫牵 连 家中 年々格 欠钱 粮 哎哟 哎嗨 哟

5 5 3 2 | i 6 i 6 6 | 5 5 6 | 2 2 2 2 6 6 | i 6 6 i 2 6 |
欠钱格 粮 搞里 一世格 冇风 光 生男 育女格 大家 爱重视

· 142 ·

2 6 i 6 6 | 5 5 6— | 5·5 6·5 5 0 | 2·3 5 0 |
最多 只好格 养半 双 哎哟 哎嗨 哟 哎嗨 哟

5 3 2 | 5 5 6 i 6 | 2 6 5 5 6 | 2 2 2 2 | 6 i i 2 6 |
养半 双 养到格半双 认真 最顶 上 养到 半双 管它男也好

i i 2 6 | i i 6 6 i | 5 5 6 | 5·5 6·5 5 | 2 2 3 5 0 |
女也 好 男々 女々格 都一 样 哎哟 哎嗨 哟 哎嗨 哟

5 3 2 | i 6 i 6 6 | 5 5 6 | 2 2 6 6 6 | i 2 6 |
哎嗨 哟 应该 男的 到女 方 应该 男家 到女 家

i i 5 5 5 | 5 i 6 | 5·5 6·5 5 | 2 2 3 5 0 |
应该 女的 来招 郎 哎哟 哎嗨 哟 哎嗨 哟，

5 5 3 2 | 6 6 i 6 i 6 6 | 5 5 6 | 2 2 2 6 6 |
来招格 郎 应家 生活 条件格 大变 样 家中 生活格

i 2 6 | i 6 6 i i i | 3 i i i 6 5 6 | 5·5 6·5 5 |
有畫 好 当过 家生 儿子格 都一 样 哎哟 哎嗨 哟

2 2 3 5 | …… ‖
哎嗨 哟。

注：斜々扒々——谋吃谋穿，到处乱钻的意思。
家厦——家中。
最顶上——最好了。

· 143 ·

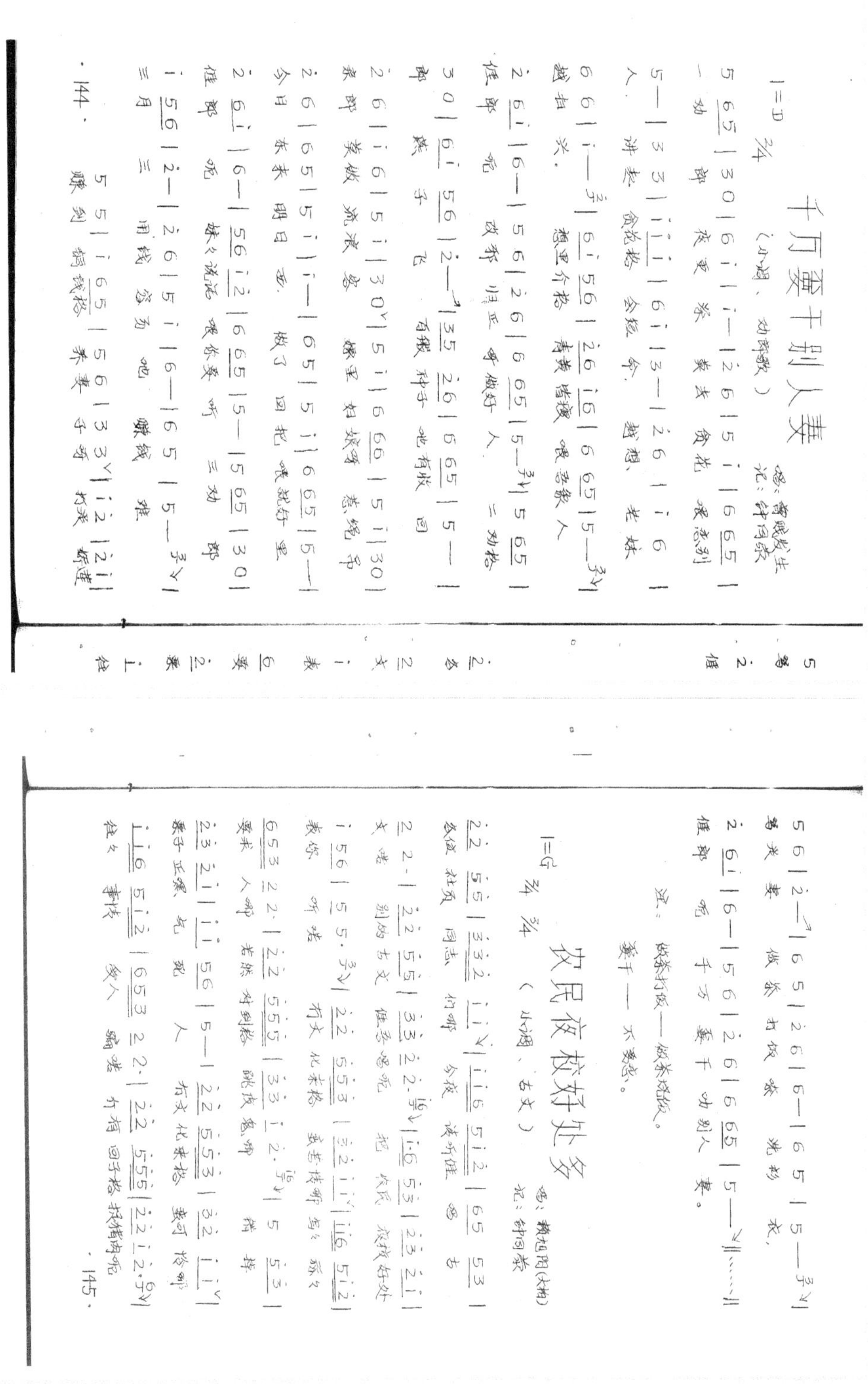

千万莫干别人妻

1=D 2/4

（小调、劝郎歌）

唱：曾贱发生
记：钟冈荣

5 65 | 3 0 | 6 i | i — | 2 6 | 5 i | 6 65 |
一 劝 郎 夜更 深 莫去 贪花 喂恋别

5 — | 3 3 | i i i | 6 i | 3 — | 2 6 | i 6 |
人. 讲起 贪花格 会短 命. 越想、 老妹

6 6 | i — | 6i 56 | 26 i6 | 6 65 | 5 — |
越扫 兴. 想里介格 青黄皆瘦 喂吾象 人

2 6i | 6 — | 5 6 | 2 6 | 6 65 | 5 — | 5 65 |
侄郎 呢 改邪 归正 呀做好 人. 二 劝格

3 0 | 6i 56 | 2 — | 35 26 | 6 65 | 5 — |
郎 燕 子 飞 有 种 种子 咃有收 回

2 6 | i 6 | 5 i | 3 0 | 5 i | 6 66 | 5 i | 3 0 |
亲郎 莫做 流浪 客 嫁里 妇娘呀 惹绳吊

2 6 | 6 5 | 5 i | i — | 6 5 | 5 i | 6 65 | 5 — |
今日 东来 明日 西. 做了 回把 喂就好 里

2 6i | 6 — | 56 i2 | 6 65 | 5 — | 5 65 | 3 0 |
侄郎 呢 妹々说话 喂你要 听 三 劝 郎

i 56 | 2 — | 2 6 | 5 i | 6 — | 6 5 | 5 — |
三月 三 用钱 容易 吧 赚钱 难

5 5 | i 65 | 5 6 | 3 3 | i 2 | 2 i |
赚到 铜钱格 养妻 子呀 打死 好莲

5 6 | 2 — | 6 5 | 2 6 | 6 — | 6 5 | 5 — |
驾 关 妻 做茶 打饭 嗏 洗衫 衣.

2 6i | 6 — | 5 6 | 2 6 | 6 65 | 5 — ||……||
侄郎 呢 千万 莫干 动别人 妻。

注：做茶打饭——做茶烧饭。

莫干——不要惹。

农民夜校好处多

1=G 2/4 3/4

（小调、古文）

唱：赖旭阳(大柏)
记：钟冈荣

22 55 | 332 ii | ii6 5i2 | 65 53 |
各位 社员 同志 们哪 今夜 请听侄 唱 古

2 2· | 22 55 | 33 2 2· | i6 53 | 23 2i |
文 唠 别的 古文 侄莫唱呢 把 农民 夜校好处

i 56 | 5 5· | 22 553 | 32 ii | ii6 5i2 |
表你 听 唠 冇文 化来格 亟苦 情哪 句々 流々

653 2 2· | 22 555 | 33 i 2· | 5 53 |
要求 人哪 若然 对到格 跳皮 鬼哪 猜 掉

23 2i | ii 56 | 5 — | 22 553 | 32 ii |
栗子 正熟 气 死 人 冇文 化来格 蛮可 怜哪

ii6 5i2 | 653 2 2· | 22 555 | 22 i 2· |
往々 事情 多人 骗 唠 介有 回子格 报猪肉呢

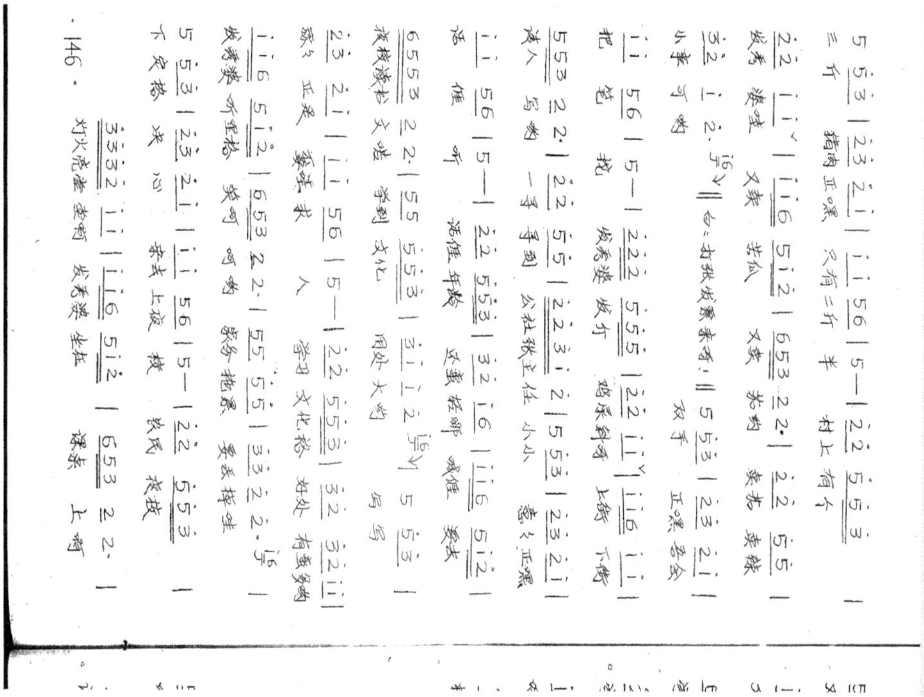

5 53 | 23 21 | 11 56 | 5— | 22 553 |
三 斤　猪肉正嘿　只有二斤　半　村上 有个

22 11 | 116 512 | 653 22· | 22 55 |
发秀 婆哇　又卖　苦瓜　又卖　茄哟　卖茄　卖辣

32 1 2· 16 ‖ 白：打张发票来呀！‖ 5 53 | 23 21 |
小事　可　哟　双手　正嘿 君会

11 56 | 5— | 222 555 | 22 11 | 116 11 |
把　笔　拢　发秀婆　发个　鸡尿斜呀　上街　下街

553 22· | 22 55 | 223i 2 | 5 53 | 23 21 |
请人　写哟　一手　手到　公社张主任　小小　意々正嘿

11 56 | 5— | 22 553 | 32 16 | 116 512 |
话　佢　听　话佢 年龄　还蛮 轻唧　喊佢　要去

6553 22· | 55 553 | 31 12 16 | 5 53 |
夜校读书 文嗟　学到 文化　用处大哟　写 写

23 21 | 11 56 | 5— | 22 553 | 32 3211 |
家々 正是　要读 求　人　学习 文化格　好处　有蛮多哟

116 512 | 653 22· | 55 55 | 33 2 2· 16 |
发秀婆 听里格　笑呵　呵 哟　家务 抛累　要去 择哇

5 53 | 23 21 | 11 56 | 5— | 22 553 |
下 定格　决　心　索去 上夜　校　农民　夜校

3332 11 | 116 512 | 653 22· |
灯火亮堂 堂呵　发秀婆 坐在　课桌　上 呵

55 553 | 32 2 2· 16 | 5 53 | 23 21 |
又认 字来　又读 书呵　又 学　文化 正嘿

11 56 | 5— | 22 553 | 32 11 | 116 512 |
又把 歌来　唱　农民 夜校　好处多哇　学文　化来

653 22· | 22 553 | 32 12· 16 | 5 53 |
学科　学呵　感谢 党妈　领导 好哇　底 个

23 21 | 11 56 | 5— | 22 553 | 3332 11 |
学习 机会　正嘿、要储 过　农民 夜校　好处多完里呀

116 512 | 653 22· | 22 553 | 33 22 |
唱得 君好　要怪　奇呀　奉劝 大家　都去 上夜

1 2· 16 | 5 53 | 23 21 | 11 56 | 5— ‖
校哇　学习　文化 正嘿、兴　风　气。

注：拢—拿。
鸡尿斜—慌々张々。
要怪奇——不要见怪的意思。

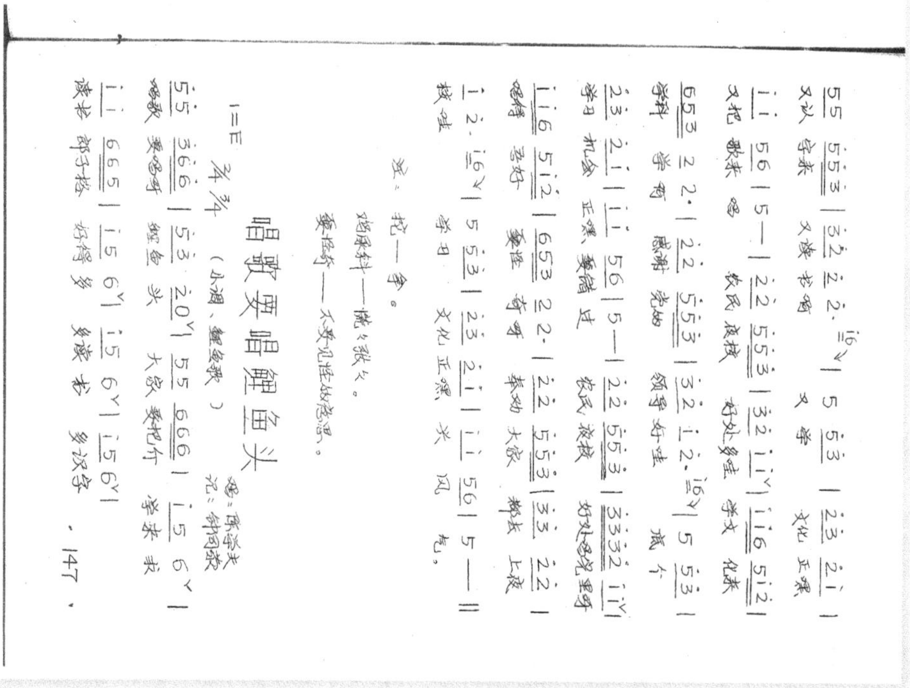

唱歌要唱鲤鱼头

1=E　2/4 3/4　（小调、鲤鱼歌）　唱：陈学夫　记：钟同荣

55 366 | 53 20 | 55 666 | 15 6 |
唱歌 要唱呀　鲤鱼 头　大家 要把个　学来 求

11 665 | 15 6 | 15 6 | 156 |
读书 郎子格　好得 多　多读 书　多识字

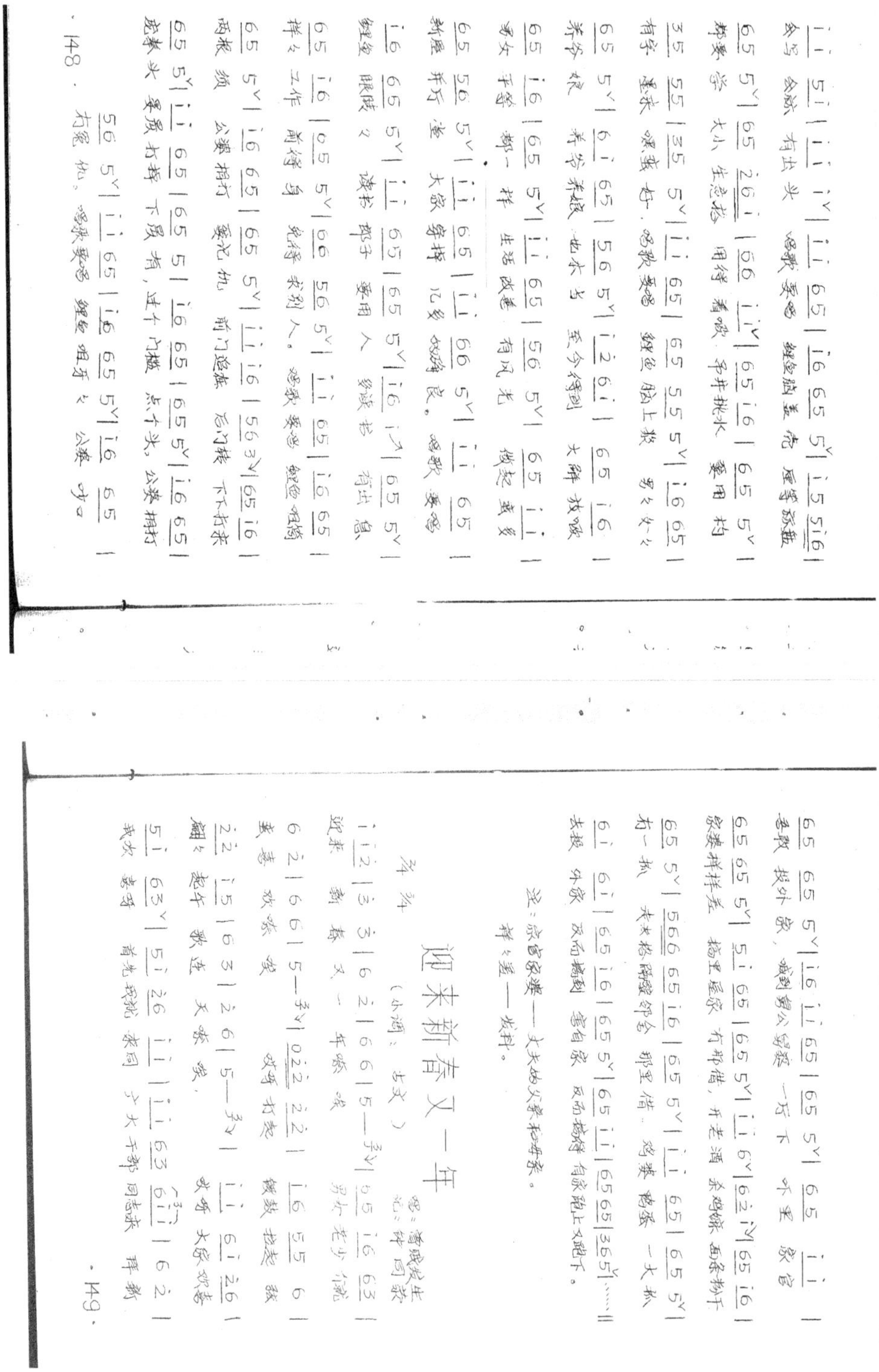

会写 会算 有出头 唱歌要唱 鲤鱼脑盖壳 硬等孙盘

都要学 大小生意搭 用得着哦 吊井挑水 要用杓

有字 墨汞 喂蚕好，唱歌要唱 鲤鱼脑上鼓 男々女々

养爷娘 养爷养娘也本当 至今得到 大解放哦

男女平等 都一样 生活改善 有风光 做起来

新屋并行塗 大家穿挥 亿多妙确良。唱歌要唱

鲤鱼眼睛々 读书郎子 要用人 多读书 有出息

样々工作 前得身 免得求别人。唱歌要唱 鲤鱼咀筒

两根须 公婆相打 要记仇 前门追在 后门转 下下打来

起拳头 要晟打挥 下晟有，过个门槛 点个头，公婆相打

有冤仇。唱歌要唱 鲤鱼咀牙々 公婆 吵口

·148·

吾敢 投外家，喊到舅公舅婆 一厅下 吓里 家官

家婆样样差 搞里屋家 冇部借，开老酒 杀鸡嫲 面条粉干

有一抓 走出格隔壁邻舍 那里借。鸡婆 鸭蛋 一大抓

去投 外家 反而搞到 害自家 反而搞得 自家跑上又跑下。

注：家官家婆——丈夫的父亲和母亲。

样々差——发料。

迎来新春又一年

2/4 3/4 （小调：古文） 唱：曾贱姣生 记：钟同歆

迎来 新春又一 年嘛 哎 男女老少 个就

喜喜 欢嘛 哎 哎呀 打起 锣鼓 拉起 弦

翩々 起舞 歌连 天嘛 哎， 哎呀 大家欢喜

我欢 喜呀 首先我就 来同 广大干部 同志来 拜新

·149·

04 第四类 · 灯歌

CATEGORY IV · LANTERN SONGS

导读

“灯歌”是与元宵、灯会及节庆表演紧密相关的歌谣，常与舞蹈、花鼓等民间艺术结合。其旋律明快，节奏鲜明，富有表演性与群体性。赣南灯歌多在庙会、节庆、婚嫁仪式中演唱，用以烘托喜庆氛围、表达祝福或调侃。歌词生动、幽默，带有即兴性，展现了民间社会的欢乐与创造力。作为节庆文化的一部分，灯歌体现了社区的凝聚力与仪式感。特别是劳动茶灯歌源自农耕社会的生产节奏与协作需要。茶农在采茶、制茶等劳动过程中即兴演唱，不仅调节节奏、减轻疲倦，也增强了集体劳动的协作氛围。歌词多以劳动过程为描绘对象，既有直叙场景，也有寓情于事的抒怀，折射出劳动者的幽默智慧与生活态度。此类歌曲常与劳动节拍高度契合，旋律简短有力，呈现出“声与事”相合的独特特征。

Introduction

“Lantern Songs” are folk songs closely associated with the Lantern Festival, lantern fairs, and festive performances, often combined with dance, flower drum plays, and other folk arts. Characterized by lively melodies and strong rhythms, they are highly performative and communal in nature. In southern Jiangxi, lantern songs were frequently sung during temple fairs, festivals, and wedding ceremonies to enhance the festive atmosphere, convey blessings, or engage in playful banter. Their lyrics are vivid, humorous, and often improvised, reflecting the joy and creativity of folk society. As an integral part of festive culture, lantern songs embody the cohesion and ritual sense of the community. In particular, Tea-Picking Lantern Songs originated from the rhythms and cooperative needs of agrarian society. Tea farmers improvised songs during the processes of tea-picking and tea-processing, serving not only to regulate work rhythm and alleviate fatigue but also to strengthen communal practice and foster a shared sense of cooperation. The lyrics often depict laboring scenes, blending direct description with emotional reflection, thereby revealing the humor, wisdom, and life attitudes of the workers. Closely aligned with the physical rhythm of labor, these songs are marked by concise and forceful melodies, presenting a distinctive feature of harmony between “sound and action.”

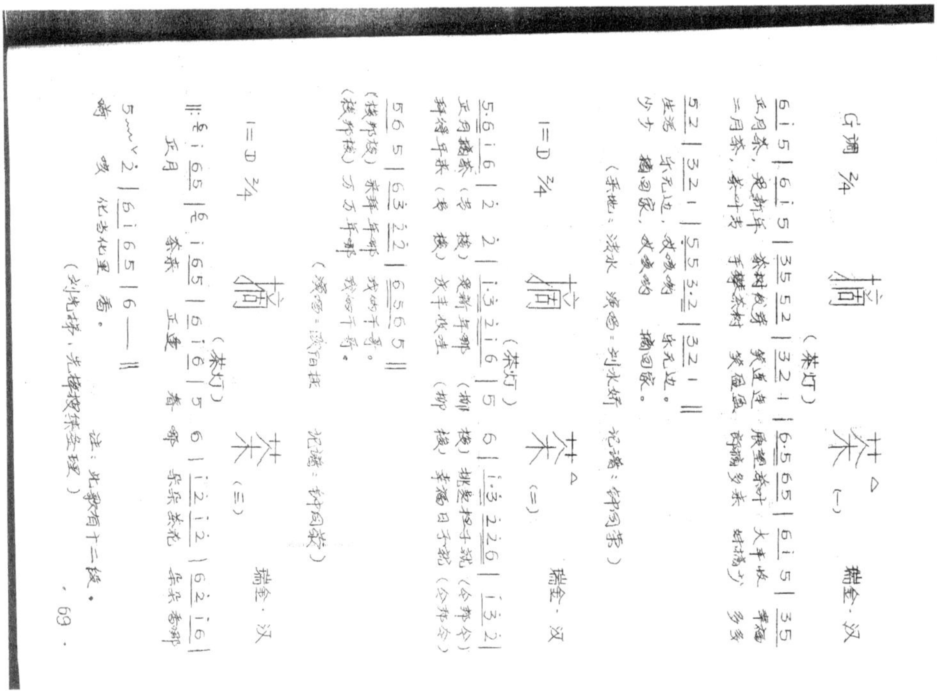

G调 2/4 摘茶△（一） 瑞金·汉

（茶灯）

6 i 5 | 6 i 5 | 35 52 | 32 1 | 6·5 65 | 6 i 5 | 35
正月茶，是新年 茶树发芽 笑连连 展望茶叶 大丰收 幸福
二月茶，茶叶青 手攀茶树 笑盈盈 郎摘多来 妹摘少 多多

52 | 32 1 | 55 3·2 | 32 1 ||
生活 乐无边，哎喨哟 乐无边。
少少 摘回家，哎喨哟 摘回家。

（采地：洁水 演唱：刘水娇 记谱：钟同荣）

1=D 2/4 摘茶△（二） 瑞金·汉

（茶灯）

5·6 i 6 | 2 2 | i·3 2i 6 | 5 6 | i·3 226 | i 3 2 |
正月摘茶（哥 梭）是新年哪（柳 梭）挑起担子就（今邦令）
拜得年来（哥 梭）庆丰收哇（柳 梭）幸福日子就（今邦令）

56 5 | 63 22 | 6565 5 ||
（梭邦梭）亲拜 年哪 我的干哥。
（梭邦梭）万万 年哪 我的干哥。

（演唱：欧阳扶 记谱：钟同荣）

1=D 2/4 摘茶（三） 瑞金·汉

（茶灯）

‖: 6 i 65 | 6 i 65 | 6 i 6 | 5 6 | i2 i2 | 62 i6 |
正月 茶来 正逢 春 哪 朵朵茶花 朵朵香哪

5～ 2 | 6i 65 | 6 — ||
嗬 哎 化当化里 香。

注：此歌有十二段。

（刘光梯、光梓搜集整理）

· 69 ·

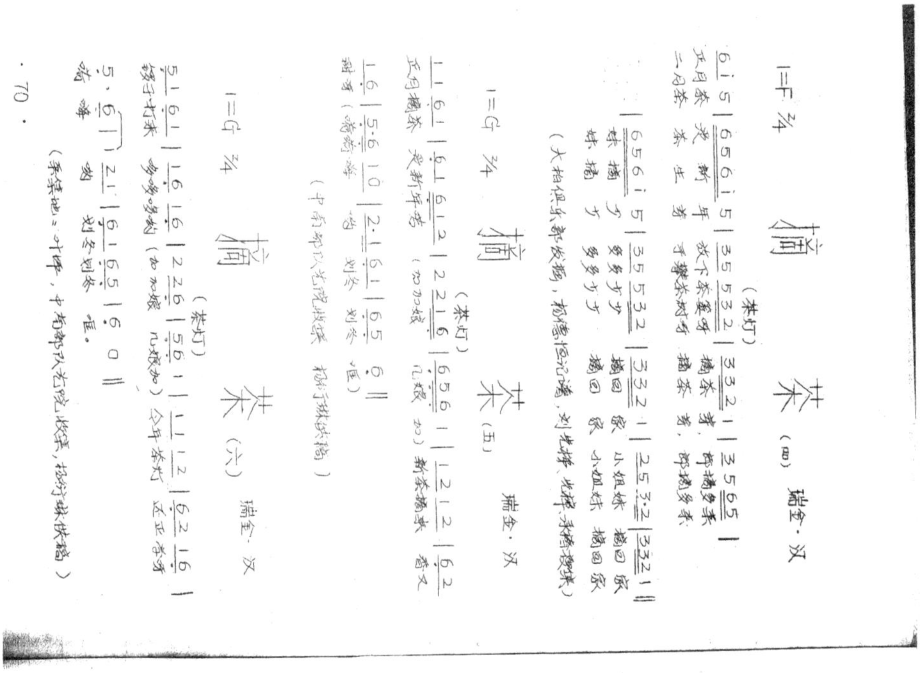

1=F 2/4 摘茶（四） 瑞金·汉

（茶灯）

6 i 5 | 656 i 5 | 35 532 | 332 1 | 35 65 |
正月茶 是 新 年 放下茶篓呀 摘茶 芽，郎摘多来
二月茶 茶 生 芽 手攀茶树呀 摘茶 芽，郎摘多来

| 656 i 5 | 35 532 | 332 1 | 25 3·2 | 332 1 ||
妹 摘 少 多多少少 摘回 家 小姐妹 摘回 家
妹 摘 少 多多少少 摘回 家 小姐妹 摘回 家

（大柏俱乐部发掘，杨德恒记谱，刘光梯、光梓、永椿搜集）

1=G 3/4 摘茶（五） 瑞金·汉

（茶灯）

11 61 | 61 612 | 2 216 | 656 1 | 12 12 | 62
正月摘茶 是新年哉 （加加娘 几娘 加）新茶摘来 香又

16 | 5·6 10 | 2·1 61 | 65 6 ||
甜呀（嗬嗬嗨 哟 刘冬 刘冬 喂）

（中南部队艺院收集 杨衍琳供稿）

1=G 2/4 摘茶（六） 瑞金·汉

（茶灯）

51 61 | 16 16 | 2 26 | 56 1 | 11 12 | 62 16 |
锣子打来 哆哆哆哟（加 加娘 几娘加）今年茶灯 还正当呀

5· 6 | 1 21 | 61 65 | 6 0 ||
嗬 嗨 哟 刘冬刘冬 喂。

（采集地：叶坪，中南部队艺院收集，杨衍琳供稿）

· 70 ·

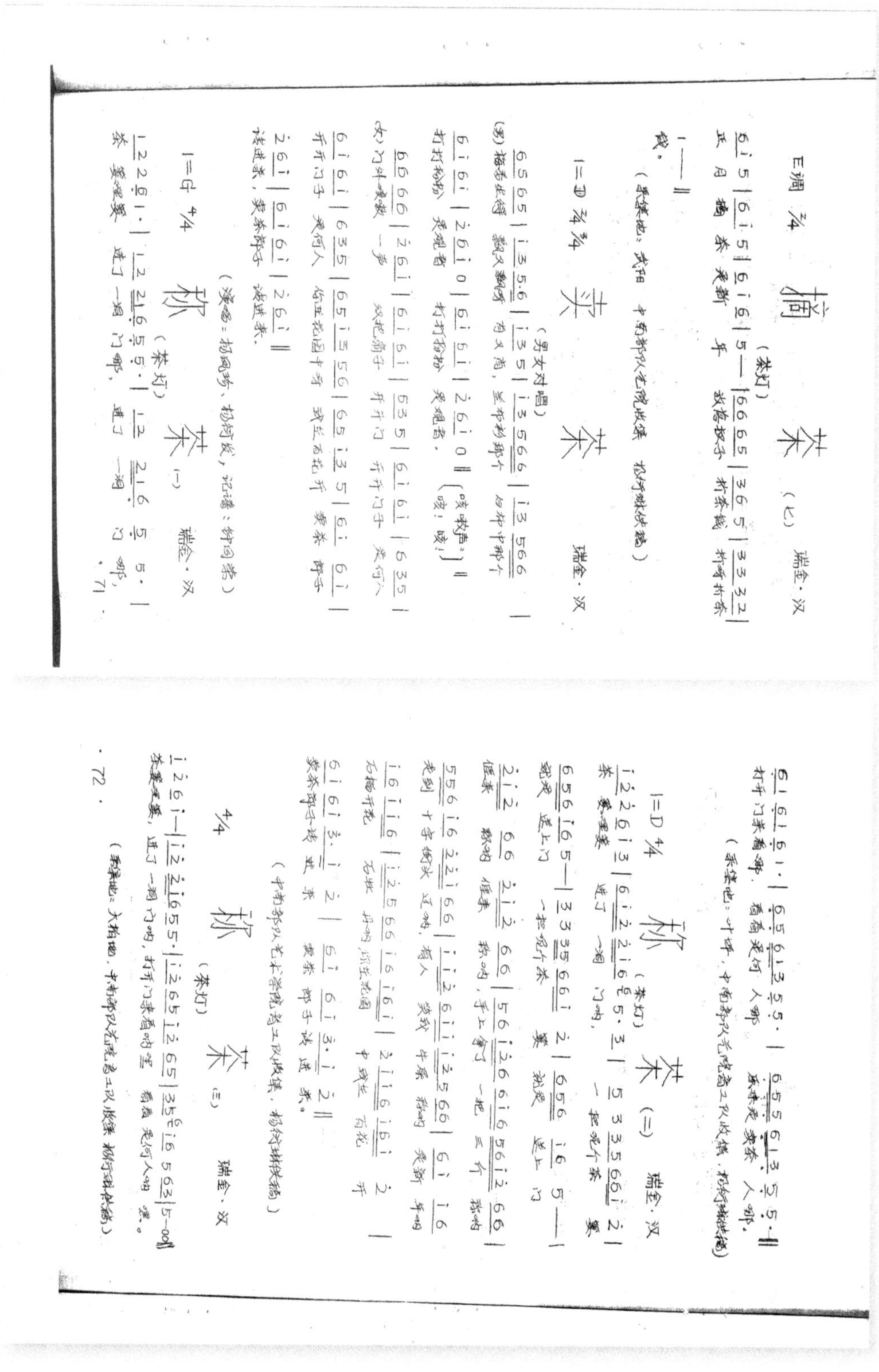

摘茶（七）

E调 2/4　　瑞金·汉

（茶灯）

正月摘茶是新年 放落杈子 折茶钱 折呀折茶钱。

（采集地：武阳　中南部队艺院收集　杨衍琳供稿）

卖茶

1=D 2/4 3/4　　瑞金·汉

（男女对唱）

（男）梅香出得 飘又飘呀 有又有，兰布衫那个 白布中那个

打打扮扮 是观音 打打扮扮 是观音。（咳啾声：咳！咳！）

（女）门外嗳嗽 一声 双把扇子 开开门 开开门子 是何人

开开门子 是何人 你在花园中呀 我在百花开 卖茶 郎子

请进来，卖茶郎子 请进来。

（演唱：杨凤玲、杨衍发，记谱：钟同荣）

称茶（一）

1=G 4/4　　瑞金·汉

（茶灯）

茶 要哩要 进了 一洞 门哪， 进了 一洞 门 哪，

·71·

打开门来看哪， 看看是何 人哪　原来是卖茶 人哪。

（采集地：叶坪，中南部队艺院舞工队收集，杨衍琳供稿）

称茶（二）

1=D 4/4　　瑞金·汉

（茶灯）

茶 要哩要 进了 一洞 门呐， 一担 砚个茶 要

就是 送上门 一担砚个茶 要 就是 送上 门

信来 称呐 信来 称呐，手上拿了 一把 三 斤 称呐

走到 十字街头 过呐，有人 笑我 牛屎 称呐 是新 年呐

石榴开花 石牡 丹呐，你在花园 中 我在 百花 开

卖茶郎子请 进 来 卖茶 郎子 请 进 来。

（中南部队艺术学院舞工队收集，杨衍琳供稿）

称茶（三）

4/4　　瑞金·汉

（茶灯）

茶要哩要，进了一洞门呐，打开门来看呐哩 看看 是何人呐 哩。

·72·

（采集地：大柏地，中南部队艺院舞工队收集　杨衍琳供稿）

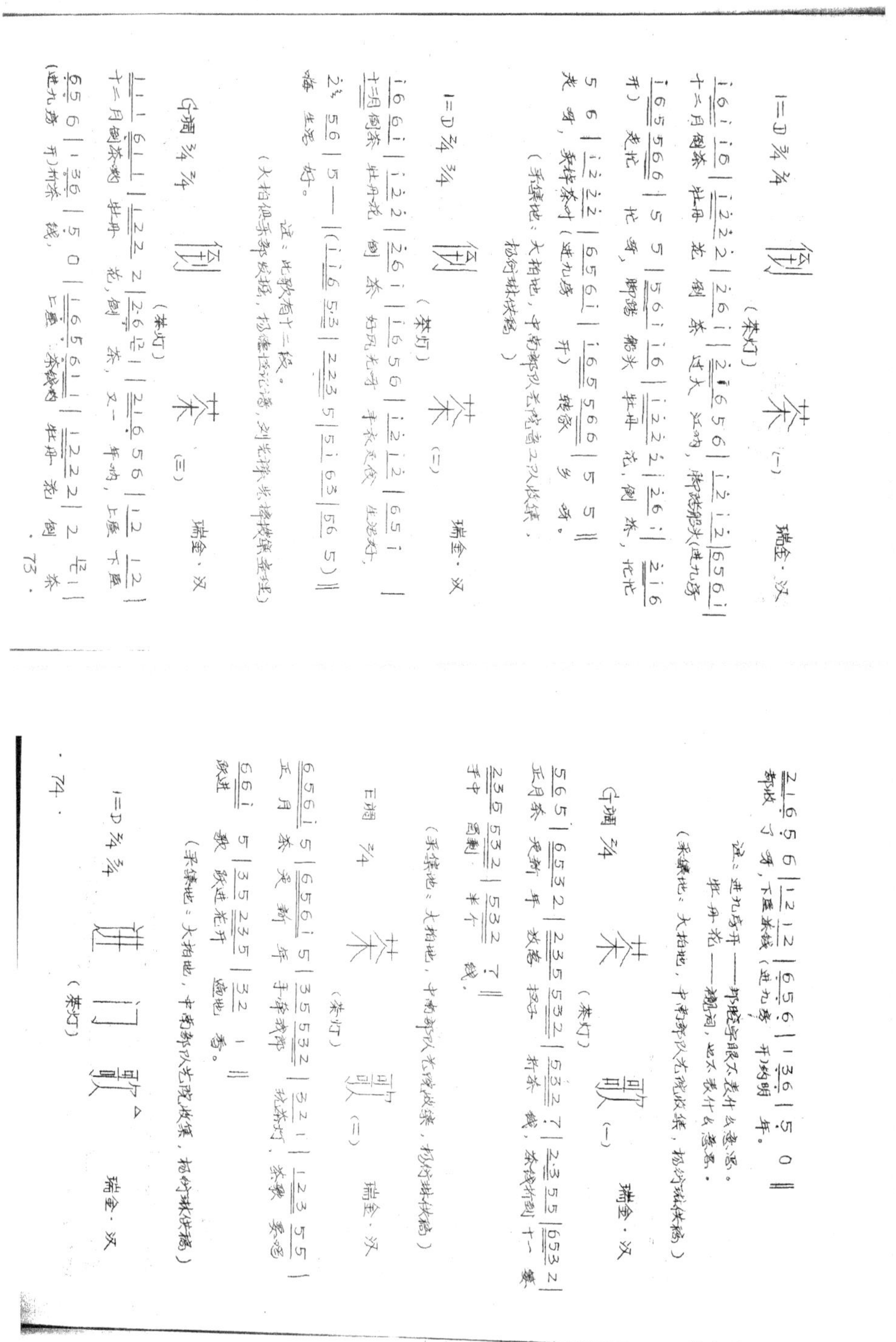

1=D 2/4 3/4 **倒 茶**（一） 瑞金·汉

（茶灯）

i6 i i6 | i 2 2 2 2 | 2 6 i | 2 i 6 5 6 | i 2 i 2 | 6 5 6 i |
十二月倒茶 牡丹 花 倒 茶 过大 江呐，脚踏船头（进九房

i 6 5 5 6 6 | 5 5 | 5 6 i i 6 | i 2 2 2 | 2 6 i | 2 i 6
开） 走忙 忙 呀，脚踏 船头 牡丹 花，倒 茶，忙忙

5 6 | i 2 2 2 | 6 5 6 i | i 6 5 5 6 6 | 5 5 ||
走 呀，采掉茶叶（进九房 开） 转家 乡 呀。

（采集地：大柏地，中南部队艺院音工队收集，杨衍琳供稿）

1=D 2/4 3/4 **倒 茶**（二） 瑞金·汉

（茶灯）

i 6 6 i | i 2 2 | 2 6 i | i 6 5 6 | i 2 i 2 | 6 5 i |
十二月倒茶 牡丹花 倒 茶 好风光呀 手衣走俊 生活好，

2 5 6 | 5 — |（i i 6 5 3 | 2 2 3 5 | 5 i 6 3 | 5 6 5）||
嗨 生活 好。

注：此歌有十二段。

（大柏地采都发掘，杨德胜记谱，刘光保光捧搜集整理）

G调 3/4 2/4 **倒 茶**（三） 瑞金·汉

（茶灯）

1 1 1 6 1 1 | 1 2 2 2 | 2 6 2 1 | 2 1 6 5 6 | 1 2 1 2 |
十二月倒茶哟 牡丹 花，倒 茶， 又一 年呐，上屋 下屋

6 5 6 | 1 3 6 | 5 0 | 1 6 5 6 1 1 | 1 2 2 2 | 2 2 1 |
（进九房 开）打茶 钱， 上屋 茶钱哟 牡丹 花 倒 茶

· 73 ·

2 1 6 5 6 | 1 2 1 2 | 6 5 6 | 1 3 6 | 5 0 ||
都收 了 呀，下屋茶钱（进九房 开）约明 年。

注：进九房开——那腔字眼不表什么意思。
牡丹花——衬词，也不表什么意思。

（采集地：大柏地，中南部队艺院收集，杨衍琳供稿）

G调 2/4 **茶 歌**（一） 瑞金·汉

（茶灯）

5 6 5 | 6 5 3 2 | 2 3 5 5 3 2 | 5 3 2 7 | 2 3 5 5 | 6 5 3 2 |
正月茶 是新 年 放客 打子 打茶 钱，茶钱打到 十一 篓

2 3 5 5 3 2 | 5 3 2 7 ||
手中 留剩 半个 钱。

（采集地：大柏地，中南部队艺院收集，杨衍琳供稿）

E调 2/4 **茶 歌**（二） 瑞金·汉

（茶灯）

6 5 6 i 5 | 6 5 6 i 5 | 3 5 5 3 2 | 3 2 1 | 1 2 3 5 5 |
正 月 茶 是 新 年 手牵我郎 玩茶灯，茶歌 要唱

6 6 i 5 | 3 5 2 3 5 | 3 2 1 ||
跃进 歌 跃进花开 遍地 香。

（采集地：大柏地，中南部队艺院收集，杨衍琳供稿）

1=D 2/4 3/4 **进 门 歌**△ 瑞金·汉

（茶灯）

· 74 ·

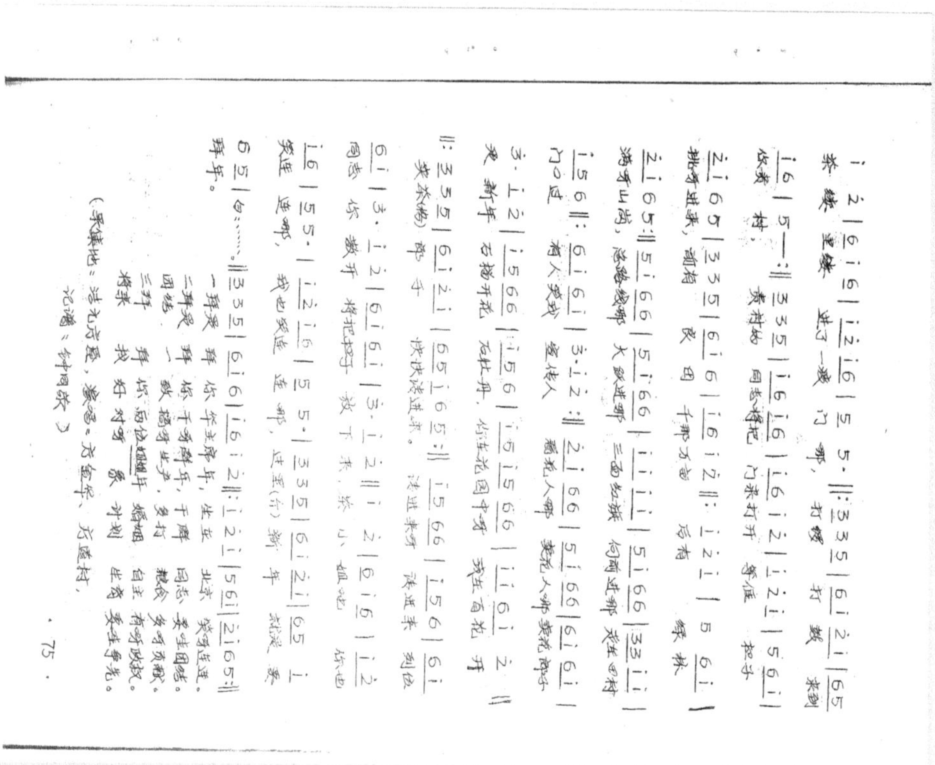

i 2̇ | 6 i 6 | i 2̇ i 6 | 5 5· ‖: 3 3 5 | 6 i 2̇ i | 6 5
茶楼 里楼 进了一道 门 哪， 打锣 打 鼓 来到

i 6 | 5 — :‖ 3 3 5 | i 6 i 6 | i 6 i 2̇ | i 2̇ i | 5 6 i |
你贵 村， 贵村的 同志将把 门来打开 等候 担子

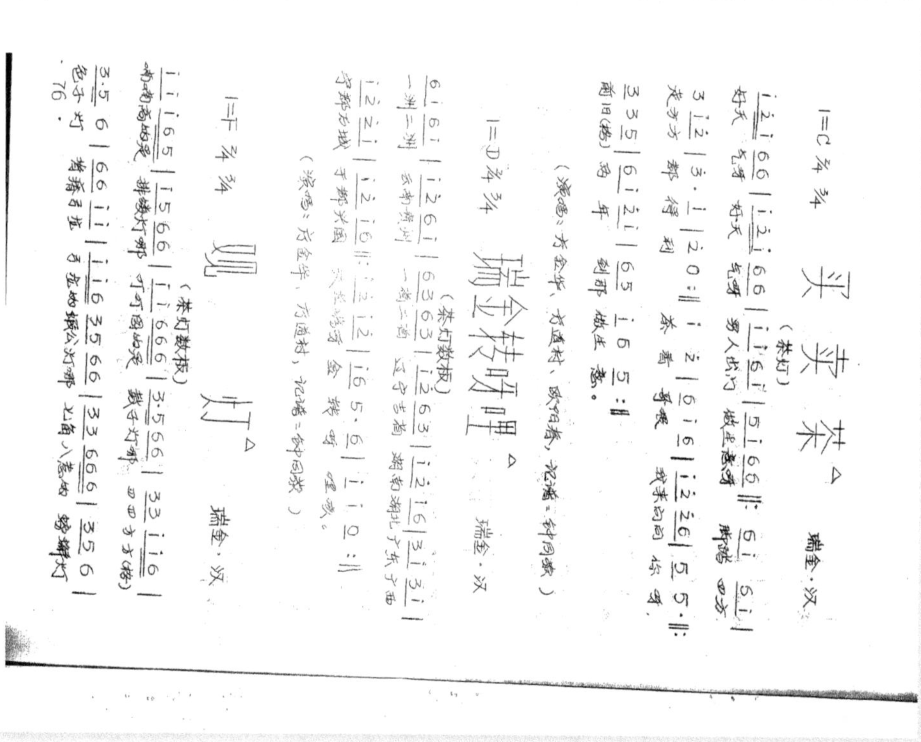

2̇ i 6 5 | 3 3 5 | 6 i 6 | i 6 i 2̇ ‖: i 2̇ i | 5 6 i |
挑呀进来，前有 良 田 千那万亩 后有 绿 林

2̇ i 6 5 :‖ 5 i 6 6 | 5 i 6 6 | i i i i | 5 i 6 6 | 3 3 i i |
满呀山岗，沿路线哪 大跃进哪 三面红旗 闪闹进那 我在四村

i 5 6 ‖: 6 i 6 i | 3· i 2̇ :‖ 2̇ i 6 6 | 5 i 6 6 | 6 i 6 i |
门口过 有人卖我 宣传人 插花人哪 卖花人哪卖花郎子

3· i 2̇ | i 5 6 6 | i 5 6 | i 5 i 5 6 6 | i i 6 i 2̇ ‖
过 新年 石榴开花 石牡丹，你在花园中呀 我在百花 开

‖: 3 3 5 | 6 i 2̇ i | 6 5 i 6 5 :‖ i 5 6 6 | i 5 6 | 6 i
卖茶(格) 郎 子 快快请进来。 请进来呀 请进来 列位

6 i | 3· i 2̇ | 6 i 6 i | 3· i 2̇ ‖ i 2̇ | 6 i 6 | i 2̇
同志 你 撒开 将把担子 放 下 来，茶 小 姐他 你也

i 6 | 5 5· | i 2̇ i 6 | 5 5· | 3 3 5 | 6 i 2̇ i | 6 5 i
笑连 连哪， 我也笑连 连 哪， 过至(介) 新 年 就是 要

6 5 | ……‖ 3 3 5 | 6 i 6 | i 6 i 2̇ ‖: i 2̇ i | 5 6 i | 2̇ i 6 5 :‖
拜年。

一拜是 拜 你 华主席年，生在 北京 笑呀连连。
二拜是 拜 你 千万群年，千群 同志 要生团结。
团结 一 致 搞呀生产，多打 粮食 多呀贡献。
三拜 拜 你 后位婚姻年 婚姻 自主 有呀政权。
将来 找 好 对呀 象 计划 生育 要在争先。

（采集地：沽元方厦，演唱：方金华、方道村，记谱：钟同歆）

· 75 ·

买卖茶△

1=C 2/4 3/4 瑞金·汉

（茶灯）

i 2̇ i 6 6 | i 2̇ i 6 6 | i i 6 i | 5 i 6 6 ‖: 6 i 5 i |
好天 气呀 好天 气呀 男人出门 做生意呀 脚踏 四方

3 i 2̇ | 3· i | 2̇ 0 :‖ i 2̇ | 6 i 6 | i 2̇ 2̇ 6 | 5 5· ‖:
走方方 都 得 利 茶 客 哥哦 我来问问 你 呀，

3 3 5 | 6 i 2̇ i | 6 5 i 6 5 :‖
前旧(格) 两 年 到那 做生 意。

（演唱：方金华、方道村、欧阳春，记谱：钟同歆）

瑞金转呀哩△

1=D 2/4 3/4 瑞金·汉

（茶灯数板）

6 i 6 i | i 2̇ 6 i | 6 3 6 3 | i 2̇ 6 3 | i 2̇ i 6 | 3 i 3 i |
一洲二洲 云南贵州 一省二省 辽宁吉省 湖南湖北广东广西

i 2̇ 2̇ i | i 2̇ i 6 ‖: i 2̇ i 2̇ | i 6 5· 6 | i i 0 :‖
宁都石城 于都兴国 [illegible] 金 转 呀 哩哦。

（演唱：方金华、方道村，记谱：钟同歆）

观灯△

1=F 2/4 3/4 瑞金·汉

（茶灯数板）

i i i 6 5 | i 5 6 6 | i i 6 6 6 | 3· 5 6 6 | 3 3 i i 6 |
喃喃高的是 排楼灯哪 可可圆的是 鼓子灯哪 四四方方(格)

3· 5 6 | 6 6 i i | i i 6 3 5 6 6 | 3 3 6 6 6 | 3 5 6 |
包子灯 剪箭弓拉 弓拉的蝦公灯哪 七角八惹的 螃蟹灯

· 76 ·

1̇2̇ 665 | 35 66 | 31̇ 31̇ | 3.5 66 | 1̇1̇ 6 66 |
胡须巴扒的 猫子灯哪 七囊七五 是龙灯哪 点着火 来是

1̇1̇ 6·6 | 61̇ 1̇66 | 1̇556 | 3333 | 1̇56 | 1̇566 |
滔滔的哪 的滔滔是 走马 灯 蜈松蜈松 狮子灯 茶篮灯哪

3566 | 1̇255 | 1̇21̇5 | 356 ‖: 1̇2̇ 1̇2̇ | 1̇61̇ 2̇6 |
茶王灯哪 姐姐手上 还有一把 扇子灯 恭来正月 十五样呢

5·6 1̇1̇ :‖
花翻哩咳。

（演唱：方金华、方道村， 记谱：钟同荣）

卖杂货△

1=D 2/4 3/4 瑞金·汉

（茶灯数板）

61̇ 61̇ | 1̇6 61̇ | 63 63 | 61̇ 1̇3 | 1̇5 66 | 1̇56 |
大包细包 三茶细椒 大捆细捆 胭脂水粉 样条巾哪 角布巾，

1̇1̇ 1̇5 66 | 1̇5 1̇56 | 1̇5 66 | 356 ‖: 1̇2̇ 1̇2̇ |
蓑衣笠姿巾哪，鞋底鞋面巾 长牙巾哪 短牙巾 还有 两包

1̇2̇ 6 | 5·6 1̇1̇ :‖
绣娘 花针哩咳。

（演唱：方金华、方道村 记谱：钟同荣）

卖菓子△

1=D 2/4 3/4 瑞金·汉

（茶灯）

1̇1̇ 1̇566 | 1̇1̇ 1̇566 | 1̇56 | 1̇56 | 1̇2 65 |
山中山荔子呀 田中田马荠呀 落花生 炒豆子 油麦 糕饼

· 77 ·

1̇56 | 2̇1̇ 65 | 1̇566 | 2̇1̇ 66 | 1̇266 ‖: 1̇2̇ 1̇2̇ |
柑桔子 人荷笑枣 柑蔗子呀 芋子芋线 竹花根哪 还有两包

1̇ 2 6 | 5·6 1̇1̇ :‖
面哩 饼子哩咳。

（演唱：方金华、方道村，记谱：钟同荣）

卖布草△

1=D 2/4 瑞金·汉

（茶灯）

1̇2 66 | 1̇2 66 | 1̇2̇ 1̇2̇ | 1̇2 61̇ | 51̇ 66 | 1̇1̇ 1̇65 |
茶香妹呀 小心记呀 听催茶呀 从头至尾 说你听哪 能能黄的是

1̇56 | 1̇2 666 | 61̇ 3 | 1̇2̇ 1̇55 | 1̇56 ‖: 1̇2̇ 1̇2̇ |
黄卡叽 兰兰色的是 士林布 花花朵朵的 花华叽 茶香妹妹

1̇ 2̇ 1̇ | 6 0 :‖
正哩合 意。

（演唱：方金华、方道村，记谱：钟同荣）

老黄茶△

1=D 2/4 3/4 瑞金·汉

（茶灯）

1̇ 2̇ | 61̇ 6 | 1̇2̇ 1̇6 | 5 5 0 | 1̇2̇ 1̇6 | 5 50 | 335 |
茶 香 哥哎 你呀听端 了哇， 我呀听端 了 哇， 名字

61̇ 2̇1̇ | 1̇ 6 6 | 5 — | 3 3 5 | 61̇ 2̇1̇ |
叫 做 老哇黄 茶 吃下 口 中

65 1̇ 6 6 | 5 — ‖
就是 好 味 烟 茶。

（演唱：方金华、方道村，记谱：钟同荣）

· 78 ·

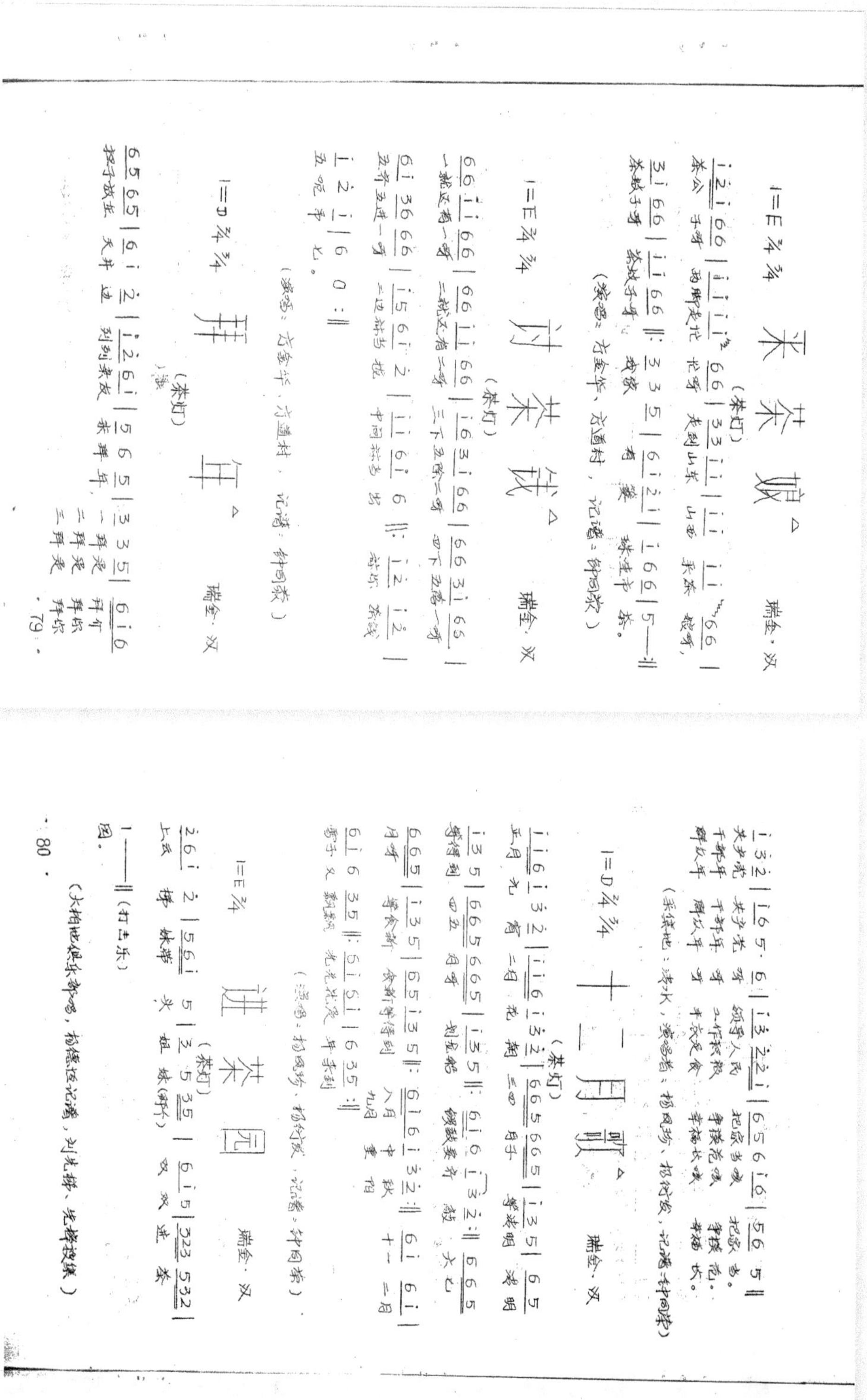

采茶娘△

1=E 2/4 3/4　　瑞金·汉

（茶灯）

i2i 66 | iii i 66 | 33 ii | ii ii 66 |
茶公 子呀 两脚走忙 忙呀 走到山东 山西 采茶 娘呀，

3i 66 | ii 66 ‖: 3 3 5 | 6i 2i | i 66 | 5— :‖
茶娘子呀 茶娘子呀 我家 有 篓 珠生节 茶。

（演唱：方金华、方通村，记谱：钟同歌）

讨茶钱△

1=E 2/4 3/4　　瑞金·汉

（茶灯）

66 ii 66 | 66 ii 66 | i6 3i 66 | 66 3i 65 |
一就还有一呀 二就还有二呀 三下五除二呀 四下五落一呀

6i 36 66 | i5 6i 2 | ii 6i 6 ‖: i2 i2 |
五齐五进一呀 二边祥当 花 中间祥当 当 祥你 茶钱

i 2 i | 6 0 :‖
五 呃 节 乜。

（演唱：方金华、方通村，记谱：钟同歌）

拜年△

1=D 2/4 3/4　　瑞金·汉

（茶灯）

65 65 | 6 i 2 | i26i | 5 6 5 | 3 3 5 | 6i6
捉子放在 天井 边 列列亲友 来 拜 年， 一拜 是 拜你
二拜 是 拜你
三拜 是 拜你

· 79 ·

i 3 2 | i6 5· 6 | i3 22i | 656 i6 | 56 5 ‖
共产党 共产党 呀 领导人民 把家当哦 把家 当。
干部年 干部年 呀 工作积极 争换花哦 争换 花。
群众年 群众年 呀 丰衣足食 幸福长哦 幸福 长。

（采集地：泱水，演唱者：杨凤珍、杨衍发，记谱：钟同荣）

十二月歌△

1=D 2/4 3/4　　瑞金·汉

（茶灯）

ii6 i 3 2 | ii6 i 3 2 | 665 665 | i3 5 | 6 5
正月 元 宵 二月 花 朝 三四 月子 等清明 清 明

i3 5 | 665 665 | i3 5 ‖: 6i 6 i 3 2 :‖ 665
等得 到 四五 月呀 划龙船 锣鼓要齐 敲 六七

665 | i3 5 | 65 i3 5 ‖: 6i 6 i 3 2 :‖ 6i 6i |
月呀 等食新 食新等得到 八月 中 秋 十一 二月
九月 重 阳

6i 6 35 ‖: 6i 6i | 6 35 :‖
雪子 又 飘飘 光光光光 年 来到

（演唱：杨凤珍、杨衍发，记谱：钟同荣）

进茶园

1=E 2/4　　瑞金·汉

（茶灯）

26i 2 | 56i 5 | 3 5 35 | 6i 5 | 323 532 |
上云 梯 妹带 头 姐 妹（呀个） 双 双 进 茶

1 —— ‖（打击乐）
园。

（大柏地俱乐部唱，杨德恒记谱，刘先梯、先梓搜集）

· 80 ·

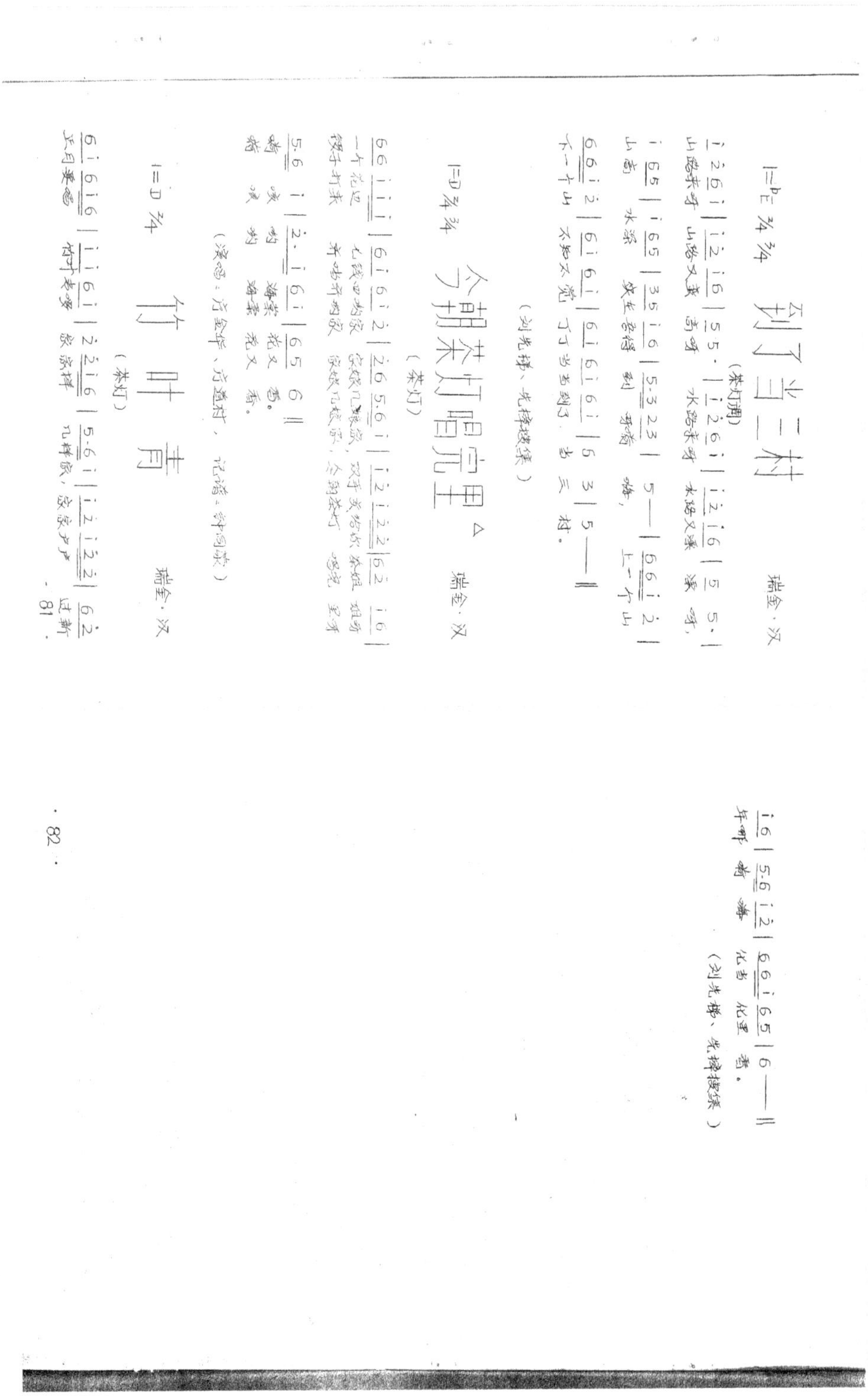

到了当三村

1=♭E 2/4 3/4 瑞金·汉

（茶灯调）

i 2 6 i | i 2 i 6 | 5 5 · | i 2 6 i | i 2 i 6 | 5 5 · |
山路来呀 山路又远 高呀 水路来呀 水路又深 深 呀，

i 6 5 | i 6 5 | 3 5 i 6 | 5·3 2 3 | 5 — | 6 6 i 2 |
山高 水深 实在吾得 到 呀当 嗨， 上一个山

6 6 i 2 | 6 i 6 i | 6 i 6 i 6 i | 5 3 | 5 — ‖
下一个山 不知不觉 丁丁当当到了 当 三 村。

（刘先梯、先梓搜集）

今朝茶灯唱完里△

1=D 2/4 3/4 瑞金·汉

（茶灯）

6 6 i i i | 6 i 6 i 2 | 2 6 5·6 i | i 2 i 2 2 | 6 2 i 6 |
一个花边 七钱四两家 家娘几娘家，双手交给你 茶姐 姐呀
锣子打来 齐哟齐哟家 家娘几娘家，今朝茶灯 唱完 里呀

5·6 i | 2· i 6 i | 6 5 6 ‖
嗬 咳 哟 海棠 花又 香。
嗬 咳 哟 海棠 花又 香。

（演唱：方金华、方道村，记谱：钟词崇）

竹叶青

1=D 2/4 瑞金·汉

（茶灯）

6 i 6 i 6 | i i 6 i | 2 2 i 6 | 5·6 i | i 2 i 2 2 | 6 2
正月要唱 竹叶老子 家家样 几样家，家家户户 过新

· 81 ·

i 6 | 5·6 i 2 | 6 6 i 6 5 | 6 — ‖
年哪 嗬 嗨 化当 化里 香。

（刘先梯、先梓搜集）

· 82 ·

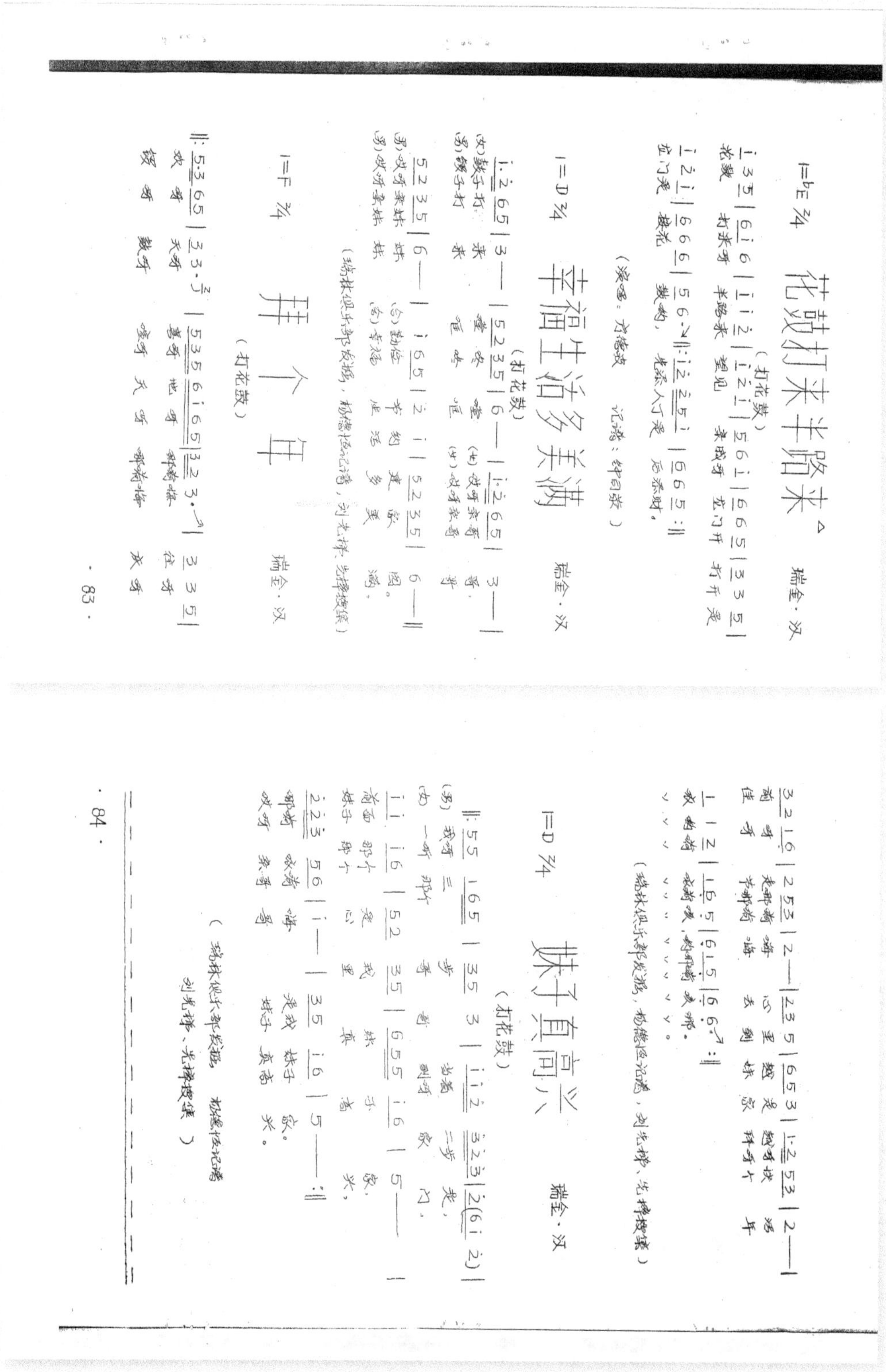

花鼓打来半路来

1=♭E 2/4　　瑞金·汉

（打花鼓）

花鼓 打来呀 半路来 望见 亲戚呀 龙门开 打开是
龙门是 接花 鼓哟， 光添人丁是 后添财。

（演唱：方德政　记谱：钟同荣）

幸福生活多美满

1=D 3/4　　瑞金·汉

（打花鼓）

(女)鼓子打 来 咚 咚 咚 (女)哎呀亲哥 哥
(男)锣子打 来 哐 哐 哐 (女)哎呀亲哥 哥
(男)哎呀亲妹 妹 (合)勤俭 节 约 建 家 园。
(男)哎呀亲妹 妹 (合)幸福 生 活 多 美 满。

（瑞林俱乐部发掘，杨德恒记谱，刘光梯、光梯搜集）

拜个年

1=F 2/4　　瑞金·汉

（打花鼓）

欢 呀 天呀 喜呀 地 呀 那荷嗨 往 呀
锣 呀 鼓呀 喧呀 天 呀 那荷嗨 庆 呀

前 呀 走那荷 嗨 心 里 越 是 越呀快 活
佳 呀 节那荷 嗨 去 到 妹 家 拜呀个 年
衣 哟 荷 衣荷 哎，哟那荷 衣 哪。

（瑞林俱乐部发掘，杨德恒记谱，刘光梯、光梯搜集）

妹子真高兴

1=D 2/4　　瑞金·汉

（打花鼓）

(男)我呀 三 步 当着 二步 走，
(女)一听 那个 哥 哥 叫呀 家 门，
前面 那个 是 我 妹 子 家，
妹子 那个 心 里 真 高 兴，
哪荷 衣荷 嗨 是我 妹子 家。
哎呀 亲哥 哥 妹子 真高 兴。

（瑞林俱乐部发掘，杨德恒记谱
刘光梯、光梯搜集）

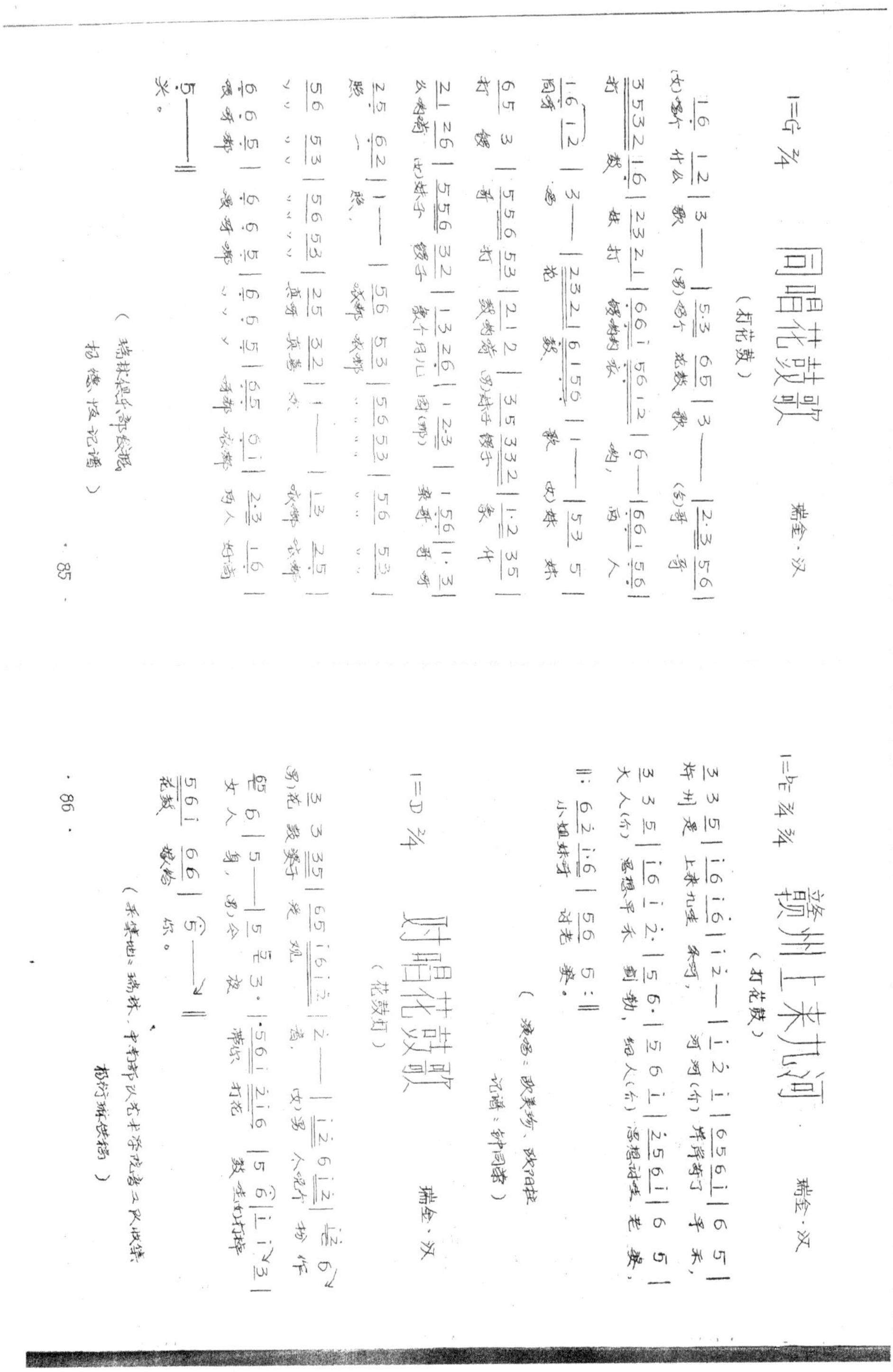

同唱花鼓歌

1=G 2/4　　　　瑞金·汉

（打花鼓）

1 6 1 2 | 3 — | 5·3 6 5 | 3 — | 2·3 5 6 |
(女)唱个 什么 歌 (男)唱个 花鼓 歌 (合)哥 哥

3 5 3 2 1 6 | 2 3 2 1 | 6 6 i 5 6 1 2 | 6 — | 6 6 1 5 6 |
打 鼓 妹 打 锣哟哟 衣 哟, 两 人

1 6 1 2 | 3 — | 2 3 2 1 6 1 5 5 | 1 — | 5 3 5 |
同呀 唱 花 鼓 歌 (女)妹 妹

6 5 3 | 5 5 6 5 3 | 2 1 2 | 3 5 3 3 2 | 1·2 3 5 |
打 锣 哥 打 鼓哟嗬 (男)妹子 锣子 象 什

2 1 2 6 | 5 5 6 3 2 | 1 3 2 6 | 1 2·3 | 1 5 6 | 1·3 |
么哟嗬 (女)妹子 锣子 象个月儿 圆(那) 亲哥 哥呀

2 5 6 2 | 1 — | 5 6 5 3 | 5 6 5 3 | 5 6 5 3 |
照 一 照, 依都 依都 〃〃〃〃 〃〃 〃〃

5 6 5 3 | 5 6 5 3 | 2 5 3 2 | 1 — | 1 3 2 5 |
〃〃 〃〃 〃〃〃〃 真呀 真喜 欢 依都 依都

6 6 5 | 6 6 5 | 6 6 5 | 6 5 6 i | 2·3 1 6 |
嗳呀 都 嗳呀 哪 〃〃〃 呀都 依都 两人 好高

5 — ||
兴。

（瑞林俱乐部发掘
杨德、恢记谱）

· 85 ·

赣州上来九河

1=♭E 2/4 3/4　　　　瑞金·汉

（打花鼓）

3 3 5 | i 6 i 6 | i 2 — | i 2 i | 6 5 6 i | 6 5 |
赣 州 是 上来九 条河， 河 河（介） 岸岸 有了 千 禾，

3 3 5 | i 6 i 2· | 5 6· | 5 6 i | 2 5 6 i | 6 5 |
大 人（介） 思想 平 禾 割 勒， 细 人（介） 思想讨 个 老 婆，

‖: 6 2 i·6 | 5 6 5 :‖
小 姐 妹呀 讨 老 婆。

（演唱：欧美珍、欧阳柱
记谱：钟同荣）

对唱花鼓歌

1=D 2/4　　　　瑞金·汉

（花鼓灯）

3 3 3 5 | 6 5 i 6 i 2 | 2 — | i 2 6 i 2 | 2 6 |
(男)花 鼓 婆子 老 观 音， (女)男 人呢个 扮 作

5 6 | 5 — | 5 5 3· | 5 6 i 2 i 6 | 5 6 | i i 3 |
女 人 身， (男)今 夜 带你 打花 鼓 唼 打样

5 6 i 6 6 | 5 — ||
花鼓 嫁给 你。

（采集地：瑞林，中南部队艺术学院音工队收集
杨衍琳供稿）

· 86 ·

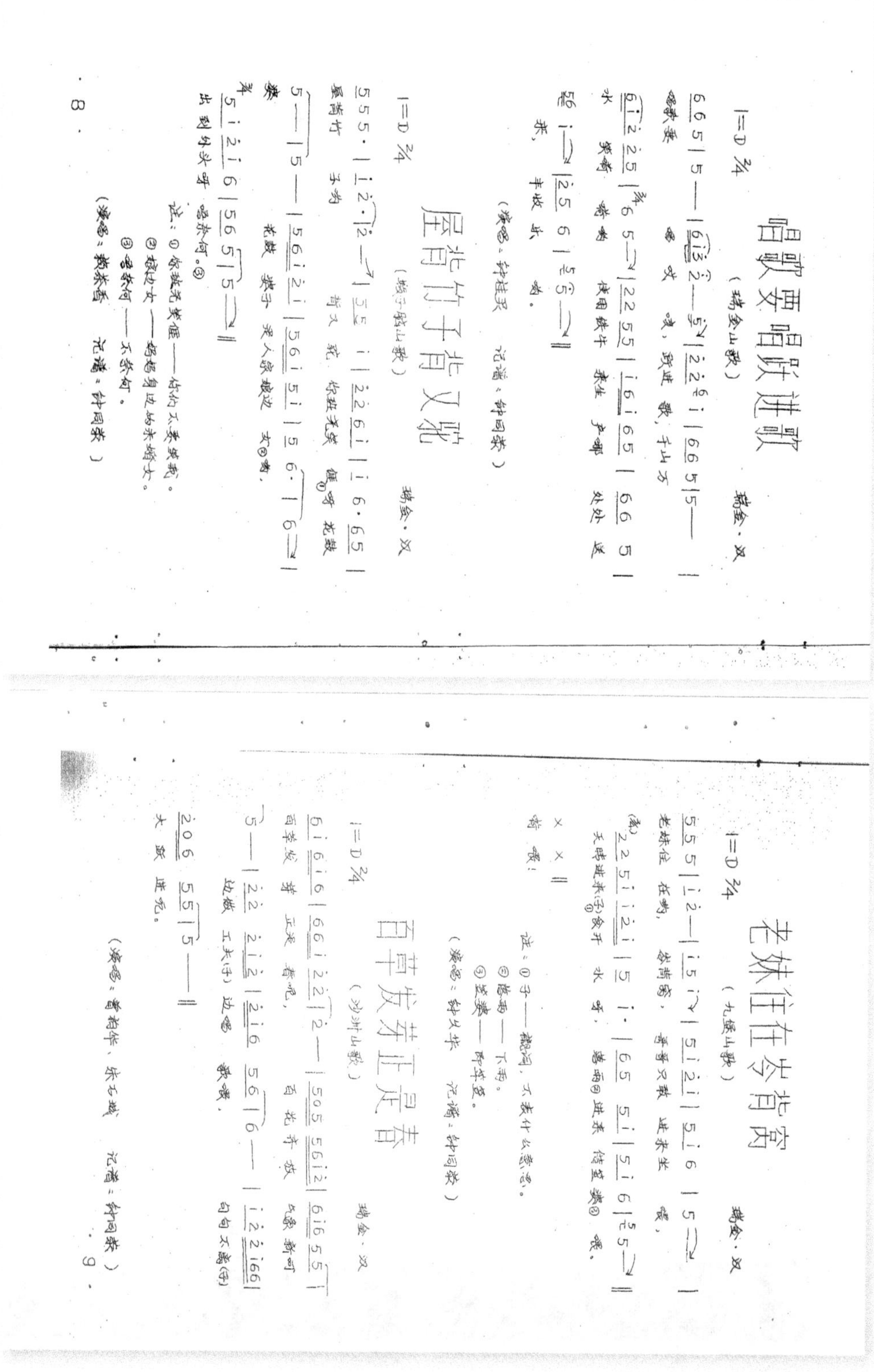

唱歌要唱跃进歌

1=D 2/4　（瑞金山歌）　瑞金·汉

6 6 5 | 5 — | 6 1 3 2 — 5 | 2 2 6 1 | 6 6 5 | 5 — |
唱歌要　　喝　哎　咳，跃进　歌，千山万

6 1 2 2 5 | 6 5 — | 2 2 5 5 | 1 6 1 6 5 | 6 6 5 |
水　笑嘀　嘀哟　使用铁牛　来生　产哪　处处　送

5 6 1 — | 2 5 6 | 5 — ‖
来，　丰收　乐　哟。

（演唱：钟桂灵　记谱：钟同荣）

屋背竹子背又驼

1=D 2/4　（蛤子脑山歌）　瑞金·汉

5 5 5 · | 1 2 · | 2 — | 5 5 1 | 2 2 6 1 | 1 6 · 6 5 |
屋背竹　子哟　　背又　驼，你班无笑　涯①呀　花鼓

5 — | 5 — | 5 6 1 2 1 | 5 6 1 5 1 | 5 6 · | 6 — |
娄　　花鼓　娄子　走人家娘边　女②哟，

5 1 2 1 6 | 5 6 5 | 5 — ‖
出到外头呀　喝奈何。③

注：① 你班无笑涯——你们不要笑我。
② 娘边女——妈妈身边的未婚女。
③ 喝奈何——不奈何。

（演唱：赖茶香　记谱：钟同荣）

· 8 ·

老妹住在岑背窝

1=D 2/4　（九堡山歌）　瑞金·汉

5 5 5 | 1 2 — | 1 5 1 | 5 1 2 1 | 5 1 6 | 5 — |
老妹住　在哟，　岑背窝，　哥哥只敢　进来坐　喂，

2 2 5 1 1 2 1 | 5 1 · | 6 5 5 1 | 5 1 6 | 5 — ‖
天晴进来（子）①食开　水　呀，　落雨②进来　借笠娄③　喂。

× × ‖
哨　喂！

注：① 子——衬词，不表什么意思。
② 落雨——下雨。
③ 笠娄——即笠笠。

（演唱：钟火华　记谱：钟同荣）

百草发芽正是春

1=D 2/4　（沙洲山歌）　瑞金·汉

6 1 6 1 6 | 6 6 1 2 2 | 2 — | 5 0 5 5 6 1 2 | 6 1 6 5 5 |
百草发　芽　正是　春呢，　　百　花齐放　气象新呵

5 — | 2 2 2 1 2 | 2 1 6 5 6 | 6 — | 1 2 2 1 6 6 |
　边做　工夫（子）边唱　歌喂，　　句句不离（子）

2 0 6 5 5 | 5 — ‖
大　跃　进呢。

（演唱：曾莉华、宋石城　记谱：钟同荣）

· 9 ·

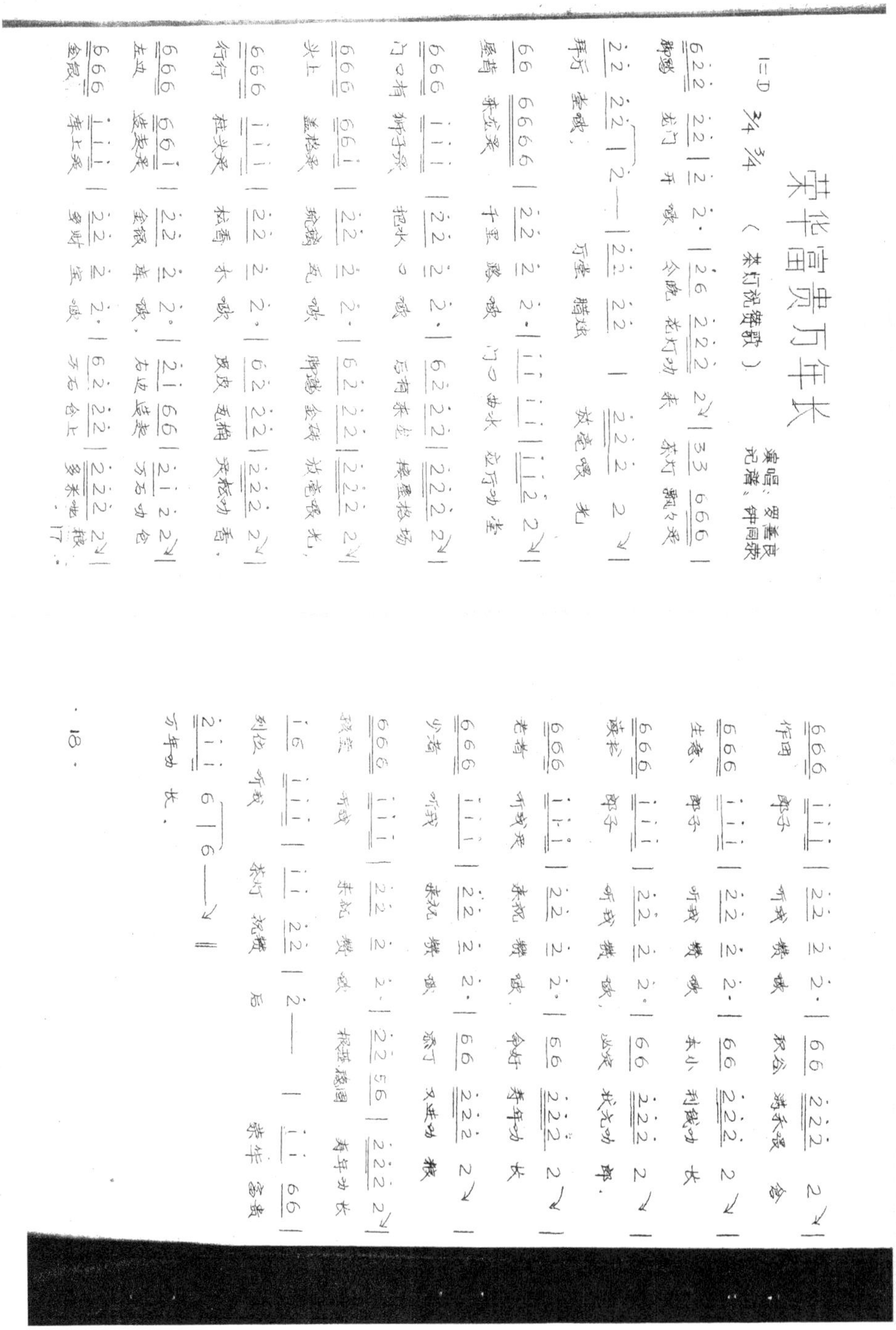

荣华富贵万年长

1=D 3/4 3/4 （茶灯祝赞歌）

演唱：罗善良
记谱：钟同荣

622 22 | 2 2· | 26 222 2↘ | 33 666 |
脚踏 龙门 开 哎 今晚 花灯 来 茶灯 飘飘来

22 22 | 2— | 22 22 | 222 2↘ |
拜厅 堂哎， 厅堂 腊烛 放毫喂 光

66 6666 | 22 2 2· | 11 11 | 112 2↘ |
屋背 来龙来 千里 路 哎 门口 曲水 过厅 堂

666 111 | 22 2 2· | 62 22 | 222 2↘ |
门口有 狮子来 把水 口 哎 后有 来龙 楼屋 格场

666 661 | 22 2 2· | 62 22 | 222 2↘ |
头上 盖格来 琉璃 瓦 哎 脚踏 金砖 放毫喂 光，

666 111 | 22 2 2· | 62 22 | 222 2↘ |
行行 柱头来 梳香 木 哎 皮皮 瓦桷 天松 香．

666 661 | 22 2 2· | 21 66 | 21 2 2↘ |
左边 造起来 金银 库 哎， 右边 造起 万石 仓

666 111 | 22 2 2· | 62 22 | 222 2↘ |
金银 库上来 多财 宝 哎 万石 仓上 多米 粮．

·17·

666 111 | 22 2 2· | 66 222 2↘ |
作田 郎子 听我 赞 哎 积谷 满禾喂 仓

666 111 | 22 2 2· | 66 222 2↘ |
生意、 郎子 听我 赞 哎 本小 利钱 长

666 111 | 22 2 2· | 66 222 2↘ |
读书 郎子 听我 赞 哎， 必定 状元 郎．

666 111 | 22 2 2· | 66 222 2↘ |
老者 听我来 来祝 赞 哎． 命好 寿年 长

666 111 | 22 2 2· | 66 222 2↘ |
少者 听我 来祝 赞 哎 添丁 又进 粮

666 111 | 22 2 2· | 22 56 | 222 2↘ |
孩童 听我 来祝 赞 哎 根基 稳固 寿年 长

16 111 | 11 22 | 2— | 11 66 |
列位 听我 茶灯 祝赞 后 荣华 富贵

211 6 | 6—↘ ‖
万年 长．

·18·

百花两朵笑微微

1=D 3/4　（瑞金茶灯、摘茶）　演唱：詹泽红　钟小青（沙洲）　记谱：钟同荣

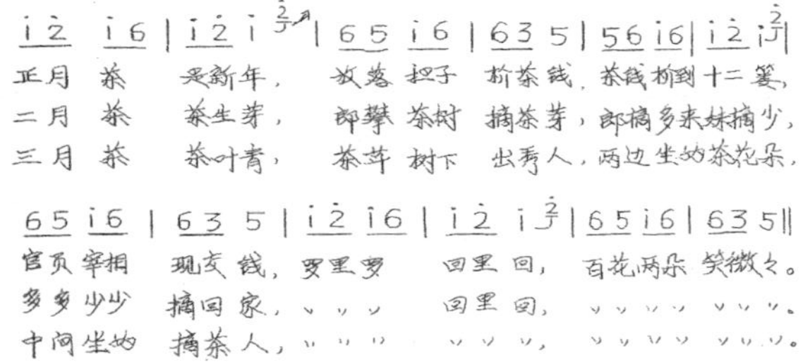

正月　茶　　是新年，　奴恋　郎子　折茶钱，茶钱折到十二宴，
二月　茶　　茶生芽，　郎攀　茶树　摘茶芽，郎摘多来妹摘少，
三月　茶　　茶叶青，　茶芽　树下　出秀人，两边坐的茶花朵，

官员宰相　现支钱，罗里罗　回里回，　百花两朵　笑微微。
多多少少　摘回家，〃〃〃　　回里回，　〃〃〃〃　〃〃〃。
中间坐的　摘茶人，〃〃〃　　〃〃〃，　〃〃〃〃　〃〃〃。

四月茶，茶叶长，犹误田冬采牛郎，前得田来茶又老，摘得茶来秧又长，罗里罗，回里回，百花两朵笑微微。

五月茶，是端阳，茶芽树下透风凉，左手挽紧老茶树，右手挽紧少年郎，罗里罗……（同上）

六月茶，暖洋洋，多插杨柳少栽桑，女人争得无用处，男人大里走四方，罗里罗……（同上）

七月茶，秋风起，搭唔妹妹织寒衣，寒衣多织三几匹，当开两匹等郎归，罗里罗……（同上）

八月茶，桂花香，风吹桂花满街香，郎子出门莫贪花，正花野花一样香，罗里罗……（同上）

九月茶，是重阳，重阳美酒一支香，老妹酒酒情哥食，一杯一盏情意长，罗里罗……（同上）

十月茶正立冬，十担茶篓九担空，茶篓放在高楼顶，明年

· 29 ·

正月再相逢，罗里罗……　（同上）

十一月茶雪子飞，雪子飞飞飘郎归，妹在家中等情郎，郎在路上想妹妹。罗里罗……　（同上）

十二月茶又一年，上村下垦讨茶钱，茶钱讨到回家转，买鱼抵肉好过年。罗里罗……　（同上）

注：罗里罗，回里回，百花两朵笑微微——均是衬词，不表什么意思。

买鱼抵肉——买鱼买肉。

脚踏紫阶大吉昌

1=D 2/4 3/4　（茶灯、祝赞）　演唱：詹先生（七堡）　记谱：钟同荣

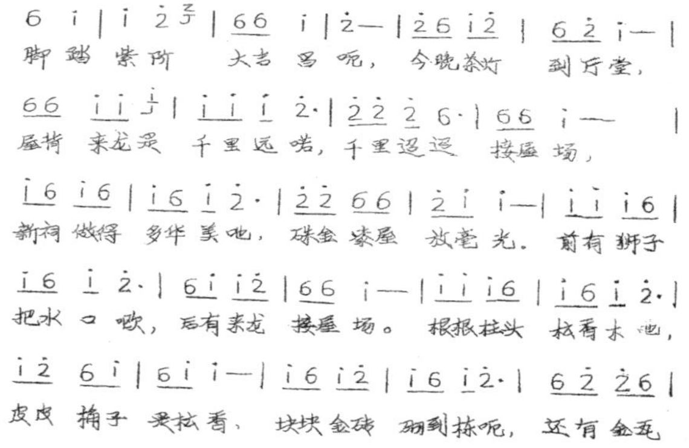

脚踏紫阶　大吉昌呢，今晚茶灯　到厅堂，
屋背　来龙　千里远呢，千里迢迢　接屋场，
新祠做得　多华美吔，珠金紫屋　放毫光。前有狮子
把水口吹，后有来龙　接屋场。根根柱头　枝香木吔，
皮皮　桷子　是栋香，块块金砖　砌到抹呢，还有金瓦

· 30 ·

盖，金对，传满，长生，听，郭，万。

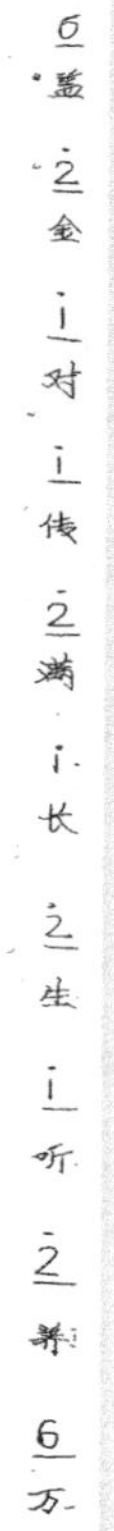

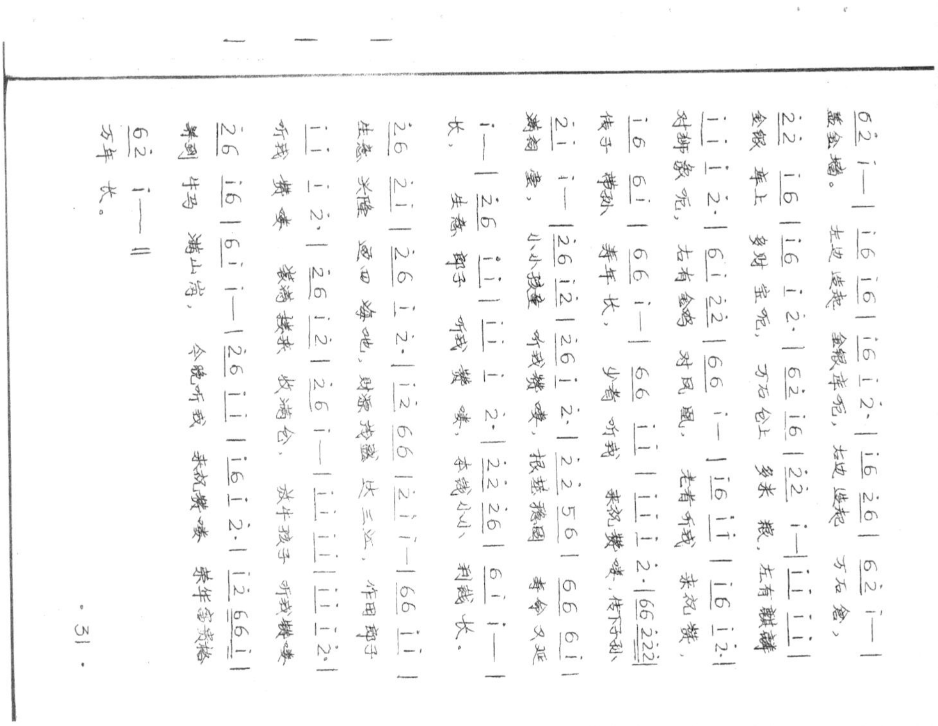

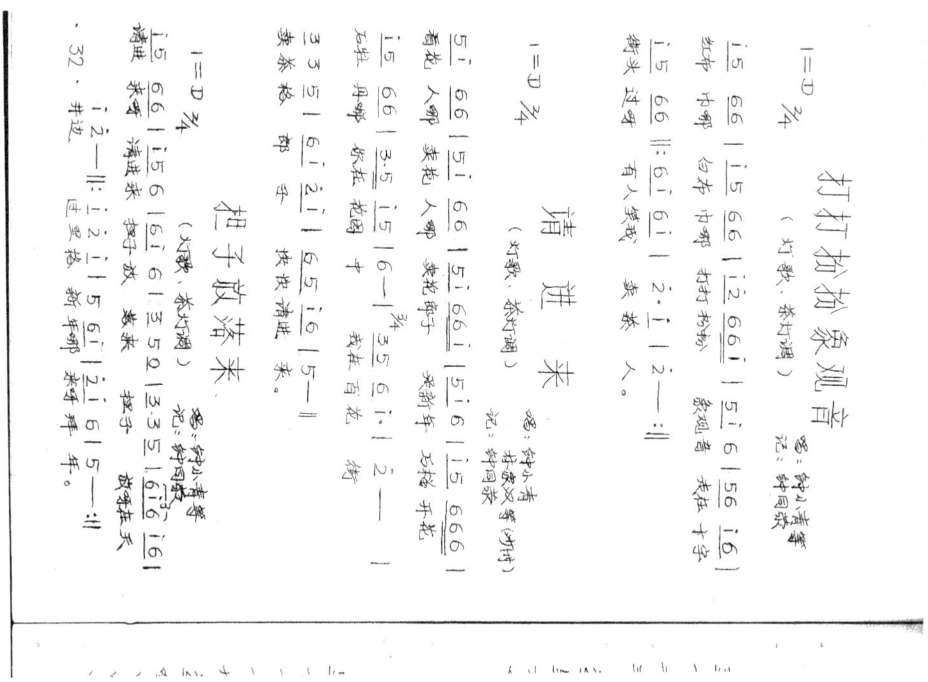

62̇ 1̇— | 1̇6 1̇6 | 1̇6 1̇ 2̇· | 1̇6 2̇6 | 62̇ 1̇— |
盖金墙。 左边造起 金银库呃，右边造起 万石仓，

2̇2̇ 1̇6 | 1̇6 1̇ 2̇· | 62̇ 1̇6 | 2̇2̇ 1̇— | 1̇1̇ 1̇1̇ |
金银 库上 多财 宝呃，万石仓上 多米 粮，左有麒麟

1̇1̇ 1̇ 2̇· | 61̇ 2̇2̇ | 66 1̇— | 1̇6 1̇1̇ | 1̇6 1̇2̇· |
对狮象呃，右有金鸡 对凤凰， 老者听我 来祝赞，

1̇6 61̇ | 66 1̇— | 66 1̇1̇ | 1̇1̇ 1̇ 2̇· | 66 2̇2̇2̇ |
传子 带孙 寿年长， 少者 听我 来祝赞喽，传下子孙

2̇1̇ 1̇— | 2̇6 1̇2̇ | 2̇6 1̇ 2̇· | 2̇2̇ 56 | 66 61̇ |
满祠 堂， 小小孩童 听我赞喽，根基稳固 寿命久延

1̇— | 2̇6 1̇1̇ | 1̇1̇ 1̇ 2̇· | 2̇2̇ 2̇6 | 61̇ 1̇— |
长， 生意 郎子 听我 赞 喽，本钱小小 利钱 长。

2̇6 2̇1̇ | 2̇6 1̇ 2̇· | 1̇2̇ 66 | 2̇1̇ 1̇— | 66 1̇1̇ |
生意 兴隆 通四 海吔，财源茂盛 达三江， 作田郎子

1̇1̇ 1̇ 2̇· | 2̇6 1̇2̇ | 2̇6 1̇— | 1̇1̇ 1̇1̇ | 1̇1̇ 1̇2̇· |
听我 赞 喽， 装满拨来 收满仓， 放牛孩子 听我赞喽

2̇6 1̇6 | 61̇ 1̇— | 2̇6 1̇1̇ | 1̇6 1̇ 2̇· | 1̇2̇ 661̇ |
养到 牛马 满山岗， 今晚听我 来祝赞喽 荣华富贵格

62̇ 1̇— ‖
万年 长。

·31·

打打扮扮象观音

1=D 2/4 （灯歌、茶灯调） 唱：钟小青等 记：钟同荣

1̇5 66 | 1̇5 66 | 1̇2̇ 661̇ | 51̇ 6 | 56 1̇6 |
红布 巾哪 白布 巾哪 打打扮扮 象观音 去在 十字

1̇5 66 ‖: 61̇ 61̇ | 2̇· 1̇ | 2̇— :‖
街头 过呀 有人笑我 卖茶 人。

请进来

1=D 2/4 （灯歌、茶灯调） 唱：钟小青 林家汉等（叶坪） 记：钟同荣

51̇ 66 | 51̇ 66 | 51̇ 661̇ | 51̇ 6 | 1̇5 666 |
看花 人哪 卖花 人哪 卖花郎子 采新年 石榴 开花

1̇5 66 | 3·5 1̇5 | 6— | 3/4 35 6 1̇· | 2̇— |
石牡 丹哪 你在 花园 中 我在 百花 街

33 5 | 61̇ 2̇1̇ | 65 1̇6 | 5— ‖
卖茶格 郎 子 快快请进 来。

担子放落来

1=D 2/4 （灯歌、茶灯调） 唱：钟小青等 记：钟同荣

1̇5 66 | 1̇5 6 | 61̇ 6 | 35 0 | 3·3 5 | 61̇6 1̇6 |
请进 来呀 请进来 担子放 落来 担子 放呀在天

1̇ 2̇— ‖: 1̇ 2̇ 1̇ | 5 61̇ | 2̇1̇ 6 | 5— :‖
井边 过 里 格 新 年哪 来呀 拜 年。

·32·

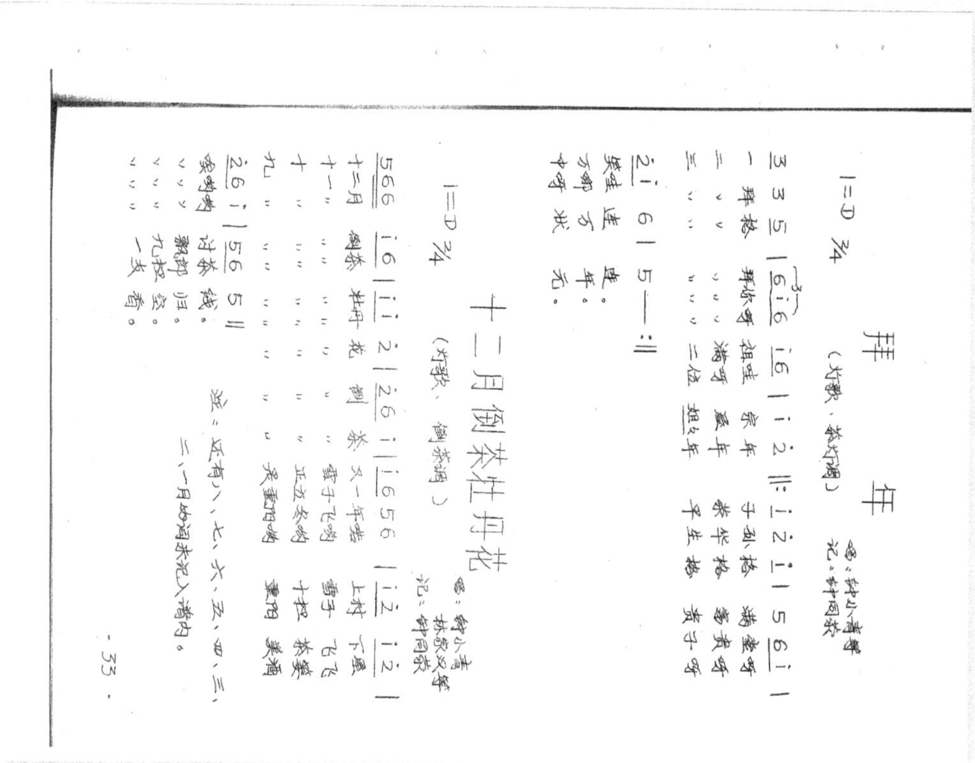

拜　年

1=D 2/4　（灯歌、茶灯调）　唱：钟小青等　记：钟同荣

3 3 5 | 6i6 i6 | i 2 ||: i 2 i | 5 6i |
一 拜 格　拜你呀 祖哇 宗 年　子孙 格　满堂呀
二 〃 〃　〃〃〃 满呀 岁 年　荣华 格　富贵呀
三 〃 〃　〃〃〃 二位 姐姐 年　平生 格　贵子呀

2i 6 | 5 — :||
笑哇 连 连。
万哪 万 年。
中呀 状 元。

十二月倒茶牡丹花

1=D 2/4　（灯歌、倒茶调）　唱：钟小青　林家汉等　记：钟同荣

566 i6 | ii 2 | 26 i | i656 | i2 i2 |
十二月 倒茶 牡丹 花 倒 茶 又一年哟 上村 下屋
十一 〃 〃〃 〃〃 〃 〃 〃 雪子飞哟 雪子 飞飞
十 〃 〃〃 〃〃 〃 〃 〃 正五冬哟 十担 茶篓
九 〃 〃〃 〃〃 〃 〃 〃 是重阳哟 重阳 美酒

26 i | 56 5 ||
实哟哟 讨茶 钱。
〃〃〃 飘郎 归。
〃〃〃 九担 空。
〃〃〃 一支 香。

注：还有八、七、六、五、四、三、二、一月的词未记入谱内。

- 33 -

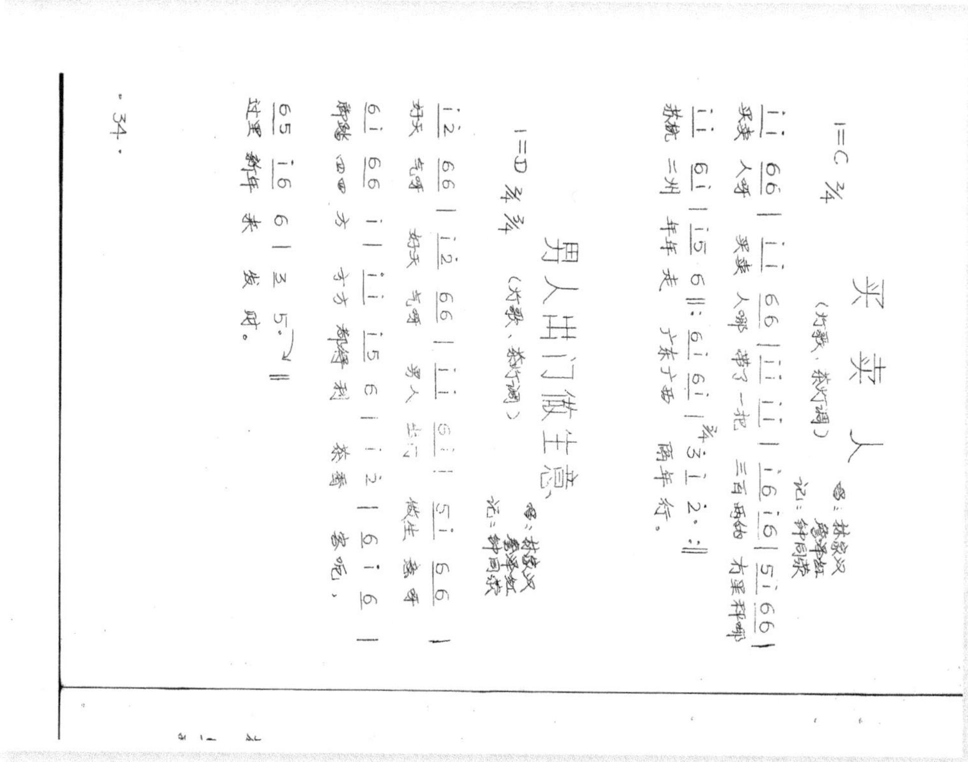

买　卖　人

1=C 2/4　（灯歌、茶灯调）　唱：林家汉　詹泽红　记：钟同荣

ii 66 | ii 66 | ii ii | i6 i6 | 5i 66 |
买卖 人呀　买卖 人哪　带了 一把　三百 两的　有星 秤哪

ii 6i | i5 6 ||: 6i 6i | 3/4 3 i 2· :||
苏杭 二州　年年 走　广东 广西　隔 年 行。

男人出门做生意

1=D 2/4 3/4　（灯歌、茶灯调）　唱：林家汉　詹泽红　记：钟同荣

i2 66 | i2 66 | ii 6i | 5i 66 |
好天 气呀　好天 气呀　男人 出门　做生 意呀

6i 66 i | ii i5 6 | i 2 | 6 i 6 |
脚踏 四四 方　方方 都得 利　茶 香　客 呢，

65 i6 6 | 3 5· ||
过里 新年 来　发 财。

- 34 -

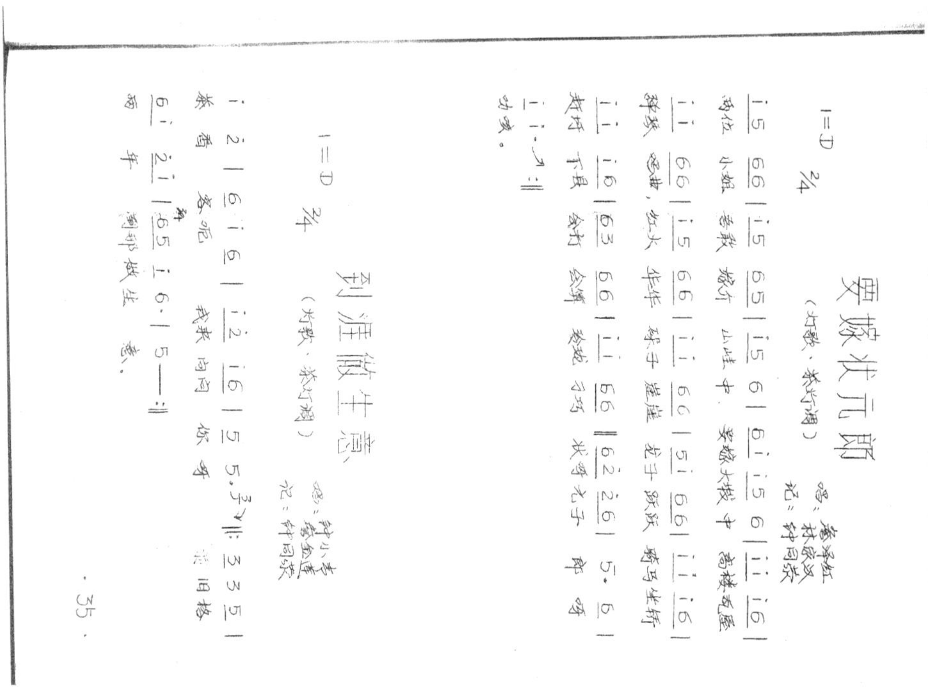

要嫁状元郎

1=D 2/4　（灯歌、茶灯调）　唱：詹泽红 林家汉　记：钟同荣

i5 66 | i5 65 | i5 6 | 6i i5 6 | ii i6 |
两位 小姐 吾载 嫁介 山岐 中。 要嫁大坝 中 高楼瓦屋

ii 66 | i5 66 | ii 66 | 5i 66 | ii i6 |
弹琴 唱曲，红火 华华 球子 崖崖 龙子 跃跃 骑马坐轿

ii i6 | 63 66 | ii 66 ‖ 62 26 | 5· 6 |
赴圩 下县 会打 会算 玲珑 子巧 状呀元子 郎 呀

i i· ↗ :‖
叻咳。

· 35 ·

到涯做生意

1=D 2/4　（灯歌、茶灯调）　唱：钟小专 詹金莲　记：钟同荣

i 2 | 6 i 6 | i2 i6 | 5 5.3 ↘‖: 3 3 5 |
茶 香 客呢 我来 问问 你 呀 前 旧 格

6i 2i | 65 i 6· | 5 — :‖
两 年 闽那 做 生 意、

一十四省飘交里

1=D 2/4　（灯歌、茶灯调）　唱：詹泽红 林家汉　记：钟同荣

i2 | 6 i 6 | i2 i6 | 5 5· | 3 3 5 | 6i 2i |
茶小 姐吔， 我来 说你 听 呀 前 旧格 两 年

65 i 6· | 5 — | 3 3 5 | 6i 2i | 65 i 6· | 5 — ‖
出外 做 生 意、 一 十 四 省 老子飘交 里。

走在瑞金转呀叻

1=D 2/4 3/4　（灯歌、茶灯调）　唱：钟小青 詹金莲（女州）　记：钟同荣

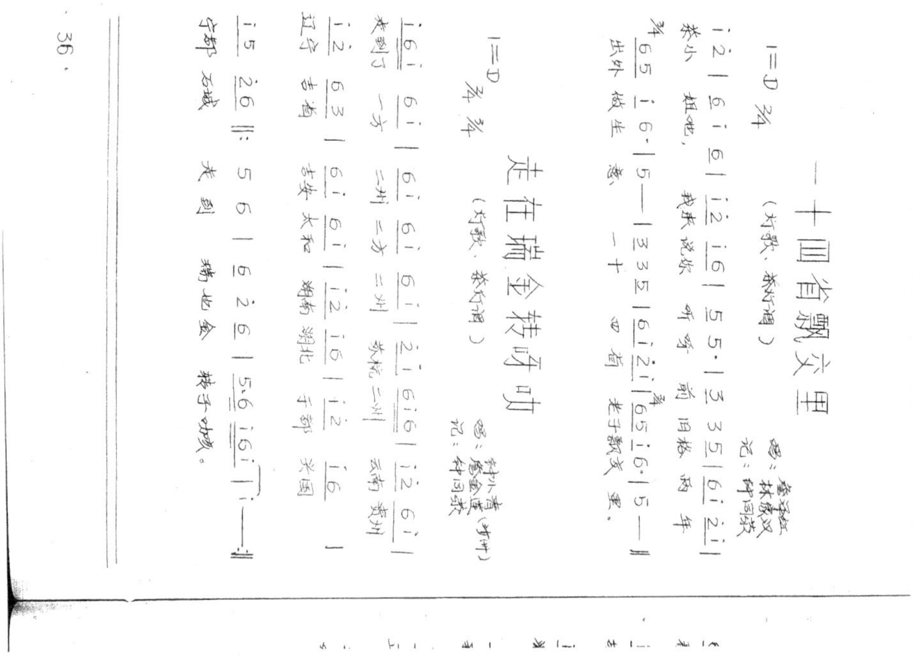

i6i 6i | 6i 6i 6i | 2i 6i6 | i2 6i |
走到了 一方 二州 二方 二州 苏杭 二州 云南 贵州

i2 63 | 6i 6i | i2 i6 | i2 i6 |
辽宁 吉省 吉安 太和 湖南 湖北 于都 兴国

i5 26 ‖: 5 6 | 6 2 6 | 5·6 i6i | i — :‖
宁都 石城 走 到 瑞也金 转子叻咳。

· 36 ·

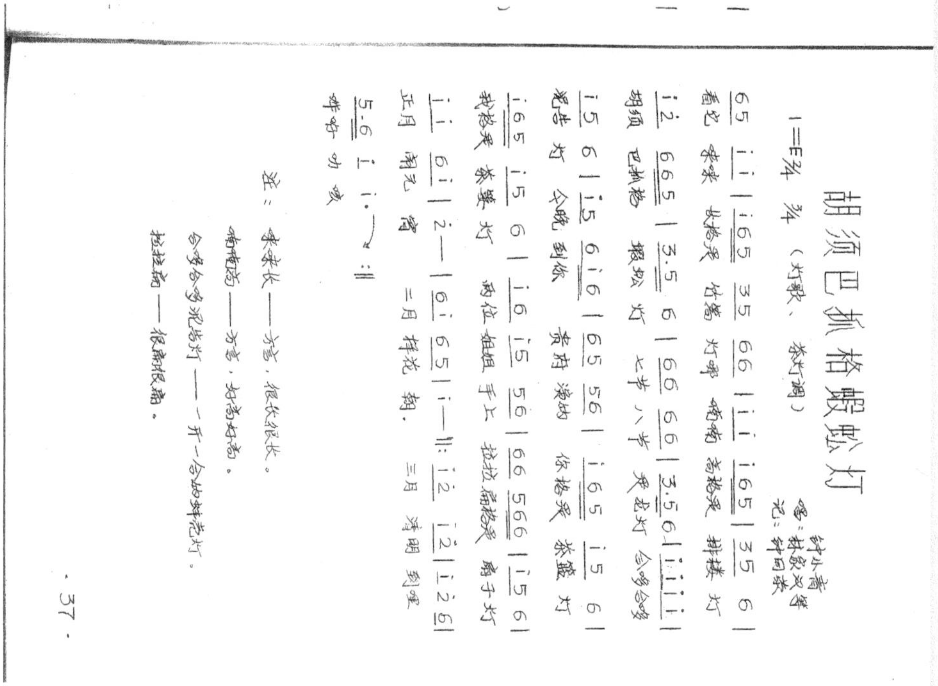

胡须巴抓格蝦蚣灯

1=E 2/4 3/4（灯歌、茶灯调）

唱：钟小青 林家双等
记：钟同荣

65 i i | i65 35 66 | i i i65 | 35 6 |
看它 来来 长格是 竹篙 灯啰 喃喃 高格是 排楼 灯

i 2 665 | 3.5 6 | 66 66 | 3.5 6 | i i i i |
胡须 巴抓格 蝦蚣 灯 七节 八节 舞龙灯 合哆合哆

i5 6 | i5 6i6 | 65 56 | i65 i5 6 |
泥告 灯 今晚 到你 贵府 演奶 你格是 茶篮 灯

i65 i5 6 | i6 i5 56 | 66 566 | i5 6 |
我格是 茶篓 灯 两位 姐姐 手上 拉拉 扇格是 扇子 灯

i i 6i | 2 — | 6i 65 | i — ‖: i2 i2 | i 2 6 |
正月 闹元 宵 二月 拜花 朝。 三月 清明 到哩

5.6 i i· :‖
咿哟 叻 咳

注：来来长——方言，很长很长。
喃喃高——方言，好高好高。
合哆合哆泥告灯——一开一合的蚌壳灯。
拉拉扁——很扁很扁。

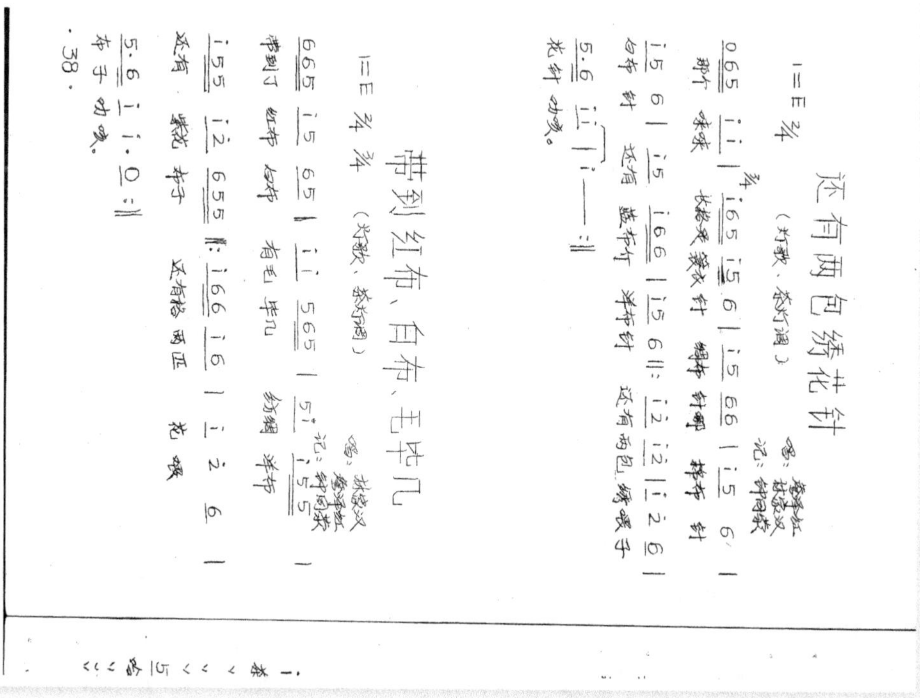

还有两包绣花针

1=E 2/4

（灯歌、茶灯调）

唱：詹泽红 林家双
记：钟同荣

065 i i | 3/4 i65 i5 6 | i5 66 | i5 6 |
那个 来来 长格是 簑衣 针 绸布 针啰 棉布 针

i5 6 | i5 i66 | i5 6 ‖: i2 i2 | i 2 6 |
白布 针 还有 蓝布个 洋布 针 还有 两包 绣哦 子

5.6 i i | i — :‖
花 针 叻 咳。

带到红布、白布、毛毕几

1=E 2/4 3/4 （灯歌、茶灯调）

唱：林家双 詹泽红
记：钟同荣

665 i5 65 | i i 565 | 5i i55 |
带到了 红布 白布 有毛 毕几 纺绸 洋布

i55 i2 655 ‖: i66 i6 | i 2 6 |
还有 紫花 布子 还有格 两匹 花 哦

5.6 i i· 0 :‖
布 子 叻 咳。

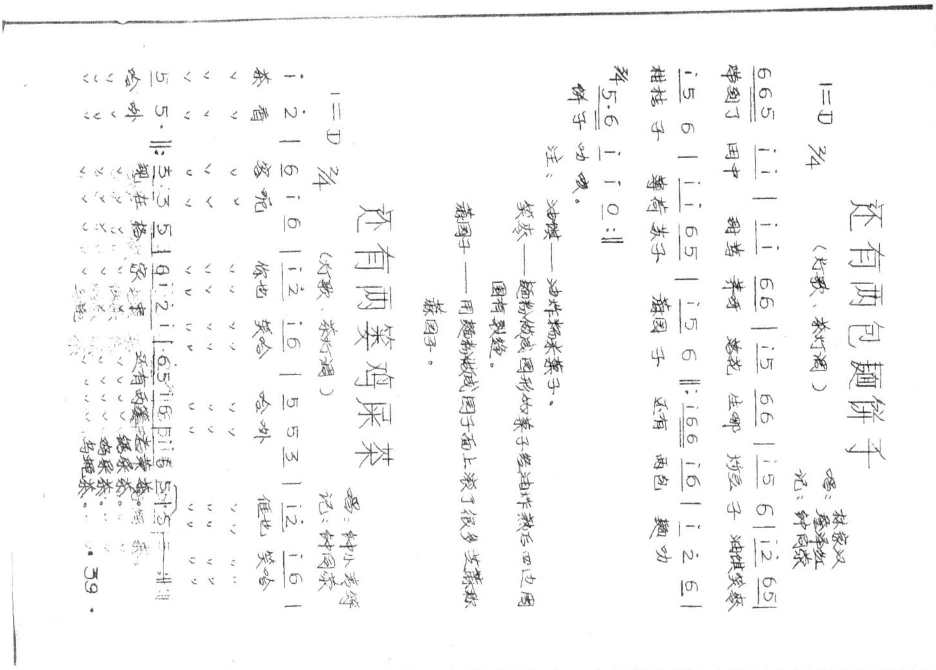

还有两包麺饼子

1=D 2/4 （灯歌、茶灯调）

唱：林家双 詹泽红
记：钟同荣

带到了 田中 甜笋 荞呀 落花 生哪 炒豆 子 油供笑枣
柑桔 子 薄荷 苏子 蒜团 子 还有 两包 麺叻
饼子 叻 咳。

注：油供——油炸粉米菓子。
笑枣——麺粉做成圆形的菓子经油炸熟后四边周围有裂缝。
蒜团子——用麺粉做成团子面上滚了很多芝蒜称蒜团子。

还有两篓鸡尿茶

1=D 2/4 （灯歌、茶灯调）

唱：钟小秀呀
记：钟同荣

茶 香 客 呢 你也 笑哈 哈 咻 佢也 笑哈
哈 咻 现在 格 家 里 还有两篓 老黄茶。
鸡尿茶。
乌蜷茶。

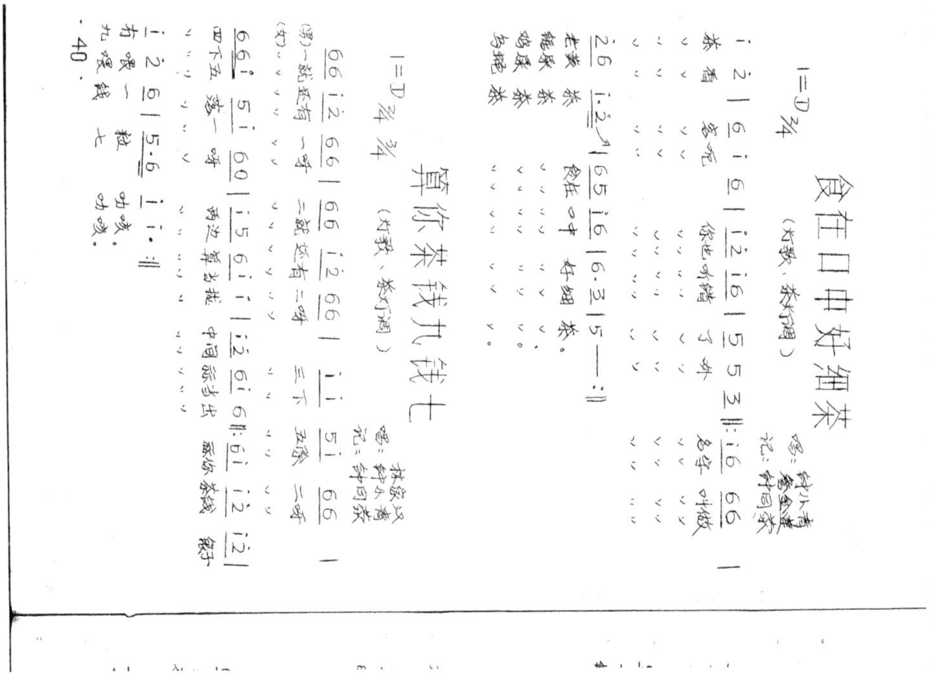

食在口中好细茶

1=D 2/4 （灯歌、茶灯调）

唱：钟小青 詹金莲
记：钟同荣

茶 香 客呢 你也听错 了 咻 名字 叫做
老黄 茶 食在 口中 好细 茶。
鸡尿 茶
鸡尿 茶
乌蜷 茶

算你茶钱九钱七

1=D 2/4 3/4 （灯歌、茶灯调）

唱：林家双 钟小青
记：钟同荣

（男）一就 还有 一呀 二就 还有 二呀 三 下 五除 二呀
（女）
四下五 落一 呀 两边 算当拢 中间 硕当出 硕你 茶钱 银子
有 喂 一 粒 叻 咳。
九 喂 钱 七 叻 咳。

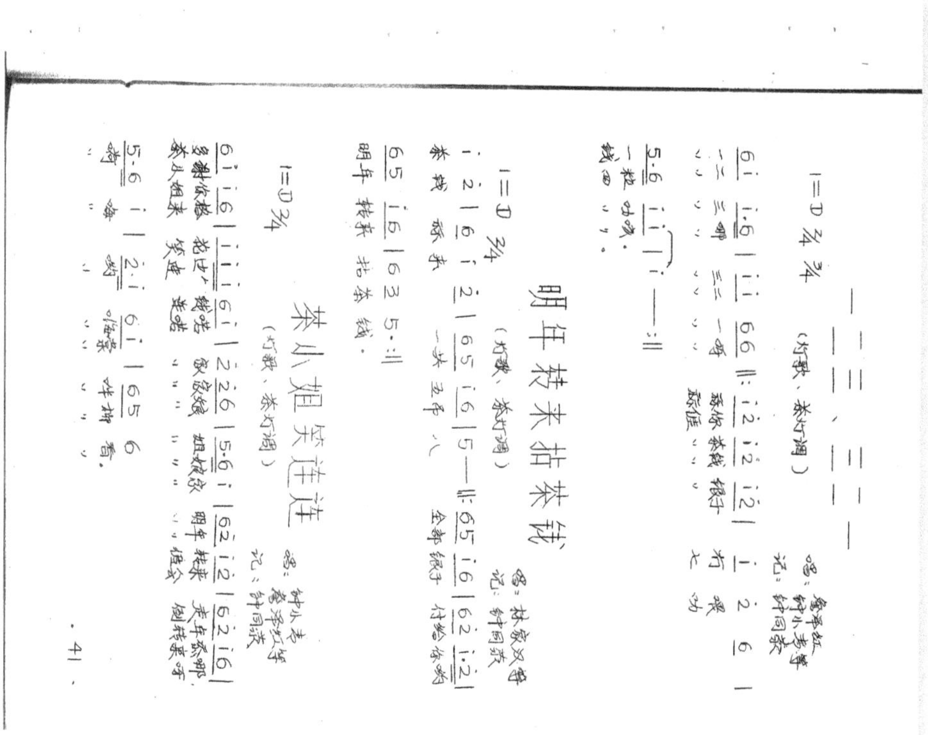

一二三、三二一

1=D 2/4 3/4　（灯歌、茶灯调）

唱：詹泽红　钟小考等
记：钟同荥

6i i.6 | ii 66 ‖: i2 i2 i2 | i 2 6 |
一二 三哪 三二 一呀 疥你 茶钱 银子 冇 喂
疥佢 七 呦

5.6 ii | i — :‖
一粒 呦哦。
钱四

明年转来拈茶钱

1=D 3/4　（灯歌、茶灯调）

唱：林家双等
记：钟同荥

i 2 | 6 i 2 | 65 i6 | 5 — ‖: 65 i6 | 62 i.2 |
茶钱 疥来 一块 五角 八 全部 银子 付给 你哟

65 i6 | 63 5 :‖
明年 转来 拈茶 钱。

茶小姐笑连连

1=D 3/4　（灯歌、茶灯调）

唱：钟小考　詹泽红等
记：钟同荥

6i i6 | iii 6i | 2 26 | 5.6 i | 62 i2 | 62 i6 |
多谢你格 花也 钱喏 叙家娘 姐娘家 明年 转来 走年 祭哪，
茶小姐来 笑连 连喏 倡会 倒转 来呀

5.6 i | 2.i 6i | 65 6
嘀 嗨 哟 嗨嗦 咩柳 香。

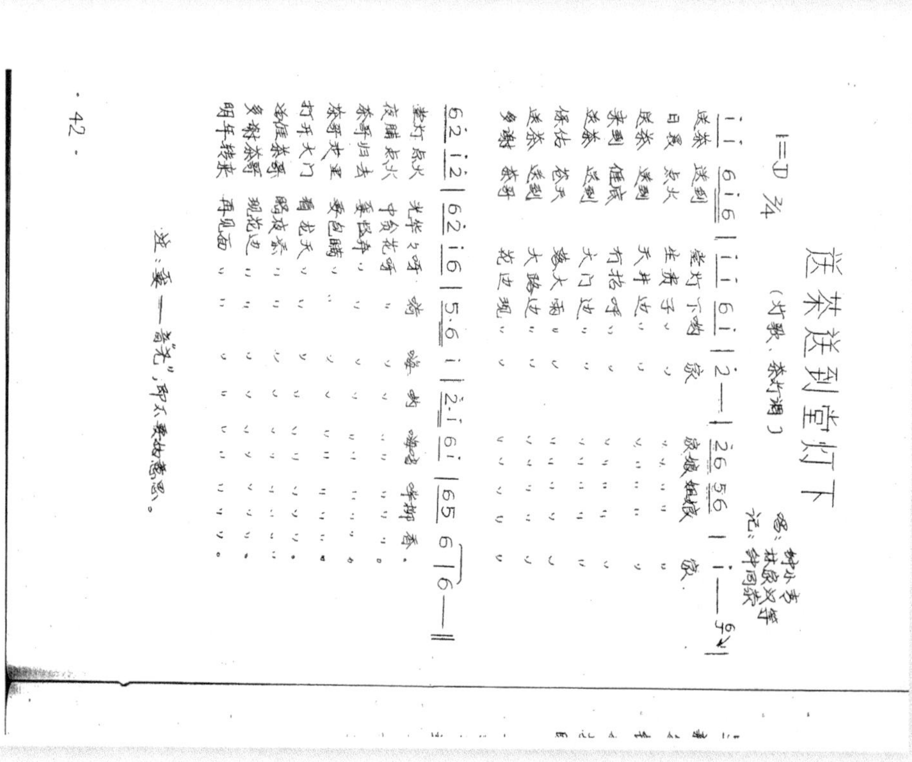

送茶送到堂灯下

1=D 2/4　（灯歌、茶灯调）

唱：钟小考　林家双等
记：钟同荥

ii 6i6 | ii 6i | 2 — | 26 56 | i — 5 |
送茶 送到 堂灯 下哟 家 家娘 姐娘 家。
日晨 点火 生贵 子
送茶 送到 天井 边
来到 佢底 冇招 呼
送茶 送到 大门 边
保佑 苍天 落大 雨
送茶 送到 大路 边
多谢 茶哥 花边 现

62 i2 | 62 i6 | 5.6 i | 2.i 6i | 65 6 | 6 — ‖
堂灯 点火 光华 々呀 嘀 嗨 哟 嗨嗦 咩柳 香。
夜晡 点火 中贵 花呀
茶哥 归去 要恼 弃
茶哥 先走 要包 睛
打开 大门 看龙 天
泌佢 茶哥 晒夜 茶
多谢 茶哥 现花 边
明年 转来 再见 面

注：要——音"无"，即不要的意思。

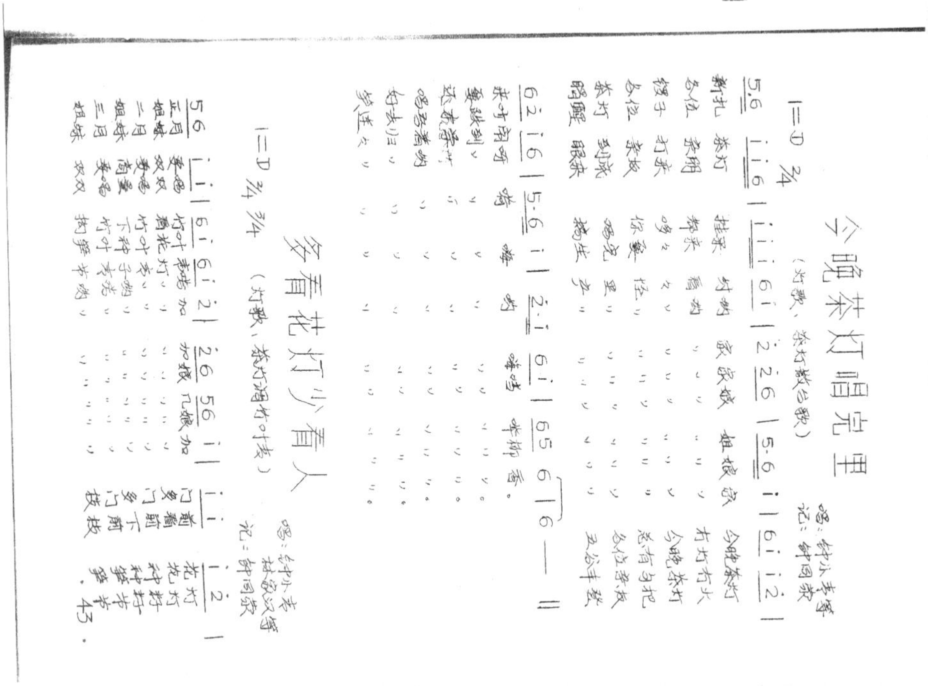

今晚茶灯唱完里

（灯歌、茶灯散台歌）

唱：钟小专等
记：钟同荣

1=D 2/4

5.6 i i 6 | i i i 6 i | 2 2 6 | 5·6 i | 6 i i 2 |

新扎 茶灯 挂采 灯哟 家家娘 姐娘家 今晚茶灯
各位 亲朋 都来 看哟 〃〃〃 〃〃〃 有灯有火
锣子 打来 哆々 々〃 〃〃〃 〃〃〃 今晚茶灯
各位 亲友 你莫 怪〃 〃〃〃 〃〃〃 总有句把
茶灯 到底 唱完 里〃 〃〃〃 〃〃〃 各位亲友
明年 眼来 搞生 产〃 〃〃〃 〃〃〃 五谷丰登

6 2 i 6 | 5·6 i | 2·i 6 i | 6 5 6 | 6 — ‖

来吋闹呀 嗬 嗨 哟 嗨哟 哗柳 香。
要跌到〃 〃 〃 〃 〃〃 〃〃〃。
还东荣吋 〃 〃 〃 〃〃 〃〃〃。
唱吾着哟 〃 〃 〃 〃〃 〃〃〃。
好去归〃 〃 〃 〃 〃〃 〃〃〃。
笑迷々〃 〃 〃 〃 〃〃 〃〃〃。

多看花灯少看人

1=D 2/4 3/4（灯歌、茶灯调竹叶青）

唱：钟小专
林家汉等
记：钟同荣

5 6 i i | 6 i 6 i 2 | 2 6 5 6 i | i i i 2 |

正月 要唱 竹叶 青哟 加 加娘 几娘 加 门前 花灯
姐妹 双双 看花 灯〃 〃 〃〃 〃〃 〃 多看 花灯
二月 要唱 竹叶 青〃 〃 〃〃 〃〃 〃 门前 种籽
姐妹 商量 下种 子哟 〃 〃〃 〃〃 〃 多下 种籽
三月 要唱 竹叶 青青 〃 〃〃 〃〃 〃 门前 笋节
姐妹 双双 掏笋 节哟 〃 〃〃 〃〃 〃 枝枝 笋节

·43·

6 2 i 6 | 5 i 2 | 6 i 6 5 6 ‖

吋纷 纷哪 嗬咳哟 满荣 花又 香。
少看 人〃 〃〃〃 〃〃〃〃 〃。
乱纷 纷〃 〃〃〃 〃〃〃〃 〃。
少求 人〃 〃〃〃 〃〃〃〃 〃。
乱纷 纷〃 〃〃〃 〃〃〃〃 〃。
拉缕 裙〃 〃〃〃 〃〃〃〃 〃。

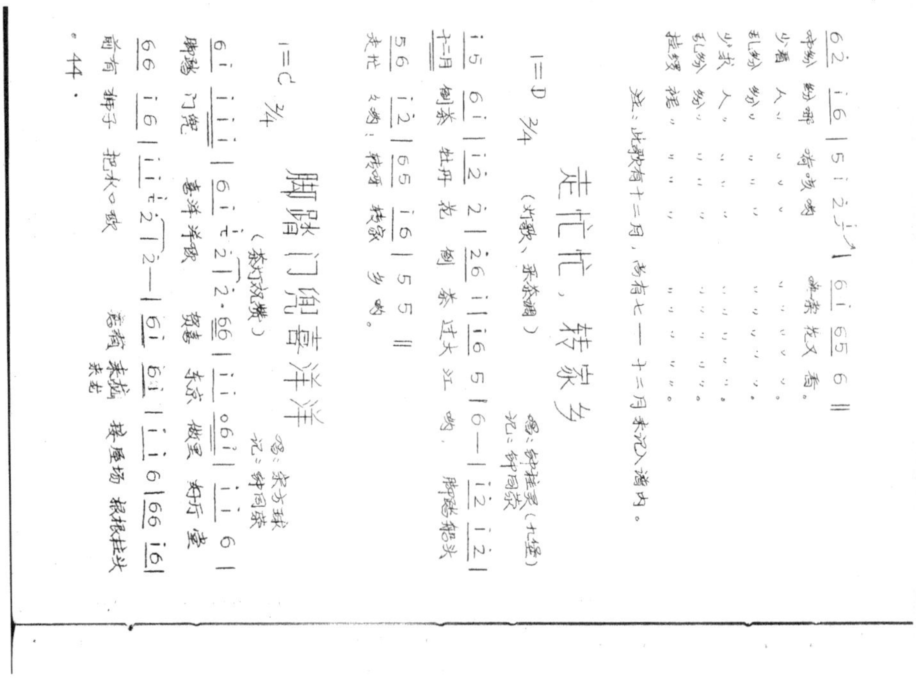

注：此歌有十二月，尚有七——十二月未记入谱内。

走忙忙，转家乡

1=D 2/4（灯歌、采茶调）

唱：钟桂灵（九堡）
记：钟同荣

i 5 6 i | i 2 2 | 2 6 i | i 6 5 | 6 — | i 2 i 2 |

十二月 倒茶 牡丹 花 倒 茶 过大 江 哟，脚踏船头

5 6 i 2 | 6 5 i 6 | 5 5 ‖

走忙 々哟！转呀 转家 乡 哟。

脚踏门兜喜洋洋

1=C 2/4

（茶灯祝赞）

唱：宋方球
记：钟同荣

6 i i i i | 6 i 2 | 2·66 | i i 06i | i i 6 |

脚踏 门兜 喜洋 洋欧 贺喜 东京 做里 好厅 堂

6 6 i 6 | i i 2 | 2 — | 6 i 6 i | i i 6 | 66 i6 |

前有 狮子 把水口欧 后有 来龙 接屋场 根根柱头

·44·

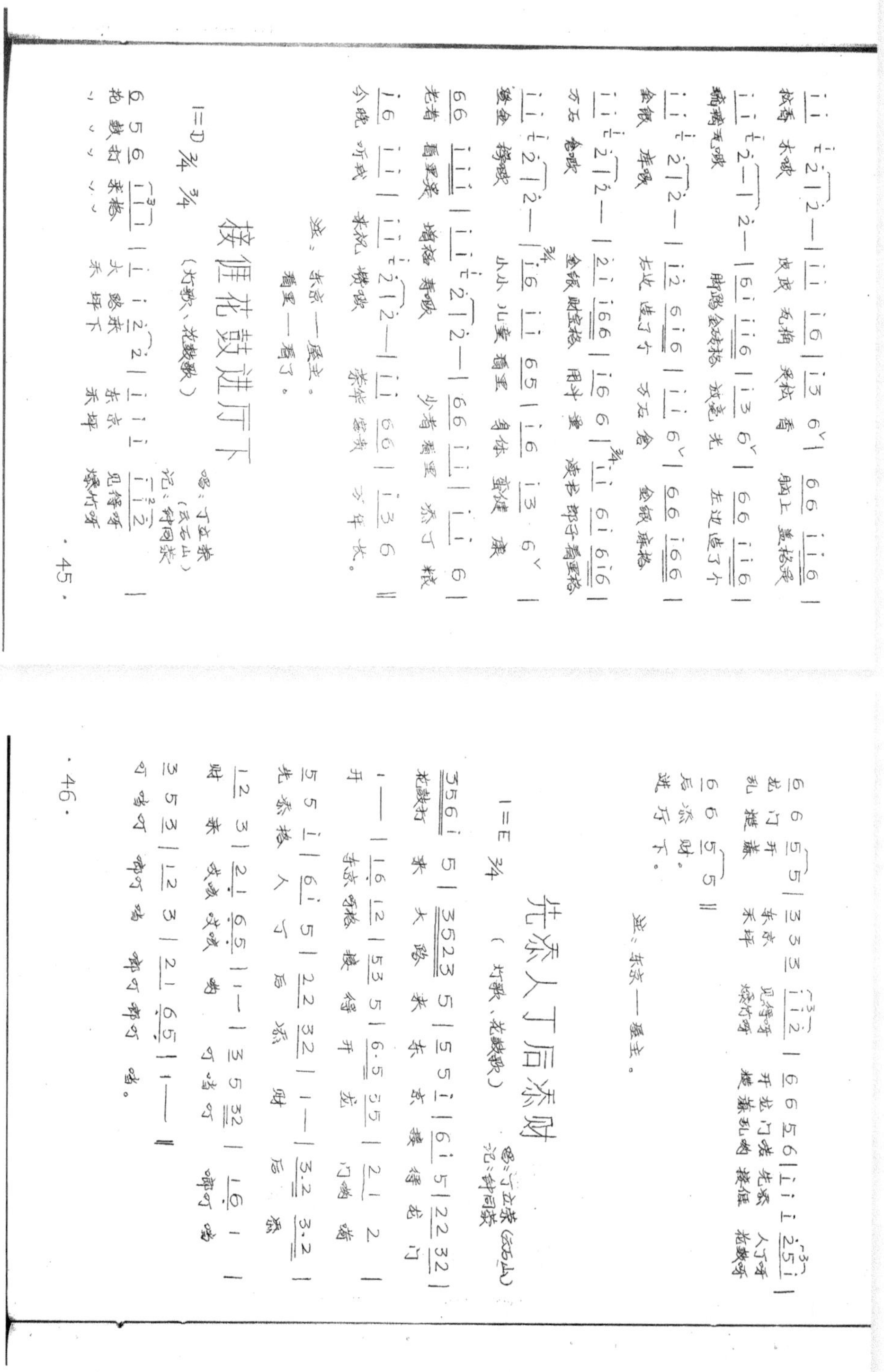

1̇1̇ 2̇ | 2̇ — | 1̇1̇ 1̇6 | 1̇3 6 | 66 1̇1̇6 |
拭香 木啵 皮皮 瓦桷 采栋 香 脑上 盖格灵

1̇1̇ 2̇ — | 2̇ — | 61̇ 1̇1̇6 | 1̇3 6 | 66 1̇1̇6 |
琉璃瓦啵 脚踏金砖格 放毫 光 左边 造了个

1̇1̇ 2̇ | 2̇ — | 1̇2̇ 61̇6 | 1̇1̇ 6 | 66 1̇66 |
金银 库啵 右边 造了个 万石 仓 金银 麻格

1̇1̇ 2̇ | 2̇ — | 2̇1̇ 1̇66 | 1̇6 6 | 3/4 1̇1̇ 61̇ 61̇6 |
万石 仓啵 金银 财宝格 用斗 量 读书 郎子 看里格

1̇1̇ 2̇ | 2̇ — | 3/4 1̇6 1̇1̇ 65 | 1̇6 1̇3 6 |
登金 榜啵 小小 儿童 看里 身体 蛮健 康

66 1̇1̇1̇ | 1̇1̇ 2̇ | 2̇ — | 66 1̇1̇ | 1̇1̇ 6 |
老者 看里是 增福 寿啵 少者 看里 添丁 粮

1̇6 1̇1̇ | 1̇1̇ 2̇ | 2̇ — | 1̇1̇ 66 | 1̇3 6 ‖
今晚 听我 来祝 赞啵 荣华 富贵 万 年 长。

注：东京——屋主。
看里——看了。

· 45 ·

接倨花鼓进厅下

1=D 2/4 3/4　（灯歌、花鼓歌）　唱：丁立荣（云石山）　记：钟同荣

6 5 6 1̇1̇1̇ | 1̇ 1̇ 2̇ 2̇ | 1̇ 1̇ 1̇ 1̇1̇2̇ |
花 鼓 打 来格 大 路 来 东 京 见得呀
〃 〃 〃 〃〃 禾 坪 下 禾 坪 爆竹呀

6 6 5 5 | 3 3 3 1̇1̇2̇ | 6 6 5 6 | 1̇ 1̇ 1̇ 2̇51̇ |
龙 门 开 东 京 见得呀 开 龙 门 啵 先添 人丁呀
乱 纷 纷 禾 坪 爆竹呀 纷 纷 乱 啲 接倨 花鼓呀

6 6 5 5 ‖
后 添 财。
进 厅 下。

注：东京——屋主。

先添人丁后添财

1=E 3/4　（灯歌、花鼓歌）　唱：丁立荣（云石山）　记：钟同荣

3561̇ 5 | 3523 5 | 5 5 1̇ | 61̇ 5 | 22 32 |
花鼓打 来 大 路 来 东 京 接 得 龙 门

1 — | 16 12 | 53 5 | 6·5 55 | 21 2 |
开 东京 呀格 接 得 开 龙 门啲 嗬

5 5 1̇ | 61̇ 5 | 22 32 | 1 — | 3·2 3·2 |
先 添 格 人 丁 后 添 财 后 添

12 3 | 21 65 | 1 — | 3 5 32 | 16 1 |
财 来 哎哦 哎哦 啲 可 嗬 可 啷可 嗬

3 5 3 | 12 3 | 21 65 | 1 — ‖
可 嗬 可 啷可 嗬 啷可 啷可 嗬。

· 46 ·

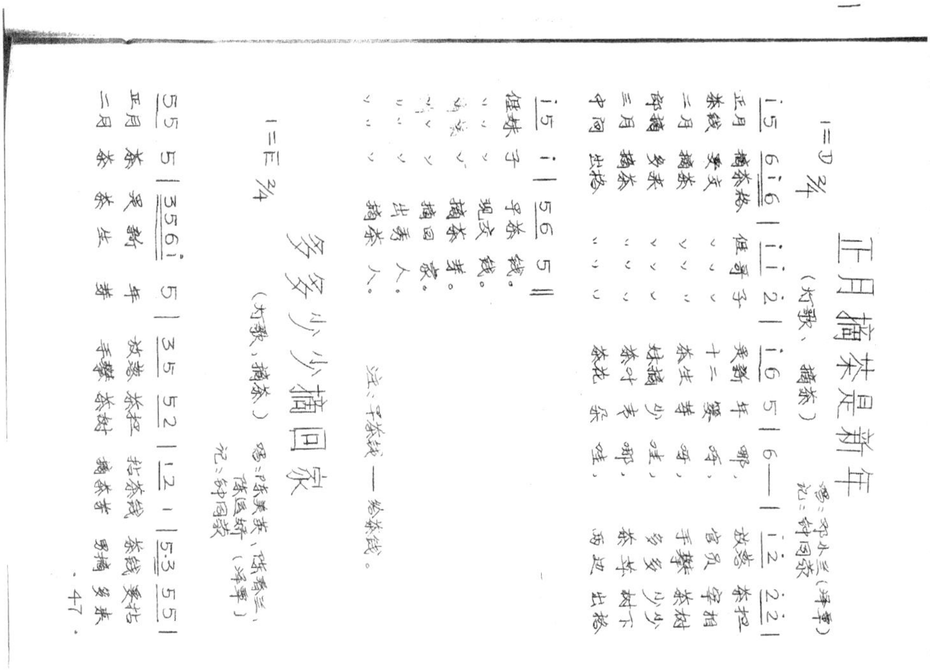

正月摘茶是新年

1=D 2/4　（灯歌、摘茶）　唱：邓小兰（泽覃）记：钟同荣

1 5 6 1 6 | 1 1 2 | 1 6 5 | 6 — | 1 2 2 2 |

正月 摘茶格 侄哥子 是新 年 哪， 放卷 茶担
茶钱 要交 ˇ ˇ ˇ 十二 箩 呀， 官员 宰相
二月 摘茶 ˇ ˇ ˇ 茶生 芽 呀， 手攀 茶树
郎摘 多来 ˇ ˇ ˇ 妹摘 少 哇， 多多 少少
三月 摘茶 ˇ ˇ ˇ 茶叶 青 哪， 茶 苹 树下
中间 出格 ˇ ˇ ˇ 茶花 朵 哇， 两边 出格

1 5 1 | 5 6 5 ‖

侄妹 子 平茶 钱。
ˇ ˇ ˇ 现交 钱。
ˇ ˇ ˇ 摘茶 芽。
ˇ ˇ ˇ 摘回 家。
ˇ ˇ ˇ 出秀 人。
ˇ ˇ ˇ 摘茶 人。

注：平茶钱——给茶钱。

多多少少摘回家

1=E 2/4　（灯歌、摘茶）　唱：陈美英、陈春兰、陈远娇（泽覃）记：钟同荣

5 5 5 | 3 5 6 1 5 | 3 5 5 2 | 1 2 1 | 5·3 5 5 |

正月 茶 是 新 年 放卷 茶担 拈茶钱 茶钱 要拈
二月 茶 茶 生 芽 手攀 茶树 摘茶芽 男摘 多来

· 47 ·

6 5 6 1 5 | 3 5 5 2 | 1 2 1 ‖

十二 箩 上交 下屋 讨现 钱。
女摘 少 多多 少少 摘回 家。

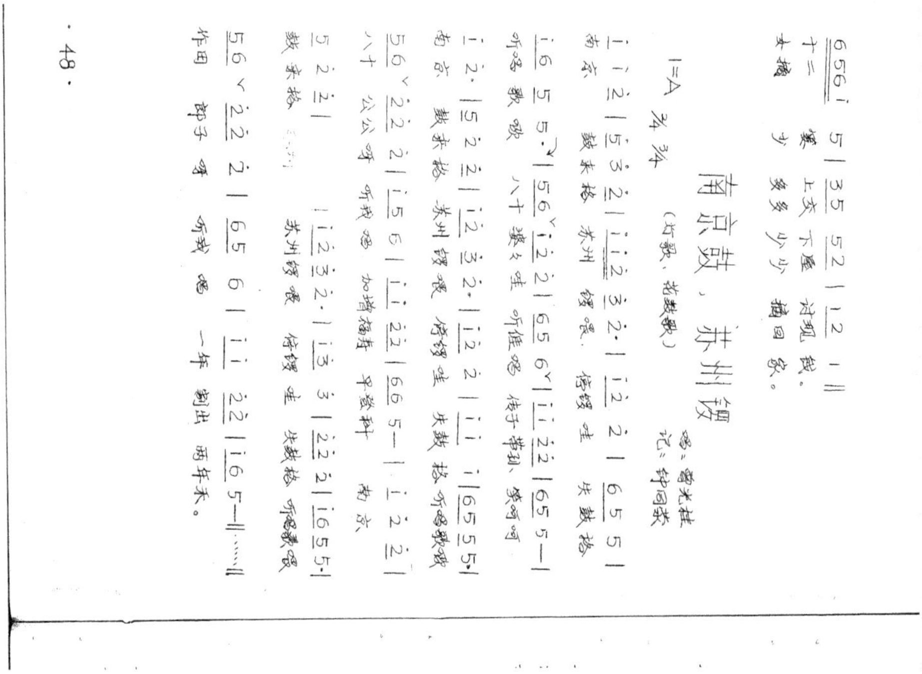

南京鼓，苏州锣

1=A 2/4 3/4　（灯歌、花鼓歌）　唱：曾光桂　记：钟同荣

1 1 2 | 5 3 2 | 1 1 2 3 2· | 1 2 2 | 6 5 5 |
南 京 鼓来格 苏州 锣喂， 侍锣 哇 失鼓 格

1 6 5 5· | 5 6 1 2 2 | 6 5 6 | 1 1 2 2 | 6 5 5 — |
听唱 歌 呦 八十 婆々 哇 听侄 唱 侍子 带孙、 笑呵 呵

1 2· | 5 2 2 | 1 2 3 2· | 1 2 2 | 1 1 1 | 6 5 5 5· |
南 京 鼓来 格 苏州 锣 喂 侍锣 哇 失鼓 格 听唱歌喂

5 6 2 2 2 | 1 5 6 | 1 1 2 2 | 6 6 5 — | 1 2 2 |
八十 公公 呀 听我 唱 加增 福寿 平登 科 南 京

5 2 2 | 1 2 3 2· | 1 3 3 | 2 2 2 | 1 6 5 5· |
鼓 来 格 苏州 锣 喂 侍锣 哇 失鼓 格 听唱歌 喂

5 6 2 2 2 | 6 5 6 | 1 1 2 2 | 1 6 5 — ‖……‖
作田 郎子 呀 听我 唱 一年 割出 两年 禾。

· 48 ·

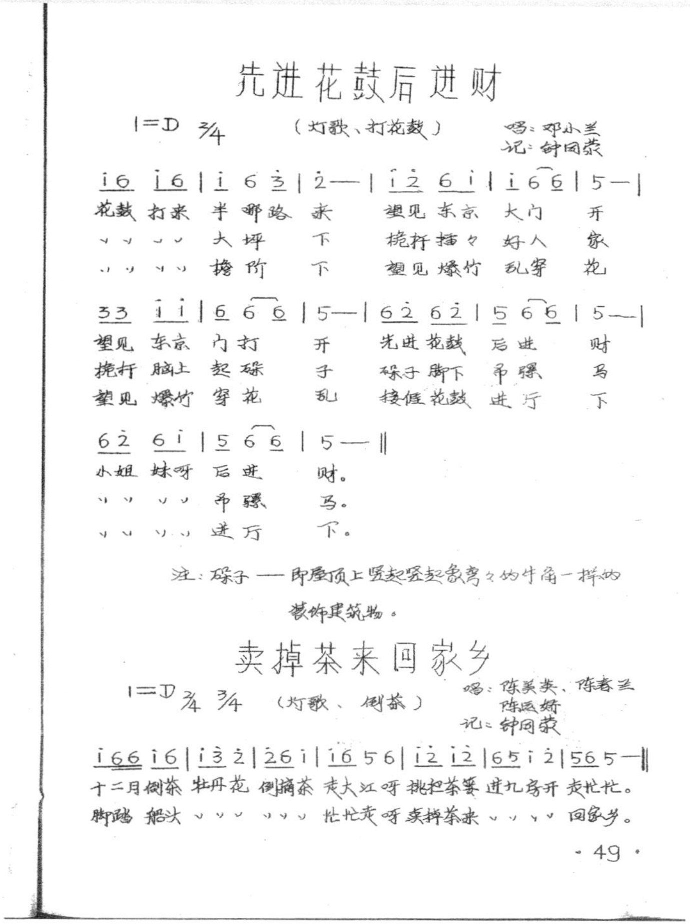

先进花鼓后进财

1=D 2/4 （灯歌、打花鼓） 唱：邓小兰 记：钟同荣

i6 i6 | i 6 3 | 2 — | i2 6i | i6 6 | 5 — |
花鼓 打来 半 哪路 来 望见 东京 大门 开
⋯ ⋯ 大 坪 下 挠打 插々 好人 家
⋯ ⋯ 檐 前 下 望见 爆竹 乱穿 花

33 ii | 6 6 6 | 5 — | 62 62 | 5 6 6 | 5 — |
望见 东京 门 打 开 先进 花鼓 后进 财
挠打 脑上 起 碌 子 碌子 脚下 吊 骡 马
望见 爆竹 穿 花 乱 接住 花鼓 进 厅 下

62 6i | 5 6 6 | 5 — ‖
小姐 妹呀 后 进 财。
⋯ ⋯ 吊 骡 马。
⋯ ⋯ 进 厅 下。

注：碌子——即屋顶上竖起竖起弯弯的牛角一样的装饰建筑物。

卖掉茶来回家乡

1=D 2/4 3/4 （灯歌、倒茶） 唱：陈美英、陈春兰、陈运娇 记：钟同荣

i66 i6 | i3 2 | 26 i | i6 5 6 | i2 i2 | 65 i 2 | 56 5 — ‖
十二月倒茶 牡丹花 倒摘茶 走大江呀 挑担茶箩 进九房开 走忙忙。
脚踏 船头 ⋯ ⋯ 忙忙走呀 卖掉茶来 ⋯ 回家乡。

·49·

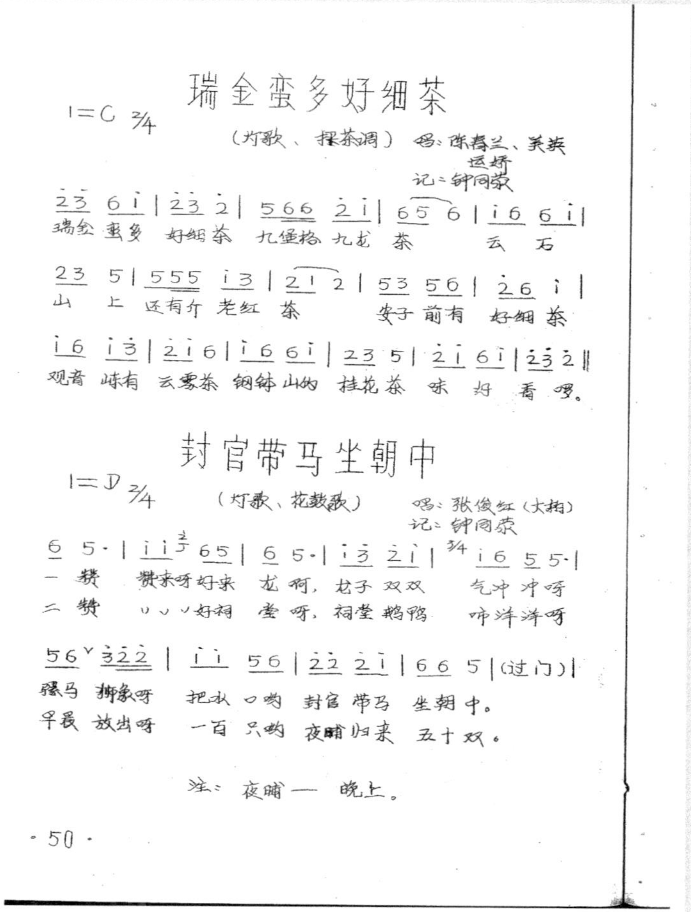

瑞金蛮多好细茶

1=C 2/4 （灯歌、探茶调） 唱：陈春兰、吴英运娇 记：钟同荣

23 6i | 23 2 | 566 2i | 65 6 | i6 6i |
瑞金 蛮多 好细茶 九堡格 九龙 茶 云 石

23 5 | 555 i3 | 21 2 | 53 56 | 26 i |
山 上 还有介 老红 茶 安子 前有 好细 茶

i6 i3 | 2i 6 | i6 6i | 23 5 | 2i 6i | 23 2 ‖
观音 峡有 云雾茶 铜钵 山的 挂花 茶 味 好 香 啰。

封官带马坐朝中

1=D 2/4 （灯歌、花鼓歌） 唱：张俊红（大柏） 记：钟同荣

6 5· | ii 65 | 6 5· | i3 2i | 3/4 i6 5 5· |
一 赞 赞来呀好来 龙 啊， 龙子 双双 气冲 冲呀
二 赞 ⋯ ⋯ 好祠 堂 呀， 祠堂 鹅鸭 咋洋洋呀

56 322 | ii 56 | 22 2i | 6 6 5 | (过门) |
骡马 排象呀 把秋 口哟 封官 带马 坐朝 中。
早晨 放出呀 一百 只哟 夜晡归来 五十 双。

注：夜晡——晚上。

·50·

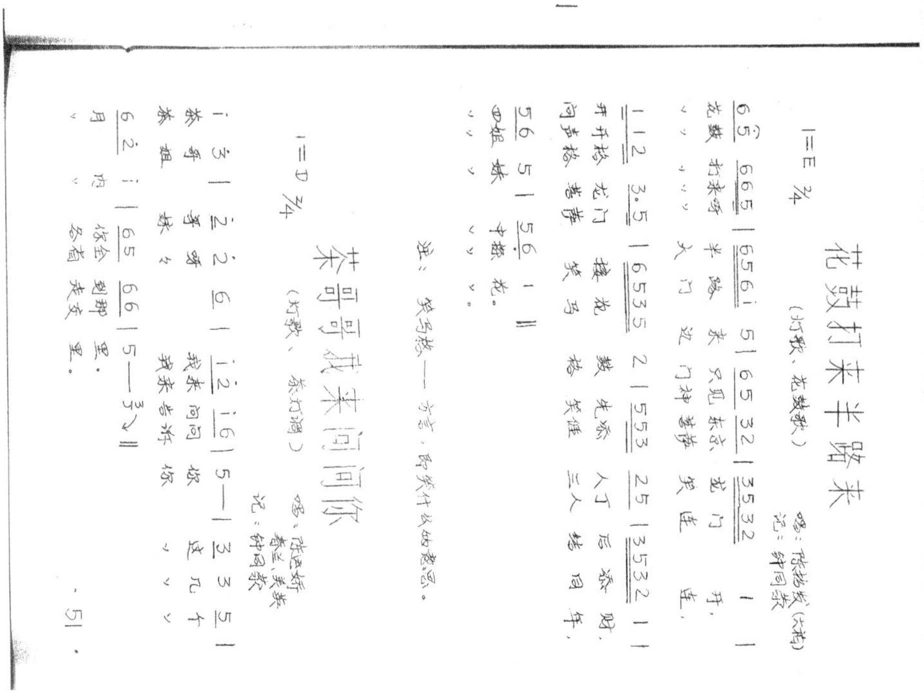

花鼓打来半路来

1=E 2/4

（灯歌、花鼓歌）

唱：陈粉发（大桥）
记：钟同荣

6 5 665 | 656i 5 | 65 32 | 3532 i |
花鼓 打来呀 半 路 来 只见东京 龙门 开，
〃〃 〃〃〃 大 门 边 门神菩萨 笑 连 连，

112 3·5 | 6535 2 | 553 25 | 3532 1 |
开开格 龙门 接 花 鼓 先添 人丁 后 添 财，
问声格 菩萨 笑 马 格 笑挂 三人 结 同 年，

56 5 | 56 1 ‖
四姐 妹 中探 花。
〃〃 〃 〃〃 〃。

注：笑马格——方言，即笑什么的意思。

茶哥哥我来问问你

1=D 2/4

（灯歌、茶灯调）

唱：陈选娇
春兰、美英
记：钟同荣

i 3 | 2 2 6 | i2 i6 | 5— | 3 3 5 |
茶 哥 哥 呀 我来 问问 你 这 几 个
茶 姐 妹 々 我来 告诉 你 〃 〃 〃

6 2 i | 65 66 | 5— ‖
月 内 你会 到那 里。
〃 〃 各有 走交 里。

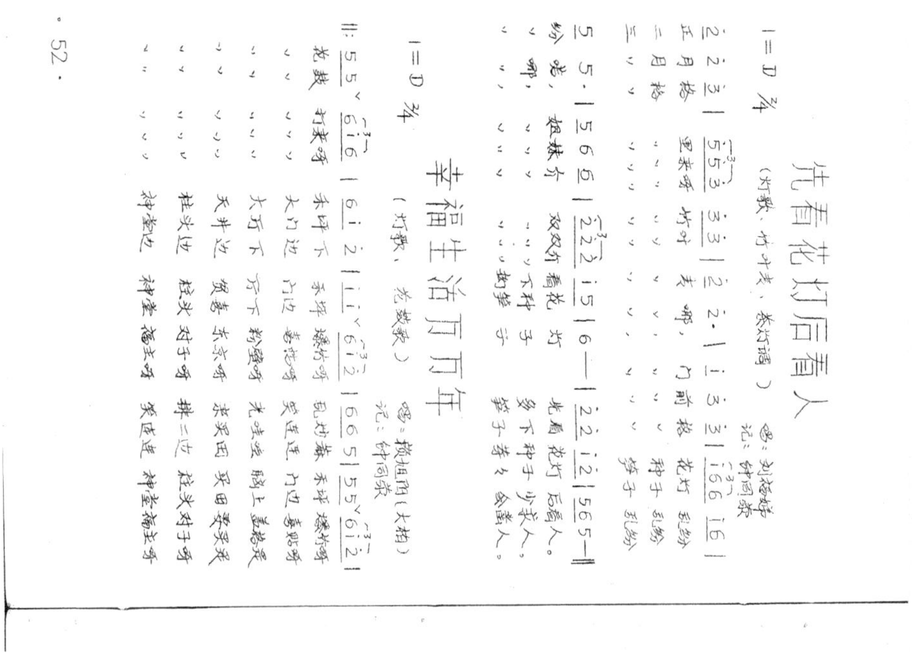

先看花灯后看人

1=D 2/4

（灯歌、竹叶表、茶灯调）

唱：刘福娣
记：钟同荣

2 2 3 | 553 33 | 2 2· | i 3 3 | i66 i6 |
正 月 格 里来呀 竹叶 表 哪， 门 前 格 花灯 乱纷
二 月 格 〃〃〃 〃〃 〃 〃， 〃 〃 〃 种子 乱纷
三 〃 〃 〃〃〃 〃〃 〃 〃， 〃 〃 〃 笋子 乱纷

5 5· | 5 6 6 | 222 i5 | 6— | 22 i2 | 565— ‖
纷 呢， 姐妹 介 双双介 看花 灯 先看 花灯 后看人。
〃 哪， 〃〃〃 〃〃〃下种 子 多下 种子 少求人，
〃 〃， 〃〃〃 〃〃〃 扮笋 子 笋子 芽々 会害人。

幸福生活万万年

1=D 2/4

（灯歌、花鼓歌）

唱：赖姐囡（大柏）
记：钟同荣

‖: 55 6i6 | 6i 2 | ii 6i2 | 665 | 55 6i2 |
花鼓 打来呀 禾坪 下 禾坪 爆竹呀 乱炒 恭 禾坪 爆竹呀
〃〃 〃〃〃 大门 边 门边 喜炮呀 笑连连 门边 喜贴呀
〃〃 〃〃〃 大厅 下 厅下 粉壁呀 光哇哇 脑上 盖格灵
〃〃 〃〃〃 天井 边 贺喜 东京呀 求买田 买田 要买灵
〃〃 〃〃〃 柱头 边 柱头 对子呀 排二边 柱头 对子呀
〃〃 〃〃〃 神堂 边 神堂 福主呀 笑连连 神堂 福主呀

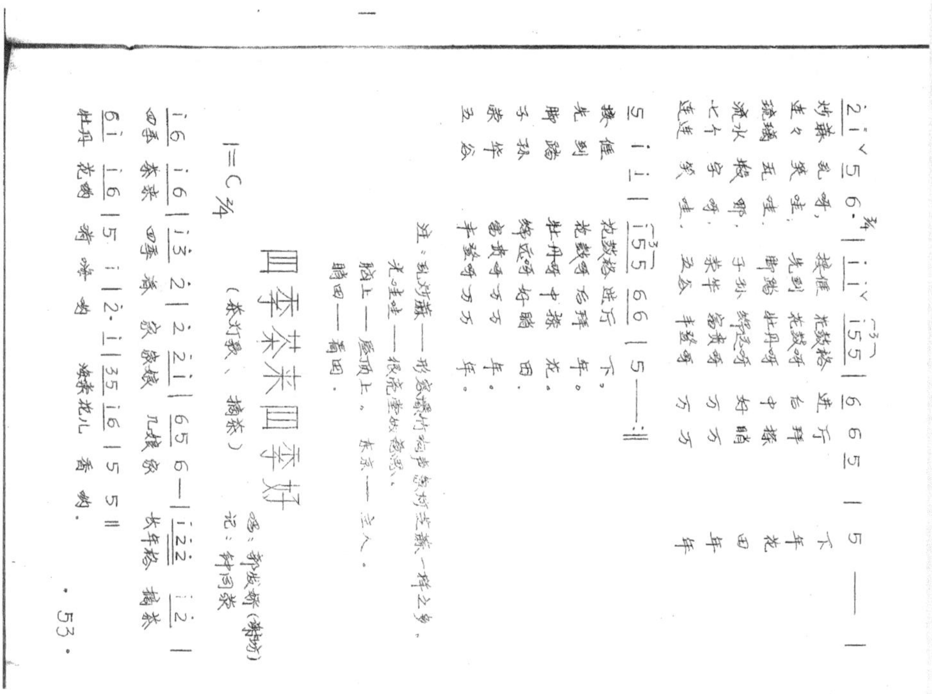

2 i 5 6· | i i i55 | 6 6 5 | 5 — |

炒蒜 乱 呀， 接偃 花鼓格 进 厅 下
连々 笑 哇， 先到 花鼓呀 后 拜 年
琉璃 瓦 哇， 脚踏 牡丹呀 中 探 花
流水 般 哪， 子孙 绵远呀 好 睛 田
七个 字 呀， 荣华 富贵呀 万 万 年
连连 笑 哇， 五谷 丰登呀 万 万 年

5 i i | i55 66 | 5—:||

接 偃 花鼓格进厅 下。
先 到 花鼓呀后拜 年。
脚 踏 牡丹呀中探 花。
子 孙 绵远呀好睛 田．
荣 华 富贵呀万万 年。
五 谷 丰登呀万万 年。

注：乱炒蒜——形容爆竹响声象炒芝蒜一样之多．
光哇哇——很亮堂的意思．
脑上——屋顶上。 东京——主人．
睛田——看田．

四季茶来四季好

1=C 2/4　（茶灯歌、摘茶）　唱：郭发娇（谢坊）　记：钟同荣

i6 i6 | i3 2 | 2 2i | 65 6— | i22 i2 |

四季 茶来 四季 将 家 家娘 几娘 家 长年格 摘茶

6i i6 | 5 i | 2· i | 35 i6 | 5 5 ||

牡丹 花哟 将 嗱 哟 海棠花儿 香 哟．

· 53 ·

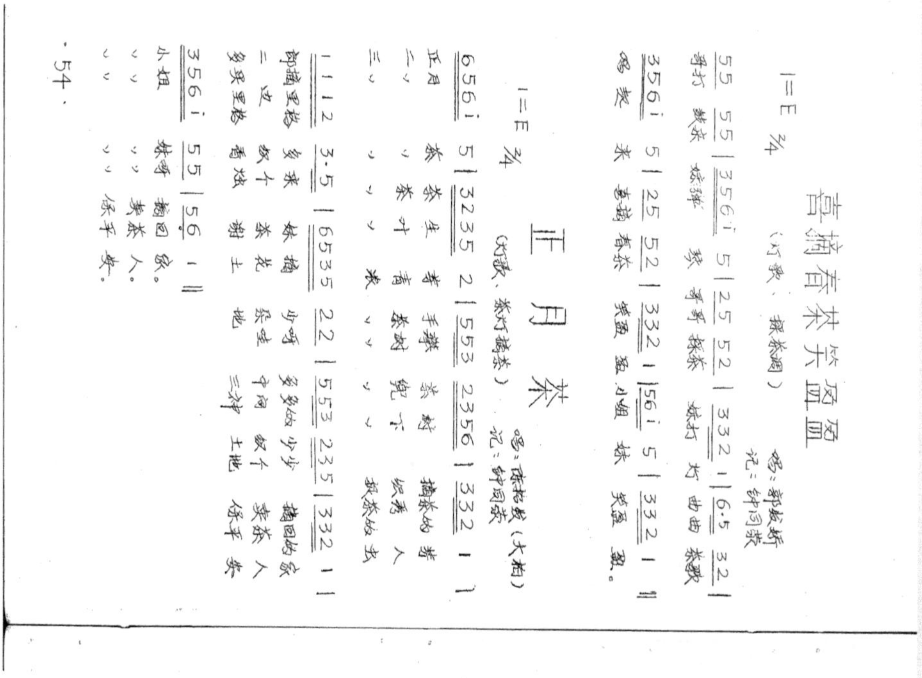

喜摘春茶笑盈盈

1=E 2/4　（灯歌、采茶调）　唱：郭发娇　记：钟同荣

55 55 | 356i 5 | 25 52 | 332 | 6·5 32 |

哥打 鼓来 妹弹 琴 哥哥 采茶 妹打 灯 曲曲 茶歌

356i 5 | 25 52 | 332 | 56i 5 | 332 ||

唱 起 来 喜摘 春茶 笑盈 盈 小姐 妹 笑盈 盈。

正月茶

1=E 2/4　（灯歌、茶灯摘茶）　唱：陈拾妹（大柏）　记：钟同荣

656i 5 | 3235 2 | 553 2356 | 332 |

正月 茶 茶生 芽 手攀 茶树 摘茶的 芽
二〃 〃 茶叶 青 茶树 兜下 织秀 人
三〃 〃 〃〃 浓 〃〃 〃〃 敬茶的 去

1112 3·5 | 6535 22 | 553 235 | 332 |

郎摘里格 多来 妹摘 少呀 多多的 少少 摘回的 家
二 边 奴个 茶花 朵哇 中间 奴个 卖茶 人
多买里格 香烛 谢土 地 三神 土地 保平 安

356i 55 | 56 ||

小姐 妹呀 摘回 家。
〃〃 〃〃 卖茶 人。
〃〃 〃〃 保平 安。

· 54 ·

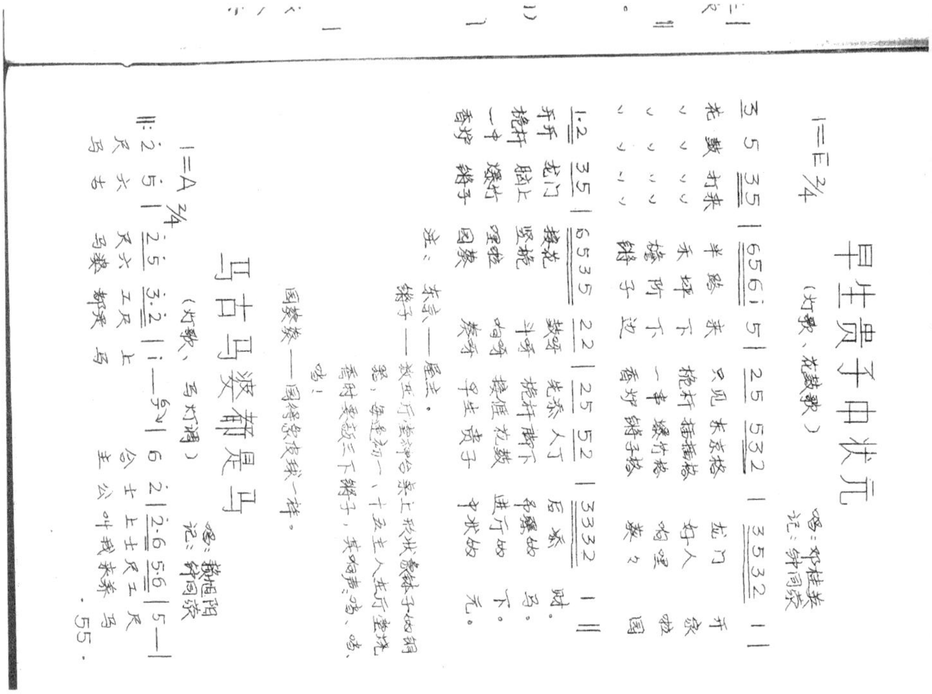

早生贵子中状元

1=E 2/4　（灯歌、花鼓歌）　唱：邓桂英　记：钟同荣

3 5 35 | 656i 5 | 25 532 | 3532 | |

花鼓打来 半路来 只见东京格 龙门 开
（同上） 禾坪下 桅杆插插格 好人 家
（同上） 檐阶下 一串爆竹格 响哩 啦
（同上） 铕子边 香炉铕子格 亲亲 国

1·2 35 | 6535 22 | 25 52 | 3332 | ||

开开 龙门 接花 鼓呀 先添 人丁 后添 财。
桅杆 脑上 竖桅 斗呀 桅杆 脚下 吊缨的 马。
一串 爆竹 哩啦 响呀 接住 花鼓 进厅的 下。
香炉 铕子 国葵 葵呀 早生 贵子 中状的 元。

注：东京——屋主。
铕子——敬在厅堂神台桌上形状象钵子的铜器，每逢初一、十五主人在厅堂烧香时要敲三下铕子，其响声：嗡、嗡、嗡！
国葵葵——圆得象皮球一样。

马古马婆都是马

1=A 2/4　（灯歌、马灯调）　唱：赖旭阳　记：钟同荣

‖: 2 5 | 25 3·2 | i — | 6 2 | 2·6 5·6 | 5 — |
尺 六 尺六 工尺 上 合 士 上士尺工 尺
马 古 马婆 都是 马 主 公 叫我来养 马

5·6 5 | 5·6 5 | 5·3 2·3 | 5·3 2·3 | 56 6 5· :‖
六士 六 尺士 尺 六士 尺士 六士 尺士 工士 五六。
侄马 夫 来养 马 牛耕 田

56 5 | 25 32 | i2 i | i — ‖
马食 谷，别人 供子 他享福。

注：供子——生子。

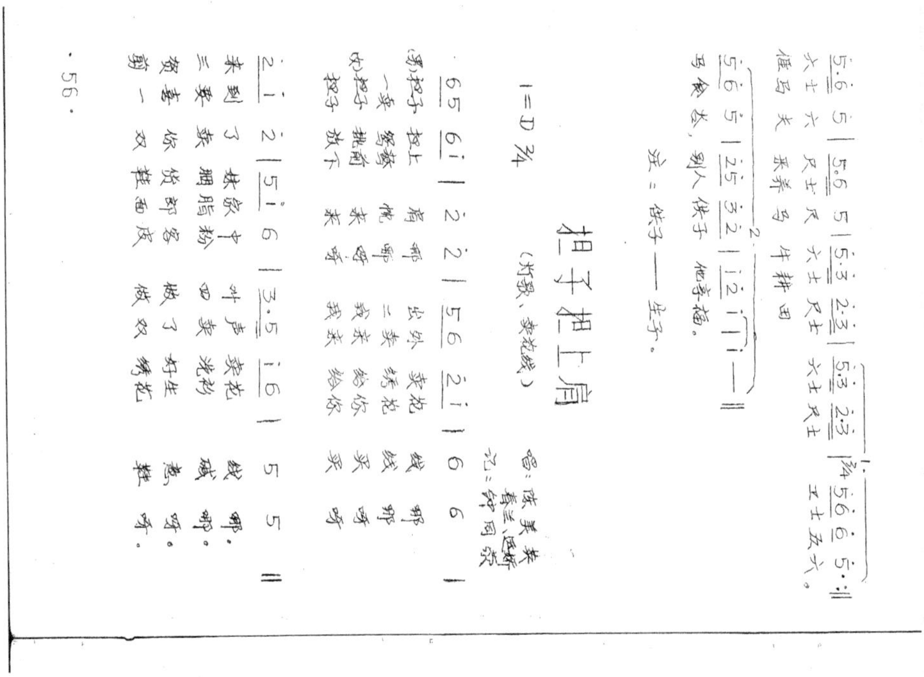

担子担上肩

1=D 2/4　（灯歌、卖花线）　唱：陈美英 春兰 廷娇　记：钟同荣

65 6i | 2 2 | 56 2i | 6 6 |

（男）担子 担上 肩 哪 出外 卖花 线 哪
一卖 鸳鸯 枕 哪 二卖 绣花 线 哪
（女）担子 挑前 来 呀 我来 给你 买 呀
担子 放下 来 呀 我来 给你 买 呀

2 i 2 | 5i 6 | 3·5 i6 | 5 5 ‖

来到 了 妹家 中 叫声 卖花 线 哪。
三要 卖 胭脂 粉 四卖 洗衫 碱 哪。
贺喜 你 货郎 客 做了 好生 意 呀。
剪一 双 鞋面 皮 做双 绣花 鞋 呀。

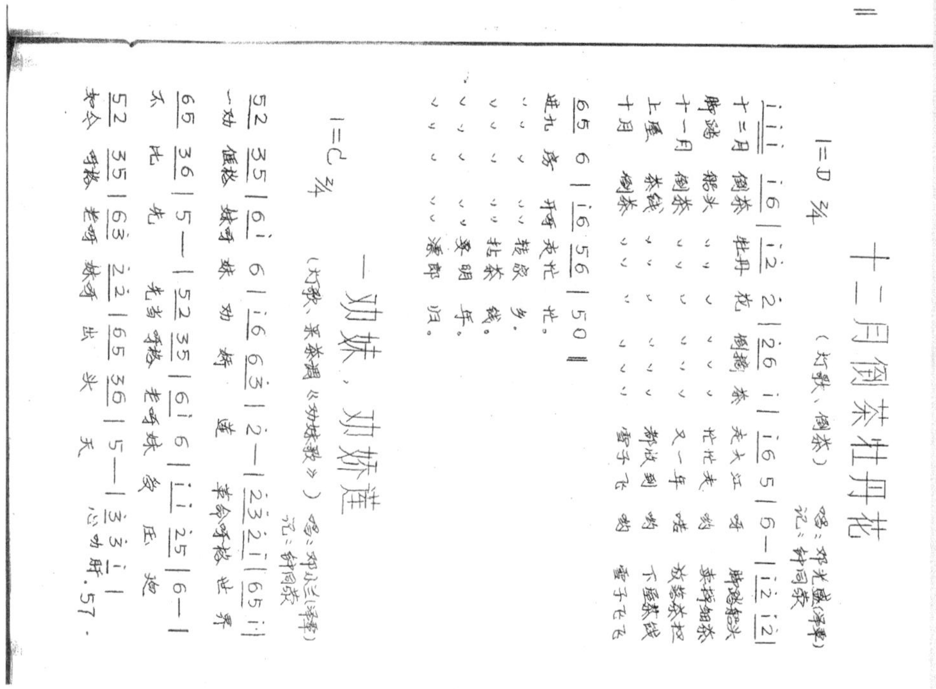

十二月倒茶牡丹花

1=D 3/4　（灯歌、倒茶）　唱：邓光盛（泽覃）
记：钟同荣

1̇1̇1̇ 1̇6 | 1̇2̇ 2̇ | 2̇6 1̇ | 1̇6 5 | 6— | 1̇2̇ 1̇2̇ |
十二月 倒茶 牡丹 花 倒摇 茶 走大江 呀 脚踏船头
脚踏 船头 〃〃 〃 〃〃〃 忙忙走 哟 卖择细茶
十一月 倒茶 〃〃 〃 〃〃〃 又一年 啰 放落茶担
上屋 茶钱 〃〃 〃 〃〃〃 都收到 哟 下屋茶钱
十月 倒茶 〃〃 〃 〃〃〃 雪子飞 哟 雪子飞飞

65 6 | 1̇6 56 | 50 ‖
进九 房 开呀 走忙 忙。
〃〃 〃 〃〃 转家 乡。
〃〃 〃 〃〃 扯茶 钱。
〃〃 〃 〃〃 买明 年。
〃〃 〃 〃〃 濛郎 归。

一劝妹，劝娇莲

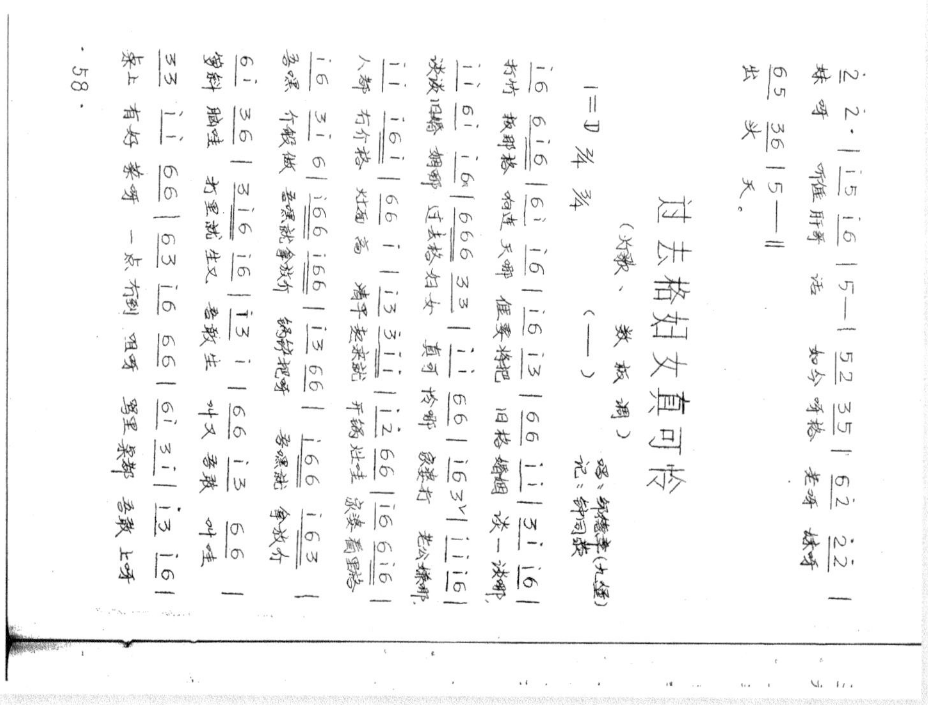

1=C 3/4
（灯歌、采茶调《劝妹歌》）　唱：邓小兰（泽覃）
记：钟同荣

52 35 | 61̇ 6 | 1̇6 63̇ | 2̇— | 2̇3̇2̇1̇ | 651̇ |
一劝 匪格 妹呀 妹 劝 娇 莲 革命呀格 世 界
65 36 | 5— | 52 35 | 61̇ 6 | 1̇1̇ 25 | 6— |
不 比 先 先当 呀格 老呀妹 受 压 迫
52 35 | 63̇ 2̇2̇ | 65 36 | 5— | 3̇3̇ 1̇ |
如今 呀格 老呀 妹呀 出 头 天 心肝

·57·

2̇ 2̇· | 1̇5 1̇6 | 5— | 52 35 | 62̇ 2̇2̇ |
妹 呀 呀匪 肝哥 活 如今 呀格 老呀 妹呀
65 36 | 5— ‖
出 头 天。

过去格妇女真可怜

（灯歌、数板调）

1=D 2/4 3/4　（一）　唱：邹德章（九堡）
记：钟同荣

1̇6 61̇6 | 61̇ 1̇6 | 1̇6 1̇3̇ | 66 1̇1̇ | 3̇1̇ 1̇6 |
打竹 板那格 响连 天哪 匪要 将把 旧格 婚姻 谈一 谈哪，
1̇1̇ 61̇ 1̇6 | 666 33 | 1̇1̇ 66 | 1̇63̇ | 1̇1̇1̇6 |
谈谈 旧婚 姻哪 过去格 妇女 真可 怜哪 家婆打 老公嫌哪，
1̇1̇ 1̇61̇ | 66 1̇ | 1̇3̇ 3̇1̇1̇ | 1̇2̇ 66 | 1̇6 61̇6 |
人都 冇介格 灶面 高 清早起来就 开锅 灶哇 家婆骂里格
1̇6 3̇1̇ 6 | 1̇66 1̇66 | 1̇3̇ 66 | 1̇66 1̇63̇ |
吾嘿 介般 做 吾嘿就拿放介 锅铲 把呀 吾嘿就 拿放介
61̇ 36 | 3̇1̇6 1̇6 | 1̇3̇ 1̇ | 66 1̇3̇ 66 |
箩斜 脑哇 打里就 生又 吾敢 生 叫又 吾敢 叫哇
33 1̇1̇ 66 | 63 1̇6 66 | 61̇ 3̇1̇ | 1̇3̇ 1̇6 |
桌上 有好 菜呀 一点 冇到 咀呀 骂里 冤都 吾敢 上呀

·58·

Note:

The expression "harmony between sound and action" (声与事相合) refers to a traditional Chinese aesthetic concept in which musical expression is directly integrated with physical activity, so that rhythm and melody resonate with the tempo of labor or ritual practice.

05 第五类 · 风俗歌与茶歌

CATEGORY V · CUSTOMARY SONGS AND TEA-PICKING SONGS

导读

风俗歌”与“茶歌”同属生活与劳动相结合的民间歌谣，前者多源于礼俗仪式与社区生活，后者则产生于农业劳动尤其是茶区的生产实践。两类歌谣都具有鲜明的地方性与口头性，体现了民众在日常与生产活动中对秩序、节奏与情感的表达方式。

“风俗歌”往往伴随婚嫁礼仪、节庆仪式、祭祀活动而唱，其歌词包含祝福、祈愿、规训或调侃，既有娱乐性，也承载社会教育与文化传承功能，折射出社区伦理与价值观。它们在民间社会中发挥着“声音的礼仪”作用，使歌声与仪式融为一体，强化了集体认同感。

“茶歌”则是劳动歌的一个重要支系，尤其盛行于赣南及周边茶区。在采茶、制茶等劳动过程中，茶农即兴演唱以调节节奏、减轻疲劳，同时增强群体协作。歌词描绘劳动场景、自然环境与生活情感，常含爱情隐喻或社会感慨。茶歌的旋律简短有力，与劳动动作紧密契合，呈现出“声与事相合”的特征，体现了劳动与艺术的内在统一。

两类歌谣的存在说明民众在不同层面上通过歌声调节生活：风俗歌强调礼仪与文化秩序，茶歌强调劳动节奏与情感抒发。二者共同构成了赣南民间音乐文化的核心版图，为研究地方社会结构、劳动文化与口头传统提供了重要材料。

Introduction

Customary Songs and *Tea-Picking Songs* both represent forms of folk singing that integrate everyday life with collective practice. The former derives largely from ritual customs and communal life, while the latter emerges directly from agricultural labor, especially in tea-growing regions. Both types are strongly localized, orally transmitted, and reveal how communities articulated order, rhythm, and emotion through song in their daily and productive activities.

Customary Songs were commonly performed during weddings, seasonal festivals, and ritual occasions. Their lyrics contain blessings, prayers, admonitions, and humorous exchanges, serving not only entertainment purposes but also functions of social instruction and cultural transmission. They acted as a form of "ritualized sound," in which singing was inseparable from ceremony, reinforcing ethical values and communal cohesion.

Tea-Picking Songs, by contrast, are a significant branch of work songs, flourishing in southern Jiangxi and surrounding tea regions. Sung spontaneously during tea-picking and tea-processing, they regulated rhythm, alleviated fatigue, and fostered collective cooperation. Their lyrics often depicted agricultural scenes, natural surroundings, and personal emotions, sometimes enriched with romantic metaphors or social reflections. Musically concise and forceful, tea-picking songs were closely aligned with the tempo of labor, embodying the principle of "harmony between sound and action."

Taken together, these two categories demonstrate how folk communities used song to structure different dimensions of life: *Customary Songs* emphasized ritual and social order, while *Tea-Picking Songs* emphasized labor rhythm and emotional expression. Together they constitute a vital core of southern Jiangxi's folk musical culture and provide key materials for the study **of social structure, labor traditions, and oral heritage in the region**.

茶歌

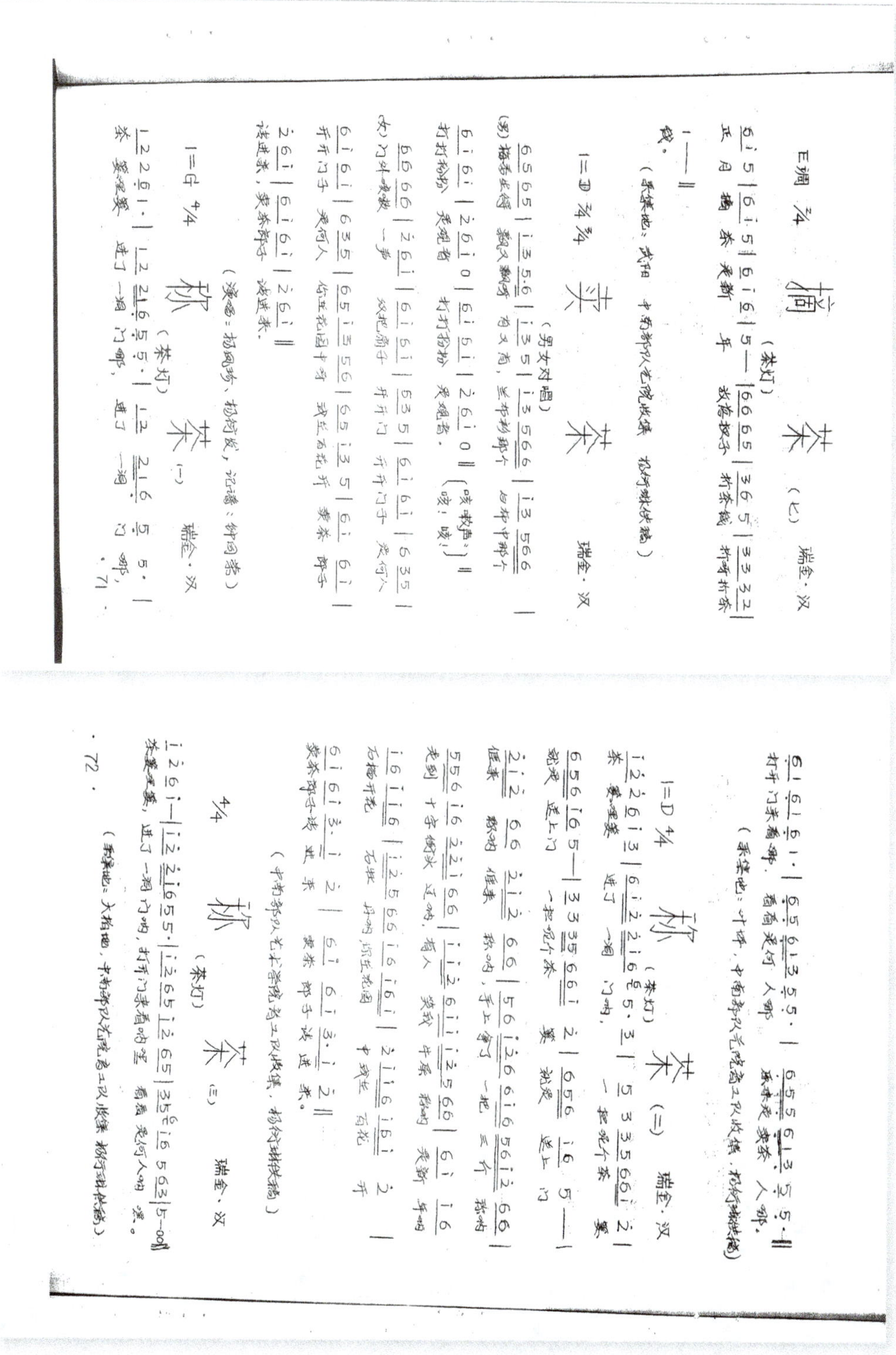

摘茶（七）

E调 2/4 瑞金·汉

（茶灯）

6 1 5 | 6 1 5 | 6 1 6 | 5 — | 66 65 | 3 6 5 | 33 32 | 1 — ‖

正 月 摘 茶 是新 年 放落裙子 折茶钱 折呀折茶 钱。

（采集地：武阳 中南部队艺院收集 杨何琳供稿）

卖茶

1=D 2/4 3/4 瑞金·汉

（男女对唱）

65 65 | 1 3 5.6 | 1 3 5 | 1 3 566 | 1 3 566 |

(男) 梅香生得 飘又飘呀 有又有，兰布衫那个 白布中那个

6 1 6 1 | 2 6 1 0 | 6 1 6 1 | 2 6 1 0 ‖ （咳 啾声：咳！咳！）‖

打打扮扮 是观音 打打扮扮 是观音。

66 66 | 2 6 1 | 6 1 6 1 | 53 5 | 6 1 6 1 | 6 35 |

(女) 门外咳嗽 一声 双把扇子 开开门 开开门子 是何人

6 1 6 1 | 6 35 | 65 1 3 56 | 65 13 5 | 6 1 6 1 |

开开门子 是何人 你在花园中呀 我在石花开 卖茶 郎子

2 6 1 | 6 1 6 1 | 2 6 1 ‖

请进来，卖茶郎子 请进来。

（演唱：杨凤玲、杨荷发，记谱：钟同荣）

称茶（一）

1=G 4/4 瑞金·汉

（茶灯）

1 2 2 6 1 · | 1 2 21 6 5 5 · | 1 2 21 6 5 5 · |

茶 叆哩叆 进了 一洞 门哪， 进了 一洞 门 哪，

· 71 ·

6 1 6 1 6 1 · | 6 5 61 3 5 5 · | 6 55 61 3 5 5 · ‖

打开门来看哪， 看看是何 人哪 原来是 卖茶 人哪。

（采集地：叶坪，中南部队艺院音工队收集，杨何琳供稿）

称茶（二）

1=D 4/4 瑞金·汉

（茶灯）

1 2 2 6 1 3 | 6 1 2 21 6 5 · 3 | 5 3 35 66 1 2 |

茶 叆哩叆 进了 一洞 门呐， 一 把呢个茶 叆

656 1 6 5 — | 3 3 35 66 1 2 | 656 1 6 5 — |

就是 送上门 一把呢个茶 叆 就是 送上 门

2 1 2 66 2 1 2 66 | 56 1 2 6 6 1 6 56 1 2 66 |

但来 称呐 但来 称呐，手上拿了 一把 三斤 称呐

556 1 6 2 2 1 66 | 1 1 2 6 1 1 1 2 5 66 | 6 1 1 6 |

走到 十字街头 过呐，有人 笑我 牛屎 秤呐 是新 年呐

1 6 1 1 6 | 1 2 5 66 1 6 1 6 1 | 2 1 1 6 1 6 1 2 |

石榴开花 石牡 丹呐，你在花园 中 我在 百花 开

6 1 6 1 3. 1 2 | 6 1 6 1 3. 1 2 ‖

卖茶郎子请 进 来 卖茶 郎子 请 进 来。

（中南部队艺术学院音工队收集，杨何琳供稿）

称茶（三）

4/4 瑞金·汉

（茶灯）

1 2 6 1 — | 1 2 21 6 5 5 · | 1 2 65 1 2 65 | 35 1 6 5 63 | 5 — 0 ‖

茶叆哩叆，进了 一洞 门呐，打开门来看呐 望 看看 是何人呐 望。

（采集地：大柏地，中南部队艺院音工队收集 杨何琳供稿）

· 72 ·

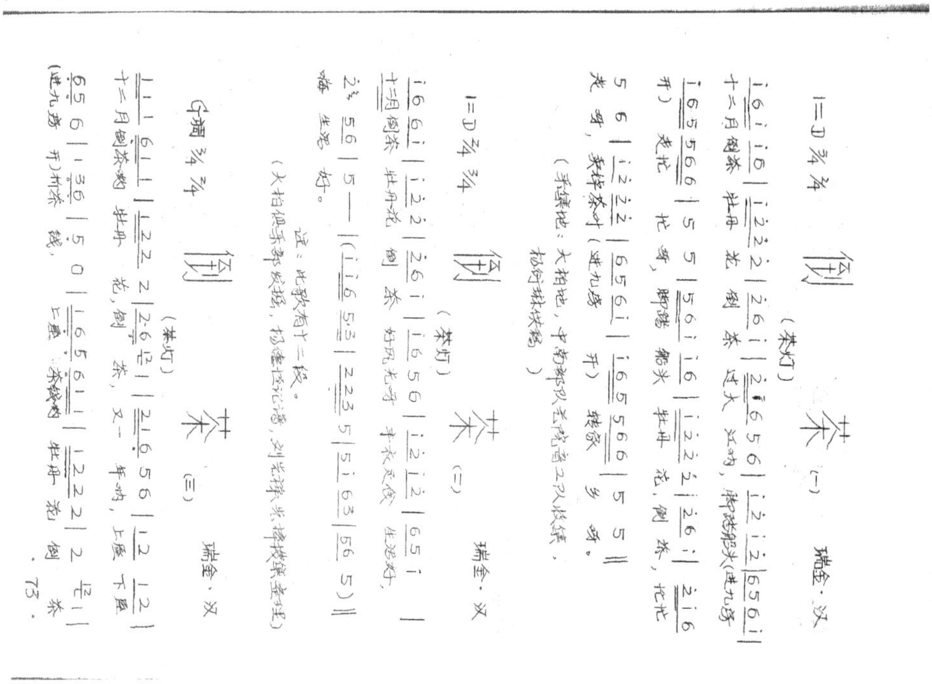

1=D 2/4 3/4 **倒　茶**（一）　瑞金·汉

（茶灯）

i6i i6 | i222 | 26i | 2i656 | i2 i2 | 656i |
十二月倒茶 牡丹 花 倒 茶 过大 江呐，脚踏船头（进九房

i65 566 | 5 5 | 56i i6 | i222 | 26i | 2i6
开） 走忙 忙 呀，脚踏 船头 牡丹 花，倒 茶，忙忙

5 6 | i2 22 | 656i | i65 566 | 5 5 ‖
走 呀，采样茶叶（进九房 开） 转路 乡 呀。

（采集地：大柏地，中南部队艺院音工队收集，杨衍琳供稿）

1=D 2/4 3/4 **倒　茶**（二）　瑞金·汉

（茶灯）

i6 6i | i22 | 26i | i656 | i2 i2 | 65i |
十二月倒茶 牡丹花 倒 茶 好风光呀 手衣足食 生活好，

2 56 | 5 — |（i i6 53 | 223 5 | 5i 63 | 56 5）‖
嗨 生活 好。

注：此歌有十二段。

（大柏地采部发掘，杨德控记谱，刘光禄、张棒搜集整理）

G调 3/4 2/4 **倒　茶**（三）　瑞金·汉

（茶灯）

111 611 | 122 2 | 2·6 i2 | 21656 | 12 12 |
十二月倒茶哟 牡丹 花，倒 茶， 又一 年呐，上屋 下屋

65 6 | 136 | 5 0 | 165 611 | 1222 | 2 i2 |
（进九房 开）折茶 钱， 上屋 茶钱哟 牡丹 花 倒 茶

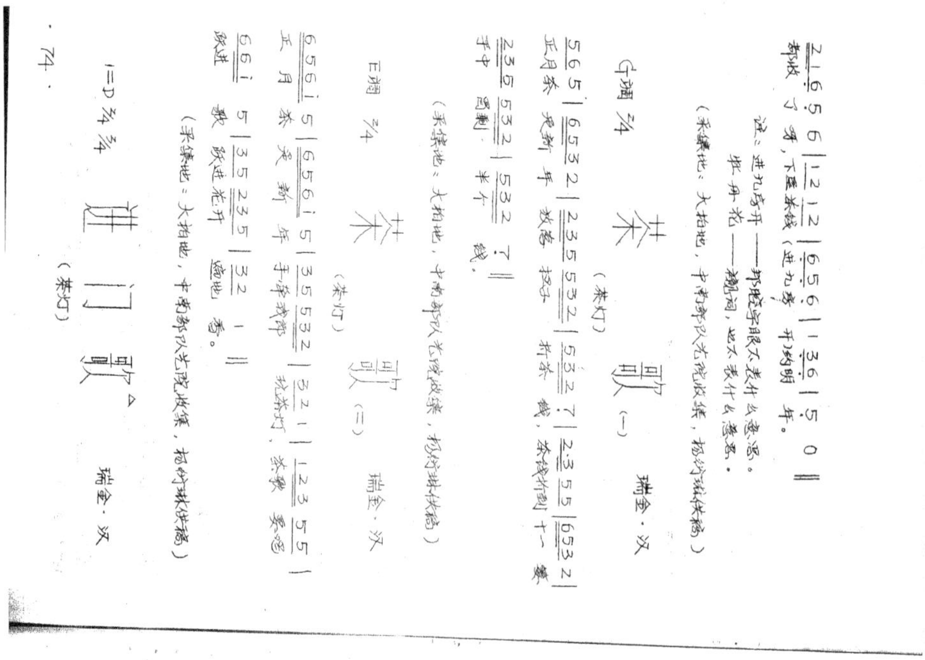

·73·

216 5 6 | 12 12 | 656 | 136 | 5 0 ‖
都收 了 呀，下屋茶钱（进九房 开）约明 年。

注：进九房开——那匹字眼不表什么意思。
牡丹花——衬词，也不表什么意思。

（采集地：大柏地，中南部队艺院收集，杨衍琳供稿）

G调 2/4 **茶　歌**（一）　瑞金·汉

（茶灯）

565 | 6532 | 235 532 | 532 7 | 2·3 55 | 653 2 |
正月茶 是新 年 放落 担子 折茶 钱，茶钱折到 十一 篓

235 532 | 532 7 ‖
子中 司剩 半个 钱。

（采集地：大柏地，中南部队艺院收集，杨衍琳供稿）

E调 2/4 **茶　歌**（二）　瑞金·汉

（茶灯）

656i 5 | 656i 5 | 35 532 | 321 | 123 55 |
正 月 茶 是 新 年 手牵我郎 玩茶灯，茶歌 要唱

66i 5 | 35 235 | 32 1 ‖
跃进 歌 跃进花开 遍地 香。

（采集地：大柏地，中南部队艺院收集，杨衍琳供稿）

1=D 2/4 3/4 **进 门 歌**△　瑞金·汉

（茶灯）

·74·

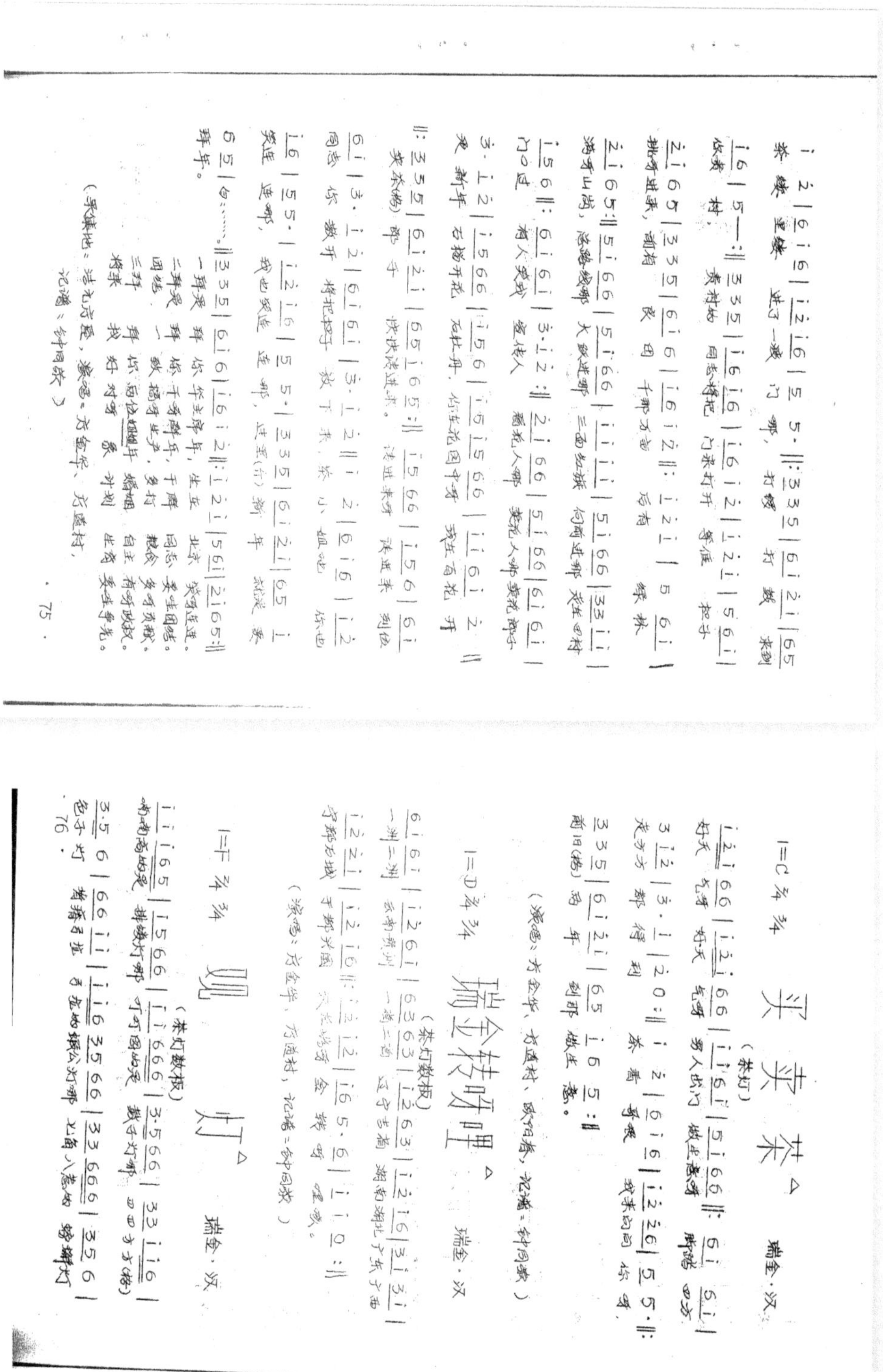

茶嫂 里嫂 进了一夜 门 哪， 打锣 打鼓 来到
你贵 村， 贵村的 同志将把 门来打开 等候 拉子
挑呀进来，请有 良 田 千那万亩 后有 绿 林
满呀山岗，落路线那 大跃进那 三面红旗 向前进那 来在四村
门口过 有人买我 宣传人 看花人哪 卖花人哪 卖花郎子
来 新年 石榴开花 石牡丹，你在花园中呀 我在百花 开
卖茶(格) 郎 子 快快请进来。 请进来呀 请进来 列位
同志 你 撒开 将把担子 放 下 来，茶 小 姐哋 你也
笑连 连哪， 我也笑连 连 哪，进来(介) 新 年 就是 要
拜年。

一拜是 拜 你 华主席年，生在 北京 笑呀连连。
二拜是 拜 你 千呀群年，干群 同志 要哇团结。
团结 一 致 搞呀生产，多打 粮食 多呀贡献。
三拜 拜 你 后位姐姐年 婚姻 自主 有呀政权。
将来 找 好 对呀 象 计划 生育 要走争先。

（采集地：洁元彷蕃，演唱：方金华、方道村，记谱：钟同歆）

· 75 ·

买卖茶△

1=C 2/4 3/4　瑞金·汉

（茶灯）

好天 气呀 好天 气呀 男人出门 做生意呀 脚踏 四方
走方方 都 得 利 茶 嵩 哥根 我来问问 你 呀，
前旧(格) 两 年 到那 做生 意。

（演唱：方金华、方道村、欧阳春，记谱：钟同歆）

瑞金转呀哩△

1=D 2/4 3/4　瑞金·汉

（茶灯数板）

一洲二洲 云南贵州 一湖二湖 辽宁吉林 湖南湖北 广东广西
宁都于城 于都兴国 [illegible] 金 转 呀 哩 哎。

（演唱：方金华、方道村，记谱：钟同歆）

观灯△

1=F 2/4 3/4　瑞金·汉

（茶灯数板）

喃喃高的是 排楼灯哪 叮叮图的是 戴子灯哪 四四方方(格)
色子 灯 [illegible] 七角八卦的 螃蟹灯

· 76 ·

12 665 | 35 66 | 31 31 | 3.5 66 | 11 6 66 |
相须巴抓呦 猫子灯哪 七囊七五 是龙灯哪 点着火 亲是

11 6·6 | 61 166 | 1556 | 3333 | 156 | 1566 |
涝涝铳哪 铳涝涝是 走马 灯 蚌松蚌松 狮子灯 茶罐灯哪

3566 | 1255 | 1215 | 356 ‖: 12 12 | 16126 |
茶兰灯哪 姐姐手上 还有二把 扁子灯 恭来正月 十五样呢

5·6 11 :‖
花朝哩咳。

（演唱：方金华、方道村， 记谱：钟同荣）

卖杂货△

1=D 2/4 3/4 瑞金·汉

（茶灯数板）

6161 | 1661 | 6363 | 61 13 | 1566 | 156 |
大包细包 三茶细椒 大捆细捆 胭脂水粉 打牙中哪 角牙中，

11 1566 | 15 156 | 1566 | 356 ‖: 12 12 |
蓑衣笠婆中哪，鞋底鞋面中 长牙中哪 短牙中 还有 两包

12 6 | 5·6 11 :‖
绣线 花针哩咳。

（演唱：方金华、方道村 记谱：钟同荣）

卖菓子△

1=D 2/4 3/4 瑞金·汉

（茶灯）

11 1566 | 11 1566 | 156 | 156 | 12 65 |
山中山荔子呀 田中田马荠呀 落花生 炒豆子 油酥 糕饼

·77·

156 | 21 65 | 1566 | 21 66 | 1266 ‖: 12 12 |
柑桔子 人荷芙蓉 柑蔗子呀 苏子芋线 竹花根哪 还有 两包

1 2 6 | 5·6 11 :‖
面 哩 饼子哩咳。

（演唱：方金华、方道村，记谱：钟同荣）

卖布草△

1=D 2/4 瑞金·汉

（茶灯）

12 66 | 12 66 | 12 12 | 12 61 | 51 66 | 11 165 |
茶香妹哥 小心记呀 听俚茶哥 从头至尾 说你听哪 佬佬黄的是

156 | 12 666 | 61 3 | 12 155 | 156 ‖: 12 12 |
黄卡叽 兰兰色的是 士林布 花花朵朵的 花华叽 茶香妹妹

1 2 1 | 6 0 :‖
正哩合 意。

（演唱：方金华、方道村，记谱：钟同荣）

老黄茶△

1=D 2/4 3/4 瑞金·汉

（茶灯）

1 2 | 616 | 12 16 | 550 | 12 16 | 5 50 | 335 |
茶 香 哥哎 你呀听端 了哇， 我呀听端 了 哇， 名字

61 21 | 1 66 | 5 — | 335 | 61 21 |
叫 做 老 鸭 黄 茶 吃下 口 中

65 1 66 | 5 — ‖
就是 好 味 道 茶。

（演唱：方金华、方道村，记谱：钟同荣）

·78·

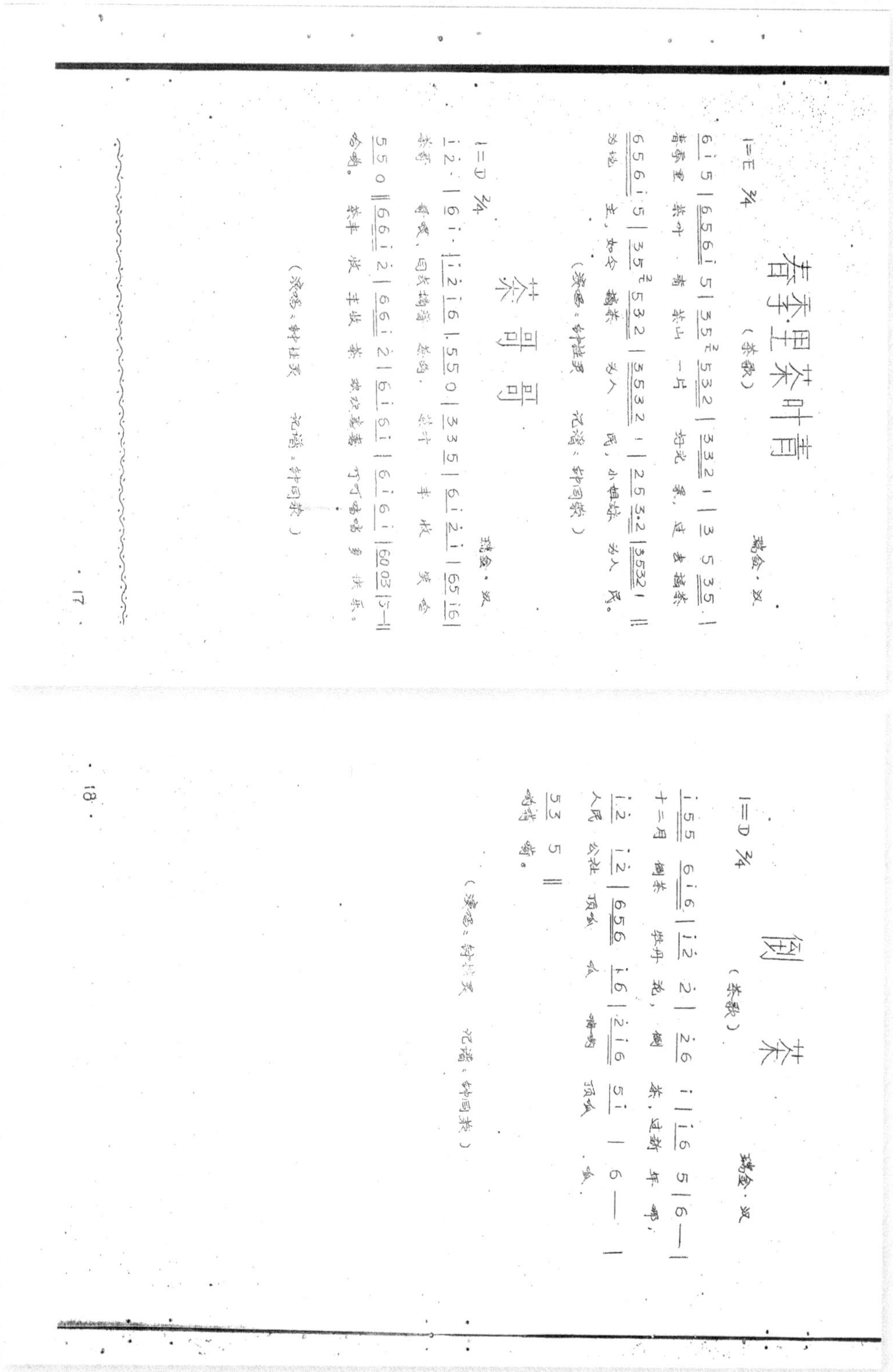

春季里茶叶青

（茶歌）

1=E 3/4　　瑞金·汉

6 i 5 | 656i 5 | 35² 532 | 332 1 | 3 5 35 . |
春季里 茶叶 青 茶山 一片 好光 景，过 去摘茶

656i 5 | 35² 532 | 3532 1 | 25 3.2 | 3532 1 ‖
为地 主，如今 摘茶 为人 民，小姐妹 为人 民。

（演唱：钟桂英　记谱：钟同荣）

茶哥哥

1=D 2/4　　瑞金·汉

i2· | 6i· | i2i6 | 550 | 335 | 6i2i | 65i6 |
茶哥 哥哦，同去摘着 茶哟， 茶叶 丰收 笑哈

550 ‖ 66i 2 | 66i 2 | 6i 5i | 6i 6i | 60 03 | 5— ‖
哈哟。 茶丰 收 丰收 茶 欢欢喜喜 丁丁咯咯 多 快乐。

（演唱：钟桂英　记谱：钟同荣）

· 17 ·

倒茶

（茶歌）

1=D 3/4　　瑞金·汉

i55 6i6 | i2 2 | 26 i | i6 5 | 6— |
十二月 倒茶 牡丹 花，倒 茶，过新 年 哪，

i2 i2 | 656 i6 | 2i6 5i | 6— |
人民 公社 顶呱 呱 嗬哟 顶呱 呱。

53 5 ‖
哟嗬 嗬。

（演唱：钟桂英　记谱：钟同荣）

· 18 ·

风俗歌

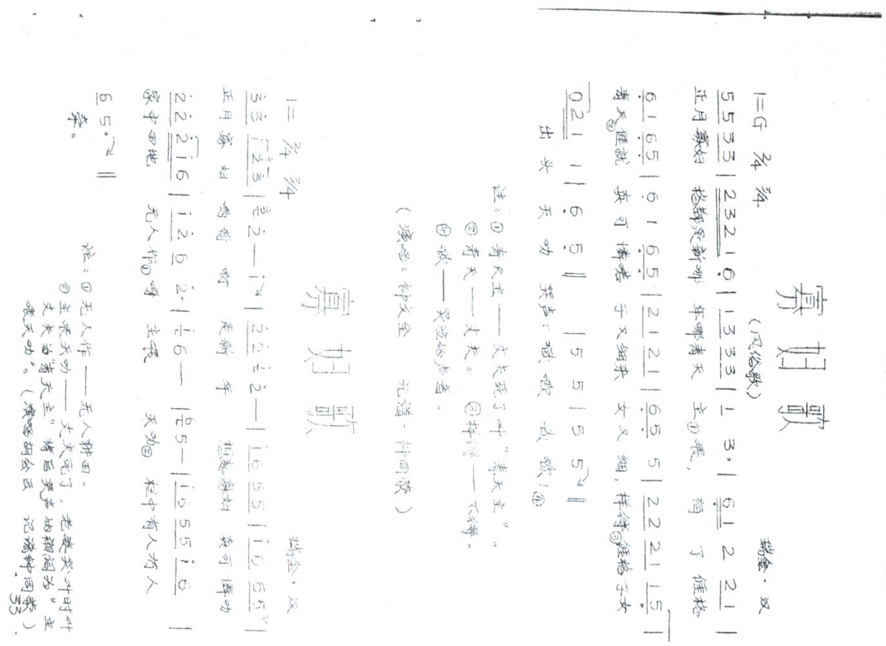

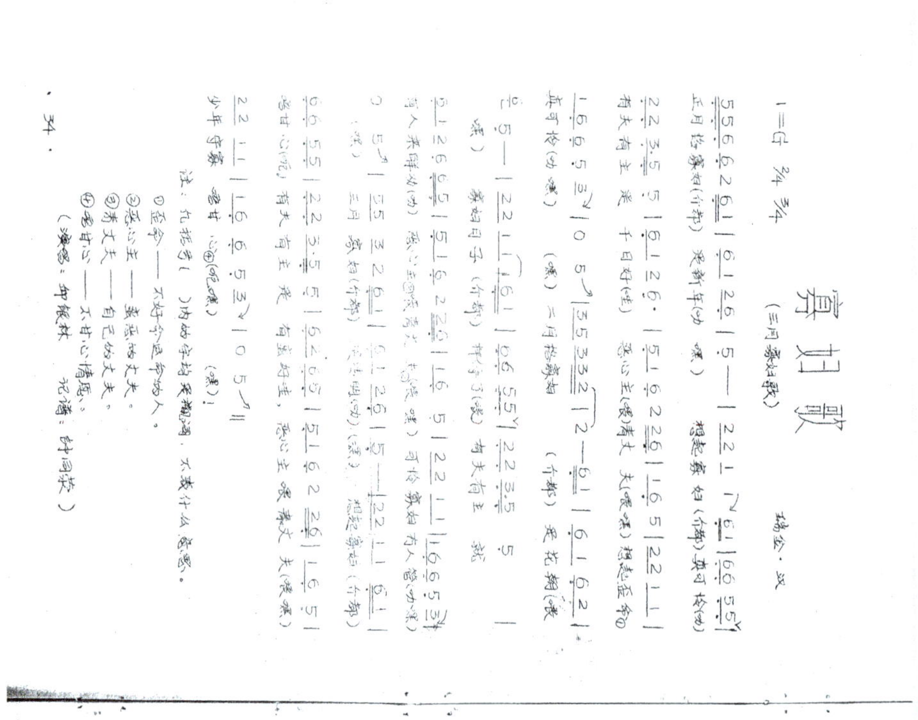

寡妇歌

（风俗歌）

1=G 2/4 3/4　　瑞金·汉

5 5 3 3 | 2 3 2 1 6 | 1 3 3 3 | 1 3· | 6 1 2 2 1 |
正月寡妇　格都是新哪　年哪青天　主①喂，　有　了　佳格

6 1 6 5 | 6 1 6 5 | 2 1 2 1 | 6 5 5 | 2 2 2 1 1 5 |
青天②佳就　真可怜嗟　子又细来　女又细，拌得③佳格子女

0 2 1 1 | 6 5 ‖ | 5 5 | 5 5 ‖
出头　天叻　哭声：哦欧　哦欧！④

注：①青天主——丈夫死了叫"青天主"。
②青天——丈夫。③拌得——不得。
④欧——哭泣的声音。

（演唱：钟文全　记谱：钟同荣）

寡妇歌

1= 2/4 3/4　　瑞金·汉

3 3 1 2 3 | 2 2 — 1 | 2 2 2 2 — | 1 6 5 5 | 1 6 6 5 |
正月寡妇　哟哥　啊　是新　年　想起寡妇　真可怜叻

2 2 2 1 6 | 1 2 6 2· | 1 6 — | 6 5 — | 1 6 5 5 1 6 |
家中田地　无人作①呀　主喂　天叻②　村中有人冇人

6 5· ‖
来。

注：①无人作——无人耕田。
②主喂天叻——丈夫死了，老婆哭叫时叫丈夫为"青天主"，背后哭声的衬词为"主喂天叻"。（演唱胡会云　记谱钟同荣）

·33·

寡妇歌

（三月寡妇歌）

1=G 2/4 3/4　　瑞金·汉

5 5 6 6 2 6 1 | 6 1 2 6 | 5 — | 2 2 1 1 6 1 | 6 6 5 5 |
正月格寡妇（介都）是新年（叻　嘿）　想起寡　妇（介都）真可　怜（叻）

2 2 3·5 5 | 6 1 2 6· | 5 1 6 2 2 6 | 1 6 5 | 2 2 1 1 |
有夫有主　是　千日好（哇）　恶心主（喂）青丈　夫（喂嘿）想起歪命①

1 6 6 5 3 | 0 5 | 3 5 3 3 2 | 2 — 6 1 | 6 1 6 2 |
真可怜（叻 嘿）　（嘿）二月格寡妇　（介都）是花朝（喂

5 — | 2 2 1 1 1 6 1 | 6 6 5 5 | 2 2 3·5 5 |
嘿）　寡妇日子（介都）拌停了（喂）有夫有主　就

6 1 2 6 6 5 | 5 1 6 2 2 6 | 1 6 5 | 2 2 1 1 | 1 6 6 5 3 |
有人来睬叻（叻）恶心主②喂青丈　夫③（喂 嘿）可怜寡妇 有人管（叻嘿）

0 5 | 5 5 3 2 6 1 | 6 1 2 6 | 5 — | 2 2 1 1 6 1 |
（嘿）　三月　寡妇（介都）　是清明（叻）（嘿）　想起寡妇（介都）

6 6 5 5 | 2 2 3·5 5 | 6 2 6 5 | 5 1 6 2 2 6 | 1 6 5 |
唔甘心（呢）有夫 有主 是　有蛮好生，恶心主 喂青丈　夫（喂嘿）

2 2 1 1 | 1 6 6 5 3 | 0 5 ‖
少年守寡　唔甘　心④（呢嘿）　（嘿）！

注：凡括号（　）内的字均是衬词，不表什么意思。
①歪命——不好命运命的人。
②恶心主——蛮恶的丈夫。
③青丈夫——自己的丈夫。
④唔甘心——不甘心情愿。
（演唱：钟银林　记谱：钟同荣）

·34·

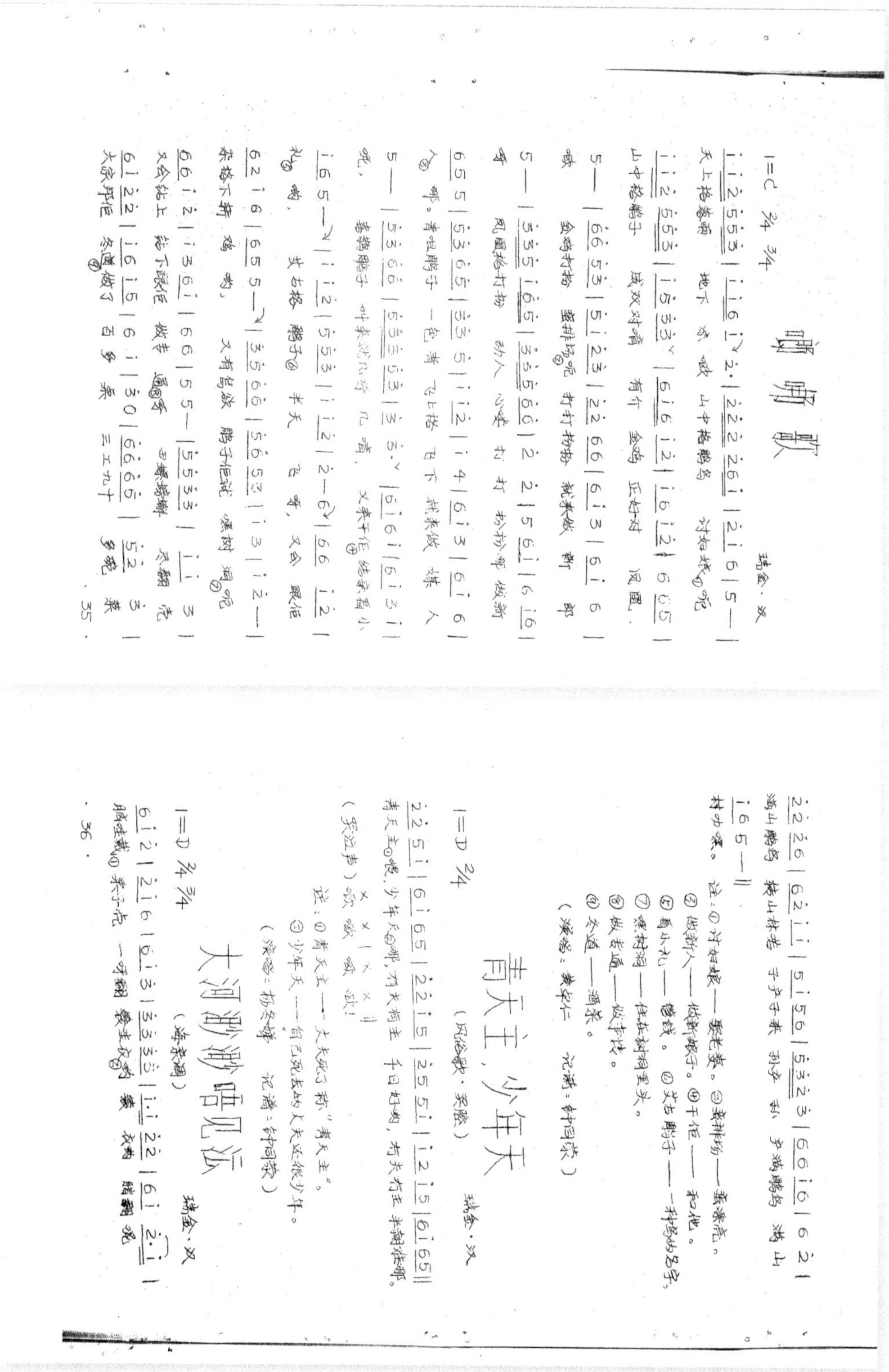

嘛嘛歌

1=C 2/4 3/4

瑞金·汉

1 1 2 5 5 3 | 1 1 6 1 2· | 2 2 2 2 6 1 | 2 1 6 | 5 — |
天上格落雨　地下　凉　啵　山中格鹏鸟　讨妇娘①呢

1 1 2 5 5 3 | 1 5 3 3 | 6 1 6 1 2 | 1 6 1 2 | 6 6 5 |
山中格鹏子　成双对嘀　有个　金鸡　正好对　凤凰，

5 — | 6 6 5 3 | 5 1 2 3 | 2 2 6 6 | 6 1 3 | 6 1 6 |
啵　金鸡打扮　蚕排场②呢　打打扮扮　就来做　新　郎

5 — | 3 3 5 1 6 5 | 3 3 5 6 6 | 2 2 | 5 6 1 | 6 1 6 |
呀　凤凰格打扮　动人　心喽　打　打　扮扮哪　做新

6 5 5 | 5 3 6 5 | 3 3 5 | 1 1 2 | 1 4 | 6 1 3 | 6 1 6 |
人③　哪。青咀鹏子　一色　青　飞上格　飞　下　就来做　媒　人

5 — | 5 3 6 6 | 5 3 3 5 3 | 3 3· | 6 1 6 1 | 6 1 3 1 |
呢，　喜鹊鹏子　叫来就几呀　几　嘀，　又来干佢④　结亲看小

1 6 5 — | 1 1 2 | 5 5 3 | 1 1 2 | 2 — 6 | 6 6 1 2 |
礼⑤　哟，　艾古格　鹏子⑥　半天　飞　呀，又会　跟佢

6 2 1 6 | 6 5 5 — | 3 5 6 6 | 5 6 5 3 | 1 3 | 1 2 — |
杂格下斩　鸡　哟，　又有乌欲　鹏子佢就　煨树　洞⑦呢

6 6 1 2 | 1 3 6 1 | 6 6 | 5 5 — | 5 5 3 3 | 1 1 3 |
又会钻上　钻下跟佢　做专　通⑧呀　田螺螃蟹　尽翻　壳

6 1 2 2 | 1 6 1 5 | 6 1 | 3 0 | 6 6 6 5 | 5 2 3 |
大家帮佢　冬道⑨做了　百　多　桌　三工九十　多碗　菜

·35·

2 2 2 6 | 6 2 1 1 | 5 1 5 6 | 5 3 2 3 | 6 6 1 6 | 6 2 |
满山鹏鸟　转山林巷　子孙子来　孙孙　孙　孙满鹏鸟　满　山

1 6 5 — ||
村动喋。

注：① 讨妇娘——娶老婆。② 蚕排场——蚕漂亮。
③ 做新人——做新娘子。④ 干佢——和他。
⑤ 看小礼——要钱。⑥ 艾古鹏子——一种鸟的名字。
⑦ 煨树洞——住在树洞里头。
⑧ 做专通——做事情。
⑨ 冬道——酒菜。

（演唱：黄卓仁　记谱：钟同荣）

青天主，少年天

1=D 2/4

（风俗歌·哭腔）

瑞金·汉

2 2 5 1 | 6 1 6 5 | 2 2 1 5 | 2 5 5 1 | 1 2 1 5 | 6 1 6 5 ||
青天主①喂，少年天②哪，有夫有主　千日好哟，有夫有主　半餬难哪。

X X | X X ||
（哭泣声）嗷　嗷　嗷　嗷！

注：① 青天主——丈夫死了称"青天主"。
② 少年天——自己死去的丈夫还很少年。

（演唱：杨冬娣　记谱：钟同荣）

大河渺渺唔见沄

1=D 2/4 3/4

（海棠调）

瑞金·汉

6 1 2 | 2 1 6 | 6 1 3 | 3 3 3 3 | 1·1 2 2 | 6 1 2·1 |
脑哇戴①　栗子壳　一呀翻　蓑生衣②的　蓑　衣的　脑翻　呢

·36·

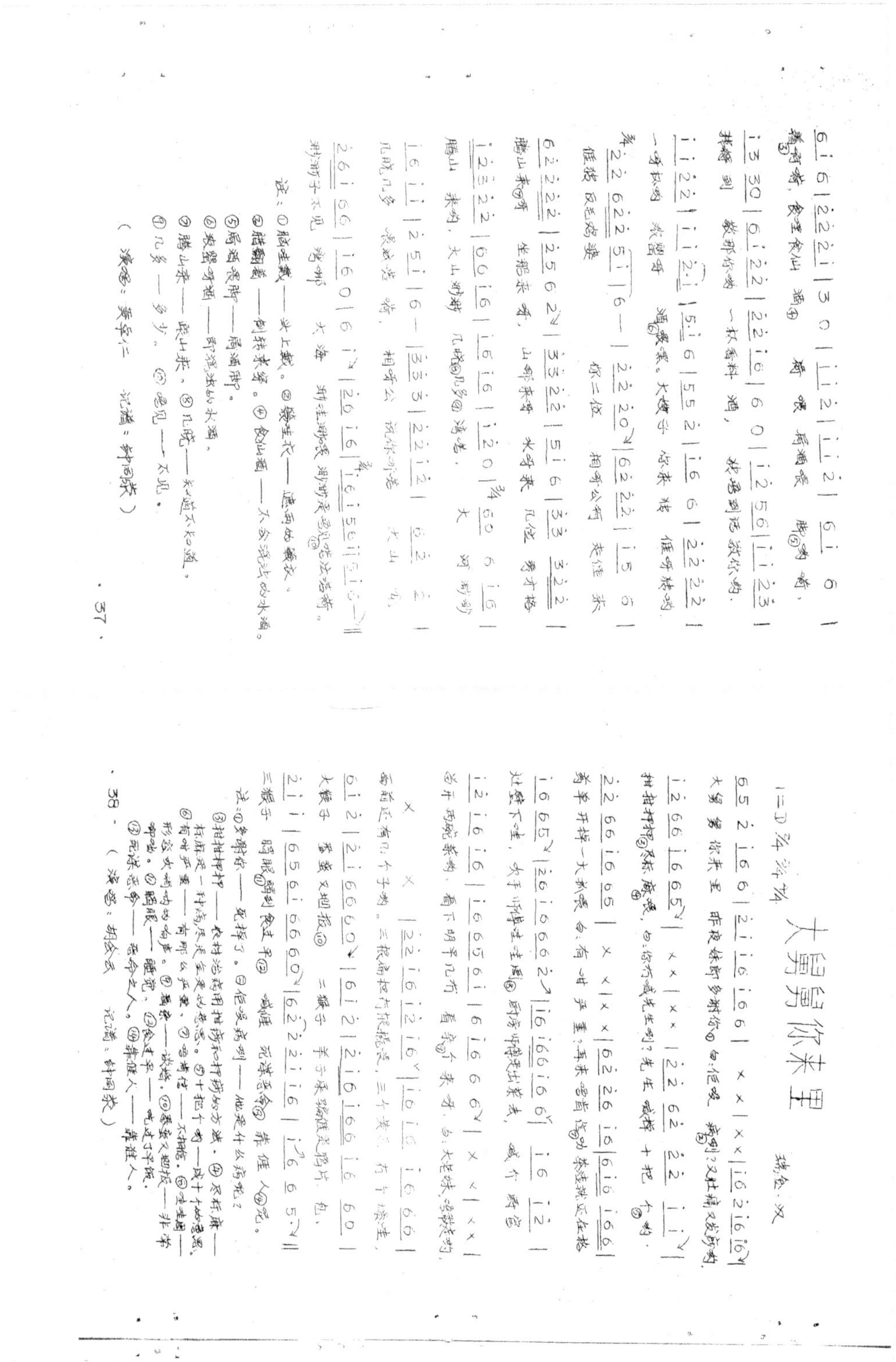

6 1 6 | 2 2 2 1 | 3 0 | 1 1 2 | 1 1 2 | 6 1 6 |
脑③哇戴，食哩食仙 酒④ 荷 喂 屙酒喂 脚⑤哟 荷。

1 3 30 | 6 1 2 2 | 2 2 1 6 | 6 0 | 1 2 5 6 | 1 1 2 3 |
拂倒 到 敬那你哟 一杯香料 酒， 被喝到话敬你哟。

1 1 2 2 | 1 1 2·1 | 5·1 6 | 5 5 2 | 1 6 6 | 2 2 2 2 |
一呀杯哟 浓嚣呀 酒⑥喂嘿。大嫂子 你来 装 佢呀装哟。

3/4 2 2 6 2 2 5 1 | 6 — | 2 2 2 0 | 6 2 2 2 | 1 5 6 |
佢装 反毛鸡婆 你二位 相呀公呵 走佢 来

6 2 2 2 2 2 | 2 5 6 2 | 3 3 2 2 | 5 1 6 | 3 3 3 2 2 |
腾山来⑦呀 坐船来 呀， 山哪来呀 水呀来 几位 秀才格

1 2 3 2 2 | 6 6 1 6 | 1 6 1 6 | 1 2 0 | 3/4 6 0 6 1 6 |
腾山 来哟，大山 渺渺 几晓⑧几多⑨ 湾哟。 大 河 渺渺

1 6 1 1 | 2 5 1 | 6 — | 3 3 3 | 2 2 1 2 | 6 2 2 |
几晓几多 喂喊哟 荷， 相呀公 说你听哟 大 山 哟

2 6 1 6 6 | 1 6 0 | 6 1 | 2 6 1 6 | 2/4 1 6 1 5 6 1 | 5 1 6 — ||
渺渺子不见 湾哪 大 海 渺哇渺喂 渺渺是唔见⑩哩法咯荷。

注：①脑哇戴——头上戴。②簑哇衣——遮雨的簑衣。
③腊翻着——倒转来穿。④食仙酒——不会混浊的水酒。
⑤屙酒喂脚——屙酒脚。
⑥浓嚣呀酒——即混浊的水酒。
⑦腾山来——跟山来。⑧几晓——知道不知道。
⑨几多——多少。⑩唔见——不见。

（演唱：黄卓仁　记谱：钟同荣）

· 37 ·

大舅舅你来里

1=D 2/4 3/4 4/4　　瑞金·双

6 5 2 1 6 6 | 2 1 1 6 1 6 6 | × × | × × | 1 6 2 1 6 1 6 |
大舅 舅 你来 里 昨夜妹郎多谢你① 白：佢哎 病咧②？又肚痛又发痧哟。

1 2 6 6 1 6 6 5 | × × | × × | 2 2 6 2 2 2 1 1 |
甜甜押押③尽标麻④喂， 白：你冇喊先生咧？先 生 喊掉 十 把 个⑤哟。

2 2 6 6 1 6 6 5 | × × | × × | 6 2 2 6 1 6 | 6 1 6 1 6 6 |
药单开掉一大抓喂 白：有 咁 严 重⑥？再来唔肯信⑦哟 茶渣就还在格

1 6 6 5 | 2 6 1 6 6 6 2 | 1 6 1 6 6 1 6 6 | 1 6 1 2 |
灶壁下哇，吹手师傅哇哇闹⑧ 厨房师傅是出菜去， 喊个 厨官

1 2 1 6 1 6 | 1 6 6 5 6 1 | 6 1 6 6 6 | × × | × × |
尚开 两碗菜哟，看下明早几冇 看亲⑨个 来 呀。白：大老妹，唔歉走哟，

× × | 2 2 1 6 1 2 1 6 | 1 6 1 6 1 6 6 6 |
面前还有几个子哟。三根扁担冇眼摇喂，三个 黄 ？ 冇 个 够哇，

6 1 2 | 2 1 6 6 6 0 | 6 1 2 | 2 1 6 1 6 6 1 6 6 0 |
大猴子 蚕蚕又坳扳⑩ 二猴子 羊子桑骗佢是鸦片 包，

2 1 1 | 6 5 6 1 6 6 6 0 | 6 2 2 2 1 1 6 | 1 6 6 5· ||
三猴子 瞓眼⑪瞓到食过平⑫ 喊佢 死谋恶命⑬ 靠佢 人⑭呢。

注：①多谢你——死掉了。②佢哎病咧——他是什么病呢？
③甜甜押押——农村治病用甜痧和押痧的方法。④尽标麻——标麻是一种病，尽是全是的意思。⑤十把个哟——成十个的意思。⑥有咁严重——有那么严重。⑦唔肯信——不相信。⑧哇哇闹——形容吹唢呐的响声。⑨看亲——谈婚。⑩蚕蚕又坳扳——非常啰唆。⑪瞓眼——睡觉。⑫食过平——吃过了平饭。⑬死谋恶命——恶命之人。⑭靠佢人——靠谁人。

· 38 ·　（演唱：胡会云　记谱：钟同荣）

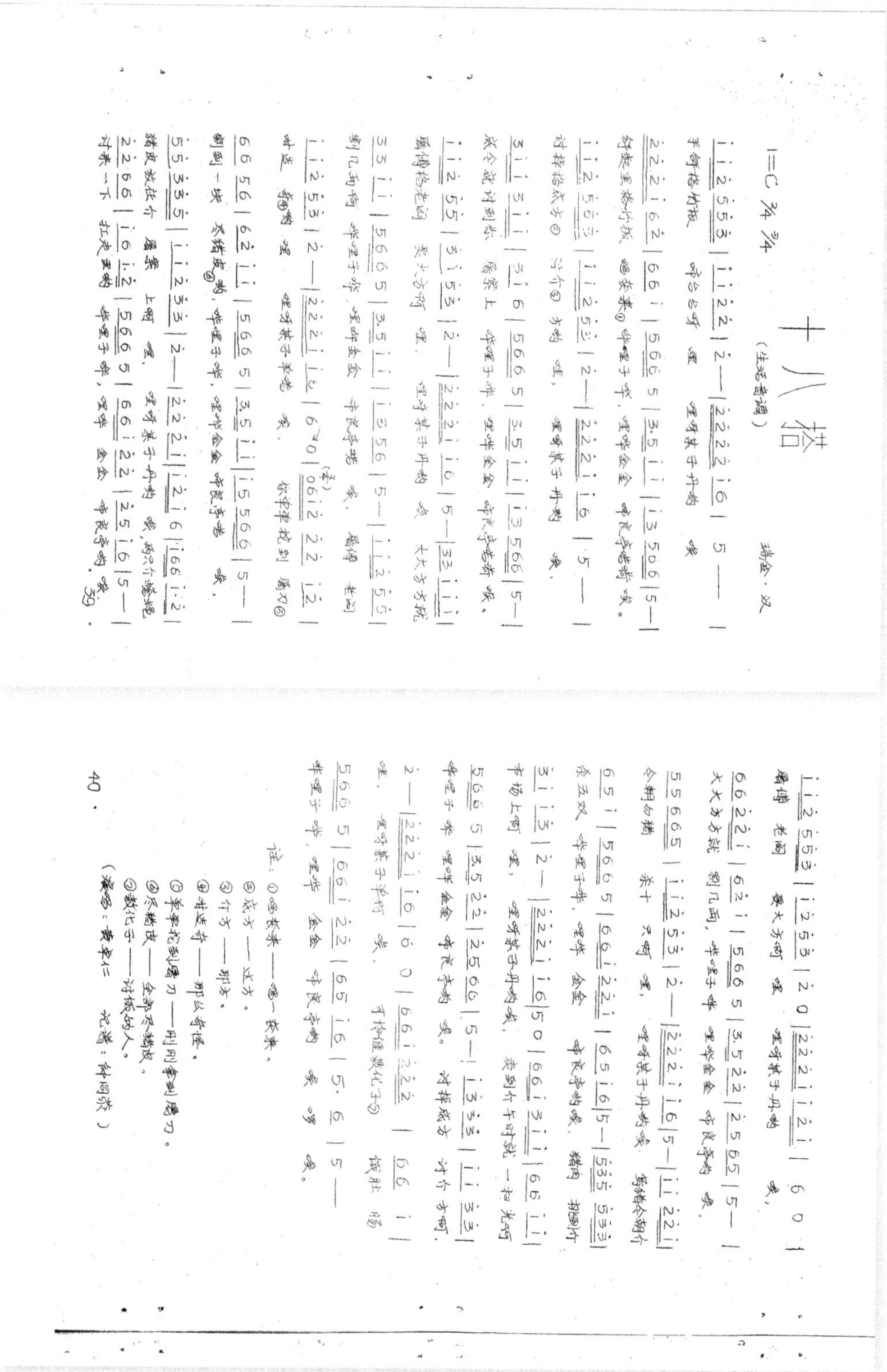

十八搭

（生活音调）

1=C 3/4 2/4　　　　瑞金·双

手钶格竹板　咘台台呀　哩　哩呀某子丹哟　唉
钶起里格竹板　唱套来① 哗哩子哗，哩哗金金　咘良亨咾嵜唉。
讨掉格底方② 讨介③ 方哟　哩，　哩呀某子丹哟　唉，
底令就讨到你　屠宗上　哗哩子哗，哩哗金金　咘良亨咾嵜唉。
屠傅格老阔　要大方阿　哩，　哩呀某子丹哟　唉　大大方方就
割几两阿　哗哩子哗　哩哗金金　咘良亨咾　唉，　屠傅　老阔
咁造　奇④哟　哩　哩呀某子单咾　唉，　你单单捉到　屠刀⑤
割到一块　尽猪皮⑥哟，哗哩子哗，哩哗金金　咘良亨咾　唉，
猪皮放在介　屠案　上啊　哩，　哩呀某子丹哟　唉，两只介蟾蜍
讨来一下　扛走里哟　哗哩子哗，哩哗　金金　咘良亨哟　唉。

39·

屠傅　老阔　要大方阿　哩　哩呀某子丹哟　唉，
大大方方就　割几两，哗哩子哗　哩哗金金　咘良亨哟　唉，
令朝白猪　杀十　只阿　哩，　哩呀某子丹哟唉　写猪令朝介
杀五双　哗哩子哗，哩哗　金金　咘良亨哟唉，猪肉　挑到介
市场上阿　哩，　哩呀某子丹哟唉，　卖到介午时就　一扫光阿
哗哩子　哗　哩哗金金　咘良亨哟　唉。　讨掉底方　讨介　方阿，
哩，　哩呀某子单阿　唉，　可怜佳数化子⑦　饿肚　肠
哗哩子哗，哩哗　金金　咘良亨哟　唉　啰　唉。

注：①唱套来——唱一套来。
②底方——这方。
③介方——那方。
④咁造奇——那么奇怪。
⑤单单捉到屠刀——刚刚拿到屠刀。
⑥尽猪皮——全部尽猪皮。
⑦数化子——讨饭的人。
（演唱：黄卓仁　　记谱：钟同荣）

40·

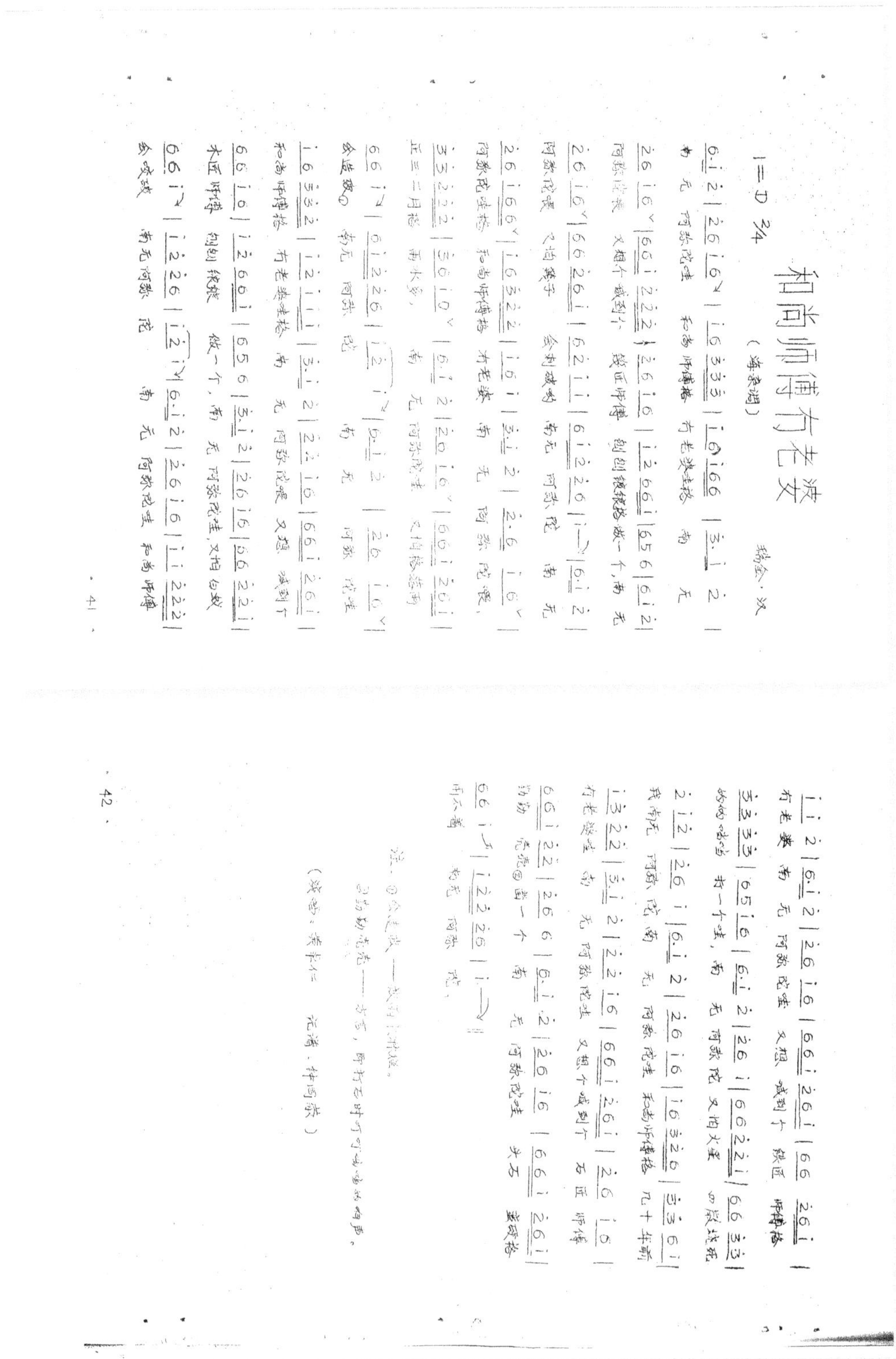

和尚师傅有老婆

1＝D 2/4

（海棠调）

瑞金·汉

6·1 2 | 26 16 | 16 333 | 16 166 | 3·1 2 |
南 无 阿弥陀哇 和尚师傅格 有老婆哇格 南 无

26 16 | 661 222 | 26 16 | 12 661 | 656 | 61 2 |
阿弥陀喂 又想个喊到个 篾匠师傅 刨刨锒锒格做一个，南 无

26 16 | 66 261 | 62 11 | 61 226 | 1— | 6·1 2 |
阿弥陀喂 又怕篾子 会刺破哟 南无 阿弥陀 南 无

26 166 | 16 322 | 16 1 | 3·1 2 | 2·6 16 |
阿弥陀哇格 和尚师傅格 有老婆 南 无 阿弥陀喂，

33 222 | 36 10 | 6·1 2 | 26 16 | 661 261 |
正三二月格 雨水多， 南 无 阿弥陀哇 又怕格落雨

66 1 | 61 226 | 12 1 | 6·1 2 | 26 16 |
会造破① 南无 阿弥 陀 南 无 阿弥 陀哇

16 332 | 12 111 | 3·1 2 | 22 16 | 661 261 |
和尚师傅格 有老婆哇格 南 无 阿弥陀喂 又想 喊到个

66 16 | 12 661 | 656 | 3·1 2 | 26 16 | 66 221 |
木匠师傅 刨刨锒锒 做一个，南 无 阿弥陀哇，又怕 白蚁

66 1 | 12 26 | 12 1 | 6·1 2 | 26 16 | 11 222 |
会咬破 南无阿弥 陀 南 无 阿弥陀哇 和尚师傅

11 2 | 6·1 2 | 26 16 | 661 261 | 66 261 |
有老婆 南 无 阿弥陀哇 又想 喊到个 铁匠 师傅格

3333 | 65 16 | 6·1 2 | 26 1 | 66 221 | 66 33 |
的的当当 打一个哇，南 无 阿弥陀 又怕火星 四散烧死

2 12 | 26 1 | 6·1 2 | 26 16 | 16 326 | 33 61 |
我南无 阿弥 陀 南 无 阿弥陀哇 和尚师傅格 几十年前

13 22 | 3·1 2 | 22 16 | 661 261 | 26 16 |
有老婆哇 南 无 阿弥陀哇 又想个喊到个 石匠 师傅

661 22 | 26 6 | 6·1 2 | 26 16 | 661 261 |
勤勤 壳壳② 凿一个 南 无 阿弥陀哇 头石 凿破格

66 1 | 122 26 | 1— ‖
雨不着 南无 阿弥 陀。

注：①会造破——[illegible]。

②勤勤壳壳——方言，即打石时叮叮当当的响声。

（演唱：黄东仁　记谱：钟同荣）

十八摸

演唱：刘承燧
记谱：钟同荣

1=D 2/4 3/4

伸手 呀重格 摸子 在 姐姐 小发 边哪，
姐姐 小发 放亮光，阵阵桂花 香 小 情 哥
做什 么 只准你 看来 不 准 摸，我 偏要格看来
偏 要 摸。

五姑姐、五姑娘

（巫见公、破胎歌）

演唱：赖光才
记谱：钟同荣

1=G 2/4 3/4

五姑 姐呀 五姑 娘 日晨 梳胸 梳个灵 盘龙
髻， 夜夜 请你 哟 姐 呀 五姑 姐
五姑 娘 夜夜 请你 上厅 嘤 堂 啊，五姑 姐
五姑 娘 今日 请你 到底来 食味 滚播 茶，

· 61 ·

五姑 姐 五姑 娘呀 哪呢 打嗷，今日 请你
到底来 食味呀 滚播 哟 茶 哟 嘅！
肮下介 泡泡 衣哟，又见介 五姑姐 五姑 娘呀
汗淋 淋 啦嘿 里 哟。

注：巫见公——一种信仰佛教的迷信者。
破胎歌——农村有一些三、五岁的小孩，面黄肌瘦多病痛，说是因为有怀孕的女人抱过了他，因此要退巫见公来烧香敬神，（破掉那女人的胎），小孩才健康，敬神烧香时唱的歌叫破胎歌。
介——那个。

叮咯啷叮咯

（向神要、盘花）

演唱：赖光才
记谱：钟同荣

1=E 2/4 3/4

叮咯 哪叮 咯 呵， 哪咯 叮哪 咯 呵，
花树 好 蜜 林 呀， 金条 子阿介 银梗 子 呀，

· 62 ·

花树 叮咯 桃花 百花 叮咯 花头 叮咯 养只 咯。

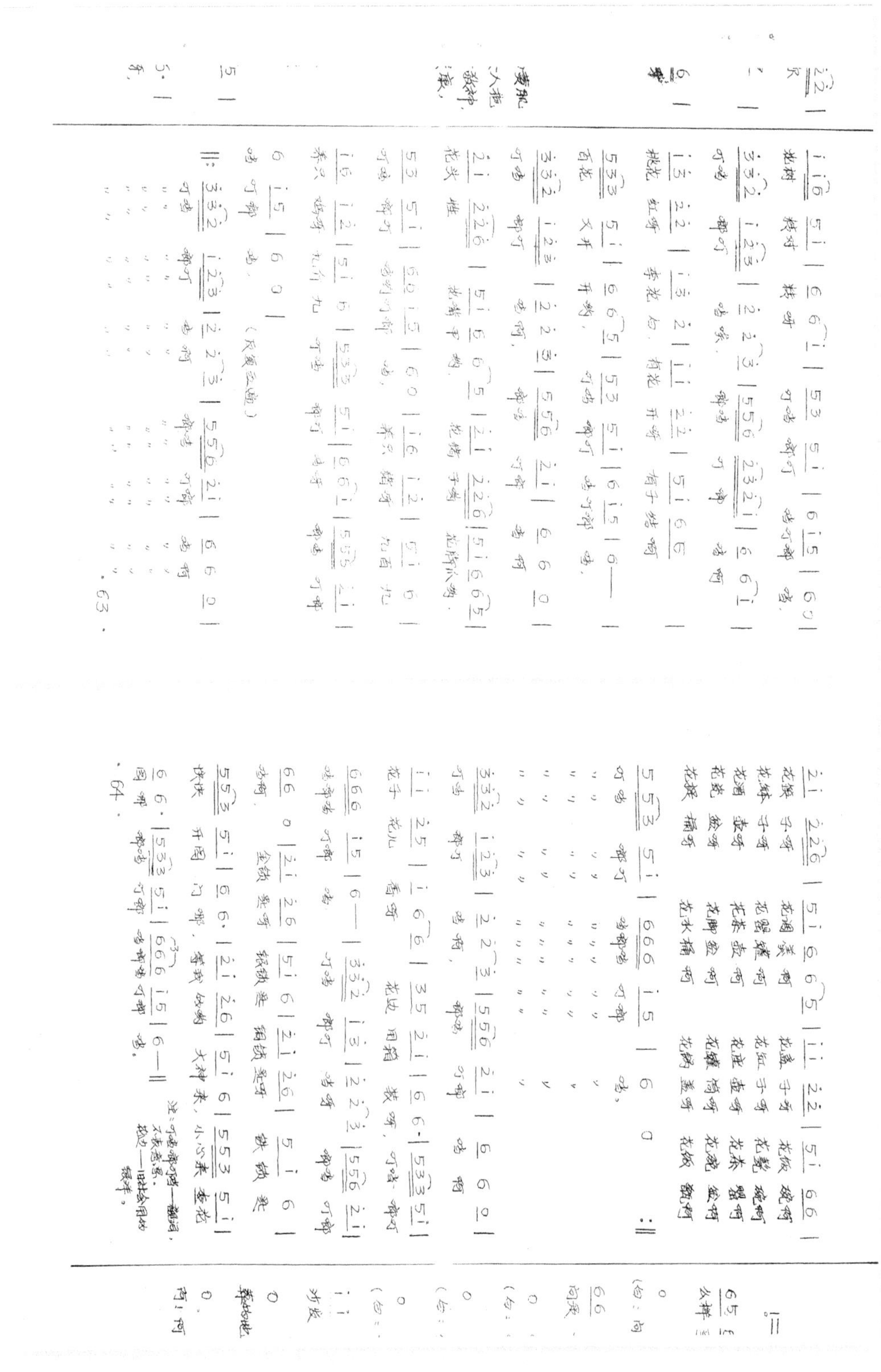

i i6 5i | 6 6 i | 53 5i | 6 i5 | 6 0 |
花树 转对 转呀 叮咚 啷叮 咚叮啷 咚。

332 i23 | 2 2 3 | 556 2321 | 6 6 i |
叮咚 啷叮 咚咳， 啷咚 叮 啷 咚 呵

i3 22 | i3 2 | ii 22 | 5i 66 |
桃花 红呀 李花 白， 有花 开呀 有子 结 呵

533 5i | 6 6 5 | 53 5i | 6 i5 | 6— |
百花 又开 开哟， 叮咚 啷叮 咚叮啷 咚。

332 i23 | 2 2 3 | 556 2i | 6 6 0 |
叮咚 啷叮 咚 呵， 啷咚 叮啷 咚 呵

2i 226 | 5i 6 6 5 | 2i 226 | 5i 665 |
花头 牲 花背 甲 哟， 花猪 子哟 花脚爪哟。

53 5i | 66 i5 | 6 0 | i6 i2 | 5i 6 |
叮咚 啷叮 咚咚叮啷 咚， 养只 猪呀 九百 九

i6 i2 | 5i 6 | 533 5i | 6 6 i | 555 2i |
养只 鸡呀 九百 九 叮咚 啷叮 咚呀 啷咚 叮啷

6 i5 | 6 0 |
咚 叮啷 咚。 （反复三遍）

||: 332 i23 | 2 2 3 | 556 2i | 6 6 0 |
叮咚 啷叮 咚 呵 啷咚 叮啷 咚 呵
〃 〃 〃 〃 〃 〃 〃 〃
〃 〃 〃 〃 〃 〃 〃 〃
〃 〃 〃 〃 〃 〃 〃 〃
〃 〃 〃 〃 〃 〃 〃 〃

·63·

2i 226 | 5i 6 6 5 | ii 22 | 5i 66 |
花铁 子呀 花调 羹 呵 花盏 子呀 花饭 碗呵
花钵 子呀 花罂 罐 呵 花缸 子呀 花鼓 碗呵
花酒 壶呀 花茶 壶 呵 花座 壶呀 花茶 罂呵
花瓷 盆呀 花脚 盆 呵 花罐 筒呀 花碗 盆呵
花提 桶呀 花水 桶 呵 花锅 盖呀 花饭 甑呵

553 5i | 666 i5 | 6 0 :||
叮咚 啷叮 咚啷咚 叮啷 咚。
〃 〃 〃 〃 〃 〃 〃 〃 〃
〃 〃 〃 〃 〃 〃 〃 〃 〃
〃 〃 〃 〃 〃 〃 〃 〃 〃
〃 〃 〃 〃 〃 〃 〃 〃 〃

332 i23 | 2 2 3 | 556 2i | 6 6 0 |
叮咚 啷叮 咚 呵， 啷咚 叮啷 咚 呵

ii 25 | i 6 6 | 35 2i | 6 6· | 5333 5i |
花子 花儿 香呀 花边 用箱 装呀， 叮咚 啷叮

666 i5 | 6— | 332 i3 | 2 2 3 | 556 2i |
咚啷咚 叮啷 咚 叮咚 啷叮 咚呀 啷咚 叮啷

66 0 | 2i 26 | 5i 6 | 2i 26 | 5 i 6 |
咚呵， 金锁 匙呀 银锁 匙 铜锁 匙呀 铁 锁 匙

553 5i | 6 6· | 2i 26 | 5i 6 | 553 5i |
快快 开困 门 哪， 等我 娘哟 大神 来， 小心 来 查花

6 6· | 533 5i | 666 i5 | 6— ||
困 哪 啷咚 叮啷 咚啷咚叮啷 咚。

注：叮咚啷叮咚——衬词，不表意思。
花边——旧社会用的银洋。

·64·

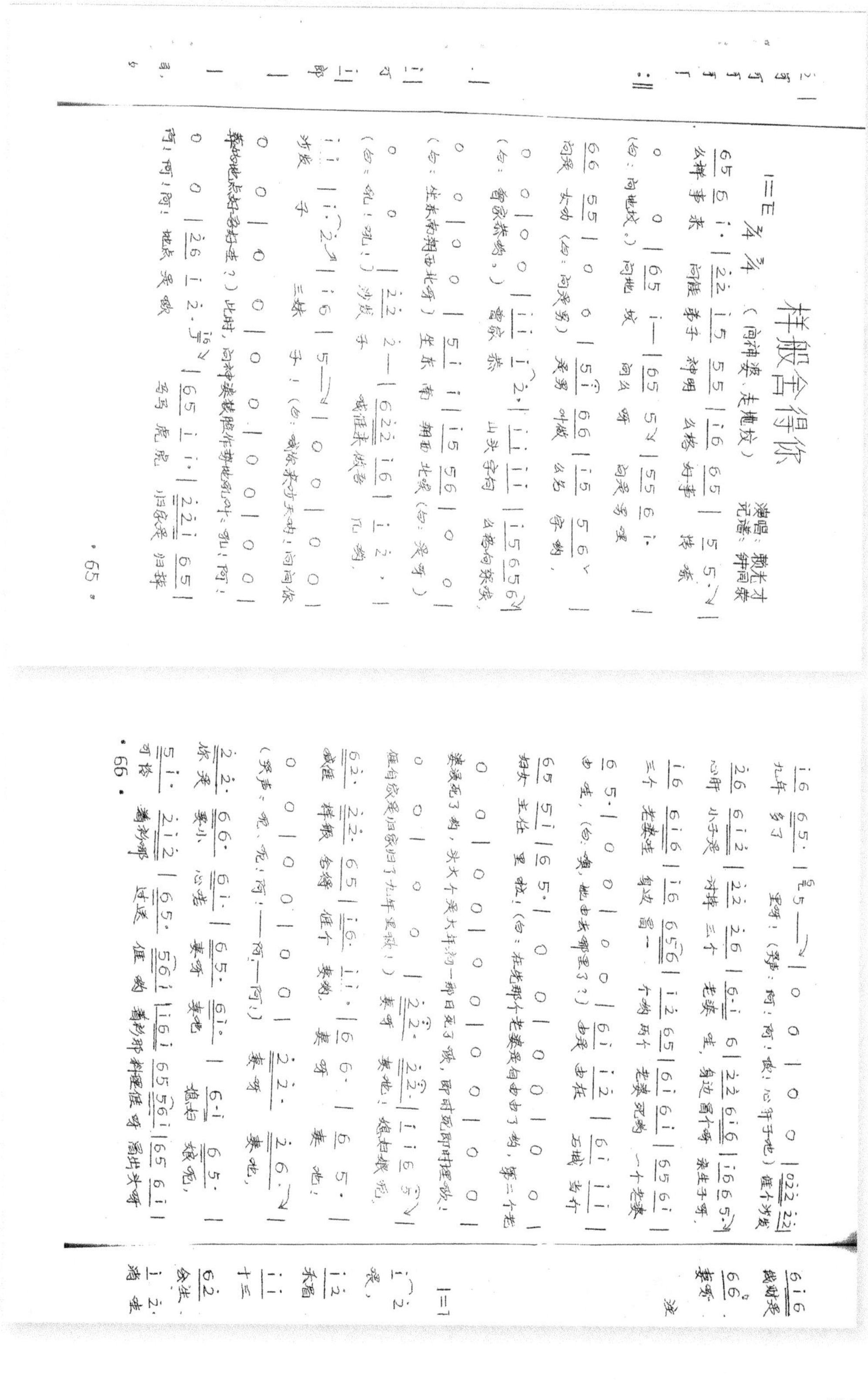

样般舍得你

1=E 2/4 3/4（向神婆、走地坟）

演唱：赖光才
记谱：钟同荣

么样事来 问佢弟子 神明 么格好事 传嗦
（白：向地坟。）向地 坟 向么 呀 向癸 另 哩
向癸 女功（白：向癸男）癸男 叫做 么名 字哟，
（白：曾家恭哟。）曾家 恭 山头字句 么格向系埃，
（白：坐东南朝西北呀）坐东 南 朝西 北埃（白：癸呀）
（白：吼！吼！）沙发 子 喊佢来做吾 几 哟。
沙发 子 三妹 子！（白：喊你来办天哟！向问你
葬的地点好吾好走？）此时，向神婆装腔作势地乱叫：吼！阿！
阿！阿！阿！地点 癸 欧 马马 虎虎 归家癸 归摔

·65·

九年 多了 里呀！（哭声：阿！阿！欸！心肝子吔）佢个沙发
心肝 小子癸 讨摔 三个 老婆 生，身边 冒个呀 亲生子呀，
三个 老婆生 身边 冒一 个哟 两个 老婆 死哟 一个老婆
由 生，（白：噢，她由去哪里了？）由癸 由在 石城 当斤
妇女 主任 里 啦！（白：在先那个老婆是自由由了哟，第二个老
婆浸死了哟，头大个癸大年初一那日死了咳，即时死即时埋欧！
佢自家癸归家归了九年里欧！）妻呀 妻吔！媳妇娘 死，
喊佢 样般 舍得 佢个 妻哟， 妻 呀 妻 吔！
（哭声：呢、呢！阿！——阿，——阿！）妻 呀 妻吔，
你 癸 要小 心些 妻呀 妻吔 媳妇 娘呢，
可 怜 着衫哪 过送 佢 哟 着衫那 料理佢 呀 冒出头呀

·66·

6 1 6 1 6 | 6 1· 6 5 | 6 2 2 1· | 6 1 1 6 5 2 1· |
钱财丢 医掉 里哟，可怜 着衫 衣哟， 着衫 过送佢哟，

6 6 6 5· ||
妻呀 妻 也！

注：问地坟——即问问神婆问家里葬人安葬的地点好不好。
么——什么。　　讨掉——娶了。
向架——方向。　　冒个——没有一个。
做哥几——做什么。　　由——自由结婚。
讨天——谈天。　　样般——怎样。
归家——死了。　　着衫——穿衣服。
佢个——我的。　　过送——照顾、护理。

海亲哥哥开门喽

1=E　　　　演唱：赖光才
渐弹　（十七、八扯）　　记谱：钟同发

1 2 | 1 2 2 2 | 1 1 2 2 2 2 1 | 2 — |
喂，　海亲 哥 喂，　九只 鸡子 佢都滴 生，

1 2 2 1 | 6 1 6 6 | 1 2 2 1 | 6 1 1 2· | 6 5· |
禾眉 鸡子 会上树树 禾眉 鹅子 会上天欧 欧……

1 1 2 2 | 1 2 2 | 1 6 1 5 1 | 2 1 2 2 1 |
十三 岁的 娓子 欧 都会 生子欧 十三两 鸡子

6 2 6 1· | 1 2· | 2 1 6 1 2 | 1 2 2 1 | 6 6 1 |
会生 蛋欧， 鸡 生， 佢九只 鸡子 崖婆 吊走 一只 啊

1 2· | 1 6 6 1 | 1 6 1 2· | 1 6 6 6 6 | 2 6 6 |
鸡 生！ 送掉 一只 给外 婆欧 全部 只数到 哦七只

· 67 ·

2 2· | 0 0 | 0 0 | 0 0 | 1 2 2 |
里 欧（白：观呀，你九只鸡子，崖婆吊走一只，佢掉 欧，还送了一只给外婆，现在总有八只了欧！）

6 6 1 2 | 2 — | 0 0 | 0 0 | 0 0 |
七只 鸡子 欧（白：崖婆吊走一只，还送了一只给外婆！）

2 6 6 6 1 | 2 6 6 1· | 2 — | 1 2 2 2· |
佢自 家还有 十一 只 欧， 喂， 海亲 哥 喂，

2 2 6 2 | 2 2· | 1 2 2 2· | 1 2 2 1 2 2 |
你有 个公 平 欧， 海亲 哥 哥， 今日里 麻烦你

2 1 2 1· | 6 1 2 | 1 2 6 1 2 | 2 1· |
开门 啰 嗬， 慢且 欧 枕头 冒寻到 欧，

1 2 2 2· | 1 2 2 1 2 | 2 1· | 6 1 2 | 2 6 1 6 |
海亲 哥 哥， 麻烦你 开门 啰 嗬， 慢且欧， 衫裤 冒脱

6 1· | 1 2 2 2· | 1 2 2 1 2 | 2 1· | 2 1 1 6 |
掉 欧， 海亲 哥 哥 麻烦你 开门 啰 嗬， 被窝 冒 背

1 2· | 1 2 2 2· | 1 2 2 2 1 | 2 1· || 0 0 ||
烧 欧， 海亲 哥 哥， 麻烦你 开门 啰 嗬，(打呼噜：呜，嗬！)

1 2 2 2· | 1 2 2 2 1 | 2 1· | 0 0 | 0 0 |
海亲 哥 哥， 麻烦 你 开门 啰 嗬！(狗叫：汪，喔喔喔喔！

0 0 | 1 2 2 2· | 1 2 2 2 1 | 2 1· | 0 0 |
喔 喔！ 海亲 哥 哥， 麻烦你 开门 啰 嗬，(打呼噜：呜，嗬！)

1 2 2 2· | 1 2 2 2 1 | 2 1 | 0 0 | 0 0 |
海亲 哥 哥， 麻烦你 开门 啰 嗬，(公鸡报晓：欧欧欧！欧！

· 68 ·

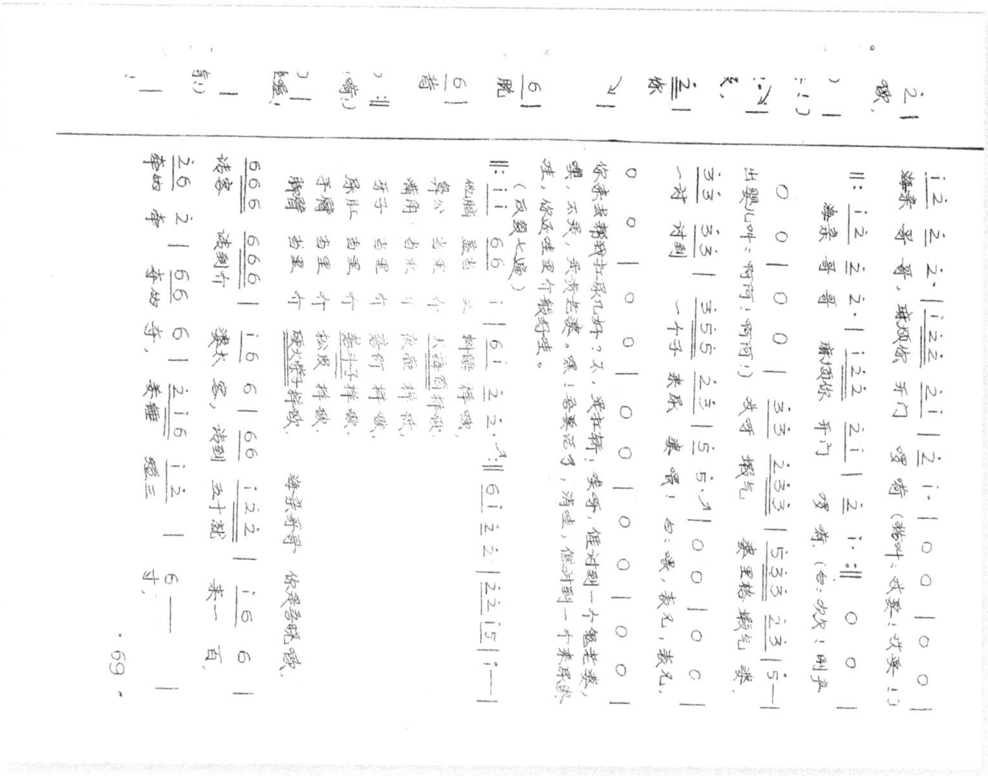

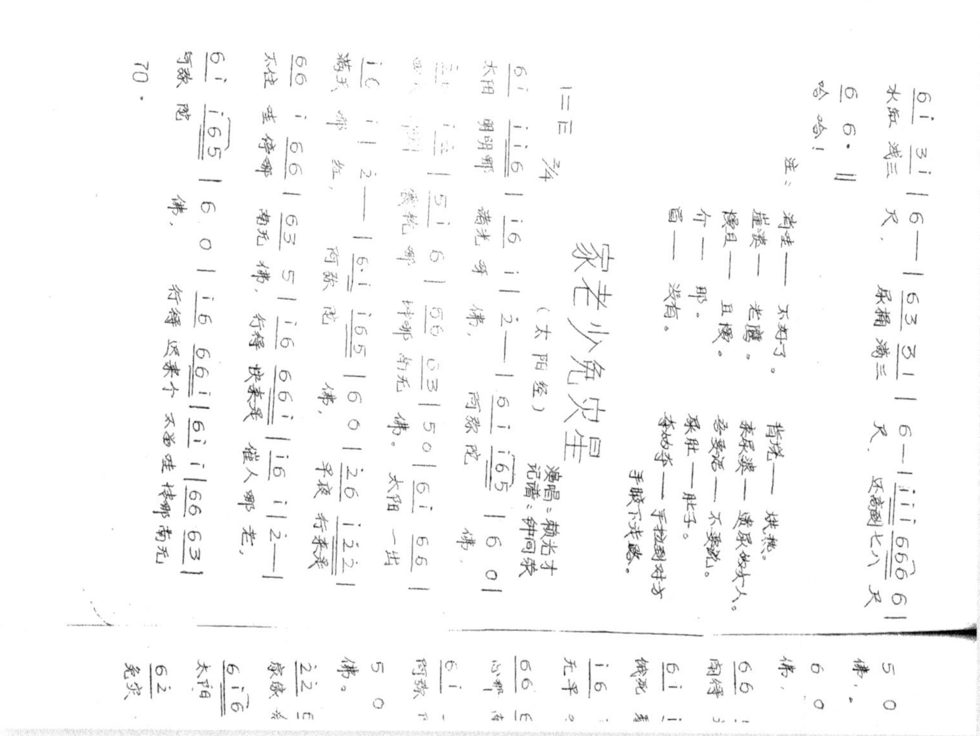

i2 2 2· | i22 2i | 2 i· | 0 0 | 0 0 |
海亲哥哥，麻烦你 开门 啰 嗬（猪叫：哎要！哎要！）

‖: i2 2 2· | i22 2i | 2 i· :‖ 0 0 |
海亲哥哥 麻烦你 开门 啰 嗬，（白：哎哎！刚产

0 0 | 0 0 | 33 233 | 533 23 | 5— |
出婴儿叫：阿阿！阿阿！）哎呀 蝦气 娄里格 蝦气 娄，

33 33 | 355 23 | 5 5· | 0 0 | 0 0 |
一讨 讨到 一个子 来尿 娄 喂！白：喂，表兄，表兄，

0 0 | 0 0 | 0 0 | 0 0 | 0 0 |
你来去帮我扛尿几好？不，是扛轿！哎呀，佢讨到一个鬼老婆，噢，不是，是贵老婆。黑！吾要活了，消哇，佢讨到一个来尿婆哇，你还哇里介般好哇。

（反复七遍）
‖: ii 66 i | 6i 2 2· :‖ 6i 2 2 | 22 i5 | i— |
脑腩 盖当 介 料箩 样哦，
鼻公 当里 介 大海筒样哦，
嘴角 当里 介 敢盆 样哦，
牙子 当里 介 簕竹 样哦，
尿肚 当里 介 盖斗子样哦，
手臂 当里 介 松皮 样哦，
脚臂 当里 介 硬火柴子样哦， 海亲哥哥 你是吾晓哦，

666 666 | i6 6 | 66 i22 | i6 6 |
诗客 诗到介 凄太 客，诗到 五十就 来一 百，

26 2 | 66 6 | 2i6 i2 | 6— |
牵奶 牵 夺奶 夺，姜锤 短三 寸，

· 69 ·

6i 3i | 6— | 63 31 | 6— | iii 666 6 |
水缸 浅三 尺， 尿桶 满三 尺， 还高到七八 尺

6 6· ‖
哈 哈！

注：消哇—— 不好了。 背烧—— 烘热。
崖婆—— 老鹰。 来尿婆—— 遗尿的女人。
懪且—— 且慢。 吾要活—— 不要讲。
介—— 那。 尿肚—— 肚子。
冇—— 没有。 牵奶牵—— 手拉到对方手腋下走路。

家老少免灾星
（太阳经）
演唱：赖光才
记谱：钟同荣

1=E 2/4
6i ii6 | i6 i | 2— | 6i i65 | 6 0 |
太阳 明明哪 诸光 呀 佛， 阿弥 陀 佛，

[illegible] | 5i 6 | 56 63 | 5 0 | 6i 66 |
[illegible] 霞轮 哪 坤哪 南无 佛。 太阳 一出

i6 i | 2— | 6·i i65 | 6 0 | 26 i22 |
满天 哪 红， 阿弥 陀 佛， 平夜 行来是

66 i 66 | 63 5 | i6 66i | i6 i | 2— |
不住 哇 停哪 南无 佛， 行得 快来是 催人 哪 老，

6i i65 | 6 0 | i6 66i | 6i i | 66 63 |
阿弥 陀 佛， 行得 迟来个 不当 哇 传哪 南无

70 ·

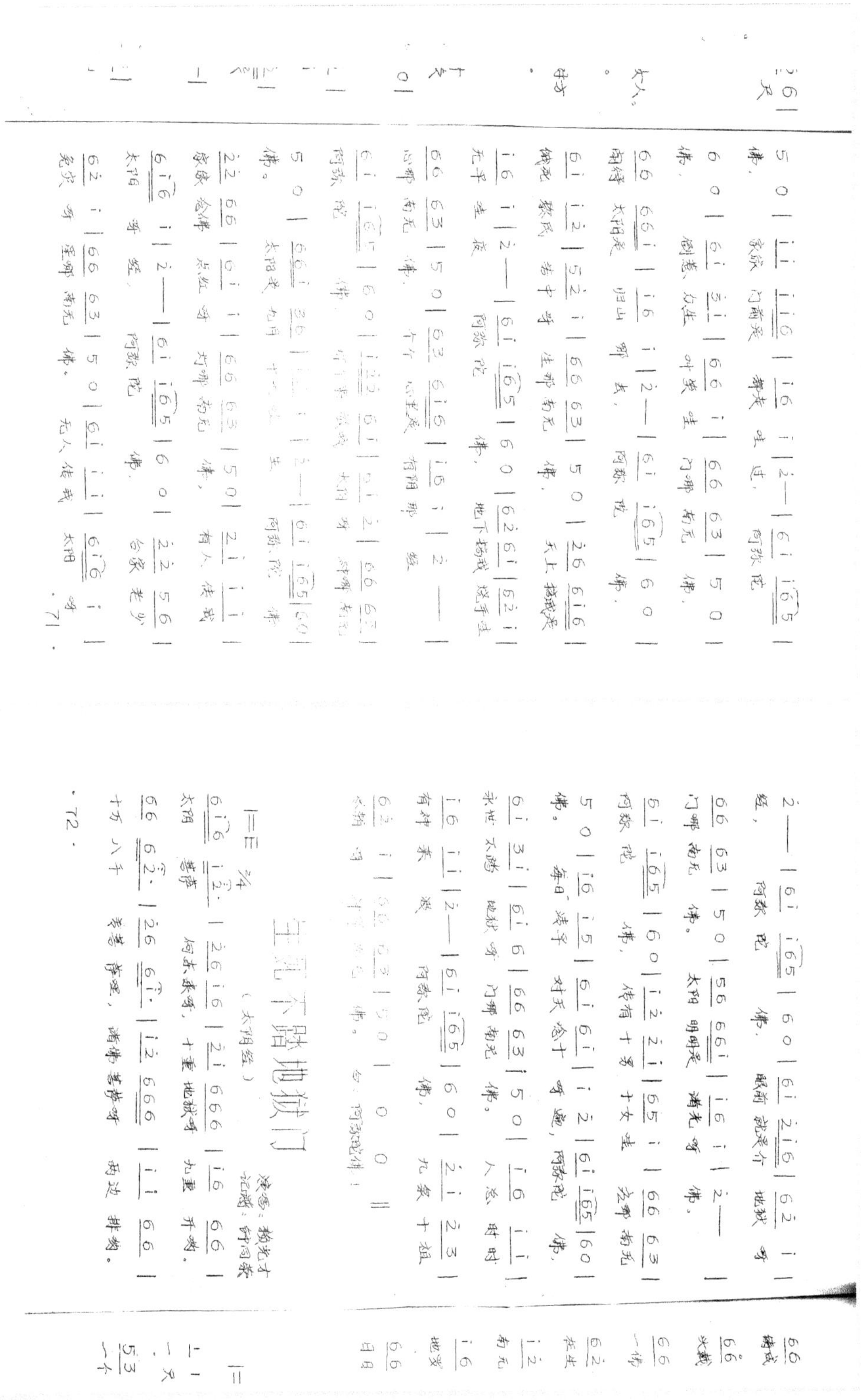

5 0 | i i i i 6 | i 6 i | 2 — | 6 i i 6 5 |
佛，家家 门前是 都来 吐 过，阿弥 陀

6 0 | 6 i 3 i | 6 6 i | 6 6 6 3 | 5 0 |
佛，倒惹、众生 叶 笑 哇 门哪 南无 佛。

6 6 6 6 i | i 6 i | 2 — | 6 i i 6 5 | 6 0 |
南镑 太阳是 归山 哪 去，阿弥 陀 佛。

6 i i 2 | 5 2 i | 6 6 6 3 | 5 0 | 2 6 6 i 6 |
饿死 黎民 苦中 呀 生哪 南无 佛。天上 搞我是

i 6 i | 2 — | 6 i i 6 5 | 6 0 | 6 2 6 i | 6 2 i |
无乎 哇 夜 阿弥 陀 佛，地下 搞我 烧手哇

6 6 6 3 | 5 0 | 6 3 6 i 6 | i 6 i | 2 — |
心哪 南无 佛。个个 心里是 有阴 那 经

6 i i 6 5 | 6 0 | i 2 2 6 i | 6 i 2 | 6 6 6 3 |
阿弥 陀 佛。[illegible] 太阳 呀 [illegible]哪 南无

5 0 | 6 6 i 3 6 | [illegible] i | 2 — | 6 i i 6 5 | 6 0 |
佛。太阳是 九月 十[illegible] 生 阿弥 陀 佛

2 2 6 6 | 6 i i | 6 6 6 3 | 5 0 | 2 i i i |
家家 念佛 点红 呀 灯哪 南无 佛，有人 传我

6 i 6 i | 2 — | 6 i i 6 5 | 6 0 | 2 2 5 6 |
太阳 呀 经，阿弥 陀 佛。合家 老少

6 2 i | 6 6 6 3 | 5 0 | 6 i i i | 6 i 6 i |
免灾 呀 星哪 南无 佛。无人 传我 太阳 呀

·71·

2 — | 6 i i 6 5 | 6 0 | 6 i 2 i 6 | 6 2 i |
经，阿弥 陀 佛。眼前 就是个 地狱 呀

6 6 6 3 | 5 0 | 5 6 6 6 i | i 6 i | 2 — |
门哪 南无 佛。太阳 明明是 诸光 呀 佛，

6 i i 6 5 | 6 0 | i 2 2 i | 6 5 i | 6 6 6 3 |
阿弥 陀 佛，传有 十男 十女 哇 [illegible]哪 南无

5 0 | i 6 i 5 | 6 i 6 i | i 2 | 6 i i 6 5 | 6 0 |
佛。每日 烧香 对天 念十 呀 遍，阿弥陀 佛，

6 i 3 i | 6 i 6 | 6 6 6 3 | 5 0 | i 6 i i |
永世 不踏 地狱 呀 门哪 南无 佛。人念 时时

i 6 i i | 2 — | 6 i i 6 5 | 6 0 | 2 i 2 3 |
有神 来 救 阿弥陀 佛，九条 十祖

6 2 i | 6 6 6 3 | 5 0 | 0 0 ‖
[illegible] 呀 [illegible] 佛。合：阿弥陀佛！

·72·

生死不踏地狱门

（太阳经）

演唱：赖光才
记谱：钟同荣

1=E 3/4

6 i 6 i 2· | 2 6 i 6 | 2 i 6 6 6 | i 6 6 6 |
太阳 菩萨 向东 来呀，十重 地狱呀 九重 开哟。

6 6 6 2· | 2 6 6 i· | i 2 6 6 6 | i i 6 6 |
十方 八千 菩萨 萨哩，诸佛 菩萨呀 两边 排哟。

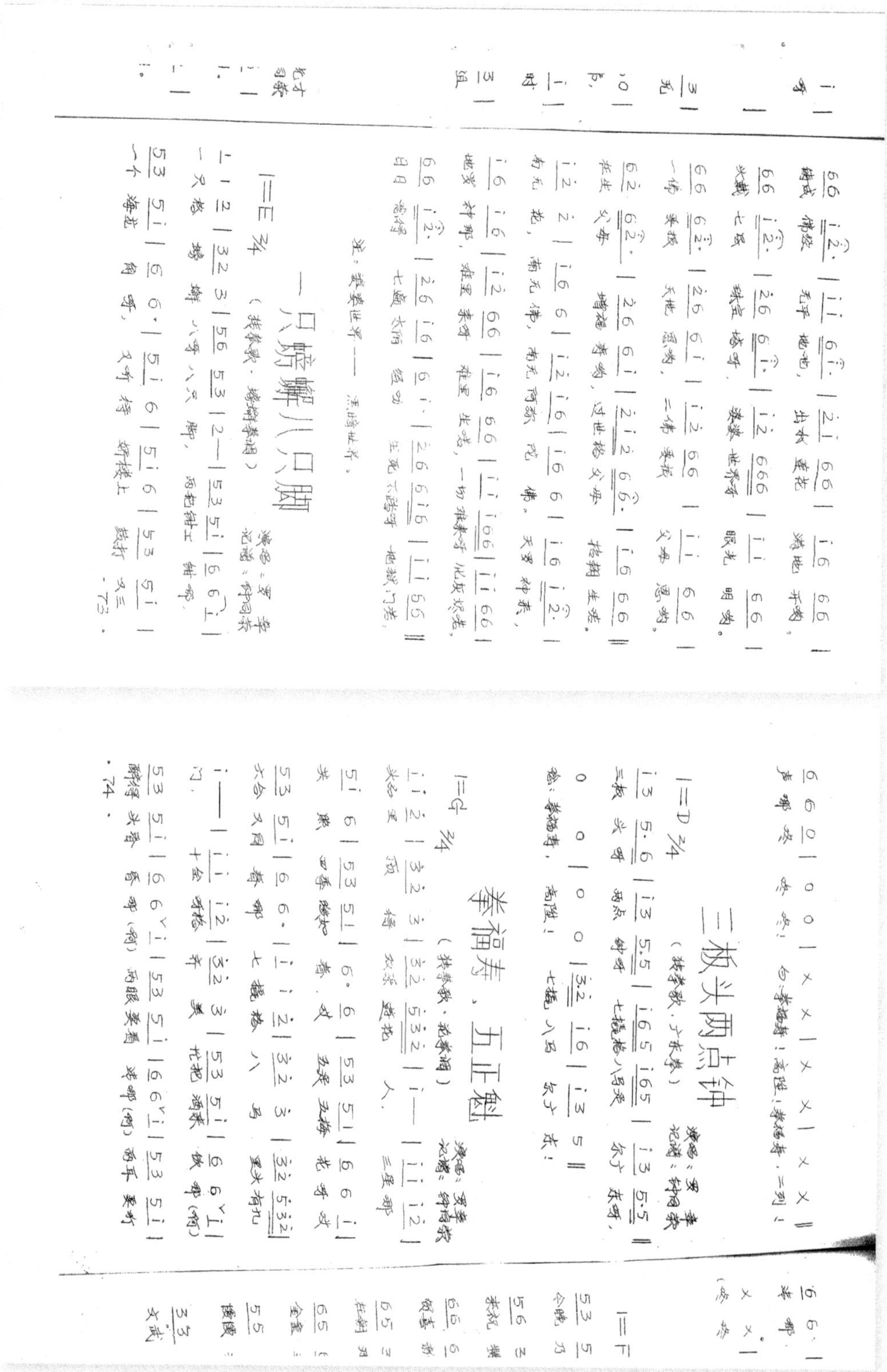

66 i2̇· | ii 6i· | 2̇i 66 | i6 66 |
铸成 佛殿 无平 地也， 出水 莲花 满地 开哟，

66 i2̇· | 2̇6 6i· | i2̇ 666 | ii 66 |
头戴 七层 珠宝 塔呀， 婆婆 世界呀 眼光 明哟。

66 62̇· | 2̇6 6i | i2̇ 66 | ii 66 |
一佛 要报 天地 恩哟， 二佛 要报 父母 恩哟。

62̇ 62̇· | 2̇6 6i | 2̇i2̇ 66· | i6 66 ||
在生 父母 增福 寿哟， 过世 格 父母 超翔 生天。

i2̇ 2̇ | i6 6 | i2̇ i6 | i6 6 | i6 i2̇· |
南无 花， 南无 佛， 南无 阿弥 陀 佛。 天罗 神表，

i6 i6 | i2̇ 66 | i6 66 | ii i66 | ii 66 |
地罗 神耶， 难里 来呀 难里 生呢， 一切 灾来呀 化灰 归尘，

66 i2̇· | 2̇6 i6 | 6 i· | 2̇6 6i6 | ii 56 ||
日月 含得 七遍 太阳 经动 生死 不踏呀 地狱 门关。

注：婆婆世界——黑暗世界。

一只螃蟹八只脚

1=E 2/4　（转拳歌·螃蟹拳调）　演唱：罗　幸　记谱：钟同荣

i i 2̇ | 32 3 | 56 53 | 2— | 53 5i | 6 6 i |
一 只 格 螃 蟹 八呀 八只 脚， 两把 钳工 钳 啊，

53 5i | 6 6· | 5i 6 | 5i 6 | 53 5i |
一个 海龙 角 呀， 又听 得 娇楼上 鼓打 又三

·73·

660 | 0 0 | x x | x x | x x ||
声哪 咚 咚 咚！ 白：拳福寿！高陞！拳福寿，二列！

三板头两点钟

1=D 2/4　（转拳歌·广东拳）　演唱：罗　幸　记谱：钟同荣

i3 5·6 | i3 5·5 | i65 i65 | i3 5·5 ||
三板 头 呀 两点 钟呀 七提格 八马来 尔广 东呀，

0 0 | 0 0 | 3·2 i6 | i3 5 ||
念：拳福寿， 高陞！ 七提 八马 尔广 东！

拳福寿、五正魁

1=G 2/4　（转拳歌·花拳调）　演唱：罗　幸　记谱：钟同荣

ii 2̇ | 32 3 | 32 532 | i— | ii i2̇ |
头品 里 顶 得 双来 莲花 人， 三星 那

5i 6 | 53 5i | 6· 6 | 53 5i | 6 6 i |
共 照 四季 发如 春， 哎 五宝 五梅 花 呀 哎

53 5i | 6 6· | i i 2̇ | 32 3 | 32 532 |
六合 又同 眷 哪 七 提 格 八 马 里头 有九

i— | ii i2̇ | 32 3 | 53 5i | 6 6ᵛi |
门， 十全 呀格 齐 美 托把 酒来 饮 那（啊）

53 5i | 6 6ᵛi | 53 5i | 66ᵛi | 53 5i |
醉得 头昏 昏 那（啊） 两眼 要看 迷 哪（啊） 两耳 要听

·74·

6 6· |
迷 哪，
x x |
（咚 咚

1=F

53 5
今晚 乃
56 3
来祝 猴
66 6
贺喜 新
65 3
红朝 习
65
全靠
55
慢慢
33
文武

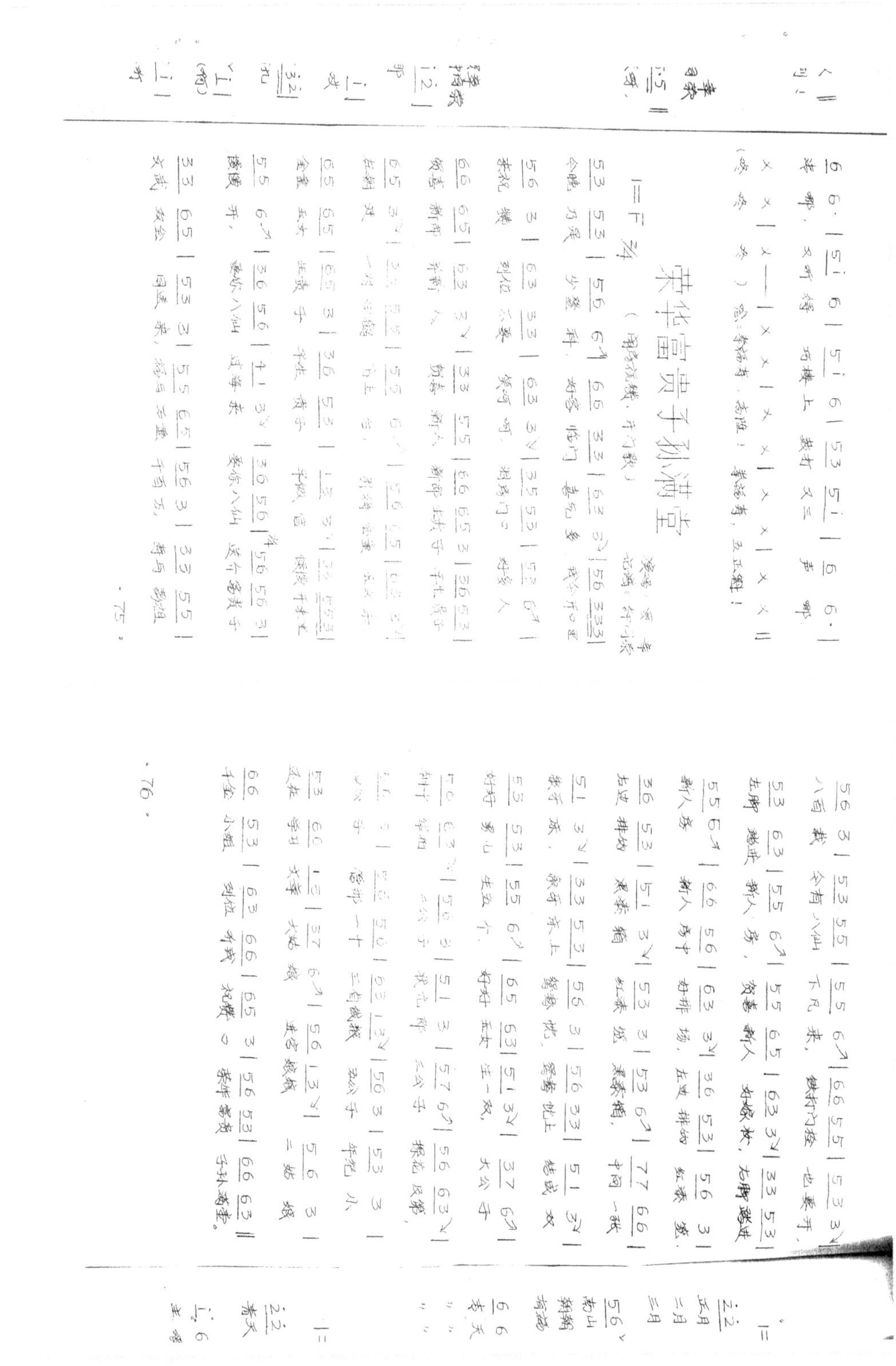

6 6· | 5i 6 | 5i 6 | 53 5i | 6 6· |
澎 哪， 又听得 巧楼上 鼓打 又三 声 哪，

X X | X — | X X | X X | X X | X X ||
（咚 咚 咚 ） 念：拳福寿，高陞！ 拳福寿，五正魁！

荣华富贵子孙满堂

1=F 2/4 （闹房祝赞、开门歌） 演唱：黄幸 记谱：钟小荣

53 53 | 56 6↗ | 66 33 | 63 3↘ | 56 333 |
今晚 乃是 少登 科， 好客 临门 喜气 多 我今开口 里

56 3 | 63 33 | 63 3↘ | 35 53 | 53 6↗ |
来祝 赞 列位 不要 笑呵 呵， 闹房门口 好多 人

66 65 | 63 3↘ | 33 55 | 66 65 3 | 36 53 |
贺喜 新郎 并新 人， 贺喜 新人 新郎 生贵子 子生贵子

65 3↘ | 33 55 | 55 6↗ | 56 65 | 63 3↘ |
左朝 对， 一对 [illegible] 台上 台， 引得 [illegible]

65 65 | 65 3 | 36 53 | 13 3↘ | 33 553 |
金童 玉女 生贵 子， 子生 贵子 子做 官 代代 [illegible]

55 6↗ | 36 56 | 41 3↘ | 36 56 | 56 56 3 |
擂鼓 开， 要你 八仙 过海 来 要你八仙 送个富贵子

33 65 | 53 3 | 55 65 | 56 3 | 33 55 |
文武 双全 同送 来， 福与 天重 千百 万， 寿与 彭祖

· 75 ·

56 3 | 53 55 | 55 6↗ | 66 55 | 53 3↘ |
八百 载 今有 八仙 下凡 来， 铁打门栓 也要 开，

53 63 | 55 6↗ | 55 65 | 63 3↘ | 33 53 |
左脚 踏进 新人 房， 贺喜 新人 好嫁妆， 右脚 踏进

55 6↗ | 66 56 | 63 3↘ | 36 53 | 56 3 |
新人房 新人 房中 好排 场， 左边 排的 红漆 箱，

36 53 | 51 3↘ | 53 3 | 53 6↗ | 77 66 |
右边 排的 黑漆 箱 红漆 箱 黑漆箱， 中间 一张

51 3↘ | 33 53 | 56 3 | 56 33 | 51 3↘ |
象牙 床， 象牙 床上 鸳鸯 枕， 鸳鸯 枕上 结成 双

53 53 | 55 6↗ | 65 63 | 51 3↘ | 37 6↗ |
好好 男儿 生五 个， 好好 玉女 生一 双， 大公 子

56 63↘ | 56 3 | 51 3 | 57 6↗ | 56 63↘ |
[illegible] 二公 子 状元 郎 三公 子 探花 及第，

56 3 | 56 56 | 63 13↘ | 56 3 | 53 3 |
[illegible] 子 总部 一十 三省 钱粮 五公子 年纪 小

53 66 13 | 37 6↗ | 56 13↘ | 56 3 |
还在 学习 文章 大姑 娘 进宫 娘娘 二姑 娘

66 53 | 63 66 | 65 3 | 56 53 | 66 63 ||
千金 小姐 列位 贺我 祝赞 口 荣华富贵 子孙满堂。

· 76 ·

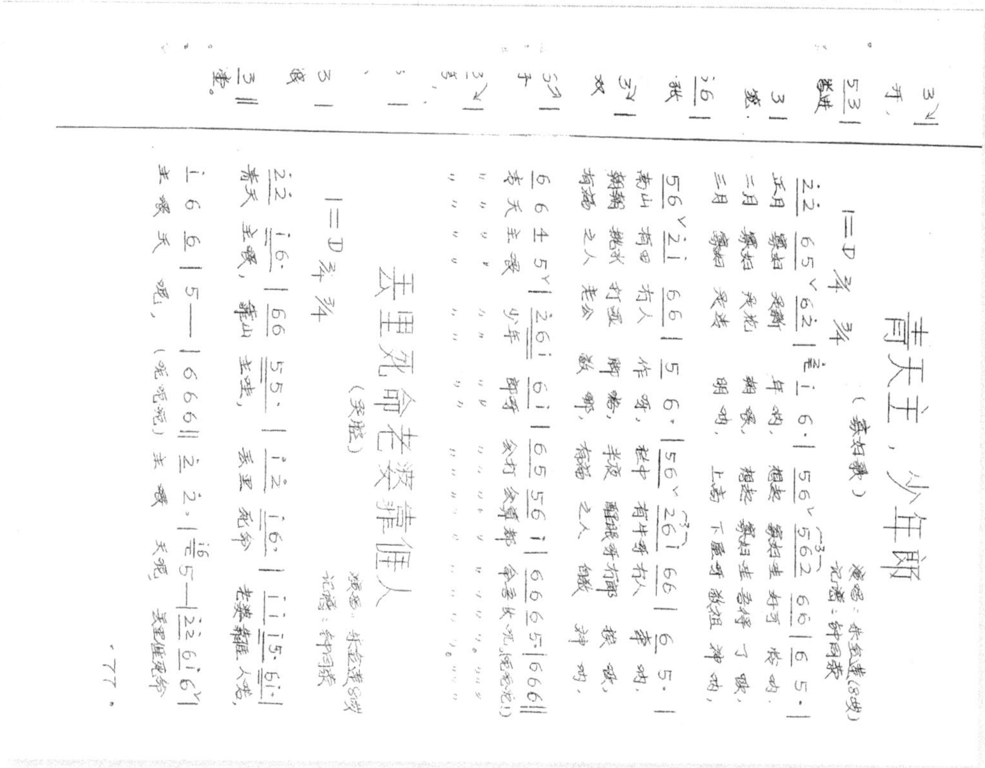

开，踏进 堂，秋 双 子 …… 喊 堂。

青天主，少年郎

（寡妇歌）

演唱：朱金莲(8岁)
记谱：钟国荣

1=D 2/4 3/4

正月 寡妇 无新 年 呐， 想起 寡妇 生 好可 怜 呐，
二月 寡妇 无花 蝴 蝶， 想起 寡妇 生 君得 了 哦，
三月 寡妇 无告 明 呐， 上高 下屋可 敬祖 神 呐，

南山 有田 有人 作 呀， 秋中 有牛呀 有人 牵 呐，
翻翻 挑水 打沤 脚 烙， 半夜 醒眼呀 有郎 换 被，
有福 之人 老公 敬 啊， 有福 之人 敬 神 呐，

青天主喂 少年 郎呀 会打 会算都 会吾长 呢，(呃呃呃！)

丢里死命老婆靠侄人

（哭腔）

演唱：朱金莲8岁
记谱：钟国荣

1=D 2/4 3/4

青天 主喂， 靠山 主哇， 丢里 死命 老婆靠侄 人哉，
主 喂 天 呢，（呃呃呃）主 喂 天呢， 丢里侄死命

·77·

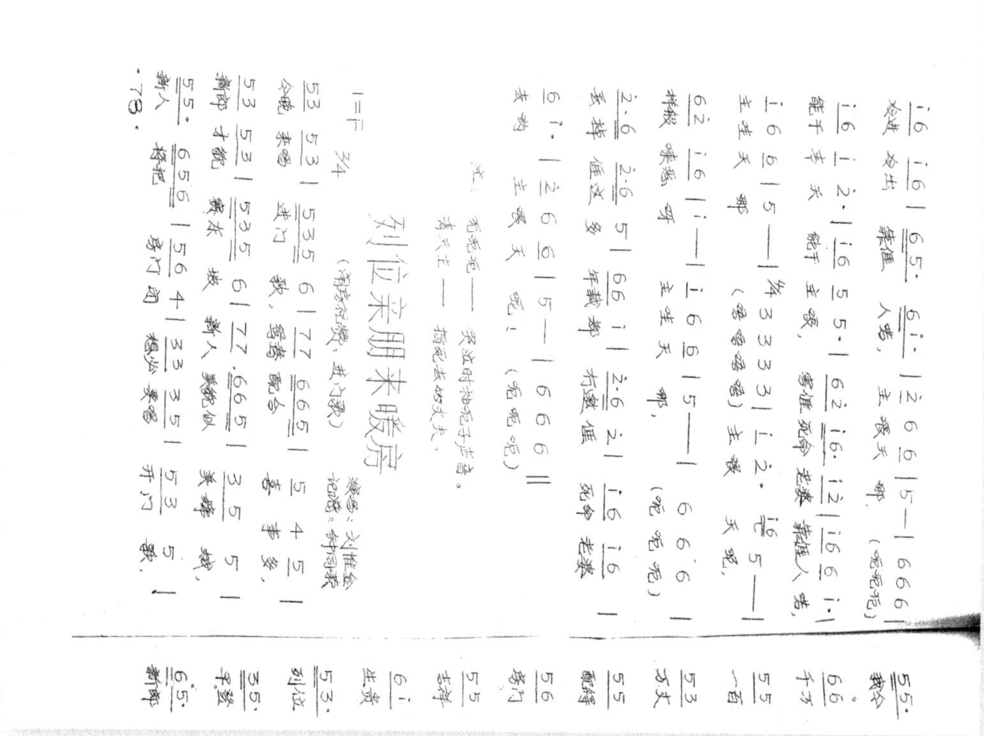

冷进 冷出 靠侄 人呀， 主 喂 天 啊，（呃呃呃）
能千 李 天 能千 主 喂， 害侄 死命 老婆 靠侄人 哉，
主 生 天 啊 （呜呜呜呜）主 喂 天 呢，
样般 嗓怎 呀 主 生 天 啊，（呃 呃 呃）
丢 掉 侄这 多 年栽 都 冇敷 侄 死命 老婆
去 呐 主 喂 天 呢！（呃 呃 呃）

注：呃呃呃——哭泣时抽泣子声音。
青天主——指死去的丈夫。

列位亲朋来暖房

（闹房祝赞、进门歌）

演唱：刘惟金
记谱：钟国荣

1=F 3/4

今晚 来唱 进门 歌， 鸳鸯 配合 喜 事 多，
新郎 才貌 赛东 坡， 新人 美貌似 美 嫦 娥，
新人 将把 房门 闭， 想必 要唱 开门 歌，

·78·

我今 千万 一百 万丈 配得 房门 吉祥 生贵 列位 早登 新郎

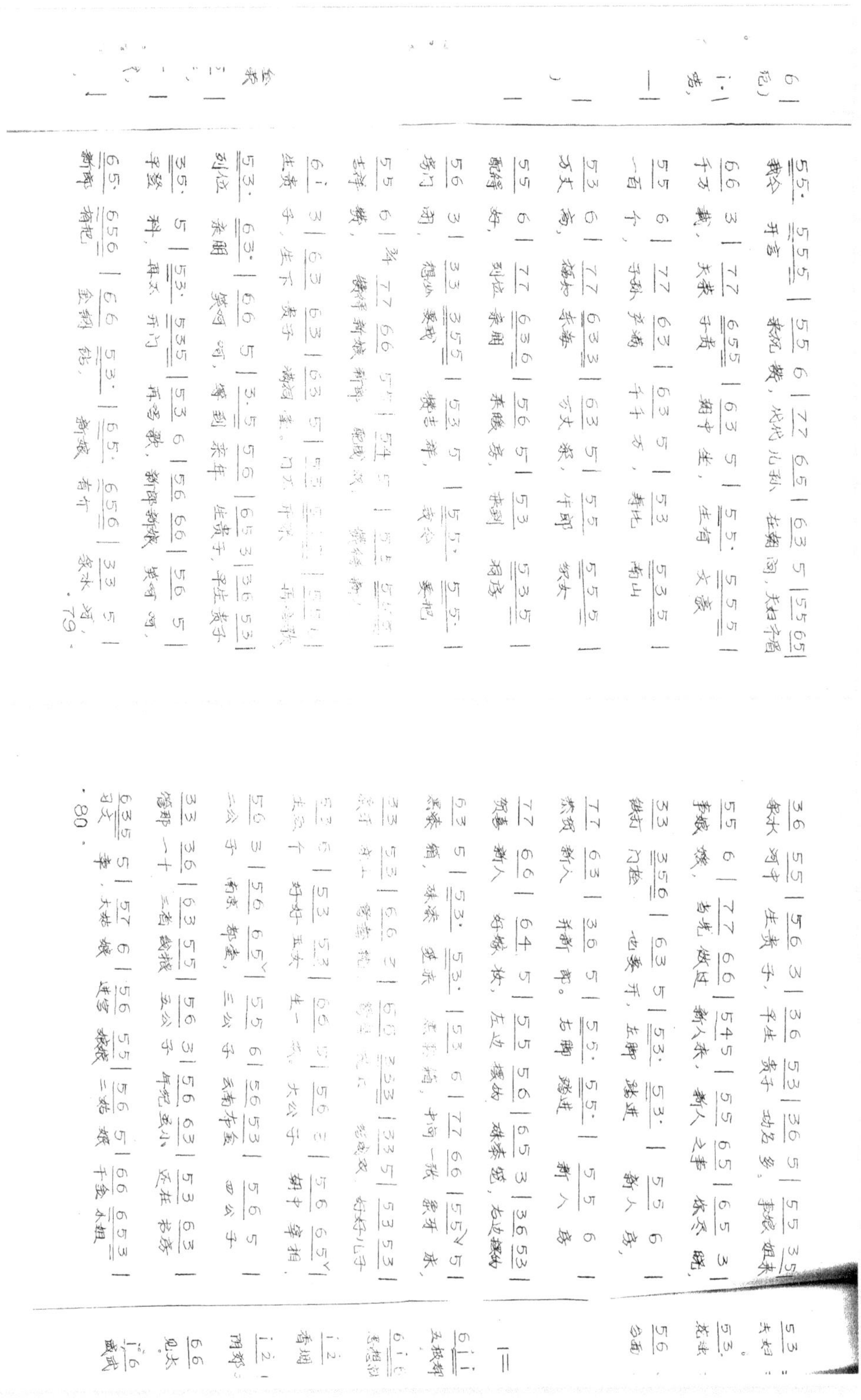

6 |
花）
i· |
若，
— |

金歌

55· 555 | 55 6 | 77 65 | 63 5 | 55 65 |
我今 开言 来祝 赞，代代 儿孙 在朝 阁，夫妇齐眉

66 3 | 77 655 | 63 5 | 55· 555 |
千万 载，夫荣 子贵 翔中 生，生有 文豪

55 6 | 77 63 | 63 5 | 53 535 |
一百 个，子孙 产满 千千 万，寿比 南山

53 6 | 77 633 | 63 5 | 55 555 |
万丈 高，福如 东海 万丈 深，牛郎 织女

55 6 | 77 636 | 56 5 | 53 535 |
配得 好，列位 亲朋 来贱 房，来到 洞房

56 3 | 33 355 | 53 5 | 55· 55· |
房门 闭，想必 要我 赞吉 祥，我今 要把

55 6 | 3/4 77 66 55 | 54 5 | [illegible] |
吉祥 赞，赞得 新娘 新郎 配成 双，赞得 新[illegible]

6i 3 | 63 63 | 63 5 | [illegible] | [illegible] |
生贵 子，生下 贵子 满洞 堂。门不 开来 再写歌

53· 63· | 66 5 | 3·5 56 | 653 | 36 53 |
列位 亲朋 笑呵 呵，等到 来年 生贵子，早生贵子

35· 5 | 53· 535 | 53 6 | 56 66 | 56 5 |
早登 科，再不 开门 再写 歌，新郎 新娘 笑呵 呵，

65· 656 | 66 53· | 65· 656 | 33 5 |
新郎 有把 金钢 钻，新娘 有个 象水 河，

·79·

36 55 | 56 3 | 36 53 | 36 5 | 55 35 |
象水 河中 生贵 子，早生 贵子 功名 多。事娘 姐来

55 6 | 77 66 | 545 | 55 65 | 65 3 |
事娘 嫁，当先 做过 新人来，新人 之事 你尽 晓，

33 356 | 63 5 | 53· 53· | 55 6 |
铁打 门栓 也要 开，左脚 踏进 新人 房，

77 63 | 36 5 | 55· 55· | 55 6 |
恭贺 新人 开新 郎。右脚 踏进 新人 房

77 66 | 64 5 | 55 56 | 65 3 | 36 53 |
贺喜 新人 好嫁 妆，左边 摆的 硃漆 笼，右边摆的

63 5 | 53· 53· | 53 6 | 77 66 | 55 5 |
黑漆 箱，硃漆 笼床 黑漆 箱，中间 一张 象牙 床，

33 53 | 66 3 | 66 333 | 33 5 | 53 53 |
象牙 床上 鸳鸯 枕 [illegible] 结成双，好好儿子

53 6 | 53 53 | 66 5 | 56 3 | 56 65 |
生六个 好好 五女 生一 [illegible]，大公 子 朝中 宰相，

56 3 | 56 65 | 55 6 | 56 53 | 56 5 |
二公 子 南京 都堂，三公 子 云南布金 四公 子

33 36 | 63 55 | 56 3 | 56 63 | 53 63 |
管那 一十 三省 钱粮 五公 子 年纪 虽小 还在 书房

635 5 | 57 6 | 56 55 | 56 5 | 66 653 |
习文 章，大姑 娘 进宫 娘娘 二姑 娘 千金 小姐

·80·

53 :
夫妇 :

53.
花虫

56
今面

1=

6i i
五根郑

6i6
思想

i2
香烟

i2
阴郑

66
见太

i6
威武

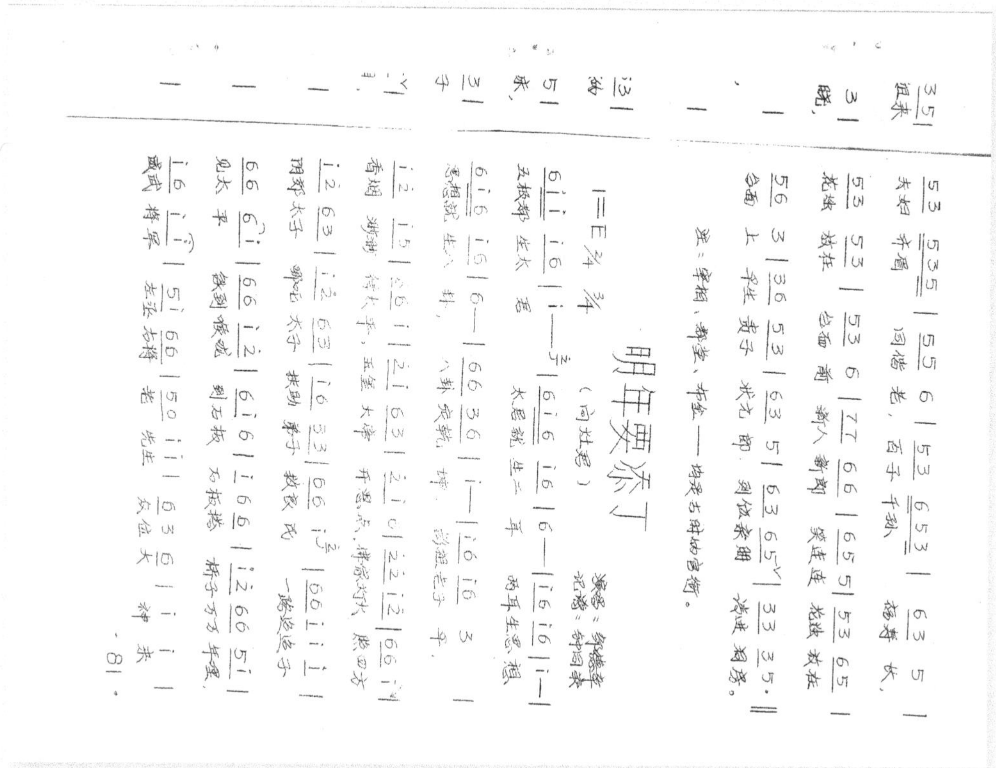

3 5 | 姐来
3 | 晓，
|
|
3 3 | 油
5 | 来，
3 | 子
| 日，
|
|
|

53 535 | 55 6 | 53 653 | 63 5 |
夫妇 齐眉 同偕 老，百子 千孙 福寿 长，

53 53 | 53 6 | 77 66 | 65 5 | 53 65 |
花烛 放在 当面 前 新人 新郎 笑连连 花烛 放在

56 3 | 36 53 | 63 5 | 63 65 | 33 35· ‖
当面 上 平生 贵子 状元 郎 列位亲朋 鸿进 洞房。

注：宰相、都堂、布金——均是古时的官衔。

明年要添丁

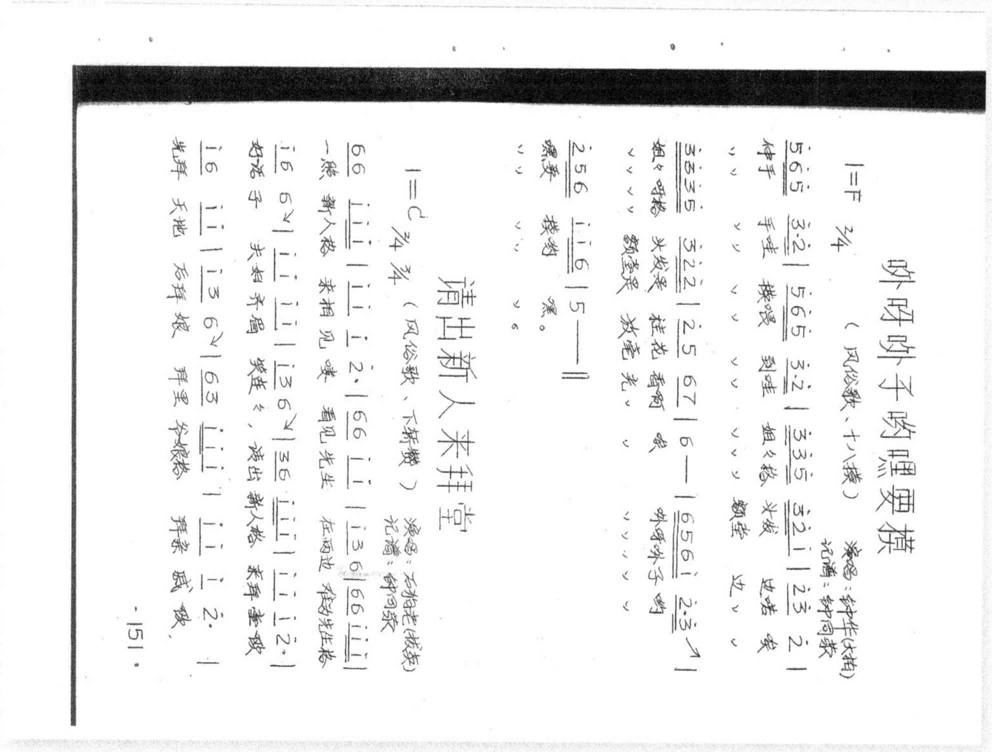

1=E 2/4 3/4　（向灶君）　演唱：邹德幸　记谱：钟同录

6i i i6 | i— | 6i6 i6 | 6— | i6 i6 | i— |
五板都 生太 君 太君就 生二 年 两耳生思 想

6i6 i6 | 6— | 66 36 | i— | i6 i6 3 |
思想就 生八 卦， 八卦 定乾 坤 尚祖老子 平，

i2 i5 | 66 i | 2i 63 | 2i 0 | 22 i2 | 66 i |
香烟 渺渺 待太 平，玉皇 大帝 开恩 点，佛家灯火 照四方

i2 63 | i2 63 | i6 53 | 66 i | 66 i i i |
阴郊 太子 哪吒 太子 扶助 弟子 救良 氏 一路追追 子

66 6i | 66 i2 | 6i 6 | i 66 | i2 66 5i |
见太 平 铁到 喉咙 到石板 石板搭 桥子万万 年坚，

i6 ii | 5i 66 | 50 ii | 63 6 | i i |
盛武 将军 左丞 右将 老 先生 众位 大 神 来

· 81 ·

吩呀吩子哟嘿要摸

1=F 2/4　（风俗歌、十八摸）　演唱：钟华(大拍)　记谱：钟同歌

565 3·2 | 565 3·2 | 335 32i | 23 2 |
伸手 手哇 摸嘿 到哇 姐々格 头发 边嗒 分
ソソ ソソ ソソ ソソ ソソソ 额堂 边ソ ソ

3335 322 | 25 67 | 6— | 6561 2·3 |
姐々呀格 头发是 桂花 香啊 哦 吩呀吩子 哟
ソソソソ 额堂是 放毫 光ソ ソ ソソソソソ

256 ii6 | 5— ‖
嘿要 摸哟 嘿。
ソソ ソソ ソ 6

请出新人来拜堂

1=C 2/4 3/4　（风俗歌、下轿赞）　演唱：石狗老(拔安)　记谱：钟同歌

66 iii | ii i 2· | 66 ii | i36 | 66 iii |
一照 新人格 来相 见 喽 看见 先生 在两边 难为先生格

i6 6 | ii ii | i36 | 36 iii | ii i2· |
好佬 子 夫妇 齐眉 笑连々，请出 新人格 来拜 堂 欧

i6 ii | i3 6 | 63 iii | ii i 2· |
先拜 天地 后拜 娘 拜里 爷娘格 拜亲 戚 欧，

· 151 ·

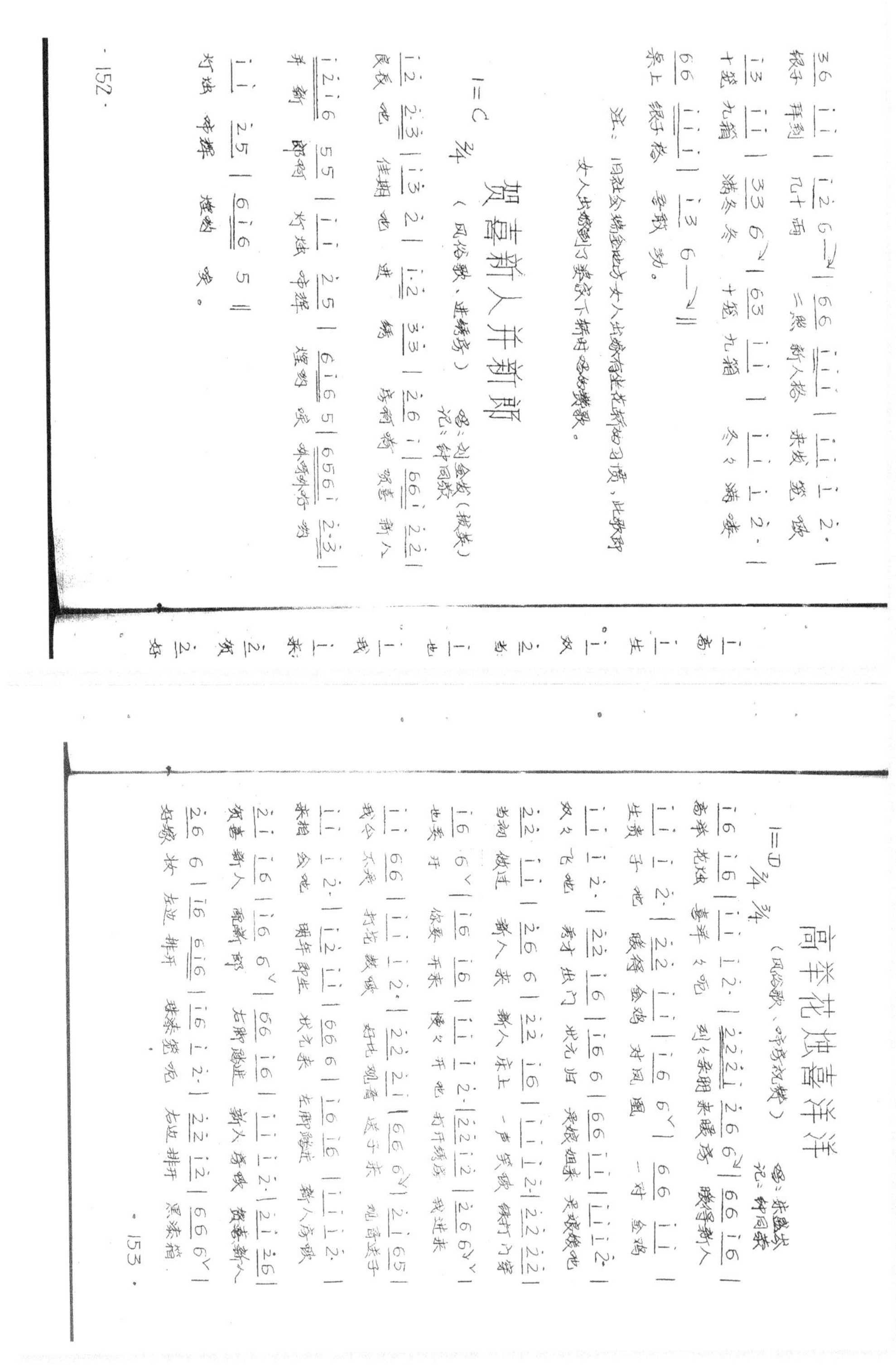

36 11 | 12 6— | 66 111 | 11 1 2· |
银子 拜到 几十两 二照 新人格 来发 笼 哎

13 11 | 33 6 | 63 11 | 11 1 2· |
十笼 九箱 满冬冬 十笼 九箱 冬冬 满 喽

66 111 | 13 6— ||
呆上 银子格 参載 劲。

注：旧社会瑞金地方女人出嫁有坐花轿的习惯，此歌即女人出嫁到了婆家下轿时唱的赞歌。

贺喜新人并新郎

1=C 2/4 （风俗歌、进绣房） 唱：刘金发（拔英） 记：钟同荣

12 23 | 13 2 | 12 33 | 26 1 | 661 22 |
良辰 吧 佳期 吧 进 绣 房 啊 啊 贺喜 新人

1216 55 | 11 25 | 6165 | 6561 23 |
并 新 郎 啊 灯 烛 辉 辉 煌 的 唉 咿呀咿呀 的

11 25 | 616 5 ||
灯烛 辉辉 煌的 唉。

高举花烛喜洋洋

1=D 2/4 3/4 （风俗歌、闹房祝赞） 唱：朱盛发 记：钟同荣

16 16 | 11 12· | 2221 26 6 | 66 16 |
高举 花烛 喜洋 々 吧 到々亲朋 来暖 房 暖得新人

11 1 2· | 22 11 | 16 6 | 66 11 |
生贵 子 吧 暖得 金鸡 对凤 凰 一对 金鸡

11 1 2· | 22 16 | 16 6 | 66 11 | 111 2· |
双々 飞 吧 秀才 出门 状元 归 来娘 姐来 来娘娘吧

22 11 | 26 6 | 22 16 | 11 1 2· | 22 22 |
当初 做过 新人 来 新人 床上 一声 笑哎 铁打门穿

16 6 | 16 16 | 11 1 2· | 22 12 | 26 6 |
也要 开 你要 开来 慢々 开 吧 打开绣房 我进来

11 66 | 11 1 2· | 22 21 | 66 6 | 21 65 |
我今 不来 打花 烛哎 好比 观音 送子 来 观音送子

11 1 2· | 12 11 | 66 6 | 16 16 | 111 2· |
来相 会 吧 明年 郎生 状元 来 左脚踏进 新人房 哎

21 16 | 16 6 | 66 16 | 11 1 2· | 21 26 |
贺喜 新人 配新 郎 右脚 踏进 新人 房哎 贺喜新人

26 6 | 16 616 | 16 1 2· | 22 12 | 66 6 |
好嫁 妆 左边 排开 珠漆 笼 吧 右边 排开 黑漆箱

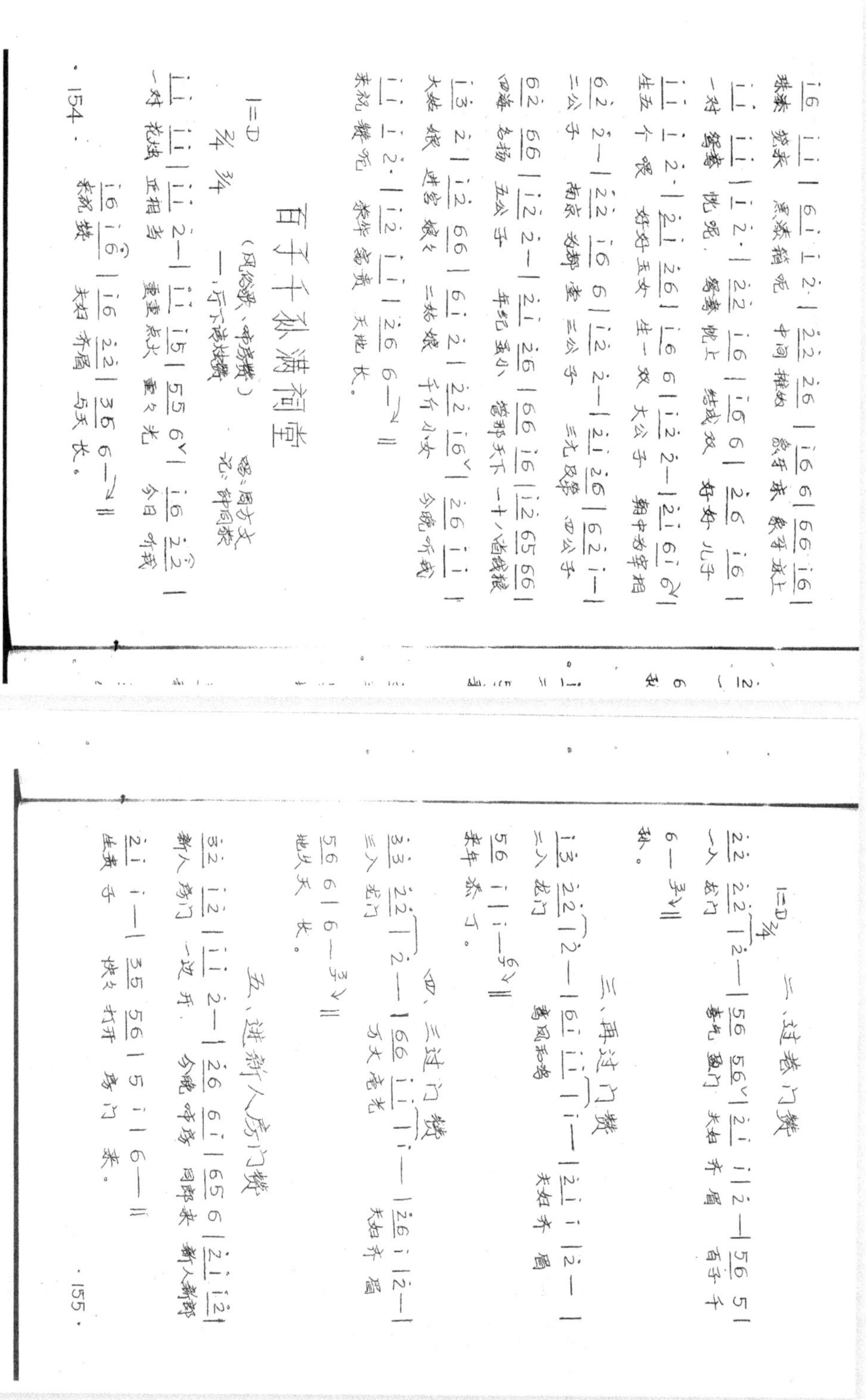

16 11 | 61 1 2· | 22 26 | 16 6 | 66 16 |
珠漆 箢来 黑漆箱呢 中间摊如 象牙床 象牙床上

11 11 | 1 2· | 22 16 | 16 6 | 26 16 |
一对 鸳鸯 忱呢， 鸳鸯 忱上 结成双 好好 儿子

11 1 2· | 21 26 | 16 6 | 12 2— | 21 61 6 |
生五 个 喂 好好玉女 生一双 大公子 朝中为宰相

62 2— | 22 16 6 | 12 2— | 21 26 | 62 1— |
二公 子 南京 为都 堂 三公子 三元及第 四公子

62 66 | 12 2— | 21 26 | 66 16 | 12 65 66 |
四海 名扬 五公 子 年纪 虽小 管那天下 一十八省钱粮

13 2 | 12 66 | 61 2 | 22 16 | 26 11 |
大姑 娘 进宫 娘々 二姑 娘 千斤小女 今晚听我

11 1 2· | 12 11 | 26 6— ||
来祝 赞呢 荣华 富贵 天地 长。

百子千孙满祠堂

1=D　（风俗歌、哞房赞）　唱：周方文
2/4 3/4　一、厅下请烛赞　记：钟同荣

11 11 | 11 2— | 11 15 | 55 6 | 16 22 |
一对 花烛 正相 当 重重点火 重々光 今日 听我

16 16 | 16 22 | 36 6— ||
来祝 赞 夫妇 齐眉 与天 长。

· 154 ·

二、过巷门赞

1=D 2/4

22 22 | 2— | 56 56 | 21 1 | 2— | 56 5 |
一入 龙门 喜气 盈门 夫妇 齐 眉 百子 千

6— ||
孙。

三、再过门赞

13 22 | 2— | 61 11 | 1— | 21 1 | 2— |
二入 龙门 鸾凤和鸣 夫妇 齐 眉

56 1 | 1— ||
来年 添 丁。

四、三过门赞

33 22 | 2— | 66 11 | 1— | 26 1 | 2— |
三入 龙门 万丈 毫光 夫妇 齐 眉

56 6 | 6— ||
地久 天 长。

五、进新人房门赞

32 12 | 11 2— | 26 61 | 65 6 | 21 12 |
新人 房门 一边 开， 今晚 哞房 同郎来 新人新郎

21 1— | 35 56 | 5 1 | 6— ||
生贵 子 快々 打开 房门 来。

· 155 ·

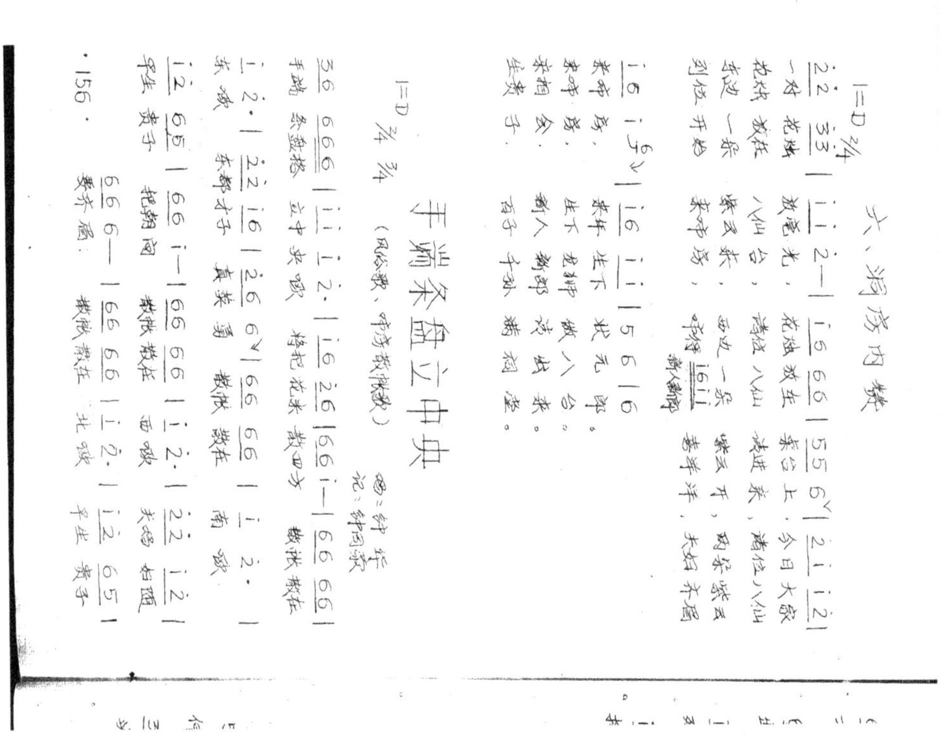

六、洞房内赞

1=D 2/4

2 2 3 3 | i i 2 — | i 6 6 6 | 5 5 6 | 2 i i 2 |
一对 花烛 放毫光， 花烛放在 桌台上， 今日大家
花烛 放在 八仙台， 请位八仙 请进来， 请位八仙
东边 一朵 紫云来， 西边一朵 紫云开， 两朵紫云
列位 开始 来闹房， 闹得 i 6 i i 新人新郎 喜洋洋， 夫妇齐眉

i 6 i 5 | i 6 i i | 5 6 | 6
来闹房， 来年生下 状元郎。
来闹房， 生下龙狮 做八台。
来相会， 新人新郎 请出来。
生贵子， 百子千孙 满祠堂。

· 156 ·

手端条盘立中央

1=D 2/4 3/4 （风俗歌、闹房散帐歌） 唱：钟华 记：钟同家

3 6 6 6 6 | i i i 2· | i 6 2 6 | 6 6 i — | 6 6 6 6 |
手端 条盘格 立中央哎 将把花米 散四方 撒帐散在

i 2· | 2 2 i 6 | 2 6 6 | 6 6 6 6 | i 2· |
东 哎 东都才子 真英勇 撒帐散在 南 哎

i 2 6 5 | 6 6 i — | 6 6 6 6 | i 2· | 2 2 i 2 |
平生 贵子 把朝间 撒帐散在 西 哎 夫唱妇随

6 6 6 — | 6 6 6 6 | i 2· | i 2 6 5 |
要齐眉， 撒帐散在 北 哎 平生 贵子

6 i 6 | 6 6 6 6 | i i i 6 | 6 i i 2· | 2 2 2 i |
万千 百 撒帐 散在 东南 西北 并中央哎 列々亲朋

6 6 i — | i 2 6 6 | i 6 i 2· | 6 i 6 3 | 6 i i — |
出绣房 明年 必定 生贵子哎 早生贵子 在中央

i 6 i 6 | i 6 i i | i 2· | 2 6 6 i | i 6 6 i |
列位 亲朋 明朝早早 起哎 早々起来 食介麻奇

i 2 i — ‖
拌勾籽。

注：此为闹房到子夜时后结束闹房时唱的歌。

麻奇拌勾籽——即糯子做的米粿拌勾籽，实际第二天早上没有此菜和给亲戚吃，而是开玩笑的一句唱词。

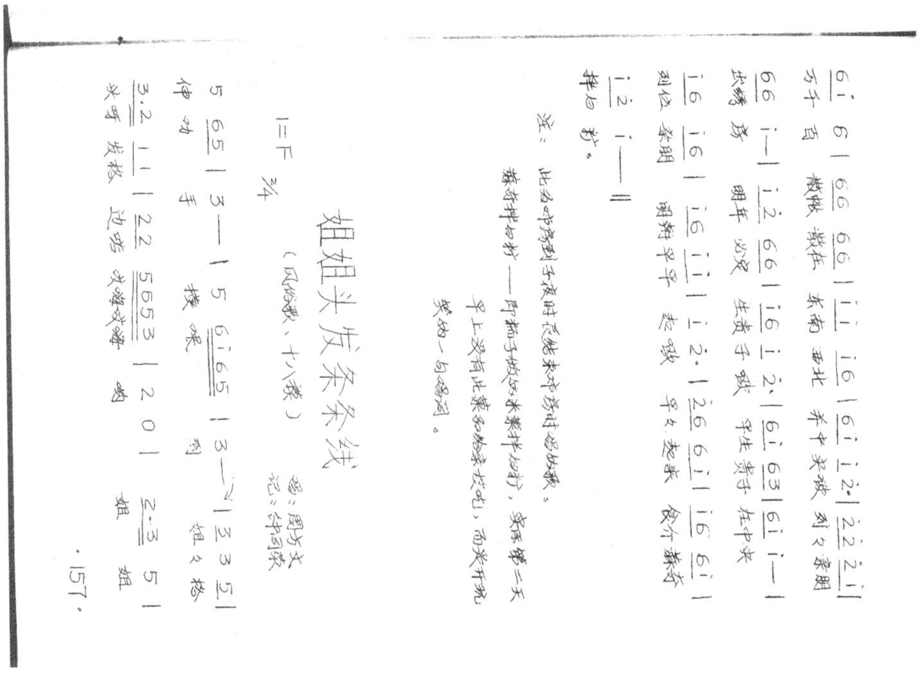

姐姐头发条条线

1=F 3/4 （风俗歌、十八摸） 唱：周方文 记：钟同荣

5 6 5 | 3 — | 5 6 i 6 5 | 3 — | 3 3 5 |
伸 动 手 摸 喂 到 姐々格

3.2 1 1 | 2 2 5 6 5 3 | 2 0 | 2·3 5 |
头呀 发格 边呀 哎嗨哎嗨 哟 姐 姐

· 157 ·

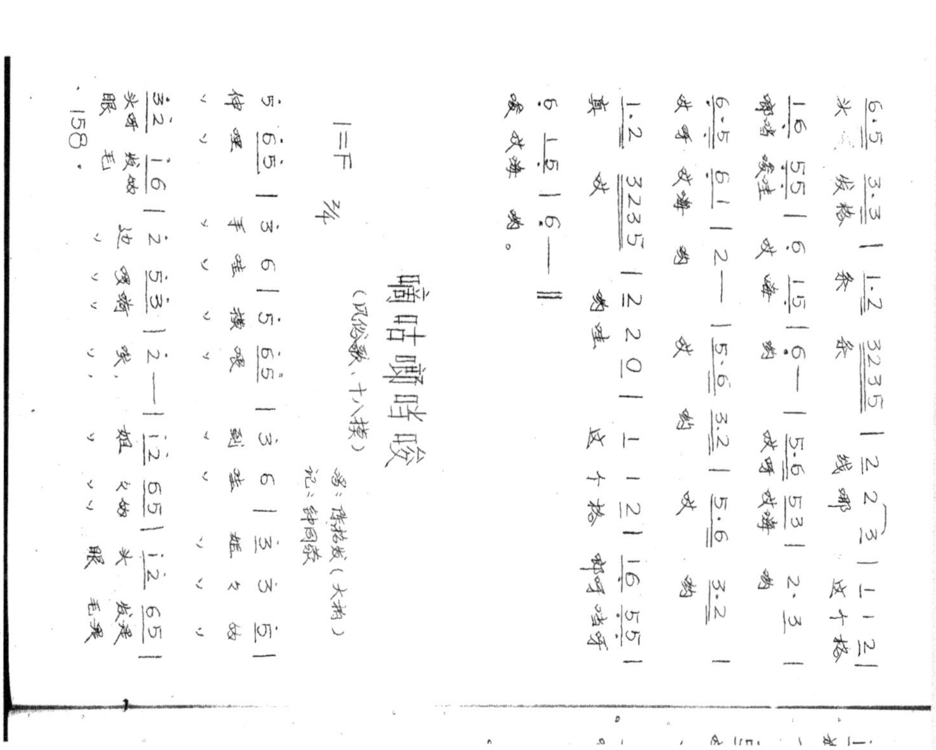

6·5 3·3 | 1·2 3235 | 2 2 3 | 1 1 2 |
头 发格 余 余 线哪 这个格

1·6 55 | 6 15 | 6 — | 5·6 53 | 2· 3 |
唧咕 唆哇 哎 嗨 哟 哎呀 哎嗨 哟

6·5 61 | 2 — | 5·6 3·2 | 5·6 3·2 |
哎 呀 哎嗨 哟 哎 哟 哎 哟

1·2 3235 | 2 2 0 | 1 1 2 | 16 55 |
真 哎 哟哇 这个格 郎呀 啥呀

6 15 | 6 — ||
唆 哎嗨 哟。

嘀咕嘀咕唆

（风俗歌、十八摸）

1=F 2/4

唱：陈拾发（大埔）
记：钟同荣

5 65 | 3 6 | 5 65 | 3 6 | 3 3 5 |
伸 哩 手 哇 摸 喂 到 哇 姐 々 的

32 16 | 2 53 | 2 — | 12 65 | 12 65 |
头呀 发的 边 喂嗬 唉， 姐 々的 头 发是
眼 毛 眼 毛是

· 158 ·

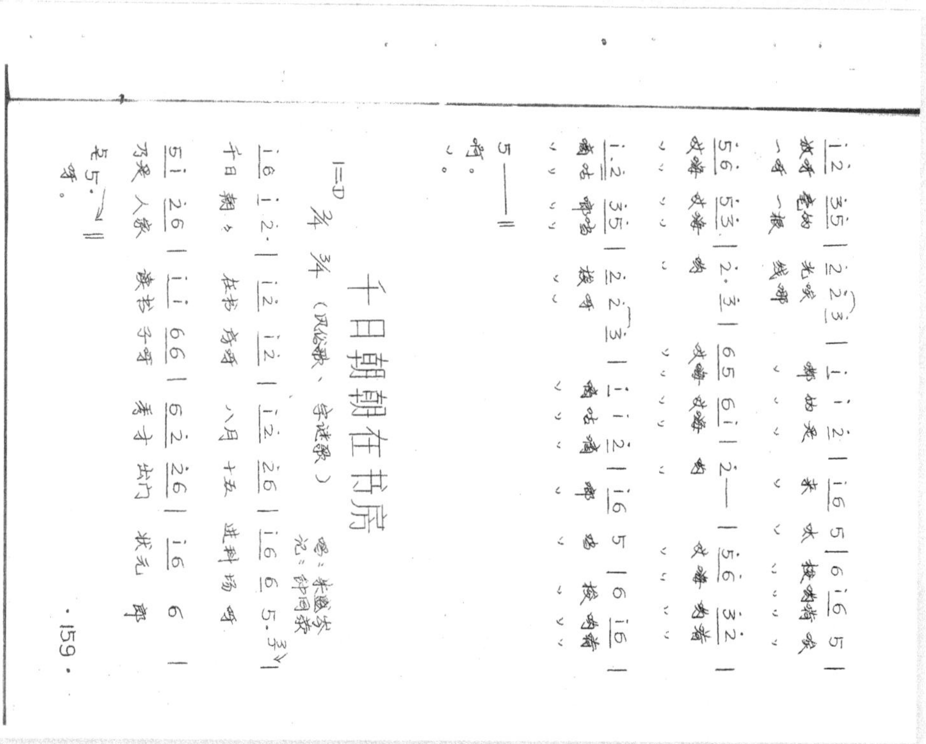

12 35 | 2 23 | 1 1 2 | 16 5 | 6 16 5 |
披呀 毫的 光唉 哪 的 是 来 哎 接哟嗬 唉
一呀 一根 线哪

56 53 | 2· 3 | 65 61 | 2 — | 56 32 |
哎嗨 哎嗨 哟 哎嗨 哎嗨 哟 哎 嗨 哟着

1·2 35 | 2 2 3 | 1 1 2 | 16 5 | 6 16 |
嘀咕 唧咕 接 呀 嘀 咕 嘀 唧 咕 接 哟嗬

5 — ||
呀。

千日朝朝在书房

1=D 2/4 3/4（风俗歌、字谜歌）

唱：朱盛岑
记：钟同荣

16 1 2· | 12 12 | 12 26 | 16 6 5·3 |
千日 朝々 在书 房呀 八月 十五 进科 场 呀

51 26 | 11 66 | 62 26 | 16 6 |
乃是 人家 读书 子呀 秀才 出门 状元 郎

2 5· ||
呀。

· 159 ·

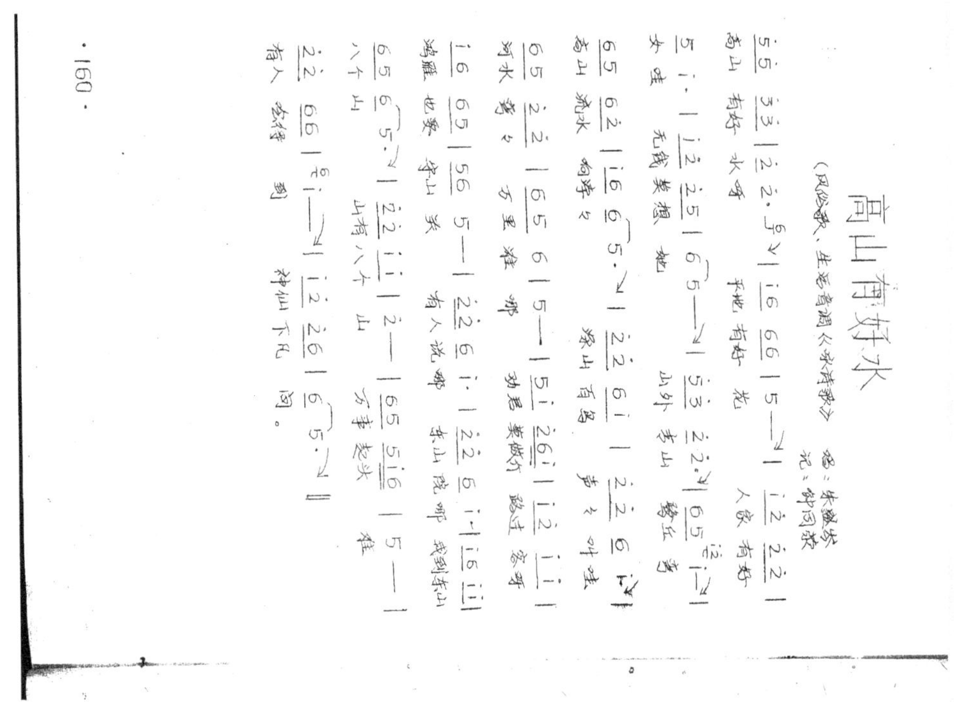
高山有好水
·160·

06 第六类 · 生活音调

CATEGORY VI · EVERYDAY MINOR TUNES

导读

“生活小调”是源自日常生活语境的民间歌谣类型，常在家庭、邻里或社区交流中演唱。与高亢奔放的山歌不同，小调旋律较为规整、形式简洁，歌词内容多涉及爱情、家庭琐事、人生感悟与市井趣事，因而贴近日常口语，富有生活气息。

在赣南地区，生活小调既可在农闲时自娱自乐，也常见于节庆、聚会和婚嫁场合。它们承载了民众的日常审美经验，表现出“以歌言事”的生活智慧。这类歌曲的普及性与亲和力，使其在代际传承中扮演重要角色，成为区域音乐文化中最具“日常性”的一支。

Introduction

Everyday Minor Tunes represent a category of folk songs rooted in the contexts of daily life, often performed within families, among neighbors, or in communal gatherings. Unlike the expansive and free-flowing *mountain songs*, minor tunes follow more regular melodic patterns and simpler forms. Their lyrics commonly address themes of love, household affairs, reflections on life, and anecdotes of ordinary people, rendered in a colloquial style that resonates with everyday experience.

In southern Jiangxi, everyday minor tunes were performed both as self-entertainment during leisure time and as part of festivals, social gatherings, and wedding celebrations. They embody the aesthetic sensibilities of ordinary life and articulate the wisdom of “speaking through song.” Their accessibility and intimacy made them widely popular, ensuring their continued transmission across generations and establishing them as one of the most “everyday” voices within the region’s folk musical culture.

啊啊仔，啊呀啊

1=G 2/4 （生活音调·摇儿歌） 瑞金·汉

12 2 | 26 1 | 12 26 | 165 6 | 12 2 |
啊啊 仔，啊呀 啊，倨格 女女① 要啊 啊，啊哇 啊，

16 1 | 1226 | 16 5 | 13 2 | 66 1 ‖
啊哇 啊，倨格女女 要啊 啊，啊哇 啊 啊哇 啊。

注：①倨格女女——我的女儿。

（演唱：杨冬娣 记谱：钟同荣）

· 45 ·

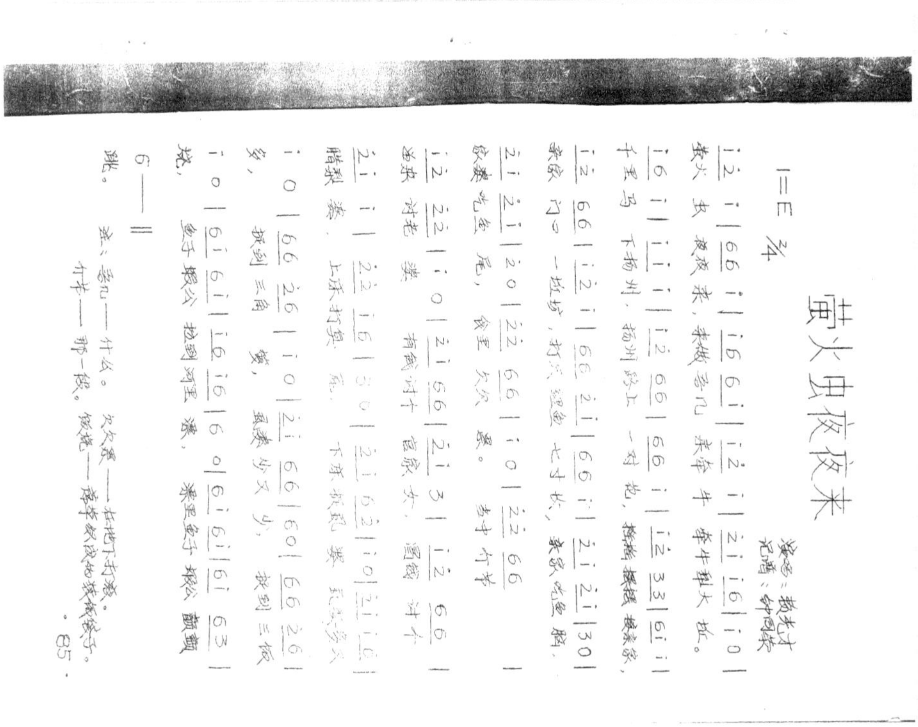

萤火虫夜夜来

1=E 2/4

演唱：赖光才
记谱：钟同荣

12 1 | 66 1 | 16 61 | 12 1 | 21 16 | 1 0 |
萤火 虫 夜夜 来，来做 吾几 来牵 牛 牵牛 犁大 坵。

16 1 | 11 1 | 12 66 | 66 1 | 12 33 | 61 1 |
千里 马 下扬 州，扬州 路上 一对 花，摇摇 摆摆 接亲家，

12 66 | 12 1 | 66 21 | 66 1 | 21 21 | 30 |
亲家 门口 一坵 塘，打只 鲤鱼 七寸 长，亲家 吃鱼 脑，

21 21 | 2 0 | 22 66 | 1 0 | 22 66 |
家婆 吃鱼 尾， 食里 欠欠 畏。 当中 竹节

12 22 | 1 0 | 21 66 | 21 3 | 12 66 |
留来 讨老 婆 有钱 讨个 官家 女， 冒钱 讨个

21 1 | 22 16 | 3 0 | 21 62 | 1 0 | 21 16 |
腊梨 婆， 上床 打臭 屁， 下床 捉虱 婆 虱婆 多又

1 0 | 66 26 | 1 0 | 21 66 | 6 0 | 66 26 |
多， 捉到 三角 篓， 虱婆 少又 少， 捉到 三饭

1 0 | 61 61 | 16 16 | 6 0 | 61 61 | 61 63 |
烧， 鱼子 虾公 拉到 河里 漂， 漂里 鱼子 虾公 颤颤

6 — ‖
跳。

注：吾几——什么。欠欠畏——在地下打滚。
竹节——那一段。饭烧——席草织成的装饭袋子。

· 85 ·

月光光救才郎

1=D 3/4

演唱：朱金莲（80岁）
记谱：钟同荣

12 2 | 61 2 | 12 6·1 | 61 6 | 53 2·1 |
月光 光 救才 郎 才郎背呀 割韭 菜 韭菜黄 呀

61 2 | 26 16 | 51 1 | 21 6·1 | 61 6 |
好干 旷 千只 鸟呀 走上 山 山有 路哇 走上 树，

61 5 | 66 21 | 61 5 | 53 22 | 61 2 |
树有 卡 跌呀 下来 做罂 井 罂井 漏呀 炒黄 豆，

53 222 | 66 5 ||
黄豆 胖呀介 煎面 烧。

月光光绢花花

1=C 2/4

演唱：朱金莲
记谱：钟同荣

12 2 | 21 6 | 56 21 | 61 6 |
月光 光 纺花 花 河下 娇莲 九有 嫁，

53 22 | 53 2 ||
肚大 了生 淌哇 淌。

·86·

乌翼子飞过河

1=D 3/4

演唱：朱金莲
记谱：钟同荣

33 2 | 13 2 | 61 65 | 66 1 |
乌翼 子 飞过 河 带娥 带女 召外 婆

33 22 | 32 16 | 21 61 | 2·1 6 | 5 — ||
外婆 还健 子女 多空 莳眠 平血 喔东 何 哇。

牛牯神

1=D 2/4

演唱：邹传秀
记谱：钟同荣

61 2 | 61 5 | 16 5 | 66 5 |
牛牯 神 快快 来 左有 转 右有 转，

62 26 | 5 62 | 26 5 | 65 12 |
铜车 车要 转 铁车 车要 转 铁打 灯芯

56 1 | 21 15 | 6 65 | 5 — ||
水要 长， 石头 种火 喂 化灰 烬。

·87·

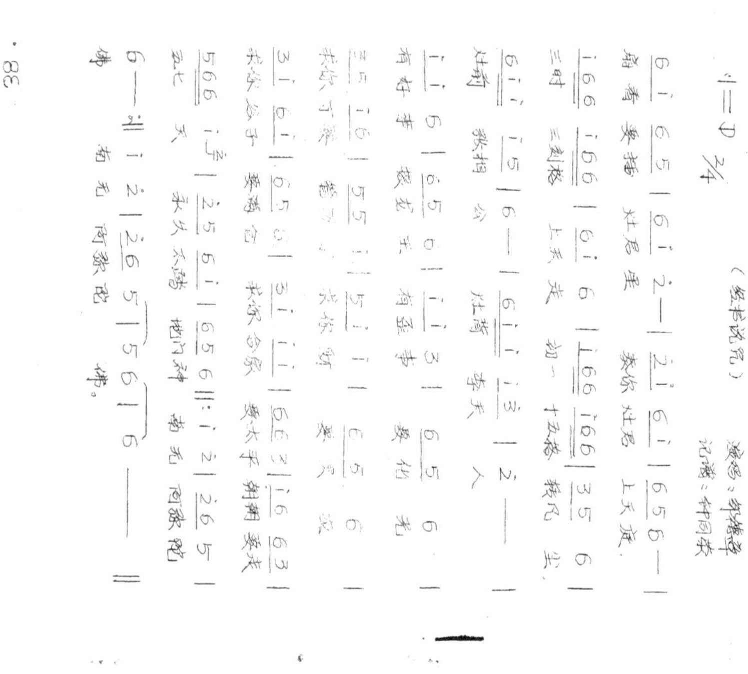

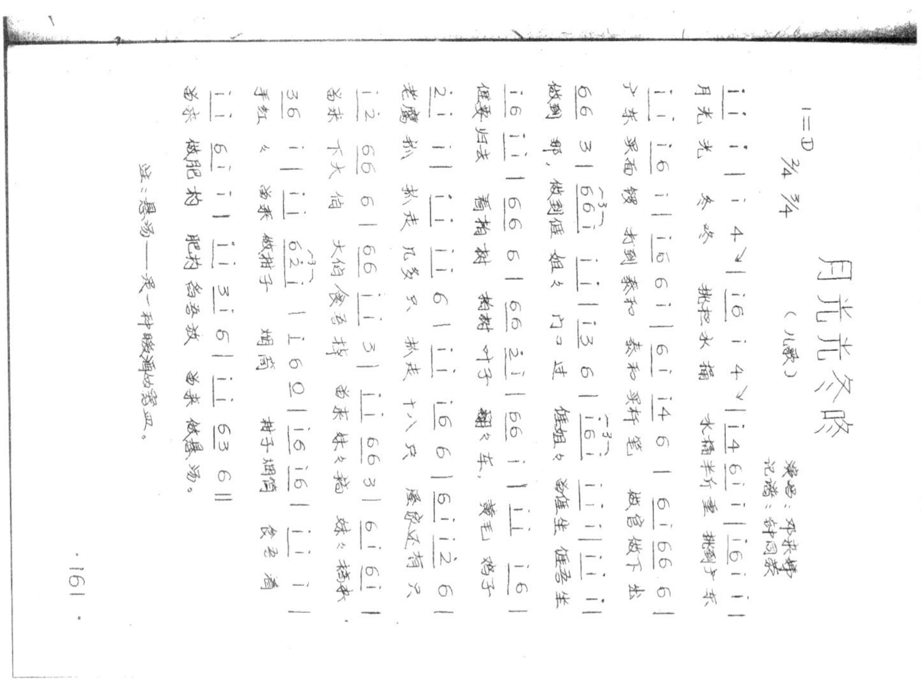

灶君星

（经书说咒）

1=D 2/4

演唱：邹禧章
记谱：钟同荣

6 1 6 5 | 6 1 2 — | 2 1 6 1 | 6 5 6 — |
扇香要插灶君星　　奉你灶君上天庭。

1 6 6 1 6 6 | 6 1 6 | 1 6 6 1 6 6 | 3 5 6 |
三时三刻格上天走初一十五格转凡尘。

6 1 1 1 5 | 6 — | 6 1 1 1 3 | 2 — |
灶前张相公　　灶背李天人

1 1 6 | 6 5 6 | 1 1 3 | 6 5 6 |
有好事报玄王有歪事要化光

3 5 1 6 | 5 5 1 | 5 1 1 | 6 5 6 |
求你丁(?)　　　　求你财要(?)

3 1 6 1 | 6 5 6 | 3 1 1 1 | 6 6 3 | 1 6 6 3 |
求你公子要满仓求你合家要太平刷刷要走

5 6 6 1 2 | 2 5 6 1 | 6 5 6 ||: 1 2 | 2 6 5 |
五七天　永久不踏地门神　南无阿弥陀

6 — :|| 1 2 | 2 6 5 | 5 6 | 6 — ||
佛　南无阿弥陀　佛。

月光光冬咚

1=D 2/4 3/4

（儿歌）

演唱：邓求娣
记谱：钟同荣

1 1 1 | 1 4 | 1 6 1 4 | 1 4 6 1 1 | 1 6 1 1 |
月光光　冬咚　挑担水桶　水桶半斤重　挑到广东

1 1 1 6 1 | 1 6 6 1 | 6 1 1 4 6 | 6 1 6 6 6 |
广东买面镘　打到泰和　泰和买杆笔　做官做下出

6 6 3 | 6 6 1 1 1 | 1 3 6 | 1 6 1 1 1 1 | 1 1 1 |
做到那，做到侄姐姐门口过　侄姐姐当侄生　侄吾生

1 6 1 1 | 6 6 6 | 6 6 2 1 | 6 6 1 | 1 1 1 6 |
侄要归去　看柏树　柏树叶子　翻翻车，黄毛鸡子

2 1 1 | 1 1 1 1 6 | 1 1 1 6 6 | 6 1 1 2 6 |
老鹰抓　抓走几多只　抓走十八只　屋家还有只

1 2 6 6 6 | 6 6 1 1 3 | 1 1 6 6 3 | 6 1 6 1 |
当来下大伯　大伯食吾掉　当来妹妹福　妹妹福来

3 6 1 | 1 1 6 2 1 | 1 6 0 | 1 6 1 6 | 1 1 1 |
手红红　当来做柑子　烟筒　柑子烟筒　食吾看

1 1 6 1 1 | 1 1 3 1 6 | 1 1 6 3 6 ||
当来做肥灼　肥灼为吾放　当来做悬汤。

注：悬汤——是一种酸酒的瓷皿。

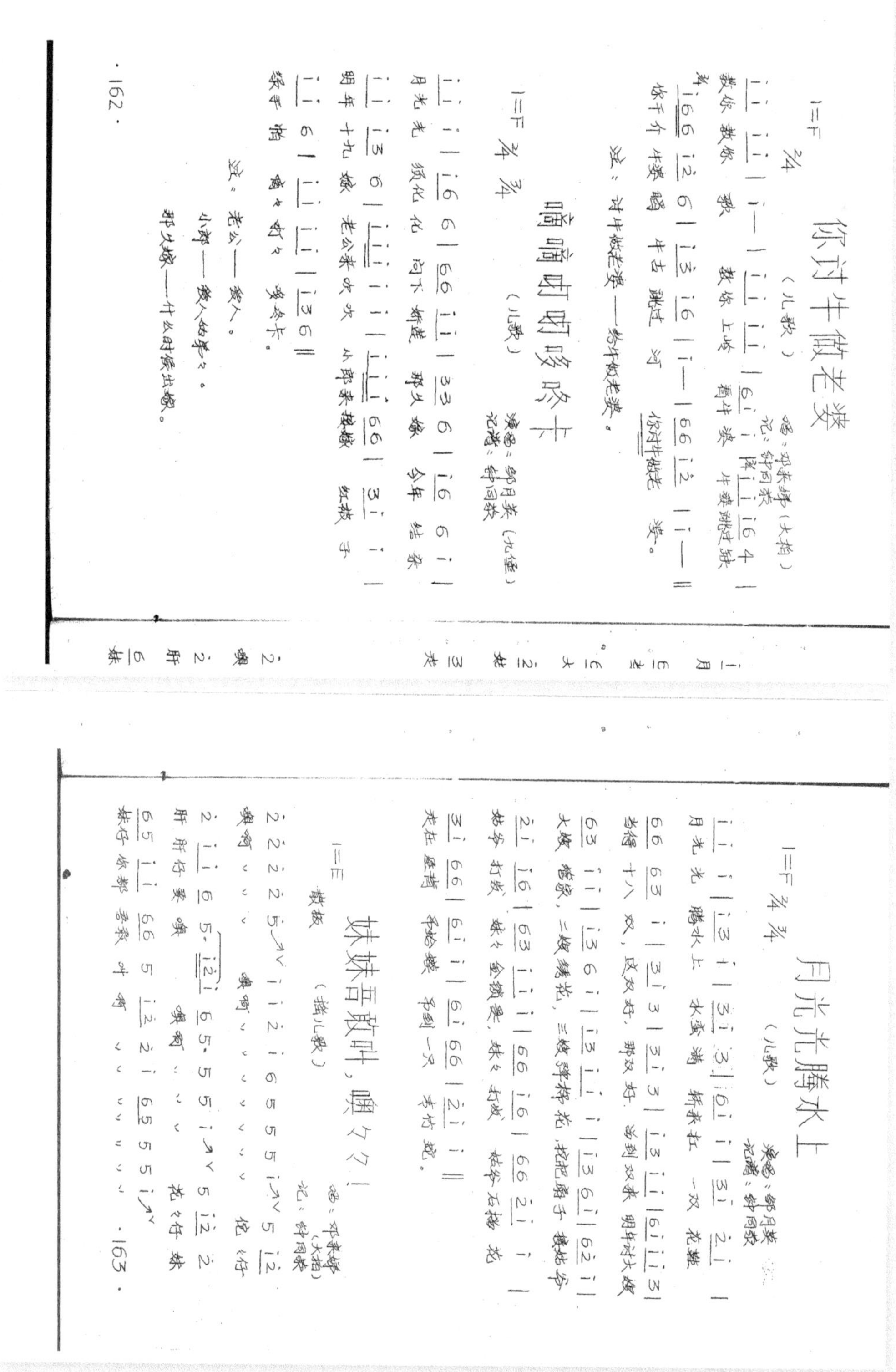

你讨牛做老婆

1=F 2/4

（儿歌）　唱：邓求娣（大拍）　记：钟同荥

教你教你　歌　教你上岭　看牛婆　牛婆跳过缺

牙你干介　牛婆瞒　牛古跳过　河　你讨牛做老　婆。

注：讨牛做老婆——找牛做老婆。

嘀嘀咐咐哆咚卡

1=F 2/4 3/4

（儿歌）　演唱：邹月英（九堡）　记谱：钟同荥

月光光　须化化　向下娇莲　那久嫁　今年结　杂

明年十九嫁　老公来吹吹　小郎来接嫁　红被子

绿手帕　嘀々打々　哆咚卡。

注：老公——爱人。
小郎——爱人的弟々。
那久嫁——什么时候出嫁。

月光光腾水上

1=F 2/4 3/4

（儿歌）　演唱：邹月英　记谱：钟同荥

月光光　腾水上　水蚕满　斩求扛　一双花鞋

当得十八双，这双好，那双好，留到双来　明年讨大嫂

大嫂管家，二嫂绣花，三嫂弹棉花，挖把扇子摇姑爷

姑爷打鼓　妹々金锁匙，妹々打鼓　姑爷石描花

走在屋背　吊蛤蟆　吊到一只　青竹蛇。

妹妹吾敢叫，噢々々！

1=E　散板

（摇儿歌）　唱：邓求娣（大拍）　记：钟同荥

噢啊 ～ ～ ～　噢啊 ～ ～ ～ ～ ～ ～ ～　佗々仔

肝肝仔要噢　噢啊 ～ ～ ～　花々仔妹

妹仔你都吾敢叫啊 ～ ～ ～ ～ ～ ～ ～

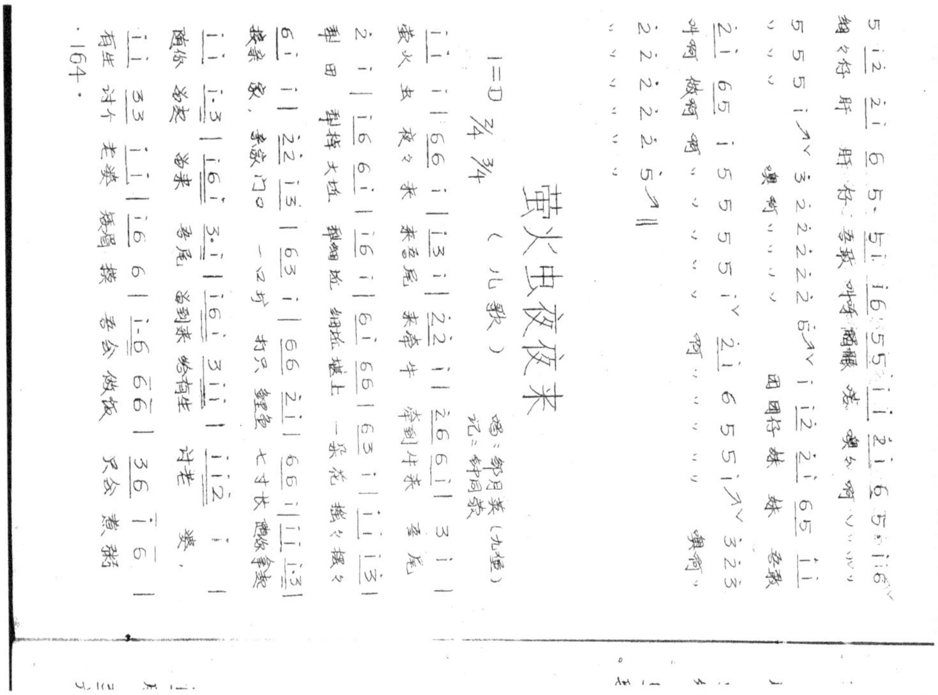

5 i2 2i 6 5· 5i i6 55 ii 2i 6 5 ii6
细々仔 肝 肝 仔 吾敢 叫呀 睏眼 烙 噢々 啊 々々々

5 5 5 i 3 2 2 2 2 2 2 6 i i2 2i 65 ii
々 々 々 噢 啊々々々々 团团仔 妹 妹 吾敢

2i 65 i 5 5 5 5 i 2i 6 5 5 i 3 2 3
叫啊 做啊 啊々 々 々 々 々 啊々 々 々 々 噢啊々

2 2 2 2 2 5 ‖
々 々 々 々 々 々

萤火虫夜夜来

（儿歌）

1=D 2/4 3/4

唱：邹月英（九堡）
记：钟同荣

ii i | 66 i | i3 i | 22 i | 266i | 3 i |
萤火 虫 夜々 来 来吾尾 来牵 牛 牵到牛来 吾尾

2 i | i6 6i | i6 i | 6i 66 | 63 i | ii i3 |
犁 田 犁掉 大坵 犁细坵 细坵 堪上 一朵花 摇々 摆々

6i i | 22 i3 | 63 i | 66 2i | 66 i | ii i3 |
接亲 家， 亲家门口 一口圹 打只 鲤鱼 七寸长 随你拿起

ii i·3 | i6i 3·i | i6i 3ii | ii2 i |
随你 拿起 拿来 吾尾 拿到来 给有生 讨老 婆，

ii 33 ii | i6 6 | i·6 66 | 36 i 6 |
有生 讨个 老婆 矮唱 挨 吾会 做饭 只会 煮粥

·164·

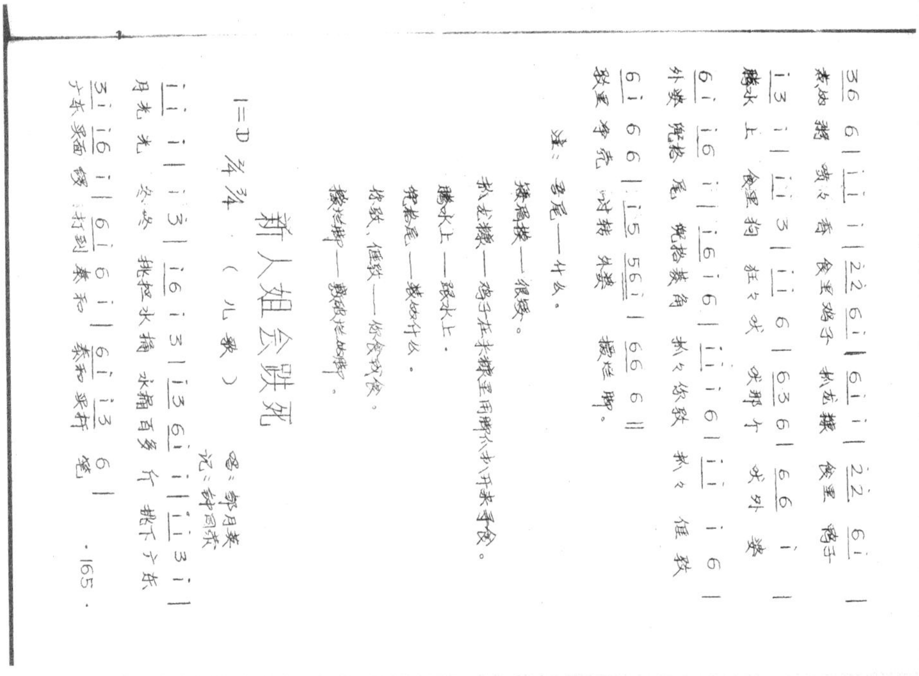

36 6 | ii i | 22 6i | 6i i | 22 6i |
煮的 粥 喷々 香 食里鸡子 扒龙糠 食里 鸭子

i3 i | ii 3 | ii 6 | 636 | 66 i |
腾水 上 食里 狗 狂々 吠 吠那个 吠外 婆

6i i6 i | i6 i 6 | ii i 6 | ii i 6 |
外婆 兜格 尾 兜格 裴角 扒々 你致 扒々 佴致

6i 66 | i5 56i | 66 6 ‖
致里 净壳 讨转 外婆 擞烂 脚。

注：吾尾——什么。
矮唱挨——很矮。
扒龙糠——鸡子在米糠里用脚爪扒开来寻食。
腾水上——跟水上。
兜格尾——装做什么。
你致、佴致——你食我食。
擞烂脚——戳破烂的脚。

新人姐会跌死

1=D 2/4 3/4

（儿歌）

唱：邹月英
记：钟同荣

ii i | i 3 | i6 i 3 | i3 6i i | ii 3 i |
月光 光 冬 冬 挑担水 桶 水桶 百多 斤 挑下 广东

3i i6 i | 6i 6 i | 6i i3 6 |
广东 买面 镜 打到 泰和 泰和 买杆 笔

·165·

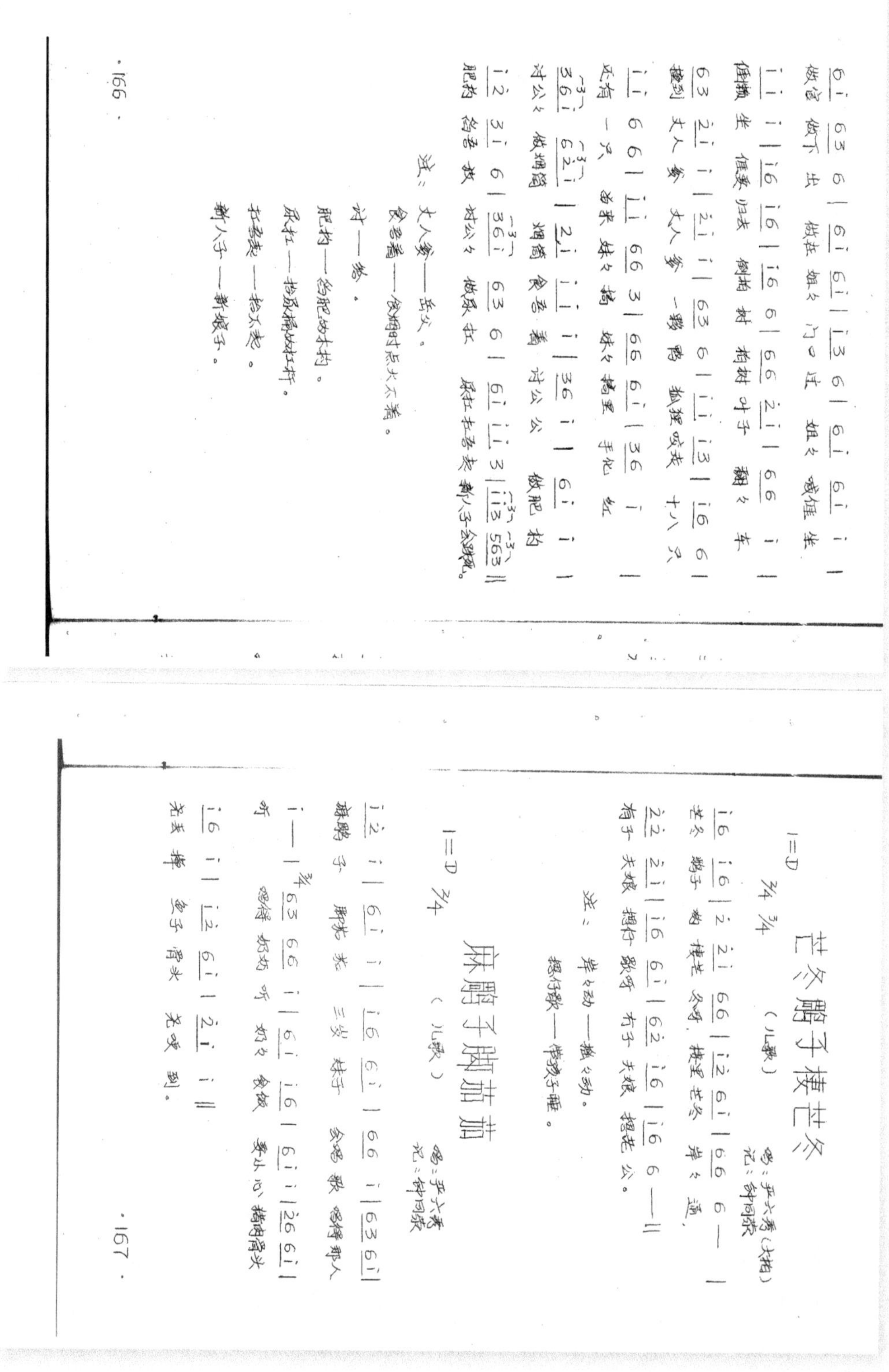

6 1̇ 6 3 6 | 6 1̇ 6 1̇ | 1̇ 3 6 | 6 1̇ 6 1̇ 1̇ |
做官 做下 出 做在 姐々 门口 过 姐々 喊佳 坐

1̇ 1̇ 1̇ | 1̇ 6 1̇ 6 | 1̇ 6 6 | 6 6 2̇ 1̇ | 6 6 1̇ |
佳懒 坐 佳要 归去 倒拘 树 拘树 叶子 翻々 车

6 3 2̇ 1̇ 1̇ | 2̇ 1̇ 1̇ | 6 3 6 | 1̇ 1̇ 1̇ 3 | 1̇ 6 6 |
撞到 丈人 爹 丈人 爹 一对 鸭 狐狸 咬去 十八 只

1̇ 1̇ 6 6 | 1̇ 1̇ 6 6 3 | 6 6 6 1̇ | 3 6 1̇ |
还有 一 只 留来 妹々 捣 妹々 捣里 手伦 红

3 6 1̇ 6 2̇ 1̇ | 2 1̇ 1̇ 1̇ 1̇ | 3 6 1̇ | 6 1̇ 1̇ |
讨公々 做烟筒 烟筒 食吾 着 讨公 公 做肥 杓

1̇ 2̇ 3 1̇ 6 | 3 6 1̇ 6 3 6 | 6 1̇ 1̇ 1̇ 3 | 1̇ 1̇ 3 5 6 3 ||
肥杓 舀吾 放 讨公々 做尿 扛 尿扛 扛吾起 新人子会踩瓦。

注：丈人爹——岳父。

食吾着——食烟时点火不着。

讨——娶。

肥杓——舀肥的木杓。

尿扛——抬尿桶的扛杆。

扛吾起——抬不起。

新人子——新娘子。

·166·

芒冬鹏子棲芒冬

1=D 3/4 3/4 （儿歌） 唱：尹六秀（大柏） 记：钟同荣

1̇ 6 1̇ 6 | 2̇ 2̇ 1̇ 6 6 | 1̇ 2̇ 6 1̇ | 6 6 6 — |
芒冬 鹏子 的 棲芒 冬呀，棲里 芒冬 岸々 通，

2̇ 2̇ 2̇ 1̇ | 1̇ 6 6 1̇ | 6 2̇ 1̇ 6 | 1̇ 6 6 — ||
有子 夫娘 摇仔 歌呀 有子 夫娘 摇老 公。

注：岸々动——摇々动。

摇仔歌——带孩子睡。

麻鹏子脚茄茄

1=D 3/4 （儿歌） 唱：尹六秀 记：钟同荣

1̇ 2̇ 1̇ | 6 1̇ 1̇ | 1̇ 6 6 1̇ | 6 6 1̇ | 6 3 6 1̇ |
麻鹏 子 脚茄 茄 三岁 妹子 会唱 歌 唱得 那人

1̇ — | 3/4 6 3 6 6 1̇ | 6 1̇ 1̇ 6 | 6 1̇ 1̇ | 2 6 6 1̇ |
听 唱得 奶奶 听 奶々 食饭 要小 心 搞肉骨头

1̇ 6 1̇ | 1̇ 2̇ 6 1̇ | 2̇ 1̇ 1̇ ||
光丢 掉 鱼子 骨头 光哽 到。

·167·

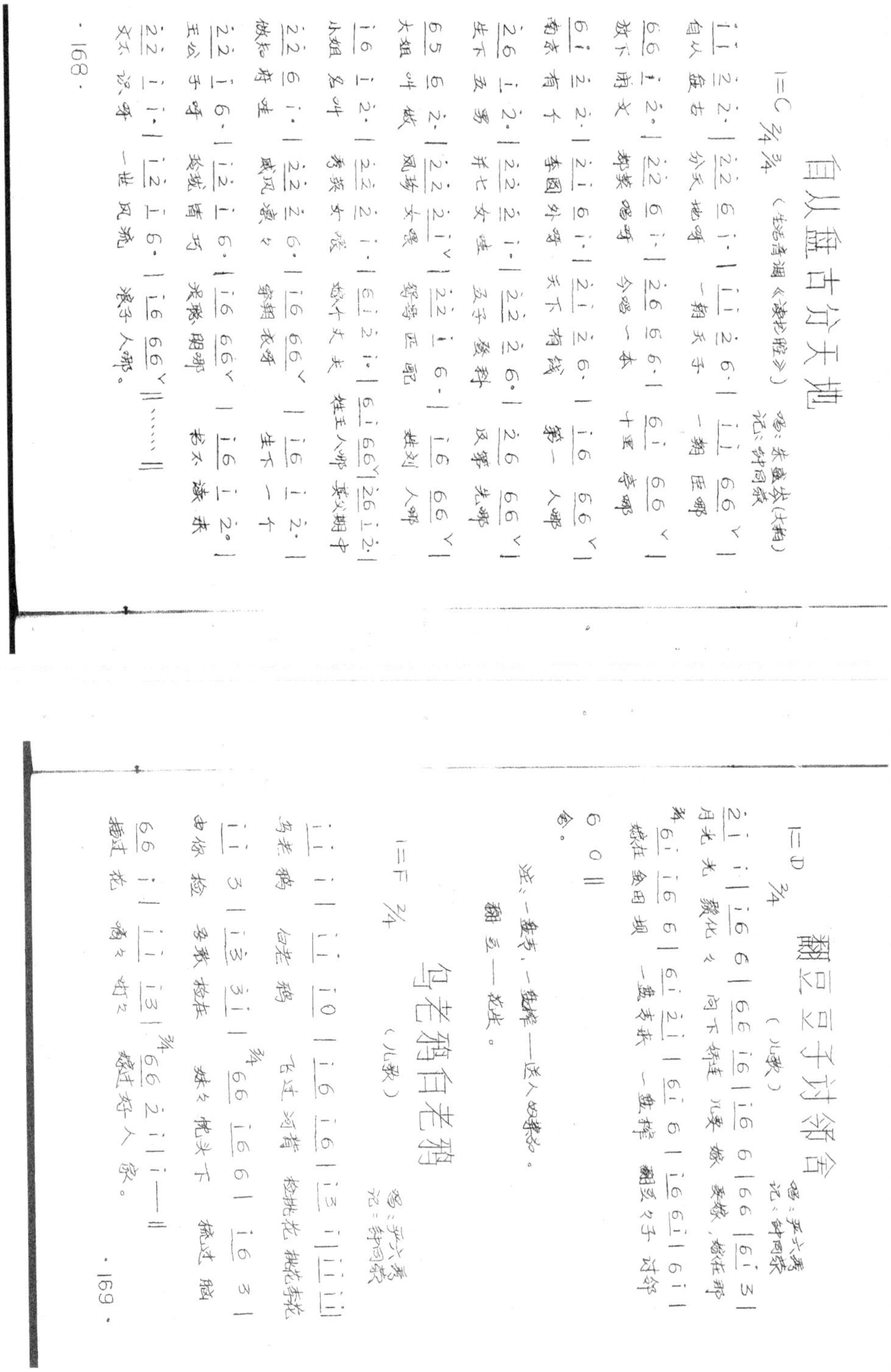

自从盘古分天地

1=C 2/4 3/4 （生活音调《读书腔》） 唱：朱盛崇（大狗） 记：钟同荣

1̇1̇ 2̇ 2̇· | 2̇2̇ 6 1̇· | 1̇1̇ 2̇ 6· | 1̇1̇ 66ᵛ |
自从 盘古 分天 地呀 一朝 天子 一朝 臣哪

66 1̇ 2̇· | 2̇2̇ 6 1̇· | 2̇6 5 6· | 61̇ 66ᵛ |
放下 雨文 都莫 唱呀 今唱 一本 十里 亭哪

61̇ 2̇ 2̇· | 2̇1̇ 6 1̇· | 2̇1̇ 2̇ 6· | 1̇6 66ᵛ |
南京 有个 李园 外呀 天下 有钱 第一 人哪

2̇6 1̇ 2̇· | 2̇2̇ 2̇ 1̇· | 2̇2̇ 2̇ 6· | 2̇6 66ᵛ |
生下 五男 并七 女哇 五子 登科 双第 先哪

65 6 2̇· | 2̇2̇ 2̇1̇ᵛ | 2̇2̇ 1̇ 6· | 1̇6 66ᵛ |
大姐 叫做 凤珍 女喂 鸳鸯 匹配 姓刘 人哪

1̇6 1̇ 2̇· | 2̇2̇ 2̇ 1̇· | 61̇ 2̇ 1̇· | 61̇ 66ᵛ | 2̇6 1̇ 2̇· |
小姐 名叫 秀英 女喂 嫁个 丈夫 姓王 人哪 其父 朝中

2̇2̇ 6 1̇· | 2̇2̇ 2̇ 6· | 1̇6 66ᵛ | 1̇6 1̇ 2̇· |
做知 府哇 威风 凛凛 穿朝 衣呀 生下 一个

2̇2̇ 1̇ 6· | 1̇2̇ 1̇ 6· | 1̇6 66ᵛ | 1̇6 1̇ 2̇· |
王公 子呀 玲珑 青巧 聪聪 明哪 书不 读来

2̇2̇ 1̇ 1̇· | 1̇2̇ 1̇ 6· | 1̇6 66ᵛ ‖……‖
文不 识呀 一世 风流 浪子 人哪。

·168·

翻豆豆子讨邻舍

1=D 3/4 （儿歌） 唱：严六秀 记：钟同荣

2̇1̇ 1̇ | 1̇6 6 | 66 1̇6 | 1̇6 6 | 66 | 61̇ 3̇ |
月光 光 凝化化 向下 娇莲 儿要 嫁 要嫁，嫁在 那

2/4 61̇ 1̇6 6 | 61̇ 2̇1̇ | 61̇ 6 | 1̇6 61̇ | 61̇ |
嫁在 金田 坝 一盘 枣来 一盘 榨 翻豆 豆子 讨邻

6 0 ‖
舍。

注：一盘枣，一盘榨——送人的礼物。

翻豆——花生。

乌老鸦白老鸦

1=F 2/4 （儿歌） 唱：严六秀 记：钟同荣

1̇1̇ 1̇ | 1̇1̇ 1̇0 | 1̇6 1̇6 | 1̇3̇ 1̇ | 1̇1̇ 1̇1̇ |
乌老 鸦 白老 鸦 飞过 河背 捡桃 花 桃花 李花

1̇1̇ 3̇ | 1̇3̇ 3̇1̇ | 3/4 66 1̇6 6 | 1̇6 3̇ |
由你 捡 多数 捡在 妹妹 枕头 下 梳过 脑

66 1̇ | 1̇1̇ 1̇3̇ | 3/4 66 2̇ 1̇ | 1̇ — ‖
插过 花 嘀嘀 哒哒 嫁过 好人 家。

·169·

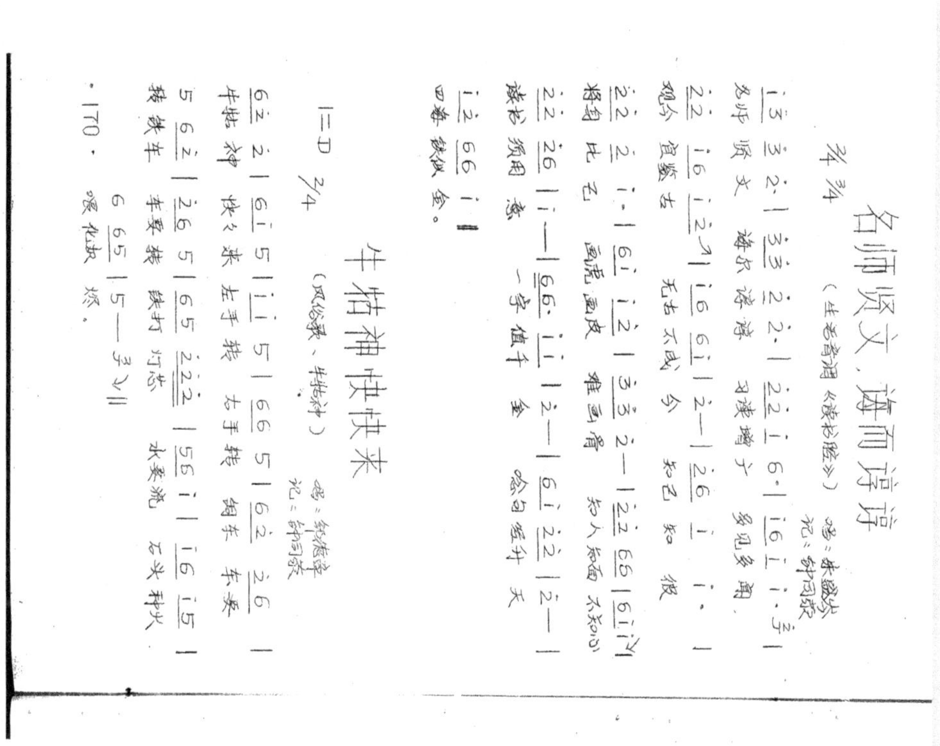

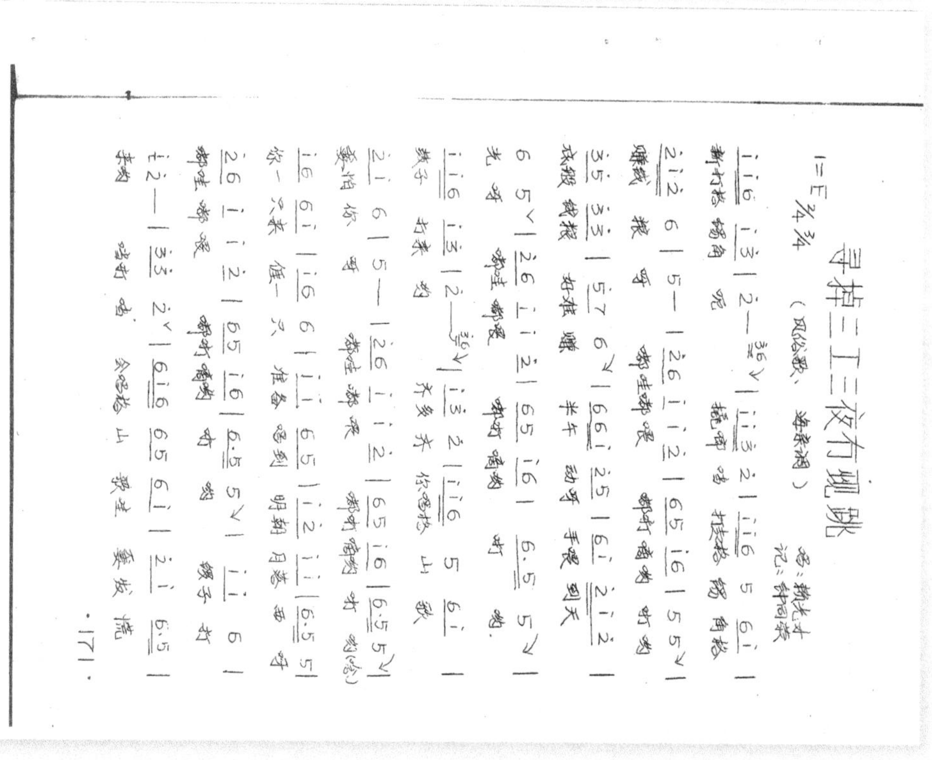

名师贤文，诲而谆谆

2/4 3/4　（生活音调《读书腔》）　唱：朱盛岑　记：钟同荣

13 3 2· | 33 2 2· | 22 1 6· | 16 1 1· 3 |
名师 贤 文　诲尔 谆 谆　习读 增 广　多见多 闻，

22 16 12 | 16 61 | 2— | 26 1 1· |
观今 宜鉴 古　无古 不成 今　知己 知 彼

22 2 1· | 61 12 | 33 2— | 22 65 | 61 1 |
将身 比 己　画虎 画皮　难画 骨　知人 知面 不知心

22 26 | 1— | 66· 11 | 2— | 61 22 | 2— |
读书 须用 意　一字 值千 金　念句 经升 天

12 66 1 ||
四海 铁似 金。

牛牯神快快来

1=D 2/4　（风俗歌、牛牯神）　唱：邹德淙　记：钟同荣

62 2 | 61 5 | 11 5 | 66 5 | 62 26 |
牛牯 神　快々 来　左手 转　右手 转　钢车 车要

5 62 | 26 5 | 65 222 | 56 1 | 16 15 |
转 铁车　车要 转　铁打 灯芯　水要 流　石头 种火

6 65 | 5— 3 ||
喂 化奴 烬。

寻掉三工三夜冇视跳

1=E 2/4 3/4　（风俗歌、婚亲调）　唱：赖光才　记：钟同荣

116 13 | 2— 35 | 113 2 | 116 5 61 |
新打格 锡角 呢　摇唧 唱　打起格 锡 角格

212 6 | 5— | 26 1 12 | 65 16 | 5 5 |
赚钱 粮 呀　嘟哇 嘟 喂　嘟打 嘀哟 叮 哟

35 33 | 57 6 | 661 25 | 61 212 |
衣服 钱粮　好难 赚　半午 动呀　手喂 到天

6 5 | 26 1 12 | 65 16 | 6.5 5 |
光 呀　嘟哇 嘟 喂　嘟打 嘀哟　叮 哟。

116 13 | 2— 35 | 13 2 | 116 5 61 |
鼓子 打来 哟　齐多 齐　你唱格 山 歌

21 6 | 5— | 26 1 12 | 65 16 | 6.5 5 |
要怕 你 呀　嘟哇 嘟 喂　嘟打 嘀哟 叮 哟（哈）

16 61 | 16 6 | 11 65 | 12 11 | 6.5 5 |
你一 只来　佢一 只　准备 唱到　明朝 月落　西 呀

26 1 12 | 65 16 | 6.5 5 | 11 6 |
嘟哇 嘟 喂　嘟打 嘀哟　叮 哟　锣子 打

12— | 33 2 | 616 65 61 | 21 6.5 |
来哟　唱打 唱　会唱格 山 歌生　要发 慌

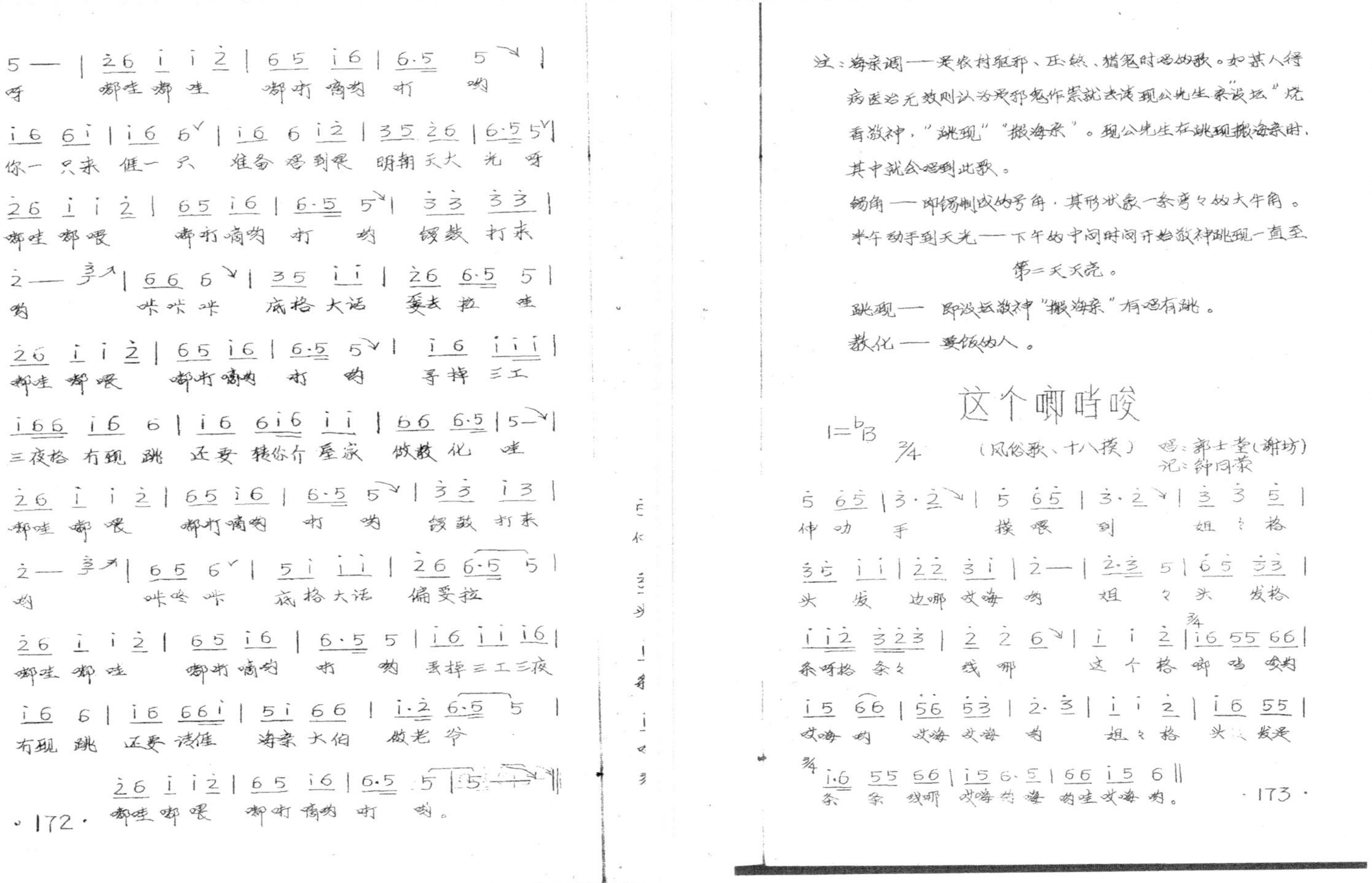

5 — | 26 1 1 2 | 65 16 | 6·5 5 |
呀 啷哇 啷哇 啷冇 嘀哟 冇 哟

16 61 | 16 6 | 16 6 12 | 35 26 | 6·5 5 |
你一 只来 佢一 只 准备 唱到哏 明朝 天大 光 呀

26 1 1 2 | 65 16 | 6·5 5 | 33 33 |
啷哇 啷哏 啷冇 嘀哟 冇 哟 锣鼓 打来

2 — 3 | 66 6 | 35 11 | 26 6·5 5 |
哟 咪咪 咪 底格 大话 耍去 拉 哇

26 1 1 2 | 65 16 | 6·5 5 | 16 111 |
啷哇 啷哏 啷冇 嘀哟 冇 哟 手拌 三工

166 16 6 | 16 616 11 | 66 6·5 | 5 — |
三夜格 有砚 跳 还要 转你介 屋家 做数 化 哇

26 1 1 2 | 65 16 | 6·5 5 | 33 13 |
啷哇 啷哏 啷冇 嘀哟 冇 哟 锣鼓 打来

2 — 3 | 65 6 | 51 11 | 26 6·5 5 |
哟 咪哆 咪 底格 大话 偏要拉

26 1 1 2 | 65 16 | 6·5 5 | 16 11 16 |
啷哇 啷哇 啷冇 嘀哟 冇 哟 丢掉 三工 三夜

16 6 | 16 661 | 51 66 | 1·2 6·5 5 |
有砚 跳 还要 请佢 海亲 大伯 做老 爷

26 1 12 | 65 16 | 6·5 5 | 5 |
啷哇 啷哏 啷冇 嘀哟 冇 哟。

注：海亲调——是农村驱邪、压煞、猎鬼时唱的歌。如某人得病医治无效则认为是邪鬼作祟就去请现公先生来"设坛"烧香敬神，"跳砚""搬海亲"。现公先生在跳砚搬海亲时，其中就会唱到此歌。

锡角——即锡制成的号角，其形状象一条弯弯的大牛角。

半午动手到天光——下午的中间时间开始敬神跳砚一直至第二天天亮。

跳砚——即设坛敬神"搬海亲"有唱有跳。

教化——要饭的人。

这个啊哇咬

1=♭B 2/4 （风俗歌、十八摸） 唱：郭士奎（谢坊） 记：钟冈荣

5 65 | 3·2 | 5 65 | 3·2 | 3 3 5 |
伸 动 手 摸 哏 到 姐 々 格

35 11 | 22 31 | 2 — | 2·3 5 | 65 33 |
头 发 边哪 哎嗨 哟 姐 々 头 发格

112 323 | 2 2 6 | 1 1 2 | 3/4 16 55 66 |
条呀格 条々 线 哪 这 个 格 啷 哒 哎哟

15 66 | 56 53 | 2· 3 | 1 1 2 | 16 55 |
哎嗨 哟 哎嗨 哎嗨 哟 姐 々 格 头 发是

3/4 1·6 55 66 | 15 6·5 | 66 15 6 ||
条 条 线哪 哎嗨 哎 嗨 哟哇 哎嗨 哟。

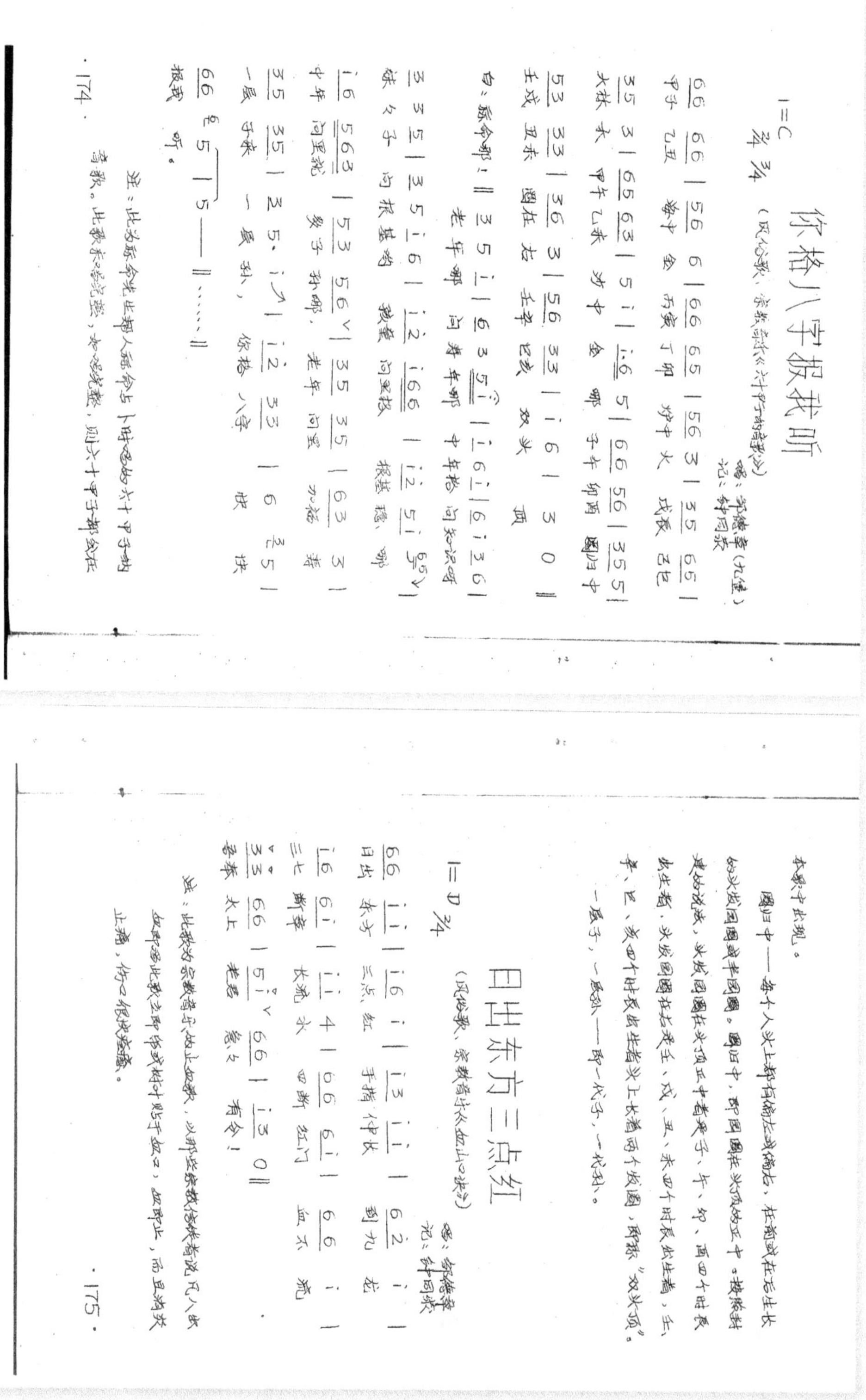

你格八字报我听

1=C
2/4 3/4　（风俗歌、宗教音乐《六十甲子的音歌》）

唱：邹德章（九堡）
记：钟同荣

66 66 | 56 6 | 66 65 | 56 3 | 35 65 |
甲子 乙丑 海中 金 丙寅 丁卯 炉中 火 戊辰 己巳

35 3 | 65 63 | 5 1̇ | 1̇6 5 | 66 56 | 35 5 |
大林 木 甲午 乙未 沙中 金 哪 子午 卯酉 囫归中

53 33 | 36 3 | 56 33 | 1̇ 6 | 3 0 ||
壬戌 丑未 圆在 右 壬辛 巳亥 双 头 面

白：算命那！‖ 3 5 1̇ | 6 3 51̇ | 1̇ 6 1̇ | 6 1̇ 3 6 |
老 年 哪 问 寿 年哪 中 年格 问知识呀

3 3 5 | 3 5 1̇ 6 | 1̇2̇ 1̇66 | 1̇2̇ 51̇ 5 |
妹 々 子 问 根 基 哟 孩童 问里极 根基 稳、哪

1̇6 563 | 53 56 | 35 35 | 63 3 |
中 年 问里就 多子 孙哪， 老年 问里 加福 寿

35 35 | 3 5. 1̇ | 1̇2̇ 33 | 6 5 |
一层 子来 一 层 孙， 你格 八字 快 快

66 5 | 5 —— ‖ …… ‖
报我 听。

注：此为算命先生帮人算命占卜时唱的六十甲子纳音歌。此歌未唱完整，如唱完整，则六十甲子都会在

· 174 ·

本歌中出现。

囫归中——每个人头上都有偏左或偏右，在前或在后生长的头发圆圈或半圆圈。囫归中，即圆圈在头顶的正中。按照封建的说法，头发圆圈在头顶正中者是子、午、卯、酉四个时辰出生者，头发圆圈在右是壬、戌、丑、未四个时辰出生者，壬、辛、巳、亥四个时辰出生者头上长着两个发圈，即称“双头顶”。

一层子，一层孙——即一代子，一代孙。

日出东方三点红

1=D 2/4　（风俗歌、宗教音乐《血山口诀》）

唱：邹德章
记：钟同荣

66 1̇1̇ | 1̇6 1̇ | 1̇3 1̇1̇ | 62̇ 1̇ |
日出 东方 三点 红 手指 仲长 到九 龙

1̇6 61̇ | 1̇1̇ 4 | 66 61̇ | 66 1̇ |
三七 断辛 长流 水 四断 红门 血不 流

33 66 | 51̇ 66 | 1̇3 0 ||
吾奉 太上 老君 急々 有令！

注：此歌为宗教音乐的止血歌，以那些宗教信徒者说凡人出血即唱此歌立即用纸或树叶贴于血口，血即止，而且消炎止痛，伤口很快痊愈。

· 175 ·

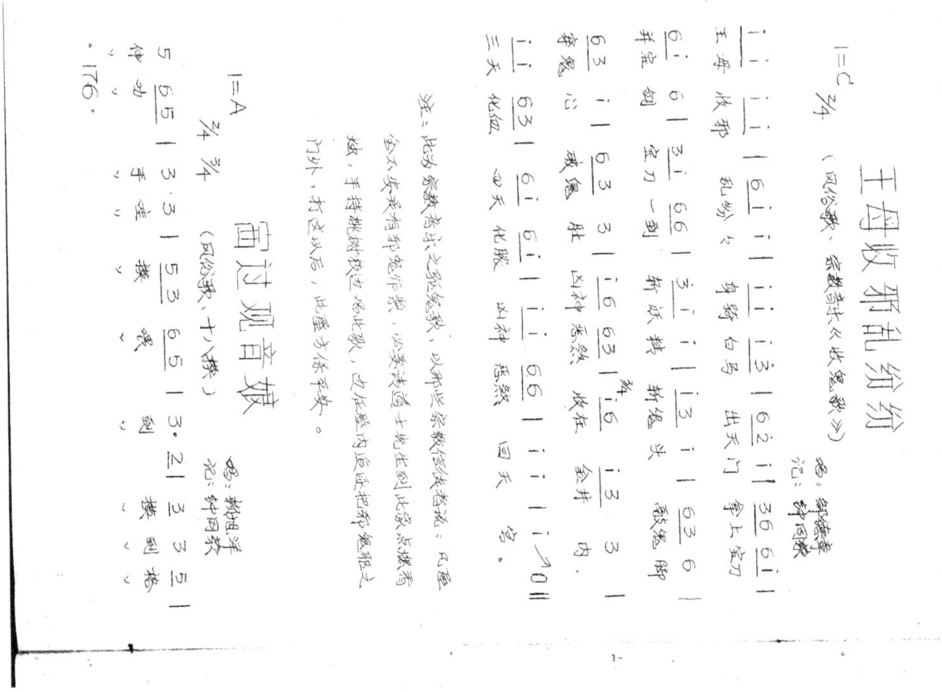

王母收邪乱纷纷

1=C 2/4　（风俗歌、宗教音乐《收鬼歌》）

唱：邹德章
记：钟同歌

i i　i i | 6 i　i | i i　i 3 | 6 2　i | 3 6　6 i |
王 母　收 邪　乱 纷 纷　身 骑　白 马　出 天 门　拿 上 宝 刀

6 i　6 | 3 i　6 6 | 3 i　i | i 3　i | 6 3　6 |
并 宝　剑　宝 刀　一 到　斩 妖 精　斩 鬼　头　敲 鬼　脚

6 3　i | 6 3　3 | i 6　6 3 | 3/4 i 6　i 3　3 |
穿 鬼　心　戒 鬼　肚　凶 神　恶 煞　收 在　金 井　内，

i i　6 3 | 6 i　6 i | i i　6 6 | i　i | i　0 ||
三 天　化 血　四 天　化 脓　凶 神　恶 煞　回 天　宫。

注：此为宗教音乐之驱鬼歌，以那些宗教信徒者说：凡屋舍不安是有邪鬼作祟，必要请道士先生到此家点燃香烛，手持桃树枝边唱此歌，边在屋内追逐把邪鬼驱之门外，打过以后，此屋方保平安。

宙过观音娘

1=A 2/4 3/4　（风俗歌、十八摸）

唱：赖旭洋
记：钟同歌

5　6 5 | 3 · 3 | 5 3　6 5 | 3 · 2 | 3　3 5 |
伸 动　手 连　摸　喂　到　摸 到 格

· 176 ·

3 2　1 1　2 2 | 5 3　2 — | 2 3　5 | 6　3 |
姐 々　头 发　边 光　哎 嗨 哟　姐 々　头 发
　　　额 堂　　　　　　　　　　　额 堂

1.2　3 5　2 2 | 1　1　2 | 1 6　5 5 | 6 — |
排　两 边　啰　生 得　格　蛮 漂　亮 呀
放　毫 光　呀　宙 过　格　观 音　娘 呀

2 1　6 · 1 | 5 · 1　6 | 2 3　3 5 | 6 · 5 | 6 — ||
哎 嗨 哟　哎 嗨 哟　生 得　蛮 漂　亮。
　　　　　　　　　　宙 过　观 音　娘。

大慈大悲观世音菩萨

1=C 2/4 3/4　（宗教音乐）

唱：余秀英（大柏）
记：钟同歌

3　2 | 2　6　i | 6 5　i | i　2 | 2　2 |
观 世　音 菩 萨　众 人 求　神 力　扶 持

i　6　i | 2　6 | 6　i | i　2　i | 5　i |
来 保 佑　佛 法　无 边　救 众 生　手 攀

i　5 | 6　5　i | i　i · | i　4 | 5　5　i |
杨 柳　阿 弥 陀　南 无　南 海　普 陀 山

i　2 | 6　6 | 6　i | 6　i | i　5　i | 6　5 — ||
游 里　世 界　大 慈　大 悲　观 世 音　菩 萨。

· 177 ·

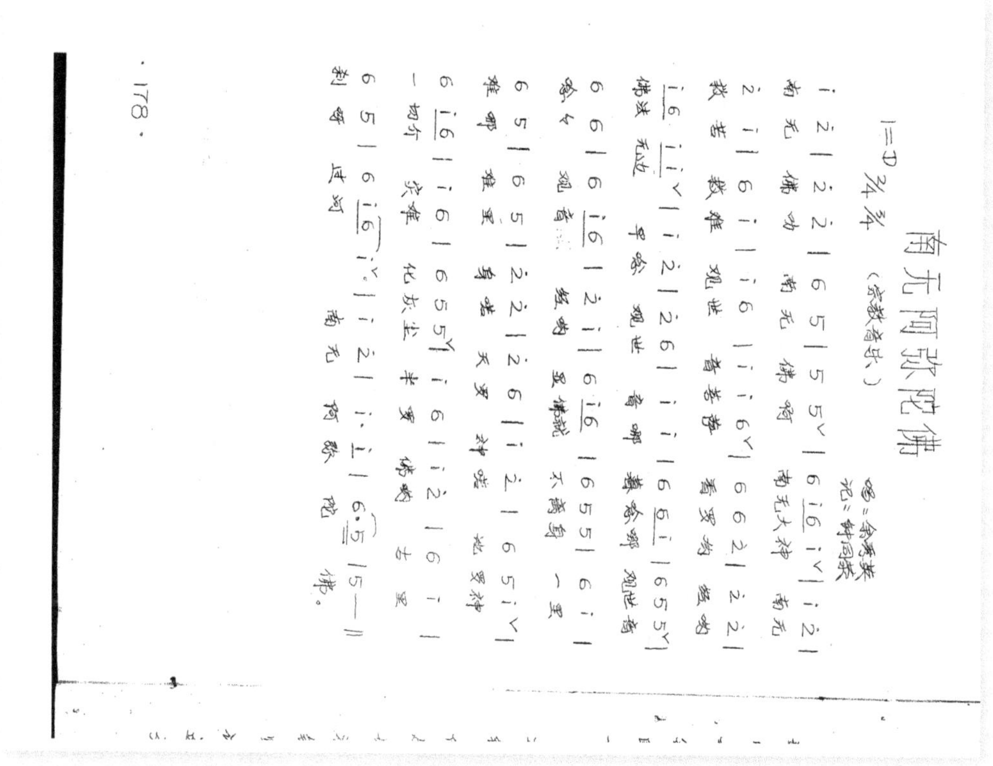

南无阿弥陀佛

1=D 2/4 3/4　（宗教音乐）

唱：余秀英
记：钟同荣

1 2 | 2 2 | 6 5 | 5 5 | 6 16 1 | 1 2 |
南 无　佛 呦　南 无　佛 啊　南无大神　南 无

2 1 | 6 1 | 1 6 | 1 1 6 | 6 6 2 | 2 2 |
救 苦　救 难　观 世　音菩萨　看罗为　经 哟

16 11 | 1 2 | 2 6 | 1 1 | 6 61 | 6 5 5 |
佛法 无边　早 念　观 世　音 哪　暮念哪　观世音

6 6 | 6 16 | 2 1 | 6 16 | 6 5 5 | 6 1 |
念 念　观 音　经 哟　显佛就　不离身　一 里

6 5 | 6 5 | 2 2 | 2 6 | 1 2 | 6 5 1 |
难 哪　难 里　身 啥　天 罗　神 啥　地罗神

6 16 | 1 6 | 6 5 5 | 1 6 | 1 2 | 6 1 |
一 切介　灾 难　化灰尘　半 罗　佛 哟　古 里

6 5 | 6 16 1 | 1 2 | 1· 1 | 6·5 | 5 — ||
刹 呀　过 河　南 无　阿 弥　陀　佛。

· 178 ·

07 第七类 · 革命历史民歌

CATEGORY VII · REVOLUTIONARY FOLK SONGS OF THE CENTRAL SOVIET AREA

导读

革命历史民歌是赣南苏区在二十世纪三十年代形成的特殊歌类。它们记录并反映了土地革命、工农武装斗争、长征征途以及红军与百姓之间的深厚情感。这类民歌以朴素语言和强烈节奏感为特征，常用于鼓舞斗志、传播革命理念、凝聚群众力量。它们既是口头文学，也是历史见证，与苏区政治生活密切交织。今天重温这些歌谣，不仅能感受到那个时代的激情与信念，也能理解民歌作为“人民历史档案”的价值。

Introduction

Revolutionary folk songs emerged in the Central Soviet Area during the 1930s as a unique genre reflecting the era of radical social change. These songs documented and reflected the land reform movement, the struggles of workers and peasants, the Long March, and the profound bond between the Red Army and the people. Characterized by plain language and a strong sense of rhythm, they served to inspire courage, spread revolutionary ideals, and unify collective strength. As both oral literature and historical testimony, these songs were deeply intertwined with the political life of the Soviet Area. Revisiting them today allows us to sense the fervor and conviction of that era, while also appreciating folk songs as “archives of the people’s history.”

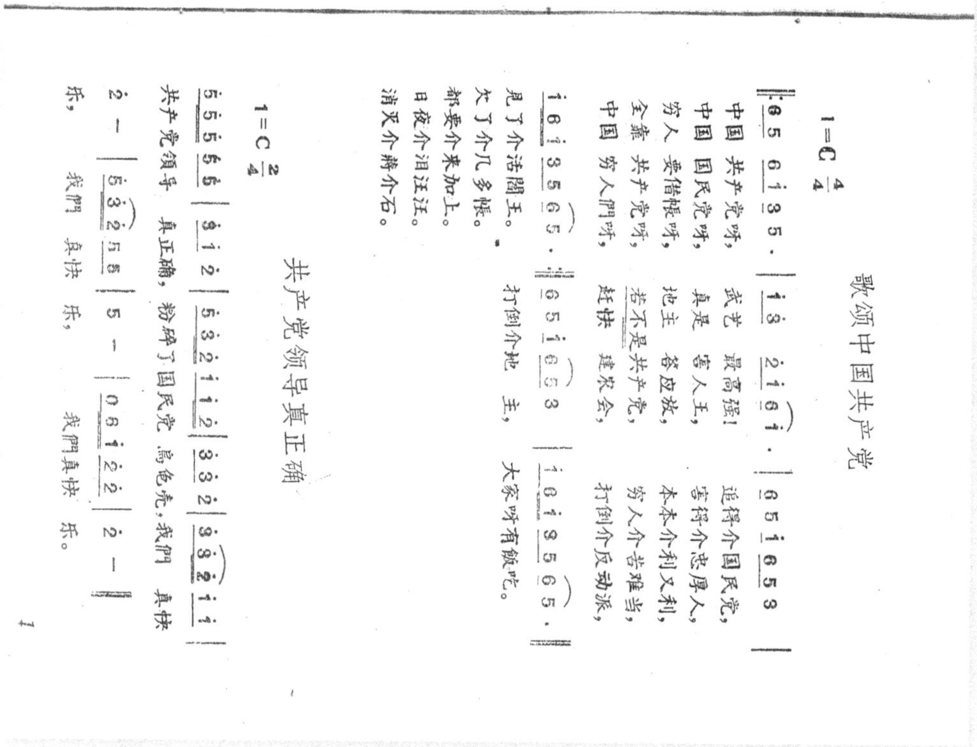

歌颂中国共产党

1=C $\frac{4}{4}$

‖: 6 5 6 i 3 5 · | i 3 2 i 6 i · | 6 5 i 6 5 3 |

中国 共产党呀， 武艺 最高强！ 追得介国民党，
中国 国民党呀， 真是 害人王， 害得介忠厚人，
穷人 要借帐呀， 地主 答应放， 本本介利又利，
全靠 共产党呀， 若不是共产党， 穷人介苦难当，
中国 穷人們呀， 赶快 建农会， 打倒介反动派，

i 6 i 3 5 6 5 · :‖ 6 5 i 6 5 3 | i 6 i 3 5 6 5 · ‖

見了介活閻王。 打倒介地 主， 大家呀有飯吃。
欠了介几多帐。
都要介来加上。
日夜介泪汪汪。
消灭介蒋介石。

共产党领导真正确

1=C $\frac{2}{4}$

5 5 5 5 5 | 3 i 2 | 5 3 2 i i 2 | 3 3 2 | 3 3 2 i i |

共产党领导 真正确，粉碎了国民党 烏龟壳，我們 真快

2 — | 5 3 2 5 5 | 5 — | 0 6 i 2 2 | 2 — ‖

乐， 我們 真快 乐， 我們真快 乐。

1

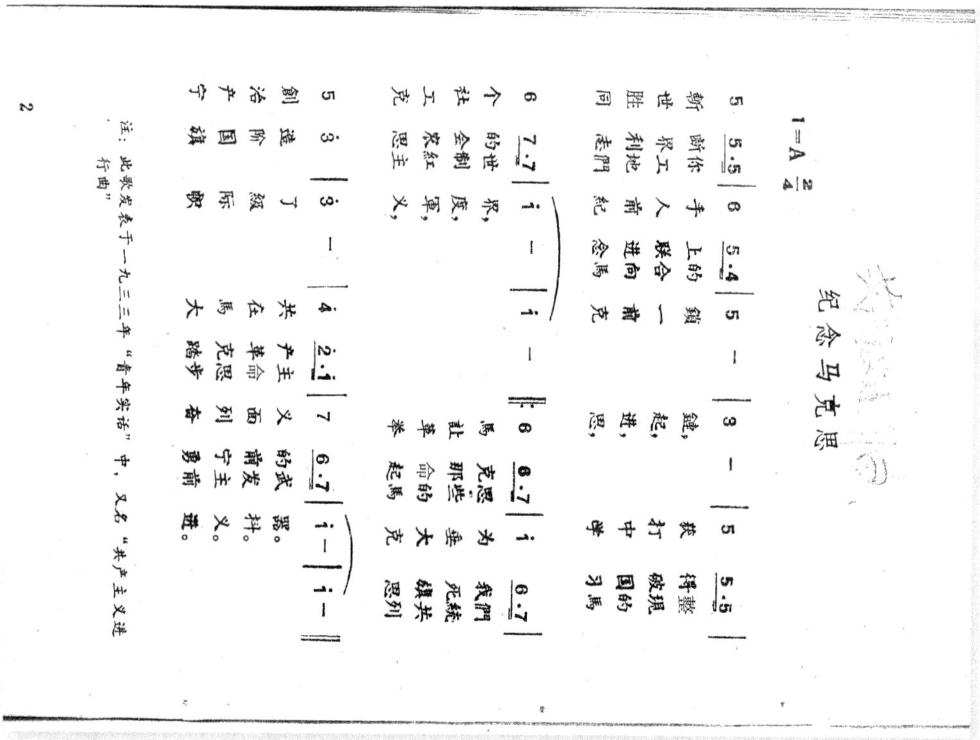

纪念马克思

1=A $\frac{2}{4}$

5 5·5 | 6 5·4 | 5 — | 3 — | 5 5·5 |

斬 断你 手 上的 鎖 鏈， 获 得整
世 界工 人 联合 一 起， 打 破現
胜 利地 前 进向 前 进， 中 国的
同 志們 紀 念馬 克 思， 学 习馬

6 7·7 | i — | i — ‖: 6 6·7 | i 6·7 |

个 的世 界， 馬 克思 为 我們
社 会制 度， 社 那些 垂 死統
工 农紅 軍， 革 命的 大 旗共
克 思主 义， 举 起馬 克 思列

5 3 | 3 — | 4 2·i | 7 6·7 | i — | i — ‖

創 造 了 共 产主 义 的武 器。
治 阶 級 在 革命 面 前发 抖。
产 国 际 馬 克思 列 宁主 义。
宁 旗 帜 大 踏步 奋 勇前 进。

注：此歌发表于一九三三年“青年实话”中，又名“共产主义进行曲”

2

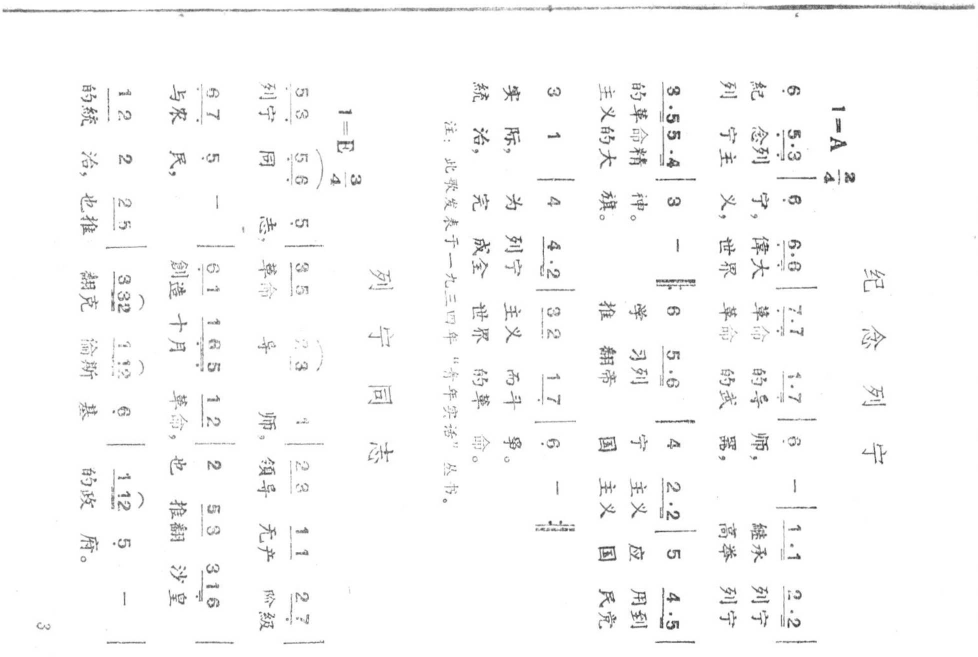

纪念列宁

1=A 2/4

6 5·3 | 6 6·6 | 7·7 1·7 | 6 — | 1·1 2·2 |
紀 念列 宁，偉大 革命 的导 师， 継承 列宁
列 宁主 义，世界 革命 的武 器， 高举 列宁

3·55·4 | 3 — ‖: 6 5·6 | 4 2·2 | 5 4·5 |
的革命精 神。 学 习列 宁 主义 应 用到
主义的大 旗。 推 翻帝 国 主义 国 民党

3 1 | 4 4·2 | 32 17 | 6 — :‖
实 际， 为 列宁 主义 而斗 争。
統 治， 完 成全 世界 的革 命。

注：此歌发表于一九三四年“青年实话”丛书。

列宁同志

1=E 3/4

53 56 5 | 35 23 1 | 23 11 27 |
列宁 同 志，革命 导 师，領导 无产 阶級

67 5 — | 61 165 12 | 2 53 316 |
与农 民， 創造 十月 革命，也 推翻 沙皇

12 2 25 | 332 112 6 | 112 5 — |
的統 治，也推 翻克 倫斯 基 的政 府。

3

35 21 6 | 15 06 2 | 32 3 56 |
革命 成 功 夺取 政 权， 解 放 工

5 21 1 | 32 3 56 | 52 3 1 ‖
人 农 民， 創造 社 会主 义苏 維 埃。

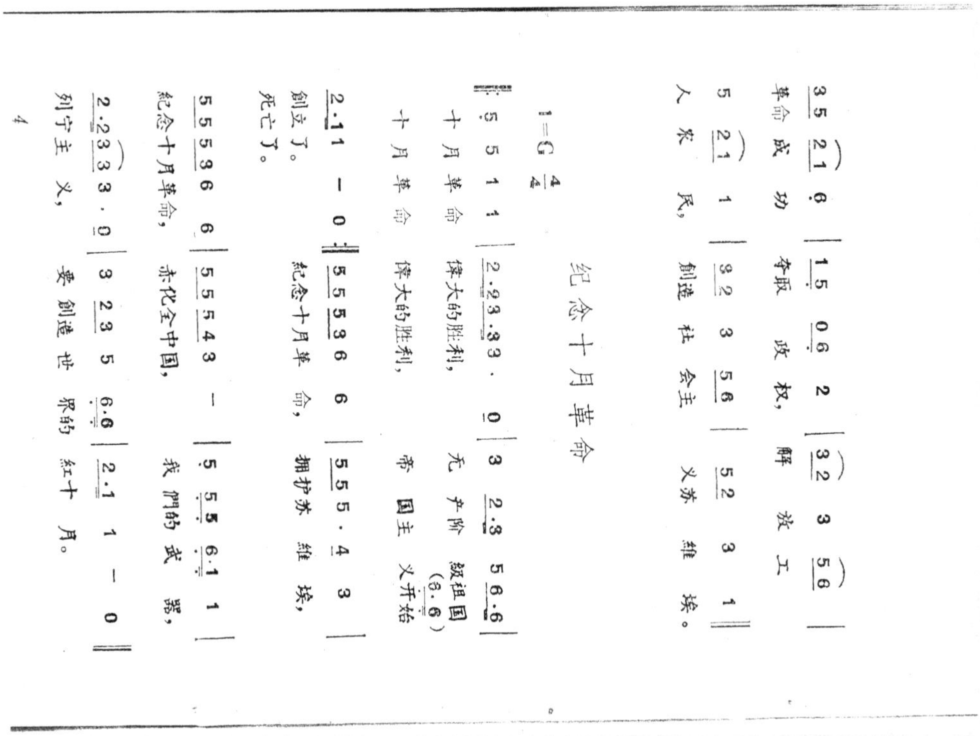

纪念十月革命

1=G 4/4

‖: 5 5 1 1 | 2·23·33· 0 | 3 2·3 5 6·6 |
十 月 革 命 偉大的胜利， 无 产阶 級祖国
(6·6)
十 月 革 命 偉大的胜利， 帝 国主 义开始

2·11 — 0 :‖ 5553 6 6 | 555·4 3 |
創立了。 紀念十月革 命， 拥护苏 維 埃，
死亡了。

5553 6 6 | 5554 3 — | 5 55 6·1 1 |
紀念十月革命， 赤化全中国， 我 們的 武 器，

2·233 3·0 | 3 23 5 6·6 | 2·1 1 — 0 ‖
列宁主 义， 要 創造 世 界的 紅十 月。

4

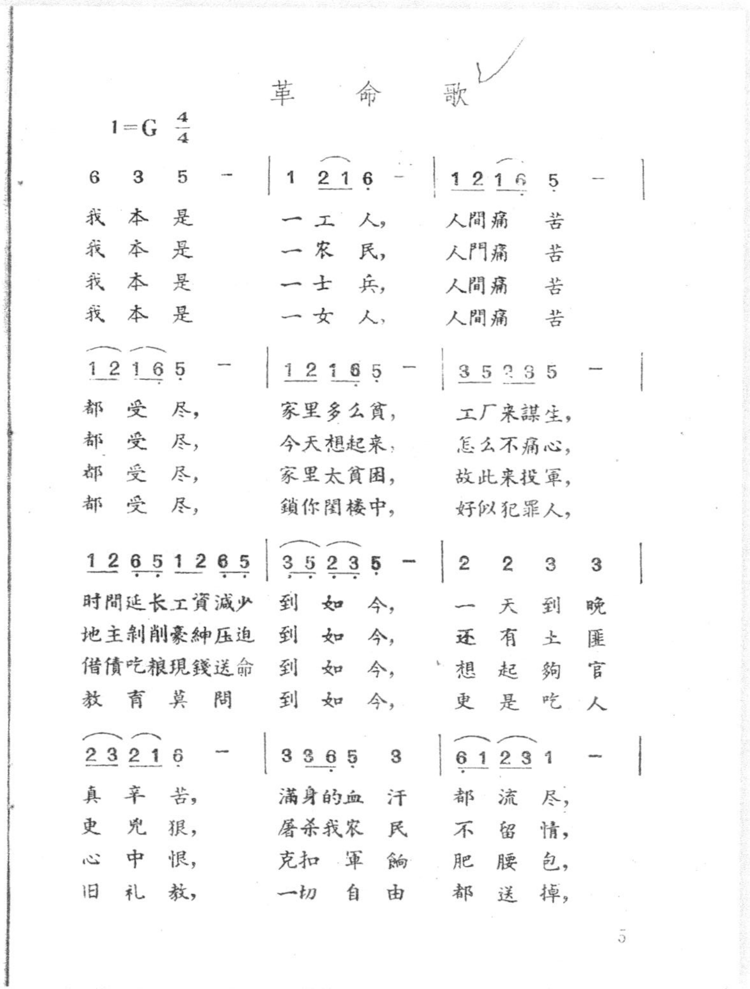

革命歌

1=G $\frac{4}{4}$

6 3 5 － | 1 2 1 6 － | 1 2 1 6 5 － |

我本是 一工人， 人間痛苦
我本是 一农民， 人門痛苦
我本是 一士兵， 人間痛苦
我本是 一女人， 人間痛苦

1 2 1 6 5 － | 1 2 1 6 5 － | 3 5 2 3 5 － |

都受尽， 家里多么貧， 工厂来謀生，
都受尽， 今天想起来， 怎么不痛心，
都受尽， 家里太貧困， 故此来投軍，
都受尽， 鎖你閨楼中， 好似犯罪人，

1 2 6 5 1 2 6 5 | 3 5 2 3 5 － | 2 2 3 3 |

时間延长工資減少 到如今， 一天到晚
地主剥削豪紳压迫 到如今， 还有土匪
借債吃粮現錢送命 到如今， 想起夠官
教育莫問 到如今， 吏是吃人

2 3 2 1 6 － | 3 3 6 5 3 | 6 1 2 3 1 － |

真辛苦， 滿身的血汗 都流尽，
吏兇狠， 屠杀我农民 不留情，
心中恨， 克扣軍餉 肥腰包，
旧礼教， 一切自由 都送掉，

5

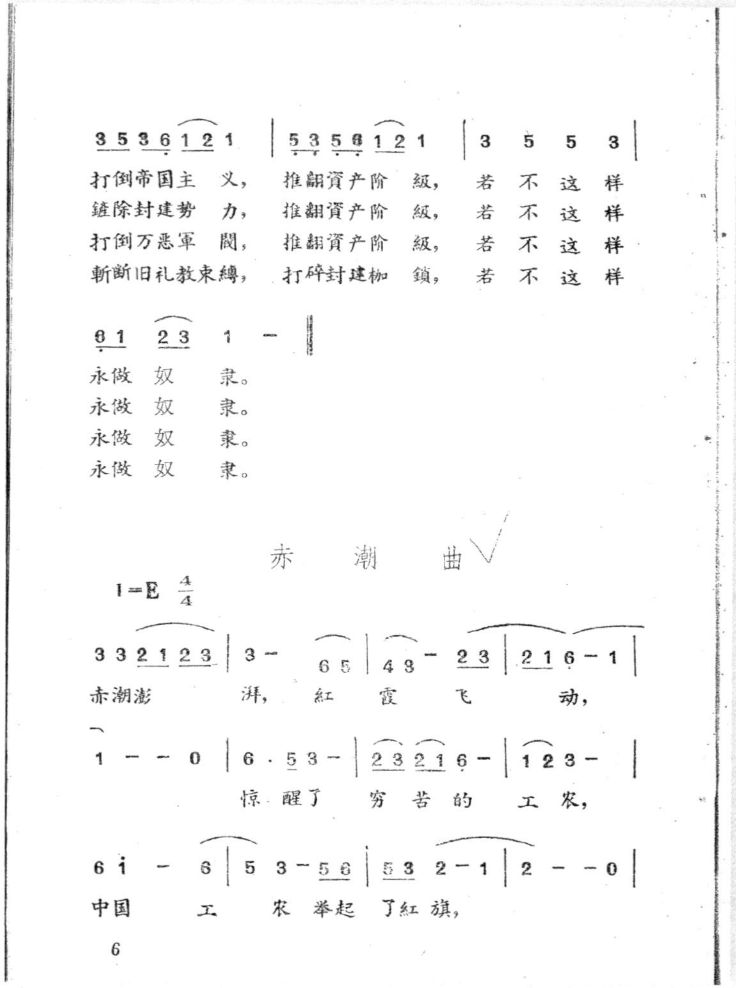

3 5 3 6 1 2 1 | 5 3 5 6 1 2 1 | 3 5 5 3 |

打倒帝国主义， 推翻資产阶級， 若不这样
鏟除封建势力， 推翻資产阶級， 若不这样
打倒万恶軍閥， 推翻資产阶級， 若不这样
斬断旧礼教束縛， 打碎封建枷鎖， 若不这样

6 1 2 3 1 － ‖

永做奴隶。
永做奴隶。
永做奴隶。
永做奴隶。

赤潮曲

1=E $\frac{4}{4}$

3 3 2 1 2 3 | 3 － 6 5 | 4 3 － 2 3 | 2 1 6 － 1 |

赤潮澎湃， 紅霞飞动，

1 － － 0 | 6 · 5 3 － | 2 3 2 1 6 － | 1 2 3 － |

惊醒了 穷苦的 工农，

6 i － 6 | 5 3 － 5 6 | 5 3 2 － 1 | 2 － － 0 |

中国工农举起了紅旗，

6

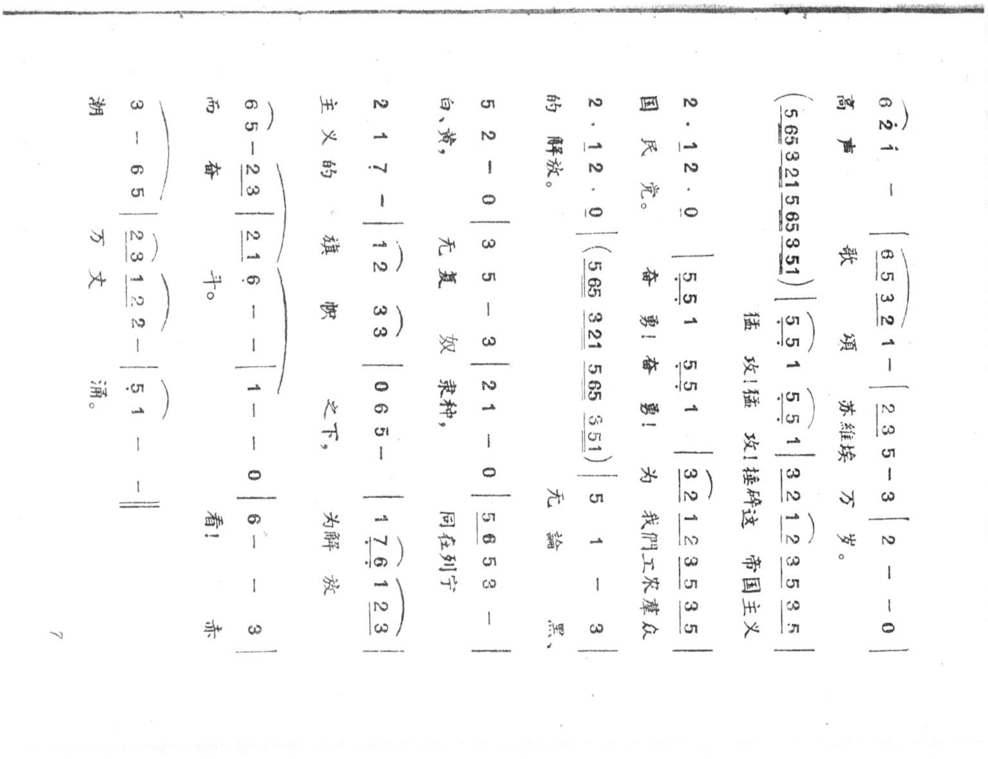

6 2 1 – | 6 5 3 2 1 – | 2 3 5 – 3 | 2 – – 0 |
高 声 歌 颂 苏維埃 万 岁。

(5 65 3 21 5 65 3 51) | 5 5 1 5 5 1 | 3 2 1 2 3 5 3 5 |
猛 攻！猛 攻！捶碎这 帝国主义

2 · 1 2 · 0 | 5 5 1 5 5 1 | 3 2 1 2 3 5 3 5 |
国 民 党。 奋 勇！奋 勇！ 为 我們工农羣众

2 · 1 2 · 0 | (5 65 3 21 5 65 3 51) | 5 1 – 3 |
的 解放。 无 論 黑、

5 2 – 0 | 3 5 – 3 | 2 1 – 0 | 5 6 5 3 – |
白、黄， 无 复 奴 隶种， 同在列宁

2 1 7 – | 1 2 3 3 | 0 6 5 – | 1 7 6 1 2 3 |
主义的 旗 帜 之下， 为解 放

6 5 – 2 3 | 2 1 6 – – | 1 – – 0 | 6 – – 3 |
而 奋 斗。 看！ 赤

3 – 6 5 | 2 3 1 2 2 – | 5 1 – – ||
潮 万 丈 涌。

7

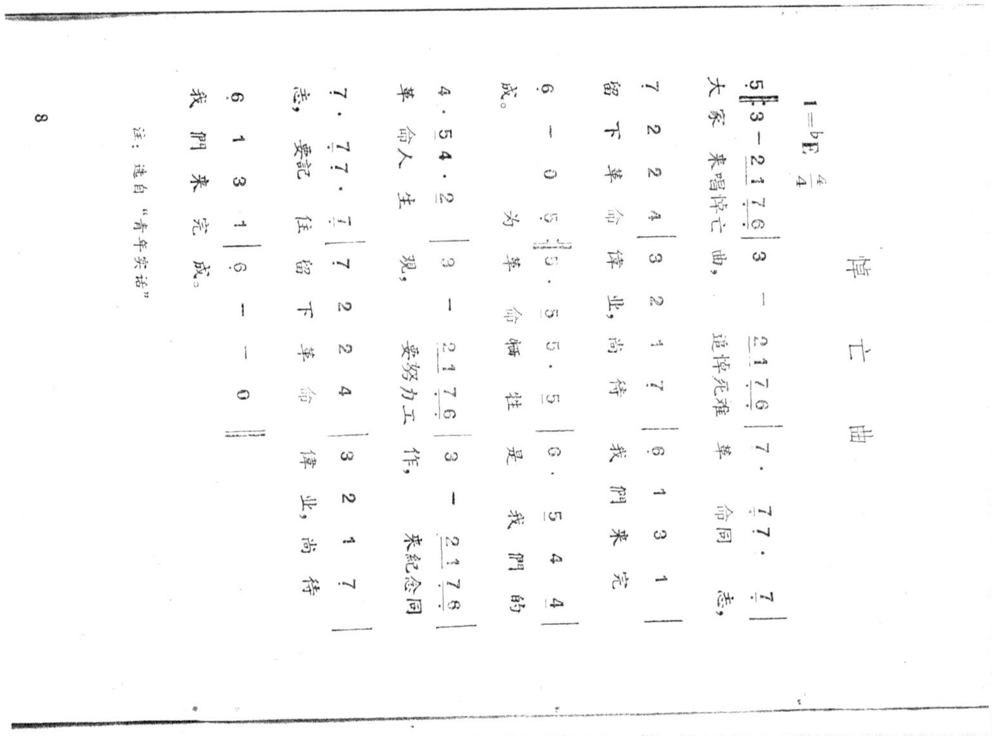

悼亡曲

1=♭E $\frac{4}{4}$

5 ‖: 3 – 2 1 7 6 | 3 – 2 1 7 6 | 7 · 7 7 · 7 |
大 家 来唱悼亡 曲， 追悼死难 革 命同 志，

7 2 2 4 | 3 2 1 7 | 6 1 3 1 |
留 下 革 命 伟 业，尚 待 我 們 来 完

6 – 0 5 :‖ 5 · 5 5 · 5 | 6 · 5 4 4 |
成。 为 革 命 牺 牲 是 我 們 的

4 · 5 4 · 2 | 3 – 2 1 7 6 | 3 – 2 1 7 6 |
革 命人 生 观， 要努力工 作， 来紀念同

7 · 7 7 · 7 | 7 2 2 4 | 3 2 1 7 |
志，要記 住 留 下 革 命 伟 业，尚 待

6 1 3 1 | 6 – – 0 ||
我 們 来 完 成。

注：选自"青年实话"

8

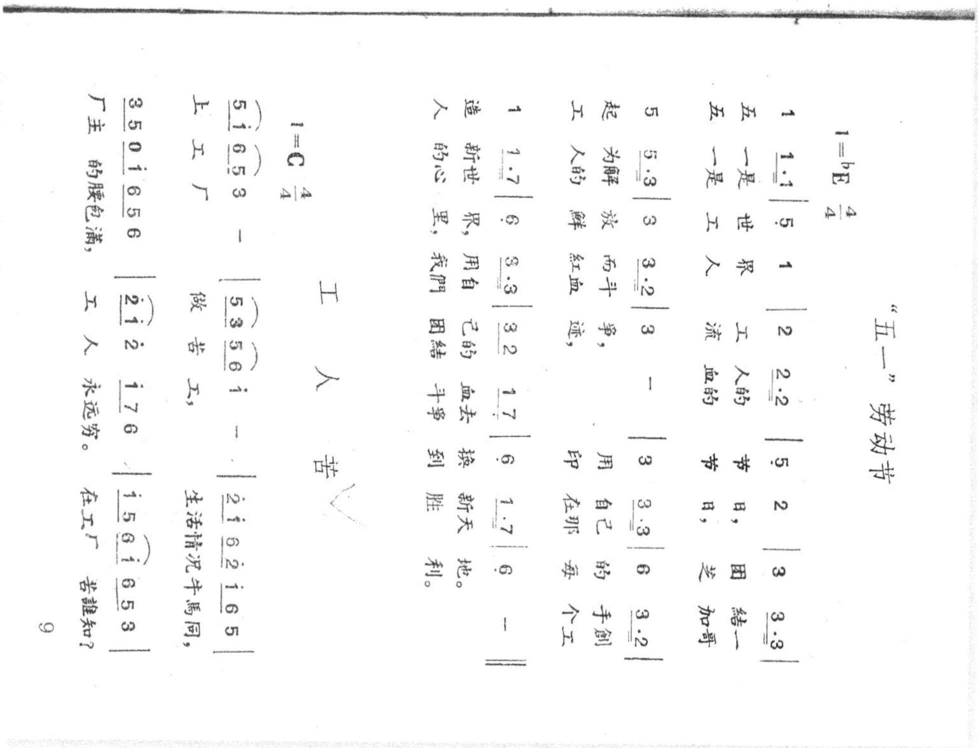

"五一"劳动节

1=♭E 4/4

1 1·1 | 5 1 | 2 2·2 | 5 2 | 3 3·3 |
五 一是 世 界 工 人的 节 日, 团 結一
五 一是 工 人 流 血的 节 日, 芝 加哥

5 5·3 | 3 3·2 | 3 — | 3 3·3 | 6 3·2 |
起 为解 放 而斗 爭, 用 自己 的 手創
工 人的 鮮 紅血 迹, 印 在那 每 个工

1 1·7 | 6 3·3 | 3 2 1 7 | 6 1·7 | 6 — ‖
造 新世 界, 用自 己的 血去 換 新天 地。
人 的心 里, 我們 团結 斗爭 到 胜 利。

9

工人苦

1=C 4/4

5 1̇ 6 5 3 — | 5 3 5 6 1̇ — | 2̇ 1̇ 6 2̇ 1̇ 6 5 |
上 工 厂 做 苦 工, 生活情况牛馬同,

3 5 0 1̇ 6 5 6 | 2̇ 1̇ 2̇ 1̇ 7 6 | 1̇ 5 6 1̇ 6 5 3 |
厂主 的腰包滿, 工 人 永远穷。 在工厂 苦誰知?

3 6 5 4 3 2 | 5 3 2 5 3 2 3 | 6 6 5 1̇ 6 3 5 |
精 疲 力 尽 难 支 持, 可怜我 工 人

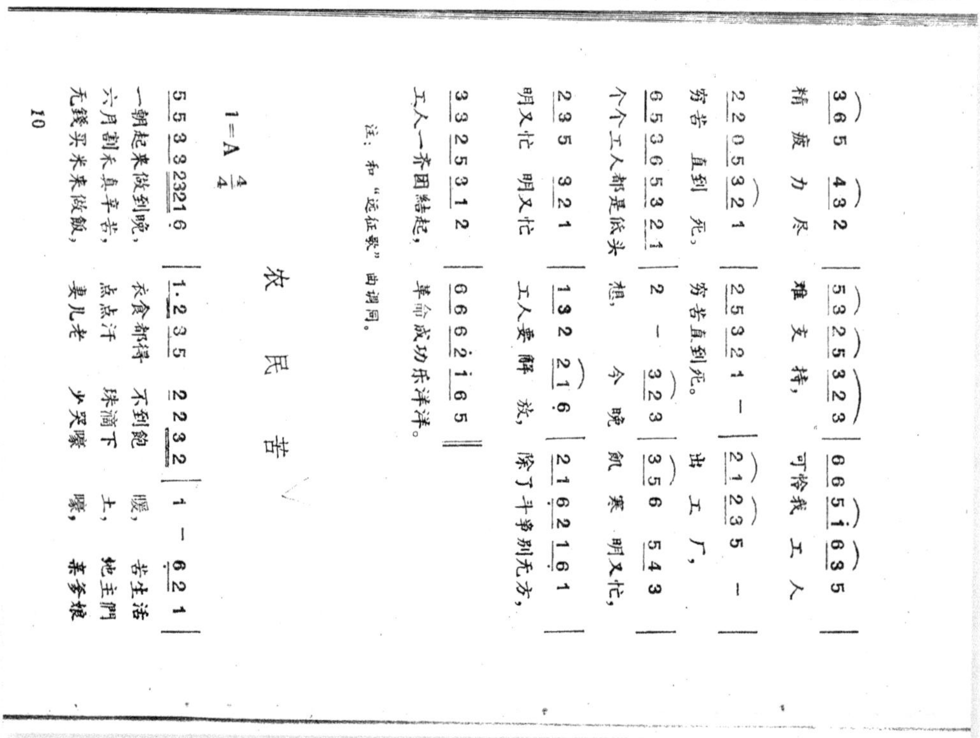

2 2 0 5 3 2 1 | 2 5 3 2 1 — | 2 1 2 3 5 — |
穷苦 直到 死, 穷苦直到死。 出 工 厂,

6 5 3 6 5 3 2 1 | 2 — 3 2 3 | 3 5 6 5 4 3 |
个个工人都是低头 想, 今 晚 飢 寒 明又忙,

2 3 5 3 2 1 | 1 3 2 2 1 6 | 2 1 6 2 1 6 1 |
明又忙 明又忙 工人要 解 放, 除了斗爭别无方,

3 3 2 5 3 1 2 | 6 6 6 2̇ 1̇ 6 5 ‖
工人一齐团結起, 革命成功乐洋洋。

注：和"远征歌"曲调同。

农民苦

1=A 4/4

5 5 3 3 2321 6 | 1·2 3 5 2 2 3 2 | 1 — 6 2 1 |
一朝起来做到晚, 衣食都得 不到飽 暖, 苦生活
六月割禾真辛苦, 点点汗 珠滴下 土, 她主們
无錢买米来做飯, 妻儿老 少哭嚎 嚎, 亲爹娘

10

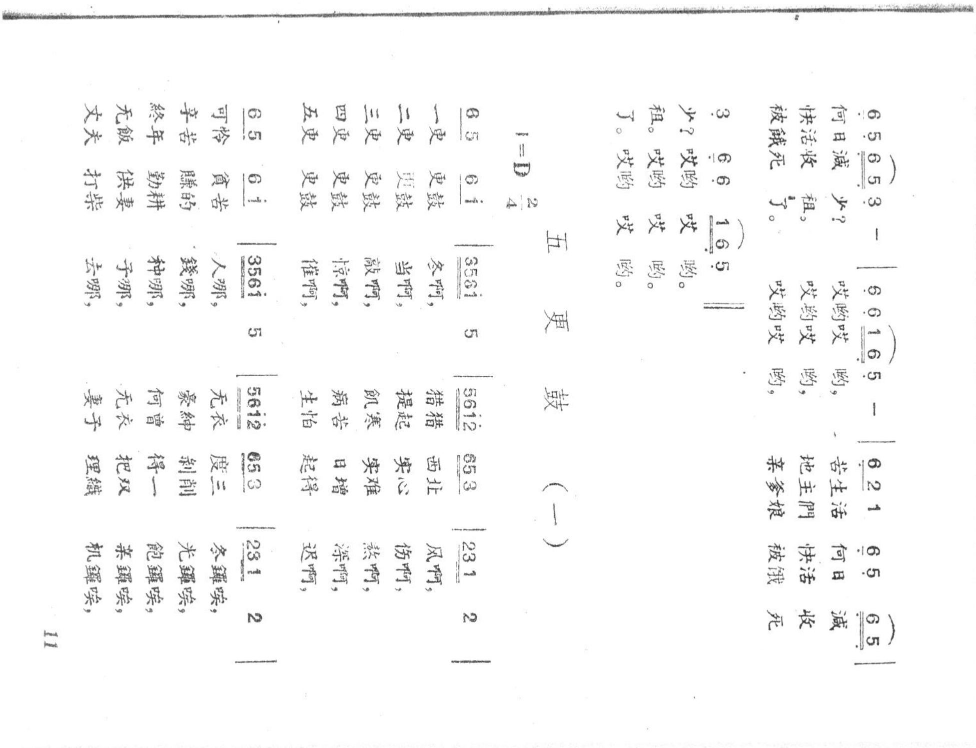

6 5 6 5 3 − | 6 6 1 6 5 − | 6 2 1 6 5 6 5 |
何日减 少？ 哎哟哎 哟， 苦生活 何日 减
快活收 租。 哎哟哎 哟， 地主們 快活 收
被餓死 了。 哎哟哎 哟， 亲爹娘 被餓 死

3 6 6 1 6 5 ‖
少？哎哟 哎 哟。
租。哎哟 哎 哟。
了。哎哟 哎 哟。

五　更　鼓　（一）

1=D $\frac{2}{4}$

6 5 6 1 | 3561 5 | 5612 653 | 231 2 |
一更 更鼓 冬啊， 猎猎 西北 风啊，
二更 更鼓 当啊， 提起 实心 伤啊，
三更 更鼓 敲啊， 飢寒 实难 熬啊，
四更 更鼓 惊啊， 病苦 日增 深啊，
五更 更鼓 催啊， 生怕 起得 迟啊，

6 5 6 1 | 3561 5 | 5612 653 | 231 2 |
可怜 貧苦 人哪， 无衣 度三 冬鑼唉，
辛苦 賺的 錢哪， 豪紳 剥削 光鑼唉，
終年 勤耕 种哪， 何曾 得一 飽鑼唉，
无飯 供妻 子哪， 无衣 把双 亲鑼唉，
丈夫 打柴 去哪， 妻子 理織 机鑼唉，

11

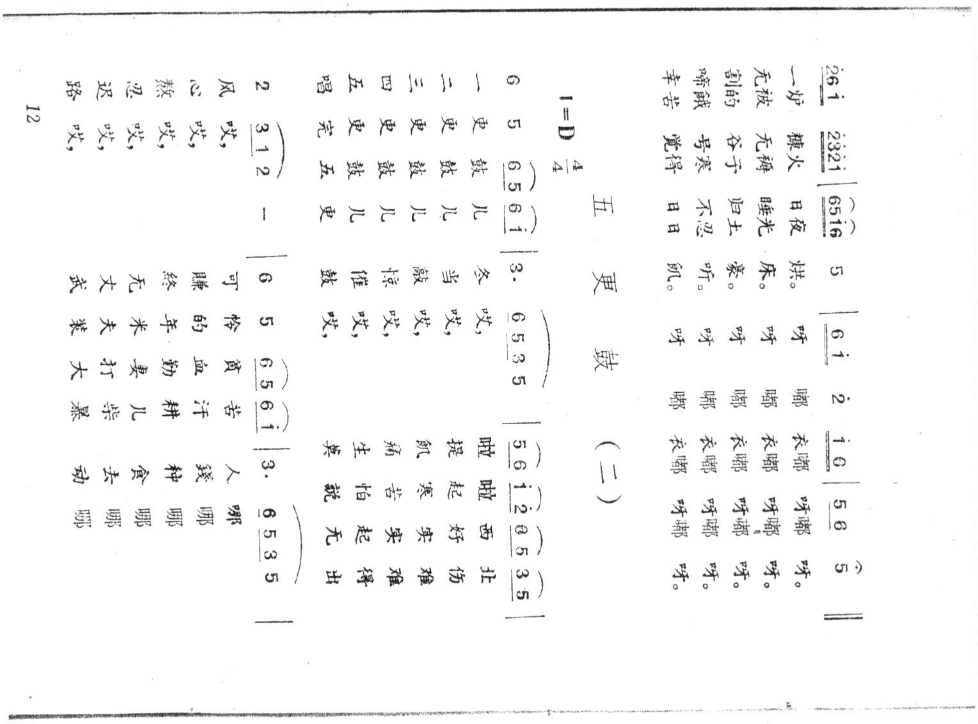

261 2321 | 6516 5 | 6 1 2 1 6 | 5 6 5 ‖
一炉 糠火 日夜 烘。 呀 嘟 衣嘟 呀嘟 呀。
无被 无褥 睡光 床。 呀 嘟 衣嘟 呀嘟 呀。
割的 谷子 归土 豪。 呀 嘟 衣嘟 呀嘟 呀。
啼餓 号寒 不忍 听。 呀 嘟 衣嘟 呀嘟 呀。
辛苦 觉得 日日 飢。 呀 嘟 衣嘟 呀嘟 呀。

五　更　鼓　（二）

1=D $\frac{4}{4}$

6 5 6 5 6 1 | 3· 6 5 3 5 | 5 6 1 2 6 5 3 5 |
一 更 鼓 儿 冬 哎， 啦 啦 西 北
二 更 鼓 儿 当 哎， 提 起 好 伤
三 更 鼓 儿 敲 哎， 飢 寒 实 难
四 更 鼓 儿 惊 哎， 痛 苦 实 难
五 更 鼓 儿 催 哎， 生 怕 起 得
唱 完 五 更 鼓 哎， 莫 説 无 出

2 3 1 2 − | 6 5 6 5 6 1 | 3· 6 5 3 5 |
风 哎， 可 怜 貧 苦 人 哪
心 哎， 賺 的 血 汗 錢 哪
熬 哎， 終 年 勤 耕 种 哪
忍 哎， 无 米 妻 儿 食 哪
迟 哎， 丈 夫 打 柴 去 哪
路 哎， 武 装 大 暴 动 哪

12

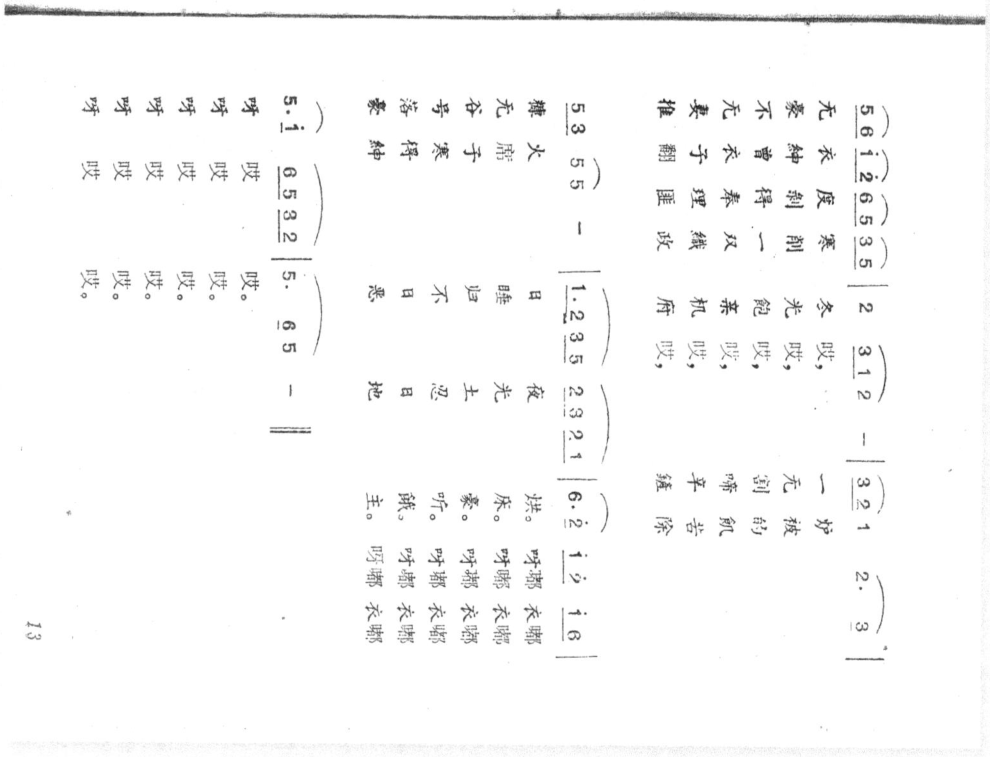

5 6 1̇ 2̇ 6 5 3 5 | 2 3 1 2 – | 3 2 1 2· 3 |

无 衣 度 寒 冬 哎，一 炉
豪 紳 剝 削 光 哎，无 被
不 曾 得 一 飽 哎，割 的
无 衣 奉 双 亲 哎，啼 飢
妻 子 理 織 机 哎，辛 苦
推 翻 匪 政 府 哎，鏟 除

5 3 5 5 – | 1·2 3 5 2 3 2 1 | 6·2̇ 1̇ 2̇ 1̇ 6 |

糠 火 日 夜 烘。呀嘟 衣嘟
无 席 睡 光 床。呀嘟 衣嘟
谷 子 归 土 豪。呀嘟 衣嘟
号 寒 不 忍 听。呀嘟 衣嘟
落 得 日 日 餓。呀嘟 衣嘟
豪 紳 恶 地 主。呀嘟 衣嘟

5·1̇ 6 5 3 2 | 5· 6 5 – ‖

呀 哎 哎。
呀 哎 哎。
呀 哎 哎。
呀 哎 哎。
呀 哎 哎。
呀 哎 哎。

13

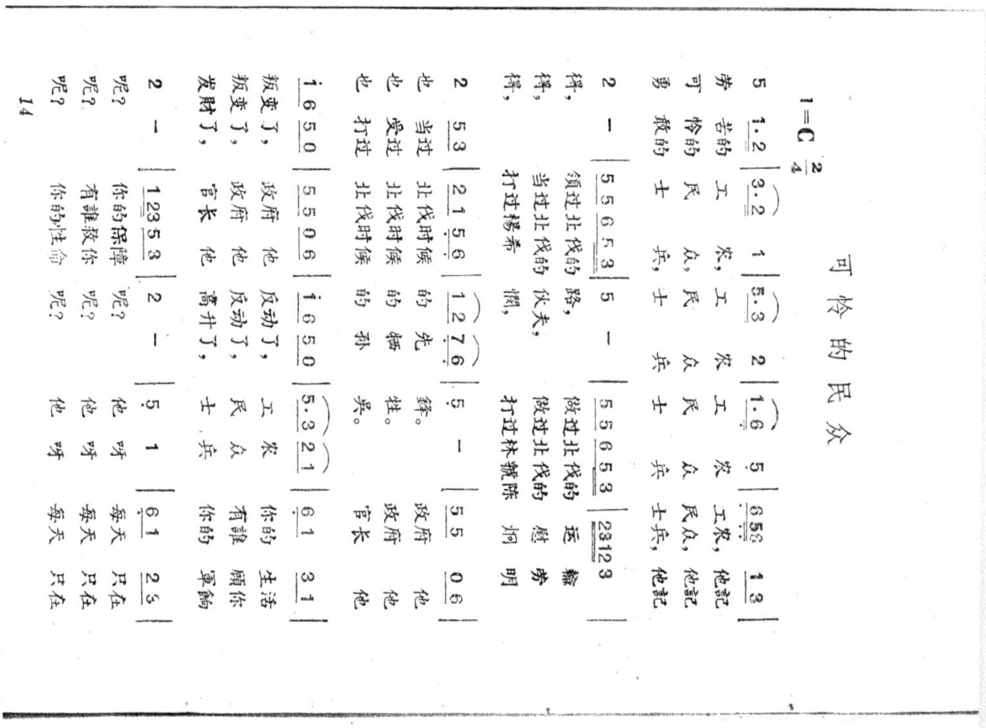

可怜的民众

1=C $\frac{2}{4}$

5 1·2 | 3·2 1 | 5·3 2 | 1·6 5 | 6 5 6 1 3 |

劳 苦的 工 农，工 农 工 农 工农，他記
可 怜的 民 众，民 众 民 众 民众，他記
勇 敢的 士 兵，士 兵 士 兵 士兵，他記

2 – | 5 5 6 5 3 | 5 – | 5 5 6 5 3 | 2 3 1 2 3 |

得， 領过北伐的 路， 做过北伐的 运 輸
得， 当过北伐的 伙夫， 做过北伐的 慰 劳
得， 打过楊希 憫， 打过林甝陈 炯 明

2 5 3 | 2 1 5 6 | 1 2 7 6 | 5 – | 5 5 0 6 |

也 当过 北伐时候 的 先 鋒。 政府 他
也 受过 北伐时候 的 牺 牲。 政府 他
也 打过 北伐时候 的 孙 吳。 官长 他

1̇ 6 5 0 | 5 5 0 6 | 1̇ 6 5 0 | 5·3 2 1 | 6 1 3 1 |

叛变了， 政府 他 反动了， 工 农 你的 生活
叛变了， 政府 他 反动了， 民 众 有誰 顾你
发財了， 官长 他 高升了， 士 兵 你的 軍餉

2 – | 1 2 3 5 3 | 2 – | 5 1 | 6 1 2 3 |

呢？ 你的保障 呢？ 他 呀 每天 只在
呢？ 有誰救你 呢？ 他 呀 每天 只在
呢？ 你的性命 呢？ 他 呀 每天 只在

14

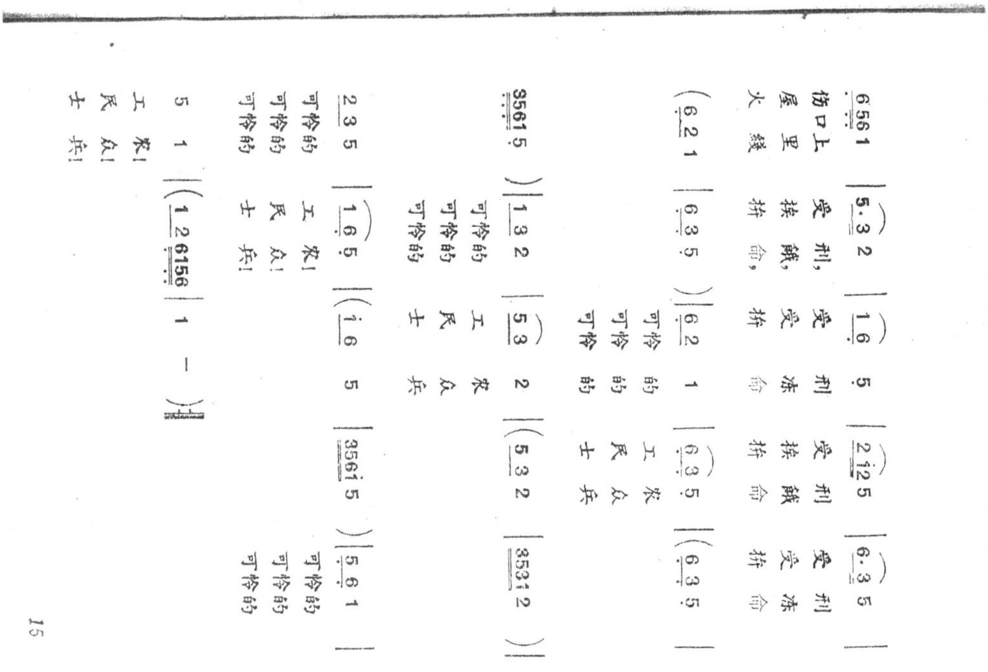

6561 | 5·3 2 | 1 6 5 | 2 1̇2 5 | 6·3 5 |
伤口上 受 刑， 受 刑 受 刑 受 刑
屋 里 挨 饿， 受 冻 挨 饿 受 冻
火 綫 拚 命， 拚 命 拚 命 拚 命

(6 2 1 | 6 3 5) | 6 2 1 | 6 3 5 | (6 3 5 |
可怜 的 工 农
可怜 的 民 众
可怜 的 士 兵

35615) | 1 3 2 | 5 3 2 | (5 3 2 | 35312) |
可怜的 工 农
可怜的 民 众
可怜的 士 兵

2 3 5 | 1 6 5 | (1̇ 6 5 | 3561̇ 5) | 5 6 1 |
可怜的 工 农！ 可怜的
可怜的 民 众！ 可怜的
可怜的 士 兵！ 可怜的

5 1 | (1 2 6156 | 1 —) ‖
工 农！
民 众！
士 兵！

15

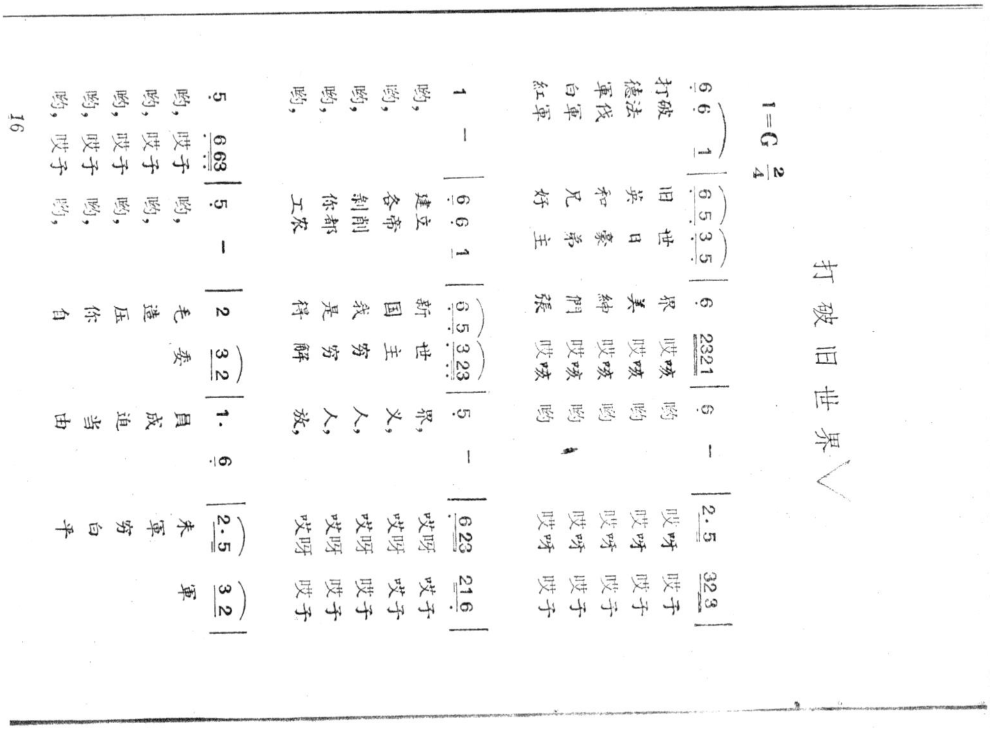

打破旧世界

1=G 2/4

6 6 1 | 6 5 3 5 | 6 2321 | 6 — | 2·5 323 |
打破 旧 世 界 哎咳 哟 哎呀 哎子
德法 英 日 美 哎咳 哟 哎呀 哎子
軍伐 和 豪 紳 哎咳 哟 哎呀 哎子
白軍 兄 弟 們 哎咳 哟 哎呀 哎子
紅軍 好 主 張 哎咳 哟 哎呀 哎子

1 — | 6 6 1 | 6 5 3 23 | 5 — | 6 23 21 6 |
哟， 建立 新 世 界， 哎呀 哎子
哟， 各帝 国 主 义， 哎呀 哎子
哟， 剥削 我 穷 人， 哎呀 哎子
哟， 你都 是 穷 人， 哎呀 哎子
哟， 工农 得 解 放， 哎呀 哎子

5 6 63 | 5 — | 2 3 2 | 1· 6 | 2·5 3 2 |
哟，哎子 哟， 毛 委 員 朱 軍
哟，哎子 哟， 造 成 軍
哟，哎子 哟， 压 迫 穷
哟，哎子 哟， 你 当 白
哟，哎子 哟， 自 由 平

16

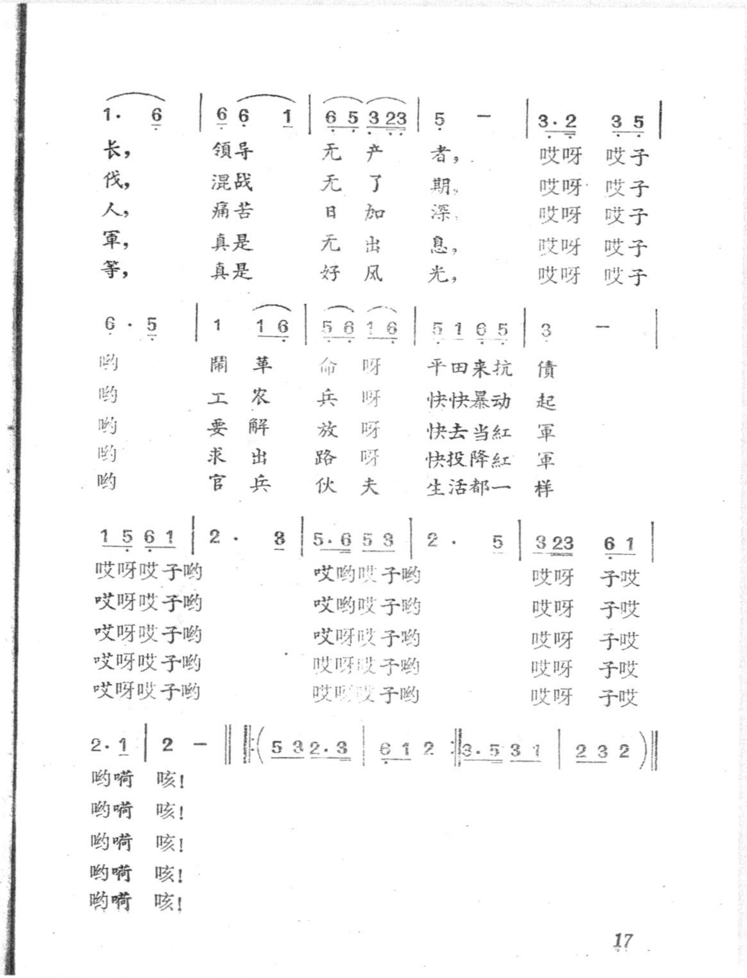

1· 6 | 6 6 1 | 6 5 3 23 | 5 — | 3·2 3 5 |
长， 领导 无 产 者， 哎呀 哎子
伐， 混战 无 了 期， 哎呀 哎子
人， 痛苦 日 加 深， 哎呀 哎子
軍， 真是 无 出 息， 哎呀 哎子
筝， 真是 好 风 光， 哎呀 哎子

6 · 5 | 1 1 6 | 5 6 1 6 | 5 1 6 5 | 3 — |
哟 鬧 革 命 呀 平田来抗 債
哟 工 农 兵 呀 快快暴动 起
哟 要 解 放 呀 快去当紅 軍
哟 求 出 路 呀 快投降紅 軍
哟 官 兵 伙 夫 生活都一 样

1 5 6 1 | 2 · 3 | 5·6 5 3 | 2 · 5 | 3 23 6 1 |
哎呀哎子哟 哎哟哎子哟 哎呀 子哎
哎呀哎子哟 哎哟哎子哟 哎呀 子哎
哎呀哎子哟 哎呀哎子哟 哎呀 子哎
哎呀哎子哟 哎呀哎子哟 哎呀 子哎
哎呀哎子哟 哎哟哎子哟 哎呀 子哎

2·1 | 2 — ‖:(5 3 2·3 | 6 1 2 :‖ 3·5 3 1 | 2 3 2) ‖
哟嗬 咳！
哟嗬 咳！
哟嗬 咳！
哟嗬 咳！
哟嗬 咳！

17

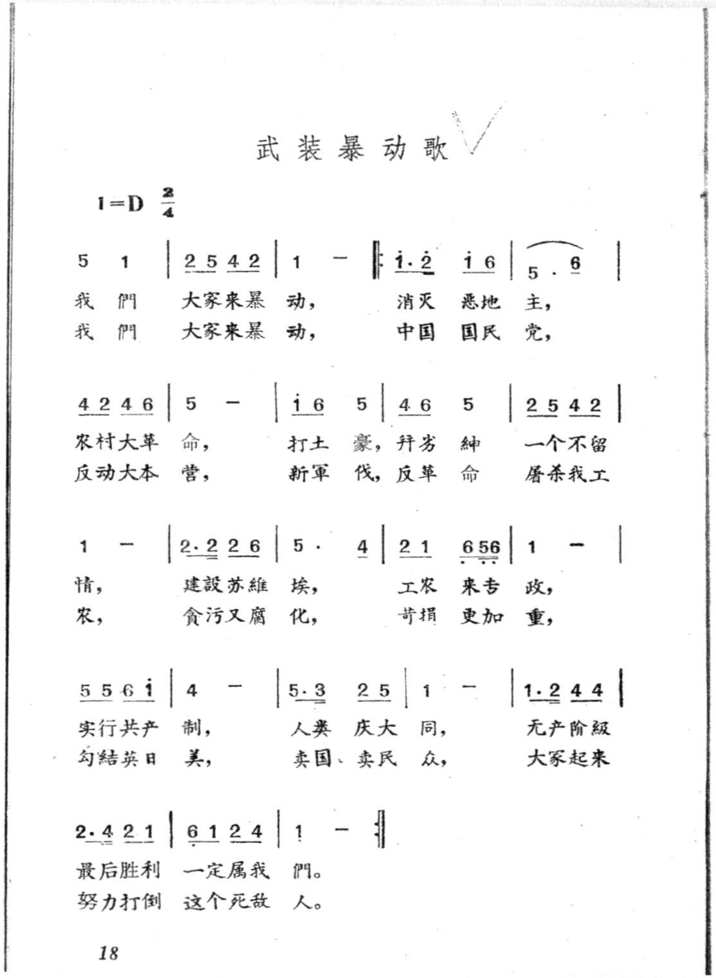

武装暴动歌

1=D $\frac{2}{4}$

5 1 | 2 5 4 2 | 1 — ‖: 1·2 1 6 | 5 · 6 |
我 們 大家来暴 动， 消灭 恶地 主，
我 們 大家来暴 动， 中国 国民 党，

4 2 4 6 | 5 — | 1 6 5 | 4 6 5 | 2 5 4 2 |
农村大革 命， 打土 豪，拜劣 紳 一个不留
反动大本 营， 新軍 伐，反革 命 屠杀我工

1 — | 2·2 2 6 | 5 · 4 | 2 1 6 56 | 1 — |
情， 建設苏維 埃， 工农 来专 政，
农， 貪污又腐 化， 苛捐 更加 重，

5 5 6 1 | 4 — | 5·3 2 5 | 1 — | 1·2 4 4 |
实行共产 制， 人类 庆大 同， 无产阶級
勾結英日 美， 卖国、卖民 众， 大家起来

2·4 2 1 | 6 1 2 4 | 1 — :‖
最后胜利 一定属我 們。
努力打倒 这个死敌 人。

18

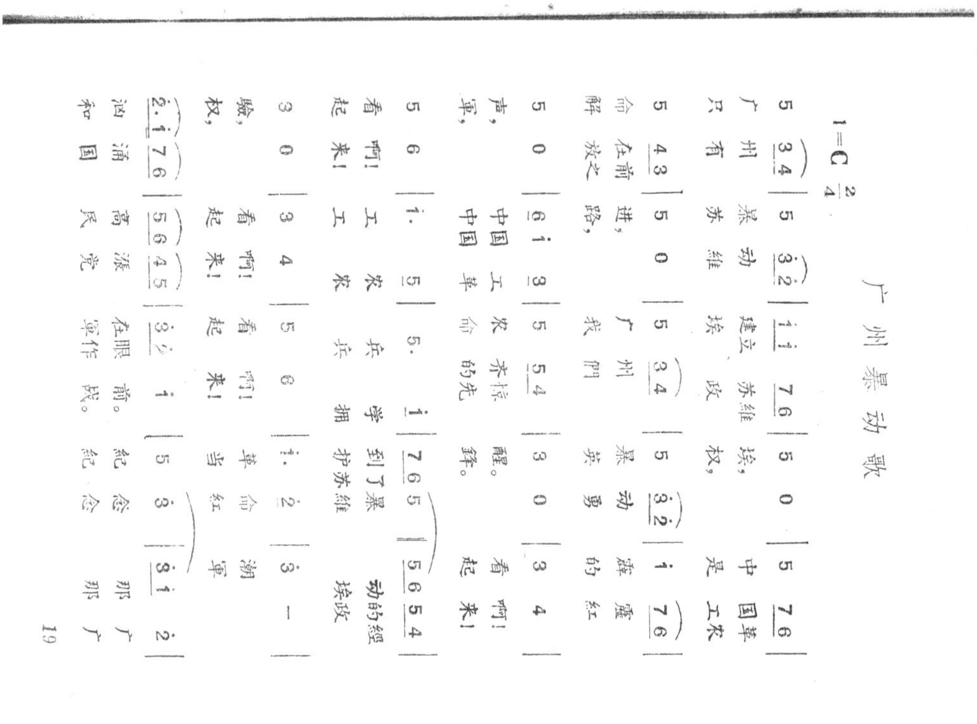

广州暴动歌

1=C 2/4

5 3 4 | 5 3̇ 2̇ | i̇ i̇ 7 6 | 5 0 | 5 7 6 |
广 州 暴 动 建立 苏维 埃， 中 国革
只 有 苏 维 埃 政 权， 是 工农

5 4 3 | 5 0 | 5 3 4 | 5 3̇ 2̇ | i̇ 7 6 |
命 在前 进， 广 州 暴 动 霹 靂
解 放之 路， 我 們 英 勇 的 紅

5 0 | 6 i̇ 3 | 5 5 4 | 3 0 | 3 4 |
声， 中国 工 农 齐惊 醒。 看 啊！
軍， 中国 革 命 的先 鋒。 起 来！

5 6 | i̇· 5 | 5· i̇ | 7 6 5 | 5 6 5 4 |
看 啊！ 工 农 兵 学 到了暴 动的經
起 来！ 工 农 兵 拥 护苏維 埃政

3 0 | 3 4 | 5 6 | i̇· 2̇ | 3̇ — |
驗， 看 啊！ 看 啊！ 革 命 潮
权， 起 来！ 起 来！ 当 紅 軍

2̇· i̇ 7 6 | 5 6 4 5 | 3̇ 2̇ i̇ | 5 3̇ | 3̇ i̇ 2̇ |
汹 涌 高 漲 在眼 前。 紀 念 那 广
和 国 民 党 軍作 战。 紀 念 那 广

19

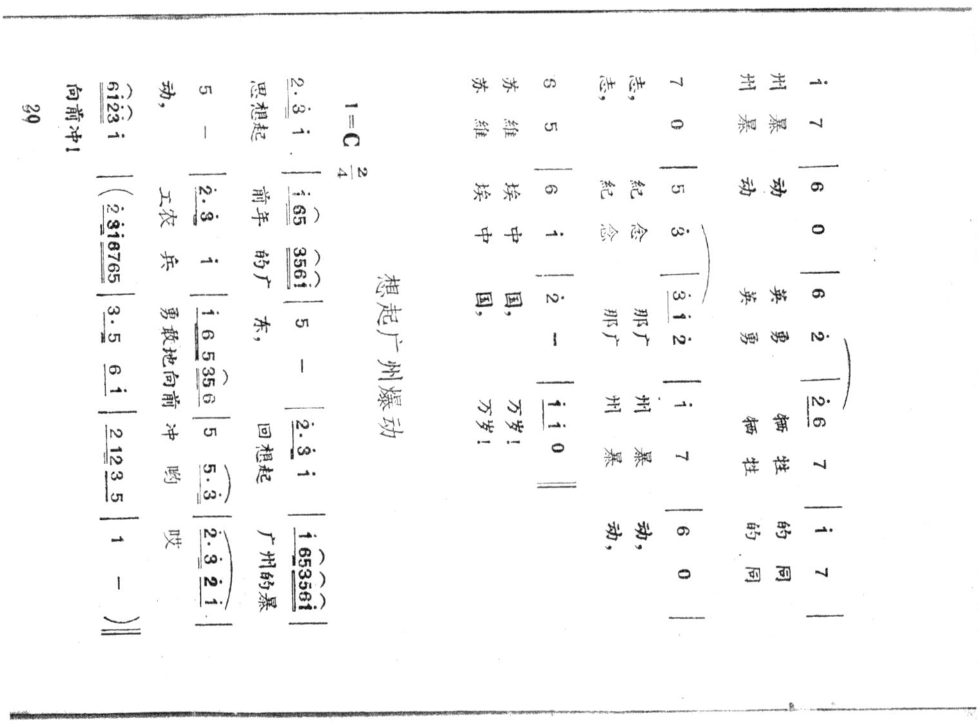

i̇ 7 | 6 0 | 6 2̇ | 2̇ 6 7 | i̇ 7 |
州 暴 动 英 勇 牺 牲 的 同
州 暴 动 英 勇 牺 牲 的 同

7 0 | 5 3̇ | 3̇ i̇ 2̇ | i̇ 7 | 6 0 |
志， 紀 念 那广 州 暴 动，
志， 紀 念 那广 州 暴 动，

6 5 | 6 i̇ | 2̇ — | i̇ i̇ 0 ||
苏 維 埃 中 国， 万岁！
苏 維 埃 中 国， 万岁！

想起广州爆动

1=C 2/4

2̇· 3̇ i̇ | i̇ 6 5 3 5 6 i̇ | 5 — | 2̇· 3̇ i̇ | i̇ 6 5 3 5 6 i̇ |
思想起 前年 的广 东， 回想起 广州的暴

5 — | 2̇· 3̇ i̇ | i̇ 6 5 3 5 6 | 5 5· 3̇ | 2̇· 3̇ 2̇ i̇ |
动， 工农 兵 勇敢地向前 冲 哟 哎

6 i̇ 2̇ 3̇ i̇ | (2̇ 3̇ i̇ 6 7 6 5 | 3· 5 6 i̇ | 2 1 2 3 5 | 1 —) ||
向前冲！

20

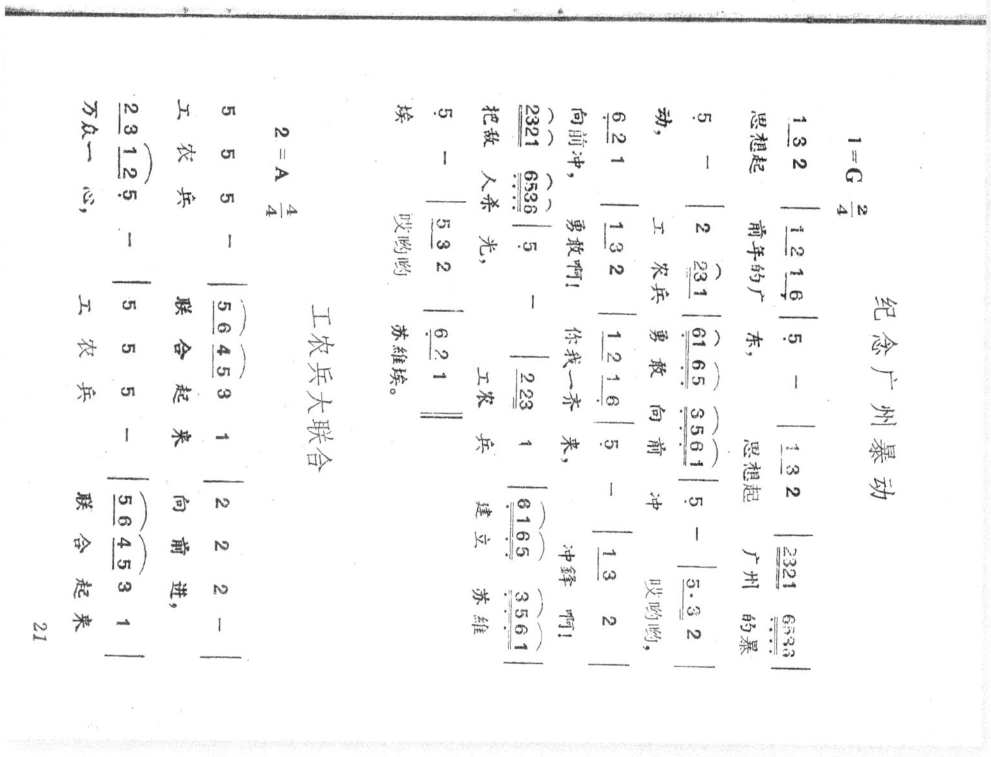

纪念广州暴动

1=G $\frac{2}{4}$

1 3 2 | 1 2 1 6 | 5 — | 1 3 2 | 2321 6533 |
思想起　前年的广　东，　思想起　广州　的暴

5 — | 2 231 | 61 65 3561 | 5 — | 5·3 2 |
动，　工　农兵　勇　敢　向　前　冲　哎哟哟，

6 2 1 | 1 3 2 | 1 2 1 6 | 5 — | 1 3 2 |
向前冲，　勇敢啊！　你我一齐　来，　冲鋒　啊！

2321 6536 | 5 — | 2 23 1 | 6165 3561 |
把敌　人杀　光，　工农　兵　建立　苏維

5 — | 5 3 2 | 6 2 1 ‖
埃　哎哟哟　苏維埃。

工农兵大联合

2=A $\frac{4}{4}$

5 5 5 — | 5 6 4 5 3 1 | 2 2 2 — |
工　农　兵　联　合　起　来　向　前　进，

2 3 1 2 5 — | 5 5 5 — | 5 6 4 5 3 1 |
万众一　心，　工　农　兵　联　合　起　来

21

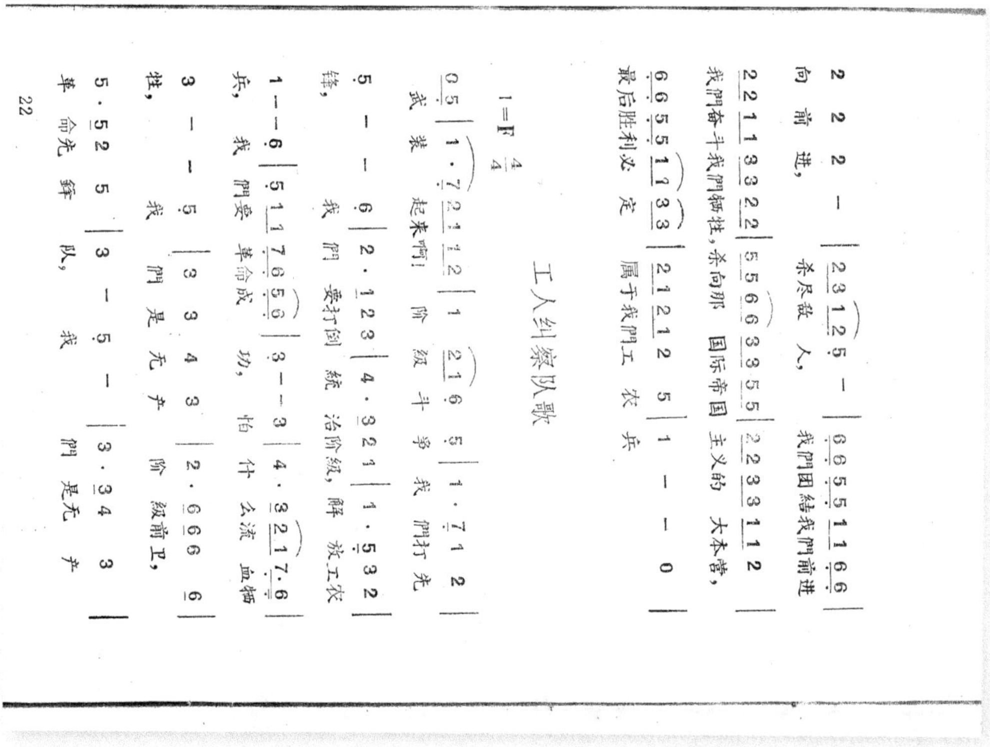

2 2 2 — | 2 3 1 2 5 — | 6 6 5 5 1 1 6 6 |
向　前　进，　杀尽敌　人，　我們团結我們前进

2 2 1 1 3 3 2 2 | 5 5 6 6 3 3 5 5 | 2 2 3 3 1 1 2 |
我們奋斗我們牺牲，杀向那　国际帝国　主义的　大本营，

6 6 5 5 1 1 3 3 | 2 1 2 1 2 5 | 1 — — 0 |
最后胜利必　定　属于我們工　农　兵

工人纠察队歌

1=F $\frac{4}{4}$

0 5 | 1 · 7 2 1 1 2 | 1 2 1 6 5 | 1 · 7 1 2 |
武　装　起来啊！　阶　級　斗　争　我　們打　先

5 — — 6 | 2 · 1 2 3 | 4 · 3 2 1 | 1 · 5 3 2 |
锋，　我　們　要打倒　統　治阶級，解　放工农

1 — — 6 | 5 1 1 7 6 5 6 | 3 — — 3 | 4 · 3 2 1 7 · 6 |
兵，　我　們要　革命成　功，　怕　什　么流　血牺

3 — — 5 | 3 3 4 3 | 2 · 6 6 6 6 |
牲，　我　們　是　无　产　阶　級前卫，

5 · 5 2 5 | 3 — 5 — | 3 · 3 4 3 |
革　命先　鋒　队，　我　們　是无　产

22

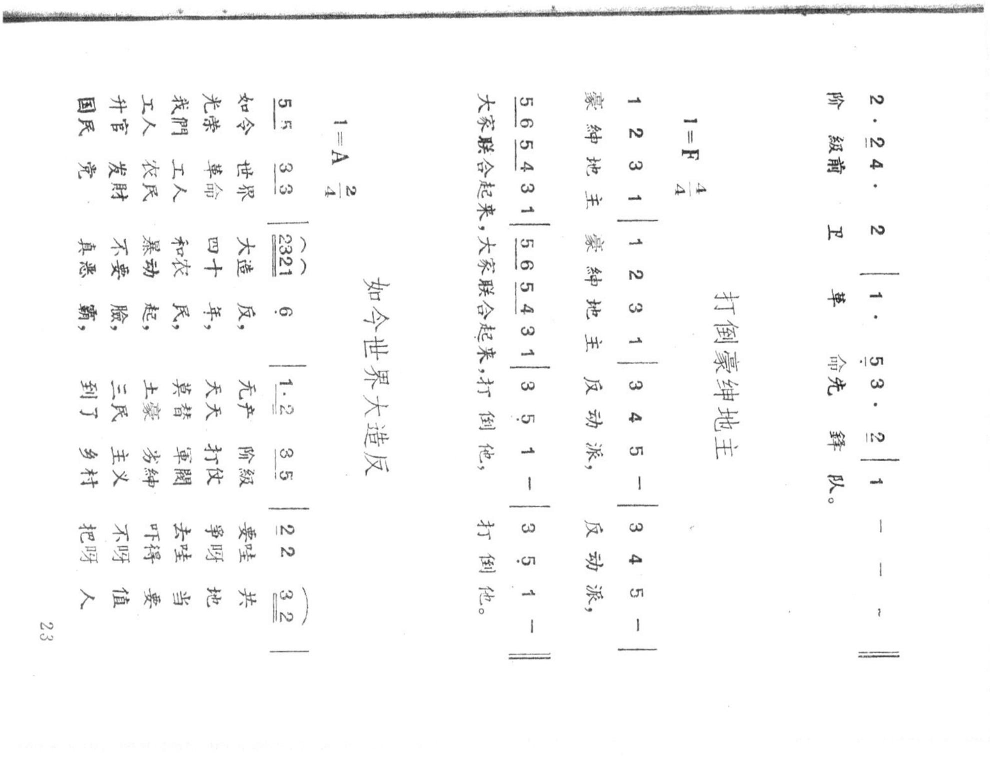

2 · 2 4 · 2 | 1 · 5 3 · 2 | 1 — — — ||
阶 級前 卫 革 命先 鋒 队。

打倒豪绅地主

1＝F 4/4

1 2 3 1 | 1 2 3 1 | 3 4 5 — | 3 4 5 — |
豪 绅 地 主 豪 紳 地 主 反 动 派， 反 动 派，

5 6 5 4 3 1 | 5 6 5 4 3 1 | 3 5 1 — | 3 5 1 — ||
大家联合起来，大家联合起来，打 倒 他， 打 倒 他。

如今世界大造反

1＝A 2/4

5 5 3 3 | 2321 6 | 1·2 3 5 | 2 2 3 2 |
如今 世界 大造 反， 无产 阶級 要哇 共
光荣 革命 四十 年， 天天 打仗 爭呀 地
我們 工人 和农 民， 莫替 軍閥 去哇 当
工人 农民 暴动 起， 土豪 劣紳 吓得 要
升官 发財 不要 臉， 三民 主义 不呀 值
国民 党 真恶 霸， 到了 乡村 把呀 人

23

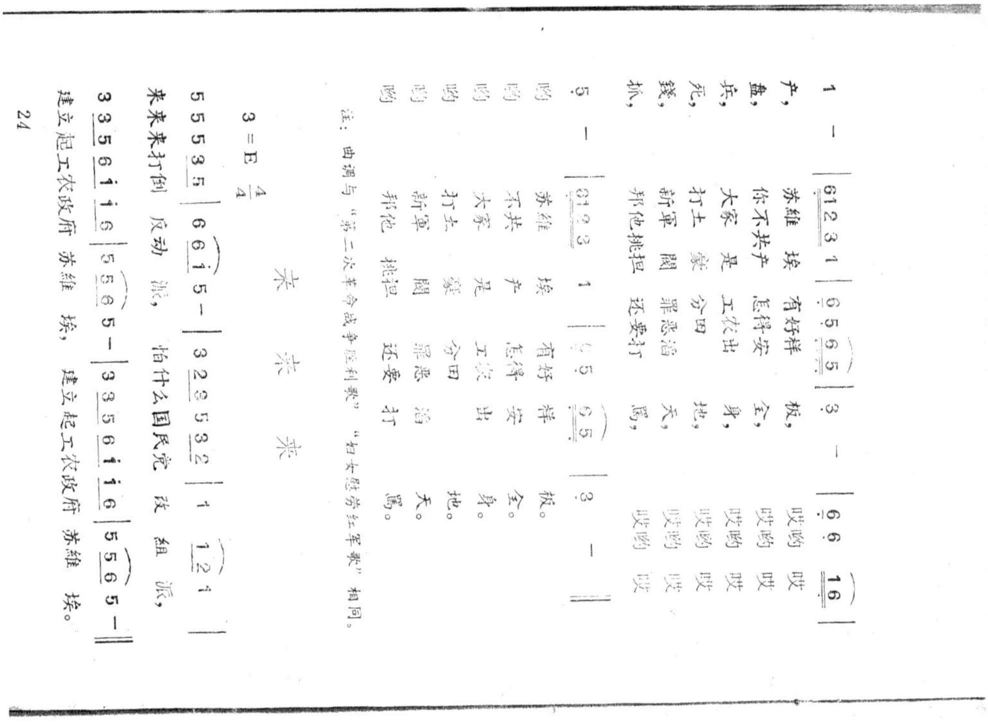

1 — | 61231 | 6565 | 3 — | 6 6 16 |
产， 苏維 埃 有好样 板， 哎哟 哎
盘， 你不共产 怎得安 全， 哎哟 哎
兵， 大家 是 工农出 身， 哎哟 哎
死， 打土 豪 分田 地， 哎哟 哎
錢， 新軍 閥 罪恶滔 天， 哎哟 哎
抓， 邦他挑担 还要打 罵， 哎哟 哎

5 — | 6123 1 | 6 5 6 5 | 3 — ||
哟 苏維 埃 有好 样 板。
哟 不共 产 怎得 安 全。
哟 大家 是 工农 出 身。
哟 打土 豪 分田 地。
哟 新軍 閥 罪恶 滔 天。
哟 邦他 挑担 还要 打 罵。

注：曲调与"第二次革命战争胜利歌""妇女慰劳红军歌"相同。

来 来 来

3＝E 4/4

5 5 5 3 5 | 6 6 i 5 — | 3 2 3 5 3 2 | 1 1 2 1 |
来来来打倒 反动 派， 怕什么国民党 改 組 派，

3 3 5 6 i i 6 | 5 5 6 5 — | 3 3 5 6 i i 6 | 5 5 6 5 — ||
建立起工农政府 苏維 埃， 建立起工农政府 苏維 埃。

24

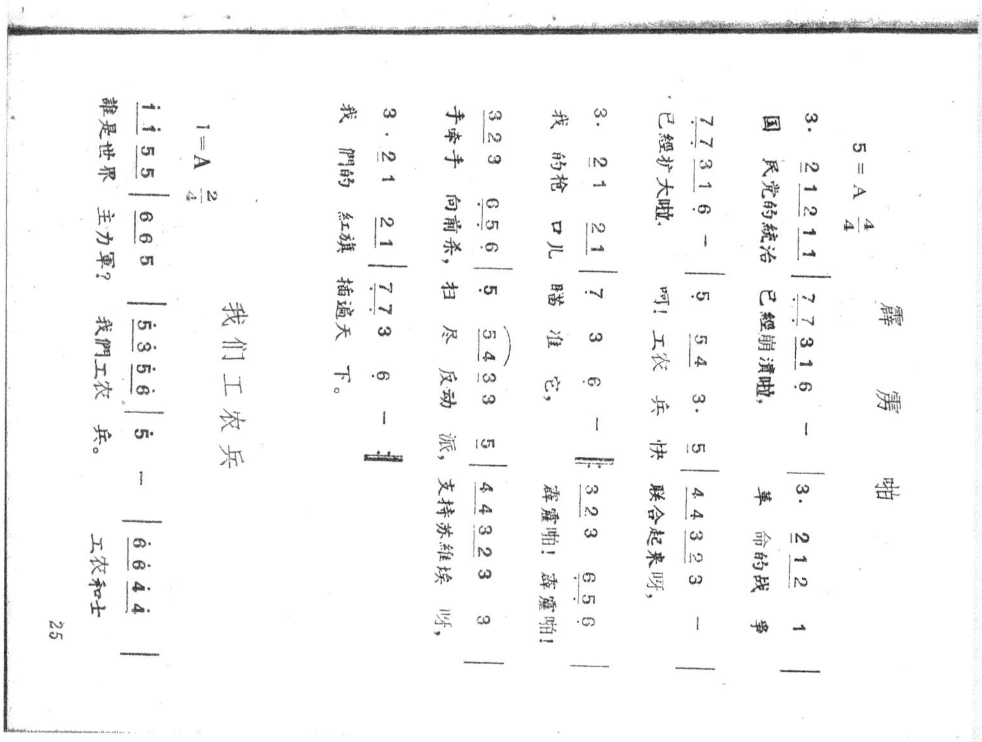

霹雳啪

5＝A $\frac{4}{4}$

3· 2 1 2 1 1 | 7 7 3 1 6 － | 3· 2 1 2 1 |
国 民党的統治 已經崩潰啦， 革 命的战 争

7 7 3 1 6 － | 5 5 4 3· 5 | 4 4 3 2 3 － |
已經扩大啦． 呵！工农 兵 快 联合起来呀，

3· 2 1 2 1 | 7 3 6 － |: 3 2 3 6 5 6 |
我 的枪 口儿 瞄 准 它， 霹靂啪！霹靂啪！

3 2 3 6 5 6 | 5 5 4 3 3 5 | 4 4 3 2 3 3 |
手牵手 向前杀，扫 尽 反动 派，支持苏維埃 呀，

3·2 1 2 1 | 7 7 3 6 － :|
我 們的 紅旗 插遍天 下。

我们工农兵

1＝A $\frac{2}{4}$

1 1 5 5 | 6 6 5 | 5 3 5 6 | 5 － | 6 6 4 4 |
誰是世界 主力軍？ 我們工农 兵。 工农和士

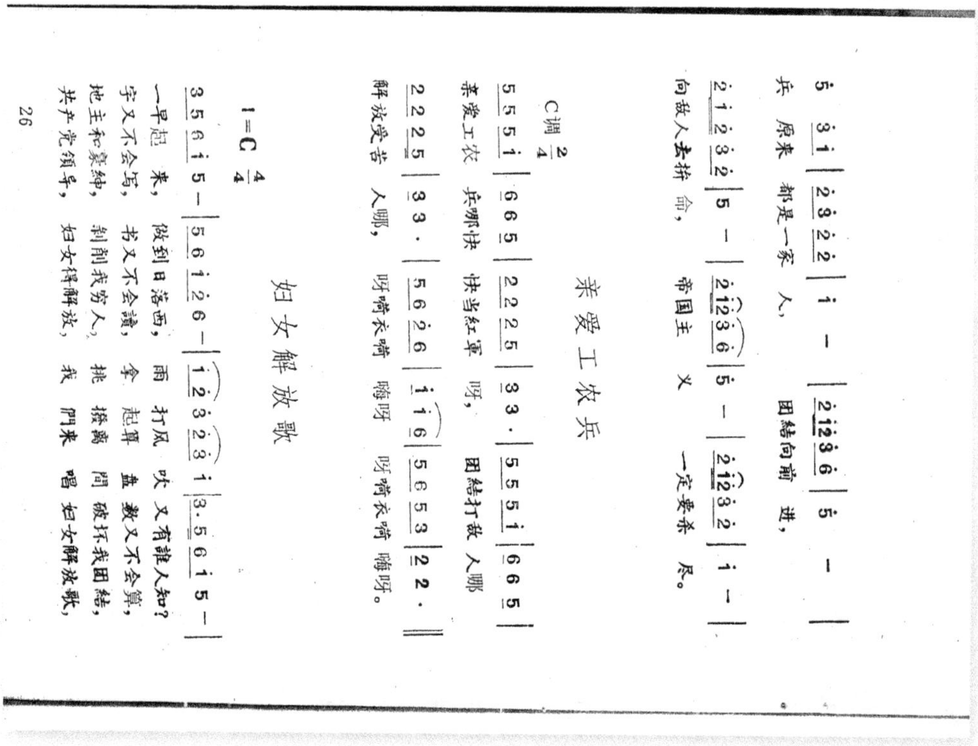

5 3 1 | 2 3 2 2 | 1 － | 2 1 2 3 6 | 5 － |
兵 原来 都是一家 人， 团結向前 进，

2 1 2 3 2 | 5 － | 2 1 2 3 6 | 5 － | 2 1 2 3 2 | 1 － |
向敌人去拚 命， 帝国主 义 一定要杀 尽。

亲爱工农兵

C调 $\frac{2}{4}$

5 5 5 1 | 6 6 5 | 2 2 2 5 | 3 3 · | 5 5 5 1 | 6 6 5 |
亲爱工农 兵哪快 快当紅軍 呀， 团結打敌 人哪

2 2 2 5 | 3 3 · | 5 6 2 6 | 1 1 6 | 5 6 5 3 | 2 2 · ||
解放受苦 人哪， 呀嗬衣嗬 嗨呀 呀嗬衣嗬 嗨呀。

妇女解放歌

1＝C $\frac{4}{4}$

3 5 6 1 5 － | 5 6 1 2 6 － | 1 2 3 2 3 1 | 3· 5 6 1 5 － |
一早起 来， 做到日落西， 雨 打风 吹 又有誰人知？
字又不会写， 书又不会讀， 拿 起算 盘 数又不会算，
地主和豪紳， 剥削我穷人， 挑 撥离 間 破坏我团結，
共产党領导， 妇女得解放， 我 們来 唱 妇女解放歌，

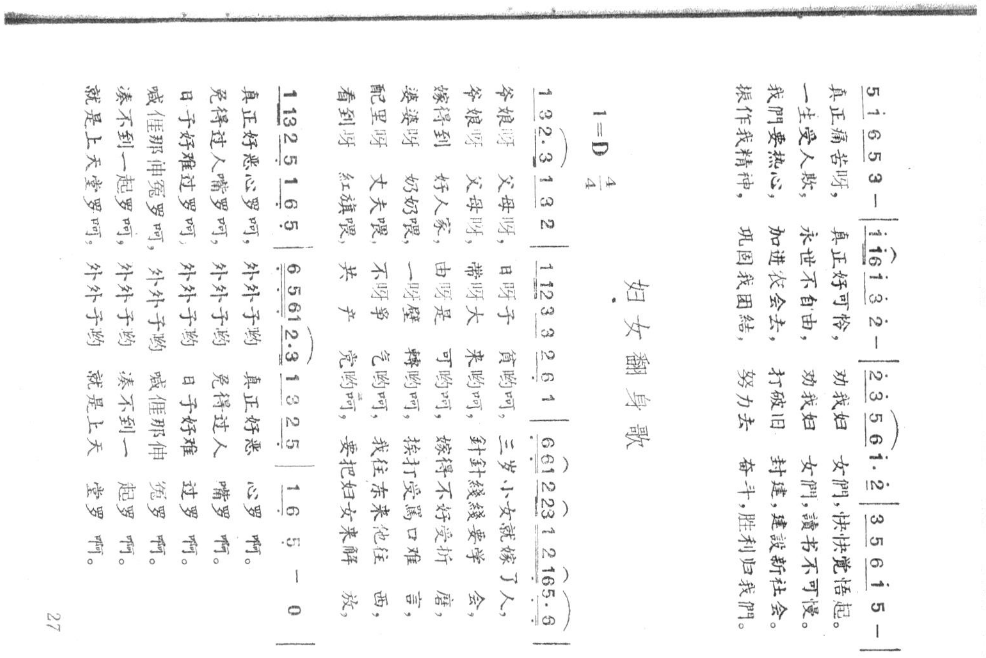

5 1̇ 6 5 3 – | 1̇ 1̇6 1̇ 3̇ 2̇ – | 2̇ 3̇ 5 6 1̇ · 2̇ | 3 5 6 1̇ 5 – |

真正痛苦呀，真正好可怜，劝我妇　女們，快快覺悟起。
一生受人欺，永世不自由，劝我妇　女們，讀书不可慢。
我們要热心，加进农会去，打破旧　封建，建設新社会。
振作我精神，巩固我团結，努力去　奋斗，胜利归我們。

妇女翻身歌

1＝D $\frac{4}{4}$

1 3 2·3 1 3 2 | 1 1 2 3 3 2 6 1 | 6 6 1 2 2 3 1 2 1 6 5·6 |

爷娘呀　父母呀，日呀子　貧哟呵，三岁小女就嫁了人，
爷娘呀　父母呀，带呀大　来哟呵，針針綫綫要学　会，
嫁得到　好人家，由呀是　可哟呵，嫁得不好受折　磨，
婆婆呀　奶奶喂，一呀壁　轉哟呵，挨打受罵口难　言，
配里呀　丈夫喂，不呀爭　气哟呵，我往东来他往　西，
看到呀　紅旗喂，共　产　党哟呵，要把妇女来解　放，

1 1 3 2 5 1 6 5 | 6 5 6 1 2·3 1 3 2 5 | 1 6 5 – 0 |

真正好恶心罗呵，外外子哟　真正好恶　心罗　啊。
免得过人嘴罗呵，外外子哟　免得过人　嘴罗　啊。
日子好难过罗呵，外外子哟　日子好难　过罗　啊。
喊佢那伸冤罗呵，外外子哟　喊佢那伸　冤罗　啊。
凑不到一起罗呵，外外子哟　凑不到一　起罗　啊。
就是上天堂罗呵，外外子哟　就是上天　堂罗　啊。

27

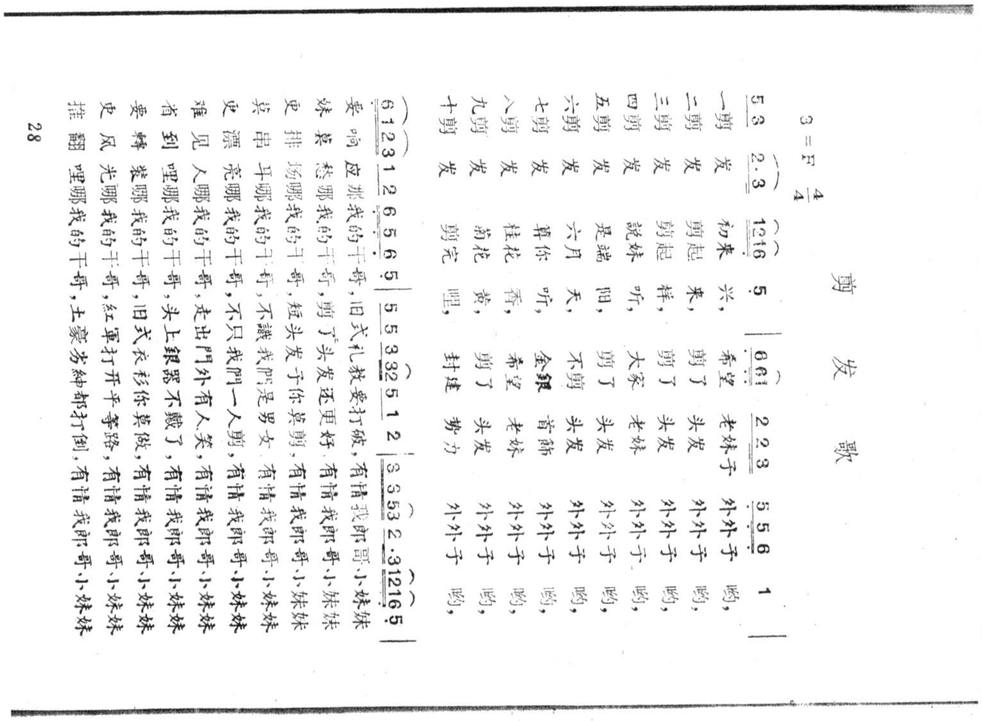

剪发歌

3＝F $\frac{4}{4}$

5 3 2·3 1 2 1 6 5 | 6 6 1 2 2 3 5 5 6 1 |

一剪　发　初来　兴，希望　老妹子　外外子　哟，
二剪　发　剪起　来，剪了　头发　外外子　哟，
三剪　发　剪起　样，剪了　头发　外外子　哟，
四剪　发　說妹　听，大家　老妹　外外子　哟，
五剪　发　是端　阳，剪了　头发　外外子　哟，
六剪　发　六月　天，不剪　头发　外外子　哟，
七剪　发　算你　听，金銀　首飾　外外子　哟，
八剪　发　桂花　香，希望　老妹　外外子　哟，
九剪　发　菊花　黄，剪了　头发　外外子　哟，
十剪　发　剪完　哩，封建　势力　外外子　哟，

6 1 2 3 1 2 6 5 6 5 | 5 5 3 3 2 5 1 2 | 3 3 5 3 2·3 1 2 1 6 5 |

要　响　应那我的干哥，旧式礼教要打破，有情我郎哥小妹妹
妹　莫　愁哪我的干哥，剪了头发还更好，有情我郎哥小妹妹
史　排　场哪我的干哥，短头发子你莫剪，有情我郎哥小妹妹
莫　串　耳哪我的干哥，不識我們是男女，有情我郎哥小妹妹
史　漂　亮哪我的干哥，不只我們一人剪，有情我郎哥小妹妹
难　见　人哪我的干哥，走出門外有人笑，有情我郎哥小妹妹
省　到　哩哪我的干哥，头上銀器不戴了，有情我郎哥小妹妹
要　轉　装哪我的干哥，旧式衣衫你莫做，有情我郎哥小妹妹
史　风　光哪我的干哥，紅軍打开平等路，有情我郎哥小妹妹
推　翻　哩哪我的干哥，土豪劣紳都打倒，有情我郎哥小妹妹

28

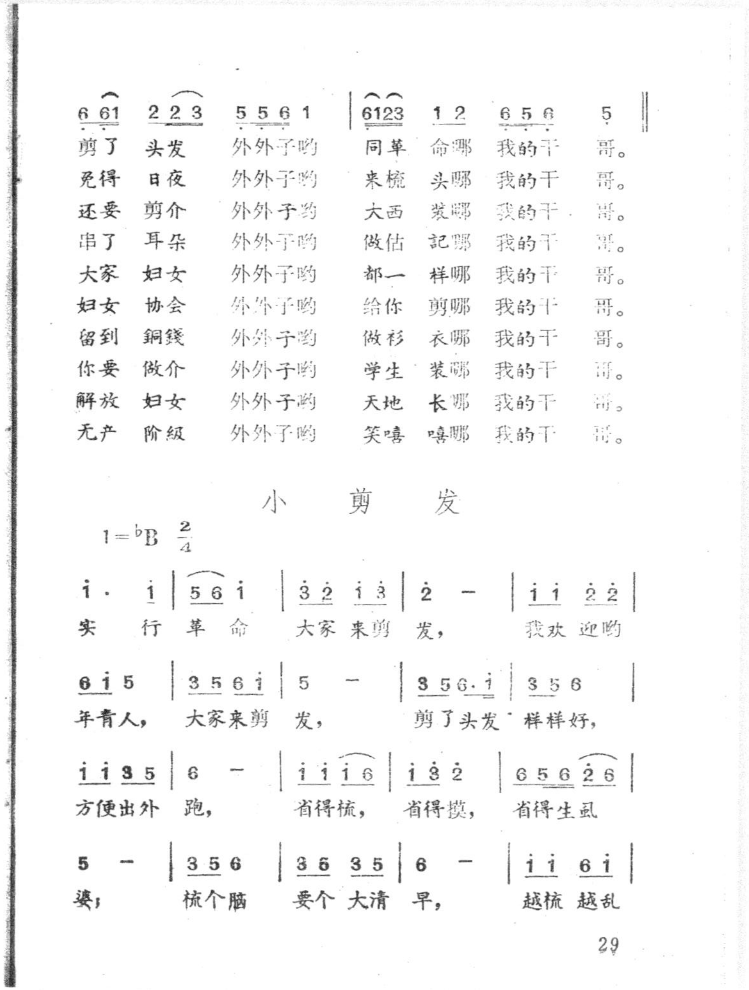

6 61 2 2 3 5 5 6 1 | 6123 1 2 6 5 6 5 ‖

剪了 头发 外外子哟 同革 命哪 我的干 哥。
免得 日夜 外外子哟 来梳 头哪 我的干 哥。
还要 剪介 外外子哟 大西 装哪 我的干 哥。
串了 耳朵 外外子哟 做估 記哪 我的干 哥。
大家 妇女 外外子哟 都一 样哪 我的干 哥。
妇女 协会 外外子哟 给你 剪哪 我的干 哥。
留到 銅錢 外外子哟 做衫 衣哪 我的干 哥。
你要 做介 外外子哟 学生 装哪 我的干 哥。
解放 妇女 外外子哟 天地 长哪 我的干 哥。
无产 阶級 外外子哟 笑嘻 嘻哪 我的干 哥。

小剪发

1 = ♭B $\frac{2}{4}$

1 · 1 | 5 6 1 | 3 2 1 3 | 2 — | 1 1 2 2 |
实 行 革 命 大家 来剪 发， 我欢 迎哟

6 1 5 | 3 5 6 1 | 5 — | 3 5 6 · 1 | 3 5 6 |
年青人， 大家来剪 发， 剪了头发 样样好，

1 1 3 5 | 6 — | 1 1 1 6 | 1 3 2 | 6 5 6 2 6 |
方便出外 跑， 省得梳， 省得摸， 省得生乱

5 — | 3 5 6 | 3 5 3 5 | 6 — | 1 1 6 1 |
婆； 梳个脑 要个 大清 早， 越梳 越乱

29

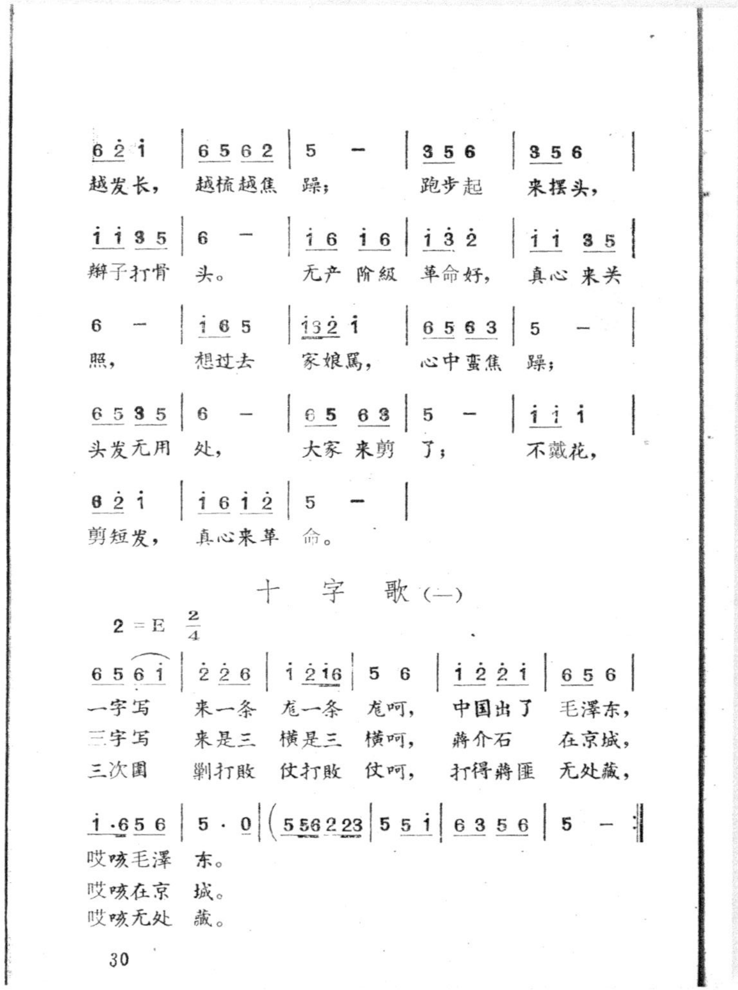

6 2 1 | 6 5 6 2 | 5 — | 3 5 6 | 3 5 6 |
越发长， 越梳越焦 躁； 跑步起 来摆头，

1 1 3 5 | 6 — | 1 6 1 6 | 1 3 2 | 1 1 3 5 |
辮子打背 头。 无产 阶級 革命好， 真心 来关

6 — | 1 6 5 | 13 2 1 | 6 5 6 3 | 5 — |
照， 想过去 家娘罵， 心中蛮焦 躁；

6 5 3 5 | 6 — | 6 5 6 3 | 5 — | 1 1 1 |
头发无用 处， 大家 来剪 了； 不戴花，

6 2 1 | 1 6 1 2 | 5 — |
剪短发， 真心来革 命。

十字歌（一）

2 = E $\frac{2}{4}$

6 5 6 1 | 2 2 6 | 1 2 16 | 5 6 | 1 2 2 1 | 6 5 6 |
一字写 来一条 龙一条 龙呵， 中国出了 毛澤东，
三字写 来是三 横是三 横呵， 蔣介石 在京城，
三次围 剿打敗 仗打敗 仗呵， 打得蔣匪 无处藏，

1 ·6 5 6 | 5 · 0 | (556223 | 5 5 1 | 6 3 5 6 | 5 — :‖
哎咳毛澤 东。
哎咳在京 城。
哎咳无处 藏。

30

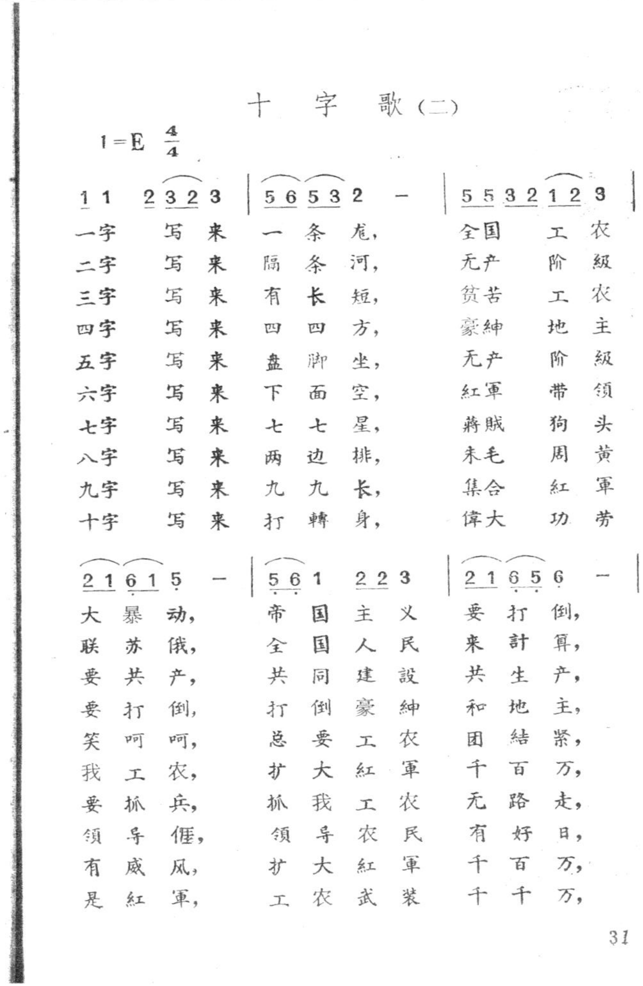

十字歌（二）

1=E 4/4

1 1 2 3 2 3 | 5 6 5 3 2 — | 5 5 3 2 1 2 3 |

一字 写来 一条龙， 全国 工农
二字 写来 隔条河， 无产 阶級
三字 写来 有长短， 贫苦 工农
四字 写来 四四方， 豪紳 地主
五字 写来 盘脚坐， 无产 阶級
六字 写来 下面空， 紅軍 带领
七字 写来 七七星， 蔣賊 狗头
八字 写来 两边排， 朱毛 周黄
九字 写来 九九长， 集合 紅軍
十字 写来 打轉身， 偉大 功劳

2 1 6 1 5 — | 5 6 1 2 2 3 | 2 1 6 5 6 — |

大暴动， 帝国主义 要打倒，
联苏俄， 全国人民 来計算，
要共产， 共同建設 共生产，
要打倒， 打倒豪紳 和地主，
笑呵呵， 总要工农 团結紧，
我工农， 扩大紅軍 千百万，
要抓兵， 抓我工农 无路走，
领导𠊎， 领导农民 有好日，
有威风， 扩大紅軍 千百万，
是紅軍， 工农武装 千千万，

6 2 1 6 5 6 1 | 2 1 6 1 5 — ‖

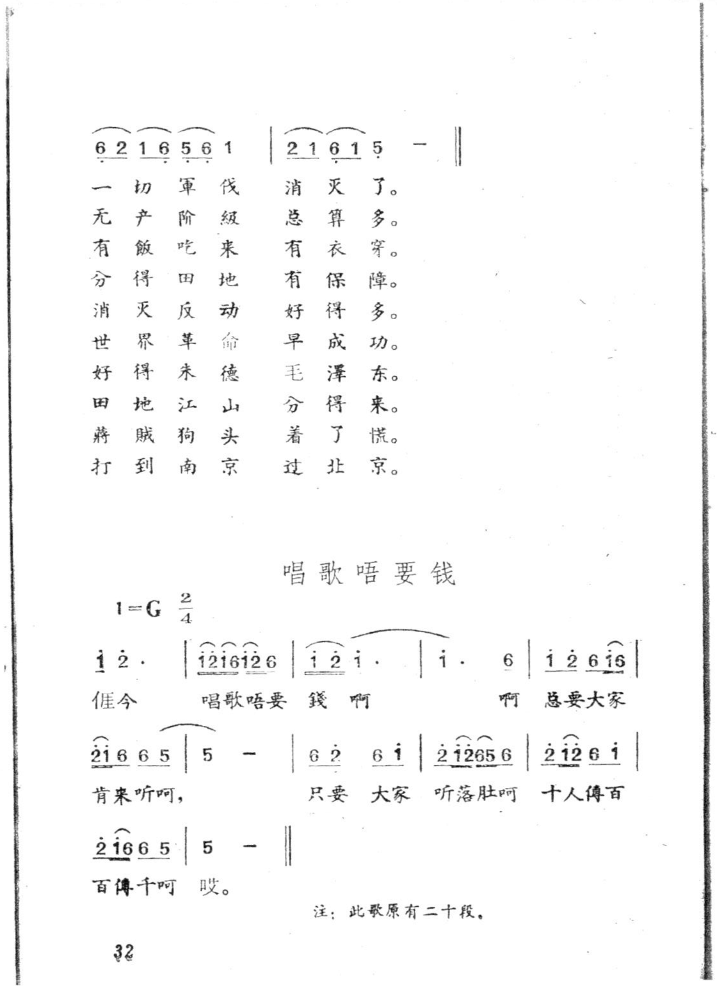

一切軍伐 消灭了。
无产阶級 总算多。
有飯吃来 有衣穿。
分得田地 有保障。
消灭反动 好得多。
世界革命 早成功。
好得朱德 毛澤东。
田地江山 分得来。
蔣賊狗头 着了慌。
打到南京 过北京。

唱歌唔要钱

1=G 2/4

1 2 · | 1 2 1 6 1 2 6 | 1 2 1 · | 1 · 6 | 1 2 6 1 6 |

𠊎今 唱歌唔要 錢 啊 啊 总要大家

2 1 6 6 5 | 5 — | 6 2 6 1 | 2 1 2 6 5 6 | 2 1 2 6 1 |

肯来听呵， 只要 大家 听落肚呵 十人傳百

2 1 6 6 5 | 5 — ‖

百傳千呵 哎。

注：此歌原有二十段。

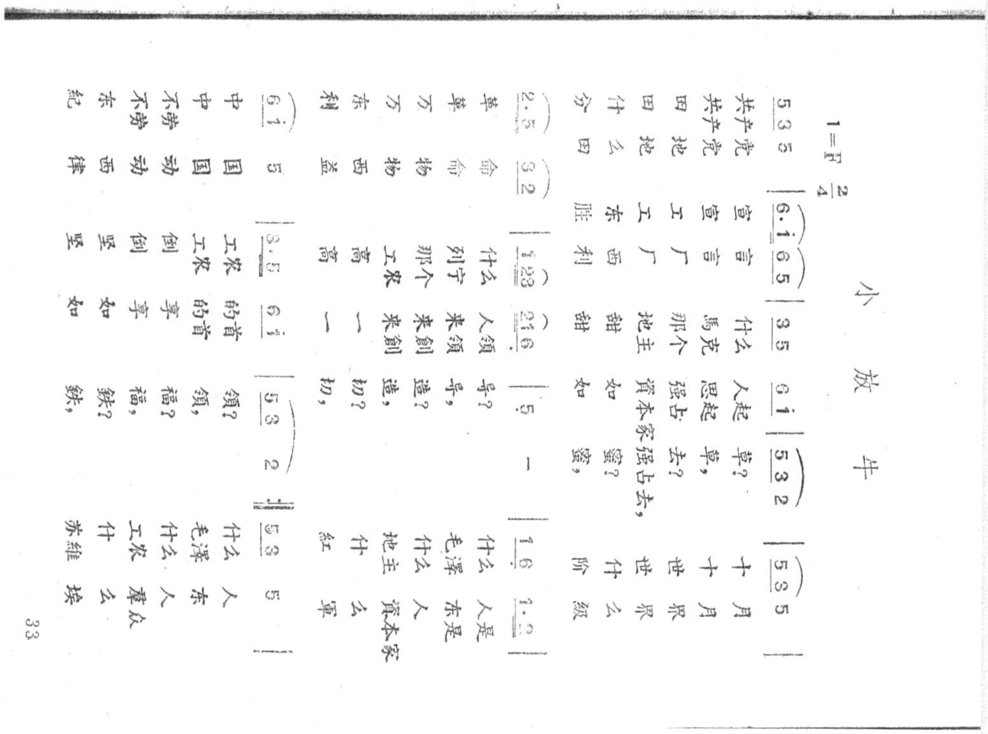

小 放 牛

1=F 2/4

5 3 5 | 6·i 6 5 | 3 5 6 i | 5 3 2 | 5 3 5 |

共产党 宣 言 什么 人起 草？ 十 月
共产党 宣 言 馬克 思起 草， 十 月
田 地 工 厂 那个 强占 去？ 世 界
田 地 工 厂 地主 資本家强占去， 世 界
什 么 东 西 甜 如 蜜？ 什 么
分 田 胜 利 甜 如 蜜， 阶 級

2·5 3 2 | i23 216 | 5 — | 1 6 1·2 |

革 命 什么 人領 导？ 什么 人是
革 命 列宁 来領 导， 毛澤 东是
万 物 那个 来創 造？ 什么 人
万 物 工农 来創 造， 地主 資本家
东 西 高 一 切？ 什 么
利 益 高 一 切， 紅 軍

6 i 5 | 3·5 6 i | 5 3 2 | 5 3 5 |

中 国 工农 的首 領？ 什么 人
中 国 工农 的首 領， 毛澤 东
不劳 动 倒 享 福？ 什么 人
不劳 动 倒 享 福， 工农 羣众
东 西 坚 如 鉄？ 什 么
紀 律 坚 如 鉄， 苏維 埃

33

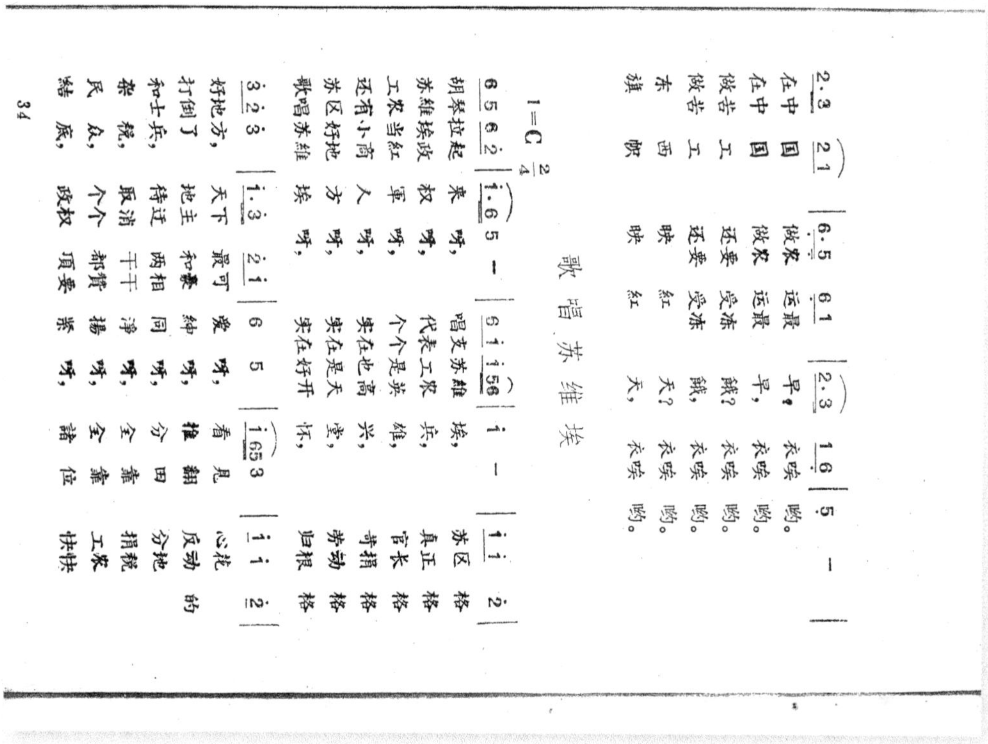

2·3 2 1 | 6·5 6 1 | 2·3 1 6 | 5 — |

在中 国 做农 运最 早， 衣唉 哟。
在中 国 做农 运最 早， 衣唉 哟。
做苦 工 还要 受冻 餓？ 衣唉 哟。
做苦 工 还要 受冻 餓， 衣唉 哟。
东 西 映 紅 天？ 衣唉 哟。
旗 帜 映 紅 天， 衣唉 哟。

歌唱苏维埃

1=C 2/4

6 5 6 2 | i·6 5 — | 6 i i56 | i — | i i 2 |

胡琴拉起 来 呀， 唱支苏維 埃， 苏区 格
苏維埃政 权 呀， 代表工农 兵， 真正 格
工农当紅 軍 呀， 个个是英 雄， 官长 格
还有小商 人 呀， 实在也高 兴， 苛捐 格
苏区好地 方 呀， 实在是天 堂， 劳动 格
歌唱苏維 埃 呀， 实在好开 怀， 归根 格

3 2 3 | i·3 2 i | 6 5 | i653 | i i 2 |

好地方， 天下 最可 爱 呀， 看 見 心花
打倒了 地主 和豪 紳 呀， 推 翻 反动 的
和士兵， 待遇 两相 同 呀， 分 田 分地
杂 税， 取消 干干 淨 呀， 全 靠 捐税
民 众， 个个 都贊 揚 呀， 全 靠 工农
結 底， 政权 頂要 紧 呀， 諸 位 快快

34

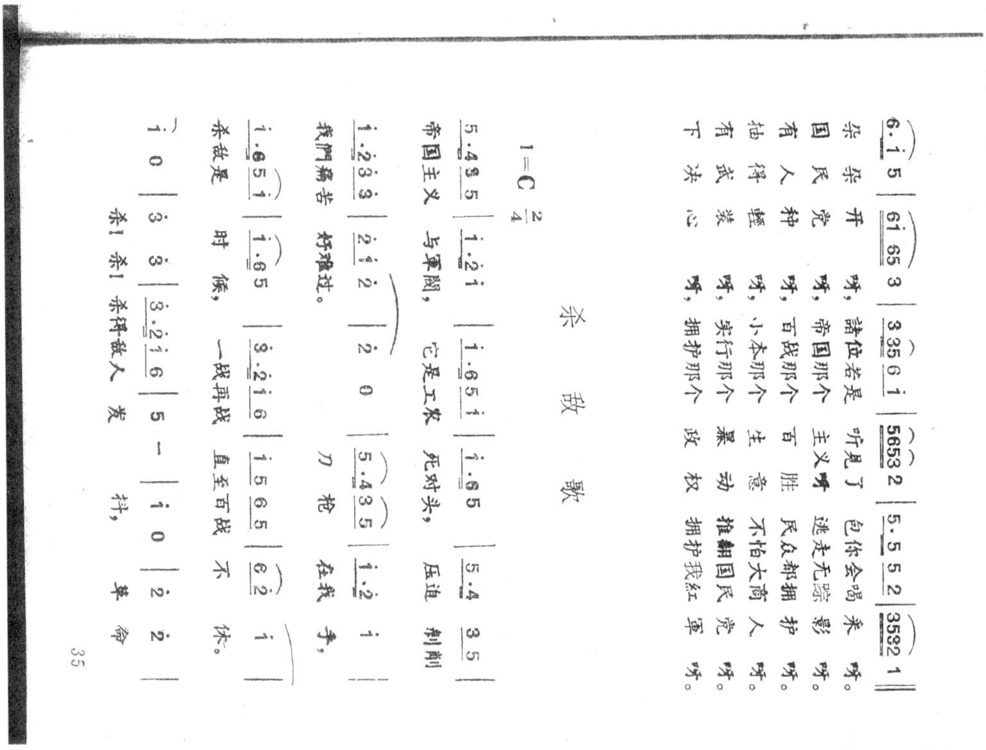

6·i 5 | 61 65 3 | 3 35 6 i | 5653 2 | 5·5 5 2 | 3532 1 ‖

朵 朵 开 呀，諸位若是 听見了 包你会唱 来 呀。
国 民 党 呀，帝国那个 主义呀 逃走无踪 影 呀。
有 人 种 呀，百战那个 百 胜 民众都拥 护 呀。
抽 得 輕 呀，小本那个 生 意 不怕大商 人 呀。
有 武 装 呀，实行那个 暴 动 推翻国民 党 呀。
下 决 心 呀，拥护那个 政 权 拥护我紅 軍 呀。

杀 敌 歌

1＝C $\frac{2}{4}$

5·43 5 | i·2 i | i·65 i | i·65 | 5·4 3 5 |
帝国主义 与軍閥， 它是工农 死对头， 压迫 剝削

i·23 3 | 2 i 2 | 2 0 | 5·43 5 | i·2 i |
我們痛苦 好难过。 刀 枪 在我 手，

i·65 i | i·65 | 3·2i 6 | i 5 6 5 | 6 2 i |
杀敌是 时 候， 一战再战 直至百战 不 休。

i 0 | 3 3 | 3·2i 6 | 5 — | i 0 | 2 2 |
杀！杀！杀得敌人 发 抖， 革 命

3·2 i 3 | 2 — | 5·43 5 | i·2 i | i·6 5 i |
精神抖 擻。 刀 枪 在我手， 向前 杀敌

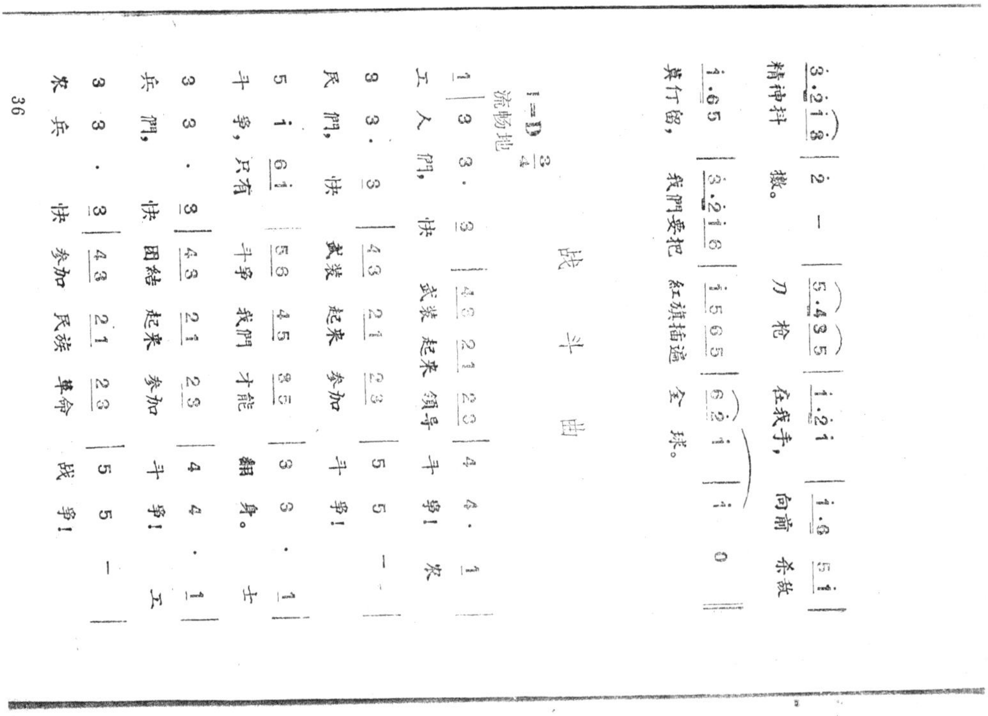

i·65 | 3·2i 6 | i 5 6 5 | 6 2 i | i 0 ‖
莫佇留， 我們要把 紅旗插遍 全 球。

战 斗 曲

1＝D $\frac{3}{4}$
流畅地

1 | 3 3· 3 | 43 21 23 | 4 4· 1 |
工 人 們， 快 武装 起来 領导 斗 爭！ 农

3 3· 3 | 43 21 23 | 5 5 — |
民 們， 快 武装 起来 参加 斗 爭！

5 i 6i | 56 45 35 | 3 3· 1 |
斗 爭，只有 斗爭 我們 才能 翻 身。 士

3 3· 3 | 43 21 23 | 4 4· 1 |
兵 們， 快 团結 起来 参加 斗 爭！ 工

3 3· 3 | 43 21 23 | 5 5 — |
农 兵 快 参加 民族 革命 战 爭！

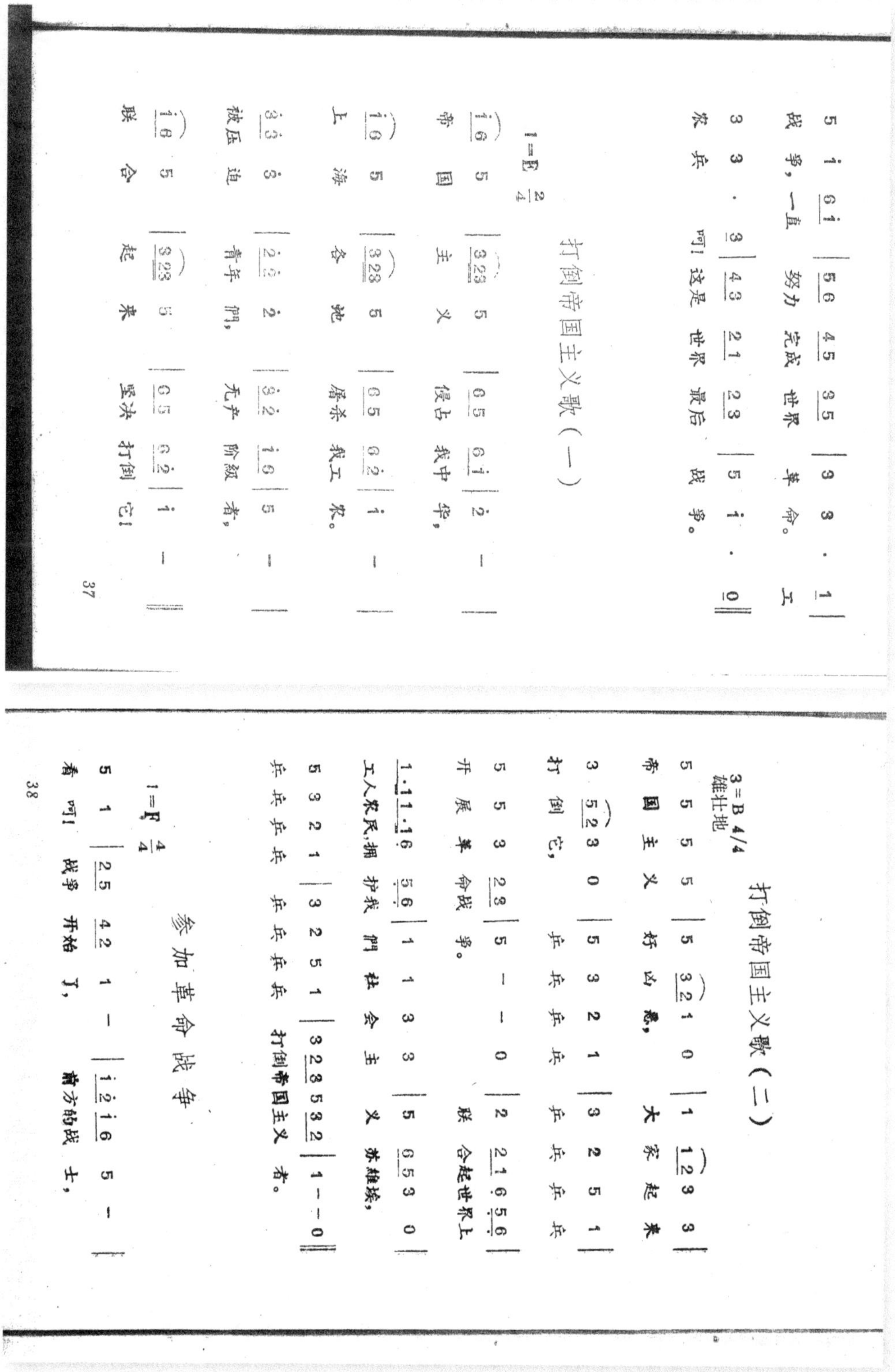

5 i 61 | 56 45 35 | 3 3 · 1 |
战 争，一直 努力 完成 世界 革 命。 工

3 3 · 3 | 43 21 23 | 5 i · 0 ‖
农 兵 呵！这是 世界 最后 战 争。

打倒帝国主义歌（一）

1＝E 2/4

i6 5 | 323 5 | 65 6i | 2 — |
帝 国 主 义 侵占 我中 华，

i6 5 | 323 5 | 65 62 | i — |
上 海 各 地 屠杀 我工 农。

33 3 | 22 2 | 32 i6 | 5 — |
被压 迫 青年 們， 无产 阶級 者，

i6 5 | 323 5 | 65 62 | i — ‖
联 合 起 来 坚决 打倒 它！

37

打倒帝国主义歌（二）

3＝B 4/4
雄壮地

5 5 5 5 | 5 32 1 0 | 1 12 3 3 |
帝 国 主 义 好 凶 恶， 大 家 起 来

3 52 3 0 | 5 3 2 1 | 3 2 5 1 |
打 倒 它， 乒 乒 乒 乒 乒 乒 乒 乒

5 5 3 23 | 5 — — 0 | 2 21 6 56 |
开 展 革 命战 争。 联 合起世界上

1·11·16 56 | 1 1 3 3 | 5 65 3 0 |
工人农民，拥 护我 們 社 会 主 义 苏維埃，

5 3 2 1 | 3 2 5 1 | 3 23 5 32 | 1 — — 0 ‖
乒 乒 乒 乒 乒 乒 乒 乒 打倒帝国主义 者。

参加革命战争

1＝F 4/4

5 1 | 25 42 1 — | i2 i6 5 — |
看 呵！ 战争 开始 了， 前方的战 士，

38

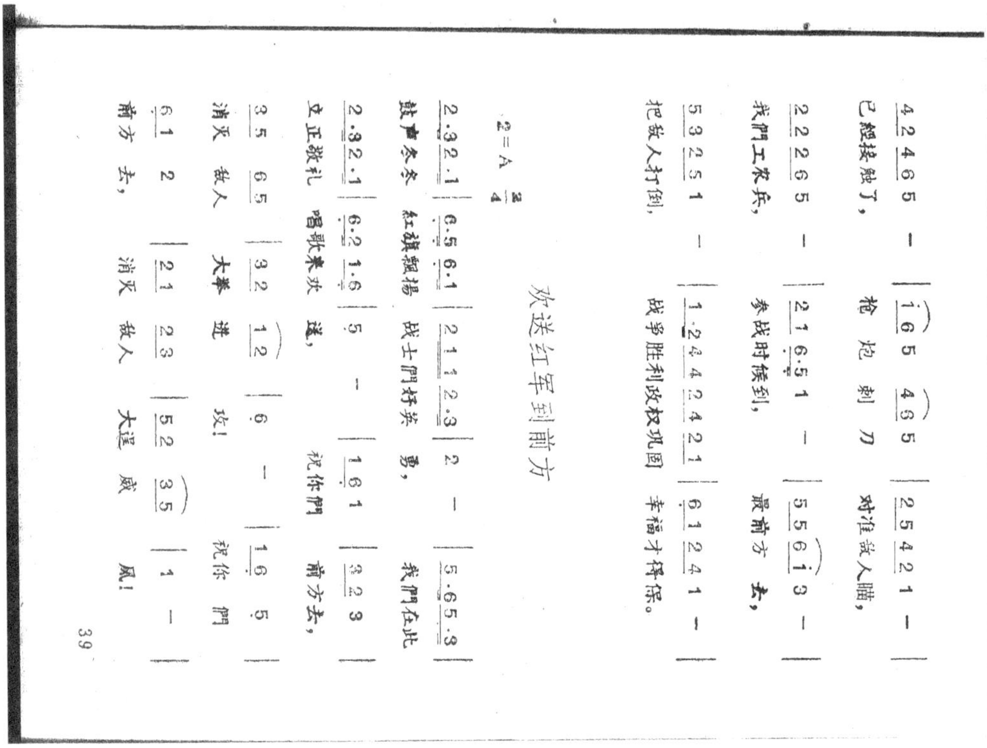

4 2 4 6 5 — | i 6 5 4 6 5 | 2 5 4 2 1 — |
已經接触了， 枪 炮 刺 刀 对准敌人瞄，

2 2 2 6 5 — | 2 1 6·5 1 — | 5 5 6 i 3 — |
我們工农兵， 参战时候到， 最前方 去，

5 3 2 5 1 — | 1·2 4 4 2 4 2 1 | 6 1 2 4 1 — |
把敌人打倒， 战爭胜利政权巩固 幸福才得保。

欢送红军到前方

2=A 2/4

2·3 2·1 | 6·5 6·1 | 2 1 1 2·3 | 2 — | 5·6 5·3 |
鼓声冬冬 紅旗飘揚 战士們好英 勇， 我們在此

2·3 2·1 | 6·2 1·6 | 5 — | 1 6 1 | 3 2 3 |
立正敬礼 唱歌来欢 送， 祝你們 前方去，

3 5 6 5 | 3 2 1 2 | 6 — | 1 6 5 |
消灭 敌人 大举 进 攻！ 祝你 們

6 1 2 | 2 1 2 3 | 5 2 3 5 | 1 — |
前方 去， 消灭 敌人 大逞 威 风！

39

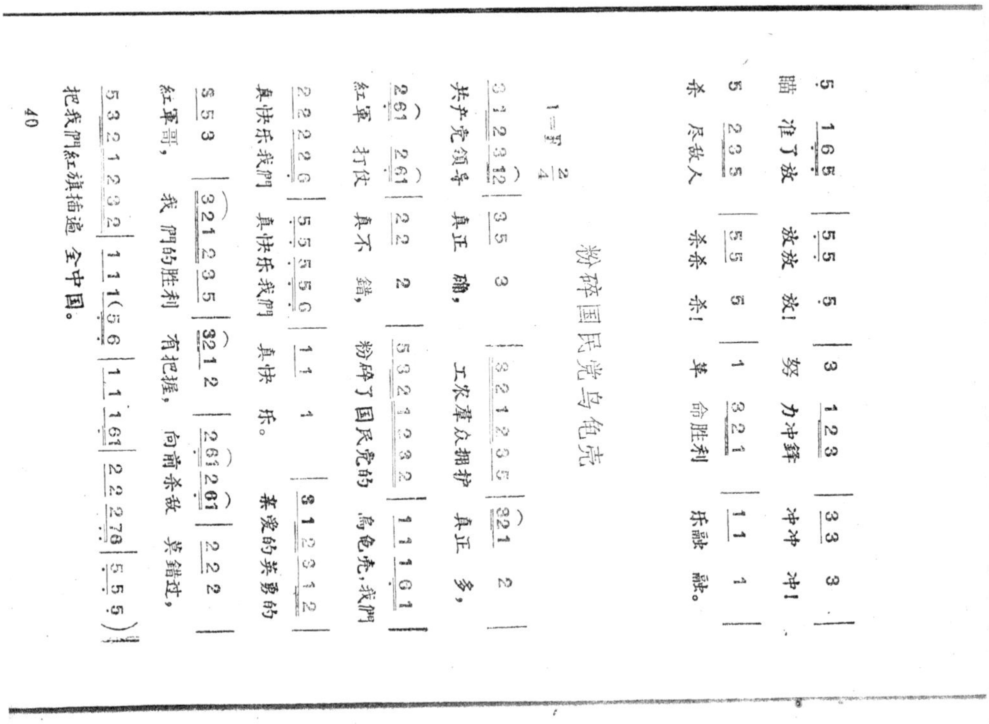

5 1 6 5 | 5 5 5 | 3 1 2 3 | 3 3 3 |
瞄 准了放 放放 放！ 努 力冲鋒 冲冲 冲！

5 2 3 5 | 5 5 5 | 1 3 2 1 | 1 1 1 |
杀 尽敌人 杀杀 杀！ 革 命胜利 乐融 融。

粉碎国民党乌龟壳

1=F 2/4

3 1 2 3 1 2 | 3 5 3 | 3 2 1 2 3 5 | 3 2 1 2 |
共产党領导 真正 确， 工农羣众拥护 真正 多，

2 6 1 2 6 1 | 2 2 2 | 5 3 2 1 2 3 2 | 1 1 1 6 1 |
紅軍 打仗 真不 錯， 粉碎了国民党的 烏龟壳，我們

2 2 2 2 6 | 5 5 5 5 6 | 1 1 1 | 3 1 2 3 1 2 |
真快乐我們 真快乐我們 真快 乐。 亲爱的英勇的

5 5 3 | 3 2 1 2 3 5 | 3 2 1 2 | 2 6 1 2 6 1 | 2 2 2 |
紅軍哥， 我 們的胜利 有把握， 向前杀敌 莫錯过，

5 3 2 1 2 3 2 | 1 1 1(5 6 | 1 1 1 6 1 | 2 2 2 7 6 | 5 5 5) |
把我們紅旗插遍 全中国。

40

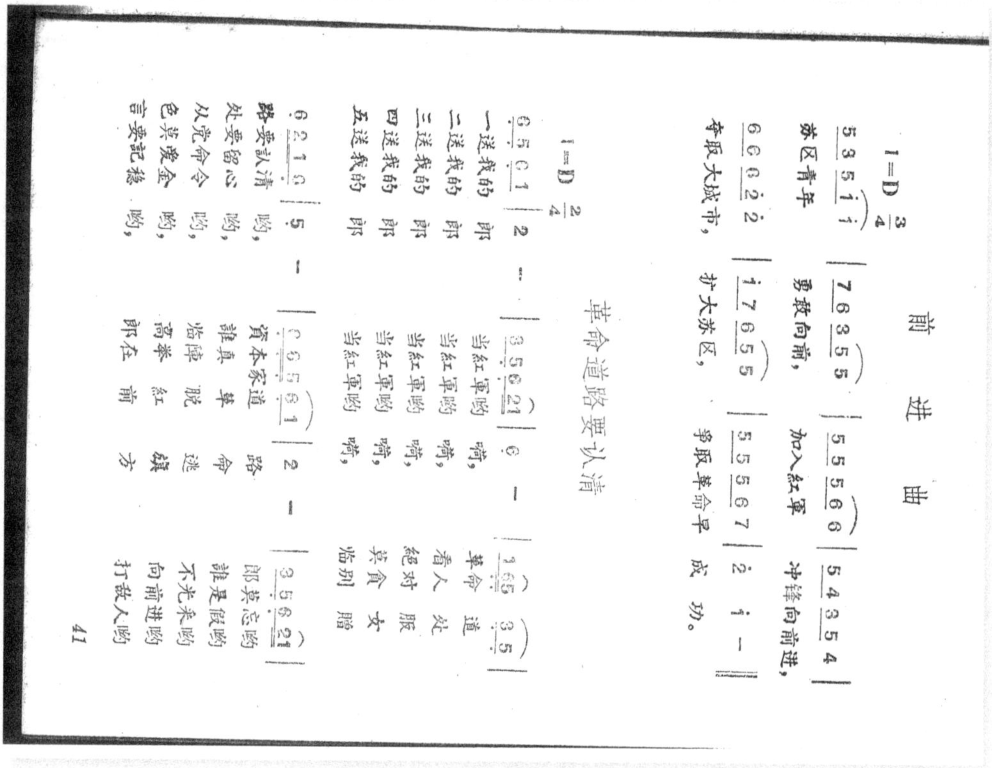

前　进　曲

1=D $\frac{3}{4}$

5 3 5 1̇ 1̇ | 7 6 3 5 5 | 5 5 5 6 6 | 5 4 3 5 4 |
苏区青年　勇敢向前，　加入紅軍　冲锋向前进，

6 6 6 2̇ 2̇ | 1̇ 7 6 5 5 | 5 5 5 6 7 | 2̇ 1̇ — ||
夺取大城市，　扩大苏区，　争取革命早　成　功。

革命道路要认清

1=D $\frac{2}{4}$

6 5 6 1 | 2 — | 3 5 6 21 | 6 — | 1 65 3 5 |
一送我的　郎　当紅軍哟　喲，　革命　道
二送我的　郎　当紅軍哟　喲，　看人　处
三送我的　郎　当紅軍哟　喲，　絕对　服
四送我的　郎　当紅軍哟　喲，　莫貪　女
五送我的　郎　当紅軍哟　喲，　临别　贈

6 2 1 6 | 5 — | 6 6 5 6 1 | 2 — | 3 5 6 21 |
路要認清　哟，　資本家道　路　郎莫忘哟
处要留心　哟，　誰真　革　命　誰是假哟
从党命令　哟，　临陣　脱　逃　不光采哟
色莫爱金　哟，　高举　紅　旗　向前进哟
言要記穩　哟，　郎在　前　方　打敌人哟

41

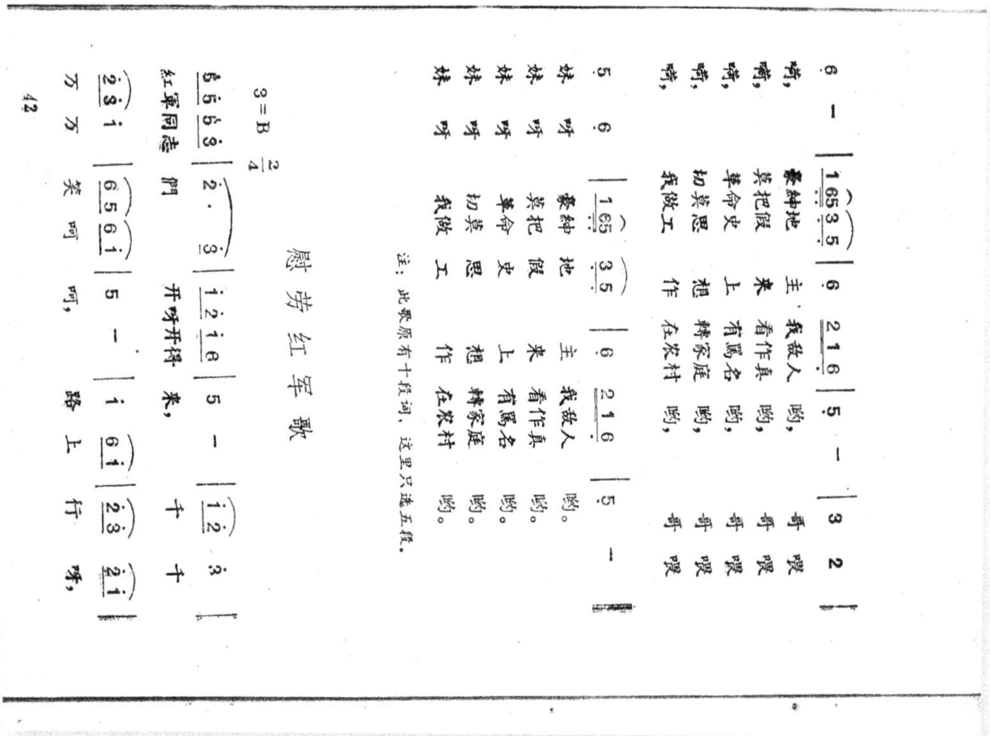

6 — | 1 65 3 5 | 6 2 1 6 | 5 — | 3 2 |
喲，　豪紳地　主　我敌人　哟，　哥　喂
喲，　莫把假　来　看作真　哟，　哥　喂
喲，　革命史　上　有罵名　哟，　哥　喂
喲，　切莫思　想　轉家庭　哟，　哥　喂
喲，　我做工　作　在农村　哟，　哥　喂

5 6 | 1 65 3 5 | 6 2 1 6 | 5 — ||
妹　呀　豪紳　地　主　我敌人　哟。
妹　呀　莫把　假　来　看作真　哟。
妹　呀　革命　史　上　有罵名　哟。
妹　呀　切莫　思　想　轉家庭　哟。
妹　呀　我做　工　作　在农村　哟。

注：此歌原有十段词，这里只选五段。

慰劳红军歌

3=B $\frac{2}{4}$

6 5 6 3 | 2· 3 | 1̇ 2̇ 1̇ 6 | 5 — | 1̇ 2̇ 3̇ |
紅軍同志　們　开呀开得　来，　千　千

2̇ 3̇ 1̇ | 6 5 6 1̇ | 5 — | 1̇ 6 1̇ | 2̇ 3̇ 2̇ 1̇ |
万　万　笑　呵　呵，　路　上　行　呀，

42

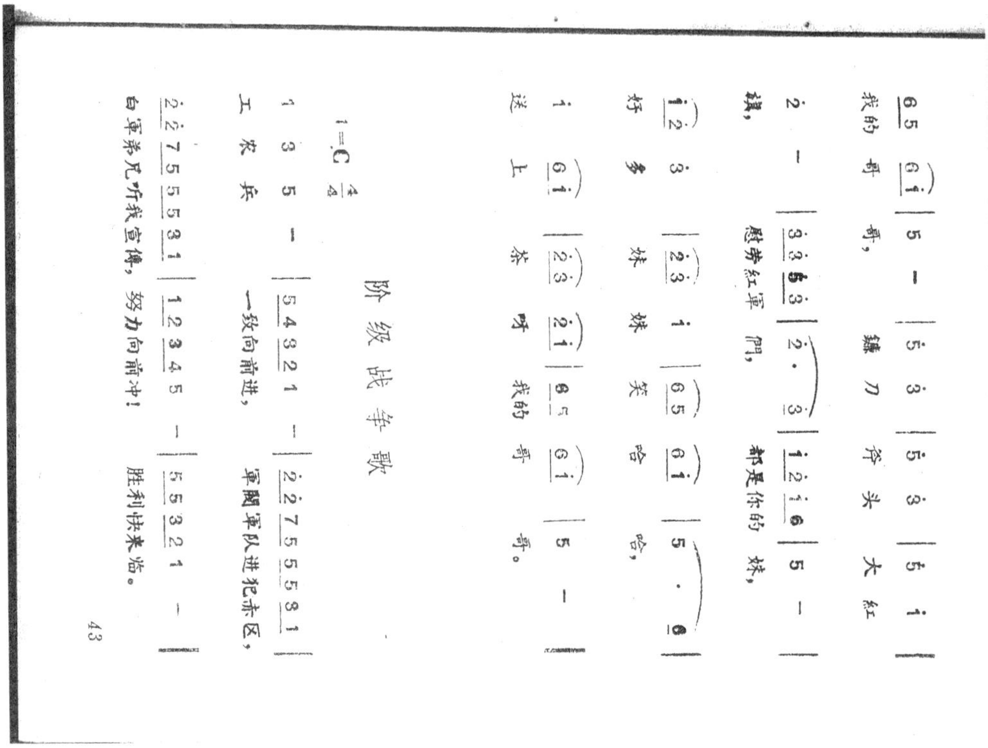

6 5 6 1 | 5 — | 5 3 | 5 3 | 5 1 |
我的哥 哥， 镰刀 斧头 大紅

2 — | 3 3 5 3 | 2 · 3 | 1 2 1 6 | 5 — |
旗， 慰劳紅軍 們， 都是你的 妹，

1 2 3 | 2 3 1 | 6 5 6 1 | 5 · 6 |
好 多 妹 妹 笑 哈 哈，

1 6 1 | 2 3 2 1 | 6 5 6 1 | 5 — |
送 上 茶 呀 我的 哥 哥。

阶级战争歌

1=C 4/4

1 3 5 — | 5 4 3 2 1 — | 2 2 7 5 5 5 3 1 |
工 农 兵 一致向前进， 軍閥軍队进犯赤区，

2 2 7 5 5 5 3 1 | 1 2 3 4 5 — | 5 5 3 2 1 — |
白軍弟兄听我宣傳， 努力向前冲！ 胜利快来临。

43

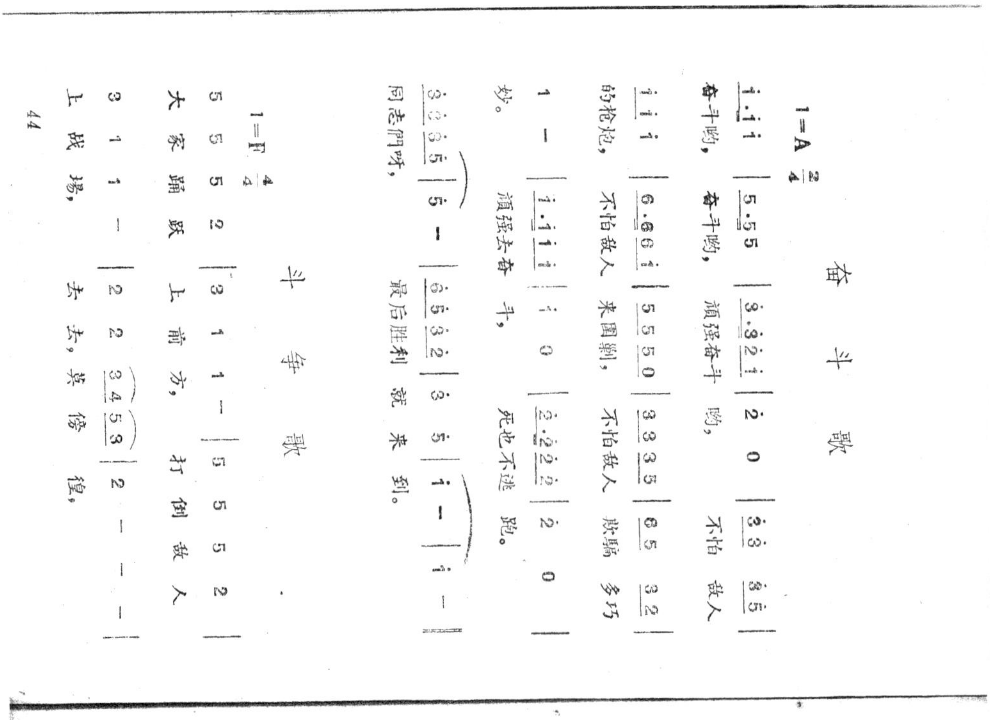

奋斗歌

1=A 2/4

1 · 1 1 | 5 · 5 5 | 3 · 3 2 1 | 2 0 | 3 3 3 5 |
奋斗哟， 奋斗哟， 頑强奋斗 哟， 不怕 敌人

1 1 1 | 6 · 6 6 1 | 5 5 5 0 | 3 3 3 5 | 6 5 3 2 |
的枪炮， 不怕敌人 来围剿， 不怕敌人 欺騙 多巧

1 — | 1 · 1 1 1 | 1 0 | 2 · 2 2 2 | 2 0 |
妙。 頑强去奋 斗， 死也不逃 跑。

3 3 3 5 | 5 — | 6 5 3 2 | 3 5 | 1 — | 1 — |
同志們呀， 最后胜利 就 来 到。

斗争歌

1=F 4/4

5 5 5 2 | 3 1 1 — | 5 5 5 2 |
大 家 踊 跃 上 前 方， 打 倒 敌 人

3 1 1 — | 2 2 3 4 5 3 | 2 — — — |
上 战 場， 去 去，莫 傍 徨，

44

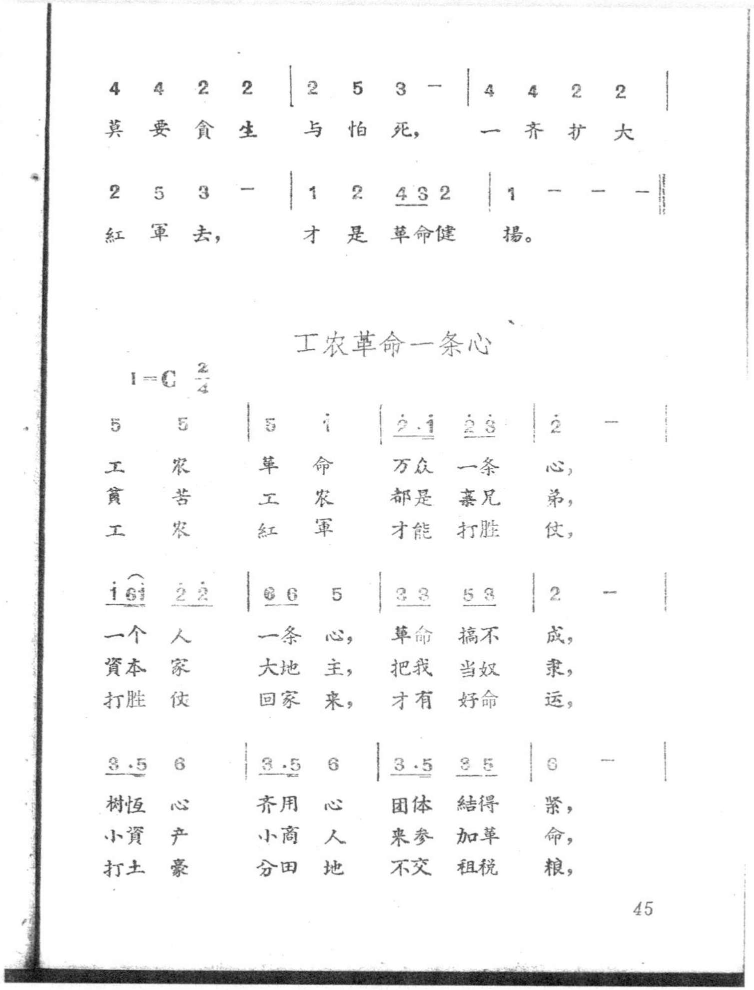

4 4 2 2 | 2 5 3 — | 4 4 2 2 |
莫 要 貪 生 与 怕 死， 一 齐 扩 大

2 5 3 — | 1 2 4 3 2 | 1 — — — ‖
紅 軍 去， 才 是 革命健 揚。

工农革命一条心

1=C $\frac{2}{4}$

5 5 | 5 i | 2·i 2 3 | 2 — |
工 农 革 命 万众 一条 心，
貧 苦 工 农 都是 弟兄 弟，
工 农 紅 軍 才能 打胜 仗，

i 6 i 2 2 | 6 6 5 | 3 3 5 3 | 2 — |
一个 人 一条 心， 革命 搞不 成，
資本 家 大地 主， 把我 当奴 隶，
打胜 仗 回家 来， 才有 好命 运，

3·5 6 | 3·5 6 | 3·5 3 5 | 6 — |
树恆 心 齐用 心 团体 結得 紧，
小資 产 小商 人 来参 加革 命，
打土 豪 分田 地 不交 租税 粮，

45

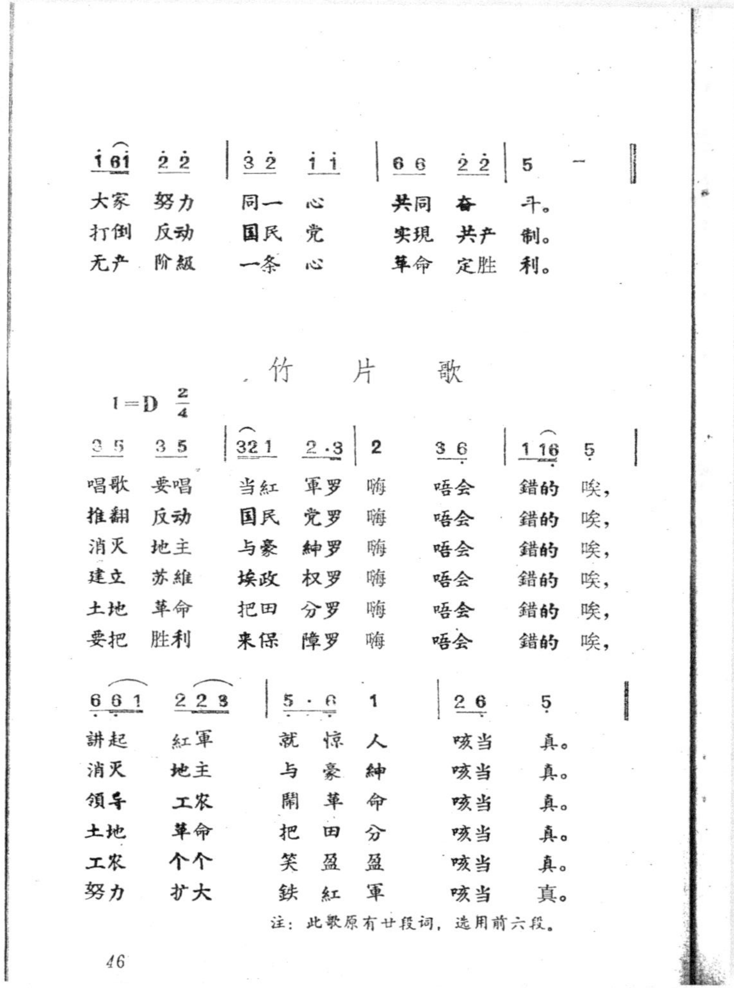

1 6 i 2 2 | 3 2 1 1 | 6 6 2 2 | 5 — ‖
大家 努力 同一 心 共同 奋 斗。
打倒 反动 国民 党 实現 共产 制。
无产 阶級 一条 心 革命 定胜 利。

竹 片 歌

1=D $\frac{2}{4}$

3 5 3 5 | 3 2 1 2·3 | 2 3 6 | 1 1 6 5 |
唱歌 要唱 当紅 軍罗 嗨 唔会 錯的 唉，
推翻 反动 国民 党罗 嗨 唔会 錯的 唉，
消灭 地主 与豪 紳罗 嗨 唔会 錯的 唉，
建立 苏維 埃政 权罗 嗨 唔会 錯的 唉，
土地 革命 把田 分罗 嗨 唔会 錯的 唉，
要把 胜利 来保 障罗 嗨 唔会 錯的 唉，

6 6 1 2 2 3 | 5·6 1 | 2 6 5 ‖
講起 紅軍 就 惊 人 咳当 真。
消灭 地主 与 豪 紳 咳当 真。
領导 工农 鬧 革 命 咳当 真。
土地 革命 把 田 分 咳当 真。
工农 个个 笑 盈 盈 咳当 真。
努力 扩大 鉄 紅 軍 咳当 真。

注：此歌原有廿段词，选用前六段。

46

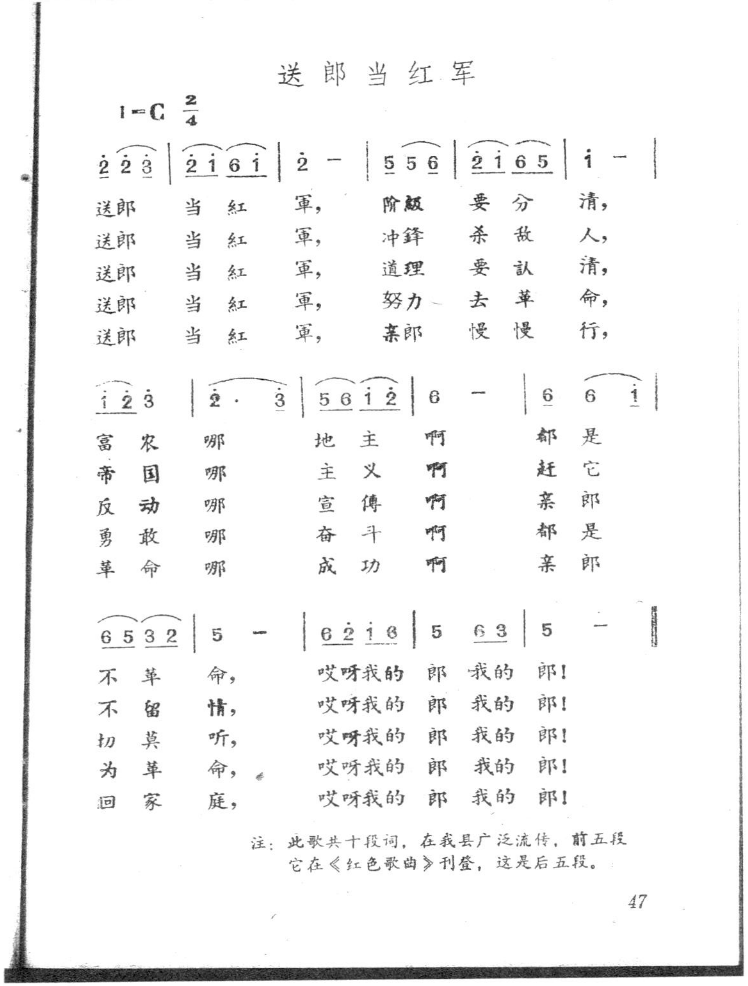

送郎当红军

1=C $\frac{2}{4}$

2 2 3 | 2 1 6 1 | 2 — | 5 5 6 | 2 1 6 5 | 1 — |

送郎 当 紅 軍， 阶級 要 分 清，
送郎 当 紅 軍， 冲鋒 杀 敌 人，
送郎 当 紅 軍， 道理 要 認 清，
送郎 当 紅 軍， 努力 去 革 命，
送郎 当 紅 軍， 亲郎 慢 慢 行，

1 2 3 | 2 · 3 | 5 6 1 2 | 6 — | 6 6 1 |

富 农 哪 地 主 啊 都 是
帝 国 哪 主 义 啊 赶 它
反 动 哪 宣 傳 啊 亲 郎
勇 敢 哪 奋 斗 啊 都 是
革 命 哪 成 功 啊 亲 郎

6 5 3 2 | 5 — | 6 2 1 6 | 5 6 3 | 5 — ‖

不 革 命， 哎呀我的 郎 我的 郎！
不 留 情， 哎呀我的 郎 我的 郎！
切 莫 听， 哎呀我的 郎 我的 郎！
为 革 命， 哎呀我的 郎 我的 郎！
回 家 庭， 哎呀我的 郎 我的 郎！

注：此歌共十段词，在我县广泛流传，前五段它在《红色歌曲》刊登，这是后五段。

47

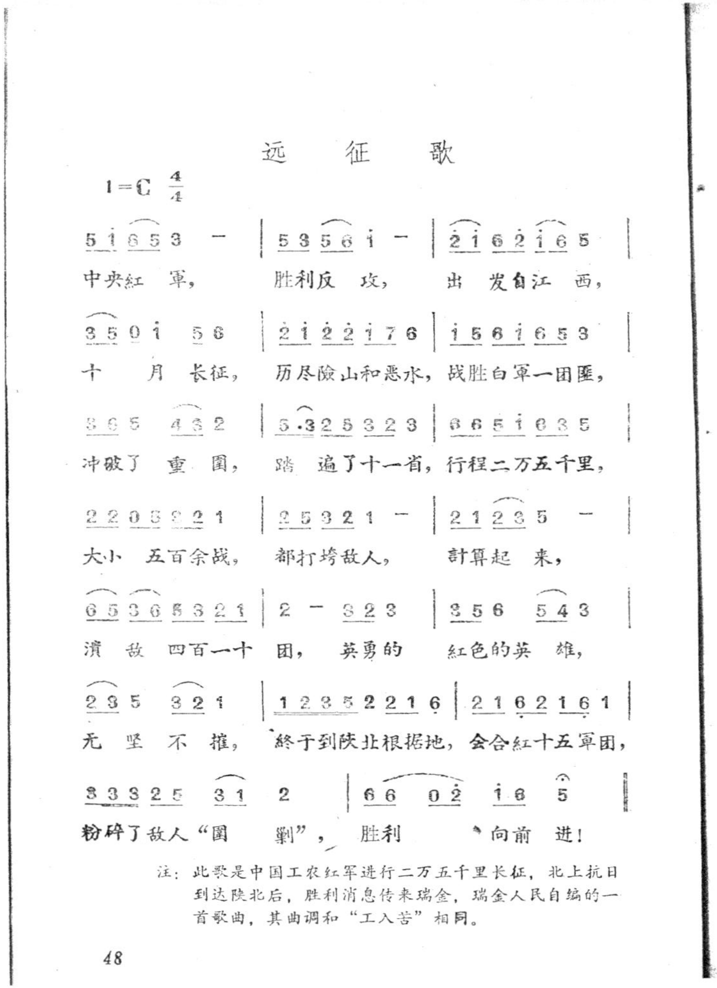

远 征 歌

1=C $\frac{4}{4}$

5 1 6 5 3 — | 5 3 5 6 1 — | 2 1 6 2 1 6 5 |

中央紅 軍， 胜利反 攻， 出 发自江 西，

3 5 0 1 5 6 | 2 1 2 2 1 7 6 | 1 5 6 1 6 5 3 |

十 月 长征， 历尽險山和恶水，战胜白軍一团匪，

3 6 5 4 3 2 | 5 ·3 2 5 3 2 3 | 6 6 5 1 6 3 5 |

冲破了 重 围， 踏 遍了十一省，行程二万五千里，

2 2 0 3 2 2 1 | 2 5 3 2 1 — | 2 1 2 3 5 — |

大小 五百余战， 都打垮敌人， 計算起 来，

6 5 3 6 5 3 2 1 | 2 — 3 2 3 | 3 5 6 5 4 3 |

潰 敌 四百一十 团， 英勇的 紅色的英 雄，

2 3 5 3 2 1 | 1 2 3 5 2 2 1 6 | 2 1 6 2 1 6 1 |

无 坚 不 摧， 終于到陕北根据地，会合紅十五軍团，

3 3 3 2 5 3 1 2 | 6 6 0 2 1 6 5 ‖

粉碎了敌人“围 剿”， 胜利 向前 进！

注：此歌是中国工农红军进行二万五千里长征，北上抗日到达陕北后，胜利消息传来瑞金，瑞金人民自编的一首歌曲，其曲调和“工人苦”相同。

48

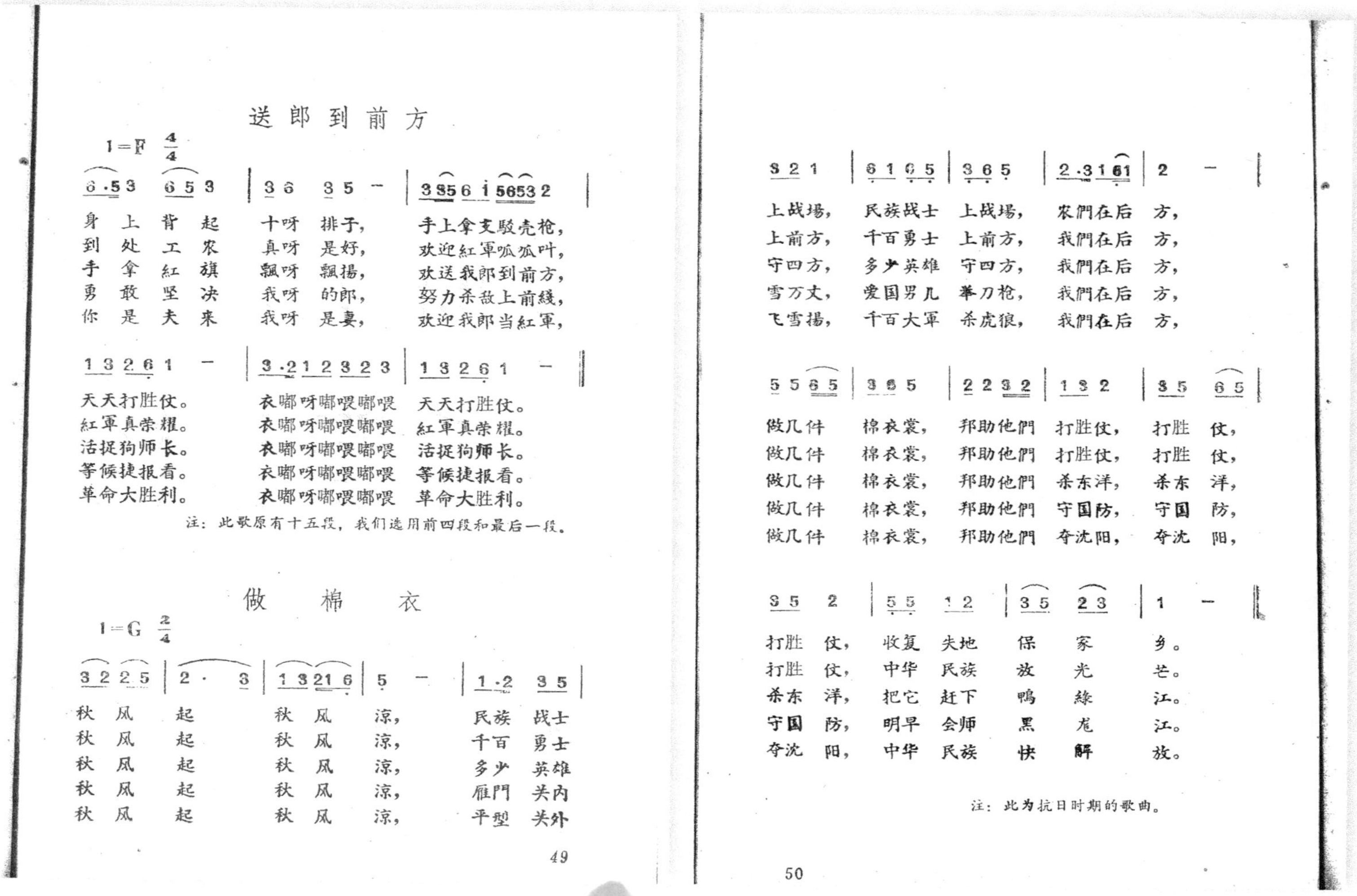

送郎到前方

1=F $\frac{4}{4}$

6.53 653 | 36 35 — | 3856 i 56532 |

身上背起　十呀排子，手上拿支駁壳枪，
到处工农　真呀是好，欢迎紅軍呱呱叫，
手拿紅旗　飘呀飘揚，欢送我郎到前方，
勇敢坚决　我呀的郎，努力杀敌上前綫，
你是夫来　我呀是妻，欢迎我郎当紅軍，

13261 — | 3.212323 | 13261 — ‖

天天打胜仗。衣嘟呀嘟喂嘟喂　天天打胜仗。
紅軍真荣耀。衣嘟呀嘟喂嘟喂　紅軍真荣耀。
活捉狗师长。衣嘟呀嘟喂嘟喂　活捉狗师长。
等候捷报看。衣嘟呀嘟喂嘟喂　等候捷报看。
革命大胜利。衣嘟呀嘟喂嘟喂　革命大胜利。

注：此歌原有十五段，我们选用前四段和最后一段。

做棉衣

1=G $\frac{2}{4}$

3225 | 2· 3 | 13216 | 5 — | 1.2 35 |

秋风起　秋风凉，民族战士
秋风起　秋风凉，千百勇士
秋风起　秋风凉，多少英雄
秋风起　秋风凉，雁門关内
秋风起　秋风凉，平型关外

321 | 6165 | 365 | 2.3161 | 2 — |

上战場，民族战士上战場，农們在后方，
上前方，千百勇士上前方，我們在后方，
守四方，多少英雄守四方，我們在后方，
雪万丈，愛国男儿拳刀枪，我們在后方，
飞雪揚，千百大軍杀虎狼，我們在后方，

5565 | 365 | 2232 | 132 | 35 65 |

做几件棉衣裳，邦助他們打胜仗，打胜仗，
做几件棉衣裳，邦助他們打胜仗，打胜仗，
做几件棉衣裳，邦助他們杀东洋，杀东洋，
做几件棉衣裳，邦助他們守国防，守国防，
做几件棉衣裳，邦助他們夺沈阳，夺沈阳，

35 2 | 55 12 | 35 23 | 1 — ‖

打胜仗，收复失地保家乡。
打胜仗，中华民族放光芒。
杀东洋，把它赶下鴨綠江。
守国防，明早会师黑龙江。
夺沈阳，中华民族快解放。

注：此为抗日时期的歌曲。

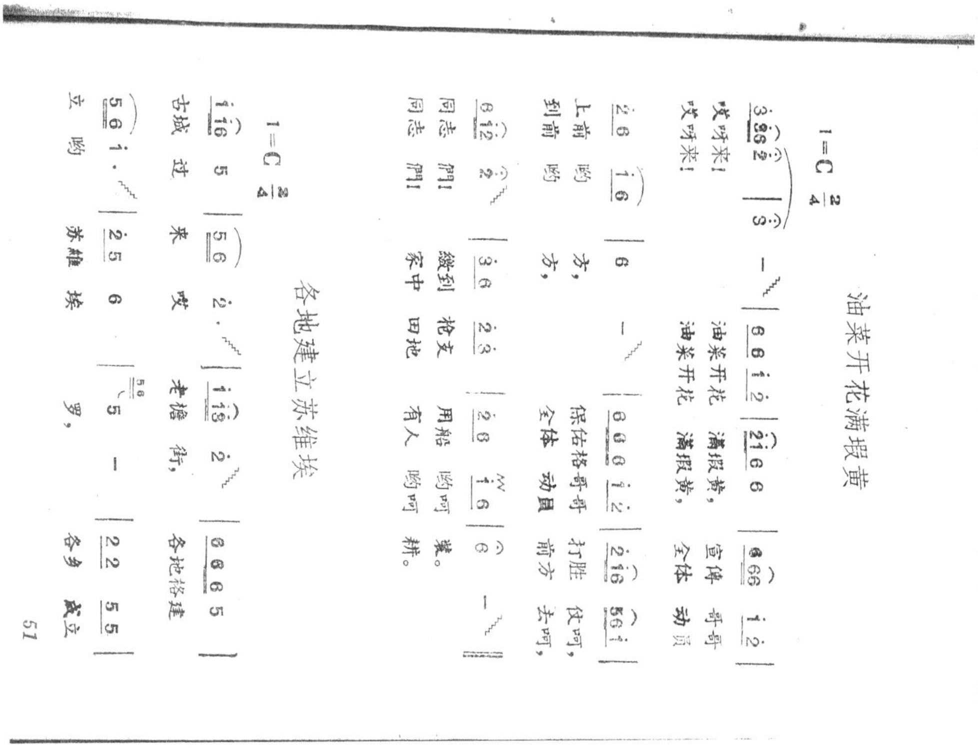

油菜开花满垠黄

1=C 2/4

3 36 2 | 3 — | 6 6 1 2 | 21 6 6 | 6 66 1 2 |
哎呀来！ 油菜开花 满垠黄， 宣傳 哥哥
哎呀来！ 油菜开花 满垠黄， 全体 动员

2 6 1 6 | 6 — | 6 6 6 1 2 | 2 16 56 1 |
上前 哟 方， 保佑格哥哥 打胜 仗呵，
到前 哟 方， 全体 动員 前方 去呵，

6 12 2 | 3 6 2 3 | 2 6 1 6 | 6 — ||
同志 們！ 繳到 枪支 用船 哟呵 裝。
同志 們！ 家中 田地 有人 哟呵 耕。

各地建立苏维埃

1=C 2/4

1 16 5 | 5 6 2 · | 1 13 2 | 6 6 6 5 |
古城 过 来 哎 老檐 街， 各地格建

5 6 1 · | 2 5 6 | 5 — | 2 2 5 5 |
立 哟 苏維 埃 罗， 各乡 成立

51

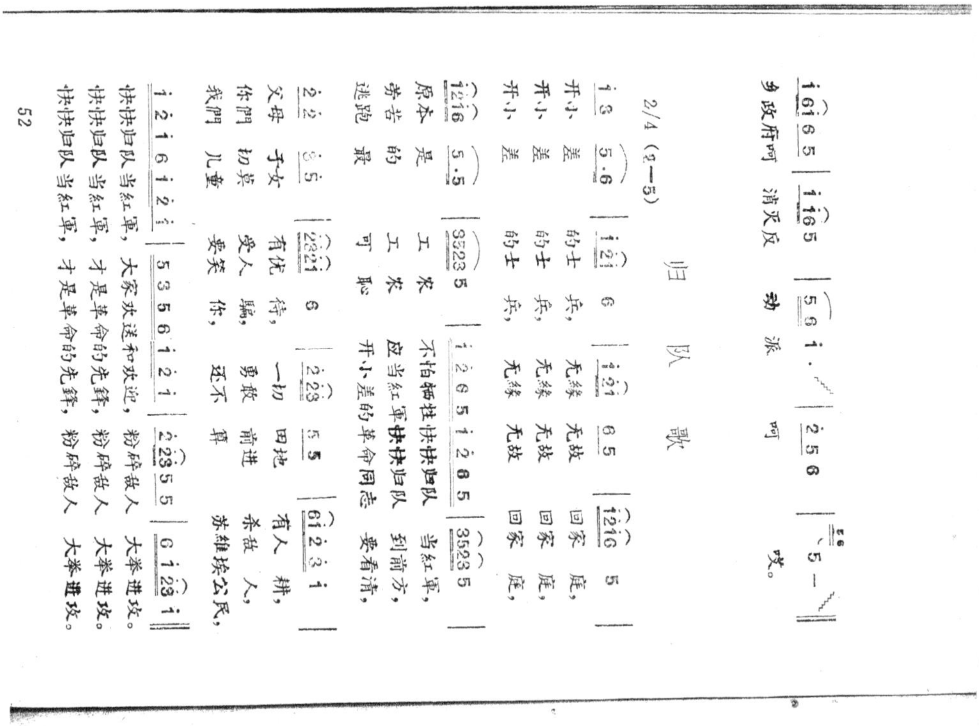

1 61 6 5 | 1 16 5 | 5 6 1 · | 2 5 6 | 5 — ||
乡政府呵 消灭反 动 派 呵 哎。

归队歌

2/4 (2—5)

1 3 5 · 6 | 1 21 6 | 1 21 6 5 | 1216 5 |
开小 差 的士 兵， 无缘 无故 回家 庭，
开小 差 的士 兵， 无缘 无故 回家 庭，
开小 差 的士 兵， 无缘 无故 回家 庭，

1216 5 · 5 | 3523 5 | 1 2 6 5 1 2 6 5 | 3523 5 |
原本 是 工 农 不怕牺牲快快归队 当紅軍，
劳苦 的 工 农 应当紅軍快快归队 到前方，
逃跑 最 可 恥 开小差的革命同志 要看清，

2 2 3 5 | 2321 6 | 2 23 5 5 | 61 2 3 1 |
父母 子女 有优 待， 一切 田地 有人 耕，
你們 切莫 受人 騙， 勇敢 前进 杀敌 人，
我們 儿童 要笑 你， 还不 算 苏維埃公民，

1 2 1 6 1 2 1 | 5 3 5 6 1 2 1 | 2 23 5 5 | 6 1 23 1 ||
快快归队当紅軍，大家欢送和欢迎，粉碎敌人 大举进攻。
快快归队当紅軍，才是革命的先鋒，粉碎敌人 大举进攻。
快快归队当紅軍，才是革命的先鋒，粉碎敌人 大举进攻。

52

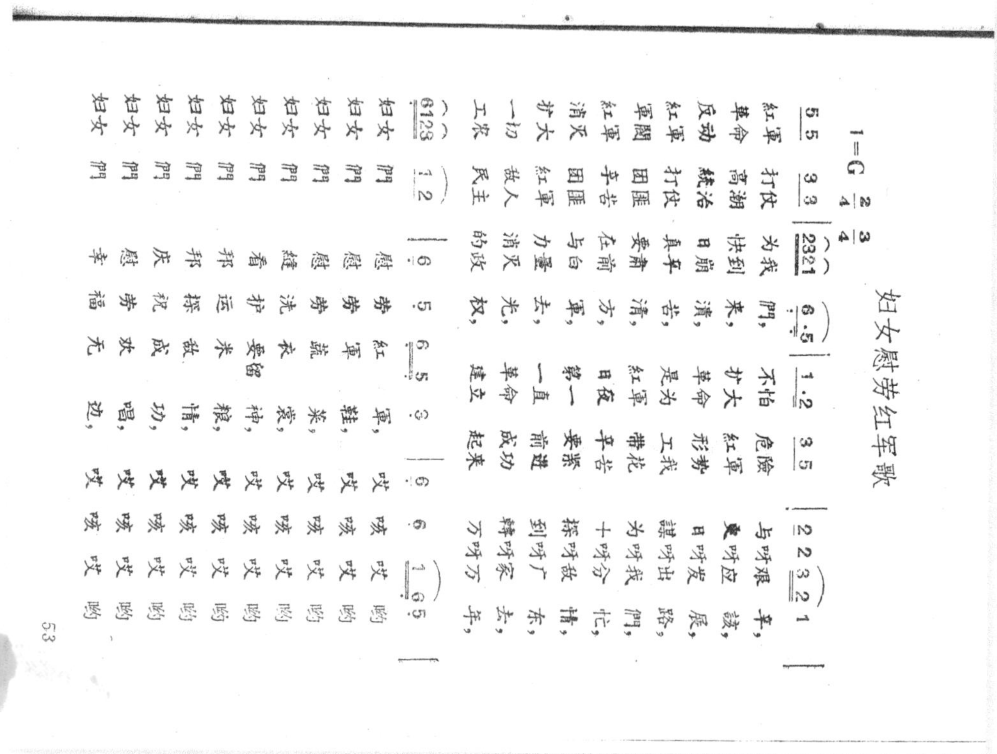

妇女慰劳红军歌

1=G 2/4 3/4

5 5 3 3 | 2321 6·5 | 1·2 3 5 | 2 2 3 2 1 |

紅軍 打仗 为我 們， 不怕 危險 与呀艰 辛，
革命 高潮 快到 来， 扩大 紅軍 更呀应 該，
反动 統治 日崩 潰， 革命 形势 日呀发 展，
紅軍 打仗 真辛 苦， 是为 工我 謀呀出 路，
軍閥 团匪 要肅 清， 紅軍 带花 为呀我 們，
紅軍 辛苦 在前 方， 日夜 辛苦 十呀分 忙，
消灭 团匪 与白 軍， 第一 要紧 探呀敌 情，
扩大 紅軍 力量 去， 一直 前进 到呀广 东，
一切 敌人 消灭 光， 革命 成功 轉呀家 去，
工农 民主 的政 权， 建立 起来 万呀万 年，

6123 1 2 | 6 5 6 5 3 | 6 6 1 65 |

妇女 們 慰 劳 紅 軍， 哎 咳 哎 哟
妇女 們 慰 劳 軍 鞋， 哎 咳 哎 哟
妇女 們 慰 劳 蔬 菜， 哎 咳 哎 哟
妇女 們 縫 洗 衣 裳， 哎 咳 哎 哟
妇女 們 看 护 要留 神， 哎 咳 哎 哟
妇女 們 邦 运 米 粮， 哎 咳 哎 哟
妇女 們 邦 探 敌 情， 哎 咳 哎 哟
妇女 們 庆 祝 成 功， 哎 咳 哎 哟
妇女 們 慰 劳 欢 唱， 哎 咳 哎 哟
妇女 們 幸 福 无 边， 哎 咳 哎 哟

53

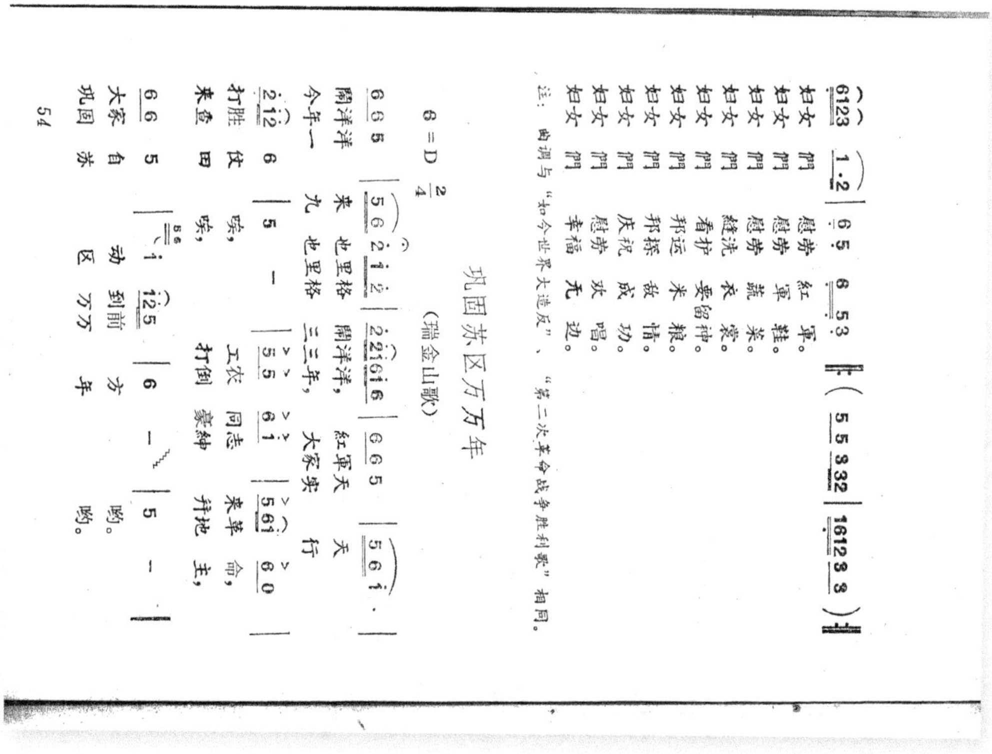

6123 1·2 | 6 5 6 53 ‖: (5 5 332 | 16123 3) :‖

妇女 們 慰劳 紅 軍。
妇女 們 慰劳 軍 鞋。
妇女 們 慰劳 蔬 菜。
妇女 們 縫洗 衣 裳。
妇女 們 看护 要留神。
妇女 們 邦运 米 粮。
妇女 們 邦探 敌 情。
妇女 們 庆祝 成 功。
妇女 們 慰劳 欢 唱。
妇女 們 幸福 无 边。

注：曲调与“如今世界大造反”、“第二次革命战争胜利歌”相同。

巩固苏区万万年

（瑞金山歌）

6=D 2/4

6 6 5 | 5 6 2 1 2 | 2 21616 | 6 6 5 | 5 6 1 · |

鬧洋洋 来 也里格 鬧洋洋， 紅軍天 天
今年一 九 也里格 三三年， 大家实 行

2 12 6 | 5 — | 5 5 6 1 | 5 61 6 0 |

打胜 仗 唉， 工农 同志 来革 命，
来查 田 唉， 打倒 豪紳 升地 主，

6 6 5 | 56 1 125 | 6 — | 5 — |

大家 自 动 到前 方 哟。
巩固 苏 区 万万 年 哟。

54

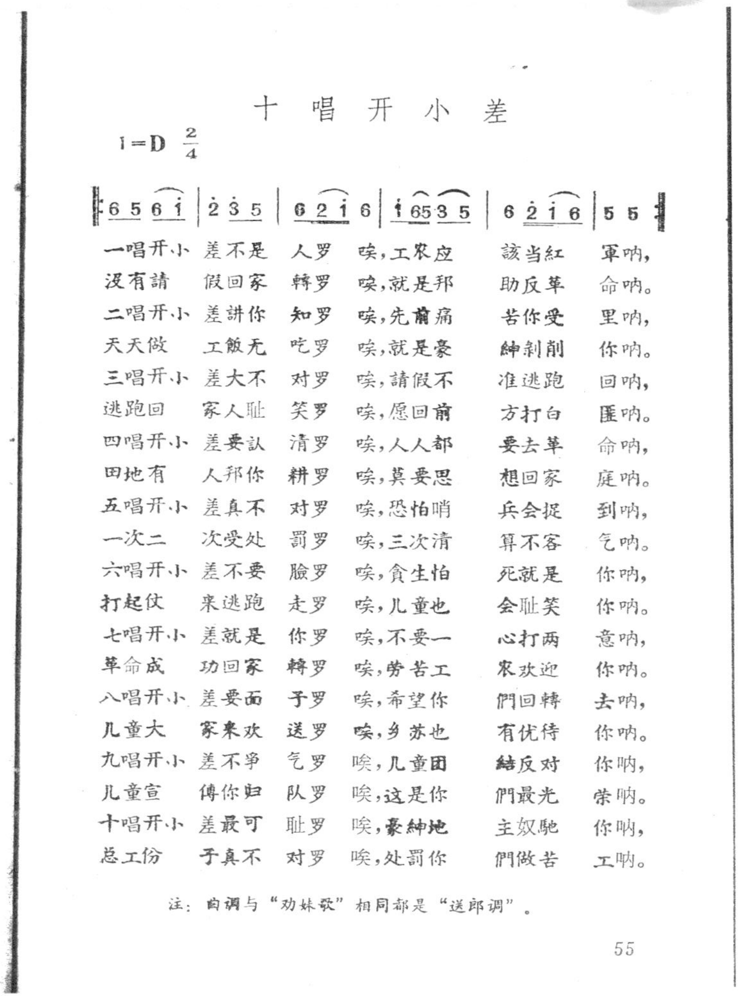

十唱开小差

1=D 2/4

| 6 5 6 1 | 2 3 5 | 6 2 1 6 | 1 65 3 5 | 6 2 1 6 | 5 5 ||

一唱开小 差不是 人罗 唉，工农应 該当紅 軍呐，
没有請 假回家 轉罗 唉，就是邦 助反革 命呐。
二唱开小 差讲你 知罗 唉，先前痛 苦你受 里呐，
天天做 工飯无 吃罗 唉，就是豪 紳剥削 你呐。
三唱开小 差大不 对罗 唉，請假不 准逃跑 回呐，
逃跑回 家人耻 笑罗 唉，愿回前 方打白 匪呐。
四唱开小 差要認 清罗 唉，人人都 要去革 命呐，
田地有 人邦你 耕罗 唉，莫要思 想回家 庭呐。
五唱开小 差真不 对罗 唉，恐怕哨 兵会捉 到呐，
一次二 次受处 罚罗 唉，三次清 算不客 气呐。
六唱开小 差不要 脸罗 唉，貪生怕 死就是 你呐，
打起仗 来逃跑 走罗 唉，儿童也 会耻笑 你呐。
七唱开小 差就是 你罗 唉，不要一 心打两 意呐，
革命成 功回家 轉罗 唉，劳苦工 农欢迎 你呐。
八唱开小 差要面 子罗 唉，希望你 們回轉 去呐，
儿童大 家来欢 送罗 唉，乡苏也 有优待 你呐。
九唱开小 差不爭 气罗 唉，儿童团 結反对 你呐，
儿童宣 傳你归 队罗 唉，这是你 們最光 荣呐。
十唱开小 差最可 耻罗 唉，豪紳地 主奴馳 你呐，
总工份 子真不 对罗 唉，处罚你 們做苦 工呐。

注：曲调与“劝妹歌”相同都是“送郎调”。

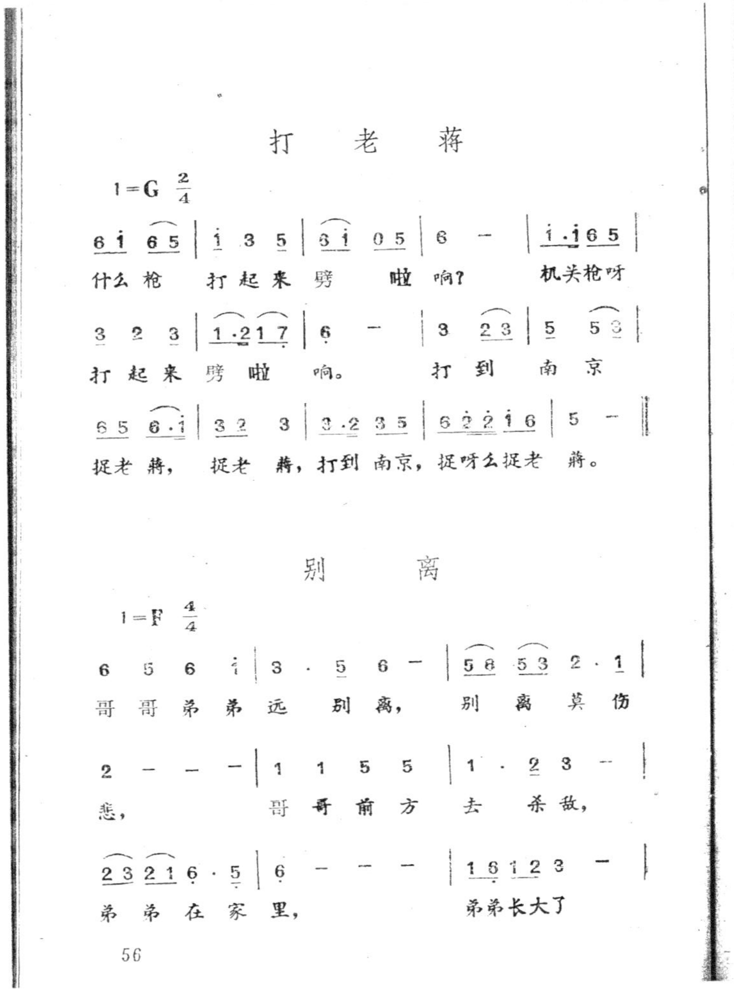

打老蒋

1=G 2/4

6 1 6 5 | 1 3 5 | 6 1 0 5 | 6 — | 1.1 6 5 |
什么 枪 打 起 来 劈 啦 响？ 机关枪呀

3 2 3 | 1.2 1 7 | 6 — | 3 2 3 | 5 5 3 |
打 起 来 劈 啦 响。 打 到 南 京

6 5 6.1 | 3 2 3 | 3.2 3 5 | 6 2 2 1 6 | 5 — ||
捉老 蒋， 捉老 蒋，打到 南京，捉呀么捉老 蒋。

别离

1=F 4/4

6 5 6 1 | 3 . 5 6 — | 5 6 5 3 2 . 1 |
哥 哥 弟 弟 远 别 离， 别 离 莫 伤

2 — — — | 1 1 5 5 | 1 . 2 3 — |
悲， 哥 哥 前 方 去 杀 敌，

2 3 2 1 6 . 5 | 6 — — — | 1 6 1 2 3 — |
弟 弟 在 家 里， 弟弟长大了

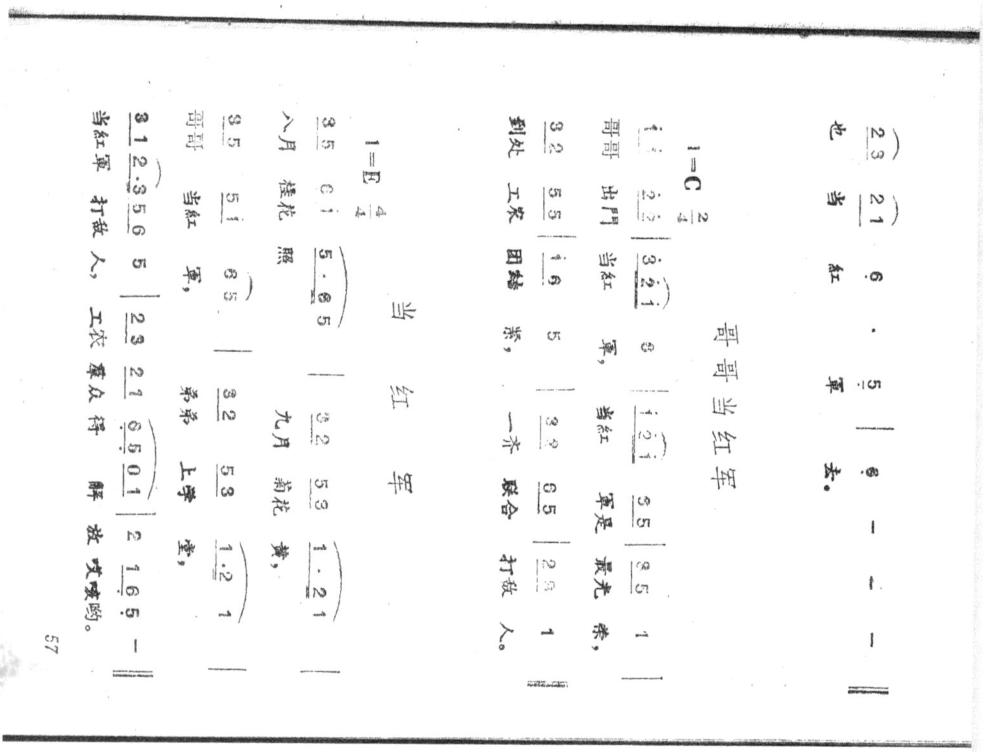

2 3 2 1 6 · 5 | 6 — — — ‖
也 当 紅 軍 去。

哥哥当红军

1=C $\frac{2}{4}$

1 1 2 2 | 3 2 1 6 | 1 2 1 3 5 | 3 5 1 |
哥哥 出門 当紅 軍， 当紅 軍是 最光 荣，

3 2 5 5 | 1 6 5 | 3 2 6 5 | 2 3 1 ‖
到处 工农 团結 紧， 一齐 联合 打敌 人。

当红军

1=E $\frac{4}{4}$

3 5 6 1 5 · 6 5 | 3 2 5 3 1 · 2 1 |
八月 桂花 照 九月 菊花 黄，

3 5 5 1 6 5 | 3 2 5 3 1 · 2 1 |
哥哥 当紅 軍， 弟弟 上学 堂，

3 1 2 · 3 5 6 5 | 2 3 2 1 6 5 0 1 | 2 1 6 5 — ‖
当紅軍 打敌 人， 工农 羣众 得 解 放 哎咳哟。

57

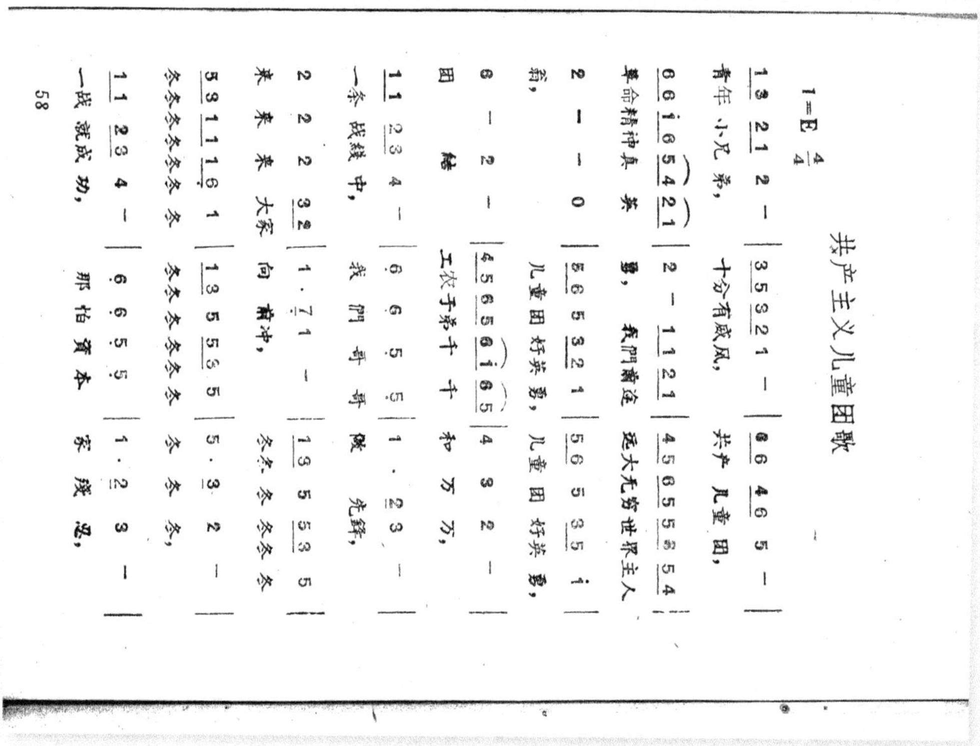

共产主义儿童团歌

1=E $\frac{4}{4}$

1 3 2 1 2 — | 3 5 3 2 1 — | 6 6 4 6 5 — |
青年 小兄 弟， 十分有威风， 共产 儿童 团，

6 6 1 6 5 4 2 1 | 2 — 1 1 2 1 | 4 5 6 5 5 6 5 4 |
革命精神真 英 勇， 我們前途 远大无穷世界主人

2 — — 0 | 5 6 5 3 2 1 | 5 6 5 3 5 1 |
翁， 儿童团 好英 勇， 儿童 团 好英 勇，

6 — 2 — | 4 5 6 5 6 1 6 5 | 4 3 2 — |
团 結 工农子弟千 千 和 万 万，

1 1 2 3 4 — | 6 6 5 5 | 1 · 2 3 — |
一条 战綫 中， 我 們 哥 哥 做 先鋒，

2 2 2 3 2 | 1 · 7 1 — | 1 3 5 5 3 5 |
来 来 来 大家 向 前冲， 冬冬 冬 冬冬 冬

5 3 1 1 1 6 1 | 1 3 5 5 3 5 | 5 · 3 2 — |
冬冬冬冬冬冬 冬 冬冬 冬 冬冬 冬 冬 冬 冬，

1 1 2 3 4 — | 6 6 5 5 | 1 · 2 3 — |
一战 就成 功， 那 怕 資 本 家 残 忍，

58

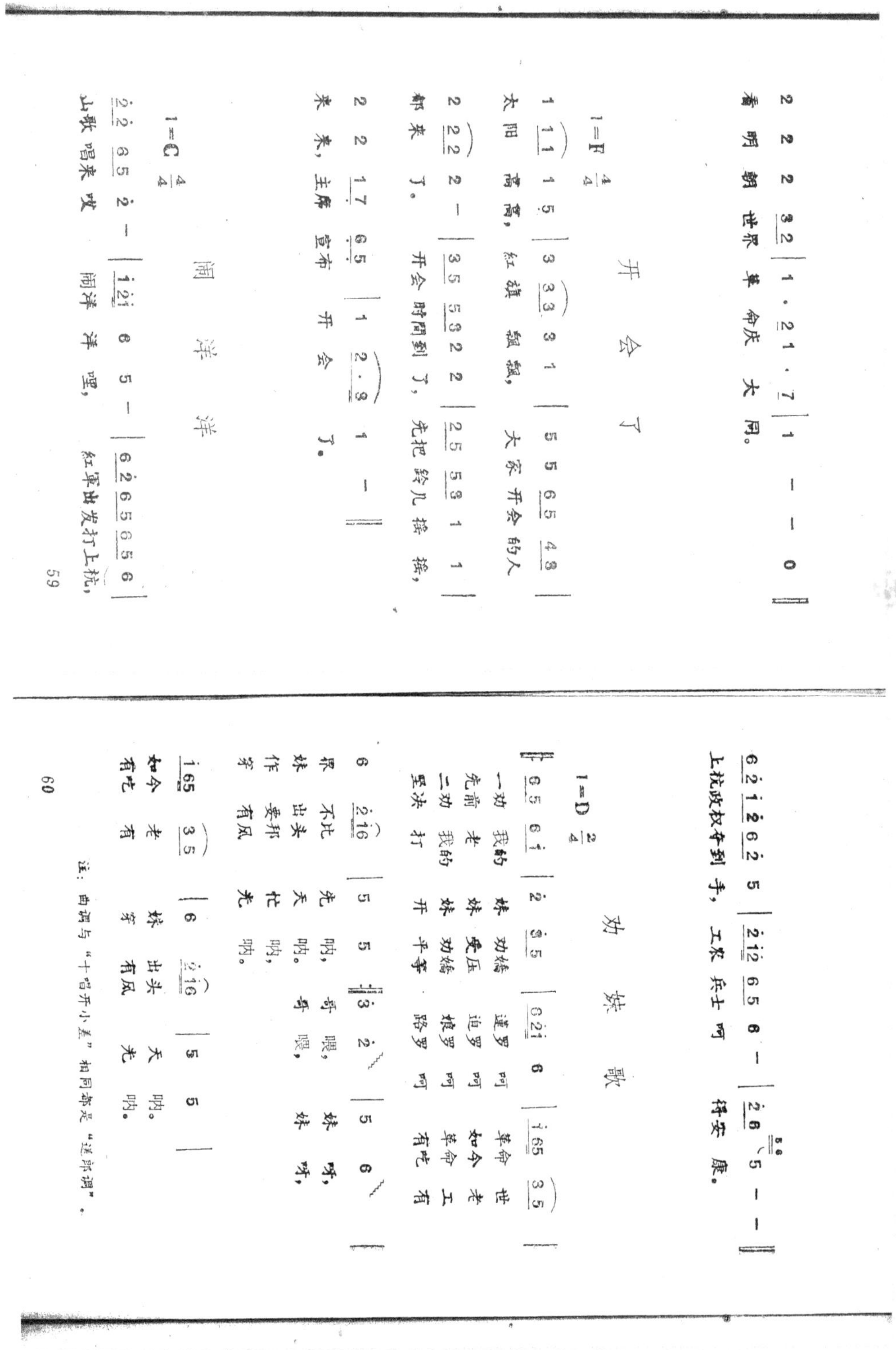

2 2 2 3 2 | 1 · 2 1 · 7 | 1 — — 0 ‖
看 明 朝 世界 革 命庆 大 同。

开 会 了

1=F 4/4

1 1 1 1 5 | 3 3 3 3 1 | 5 5 6 5 4 3 |
太 阳 高 高， 紅 旗 飄 飄， 大 家 开会 的人

2 2 2 2 — | 3 5 5 3 2 2 | 2 5 5 3 1 1 |
都 来 了。 开会 時間到 了， 先把 鈴儿 搖 搖，

2 2 1 7 6 5 | 1 2 · 3 1 — ‖
来 来，主席 宣布 开 会 了。

闹 洋 洋

1=C 4/4

2 2 6 5 2 — | 1 2 1 6 5 — | 6 2 6 5 6 5 6 |
山歌 唱来 哎 闹洋 洋 哩， 紅軍出发打上杭，

59

6 2 1 2 6 2 5 | 2 1 2 6 5 6 — | 2 6 5 — — ‖
上杭政权夺到 手， 工农 兵士 呵 得安 康。

劝 妹 歌

1=D 2/4

‖: 6 5 6 1 | 2 3 5 | 6 2 1 6 | 1 6 5 3 5 |
一劝 我的 妹 劝嬌 蓮罗 呵 革命 世
先前 老 妹 受压 迫罗 呵 如今 老
二劝 我的 妹 劝嬌 娘罗 呵 革命 工
坚决 打 开 平等 路罗 呵 有吃 有

6 2 1 6 | 5 5 :‖ 3 2 | 5 6 |
界 不比 先 吶， 哥 喂， 妹 呀，
妹 出头 天 吶。 哥 喂， 妹 呀，
作 要邦 忙 吶，
穿 有风 光 吶。

1 6 5 3 5 | 6 2 1 6 | 5 5 |
如今 老 妹 出头 天 吶。
有吃 有 穿 有风 光 吶。

注：曲调与“十唱开小差”相同都是“送郎调”。

60

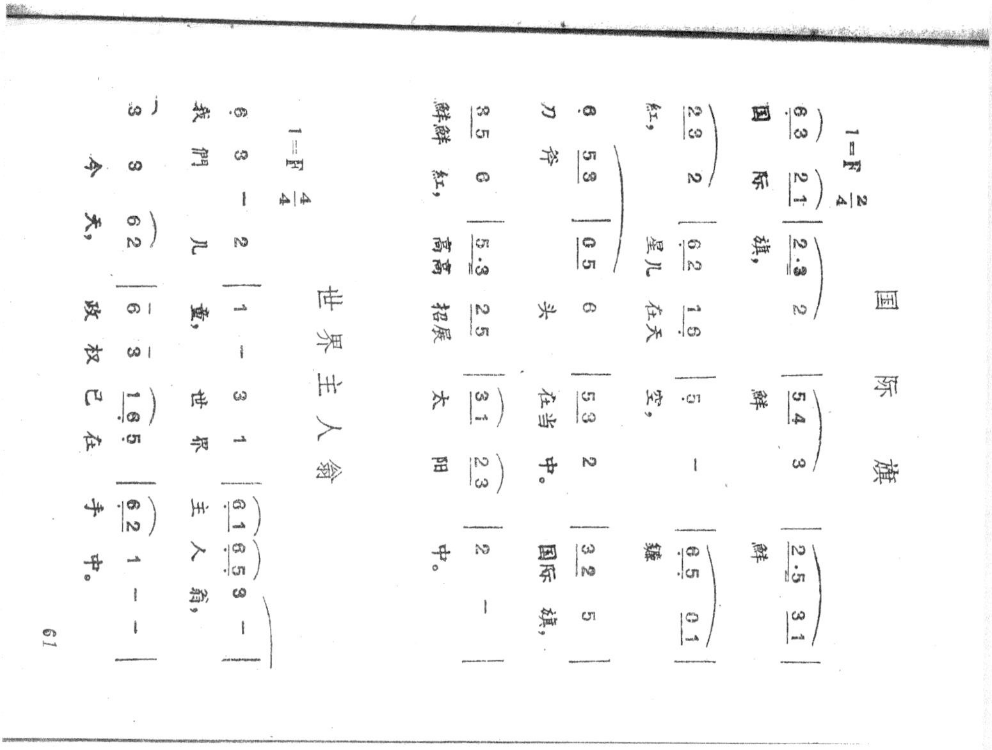

国　际　旗

1=F $\frac{2}{4}$

6 3　2 1 | 2·3　2 | 5 4　3 | 2·5　3 1 |
国　际　旗，　鲜　鲜

2 3　2 | 6 2　1 6 | 5　— | 6 5　0 1 |
紅，　星儿　在天　空，　镰

6　5 3 | 0 5　6 | 5 3　2 | 3 2　5 |
刀　斧　头　在当　中。　国际　旗，

3 5　6 | 5·3　2 5 | 3 1　2 3 | 2　— |
鲜鲜　紅，　高高　招展　太　阳　中。

世界主人翁

1=F $\frac{4}{4}$

6　3　—　2 | 1　—　3　1 | 6 1　6 5　3　— |
我　們　儿　童，　世　界　主　人　翁，

3　3　6 2 | 6　3　1 6 5 | 6 2　1　—　— |
今　天，　政　权　已　在　手　中。

61

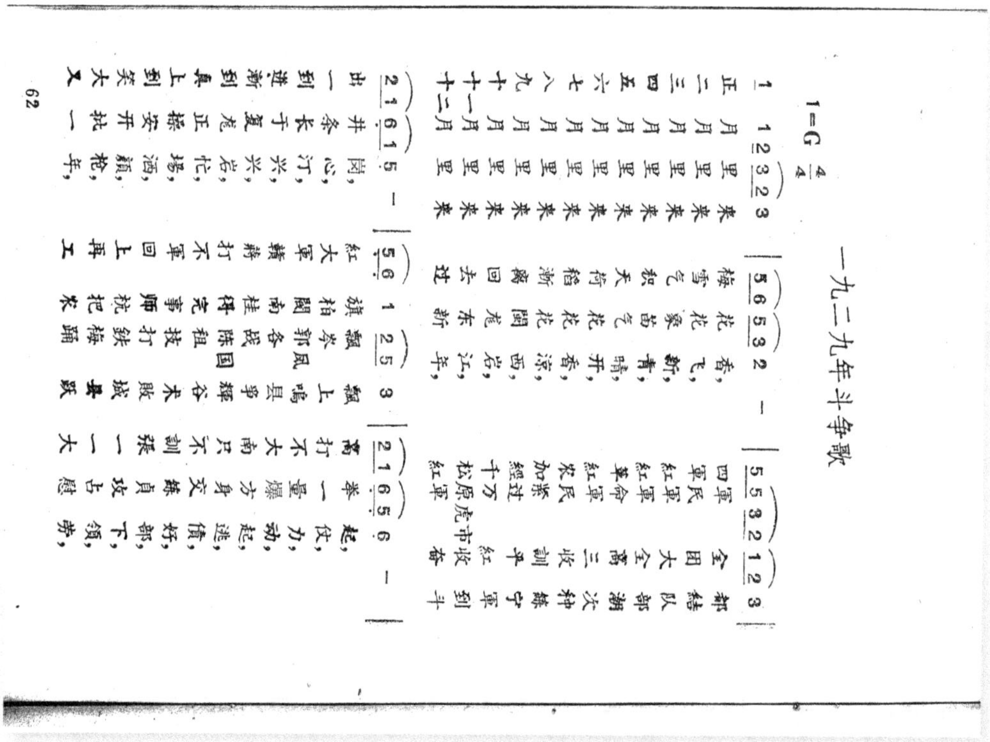

一九二九年斗争歌

1=G $\frac{4}{4}$

1　1 2　3 2　3 | 5 6　5 3　2　— | 5 5　3 2　1 2　3 |

正月里来　梅花香，　四軍全都
二月里来　雪花飞，　軍民团结
三月里来　气象新，　紅軍大队
四月里来　积苗青，　紅軍全部
五月里来　天气晴，　革命高潮
六月里来　荷花开，　紅軍三次
七月里来　稻花香，　农民收种
八月里来　渐花凉，　加紧訓練
九月里来　离闽西，　經过平宁
十月里来　回龙岩，　千万紅軍
十一月里来　去东江，　松原虎市收到
十二月里来　过新年，　紅軍奋斗

2 1　6 1　5　— | 5 6　1　2 5　3 | 2 1　6 5　6　— |

出井岗，　紅旗飄飄　高举起，
一条心，　大柏岑上　打一仗，
到长汀，　大軍闘郭凤鳴　不量力，
进于兴，　赣南各县　大爆动，
渐复兴，　蔣桂战争　南方起，
到龙岩，　打得陈国輝　只身逃，
真正忙，　不完租谷　不交債，
上操場，　軍事技术　訓練好，
到安酒，　回师打敗　張貞部，
笑开顔，　上杭鉄城　一攻下，
大扯枪，　再把梅县　一占領，
又一年，　工农踊跃　大慰劳，

62

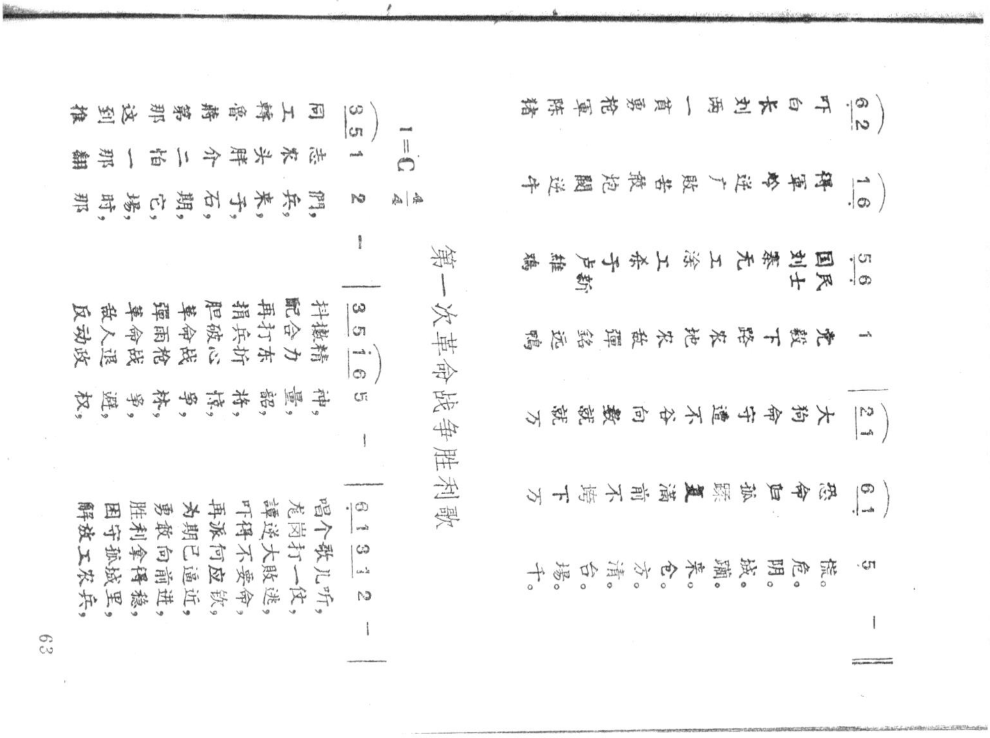

6 2	1 6	5 6	1	2 1	6 1	5 — ‖
吓	得	国民	党	大	恐	慌。
白	軍	刘士	毅	狗	命	危。
长	岭	搴	下	命	归	阴。
刘	逆	无	路	守	孤	城。
两	广	工	农	遭	蹂	躏。
一	败	涂	地	不	复	来。
貧	苦	工	农	谷	满	仓。
勇	敢	杀	敌	向	前	方。
枪	炮	于	彈	数	不	清。
軍	閥	卢新	銘	就	垮	台。
陈	逆	維	远	就	下	場。
猪	牛	鸡	鴨	万	万	千。

第一次革命战争胜利歌

1=C $\frac{4}{4}$

3 5 1 2 —	3 5 1̇ 6 5 —	6 1 3 1 2 —
同 志 們，	抖擻精 神，	唱个歌儿听，
工 农 兵，	配合力 量，	龙岗打一仗，
轉 头 来，	再打东 韶，	譚逆大敗逃，
魯 胖 子，	损兵折 将，	吓得不要命，
蔣 介 石，	胆破心 惊，	再派何应钦，
第 二 期，	革命战 争，	为期已逼近，
那 怕 它，	彈雨枪 林，	勇敢向前进，
这 一 場，	革命战 争，	胜利拿得稳，
到 那 时，	敌人退 避，	困守孤城里，
推 翻 那	反动政 权，	解放工农兵，

63

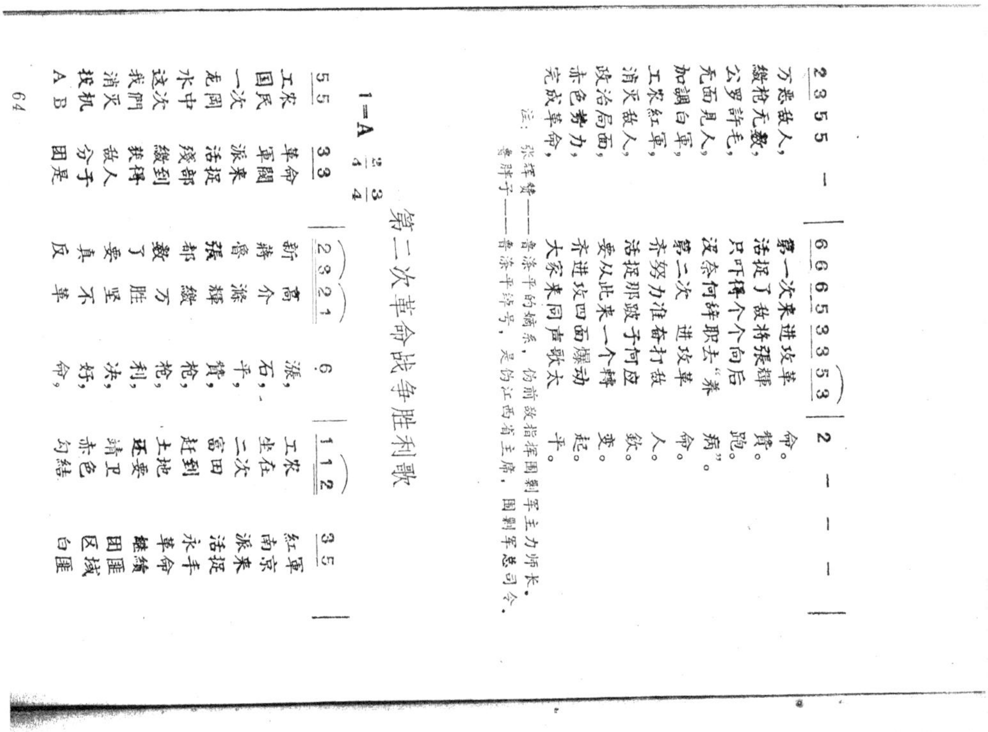

2 3 5 5 —	6 6 6 5 3 3 5 3	2 — — —
万恶敌人，	第一次来进攻革	命。
繳枪无数，	活捉了敌将張輝	瓚。
公罗許毛，	只吓得个个向后	跑。
无面見人，	没奈何辞职去“养	病”。
加調白軍，	第二次 进攻革	命。
工农紅軍，	齐努力准备打敌	人。
消灭敌人，	活捉那跛子何应	欽。
政治局面，	要从此来一个轉	变。
赤色势力，	齐进攻四面爆动	起。
完成革命，	大家来同声歌太	平。

注：张辉赞——鲁涤平的嫡系，伪前敌指挥围剿军主力师长。
鲁胖子——鲁涤平绰号，是伪江西省主席，围剿军总司令。

第二次革命战争胜利歌

1=A $\frac{2}{4}$ $\frac{3}{4}$

5 5	3 3	2 3 2 1	6	1 1 2	3 5
工农	革命	新 高	涨，	工农	紅軍
国民	軍閥	蔣 介	石，	坐在	南京
一次	派来	魯 滌	平，	二次	派来
龙岡	活捉	張 輝	瓚，	富田	活捉
水中	殘部	都 繳	枪，	赶到	永丰
这次	繳到	数 万	枪，	土地	革命
我們	获得	了 胜	利，	还要	継續
消灭	敌人	要 坚	决，	靖卫	团匪
投机	分子	真 不	好，	赤色	区域
A B	团是	反 革	命，	勾結	白匪

64

2 2 3 2 1 | 6 1 2 3 1 | 6 5 6 5 3 |

有呀 力 量，共 产 党，最 好 主 張。
大呀 害 怕，到 江 西，調 兵 鎮 压。
何呀 应 欽，到 江 西，屠 杀 革 命。
公呀 秉 蕃，我 紅 軍，追 到 水 南。
打呀 敌 人，多 繳 枪，发 給 貧 民。
更呀 保 障，苏 維 埃，牢 固 发 展。
向呀 前 进，把 敌 人，完 全 肃 清。
要呀 肃 清，免 得 他，搞 乱 革 命。
来呀 造 謠，調 查 到，把 他 打 倒。
打呀 紅 軍，他 想 来，破 坏 革 命。

6 6 1 6 5 | 6 1 2 3 1 | 6 5 6 5 3 |

哎哟 哎 哟 共 产 党 最 好 主 張。
哎哟 哎 哟 到 江 西 調 兵 鎮 压。
哎哟 哎 哟 到 江 西 屠 杀 革 命。
哎哟 哎 哟 我 紅 軍 追 到 水 南。
哎哟 哎 哟 多 繳 枪 发 給 貧 民。
哎哟 哎 哟 苏 維 埃 牢 固 发 展。
哎哟 哎 哟 把 敌 人 完 全 肃 清。
哎哟 哎 哟 免 得 他 搗 乱 革 命。
哎哟 哎 哟 調 查 到 把 他 打 倒。
哎哟 哎 哟 他 想 来 破 坏 革 命。

注：曲调与"如今世界大造反"、"妇女慰劳红军歌"相同。

65

红军胜利万万岁

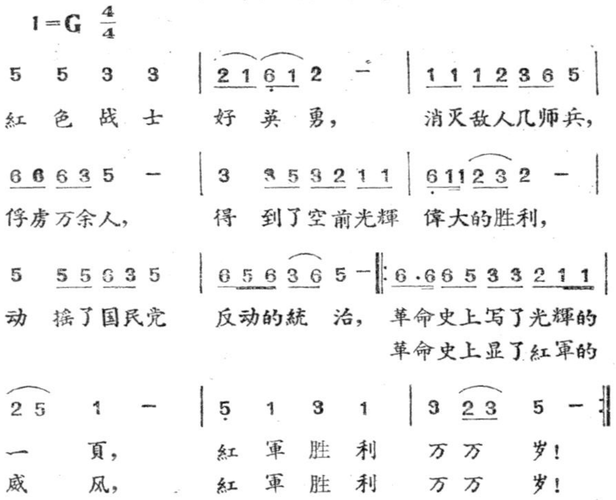

1=G $\frac{4}{4}$

5 5 3 3 | 2 1 6 1 2 - | 1 1 1 2 3 6 5 |

紅 色 战 士 好 英 勇，消灭敌人几师兵，

6 6 6 3 5 - | 3 3 5 3 2 1 1 | 6 1 1 2 3 2 - |

俘虏万余人，得 到了空前光輝 偉大的胜利，

5 5 5 6 3 5 | 6 5 6 3 6 5 - ‖: 6·6 6 5 3 3 2 1 1 |

动 摇了国民党 反动的統 治，革命史上写了光輝的
革命史上显了紅軍的

2 5 1 - | 5 1 3 1 | 3 2 3 5 - :‖

一 頁，紅 軍 胜 利 万 万 岁！
威 风，紅 軍 胜 利 万 万 岁！

粉碎敌人第五次"围剿"

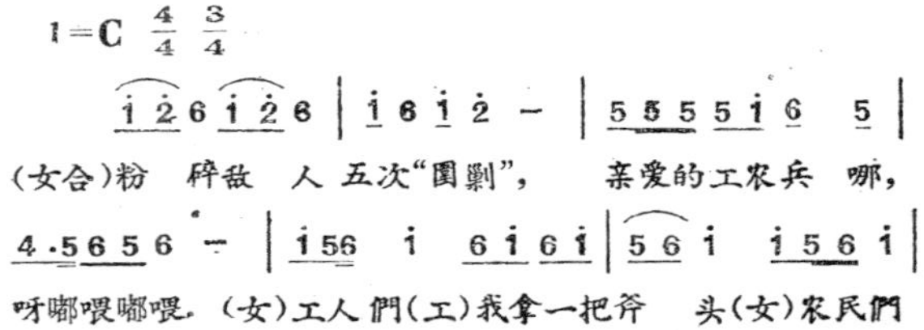

1=C $\frac{4}{4}$ $\frac{3}{4}$

i 2 6 i 2 6 | i 6 i 2 - | 5 5 5 5 i 6 5 |

(女合)粉 碎敌 人 五次"围剿"，亲爱的工农兵 哪，

4·5 6 5 6 - | i 5 6 i 6 i 6 i | 5 6 i i 5 6 i |

呀嘟喂嘟喂，(女)工人們(工)我拿一把斧 头(女)农民們

66

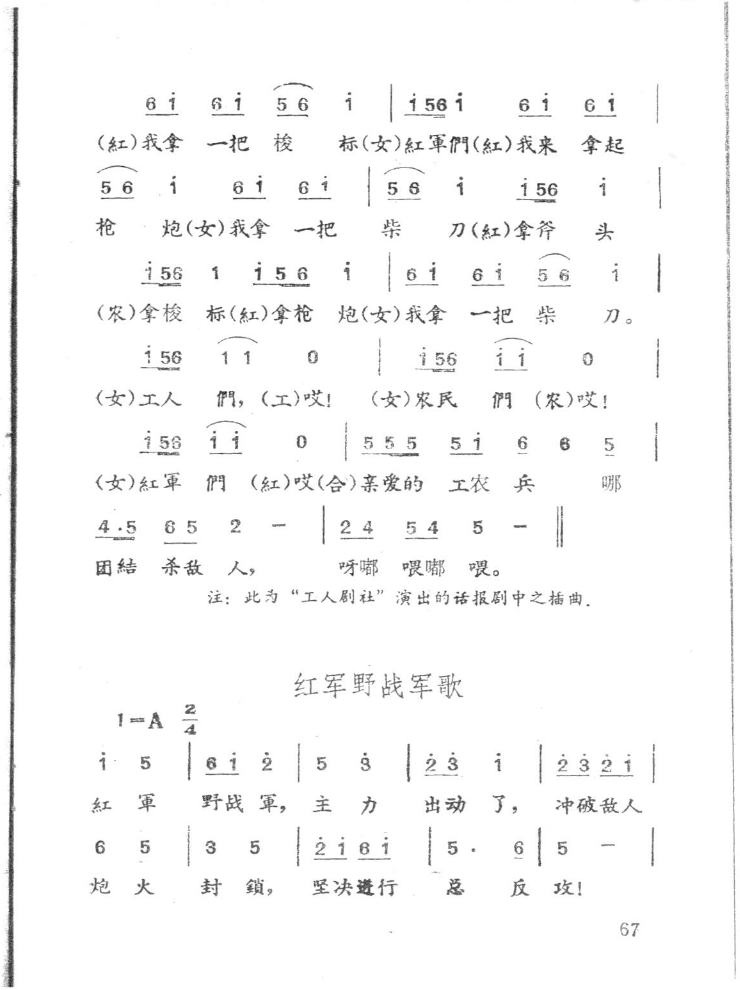

6 1̇ 6 1̇ 5 6 1̇ | 1̇ 5 6 1̇ 6 1̇ 6 1̇ |
(紅)我拿 一把 梭 标(女)紅軍們(紅)我來 拿起
5 6 1̇ 6 1̇ 6 1̇ | 5 6 1̇ 1̇ 5 6 1̇ |
枪 炮(女)我拿 一把 柴 刀(紅)拿斧 头
1̇ 5 6 1 1̇ 5 6 1̇ | 6 1̇ 6 1̇ 5 6 1̇ |
(农)拿梭 标(紅)拿枪 炮(女)我拿 一把 柴 刀。
1̇ 5 6 1 1 0 | 1̇ 5 6 1̇ 1̇ 0 |
(女)工人 們，(工)哎！ (女)农民 們 (农)哎！
1̇ 5 6 1̇ 1̇ 0 | 5 5 5 5 1̇ 6 6 5 |
(女)紅軍 們 (紅)哎(合)亲爱的 工农 兵 哪
4·5 6 5 2 — | 2 4 5 4 5 — ||
团結 杀敌 人， 呀嘟 喂嘟 喂。

注：此为“工人剧社”演出的话报剧中之插曲.

红军野战军歌

1=A $\frac{2}{4}$

1̇ 5 | 6 1̇ 2̇ | 5 3̇ | 2̇ 3̇ 1̇ | 2̇ 3̇ 2̇ 1̇ |
紅 軍 野战 軍， 主 力 出动 了， 冲破敌人
6 5 | 3 5 | 2̇ 1̇ 6 1̇ | 5 · 6 | 5 — |
炮 火 封 鎖， 坚决進行 总 反 攻！

67

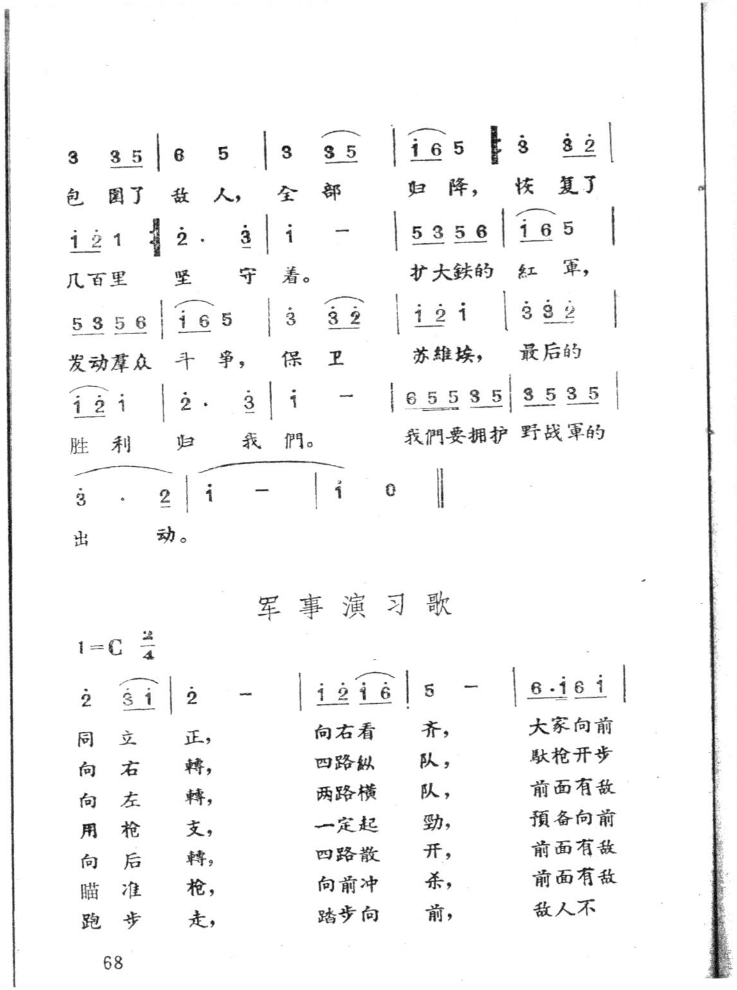

3 3 5 | 6 5 | 3 3̇ 5 | 1̇ 6 5 3̇ 3̇ 2̇ |
包 围了 敌 人， 全 部 归 降， 恢 复了
1̇ 2̇ 1 2̇ · 3̇ | 1̇ — | 5 3 5 6 | 1̇ 6 5 |
几百里 坚 守 着。 扩大鉄的 紅 軍，
5 3 5 6 | 1̇ 6 5 | 3̇ 3̇ 2̇ | 1̇ 2̇ 1̇ | 3̇ 3̇ 2̇ |
发动羣众 斗 争， 保 卫 苏維埃， 最后的
1̇ 2̇ 1̇ | 2̇ · 3̇ | 1̇ — | 6 5 5 3 5 | 3 5 3 5 |
胜 利 归 我 們。 我們要拥护 野战軍的
3̇ · 2̇ | 1̇ — | 1̇ 0 ||
出 动。

军事演习歌

1=C $\frac{2}{4}$

2̇ 3̇ 1̇ | 2̇ — | 1̇ 2̇ 1̇ 6̇ | 5 — | 6 · 1̇ 6 1̇ |
同 立 正， 向右看 齐， 大家向前
向 右 轉， 四路縱 队， 駄枪开步
向 左 轉， 两路横 队， 前面有敌
用 枪 支， 一定起 劲， 預备向前
向 后 轉， 四路散 开， 前面有敌
瞄 准 枪， 向前冲 杀， 前面有敌
跑 步 走， 踏步向 前， 敌人不

68

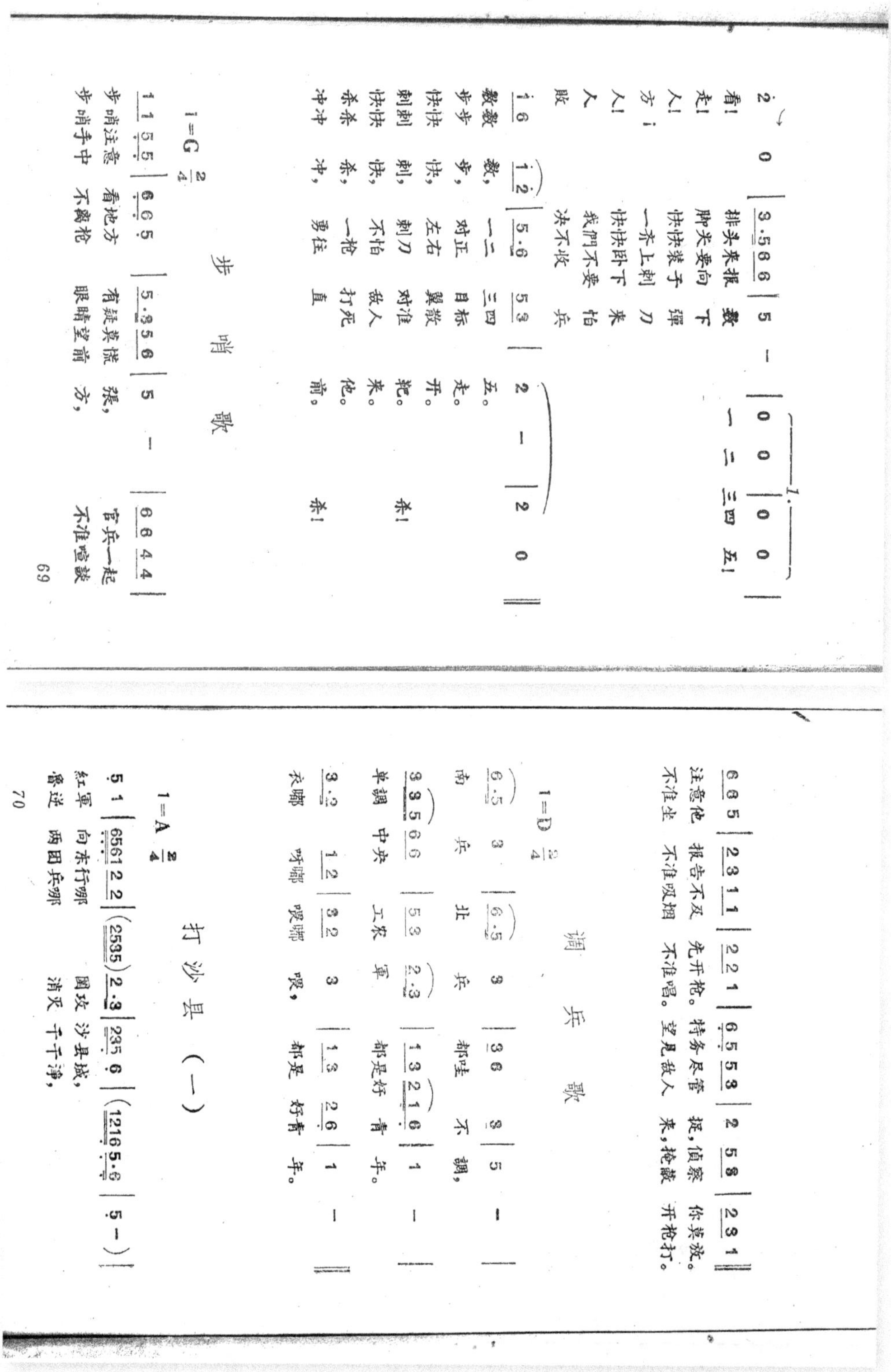

2 0 | 3·566 | 5 — | 0 0 | 0 0 |

看！　排头来报　数　一　二　三四　五！
走！　脚尖要向　下
人！　快快装子　彈
方 i　一齐上刺　刀
人！　快快卧下　来
人　我們不要　怕
敗　决不收　兵

16 12 | 5·6 53 | 2 — | 2 0 ‖

数数　数，　一二　三四　五。
步步　步，　对正　目标　走。
快快　快，　左右　翼散　开。
刺刺　刺，　刺刀　对准　靶。　杀！
快快　快，　不怕　敌人　来。
杀杀　杀，　一枪　打死　他。
冲冲　冲，　勇往　直　前。　杀！

步　哨　歌

1=G $\frac{2}{4}$

1155 | 665 | 5·356 | 5 — | 6644 |

步哨注意　看地方　有疑莫慌　張，　官兵一起
步哨手中　不离枪　眼睛望前　方，　不准喧談

69

685 | 2311 | 221 | 6553 | 2 58 | 231 ‖

注意他　报告不及　先开枪。特务尽管　捉，偵察　你莫放。
不准坐　不准吸烟　不准唱。望見敌人　来，掩蔽　开枪打。

调　兵　歌

1=D $\frac{2}{4}$

6·5 3 | 6·5 3 | 36 3 | 5 — |

南　兵　北　兵　都哇　不　調，

33566 | 53 2·3 | 13216 | 1 — |

单調　中央　工农　軍　都是好　青　年。

3·2 12 | 32 3 | 13 26 | 1 — ‖

衣嘟　呀嘟　喂嘟　喂，　都是　好青　年。

打沙县（一）

1=A $\frac{2}{4}$

5 1 | 6561 2 2 | (2535) 2·3 | 235 6 | (1216 5·6 | 5 —) |

紅軍　向东行哪　　圍攻　沙县城，
魯逆　两团兵哪　　消灭　干干淨，

70

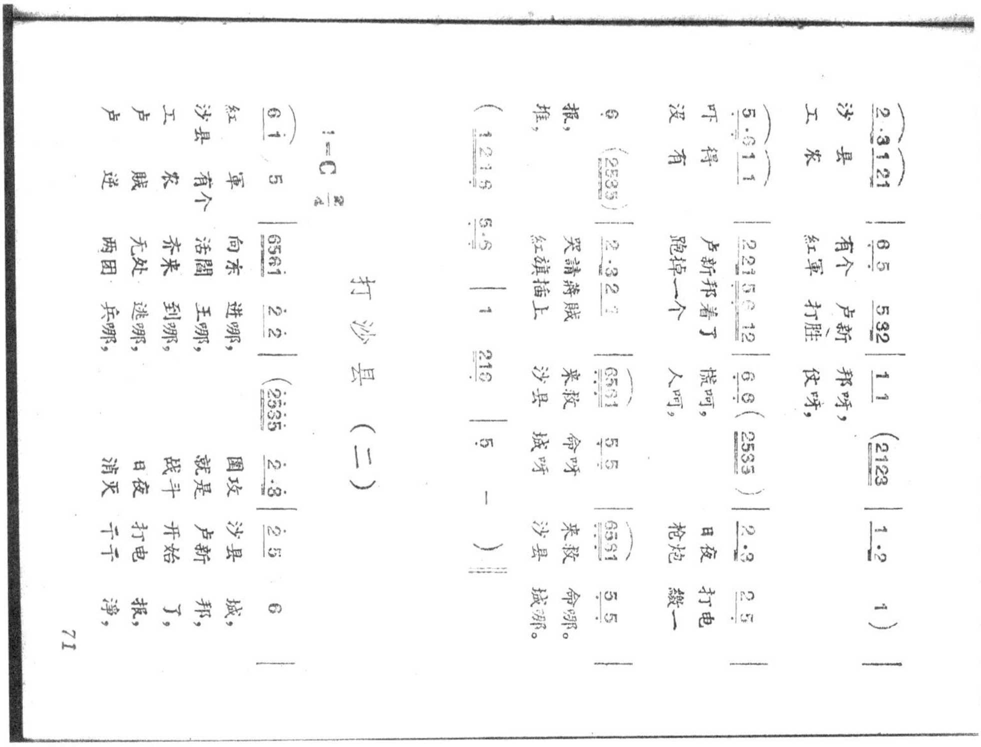

2·3 1 21 | 6 5 5 32 | 1 1 (2123 | 1·2 1) |
沙 县 有个 卢新 邦呀，
工 农 紅軍 打胜 仗呀，

5·6 1 1 | 2 21 5 6 12 | 6 6 (2535) | 2·3 2 5 |
吓 得 卢新邦着了 慌呵， 日夜 打电
沒 有 跑掉一个 人呵， 枪炮 繳一

6 (2535) | 2·3 2 1 | 6561 5 5 | 6561 5 5 |
报， 哭請蔣賊 来救 命呀 来救 命哪。
堆， 紅旗插上 沙县 城呀 沙县 城哪。

(1216 5·6 | 1 216 | 5 —) ||

71

打沙县（二）

1=C $\frac{2}{4}$

6 1 5 | 6561 2 2 | (2535 2·3 | 2 5 6 |
紅 軍 向东 进哪， 围攻 沙县 城，
沙县 有个 活閻 王哪， 就是 卢新 邦，
工 农 齐来 到哪， 战斗 开始 了，
卢 賊 无处 逃哪， 日夜 打电 报，
卢 逆 两团 兵哪， 消灭 干干 淨，

(1216 5·6 | 1 —) | 2·3 2 1 | 6561 5 5 | (1216 5·6 |
打倒土豪 把田分哪。
压迫穷人 如豺狼呀。
看你卢賊 那里逃？
哭請蔣賊 来救命；
沒有跑掉 一个人。

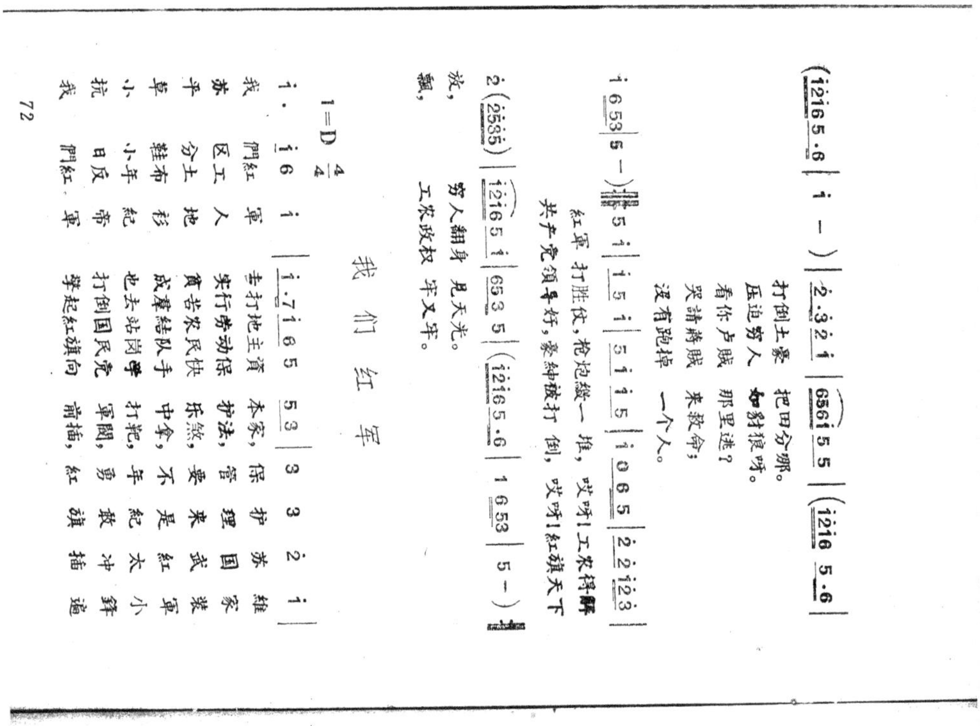

1 6 53 | 5 —) |: 5 1 | 1 5 1 | 5 1 1 5 | 1 0 6 5 | 2 2 12 3 |
紅軍 打胜仗，枪炮繳一 堆， 哎呀！工农得解
共产党領导好，豪紳被打 倒， 哎呀！紅旗天下

2 (2535) | 1216 5 1 | 65 3 5 | (1216 5·6 | 1 6 53 | 5 —) :|
放， 穷人翻身 見天光。
飄， 工农政权 牢又牢。

我 们 红 军

1=D $\frac{4}{4}$

1· 1 6 1 | 1·7 1 6 5 5 3 | 3 3 2 1 |
我 們紅 軍 专打地主資 本家，保 护 苏 維
苏 区工 人 实行劳动保 护法，管 理 国 家
平 分土 地 貧苦农民快 乐煞，要 来 武 裝
草 鞋布 衫 成羣結队手 中拿，不 是 紅 軍
小 小年 紀 也去站岗学 打靶，年 紀 太 小
抗 日反 帝 打倒国民党 軍閥，勇 敢 冲 鋒
我 們紅 軍 擎起紅旗向 前插，紅 旗 插 遍

72

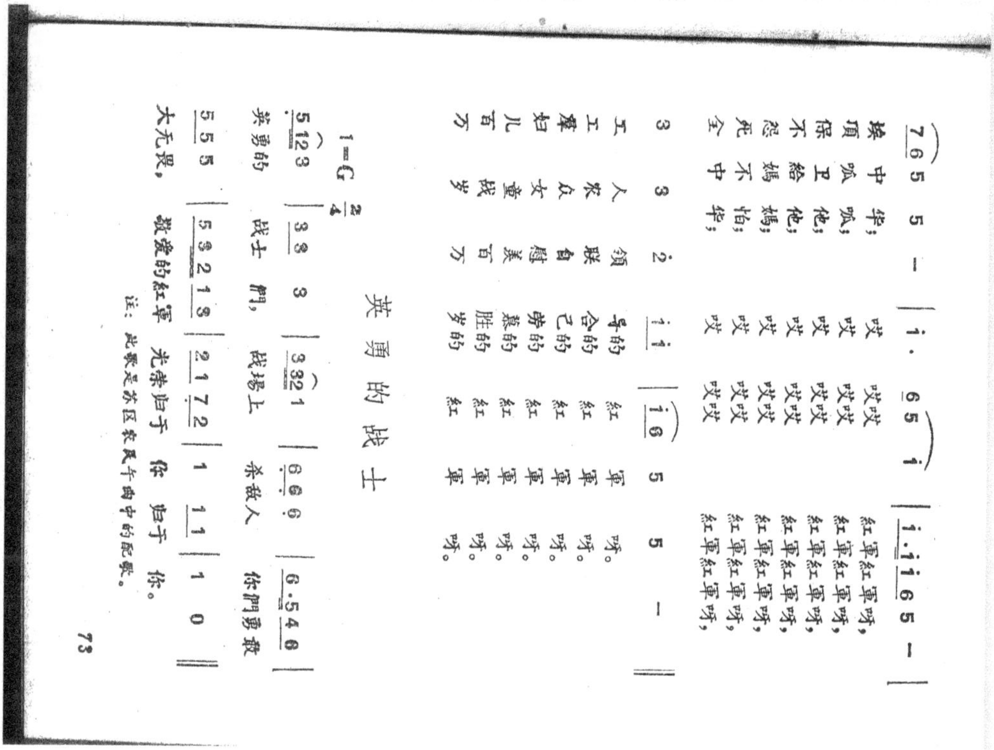

7 6 5　5　－ | i · 6 5 i | i · i i 6 5 － |

埃中华；　哎　哎哎　紅軍紅軍呀，
項呱呱；　哎　哎哎　紅軍紅軍呀，
保卫他；　哎　哎哎　紅軍紅軍呀，
不給他；　哎　哎哎　紅軍紅軍呀，
怨媽媽；　哎　哎哎　紅軍紅軍呀，
死不怕；　哎　哎哎　紅軍紅軍呀，
全中华；　哎　哎哎　紅軍紅軍呀，

3　3　2　i i | i 6　5　5　－ ‖

工人領导的紅軍呀。
工农联合的紅軍呀。
羣众自己的紅軍呀。
妇女慰劳的紅軍呀。
儿童羡慕的紅軍呀。
百战百胜的紅軍呀。
万岁万岁的紅軍呀。

英勇的战士

1=G $\frac{2}{4}$

5 1 2 3 | 3 3　3 | 3 3 2 1 | 6 6 6 | 6 · 5 4 6 |

英勇的　战士　們，　战場上　杀敌人　你們勇敢

5 5 5 | 5 3 2 1 3 | 2 1 7 2 | 1　1 1 | 1　0 ‖

大无畏，　敬爱的紅軍　光荣归于　你　归于　你。

注：此歌是苏区农民午曲中的配歌。

73

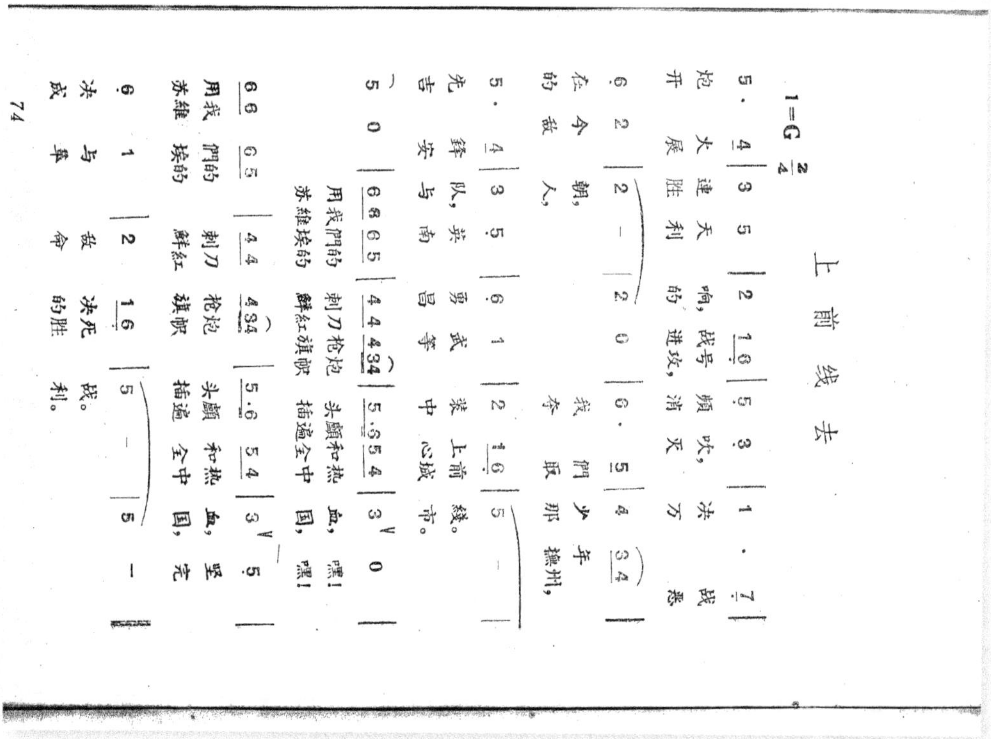

上前线去

1=G $\frac{2}{4}$

5 · 4 | 3　5 | 2　1 6 | 5　3 | 1　·　7 |

炮火連天响，战号頻吹，决战
开展胜利的进攻，消灭万恶

6　2 | 2　－ | 2　0 | 6 · 5 | 4　3 4 |

在今朝，我們少年
的敌人，夺取那撫州，

5 · 4 | 3　5 | 6　1 | 2　1 6 | 5　－ |

先鋒队，英勇武装上前綫。
吉安与南昌等中心城市。

5　0 | 6 6 6 5 | 4 4 4 3 4 | 5 · 6 5 4 | 3　0 |

用我們的刺刀枪炮头顱和热血，嘿！
苏維埃的鮮紅旗帜插遍全中国，嘿！

6 6　6 5 | 4 4　4 3 4 | 5 · 6　5 4 | 3　5 |

用我們的刺刀枪炮头顱和热血，坚
苏維埃的鮮紅旗帜插遍全中国，完

6　1 | 2　1 6 | 5　－ | 5　－ |

决与敌决死战。
成革命的胜利。

74

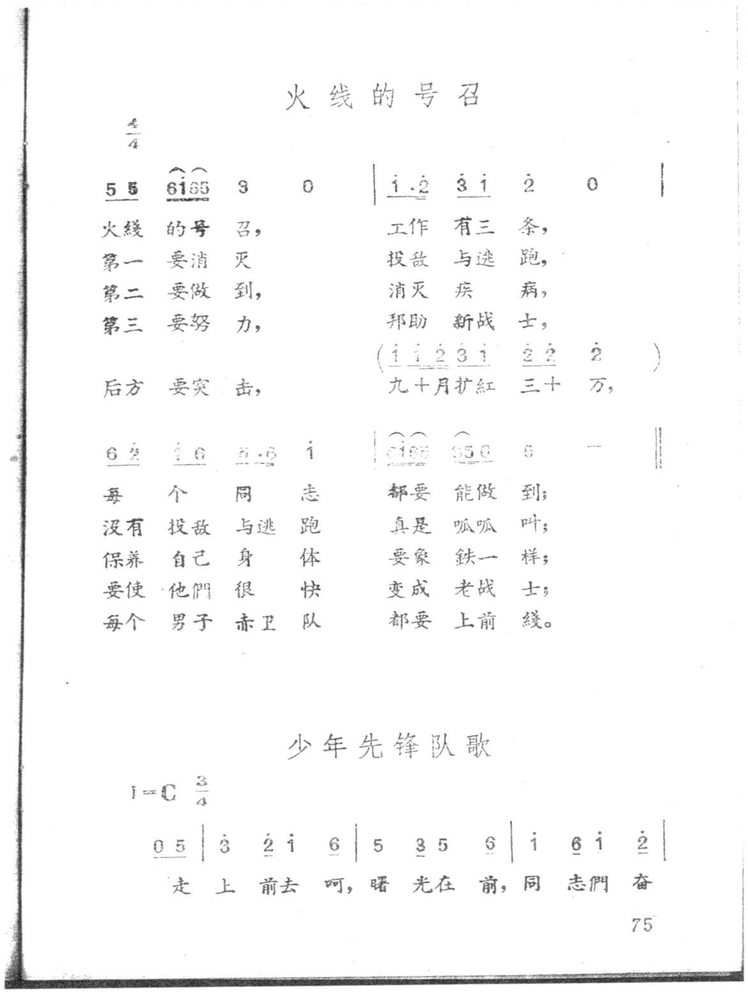

火线的号召

4/4

5 5 6i65 3 0 | i·2 3i 2 0 |

火綫 的号 召， 工作 有三 条，
第一 要消 灭 投敌 与逃 跑，
第二 要做 到， 消灭 疾 病，
第三 要努 力， 邦助 新战 士，
(i i 2 3 i 2 2 2)
后方 要实 击， 九十月扩紅 三十 万，

6 2 i 6 5·6 i | 6i65 650 5 — ||

每 个 同 志 都要 能做 到；
沒有 投敌 与逃 跑 真是 呱呱 叫；
保养 自己 身 体 要象 鉄一 样；
要使 他們 很 快 变成 老战 士；
每个 男子 赤卫 队 都要 上前 綫。

少年先锋队歌

1=C 3/4

0 5 | 3 2 i 6 | 5 3 5 6 | i 6 i 2 |
走 上 前去 呵，曙 光在 前，同 志們 奋

75

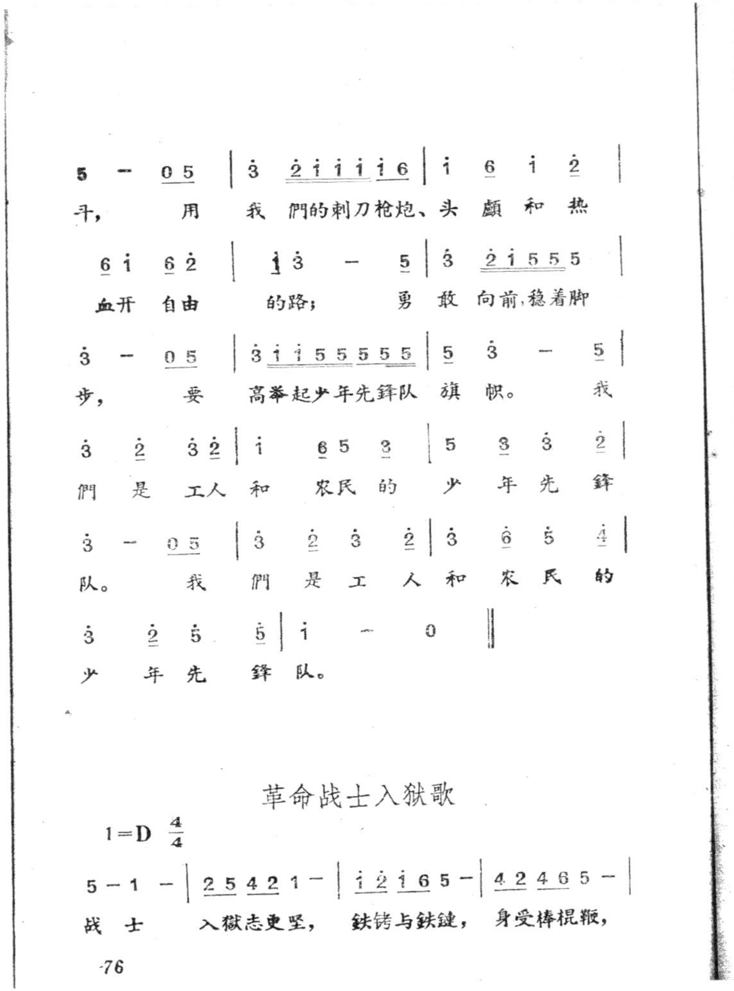

5 — 0 5 | 3 2 i i i i 6 | i 6 i 2 |
斗， 用 我 們的刺刀枪炮、头 顱 和 热

6 i 6 2 | i 3 — 5 | 3 2 i 5 5 5 |
血开 自由 的路； 勇 敢 向前,稳着脚

3 — 0 5 | 3 i i 5 5 5 5 5 | 5 3 — 5 |
步， 要 高举起少年先鋒队 旗 帜。 我

3 2 3 2 | i 6 5 3 | 5 3 3 2 |
們 是 工人 和 农民 的 少 年 先 鋒

3 — 0 5 | 3 2 3 2 | 3 6 5 4 |
队。 我 們 是 工 人 和 农 民 的

3 2 5 5 | i — 0 ||
少 年 先 鋒 队。

革命战士入獄歌

1=D 4/4

5 — 1 — | 2 5 4 2 1 — | i 2 i 6 5 — | 4 2 4 6 5 — |
战 士 入獄志更坚， 鉄铐与鉄鏈， 身受棒棍鞭，

76

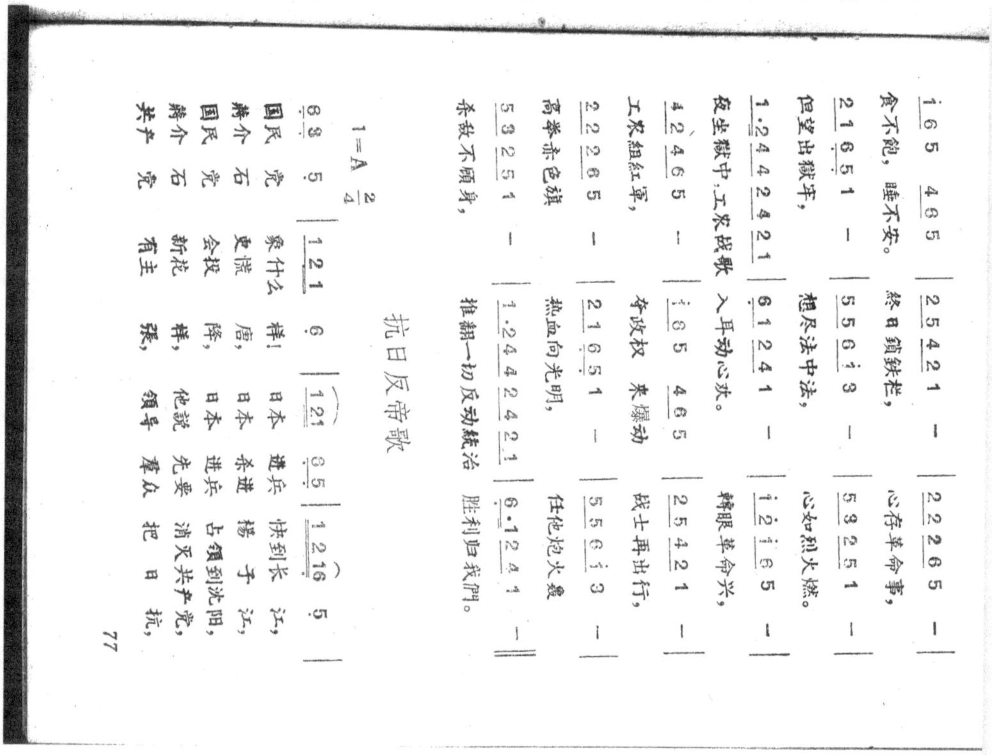

1̇ 6 5　4 6 5 | 2 5 4 2 1 — | 2 2 2 6 5 — |
食不飽，睡不安。終日鎖鉄栏，心存革命事，

2 1 6 5 1 — | 5 5 6 1̇ 3 — | 5 3 2 5 1 — |
但望出獄牢，想尽法中法，心如烈火燃。

1·2 4 4 2 4 2 1 | 6 1 2 4 1 — | 1̇ 2̇ 1̇ 6 5 — |
夜坐獄中，工农战歌入耳动心欢。轉眼革命兴，

4 2 4 6 5 — | 1̇ 6 5　4 6 5 | 2 5 4 2 1 — |
工农組紅軍，夺政权　来爆动　战士再出行，

2 2 2 6 5 — | 2 1 6 5 1 — | 5 5 6 1̇ 3 — |
高举赤色旗　热血向光明，任他炮火轟

5 3 2 5 1 — | 1·2 4 4 2 4 2 1 | 6·1 2 4 1 — ‖
杀敌不顾身，推翻一切反动統治　胜利归我們。

抗日反帝歌

1＝A 2/4

6 3　5 | 1 2 1　6 | 1 2 1　6 5 | 1 2 1 6　5 |
国民　党　象什么　样！日本　进兵　快到长　江，
蔣介　石　史慌　唐，日本　杀进　楊子　江，
国民　党　会投　降，日本　进兵　占領到沈阳，
蔣介　石　新花　样，他說　先要　消灭共产党，
共产　党　有主　張，領导　羣众　把　日　抗，

1 2 1 6　5 | 3 5 2 3　5 | 1 2 6 5　1 2 6 5 |
誰都不抵　抗，誰也不打　仗，节节退让，节节退让，
不准放一　枪，不准去打　仗，国民政府，赶快搬家，
到处燒房　屋，見人就开　枪，飞机大炮，屠杀工农，
才能去打　仗，才能把日　抗，四次圍剿，大举进攻，
工农背武　器，一齐上战　場，百战百胜，鉄的紅軍，

3 5 2 3　5 | 2 2　3 5 | 1 2 1　6 |
退到石家　庄。張　学良精兵　二十多　万，
搬到洛　阳。十九路的士兵　孤軍奋　战，
如　虎　狼。义　勇　軍　抗日經百　战，
逞　瘋　狂。七　分　政治　三分軍　事，
真　坚　强。若　要收回　我們东山　省，

3 3 6　5 3 | 6 1 2 3　1 | 3 5 5 6　1 2 1 |
全不　抵抗　只会繳　枪，好个卖国的国民党，
蔣介石　还要　繳他的　枪，好个卖国的国民党，
蔣介石　还要　繳他的　枪，国民党政府真慌唐，
随便送給紅軍　三万多支　枪，无可奈何　到南昌，
先要打　进攻　苏区国民　党，中国民族　方解放，

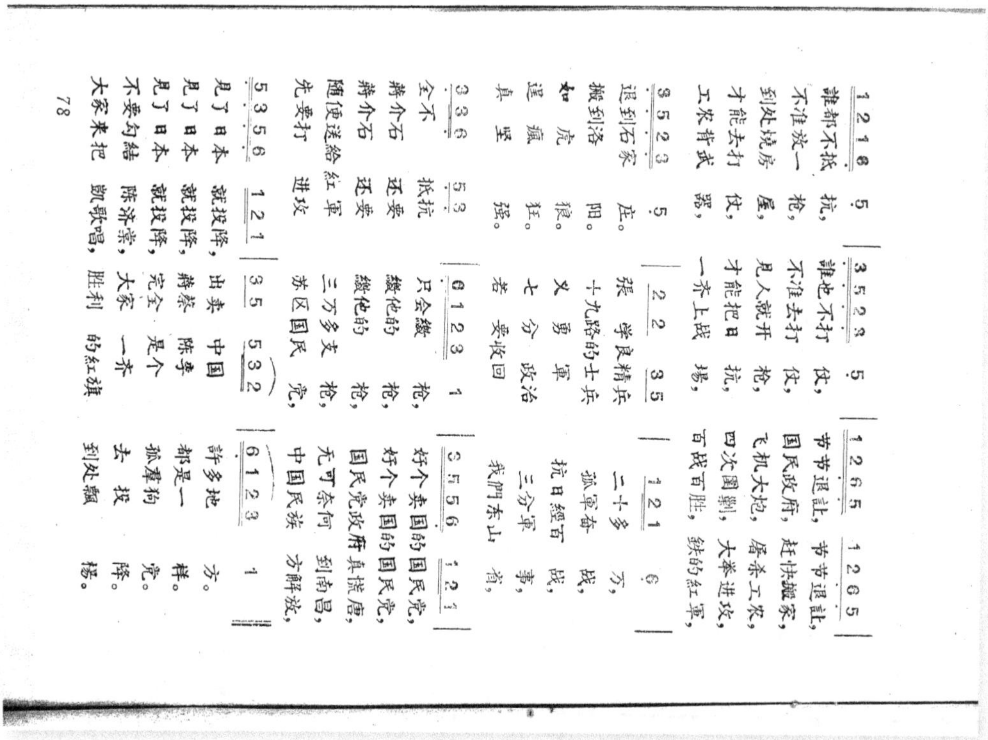

5 3 5 6　1 2 1 | 3 5　5 3 2 | 6 1 2 3　1 ‖
見了日本　就投降，出卖　中国　許多地　方。
見了日本　就投降，蔣蔡　陈李　都是一　样。
見了日本　就投降，完全　是个　孤羣狗　党。
不要勾結　陈济棠，大家　一齐　去　投　降。
大家来把　凱歌唱，胜利　的紅旗　到处飄　揚。

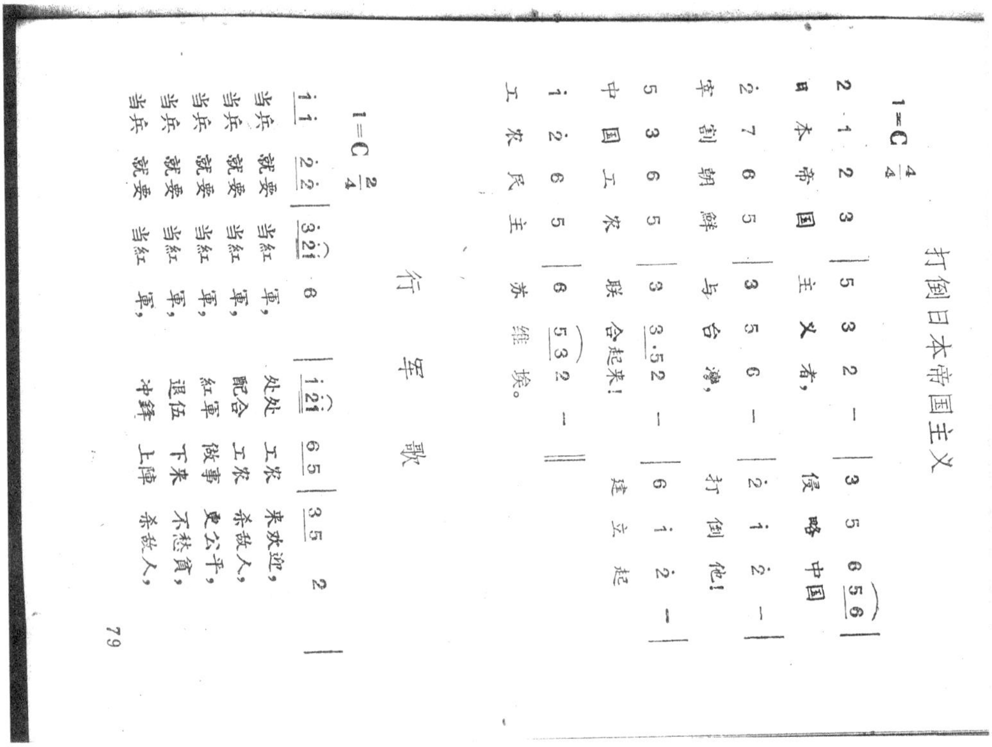

打倒日本帝国主义

1=C $\frac{4}{4}$

2 1 2 3 | 5 3 2 — | 3 5 6 56 |
日本帝国 主义者， 侵略中国

2̇ 7 6 5 | 3 5 6 — | 2̇ 1̇ 2̇ — |
宰割朝鲜 与台灣， 打倒他！

5 3 6 5 | 3 3.52 — | 6 1̇ 2̇ — |
中国工农 联合起来！ 建立起

1̇ 2̇ 6 5 | 6 532 — ||
工农民主 苏维埃。

行军歌

1=C $\frac{2}{4}$

1̇1̇ 2̇2̇ | 3̇2̇1̇ 6 | 1̇2̇1̇ 65 | 35 2 |
当兵 就要 当紅 軍， 处处 工农 来欢迎，
当兵 就要 当紅 軍， 配合 工农 杀敌人，
当兵 就要 当紅 軍， 紅軍 做事 更公平，
当兵 就要 当紅 軍， 退伍 下来 不愁貧，
当兵 就要 当紅 軍， 冲鋒 上陣 杀敌人，

79

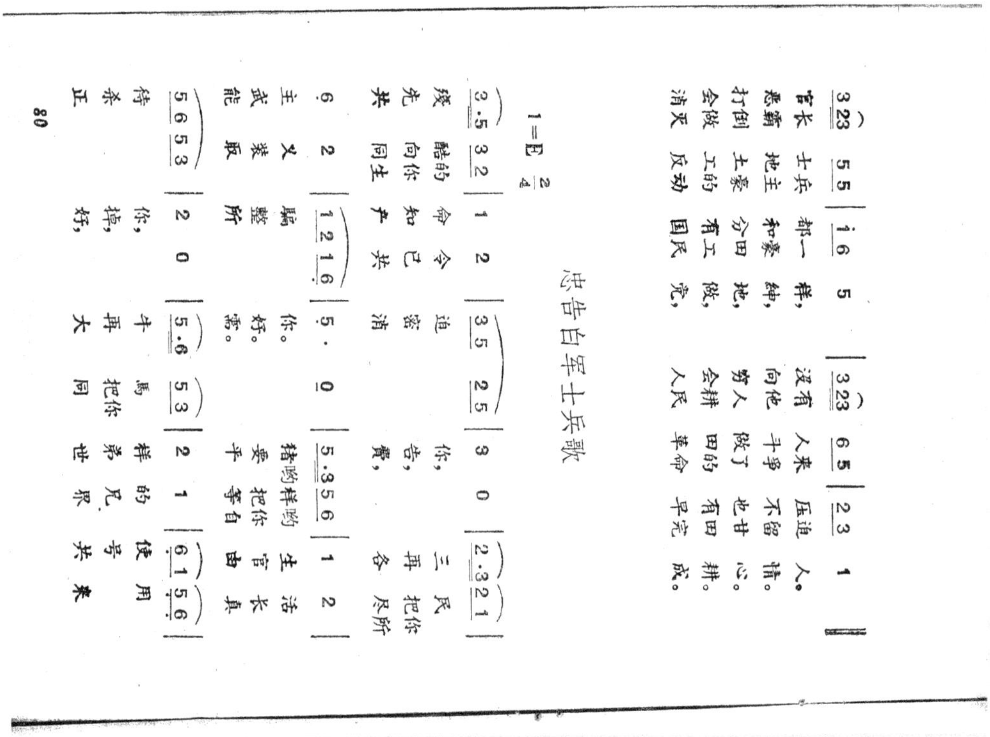

323 55 | 1̇6 5 | 323 65 | 23 1 ||
官长 士兵 都一 样， 没有 人来 压迫 人。
恶霸 地主 和豪 紳， 向他 斗爭 不留 情。
打倒 土豪 分田 地， 穷人 做了 也甘 心。
会做 工的 有工 做， 会耕 田的 有田 耕。
消灭 反动 国民 党， 人民 革命 早完 成。

忠告白军士兵歌

1=E $\frac{2}{4}$

3.5 32 | 1 2 | 35 25 | 3 0 | 2.321 |
残 酷的 命 令 迫 你， 三 民
先 向你 知 已 密 告， 再 把你
共 同生 产 共 消 費， 各 尽所

6 2 | 1216 | 5. 0 | 5.356 | 1 2 |
主 义 騙 你。 猪哟样哟 生 活
武 装 整 好。 要 把你 官 长
能 取 所 需。 平 等自 由 真

5653 | 2 0 | 5.6 53 | 2 1 | 6156 |
待 你， 牛 馬 样 的 使 用
杀 掉， 再 把你 弟 兄 号
正 好， 大 同 世 界 共 来

80

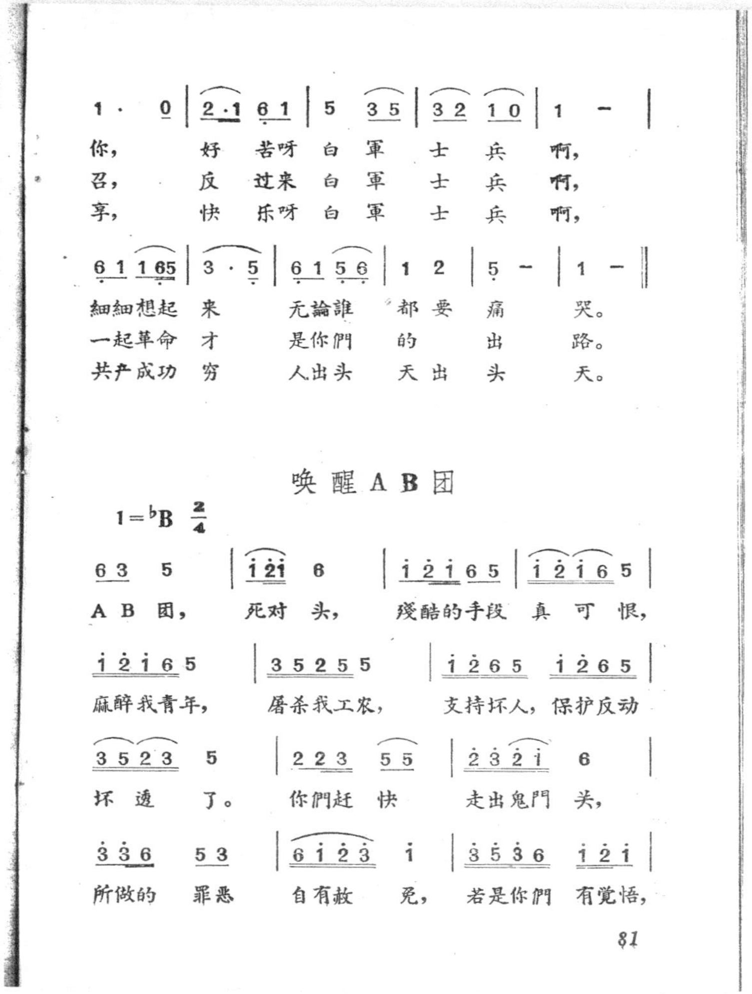

1 · 0 | 2·1 6 1 | 5 3 5 | 3 2 1 0 | 1 — |
你，　好　苦呀　白　軍　士　兵　啊，
召，　反　过来　白　軍　士　兵　啊，
享，　快　乐呀　白　軍　士　兵　啊，

6 1 1 65 | 3 · 5 | 6 1 5 6 | 1 2 | 5 — | 1 — ‖
細細想起　来　无論誰　都要　痛　哭。
一起革命　才　是你們　的　出　路。
共产成功　穷　人出头　天出　头　天。

唤醒AB团

1=♭B $\frac{2}{4}$

6 3 5 | 1̇ 2̇ 1̇ 6 | 1̇ 2̇ 1̇ 6 5 | 1̇ 2̇ 1̇ 6 5 |
A B 团，　死对　头，　殘酷的手段　真　可　恨，

1̇ 2̇ 1̇ 6 5 | 3 5 2 5 5 | 1̇ 2̇ 6 5 1̇ 2̇ 6 5 |
麻醉我青年，　屠杀我工农，　支持坏人，保护反动

3 5 2 3 5 | 2 2 3 5 5 | 2̇ 3̇ 2̇ 1̇ 6 |
坏　透　了。　你們赶　快　走出鬼門　关，

3̇ 3̇ 6 5 3 | 6 1̇ 2̇ 3̇ 1̇ | 3̇ 5̇ 3̇ 6 1̇ 2̇ 1̇ |
所做的　罪恶　自有救　兄，　若是你們　有觉悟，

81

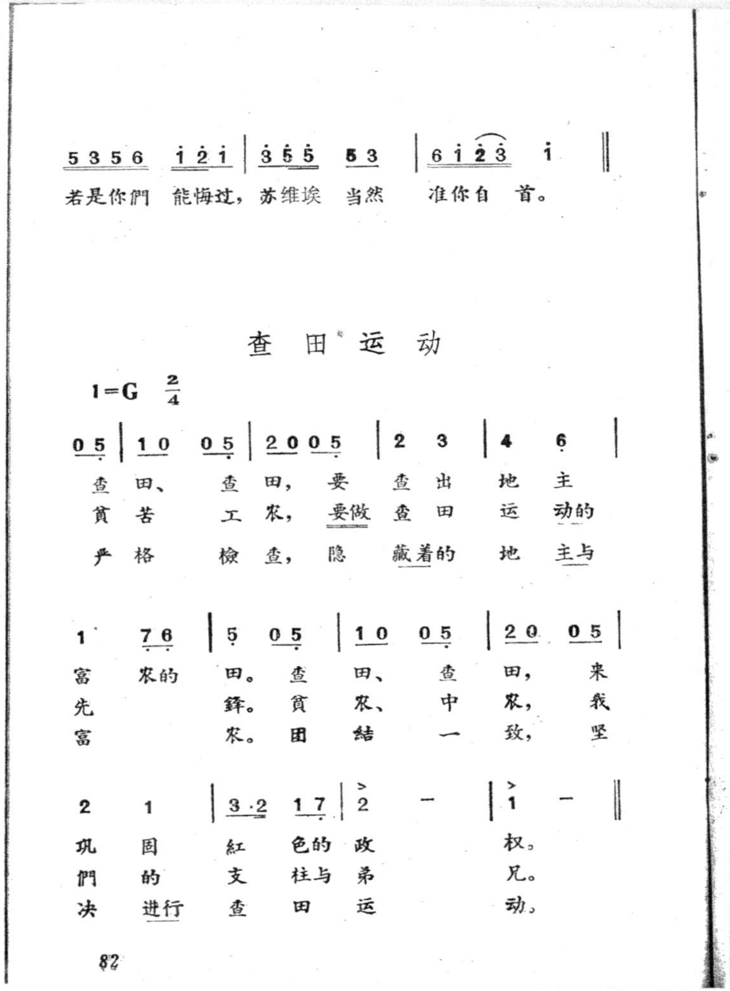

5 3 5 6 1̇ 2̇ 1̇ | 3̇ 5̇ 5̇ 5 3 | 6 1̇ 2̇ 3̇ 1̇ ‖
若是你們　能悔过，苏维埃　当然　准你自　首。

查田运动

1=G $\frac{2}{4}$

0 5 | 1 0 0 5 | 2 0 0 5 | 2 3 | 4 6 |
查　田、　查　田，　要　查　出　地　主
貧　苦　工　农，　要做　查　田　运　动的
严　格　檢　查，　隐　藏着的　地　主与

1 7 6 | 5 0 5 | 1 0 0 5 | 2 0 0 5 |
富　农的　田。　查　田、　查　田，　来
先　　　鋒。　貧　农、　中　农，　我
富　　　农。　团　結　一　致，　坚

2 1 | 3·2 1 7 | 2̂ — | 1̂ — ‖
巩　固　紅　色的　政　权。
們　的　支　柱与　弟　兄。
决　进行　查　田　运　动。

82

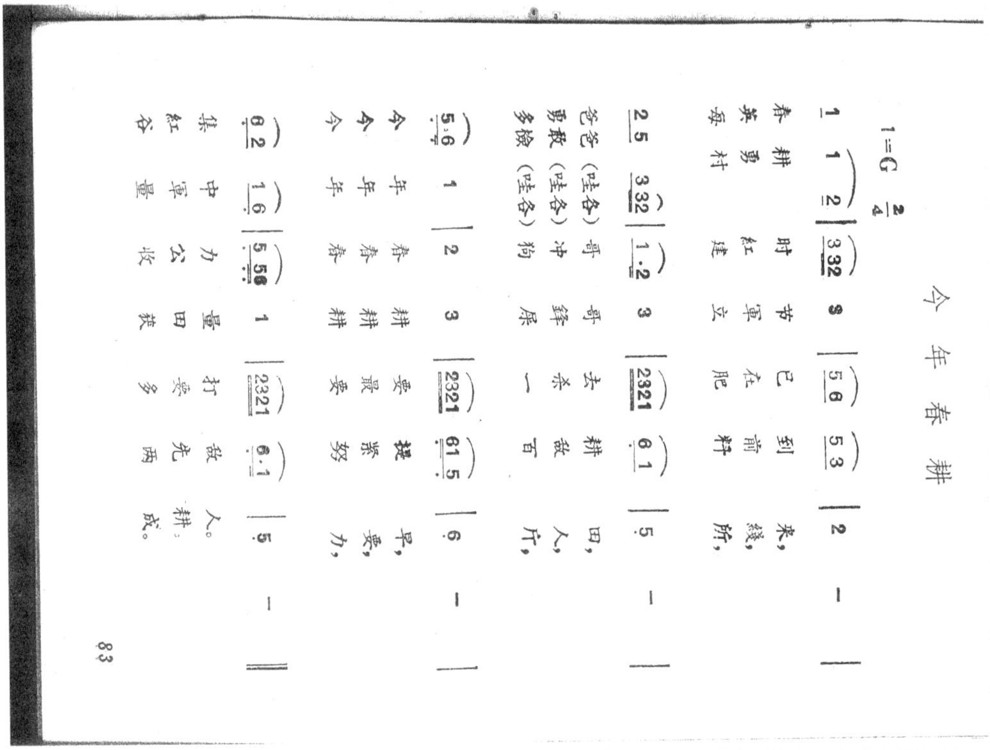

今年春耕

1=G $\frac{2}{4}$

1 1 2 | 3 32 3 | 5 6 5 3 | 2 — |

春耕　时　节　已　到　来，
英勇　紅　軍　在　前　綫，
每村　建　立　肥　料　所，

2 5 3 32 | 1·2 3 | 2321 6 1 | 5 — |

爸爸（哇各）哥　哥　去　耕　田，
勇敢（哇各）冲　鋒　杀　敌　人，
多檢（哇各）狗　屎　一　百　斤，

5·6 1 | 2 3 | 2321 61 5 | 6 — |

今　年　春　耕　要　提　早，
今　年　春　耕　最　紧　要，
今　年　春　耕　要　努　力，

6 2 1 6 | 5 56 1 | 2321 6·1 | 5 — ‖

集　中　力　量　打　敌　人。
紅　軍　公　田　要　先　耕。
谷　量　收　获　多　两　成。

83

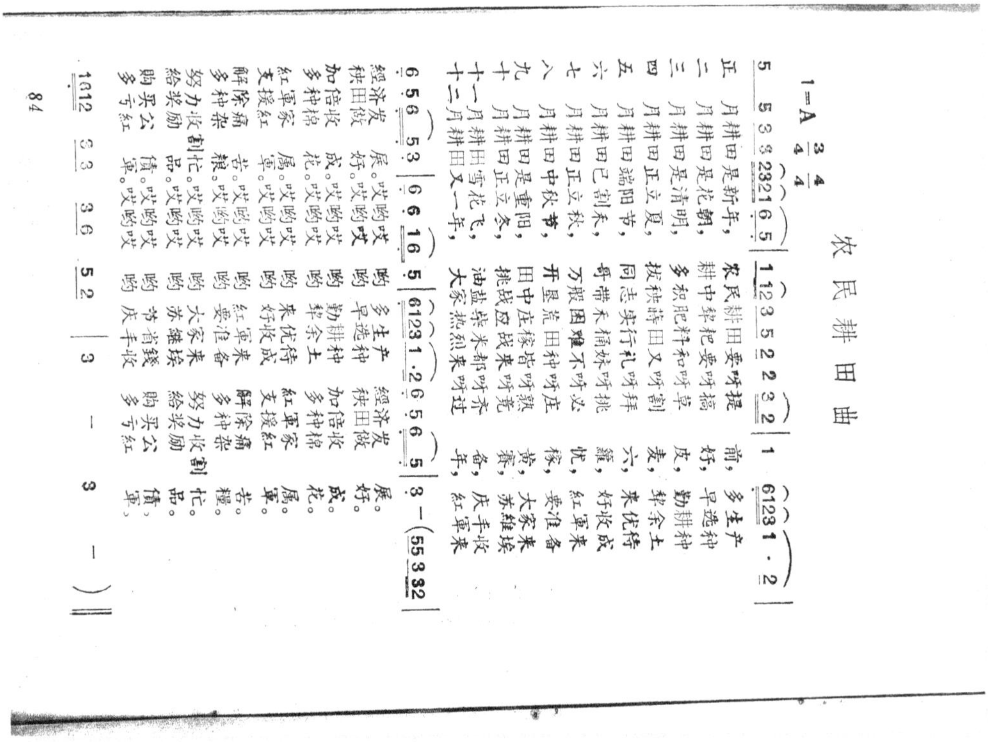

农民耕田曲

1=A $\frac{3}{4}$ $\frac{4}{4}$

5 5 3 3 2321 6 5 | 1 12 3 5 2 2 3 2 | 1 6123 1 · 2 |

正　月耕田是新年，农民耕田要呀提　前，多生产
二　月耕田是花朝，耕中犁耙要呀搞　好，早选种
三　月耕田是清明，多积肥料和呀草　皮，勤耕种
四　月耕田正立夏，拔秧蒔田又呀割　麦，犁余土
五　月耕田端阳节，同志实行礼呀拜　六，来优待
六　月耕田已割禾，哥带禾桶妹呀挑　籮，好收成
七　月耕田正立秋，万般困难不呀必　忧，紅軍来
八　月耕田中秋节，开垦荒田种呀庄　稼，要准备
九　月耕田是重阳，田中庄稼皆呀熟　黄，大家来
十　月耕田正立冬，挑战应战来呀竞　賽，苏維埃
十一月耕田雪花飞，油盐柴米都呀齐　备，庆丰收
十二月耕田又一年，大家热烈来呀过　年，紅軍来

6 56 5 3 | 6 6 16 5 | 6123 1·2 6 5 6 5 | 3 — (55 3 32 |

經济发　展。哎哟哎　哟　多生产　經济发　展。
秧田做　好。哎哟哎　哟　早选种　秧田做　好。
加倍收　成。哎哟哎　哟　勤耕种　加倍收　成。
多种棉　花。哎哟哎　哟　犁余土　多种棉　花。
紅軍家　属。哎哟哎　哟　来优待　紅軍家　属。
支援紅　軍。哎哟哎　哟　好收成　支援紅　軍。
解除痛　苦。哎哟哎　哟　紅軍来　解除痛　苦。
多种杂　粮。哎哟哎　哟　要准备　多种杂　糧。
努力收割忙。哎哟哎　哟　大家来　努力收割　忙。
給奖励　品。哎哟哎　哟　苏維埃　給奖励　品。
购买公　債。哎哟哎　哟　节省錢　购买公　債。
多亏紅　軍。哎哟哎　哟　庆丰收　多亏紅　軍。

1612 3 3 3 6 5 2 | 3 — 3 —) ‖

84

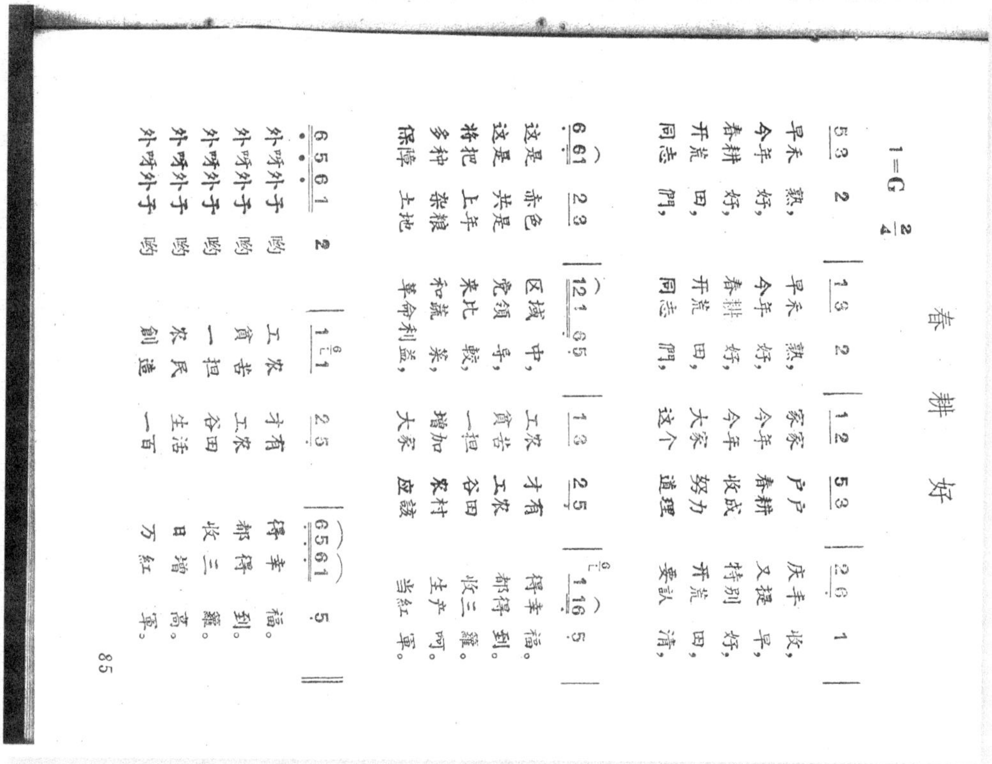

春耕好

1=G 2/4

53 2 | 13 2 | 12 53 | 26 1 |

早禾熟，早禾熟，家家户户庆丰收，
今年好，今年好，今年春耕又提早，
春耕好，春耕好，今年收成特别好，
开荒田，开荒田，大家努力开荒田，
同志們，同志們，这个道理要認清，

661 23 | 121 65 | 13 25 | 116 5 |

这是赤色区域中，工农才有得幸福。
这是共是党領导，貧苦工农都得到。
将把上年来比較，一担谷田收三籮。
多种杂粮和蔬菜，增加农村生产呵。
保障土地革命利益，大家应該当紅軍。

6561 2 | 11 25 | 6561 5 ||

外呀外子哟 工农才有得幸福。
外呀外子哟 貧苦工农都得到。
外呀外子哟 一担谷田收三籮。
外呀外子哟 农民生活日增高。
外呀外子哟 創造一百万紅軍。

85

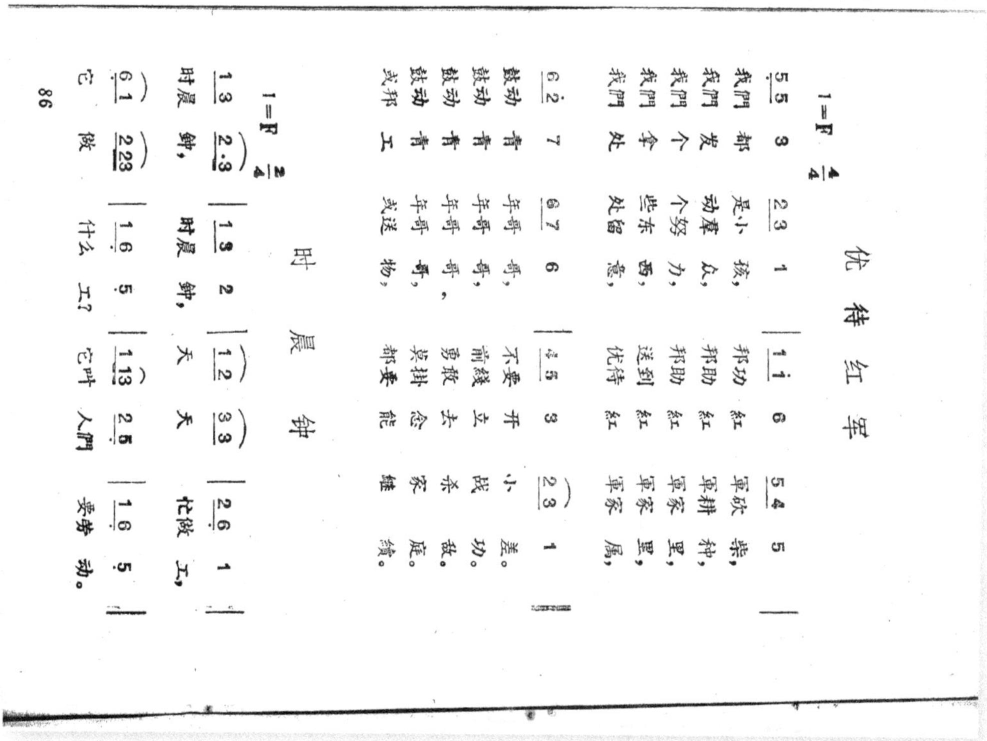

优待红军

1=F 4/4

55 3 23 1 | 11 6 54 5 |

我們都是小孩，邦功紅軍砍柴，
我們发动群众，邦助紅軍耕种，
我們个个努力，邦助紅軍家里，
我們拿些东西，送到紅軍家里，
我們处处留意，优待紅軍家属，

62 7 67 6 | 45 3 23 1 ||

鼓动青年哥哥，不要开小差。
鼓动青年哥哥，前綫立战功。
鼓动青年哥哥，勇敢去杀敌。
鼓动青年哥哥，莫掛念家庭。
或邦工或送物，都要能继續。

时晨钟

1=F 2/4

13 2·3 | 13 2 | 12 33 | 26 1 |

时晨钟，时晨钟，天天忙做工，

61 223 | 16 5 | 113 25 | 16 5 |

它做什么工？它叫人們要劳动。

86

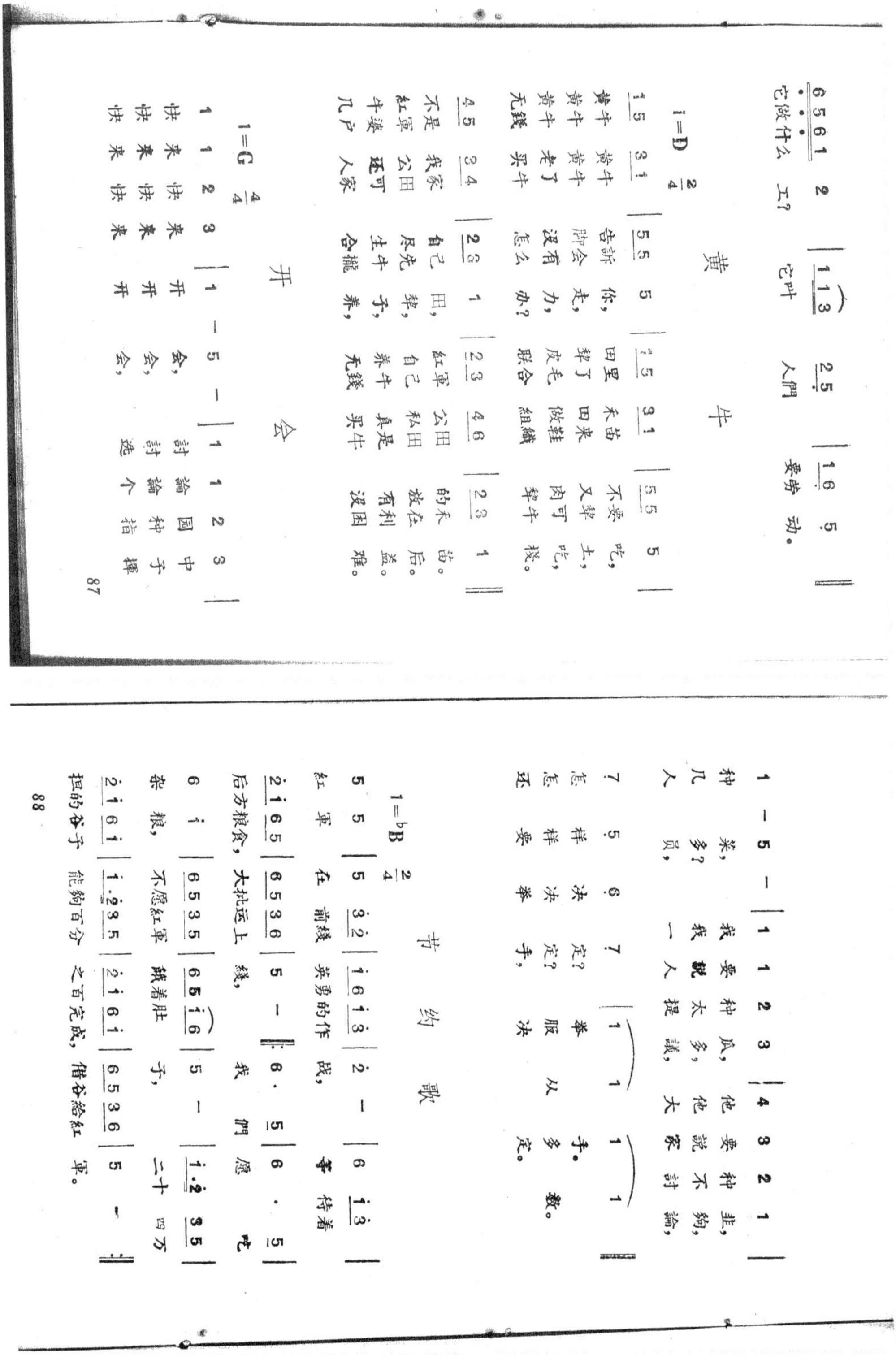

6 5 6 1 2 | 1 1 3 2 5 | 1 6 5 ‖
它做什么 工？ 它叫 人們 要劳 动。

黄　牛

1=D 2/4

1 5 3 1 | 5 5 5 | 1 5 3 1 | 5 5 5 |
黄牛 黄牛 告訴 你， 田里 禾苗 不要 吃，
黄牛 黄牛 脚会 走， 犁了 田来 又犁 土，
黄牛 老了 没有 力， 皮毛 做鞋 肉可 吃，
无錢 买牛 怎么 办？ 联合 組織 犁牛 楼。

4 5 3 4 | 2 3 1 | 2 3 4 6 | 2 3 1 ‖
不是 我家 自己 田， 紅軍 公田 的禾 苗。
紅軍 公田 尽先 犁， 自己 私田 放在 后。
牛婆 还可 生牛 子， 养牛 真是 有利 益。
几户 人家 合攏 养， 无錢 买牛 没困 难。

开　会

1=G 4/4

1 1 2 3 | 1 — 5 — | 1 1 2 3 |
快 来 快 来 开 会， 討 論 园 中
快 来 快 来 开 会， 討 論 种 子
快 来 快 来 开 会， 选 个 指 揮

87

1 — 5 — | 1 1 2 3 | 4 3 2 1 |
种 菜， 我 要 种 瓜， 他 要 种 韭，
几 多？ 我 說 太 多， 他 說 不 夠，
人 員， 一 人 提 議， 大 家 討 論，

7 5 6 7 | 1 1 1 1 ‖
怎 样 决 定？ 举 手。
怎 样 决 定？ 服 从 多 数。
还 要 举 手， 决 定。

节　约　歌

1=♭B 2/4

5 5 | 5 3 2 | 1 6 1 3 | 2 — | 6 1 3 |
紅 軍 在 前綫 英勇的作 战， 等 待着

2 1 6 5 | 6 5 3 6 | 5 — |: 6 · 5 | 6 · 5 |
后方粮食， 大批运上 綫， 我 們 愿 吃

6 1 | 6 5 3 5 | 6 5 1 6 | 5 — | 1 ·2 3 5 |
杂 粮， 不愿紅軍 餓着肚 子， 二十 四万

2 1 6 1 | 1 ·2 3 5 | 2 1 6 1 | 6 5 3 6 | 5 — :‖
担的谷子 能夠百分 之百完成， 借谷給紅 軍。

88

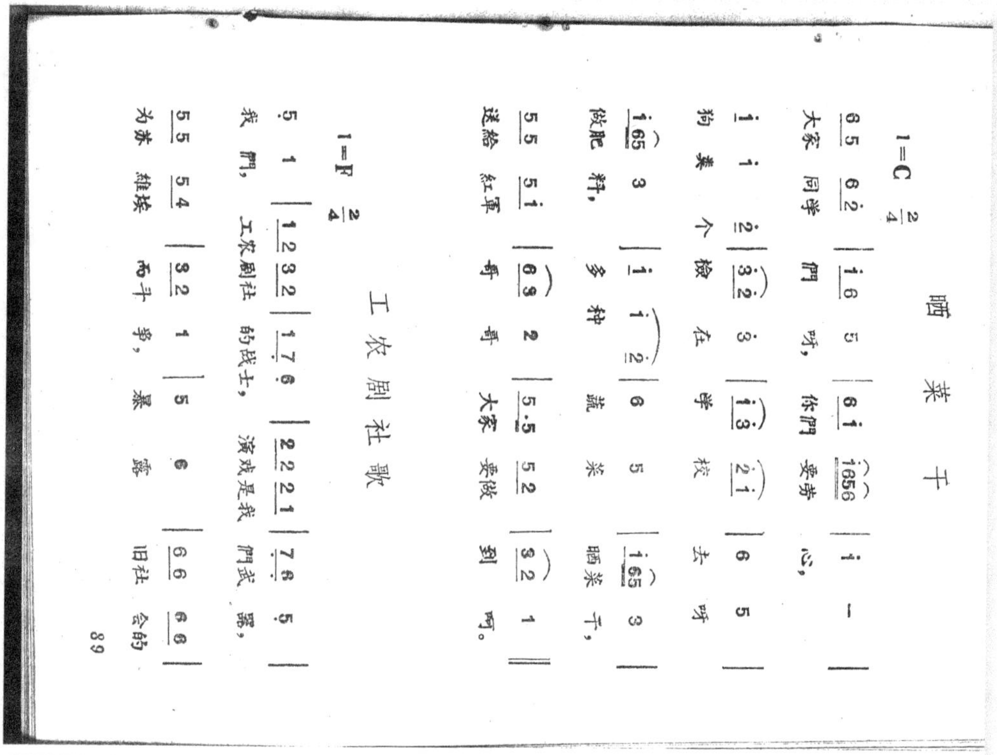

晒 菜 干

1=C 2/4

6 5 6 2 | 1 6 5 | 6 1 1656 | 1 — |
大家 同学 們 呀， 你們 要劳 心，

1 1 2 | 3 2 3 | 1 3 2 1 | 6 5 |
狗 粪 个 撿 在 学 校 去 呀

1 65 3 | 1 1 2 | 6 5 | 1 65 3 |
做肥 料， 多 种 蔬 菜 晒菜 干，

5 5 5 1 | 6 3 2 | 5·5 5 2 | 3 2 1 ||
送給 紅軍 哥 哥 大家 要做 到 呵。

工 农 剧 社 歌

1=F 2/4

5 1 | 1 2 3 2 | 1 7 6 | 2 2 2 1 | 7 6 5 |
我 們， 工农剧社 的战士， 演戏是我 們武 器，

5 5 5 4 | 3 2 1 | 5 6 | 6 6 6 6 |
为苏 維埃 而斗 爭， 暴 露 旧社 会的

89

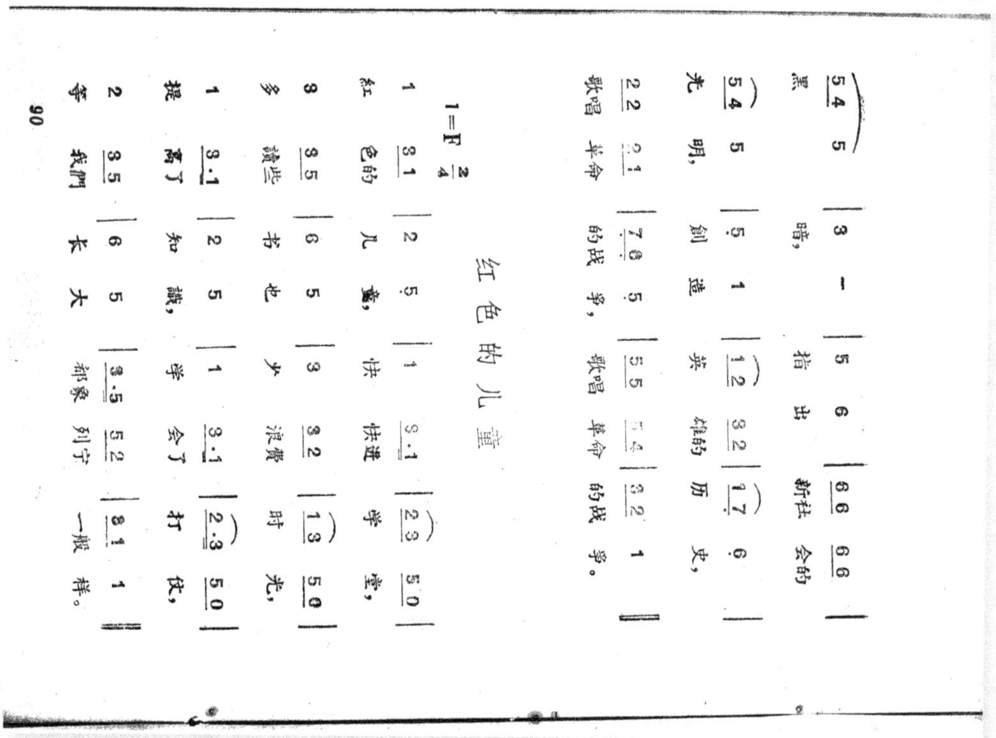

5 4 5 | 3 — | 5 6 | 6 6 6 6 |
黑 暗， 指 出 新社 会的

5 4 5 | 5 1 | 1 2 3 2 | 1 7 6 |
光 明， 創 造 英 雄的 历 史，

2 2 2 1 | 7 6 5 | 5 5 5 4 | 3 2 1 ||
歌唱 革命 的战 爭， 歌唱 革命 的战 爭。

红 色 的 儿 童

1=F 2/4

1 3 1 | 2 5 | 1 3·1 | 2 3 5 0 |
紅 色的 儿 童， 快 快进 学 堂，

3 3 5 | 6 5 | 3 3 2 | 1 3 5 0 |
多 讀些 书 也 少 浪費 时 光，

1 3·1 | 2 5 | 1 3·1 | 2·3 5 0 |
提 高了 知 識， 学 会了 打 仗，

2 3 5 | 6 5 | 3·5 5 2 | 3 1 1 ||
等 我們 长 大 都象 列宁 一般 样。

90

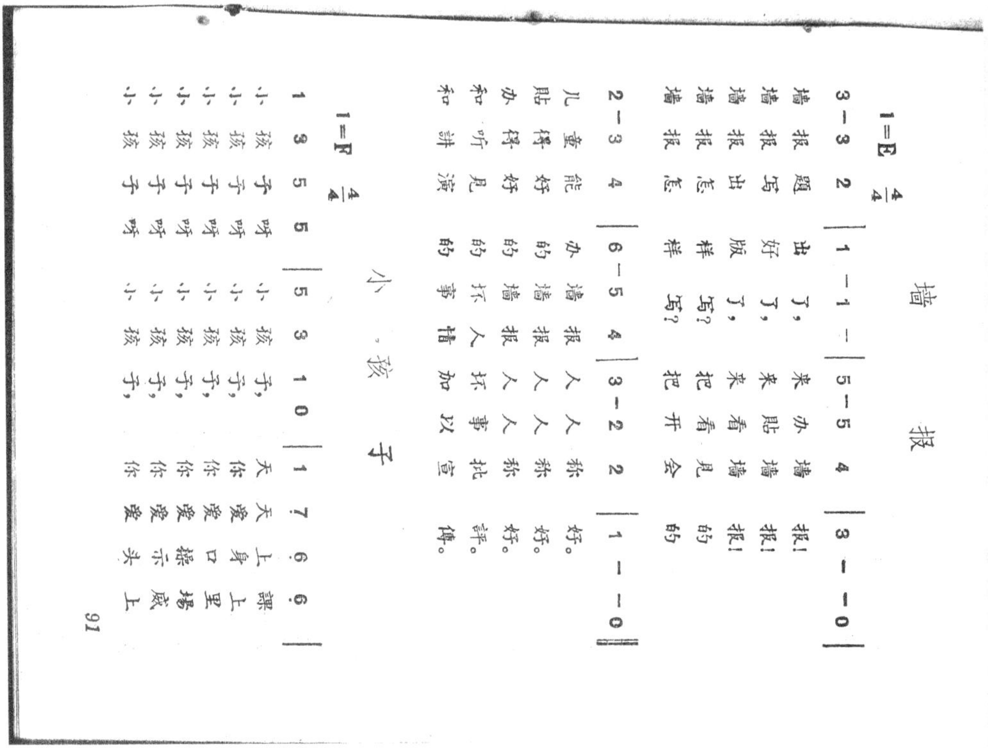

墙　报

1=E $\frac{4}{4}$

3 – 3 2 | 1 – 1 – | 5 – 5 4 | 3 – – 0 |

墙报题 出了， 来办墙 报！
墙报写 好了， 来贴墙 报！
墙报出 版了， 来看墙 报！
墙报怎 样写？ 把看見 的
墙报怎 样写？ 把开会 的

2 – 3 4 | 6 – 5 4 | 3 – 2 2 | 1 – – 0 ‖

儿童能 办墙报 人人称 好。
貼得好 的墙报 人人称 好。
办得好 的墙报 人人称 好。
和听見 的坏人 坏事批 評。
和講演 的事情 加以宣 傳。

小孩子

1=F $\frac{4}{4}$

1 3 5 5 | 5 3 1 0 | 1 7 6 6 |

小孩子呀 小孩子， 天天上課
小孩子呀 小孩子， 你爱身上
小孩子呀 小孩子， 你爱口里
小孩子呀 小孩子， 你爱操場
小孩子呀 小孩子， 你爱示威
小孩子呀 小孩子， 你爱头上

91

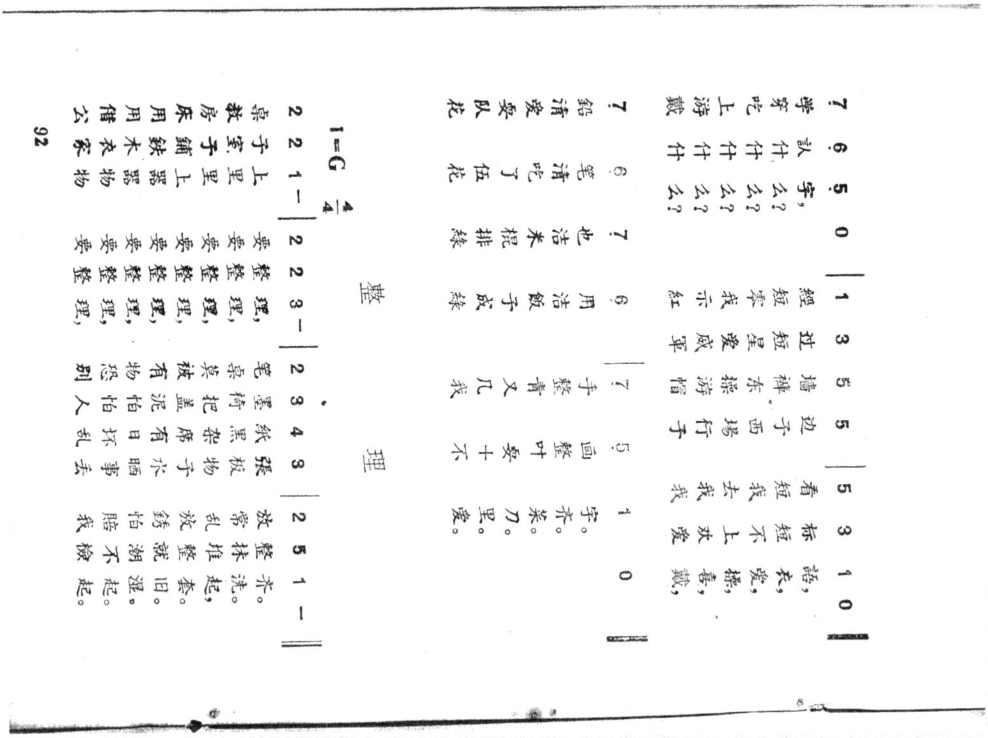

7 6 5 0 | 1 3 5 5 | 5 3 1 0 ‖

学認字， 經过墙边 看标語，
穿什么？ 短短褲子 短短衣，
吃什么？ 零星东西 我不爱，
上什么？ 我爱操場 去上操，
游什么？ 示威游行 我欢喜，
戴什么？ 紅軍帽子 我爱戴，

7 6 7 6 | 7 5 1 0 ‖

鉛笔也用 手画字。
清清洁洁 整整齐。
爱吃米飯 青叶菜。
要了棍子 又要刀。
队伍排成 几十里。
花花綠綠 我不爱。

整　理

1=G $\frac{4}{4}$

2 2 1 – | 2 2 3 – | 2 3 4 3 | 2 5 1 – ‖

桌子上 要整理， 笔墨紙張 放整齐。
教室里 要整理， 桌椅黑板 常抹洗。
房子里 要整理， 莫把杂物 乱堆起，
床鋪上 要整理， 被盖席子 放整套。
用鉄器 要整理， 有泥有水 銹就旧。
用木器 要整理， 物怕日晒 怕潮湿。
借衣物 要整理， 恐怕坏事 賠不起。
公家物 要整理， 別人乱丢 我檢起。

92

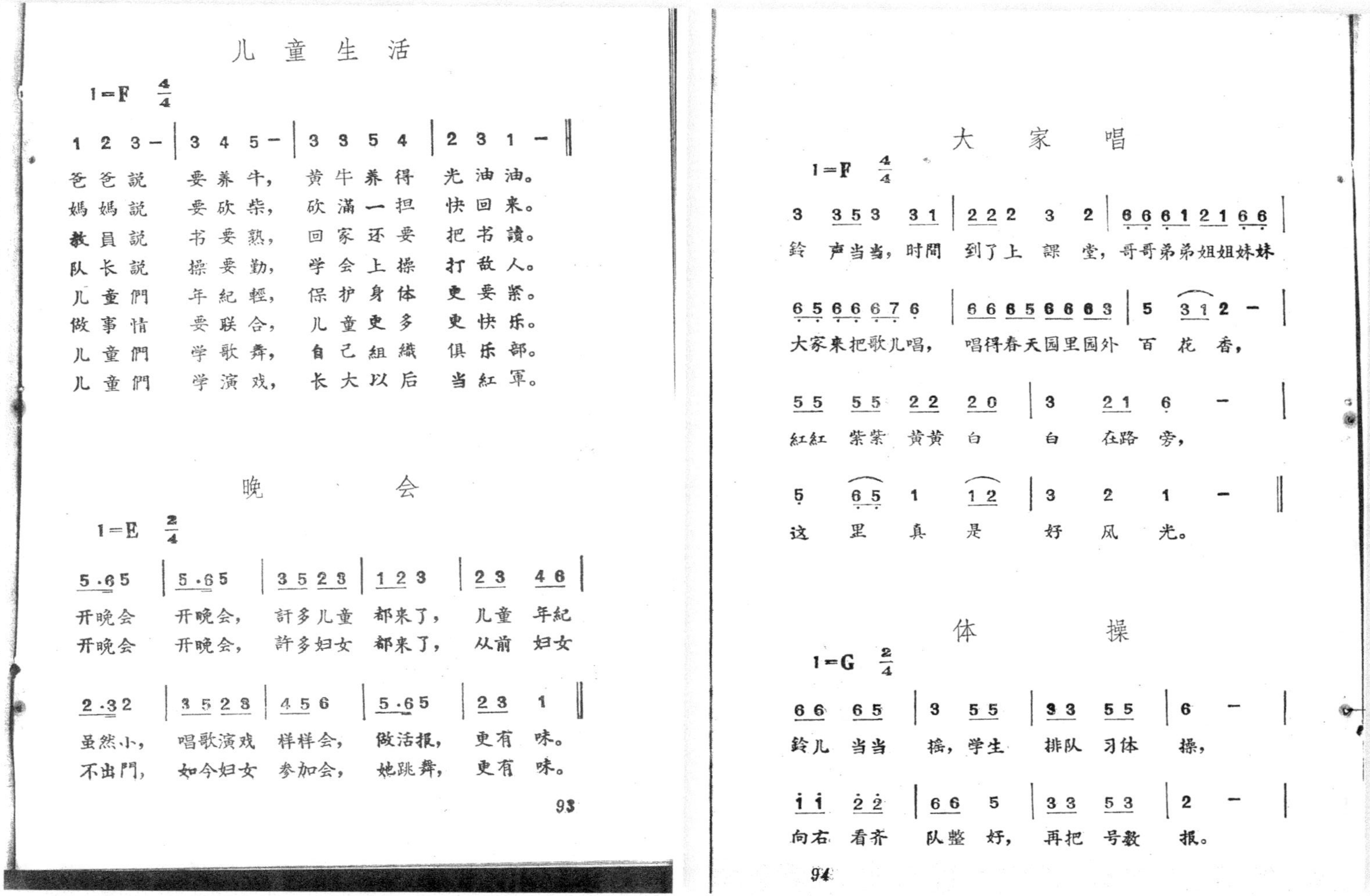

儿童生活

1=F 4/4

1 2 3 – | 3 4 5 – | 3 3 5 4 | 2 3 1 – ‖

爸爸説　要养牛，黄牛养得　光油油。
媽媽説　要砍柴，砍滿一担　快回来。
教員説　书要熟，回家还要　把书讀。
队长説　操要勤，学会上操　打敌人。
儿童們　年紀輕，保护身体　更要紧。
做事情　要联合，儿童更多　更快乐。
儿童們　学歌舞，自己組織　俱乐部。
儿童們　学演戏，长大以后　当紅軍。

晚　会

1=E 2/4

5·65 | 5·65 | 3523 | 123 | 23 46 |

开晚会　开晚会，許多儿童　都来了，儿童　年紀
开晚会　开晚会，許多妇女　都来了，从前　妇女

2·32 | 3523 | 456 | 5·65 | 23 1 ‖

虽然小，唱歌演戏　样样会，做活报，更有　味。
不出門，如今妇女　参加会，她跳舞，更有　味。

93

大　家　唱

1=F 4/4

3 353 31 | 222 3 2 | 66 61 21 66 |

鈴　声当当，时間　到了上　課　堂，哥哥弟弟姐姐妹妹

65 66 67 6 | 66 65 66 63 | 5 31 2 – |

大家来把歌儿唱，唱得春天园里园外　百　花　香，

55 55 22 20 | 3 21 6 – |

紅紅　紫紫　黄黄　白　自　在路　旁，

5 65 1 12 | 3 2 1 – ‖

这　里　真　是　好　风　光。

体　操

1=G 2/4

66 65 | 3 55 | 33 55 | 6 – |

鈴儿　当当　摇，学生　排队　习体　操，

11 22 | 66 5 | 33 53 | 2 – |

向右　看齐　队整　好，再把　号数　报。

94

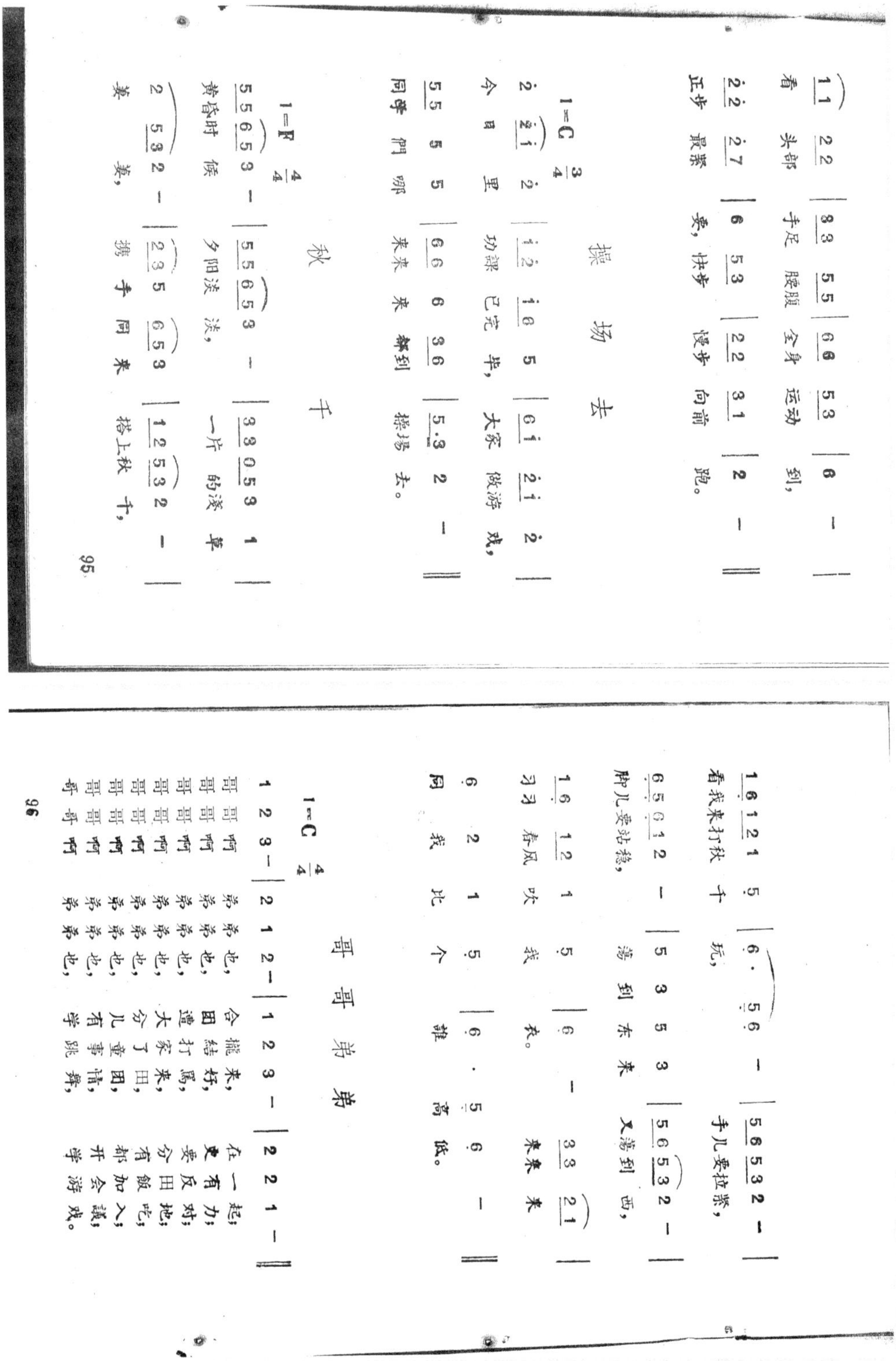

1 1 2 2 | 3 3 5 5 | 6 6 5 3 | 6 — |
看 头部 手足 腰腹 全身 运动 到，

2̇ 2̇ 2̇ 7 | 6 5 3 | 2 2 3 1 | 2 — ‖
正步 最紧 要，快步 慢步 向前 跑。

操场去

1=C 3/4

2̇ 2̇ 1̇ 2̇ | 1̇ 2̇ 1̇ 6 5 | 6 1̇ 2̇ 1̇ 2̇ |
今 日 里 功課 已完 毕，大家 做游 戏，

5 5 5 5 | 6 6 6 3 6 | 5·3 2 — ‖
同學 們 哪 来来 来 都到 操場 去。

秋千

1=F 4/4

5 5 6 5 3 — | 5 5 6 5 3 — | 3 3 0 5 3 1 |
黄昏时 候 夕阳淡 淡， 一片 的淺 草

2 5 3 2 — | 2 3 5 6 5 3 | 1 2 5 3 2 — |
萋 萋， 携 手 同 来 搭上秋 千，

95

1 6 1 2 1 5 | 6 · 5 6 — | 5 6 5 3 2 — |
看我来打秋 千 玩， 手儿要拉紧，

6 5 6 1 2 — | 5 3 5 3 | 5 6 5 3 2 — |
脚儿要站稳， 蕩 到 东 来 又蕩到 西，

1 6 1 2 1 5 | 6 — 3 3 2 1 |
习习 春风 吹 我 衣。 来来 来

6 2 1 5 | 6 · 5 6 — ‖
同 我 比 个 誰 高 低。

哥哥弟弟

1=C 4/4

1 2 3 — | 2 1 2 — | 1 2 3 — | 2 2 1 — ‖

哥哥啊 弟弟也， 合攏来， 在一起；
哥哥啊 弟弟也， 团结好， 更有力；
哥哥啊 弟弟也， 遭打罵， 要反对；
哥哥啊 弟弟也， 大家来， 分田地；
哥哥啊 弟弟也， 分了田， 有飯吃；
哥哥啊 弟弟也， 儿童团， 都加入；
哥哥啊 弟弟也， 有事情， 开会議；
哥哥啊 弟弟也， 学跳舞， 学游戏。

96

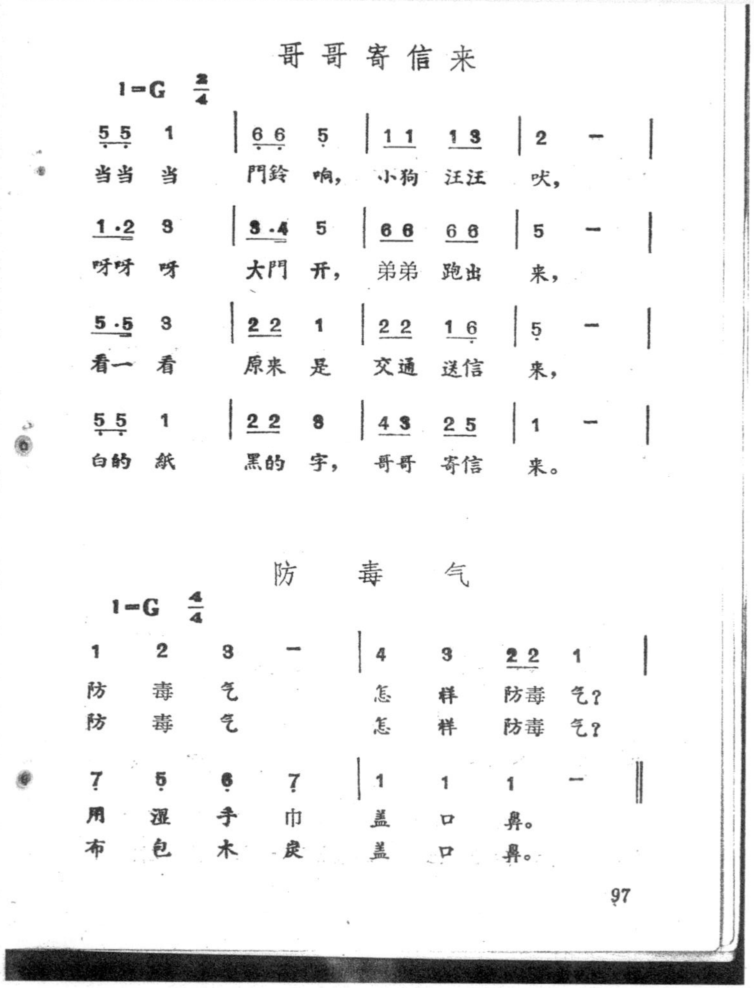

哥哥寄信来

1=G 2/4

5 5 1 | 6 6 5 | 1 1 1 3 | 2 — |
当当 当　門鈴 响，小狗 汪汪 吠，

1·2 3 | 3·4 5 | 6 6 6 6 | 5 — |
呀呀 呀　大門 开，弟弟 跑出 来，

5·5 3 | 2 2 1 | 2 2 1 6 | 5 — |
看一 看　原来 是　交通 送信 来，

5 5 1 | 2 2 3 | 4 3 2 5 | 1 — |
白的 紙　黑的 字，哥哥 寄信 来。

防毒气

1=G 4/4

1 2 3 — | 4 3 2 2 1 |
防 毒 气　怎 样 防毒 气？
防 毒 气　怎 样 防毒 气？

7 5 6 7 | 1 1 1 — ‖
用 湿 手 巾　盖 口 鼻。
布 包 木 炭　盖 口 鼻。

97

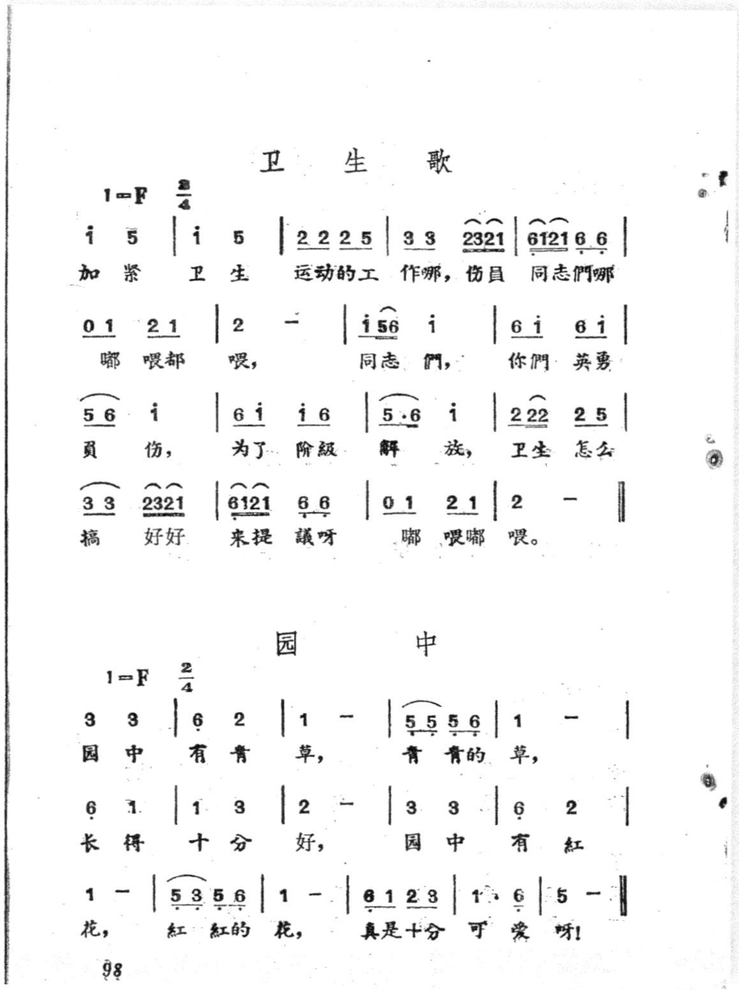

卫生歌

1=F 2/4

i 5 | i 5 | 2 2 2 5 | 3 3 2321 | 6121 6 6 |
加 紧　卫 生　运动的工　作哪，伤員　同志們哪

0 1 2 1 | 2 — | i56 i | 6 i 6 i |
嘟 喂都　喂，　同志 們，你們 英勇

5 6 i | 6 i i 6 | 5·6 i | 2 22 2 5 |
負 伤，为了 阶級　解 放，卫生 怎么

3 3 2321 | 6121 6 6 | 0 1 2 1 | 2 — ‖
搞 好好　来提 議呀　嘟 喂嘟　喂。

园中

1=F 2/4

3 3 | 6 2 | 1 — | 5 5 5 6 | 1 — |
园 中　有 青　草，　青 青的　草，

6 1 | 1 3 | 2 — | 3 3 | 6 2 |
长 得　十 分　好，　园 中　有 紅

1 — | 5 3 5 6 | 1 — | 6 1 2 3 | 1 6 | 5 — ‖
花，　紅 紅的　花，　真是十分　可 爱　呀！

98

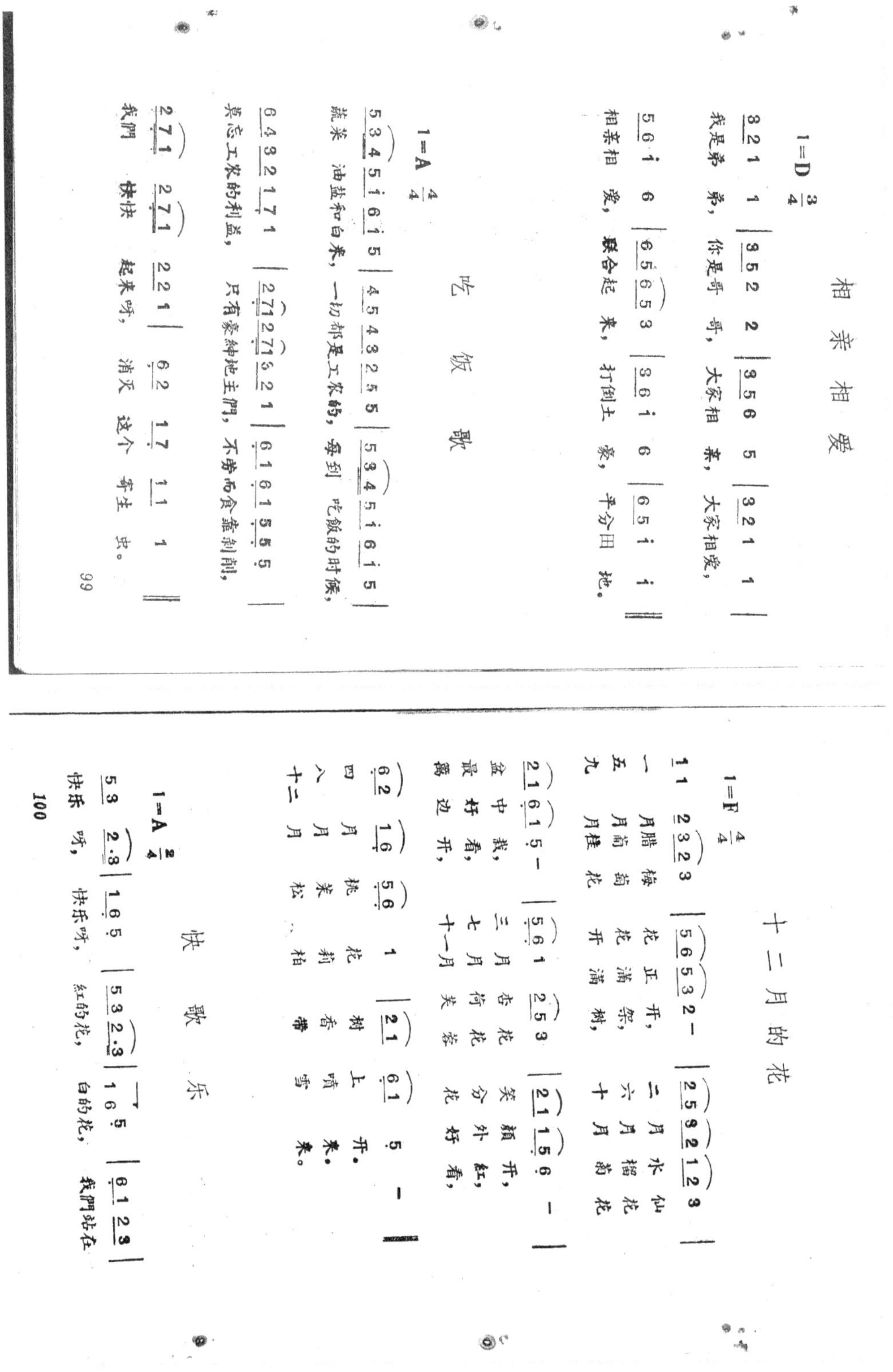

相亲相爱

1=D $\frac{3}{4}$

3 2 1　1 | 3 5 2　2 | 3 5 6　5 | 3 2 1　1 |

我是弟　弟，你是哥　哥，大家相　亲，大家相爱，

5 6 i　6 | 6 5 6 5 3 | 3 6 i　6 | 6 5 i　i ‖

相亲相　爱，联合起　来，打倒土　豪，平分田　地。

吃饭歌

1=A $\frac{4}{4}$

5 3 4 5 i 6 i 5 | 4 5 4 3 2 5 5 | 5 3 4 5 i 6 i 5 |

蔬菜　油盐和白米，一切都是工农的，每到　吃飯的时候，

6 4 3 2 1 7 1 | 2 71 2 71 6 2 1 | 6 1 6 1 5 5 5 |

莫忘工农的利益，　只有豪紳地主們，不劳而食靠剝削，

2 7 1　2 7 1　2 2 1 | 6 2　1 7　1 1　1 ‖

我們　快快　起来呀，消灭　这个　寄生　虫。

99

十二月的花

1=F $\frac{4}{4}$

1 1　2 3 2 3 | 5 6 5 3 2 — | 2 5 3 2 1 2 3 |

一　月腊　梅　花　正　开，　二　月　水　仙
五　月葡　萄　花　滿　架，　六　月　榴　花
九　月桂　花　开　滿　树，　十　月　菊　花

2 1 6 1 5 — | 5 6 1　2 5 3 | 2 1 1 5 6 — |

盆　中　栽，　三　月　杏　花　笑　顏　开，
最　好　看，　七　月　荷　花　分　外　紅，
籬　边　开，　十一月　芙　蓉　花　好　看，

6 2　1 6　5 6　1 | 2 1　6 1　5 — ‖

四　月　桃　花　树　上　开。
八　月　茉　莉　香　噴　来。
十二　月　松　柏　带　雪　来。

快歌乐

1=A $\frac{2}{4}$

5 3　2 . 3 | 1 6 5 | 5 3 2 . 3 | 1 6 5 | 6 1 2 3 |

快乐　呀，　快乐呀，　紅的花，　白的花，　我們站在

100

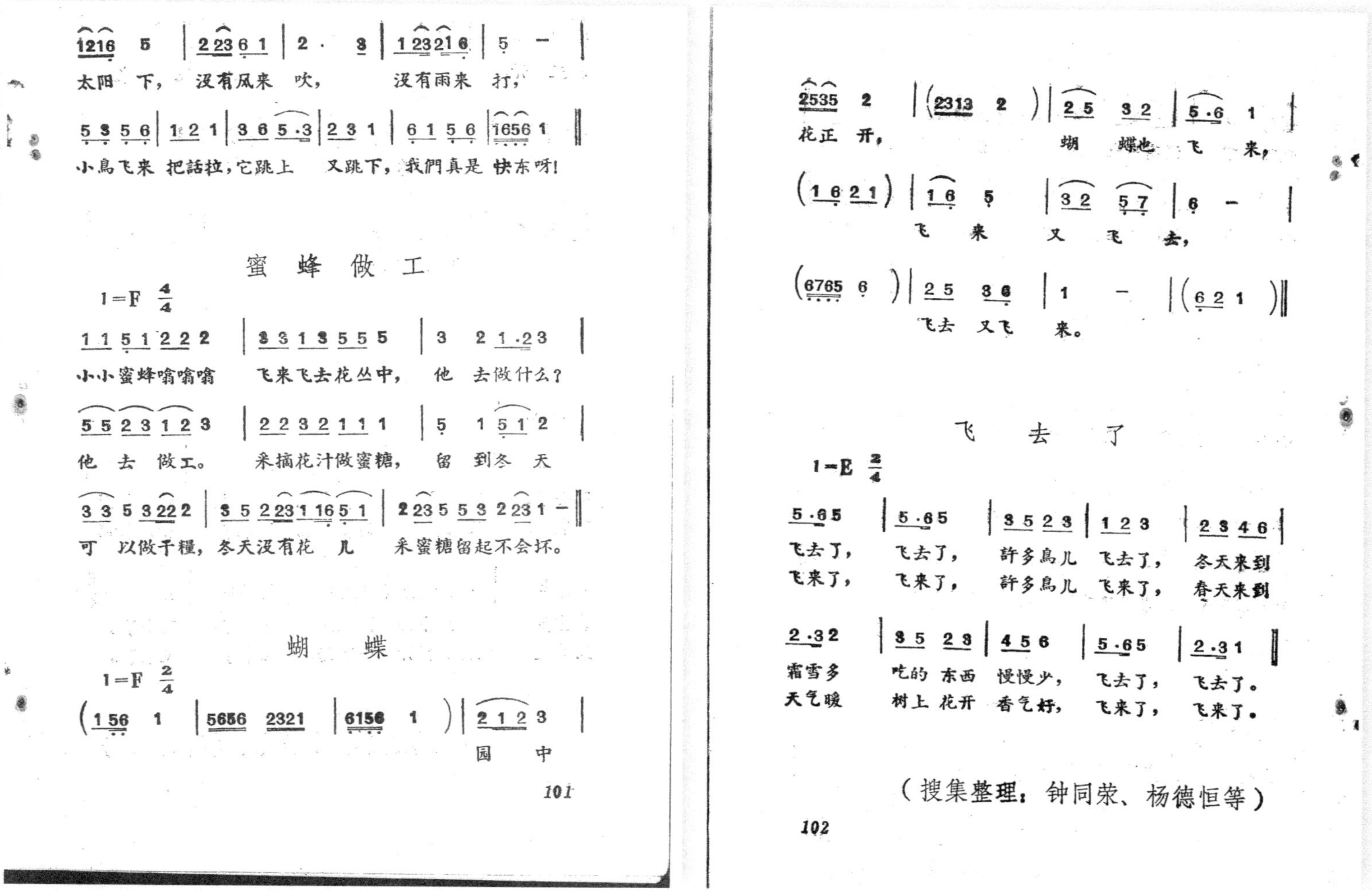

1216 5 | 2 23 6 1 | 2 · 3 | 1 23 21 6 | 5 — |
太阳 下， 没有风来 吹， 没有雨来 打，

5 3 5 6 | 1 2 1 | 3 6 5·3 | 2 3 1 | 6 1 5 6 | 1656 1 ‖
小鳥飞来 把話拉，它跳上 又跳下，我們真是 快乐呀！

蜜 蜂 做 工

1=F $\frac{4}{4}$

1 1 5 1 2 2 2 | 3 3 1 3 5 5 5 | 3 2 1·2 3 |
小小蜜蜂嗡嗡嗡 飞来飞去花丛中， 他 去做什么？

5 5 2 3 1 2 3 | 2 2 3 2 1 1 1 | 5 1 5 1 2 |
他 去 做工。 采摘花汁做蜜糖， 留 到冬 天

3 3 5 3 22 2 | 3 5 2 23 1 16 5 1 | 2 23 5 5 3 2 23 1 — ‖
可 以做干糧，冬天没有花 儿 采蜜糖留起不会坏。

蝴 蝶

1=F $\frac{2}{4}$

(1 56 1 | 5656 2321 | 6156 1) | 2 1 2 3 |
园 中

101

2535 2 | (2313 2) | 2 5 3 2 | 5·6 1 |
花正 开， 蝴 蝶也 飞 来，

(1 6 2 1) | 1 6 5 | 3 2 5 7 | 6 — |
飞 来 又 飞 去，

(6765 6) | 2 5 3 6 | 1 — | (6 2 1) ‖
飞去 又飞 来。

飞 去 了

1=E $\frac{2}{4}$

5·65 | 5·65 | 3 5 2 3 | 1 2 3 | 2 3 4 6 |
飞去了， 飞去了， 許多鳥儿 飞去了， 冬天来到
飞来了， 飞来了， 許多鳥儿 飞来了， 春天来到

2·32 | 3 5 2 3 | 4 5 6 | 5·65 | 2·3 1 ‖
霜雪多 吃的 东西 慢慢少， 飞去了， 飞去了。
天气暖 树上 花开 香气好， 飞来了， 飞来了。

（搜集整理：钟同荣、杨德恒等）

102

06

第六章　革命历史民歌的艺术特征

Chapter Six: Artistic Characteristics of Revolutionary Historical Folk Songs

第一节 抒情与叙事的交织

SECTION ONE: THE INTERWEAVING OF LYRICISM AND NARRATIVE

引言 / Introduction

在中国民间歌谣的传统之中，抒情与叙事始终是两条并行的艺术脉络。前者重在情感的直抒胸臆，后者强调事件的铺陈与历史的讲述。然而，在中央苏区的革命历史民歌中，这两条脉络却以一种极为紧密的方式交织在一起，形成了一种特殊的艺术生态。民歌既是普通百姓的情感出口，又是革命历史的口头载体。换言之，这些作品既承载了个体的悲欢离合，也构筑了群体的精神史诗。

苏区的革命历史民歌因而不同于单纯的山歌或劳动号子。它们往往在一首歌中同时呈现情感与叙事的双重维度，使歌声既能抚慰人心，又能动员人心。在今天回望这些歌谣时，我们不应仅仅把它们理解为政治宣传的工具，而更应看到其背后深厚的民间性与历史语境。

Within the tradition of Chinese folk songs, lyricism and narrative have always functioned as two parallel artistic threads. The former emphasizes the direct outpouring of personal emotion, while the latter highlights the unfolding of events and the recounting of history. In the revolutionary historical folk songs of the Central Soviet Area, however, these two threads are woven together in an unusually tight manner, forming a distinctive artistic ecology. These songs serve not only as an outlet for the emotions of ordinary people, but also as oral carriers of revolutionary history. In other words, they both embody the joys and sorrows of individuals and construct a collective spiritual epic.

For this reason, the revolutionary folk songs of the Soviet Area differ significantly from simple mountain songs or work chants. They often present, within a single song, both emotional and narrative dimensions at once, allowing the singing to both console and mobilize. When we look back on these songs today, we should not understand them merely as tools of political messaging; rather, we must recognize the profound popular foundations and historical contexts that underlie them.

01 旋律中的抒情性

THE LYRICISM IN MELODY

首先，革命历史民歌继承了赣南客家山歌的旋律传统，强调**长腔慢板**与**自由延展**。许多歌曲在结构上不拘泥于严格的节拍，而是随歌者情绪自由起伏。这种旋律特征本身即是情感的体现：歌声像叹息一样延长，像呼喊一样上扬，带着浓烈的主观色彩。

例如《哭别歌》的一段旋律，常常以小二度、三度的下行构成，营造出近似啜泣的氛围。即使没有歌词，仅凭旋律的跌宕，也能让人感受到离愁与痛苦。这样的旋律语言，赋予歌曲高度的抒情性，使个体心声能够被音乐直接传递。

与此同时，某些歌曲会在句末加入“拖腔”，延长一个音节，使情绪久久不散。这种唱法带有鲜明的地方特色，也是民歌歌手在即兴演唱中常用的技巧。可以说，旋律的宽广性与自由性，为个体抒情提供了最基本的音乐条件。

First, revolutionary historical folk songs inherited the melodic tradition of Hakka mountain songs in southern Jiangxi, characterized by long phrases, slow tempos, and free extension. Many songs are not bound to strict rhythmic measures but instead rise and fall freely with the singer's emotions. This melodic feature itself is a manifestation of sentiment: the singing stretches like a sigh, soars like a cry, and carries strong subjective coloring.

For example, in one passage of the song *"Farewell in Tears"* (*Ku Bie Ge*), the melody often descends in minor seconds or thirds, creating an atmosphere akin to sobbing. Even without lyrics, the fluctuation of the melody alone conveys feelings of sorrow and pain. Such a musical language grants the song a high degree of lyricism, enabling personal emotions to be transmitted directly through music.

At the same time, some songs add a "dragged note" (*tuo qiang*) at the end of a phrase, prolonging a syllable so that the emotion lingers on. This singing style bears a strong regional character and is a common technique in the improvisational performances of folk singers. In short, the expansiveness and freedom of the melody provide the most fundamental musical conditions for lyrical expression.

02 节奏中的叙事性

THE NARRATIVITY IN RHYTHM

与旋律的抒情性相对应，节奏则更多服务于叙事。许多革命历史民歌采用整齐的二拍子或四拍子，与步伐和劳动动作紧密契合。特别是在行军歌、号子类作品中，这种节奏稳定的特征尤其明显。

以《行军歌》为例：

“红旗飘飘迎风展，革命队伍往前赶。
山高路远不怕难，万水千山脚下穿。”

歌词简短有力，节奏与脚步一致，使得歌曲不仅仅是叙述行军场景，更成为实际行动的伴奏。这里的叙事并非纸面上的“讲故事”，而是一种“身体叙事”，通过节奏直接进入集体的行动逻辑。

这种规律化的节奏，使民歌具备了超越个体的功能：它能够统一步伐、增强士气，同时把集体的历史经验镶嵌在歌声中，成为一种可传唱的叙事方式。

In contrast to the lyricism conveyed through melody, rhythm in revolutionary historical folk songs primarily serves the purpose of narration. Many of these songs adopt steady duple or quadruple meters, closely synchronized with marching steps or labor movements. This rhythmic stability is especially prominent in works such as marching songs and work chants.

Take the *“Marching Song”* (*Xing Jun Ge*) as an example:

“The red flag waves proudly in the wind,
The revolutionary troops advance ahead.
Though the mountains are high and the roads are long,
We will cross all rivers and climb all peaks under our feet.”

The lyrics are short and forceful, and the rhythm aligns with the footsteps, making the song not only a description of the marching scene but also an actual accompaniment to the movement itself. Here, narration is not merely “telling a story” on paper but rather a kind of "embodied narration" that directly enters the collective's logic of action through rhythm.

This regularized rhythm enables the folk songs to perform functions beyond the individual: it unifies steps, boosts morale, and embeds collective historical experiences within the singing, transforming them into a transmittable form of narration.

03 歌词的双重结构

THE DUAL STRUCTURE OF LYRICS

歌词是抒情与叙事结合最直观的层面。许多歌曲在前半部分呈现浓烈的私人情感，而在后半部分则迅速转入宏大的集体叙事。这种"情感到历史"的过渡几乎成了一种固定结构。

例一：《送别歌》

"送郎送到大路口，眼泪落在黄泥沟；

盼郎早日回苏区，同把红旗举高头。"

这里前两句描写的是细腻的离愁别绪，属于典型的抒情语境；而后三句则立刻引入集体事业，把私人情感升华为革命目标。个体的情绪被纳入集体叙事，这正是苏区民歌的独特逻辑。

例二：《劳动歌》

"锄头当枪挑黄土，汗珠落地变珍珠；

劳动也是打胜仗，田里田外有功夫。"

此歌表面上是叙述劳动场景，但"汗珠变珍珠"的比喻使劳动具备了诗意的抒情色彩。歌曲通过修辞把沉重劳作转化为美丽意象，从而在叙事中注入情感的温度。

这种双重结构的存在，说明苏区民歌并非简单的政治宣传口号，而是在"个体感情"与"历史叙事"的交汇处自然生成的艺术表达。

Lyrics are the most direct level at which lyricism and narration are combined. Many songs begin with an intense expression of private emotions in the first half, and then swiftly shift to a grand collective narrative in the latter half. This transition from "emotion to history" almost became a fixed structural pattern.

Example 1: *"Farewell Song"* (*Song Bie Ge*)

"I walk my beloved to the crossroads,

My tears fall into the yellow clay ditch.

I long for his early return to the Soviet Area,

So together we may raise the red flag high."

The first two lines depict delicate emotions of parting sorrow, a typical lyrical setting. Yet the final two lines immediately introduce the collective cause, elevating private sentiment into a revolutionary goal. Individual emotion is absorbed into collective narration—this is the unique logic of Soviet Area folk songs.

Example 2: *"Labor Song"* (*Lao Dong Ge*)

"The hoe becomes a gun to lift the yellow earth,

Sweat drops to the ground and turns into pearls.

Labor, too, is winning a battle,

Both in the fields and beyond, skill brings merit."

On the surface, this song narrates a scene of labor, but the metaphor of "sweat turning into pearls" imbues the toil with poetic lyricism. Through figurative language, heavy physical work is transformed into beautiful imagery, thereby infusing narrative with emotional warmth.

The existence of such dual structures shows that Soviet Area folk songs were not simply political slogans, but artistic expressions that naturally emerged at the intersection of "individual emotions" and "historical narratives."

04 历史语境与功能

HISTORICAL CONTEXT AND FUNCTION

这种艺术特征背后，有其深刻的社会与历史原因。在战争与动荡的环境中，个体情感无法游离于公共生活之外。离愁、思乡、爱情、亲情等私人情绪，往往在歌声中被重新编码，成为革命叙事的一部分。

民歌在这一过程中承担了两重功能：

心理调适——民众通过歌声抒发痛苦与离愁，获得精神释放；

政治动员——个体情绪被转化为集体目标，使群众在情感认同中投身事业。

这种功能的双重性，使革命历史民歌不仅是艺术作品，更是社会心理的调节器。它既安抚了人心，又激发了斗志，成为苏区社会凝聚力的重要来源。

Behind these artistic characteristics lie profound social and historical reasons. In times of war and upheaval, individual emotions could not exist apart from public life. Feelings of parting, homesickness, love, and kinship were often re-encoded within the songs, becoming part of the revolutionary narrative.

In this process, folk songs carried a dual function:

Psychological adjustment — Through singing, the people expressed their pain and sorrow, finding emotional release.

Political mobilization — Individual emotions were transformed into collective goals, enabling the masses to devote themselves to the revolutionary cause through shared emotional identification.

This dual functionality made revolutionary historical folk songs not only works of art but also regulators of social psychology. They both comforted the people and aroused their fighting spirit, becoming an important source of cohesion within the Soviet Area society.

05 集体记忆与叙事诗学

COLLECTIVE MEMORY AND THE POETICS OF NARRATIVE

从文化记忆研究的角度看，革命历史民歌是“口头叙事记忆”的典型样态。法国社会学家阿尔布瓦赫指出，集体记忆必须依赖社会框架才能保存与延续。在苏区，民歌正是这种框架之一。

歌曲中的抒情元素，使记忆生动、感人；叙事元素，则确保记忆的连续性和方向性。二者结合，使得这些歌不仅仅是民间娱乐作品，而是携带历史记忆的声音档案。

从叙事学的角度看，革命历史民歌接近于“歌唱的叙事诗”。它们通过简洁的结构、重复的节奏、直白的意象，完成对重大历史事件的口头记录。与文字史料不同，民歌以声音的方式传递历史，使之更容易在大众中传播与铭记。

From the perspective of cultural memory studies, revolutionary historical folk songs represent a typical form of “oral narrative memory.” The French sociologist Maurice Halbwachs emphasized that collective memory must rely on social frameworks in order to be preserved and transmitted. In the Central Soviet Area, folk songs constituted precisely such a framework.

The lyrical elements within these songs made memory vivid and moving, while the narrative elements ensured its continuity and direction. The fusion of the two meant that these works were not merely popular entertainment, but sonic archives carrying historical memory.

From the standpoint of narratology, revolutionary historical folk songs resemble “sung narrative poems.” Through concise structures, repetitive rhythms, and straightforward imagery, they accomplished the oral recording of significant historical events. Unlike written documents, these folk songs transmitted history through sound, making it easier for the broader public to spread and remember.

06 艺术的张力与意义

ARTISTIC TENSION AND SIGNIFICANCE

抒情与叙事的结合，使这些民歌既具备艺术的美感，又承载历史的厚重。它们不是孤立的“艺术品”，而是活生生的社会实践。

从艺术角度看，抒情元素保证了歌曲的感性魅力，使人能够产生共鸣；

从历史角度看，叙事元素保证了歌曲的史诗色彩，使之成为时代的记录。

这种双重价值，使革命历史民歌在今天依然具有意义。它们不仅帮助我们理解苏区的历史经验，也让我们看到普通人在动荡岁月中如何通过歌声建构意义。

中央苏区的革命历史民歌在艺术结构上表现出明显的**抒情—叙事双重性**。旋律的自由与节奏的规整，歌词的情感与叙事，历史语境的私人性与公共性，共同塑造了这一独特的音乐现象。这些歌曲既让个人的哭泣与欢笑在歌声中得到安放，又把它们融入革命的历史叙事，成为民族记忆的一部分。因而，它们既是艺术的创造，也是历史的见证，更是精神的纽带。

The combination of lyricism and narration endowed these folk songs with both aesthetic beauty and historical weight. They were not isolated “artworks” but living forms of social practice.

From an artistic perspective, the lyrical elements ensured the songs’ emotional appeal, allowing audiences to resonate with them.

From a historical perspective, the narrative elements gave the songs an epic quality, turning them into records of their era.

This dual value makes revolutionary historical folk songs meaningful even today. They not only help us better understand the historical experience of the Soviet Area but also show how ordinary people, in times of turbulence, constructed meaning through singing.

the revolutionary historical folk songs of the Central Soviet Area display a distinct duality of **lyricism and narration** in their artistic structure. The freedom of melody and the regularity of rhythm, the interplay of emotional and narrative lyrics, and the tension between private and public dimensions within their historical context—all together shaped this unique musical phenomenon.

These songs allowed individual tears and laughter to find expression in music, while at the same time incorporating them into the revolutionary historical narrative, thus becoming part of the nation's collective memory. In this way, they are not only creations of art but also witnesses of history and bonds of spiritual connection.

第二节　象征与隐喻的艺术语言

SECTION TWO: THE ARTISTIC LANGUAGE OF SYMBOL AND METAPHOR

引言 / Introduction

在中央苏区的革命历史民歌中，象征与隐喻构成了最为鲜明的艺术特征之一。作为一种主要依托口头传播的民间文艺形态，民歌创作者多为普通劳动者，他们并不具备系统化的诗学训练，却凭借生活经验、审美直觉以及集体性的想象力，创造出极具表现力的艺术语言。这些语言往往通过象征物与隐喻性的表达，把复杂的社会矛盾、深沉的家国情感和革命信念，转化为平易近人而又寓意丰富的歌唱形式。

In the revolutionary historical folk songs of the Central Soviet Area, symbolism and metaphor form some of the most striking artistic features. As a form of folk art primarily reliant on oral transmission, most of the creators of these songs were ordinary laborers. Although they lacked systematic training in poetics, they relied on life experience, aesthetic intuition, and collective imagination to craft highly expressive artistic language. Such language often employed symbolic objects and metaphorical expressions to transform complex social contradictions, profound patriotic emotions, and revolutionary beliefs into accessible yet richly meaningful songs.

01 自然意象的象征性转化

THE SYMBOLIC TRANSFORMATION OF NATURAL IMAGERY

在这些民歌中，自然界的动植物、山川河流往往成为最常见的意象。例如“青松”“黄河”“红花”等，不仅仅是客观存在的自然物象，更承载着坚韧、浩荡与热烈的象征意义。青松常常被用来比拟革命战士的坚贞不屈，红花则寓意流血牺牲后的新生与希望。这样的转换，使得听众能够在熟悉的自然景物中感受到革命叙事的力量，实现了从日常生活到精神追求的过渡。

In these folk songs, elements of nature—plants, animals, mountains, and rivers—appear as some of the most common images. For example, “green pine,” “Yellow River,” and “red flower” are not simply natural objects but bear symbolic meanings of resilience, grandeur, and passion. The green pine often symbolizes the unyielding spirit of revolutionaries, while the red flower represents renewal and hope born out of bloodshed and sacrifice. Such transformations allowed listeners to perceive the power of revolutionary narratives through familiar natural imagery, bridging daily life and spiritual pursuit.

02 生活物件的隐喻功能

THE METAPHORICAL FUNCTION OF EVERYDAY OBJECTS

除了自然景物，衣食住行中的日常物件，也在歌谣中被赋予新的隐喻功能。例如，箩筐、锄头、红被单等，看似普通，却在民歌中与阶级斗争、爱情守望、信仰坚持联系在一起。尤其是“红被单”这样的意象，在若干歌谣中既是爱情的见证，也是革命信念的符号化承载。通过这种双重指涉，民歌有效地将个体情感与集体理想连接在一起，形成了独特的叙事张力。

Beyond natural scenery, ordinary objects from daily life—such as baskets, hoes, or red quilts—were also endowed with new metaphorical meanings in the songs. These simple items, in folk lyrics, became associated with class struggle, the longing of love, and the perseverance of faith. Especially the image of the "red quilt," which in some songs served both as a witness to love and as a symbolic bearer of revolutionary belief. Through such dual references, folk songs effectively linked personal emotions with collective ideals, creating a distinctive narrative tension.

03 动物意象与拟人化表达
ANIMAL IMAGERY AND PERSONIFICATION

革命民歌中，动物意象也频繁出现，例如“雄鸡”“黄牛”“麻雀”等。雄鸡报晓常被歌者隐喻为革命即将到来之时，黄牛的沉稳与勤劳则对应着劳动人民的坚韧品格，而麻雀虽小却敢于抗争，暗合弱者不屈服的精神。通过拟人化的修辞，这些动物形象不仅充满生动感，也在集体记忆中强化了革命叙事的寓言性特征。

Animal images also appear frequently in revolutionary folk songs—for instance, the rooster, the ox, or the sparrow. The crowing rooster is often used as a metaphor for the imminent arrival of revolution; the ox's steadiness and diligence correspond to the resilient qualities of the working people; the sparrow, though small, dares to resist, embodying the indomitable spirit of the weak. Through personification, these animal figures became vivid and lively, reinforcing the allegorical qualities of revolutionary narratives within collective memory.

04 双关与暗示的含蓄表达

SUBTLE EXPRESSION THROUGH DOUBLE MEANINGS AND ALLUSIONS

由于历史处境特殊，许多歌曲不得不采用委婉曲折的表达方式，以避免直接的政治风险。于是，双关、暗喻、转喻等修辞手法成为常见的表达策略。比如，用“送郎上山”暗指参加红军，用“割稻打谷”暗示对敌斗争。这些隐含的语义一方面保证了歌谣的传播安全，另一方面也提升了作品的审美张力，使其在含蓄与明示之间产生了耐人寻味的多重解读空间。

Given the special historical circumstances, many songs had to adopt indirect and euphemistic expressions to avoid political risk. Hence, rhetorical devices such as puns, metaphors, and metonymy became common strategies. For example, “sending my beloved up the mountain” implied joining the Red Army, while “harvesting rice and threshing grain” alluded to struggles against the enemy. These hidden meanings not only ensured the safe circulation of songs but also enhanced their aesthetic tension, creating layers of interpretation between concealment and revelation.

05 集体认同的象征建构

THE CONSTRUCTION OF COLLECTIVE IDENTITY THROUGH SYMBOLS

象征与隐喻不仅是艺术修辞，更是建构集体认同的重要手段。通过“红花”“青松”等不断重复的意象，民歌在集体记忆中逐渐形成了稳定的符号系统，进而强化了共同体意识。对于当时的劳动大众而言，这些象征物既是美学符号，也是社会动员的媒介，使个人情感自然融入集体的价值追求。

Symbol and metaphor were not merely artistic techniques but also crucial tools for constructing collective identity. Through the repeated use of images such as "red flower" and "green pine," folk songs gradually built a stable system of symbols within collective memory, thereby reinforcing community consciousness. For the working masses at the time, these symbols were not only aesthetic signs but also media of social mobilization, allowing individual emotions to merge naturally into collective values.

06 历史语境下的再解读

REINTERPRETATION WITHIN HISTORICAL CONTEXT

今天回望这些歌曲，我们更应当从历史语境出发，理解象征与隐喻的生成逻辑。它们不仅是革命时期的宣传手段，更是民众情感与生活智慧的真实流露。正是在这种象征化、隐喻化的艺术语言中，革命历史民歌突破了口头诗歌的局限，成为连接个体与时代的重要文化见证。若将其单纯解读为政治动员文本，未免失之偏颇；而当我们把它们置于文化人类学与文学史的维度加以考察时，则更能体会到这些作品所蕴含的深厚审美价值与象征意义。

Looking back today, we should interpret these songs within their historical context in order to understand the logic behind their symbolic and metaphorical language. They were not only tools of revolutionary propaganda but also authentic expressions of popular sentiment and life wisdom. Through symbolic and metaphorical artistic language, revolutionary historical folk songs transcended the limitations of oral poetry to become vital cultural testimonies connecting individuals and their era. To interpret them solely as political mobilization texts would be reductive; when examined through the lenses of cultural anthropology and literary history, their profound aesthetic value and symbolic significance become far more apparent.

第三节 即兴与口传的创作机制

SECTION THREE: THE CREATIVE MECHANISM OF IMPROVISATION AND ORAL TRANSMISSION

中央苏区的革命历史民歌，和所有传统民歌一样，最突出的特点便是其口头性与即兴性。它们并非出自单一作者之手，而是在特定的社会情境中，由群众在劳动、行军、集会乃至日常交流的过程中自发唱出，并在不断传唱与再创作中逐渐定型。这种创作机制不仅反映了民众的集体智慧，更折射出革命年代独特的传播生态与文化活力。

Like all traditional folk songs, the revolutionary historical folk songs of the Central Soviet Area are most notable for their oral and improvisational nature. They were not composed by a single author but emerged spontaneously within specific social contexts—during labor, marching, gatherings, or even daily conversations. Over time, through repeated performance and re-creation, they gradually took shape. This creative mechanism not only reflects the collective wisdom of the people but also mirrors the unique ecology of dissemination and cultural vitality in the revolutionary era.

01 即兴创作的动因

MOTIVATIONS FOR IMPROVISED CREATION

革命历史民歌往往产生于瞬间的生活场景中。农民在田间劳作时，红军在行军途中，妇女在纺织或汲水的间隙，都可能随口唱出几句。即兴性源于民众急切表达内心感受的需求：或抒发离别之情，或歌颂战斗英雄，或讽刺敌人。正因为这种创作并不依赖纸笔，而是直接依靠语言与旋律的即时组合，它才能以最快的速度回应现实，并在广泛传播中形成强烈的现场感与生命力。

Revolutionary folk songs often arose out of immediate life situations. Farmers might sing while working in the fields, soldiers while marching, or women while weaving or fetching water. Improvisation stemmed from people's urgent need to express their emotions—whether longing at parting, praise for heroes, or satire of the enemy. Because this creation relied not on pen and paper but directly on the instant combination of language and melody, the songs could respond swiftly to reality and spread widely, carrying a strong sense of presence and vitality.

02 口传中的再创造

RE-CREATION THROUGH ORAL TRANSMISSION

在口头传统中，民歌并非以“定稿”的形式存在，而是每一次传唱都可能发生变化。歌词的细节、曲调的走向、甚至节奏的安排，都可能因演唱者的经验与情感而发生调整。这种口传—再创造的机制，使得民歌始终处于动态的生成状态。例如同一首《十送红军》，在不同村落中就有多种唱法和版本，每一次演唱都带着个人印记，却依然保持着共同的核心主题。

Within the oral tradition, folk songs did not exist in a “finalized” form; every performance could bring changes. Details of the lyrics, the melodic contour, or even the rhythmic arrangement might shift according to the singer's experiences and feelings. This mechanism of oral transmission and re-creation kept the songs in a dynamic state of evolution. For example, the well-known *“Ten Farewells to the Red Army”* (*Shi Song Hong Jun*) exists in many versions across different villages, with each rendition carrying personal imprints yet retaining the same core theme.

03 集体记忆的协作模式

A COLLABORATIVE MODE OF COLLECTIVE MEMORY

即兴与口传并非个体行为，而是一种集体性的文化实践。人们在公共场合中轮流唱、对唱或合唱，某人唱出的句子可能立刻被他人补充、改造或续写。久而久之，歌谣逐渐凝固为群体认可的“固定版本”，而那些未被接受的唱法则自然被淘汰。这种机制与其说是“作者创作”，不如说是“群体筛选”，它体现了口头传统的民主性与开放性。

Improvisation and oral transmission were not individual acts but collective cultural practices. In public spaces, people would sing alternately, in dialogue, or in chorus. A line sung by one person might be immediately supplemented, revised, or continued by others. Over time, certain versions were accepted by the group and solidified as “fixed” forms, while less favored variants naturally faded away. This process was less about “individual authorship” than about “collective selection,” embodying the democratic and open nature of oral traditions.

04 口传中的简约与重复

SIMPLICITY AND REPETITION IN ORAL TRANSMISSION

由于依靠记忆传递，民歌往往追求结构上的简约与内容上的重复。常见的叠词、套语和排比句，既有助于记忆，也增强了节奏感和感染力。例如“山山水水”“夜夜朝朝”“一心一意”等表达，不仅朗朗上口，还在重复中强化了情感的真挚与主题的突出。这种简洁明快的语言风格，与革命年代需要快速传播的现实需求高度契合。

Because the songs were passed down through memory, they often pursued structural simplicity and linguistic repetition. Common devices included reduplication, formulaic expressions, and parallelism, which not only aided memorization but also heightened rhythm and emotional power. Phrases such as "mountain after mountain," "night after night," or "wholeheartedly" were easy to recite and, through repetition, reinforced sincerity and thematic emphasis. This concise and lively style matched the revolutionary need for rapid dissemination.

05 口传与旋律的适应性

THE ADAPTABILITY OF MELODY IN ORAL TRADITION

歌词的变化往往伴随着旋律的自由调整。苏区的民歌旋律多源于客家山歌、小调等地方音乐传统，结构宽松，便于插入不同的歌词。民众在口传过程中，会根据演唱环境与听众反应，灵活延长、缩短或变换旋律。这种高度的适应性，使得民歌不仅是文本的传递，更是现场表演的一部分，其生命力正是在不断的表演实践中得以延续。

Changes in lyrics were often accompanied by flexible adjustments in melody. The tunes of Soviet Area folk songs drew heavily on Hakka mountain songs and local ditties, with loose structures that made it easy to insert new lines. During oral transmission, singers would adapt the melody according to the performance environment and audience response, lengthening, shortening, or altering phrases as needed. This high adaptability meant that the songs were not only texts but also live performances, whose vitality was sustained through constant enactment.

06 革命语境下的功能转化

FUNCTIONAL TRANSFORMATION IN THE REVOLUTIONARY CONTEXT

即兴与口传的创作机制，本来就是民歌文化的内在规律。在革命语境下，这一规律被赋予新的功能：它加快了歌曲的传播速度，使其迅速在广大群众中流行；同时也让歌曲能够随时吸收新的事件、人物与口号，保持内容的鲜活性。正因如此，革命历史民歌才能在短短数年间，积累出数量庞大、题材多样的作品群体。

Improvisation and oral transmission were intrinsic to folk culture. In the revolutionary context, however, these traits acquired new functions: they accelerated the dissemination of songs, enabling them to spread rapidly among the masses; at the same time, they allowed the songs to absorb new events, figures, and slogans in real time, keeping the content fresh. For this reason, within just a few years, revolutionary folk songs accumulated in large numbers and covered a wide range of themes.

07 当代视角的再阐释

CONTEMPORARY REINTERPRETATIONS

今天重新审视这些即兴与口传的机制，我们不应仅仅将其理解为“革命宣传”的工具，而更应看到其作为口头文学与表演艺术的独特价值。这些作品记录了人民在历史转折中的情感与创造力，展现了口头传统在现代社会剧烈变动中的适应性。它们既是革命历史的文化见证，也是口头诗学的重要文本，为我们理解民间文艺的生成逻辑提供了生动案例。

Re-examining these mechanisms today, we should not see them merely as tools of "revolutionary propaganda," but also recognize their unique value as oral literature and performance art. These songs recorded the emotions and creativity of the people during historical upheavals, demonstrating how oral traditions adapted to the dramatic changes of modern society. They are both cultural testimonies of revolutionary history and significant texts of oral poetics, offering vivid examples for understanding the generative logic of folk art.

第四节　叙事与抒情的交织结构

SECTION FOUR: THE INTERWOVEN STRUCTURE OF NARRATIVE AND LYRICISM

引言 / Introduction

在中央苏区的革命历史民歌中，叙事与抒情始终呈现出紧密交织的状态。民歌既要叙述具体的事件、人物与情境，又要传达歌者与群体的情感体验。叙事提供了内容的骨架，而抒情则赋予了歌曲生命的温度，两者相辅相成，共同构成了这一类民歌的独特艺术风格。

In the revolutionary historical folk songs of the Central Soviet Area, narrative and lyricism are always tightly interwoven. The songs must recount concrete events, characters, and circumstances, while simultaneously conveying the emotions of the singers and their community. Narrative provides the skeletal framework of content, while lyricism infuses the songs with warmth and vitality. The two complement each other, together shaping the distinctive artistic style of this genre.

01 叙事的基础功能
THE FUNDAMENTAL FUNCTION OF NARRATIVE

许多革命历史民歌源于真实的生活事件，例如红军长征途中的送别、战斗中的牺牲、根据地中的生产场景等。歌词常常以时间顺序或空间线索为结构，清晰地勾勒出事件的经过。例如《十送红军》通过十次送别的场景，层层递进地叙述了军民分别的全过程。这样的叙事性不仅帮助听众理解故事情境，也为后续的情感表达提供了框架。

Many revolutionary folk songs originated from real-life events—for example, farewells during the Red Army's Long March, sacrifices in battle, or scenes of production in the revolutionary bases. Lyrics often follow chronological or spatial sequences, clearly outlining the course of events. For instance, *"Ten Farewells to the Red Army"* (*Shi Song Hong Jun*) narrates the process of parting through ten successive farewell scenes. This narrative element not only helps audiences grasp the story's context but also provides a framework for subsequent emotional expression.

02 抒情的核心地位
THE CENTRAL ROLE OF LYRICISM

虽然有较强的叙事背景，但这些民歌的真正力量在于抒情。歌者通过简单直接的语言，将离别的痛苦、战斗的豪情、对未来的憧憬倾注于歌声之中。例如“十里长亭送红军，热泪双双洒衣襟”一句，尽管叙述了送别的情景，但更突出的是情感的浓烈。由此可见，叙事往往只是抒情的载体，民歌的最终指向是情感的共鸣。

Although the songs have strong narrative backgrounds, their true power lies in lyricism. Through simple and direct language, singers infused their songs with the pain of separation, the fervor of battle, and the hope for the future. For example, the line *"At the long pavilion, I see the Red Army off; hot tears stream down, soaking our sleeves"* depicts a farewell scene but emphasizes even more strongly the depth of emotion. Thus, narrative often serves merely as a vehicle for lyricism, and the ultimate aim of folk songs is to evoke emotional resonance.

03 叙事与抒情的交错方式

THE ALTERNATION OF NARRATIVE AND LYRICISM

在具体的表现手法上，苏区民歌常常在叙事与抒情之间来回切换。歌曲可能从讲述一件小事开始，如红军行军过村，接着立即转入群众的感受，如“看到红军心里喜”，再返回叙事，描绘红军与群众一起挑粮、挖战壕。这种交替，使得歌曲既不流于单纯的叙事，也避免了情感的抽象化。它让历史事件被赋予情感色彩，而个人情感也因事件而具体化。

In practice, Soviet Area folk songs frequently shift back and forth between narrative and lyricism. A song might begin by describing a small incident—such as Red Army troops passing through a village—then immediately turn to the villagers' feelings, for example, *"seeing the Red Army makes our hearts rejoice"*, before returning again to narrative, depicting soldiers and villagers carrying grain or digging trenches together. This alternation prevents the songs from being mere narration or abstract sentiment. Instead, it imbues historical events with emotional color while grounding personal feelings in concrete circumstances.

04 细节描写中的叙事化倾向

NARRATIVE TENDENCIES IN DETAILED DESCRIPTION

为了增强真实感，民歌往往注重细节描写。这些细节既是叙事的组成部分，也是抒情的触发点。例如歌曲中对地名的提及（瑞金沙洲坝、长汀、宁都等），对人物身份的描绘（红军小哥哥、游击队阿妹），都让歌曲具有了鲜明的地方感与现场感。这种细节不仅承载了记忆功能，还强化了民众的情感投射。

To enhance realism, folk songs often rely on detailed descriptions. These details are both components of narration and triggers for lyricism. References to place names (such as Ruijin's Shazhouba, Changting, or Ningdu) and portrayals of character identities (the "Red Army brother" or the "guerrilla sister") give the songs a vivid sense of locality and immediacy. Such details not only preserve memory but also intensify emotional projection among the people.

05 情感节奏中的抒情化扩展

LYRIC EXPANSION WITHIN EMOTIONAL RHYTHM

在抒情部分，民歌常借助节奏与旋律的延展，将情感推向高潮。叠字、反复和长音的使用，往往不承担新的叙事任务，而是反复强化情绪的表达。例如"送郎送到大路口，口口声声叮咛嘱"，一句叙事之后，通过重复和拖腔，逐渐转化为深情的抒发。这种抒情化扩展让歌曲更具感染力，也延长了听众的情感停留。

In their lyrical sections, folk songs frequently employ rhythm and melody to extend emotion to its peak. The use of reduplication, repetition, and sustained tones often does not serve new narrative tasks but instead reinforces the expression of feeling. For instance, the line *"I walk my beloved to the crossroads, repeating words of exhortation"* begins with narration but, through repetition and drawn-out syllables, gradually transforms into a deeply emotional outpouring. This lyrical expansion strengthens the song's expressive power and prolongs the audience's emotional engagement.

06 集体叙事与个人抒情的融合

THE FUSION OF COLLECTIVE NARRATIVE AND PERSONAL LYRICISM

革命历史民歌的叙事常常涉及群体经验，如红军过境、村庄支援等，但抒情部分却往往回到个体情感，如一位母亲的不舍、一对情侣的离愁。这种“集体叙事”与“个人抒情”的结合，使得歌曲既能代表宏大的历史，又能触及个体的内心。正因如此，这些歌曲才在群众中广泛流传，因为它们不仅讲述历史，更讲述了每一个人可能经历的情感。

The narrative content of revolutionary folk songs often reflects collective experience—such as the Red Army's passage or the villagers' support—while the lyrical sections frequently return to individual emotions, such as a mother's reluctance or lovers' sorrow at parting. The integration of "collective narrative" and "personal lyricism" allowed the songs to represent grand historical themes while also touching the hearts of individuals. This explains why they spread so widely among the people: they narrated history while also articulating emotions that everyone might experience.

07 叙事—抒情交织的艺术意义

THE ARTISTIC SIGNIFICANCE OF INTERWOVEN NARRATIVE AND LYRICISM

这种叙事与抒情交织的结构，既是口头文学的普遍规律，也是革命语境下民歌能够动员群众的原因之一。从艺术史的角度看，它展现了口头叙事诗与抒情歌谣的互融，为我们理解口头传统的多样性提供了新的范例。从文化记忆的角度看，它让革命历史以“带情感的叙事”形式被记住和传承，而不仅仅是冷冰冰的史实。

This structure, in which narrative and lyricism are interwoven, is not only a general pattern of oral literature but also one of the reasons revolutionary folk songs were able to mobilize the masses. From the perspective of art history, it reveals the fusion of oral narrative poetry and lyrical song, providing a new model for understanding the diversity of oral traditions. From the perspective of cultural memory, it allowed revolutionary history to be remembered and transmitted in the form of “emotion-laden narrative,” rather than as cold, detached facts.

第五节　地域风格与音乐元素

SECTION FIVE: REGIONAL STYLES AND MUSICAL ELEMENTS

引言 / Introduction

中央苏区的革命历史民歌不仅是政治与社会生活的写照，更深深扎根于赣南、闽西、湘南等地的民间文化传统。它们在语言、旋律、节奏和表演形态上，都带有鲜明的地域印记。这些地方性的音乐元素既保证了歌曲的亲切感和可接受性，也使其在艺术风格上展现出多样化的面貌。

The revolutionary historical folk songs of the Central Soviet Area were not only reflections of political and social life but were also deeply rooted in the folk cultural traditions of southern Jiangxi, western Fujian, and southern Hunan. In their language, melody, rhythm, and performance forms, they all bore distinctive regional imprints. These local musical elements ensured that the songs felt familiar and approachable, while also giving them stylistic diversity in artistic expression.

01 语言与方言特色

LINGUISTIC AND DIALECTAL FEATURES

赣南客家方言、闽西方言和湘南土语在民歌中被广泛保留。方言的使用不仅增强了歌曲的口语化和生活气息，也在声韵和节奏上提供了特殊的音乐效果。例如赣南客家话中大量入声字，使得歌词在演唱时具有短促有力的节奏感，非常契合战斗与号召的氛围。而一些闽西方言中的叠词、拟声词，则增强了歌词的抒情和诙谐效果。语言的地域性不仅体现了文化身份的差异，也成为苏区民歌鲜明的“声腔标记”。

Hakka dialects of southern Jiangxi, the dialects of western Fujian, and the vernaculars of southern Hunan were widely preserved in the songs. The use of dialect not only enhanced the songs' colloquial and lifelike quality but also provided unique musical effects in sound and rhythm. For example, the abundance of entering-tone syllables in the Hakka dialect of Jiangxi created a short, forceful rhythmic feel when sung—well-suited to the atmosphere of battle and mobilization. Meanwhile, reduplications and onomatopoeic words in western Fujian dialects enriched the songs' lyricism and humor. Thus, dialectal language not only embodied regional identity but also became distinctive "vocal markers" of Soviet Area folk songs.

02 旋律的地域流变

REGIONAL VARIATIONS IN MELODY

中央苏区地处赣、闽、粤交界，民间音乐资源丰富多元。其革命历史民歌大量吸收了当地传统山歌、小调、灯歌的旋律结构，因而旋律既简洁又富有地方色彩。例如，赣南山歌常用的五声调式被广泛继承，旋律舒展、自然流畅，易于传唱；而闽西灯歌旋律灵动、节奏鲜明，为一些鼓动性强的歌曲提供了借鉴。这种“在地化”的旋律结构，使民歌能够在群众中迅速传播并形成共鸣。

Situated at the junction of Jiangxi, Fujian, and Guangdong, the Central Soviet Area was rich in diverse folk musical resources. Revolutionary folk songs absorbed heavily from local traditions such as mountain songs, ditties, and lantern songs, resulting in melodies that were both simple and rich in regional color. For instance, the pentatonic modes common in Jiangxi mountain songs were widely adopted, producing melodies that were smooth, natural, and easy to sing. Meanwhile, the lively, rhythmically sharp melodies of western Fujian lantern songs influenced more rousing revolutionary pieces. This "localized" melodic structure enabled the songs to spread quickly and resonate strongly among the masses.

03 节奏与劳动场景的关系

RHYTHM AND ITS RELATION TO LABOR SCENES

许多歌曲的节奏模式，直接来自于劳动号子或生产歌谣。例如挑担号子、打谷歌、车水号等，往往有规律的节奏，与劳动动作保持一致。红军歌曲吸收了这一传统，使得演唱与群体劳动能够同步进行，增强了团队协作感。例如在挑粮支前的歌声中，强拍落在“抬”或“走”的动作上，音乐成为身体劳动的节律框架。这种节奏—动作的结合，使得革命民歌不仅是娱乐或抒情工具，更是实际生产和战斗中的功能性声音资源。

The rhythmic patterns of many songs derived directly from work chants or production songs. Examples include carrying chants, threshing songs, and waterwheel chants, all of which featured regular rhythms synchronized with labor movements. Red Army songs drew on this tradition so that singing could accompany collective labor, enhancing teamwork. For instance, in supply-carrying songs, strong beats fell on movements such as “lift” or “walk,” making the music a rhythmic framework for bodily action. This union of rhythm and movement made revolutionary folk songs not only tools of entertainment or lyricism but also functional sound resources in production and combat.

04 音区与声腔的地域差异

REGIONAL DIFFERENCES IN VOCAL RANGE AND SINGING STYLE

在苏区不同的区域，民歌的音区和演唱方式也有所差别。赣南客家山歌多为高亢声腔，适合在山野、田间传唱；闽西灯歌则更强调低声区的婉转与连绵，常见于夜晚或节庆场合。革命历史民歌在传播过程中，往往根据场合需要在声腔上灵活调整：既可以采用高亢激越的唱法，鼓舞士气；也可以使用婉转细腻的腔调，表现离别与思念。声腔的多样化，既延续了地方传统，又赋予了民歌跨场景的适应性。

In different parts of the Soviet Area, folk songs varied in vocal range and performance style. Jiangxi Hakka mountain songs often employed high-pitched voices, suited to singing across mountains and fields; western Fujian lantern songs emphasized lower registers with flowing, lingering tones, more common at night or during festivals. Revolutionary folk songs, as they spread, adapted flexibly: adopting vigorous, high-pitched styles to inspire morale in battle, or tender, restrained tones to express parting and longing. This diversity of vocal timbre both continued regional traditions and allowed the songs to adapt to varied contexts.

05 表演与群体互动

PERFORMANCE AND COLLECTIVE INTERACTION

地域风格还体现在表演形态上。赣南一带的民歌常以对唱、问答形式出现，这种表演结构在革命历史民歌中被广泛吸收，使得歌曲成为群众互动的一部分。例如村民与红军之间的“唱问唱答”，不仅是艺术表现，也是一种社会交往。闽西灯歌则习惯在节庆场合以舞蹈、动作配合演唱，这一传统也被革命歌曲继承，用于集会、动员与庆典。群体性的表演让歌曲超越了单纯的听觉作品，而成为一种社会仪式。

Regional style was also evident in performance practices. In Jiangxi, folk songs often appeared in antiphonal singing or question-and-answer forms, which revolutionary folk songs widely absorbed, making them integral to communal interaction. For example, the Red Army and villagers would engage in “call-and-response” singing, which was not only an artistic form but also a mode of social communication. In western Fujian, lantern songs were traditionally performed with dance and movement during festivals; revolutionary songs adopted similar elements for rallies, mobilizations, and celebrations. Such collective performances elevated the songs beyond auditory works, transforming them into social rituals.

06 音乐元素的跨界融合

CROSS-REGIONAL FUSION OF MUSICAL ELEMENTS

苏区革命历史民歌并非封闭的地方艺术，而是在不同地域传统的交汇处进行创新的产物。赣南山歌的舒展、闽西灯歌的灵动、湘南小调的婉转在这里相互渗透。更重要的是，这些地方元素与新的革命主题结合，产生了兼具地方特色与时代感的音乐风格。正是在这种跨界融合的过程中，革命历史民歌既保持了地域性，又形成了超越地域的普遍感染力。

The revolutionary folk songs of the Soviet Area were not enclosed local art forms but products of innovation at the intersection of multiple traditions. The expansiveness of Jiangxi mountain songs, the liveliness of Fujian lantern songs, and the tenderness of Hunan ditties intermingled here. More importantly, these regional elements were fused with new revolutionary themes, producing a musical style that combined local characteristics with a strong sense of the times. Through this cross-regional fusion, the songs retained their local identity while gaining universal appeal.

07 地域风格的历史与文化意义

THE HISTORICAL AND CULTURAL SIGNIFICANCE OF REGIONAL STYLES

将这些音乐元素放在更大的历史语境中，可以看到它们体现了文化的延续与转化。革命历史民歌并非凭空产生，而是对传统民间音乐资源的再利用和再创造。地方音乐元素的保留，使这些歌曲成为区域文化身份的象征；而这些元素被赋予新的政治与社会意义，则体现了文化在历史转型期的再生。由此，苏区民歌既是地方文化的延续，也是历史语境下的创造性回应。

Placed in a broader historical context, these musical elements embody both cultural continuity and transformation. Revolutionary folk songs did not arise from nothing; they were reuses and re-creations of traditional folk music resources. The preservation of local musical elements made them symbols of regional cultural identity, while their endowment with new political and social meanings reflected the regeneration of culture in a time of historical transition. Thus, Soviet Area folk songs were both continuations of local culture and creative responses to their historical context.

第六节 文化记忆与历史语境

SECTION SIX: CULTURAL MEMORY AND HISTORICAL CONTEXT

引言 / Introduction

中央苏区的革命历史民歌，并不仅仅是历史事件的附属物，它们在更深层次上承载着一种文化记忆。这种记忆既包含了个人的生命体验与情感表达，也反映了群体在特定历史时期的共同心声。若将这些歌曲仅仅理解为政治宣传，显然会低估其文化厚度与艺术价值。只有将其放置在历史语境中，才能更为全面地理解它们的意义。

The revolutionary historical folk songs of the Central Soviet Area were not merely appendages to historical events. On a deeper level, they carried cultural memory. This memory encompassed not only individual life experiences and emotional expressions but also reflected the collective voices of the people during a specific historical period. To interpret these songs solely as political propaganda would be to underestimate their cultural depth and artistic value. Only by situating them within their historical context can we fully grasp their significance.

01 民间叙事与集体记忆

FOLK NARRATIVES AND COLLECTIVE MEMORY

革命历史民歌往往以民间叙事的方式流传。它们并不遵循官方史书的书写逻辑，而是通过歌声记录日常生活的片段——征兵的离别、支前的劳作、村庄的动员、亲人的思念。这些歌声所保存的，是普通人在历史洪流中的生命经验。作为集体记忆的一部分，它们见证了苏区百姓如何以自己的声音回应时代。

Revolutionary folk songs were transmitted through modes of folk narration. Rather than following the logic of official historiography, they recorded fragments of everyday life through song—farewells at conscription, labor in support of the front, village mobilizations, and the longing for loved ones. What these songs preserved were the life experiences of ordinary people within the torrents of history. As part of collective memory, they bore witness to how the people of the Soviet Area responded to their era with their own voices.

02 历史语境的双重维度

THE DUAL DIMENSIONS OF HISTORICAL CONTEXT

这些民歌必须放在两个层面来理解：一是**地方文化的延续**，二是**历史环境的回应**。

从文化延续的角度看，它们继承了赣南、闽西等地的山歌、小调、号子传统，延续了世代相传的声音表达方式。

从历史回应的角度看，它们又是特定政治环境下的产物，用以表达对新社会、新生活的想象和呼唤。正是这种双重性，使得革命历史民歌既是“旧文化”的延伸，也是“新历史”的见证。

These songs must be understood on two levels: as continuations of local culture, and as responses to historical circumstances.

From the perspective of cultural continuity, they inherited traditions of mountain songs, ditties, and work chants from regions such as southern Jiangxi and western Fujian, thus extending long-standing vocal practices.

From the perspective of historical response, they were products of specific political environments, expressing the people's imagination of, and longing for, a new society and a new life.

It was precisely this duality that made revolutionary folk songs both extensions of "old culture" and witnesses of "new history."

03 记忆与遗忘的张力

THE TENSION BETWEEN MEMORY AND FORGETTING

在当下回望时，我们会发现这些歌曲中既有永恒的情感主题（如亲情、爱情、乡愁），也有特定历史语境下的政治口号。随着时间推移，部分口号性的内容逐渐淡化，但情感性的元素依旧动人。记忆与遗忘之间的张力，使这些民歌既是历史文献，也是文化遗产。我们今日的整理与呈现，不是为了重现政治口号，而是为了保留那份声音中最本质的人类经验与情感记忆。

Looking back today, we find that these songs contain both timeless emotional themes—such as kinship, love, and homesickness—and historically specific political slogans. Over time, much of the slogan-like content has faded, yet the emotional elements remain moving. The tension between memory and forgetting makes these folk songs both historical documents and cultural heritage. Our present-day efforts at collection and presentation are not about reproducing political slogans but about preserving the most essential human experiences and emotional memories carried in these voices.

04 声音的象征与文化断裂

THE SYMBOLISM OF SOUND AND CULTURAL RUPTURE

许多歌曲原本以口耳相传的方式流布，声音本身是最重要的载体。但随着时间的推移，声音逐渐消逝，只留下手稿、歌词和部分乐谱。这种“声音的缺席”，本身就成为文化断裂的象征。我们在整理、出版、再演绎这些歌曲的过程中，实际上是在尝试弥补这一断裂，让历史的声音以另一种方式重新回到当下。

Many songs were originally disseminated orally, with sound itself as the most important carrier. Yet as time passed, the voices gradually disappeared, leaving behind only manuscripts, lyrics, and partial scores. This “absence of sound” became a symbol of cultural rupture. In the processes of collecting, publishing, and reinterpreting these songs, we are in fact attempting to mend that rupture—allowing the voices of history to return in another form to the present.

05 历史语境化的再诠释

REINTERPRETATION THROUGH HISTORICAL CONTEXTUALIZATION

将这些民歌放置在“历史语境化”的框架中，可以弱化它们单一的政治性，而突出其文化多重性：

它们是**地方文化的见证**：通过语言、旋律、节奏保存了区域特色；

它们是**民间社会的叙事**：普通人以歌声书写了自己的生活与苦乐；

它们是**历史转型的声音**：在旧秩序瓦解、新秩序建立的过渡期，歌声成为集体身份的象征。

Placing these folk songs within the framework of "historical contextualization" allows us to move beyond a narrow political reading and to highlight their cultural multiplicity:

They are **witnesses of local culture**, preserving regional features through language, melody, and rhythm.

They are **narratives of folk society**, in which ordinary people wrote their own lives and struggles in song.

They are **voices of historical transition**, embodying collective identity during the collapse of the old order and the emergence of the new.

06 当代意义与文化再生产

CONTEMPORARY SIGNIFICANCE AND CULTURAL REPRODUCTION

在今天重读这些民歌，不应只是历史学的考据，而更应看到它们在文化再生产中的价值。它们既可以作为音乐学、民俗学、社会学的研究对象，也可以作为非物质文化遗产进入公共记忆体系。在数字化保存、跨文化传播的语境中，革命历史民歌有可能成为一种新的文化资源——既是历史的遗存，也是未来的创造。

Re-reading these songs today should not be limited to historical inquiry; we must also recognize their value in cultural reproduction. They can serve as research objects in musicology, folklore, and sociology, while also entering public memory systems as intangible cultural heritage. Within the frameworks of digital preservation and cross-cultural transmission, revolutionary historical folk songs may become new cultural resources—not only relics of history but also creative foundations for the future.

小结 / Conclusion

“文化记忆与历史语境”的视角，帮助我们超越了革命历史民歌的政治表层，而深入到其文化和人文核心。它们既是地方社会在特定历史条件下的创造，也是跨代传承的重要文化遗产。通过历史语境化的理解，我们得以在今天重新聆听那段历史的回响，并将其转化为对未来文化对话。

The perspective of “cultural memory and historical context” allows us to move beyond the political surface of revolutionary historical folk songs and approach their cultural and humanistic core. They were creations of local society under specific historical conditions, and they remain important cultural heritage for intergenerational transmission. By situating them within their historical contexts, we can once again hear the echoes of that era today and transform them into resources for future cultural dialogue.

结语 在歌声中聆听历史与未来
Conclusion: Listening to History and the Future through Songs

在本书的整理、编纂与书写过程中，我们一路追随瑞金民歌的足迹，走过田野与档案，走过岁月与记忆。从七大类传统民歌的生活智慧，到革命历史歌曲的历史语境，我们不仅看见了声音如何见证过去，更看见了声音如何持续塑造今天的身份与文化认同。

瑞金民歌并非只是地域性的歌谣，它在本质上是一种**集体记忆的艺术表达**。它把农耕生活的劳作节奏、婚丧嫁娶的仪式秩序、山水自然的生命寓意，都凝聚进一个个简洁却意味深长的曲调与歌词之中。尤其是在中央苏区的历史语境下，这些歌谣又被赋予了新的政治性与集体动员力量，成为那个特殊年代里人们的心灵寄托与精神支撑。

然而，时间的流逝并没有使这些歌声褪色。相反，它们的多重层次——从民俗到历史、从日常到政治、从地域到民族——构成了一种独特的文化复合体。在今天的语境中，当我们重新整理与出版这些歌谣时，实际上是在进行一种**文化的再发现**。这既是对祖辈心血的回响，也是对未来跨文化对话的奠基。

01 声音作为非物质文化遗产

联合国教科文组织在“非物质文化遗产”保护的理念中，特别强调**口传传统与表演艺术**的重要性。瑞金民歌恰恰以最典型的方式回应了这一点。它没有被刻意雕琢，却因代代传唱而生生不息。它既没有文字的固定，却因旋律与语音的流转而保留下来。

通过对瑞金民歌的系统整理，我们不仅保存了一批“文本化”的歌词，更重要的是保存了**承载这些歌声的文化语境**。在这个过程中，我们清醒地意识到：非遗保护不仅是“留住一首首歌”，而是要留住**人与歌、与土地、与时代的记忆**。

02 从地域到世界

在今天的全球化背景下，瑞金民歌所展现的意义，已经远远超越了赣南山区的地理边界。它们承载的，是一种能够与全世界对话的文化力量。

无论是与爱尔兰的民间叙事歌谣相对照，还是与非洲的口传史诗对比，瑞金民歌都显示出一种**普遍的人类情感共鸣**。这些歌谣中关于劳作、爱情、别离、家园的主题，跨越语言与国界，能够与世界上无数民族的歌声互相呼应。与此同时，它们又具有鲜明的地域性与历史性，使得这种对话带有独特的“瑞金印记”。

因此，《听见瑞金》不仅是对一段地方文化的保存，也是对**跨文化传播可能性**的一次探索。我们希望在未来，通过数字化、学术研究与国际交流，让这些歌声走得更远，成为全球文化语境中的重要声音。

03 数字化与再表达

在技术高度发展的今天，声音档案的数字化、乐谱的重建与 AI 技术的辅助演绎，为我们提供了全新的可能性。瑞金民歌的保护与传播，不应止步于纸面出版，而应延展至**数字音乐、互动媒体与跨界艺术**的更广阔领域。

这意味着，我们不仅要“保存”这些歌，更要让它们“活起来”。未来的听众，或许可以在虚拟展厅里，随着一首瑞金山歌的旋律走进 20 世纪三十年代的中央苏区；也可以在跨国音乐节的舞台上，听见瑞金民歌与非洲鼓点、欧洲弦乐的对话；更可以在学术研究的跨学科平台上，把瑞金民歌作为案例，探讨声音、人类学、记忆研究的多重议题。

04 传承与未来

最重要的是，瑞金民歌是一种**活的文化**。它不是博物馆里的静态展品，而是活在人们口耳之间的生命形态。它提醒我们，文化的价值不在于被封存，而在于被不断传唱、被赋予新的意义。

在整理这批歌谣的过程中，我们深切体会到：真正的传承，不是复制，而是创造性的延续。新一代年轻人可以用他们的方式去理解、去再唱瑞金民歌——哪怕是用流行乐的旋律、说唱的节奏、数字影像的形式。只要其中保留了那份情感与精神的核心，就依然是对祖辈的回应。

05 聆听历史，也聆听未来

《听见瑞金》最终想要传达的，是一种**穿越时空的聆听**。我们聆听的不仅是过去的声音，也是我们自身与未来的声音。

当我们在书页中读到一首首歌谣时，不妨设想，它们并不是“被完成”的历史，而是“正在发生”的文化。每一次阅读与传唱，都是一次重新激活。这种激活让我们看到：民歌并不是遥远的遗产，而是此刻仍能塑造身份、连接世界、启发未来的力量。

因此，我们以本书作为阶段性的成果，既是对过往的致敬，也是对未来的召唤。希望《听见瑞金》能够成为一座桥梁，让过去的声音在今天被重新听见，让今天的声音也能在未来留下回响。

In the process of compiling, editing, and writing this book, we have followed the footprints of Ruijin folk songs—through the fields and the archives, across years and memories. From the life wisdom embedded in the seven categories of traditional folk songs to the historical context of revolutionary songs, we not only witness how voices bear testimony to the past but also how they continue to shape identities and cultural consciousness today.

Ruijin folk songs are not merely local ballads; at their core, they are an artistic expression of collective memory. They condense the rhythms of agricultural labor, the rituals of marriage and mourning, and the symbolic meanings of nature into concise yet profound melodies and lyrics. Particularly within the historical context of the Central Soviet Area, these songs were endowed with new political functions and mobilizing power, becoming a source of solace and spiritual strength in that extraordinary era.

Yet the passage of time has not diminished their resonance. On the contrary, their multiple layers—from folklore to history, from daily life to politics, from locality to nationhood—have formed a unique cultural complex. In today's context, the re-compilation and publication of these songs are in fact a process of cultural rediscovery. It is both an echo of our ancestors' devotion and a foundation for future cross-cultural dialogues.

01 Voices as Intangible Cultural Heritage

UNESCO's concept of "intangible cultural heritage" emphasizes the importance of **oral traditions and performing arts**. Ruijin folk songs exemplify this in the most vivid way. They are neither artificially refined nor textually fixed, yet their vitality endures through generations of oral transmission.

By systematically compiling Ruijin folk songs, we have not only preserved a corpus of "textualized" lyrics but also safeguarded the cultural contexts in which these songs once lived. This process reminds us that protecting intangible heritage is not simply about "keeping the songs," but about preserving the memories among people, their voices, the land, and the times.

02 From the Local to the Global

In today's globalized world, the significance of Ruijin folk songs extends far beyond the geographic boundaries of southern Jiangxi. They embody a cultural force capable of engaging in dialogue with the world.

Placed alongside Irish narrative ballads or compared with African oral epics, Ruijin folk songs reveal a **universal resonance of human emotions**. Themes of labor, love, parting, and homeland transcend languages and borders, echoing with the songs of countless other peoples worldwide. At the same time, their distinct regional and historical characteristics lend a unique "Ruijin imprint" to this dialogue.

Thus, *Listening to Ruijin* is not only a preservation of local culture but also an exploration of the possibilities of **cross-cultural communication**. Looking ahead, through digital preservation, scholarly research, and international exchange, we hope these voices will travel further and become an important presence in global cultural discourse.

03 Digitalization and Re-expression

With the advancement of technology, digital archiving of sounds, reconstruction of scores, and AI-assisted interpretation offer new possibilities. The protection and dissemination of Ruijin folk songs should not be confined to print publication, but should also extend into the broader realms of **digital music, interactive media, and cross-disciplinary art**.

This means we should not only "preserve" the songs but also "bring them to life." Future audiences may enter a virtual exhibition and, guided by the melody of a Ruijin mountain song, step back into the Central Soviet Area of the 1930s. They may hear Ruijin folk songs conversing with African drums or European strings on a world music stage. They may also encounter them in interdisciplinary scholarship, where the songs serve as case studies in sound studies, anthropology, and memory research.

04 Transmission and the Future

Most importantly, Ruijin folk songs are a **living culture**. They are not static artifacts in a museum, but a living form sustained in the oral traditions of people. They remind us that the value of culture lies not in its being sealed away but in its continued singing and the creation of new meanings.

In compiling these songs, we have come to realize that true transmission is not replication but **creative continuation**. Younger generations may interpret and sing Ruijin folk songs in their own ways—through the melodies of popular music, the rhythms of rap, or the forms of digital media. As long as the core emotions and spirit remain, the response to our ancestors will endure.

V. Listening to History, Listening to the Future

What **Listening to Ruijin** *ultimately seeks to convey is a listening that transcends time. What we hear is not only the voices of the past, but also the echoes of ourselves and the future.*

When we encounter these songs on the page, we might imagine that they are not a "completed" history, but a culture still "in the making." Each act of reading and singing is a reactivation—one that shows us that folk songs are not distant relics, but living forces that can continue to shape identities, connect worlds, and inspire futures.

Thus, we present this book as a milestone, both as a tribute to the past and as a call toward the future. We hope that *Listening to Ruijin* may serve as a bridge: allowing the voices of the past to be heard anew today, and ensuring that today's voices may in turn resonate into the future.

参考文献 References

1. 江西瑞金革命纪念馆 [Revolutionary Memorial Hall of Ruijin]. *《中华苏维埃共和国临时中央政府史料》 Zhonghua Suwei'ai Gongheguo Linshi Zhongyang Zhengfu Shiliao* [Historical Materials of the Provisional Central Government of the Chinese Soviet Republic]. 1981.
2. 林给生 [Lin, Geisheng]. *《中央苏区音乐史话》 Zhongyang Suqu Yinyue Shihua* [A Historical Narrative of Music in the Central Soviet Area]. 江西师范大学.
3. 《红色中华》及副刊《赤焰》 [*Hongse Zhonghua* and *Chiyan* / *Red China* and *Red Flame*]. 1931–1934.
4. 张怀智 [Zhang, Huaizhi]. "瞿秋白与《赤潮曲》 Qu Qiubai yu 'Chichao Qu' [Qu Qiubai and the 'Song of the Red Tide']." *《中国音乐》 Zhongguo Yinyue* [Chinese Music], no. 3 (1988).
5. 钟同荥, 杨德恒 [Zhong, Tongying, and Yang, Deheng], eds. *《中央苏区革命歌曲选》 Zhongyang Suqu Geming Gequ Xuan* [Selected Revolutionary Songs of the Central Soviet Area]. 瑞金文化馆, 1979.
6. 瑞金县委宣传教育部 [Propaganda and Education Department of the Ruijin County Committee]. *《苏区文艺绘编》第一辑 Suqu Wenyi Huibian, Di 1 Ji* [Collected Literary and Artistic Works of the Soviet Area, Vol. 1]. 1958.
7. 汪毓和 [Wang, Yuhé]. *《中国近代音乐史》 Zhongguo Jindai Yinyue Shi* [A History of Modern Chinese Music].
8. 毛泽东 [Mao, Zedong]. *《湖南农民运动考察报告》 Hunan Nongmin Yundong Kaocha Baogao* [Report on an Investigation of the Peasant Movement in Hunan]. 1927.
9. 江西人民出版社 [Jiangxi People's Publishing House]. *《江西人民革命史资料》 Jiangxi Renmin Geming Shi Ziliao* [Historical Materials of the Jiangxi People's Revolutionary Movement].

www.ingramcontent.com/pod-product-compliance
Lightning Source LLC
Chambersburg PA
CBHW060413010526
44107CB00006B/671

* 9 7 8 1 9 7 0 3 1 6 0 5 6 *